The Opera Reader

Books by Louis Biancolli

THE BOOK OF GREAT CONVERSATIONS
(FROM SOCRATES TO SHAW)
MARY GARDEN'S STORY
THE FLAGSTAD MANUSCRIPT
THE ANALYTICAL CONCERT GUIDE
THE OPERA READER

with Robert Bagar

THE CONCERT COMPANION
THE VICTOR BOOK OF OPERAS

The Opera Reader

Compiled and Edited by

LOUIS BIANCOLLI

McGRAW-HILL BOOK COMPANY, INC.

NEW YORK   TORONTO   LONDON

Library of Congress Catalog Card Number: 53–9008.

Published by the McGraw-Hill Book Company, Inc.
Printed in the United States of America.

LIST OF COPYRIGHTS

APPLETON-CENTURY-CROFTS, INC. From *A Thousand and One Nights of Opera* by Frederick H. Martens. Copyright 1926 D. Appleton & Company. Reprinted by permission of the publishers Appleton-Century-Crofts, Inc.

BOSTON SYMPHONY ORCHESTRA. From selections by John N. Burk in the "Boston Symphony Program." Copyright 1947 by the Boston Symphony Orchestra. Reprinted by permission of John N. Burk and the Boston Symphony Orchestra.

From selections by Philip Hale in the Boston Symphony Program. Reprinted by permission of John N. Burk and the Boston Symphony Orchestra.

BROADCAST MUSIC, INC. From *Ten Operatic Masterpieces* by Olin Downes. Copyright 1952 by Broadcast Music, Inc. Reprinted by permission of Broadcast Music, Inc.

CHATTO & WINDUS. From *Gluck* by Martin Cooper. Copyright 1935 by Chatto & Windus. Reprinted by permission of Chatto & Windus.

J. M. DENT & SONS, LTD. From *Gluck* by Alfred Einstein, translated by Eric Blom. Copyright 1936 by J. M. Dent & Sons, Ltd., London. Reprinted by permission of J. M. Dent & Sons, Ltd.

DODD, MEAD & COMPANY, INC. Reprinted by permission of Dodd, Mead & Company from *The International Cyclopedia of Music and Musicians*. Copyright 1938 by Dodd, Mead & Company, Inc.

DOUBLEDAY & COMPANY, INC. From *The Music Lovers' Almanac* by William Hendelson and Paul Zucker. Copyright 1943 by Doubleday & Company, Inc.

From *Music Lovers' Encyclopedia,* compiled by Rupert Hughes, edited by Deems Taylor. Copyright 1939 by Doubleday & Company, Inc.

E. P. DUTTON & CO., INC. From *Lives of the Great Composers* by A. L. Bacharach. Published 1936 by E. P. Dutton & Co., Inc., New York. Reprinted by permission of E. P. Dutton & Co., Inc.

ENCYCLOPAEDIA BRITANNICA. For material on Berlioz and Donizetti from the *Encyclopaedia Britannica, 13th Edition.* Copyright 1926 by the Encyclopaedia Britannica. Reprinted by permission of the publisher.

VICTOR GOLLANCZ, LTD. From chapter on opera (one-third of the original version) by Edward J. Dent from *The Musical Companion,* edited by A. L. Bacharach. Copyright 1934 by Victor Gollancz, Ltd. Reprinted by permission of Edward J. Dent, A. L. Bacharach, and Victor Gollancz, Ltd.

A. K. HOLLAND. From *Purcell* by A. K. Holland published by George Bell & Sons. Copyright 1932 by George Bell & Sons. Copyright 1948 Penguin Books, Ltd. Reprinted by permission of the publisher and author.

HENRY HOLT AND COMPANY, INC. From *Bolero, The Life of Maurice Ravel* by Madeleine Goss. Copyright 1940 by Henry Holt and Company, Inc. Used by permission of the publishers.

JOHN LANE THE BODLEY HEAD LTD. From *Mozart's "Così Fan Tutte"* (published in the Sadler's Wells Opera Books) by kind permission of Messrs. John Lane The Bodley Head Ltd., London.

ALFRED A. KNOPF, INC. From *Stories of the Great Operas* by Ernest Newman by permission of Alfred A. Knopf, Inc. Copyright 1929 by Alfred A. Knopf, Inc.

From *Stories of the Great Operas* by Ernest Newman by permission of Alfred A. Knopf, Inc. Copyright 1930 by Alfred A. Knopf, Inc.

From *More Stories of Famous Operas* by Ernest Newman by permission of Alfred A. Knopf, Inc. Copyright 1943 by Alfred A. Knopf, Inc.

From *Rossini: A Study in Tragi-Comedy* by Francis Toye by permission of Alfred A. Knopf, Inc. Copyright 1934 by Alfred A. Knopf, Inc.

From *Giuseppe Verdi: His Life and Works* by Francis Toye by permission of Alfred A. Knopf, Inc. Copyright 1946 by Alfred A. Knopf, Inc.

This book is respectfully dedicated to

THE METROPOLITAN OPERA
The house,
The institution,
The symbol,
and to

The thousands of named and unnamed workers, artists, and benefactors who have maintained its proud tradition of service and allegiance to a noble ideal.

Preface

Whatever else may be said of the musical cupboard it is not bare of opera books. Quite the contrary. Today there are at least a dozen excellent guides available in bookstores or libraries for those who cherish a well-told opera tale. In the hands of an Ernest Newman the opera "synopsis" has become a remarkable blend of science and beauty. Thanks to Herbert F. Peyser the opera "analysis" is now the adroit and thorough thing that the symphonic "program note" has long been with the best annotators, Mr. Peyser himself among them. Moreover, there have been histories of opera—to my thinking none superior to *The Opera* of Wallace Brockway and Herbert Weinstock. For the story of the Metropolitan Opera House there is scarcely a chance that Irving Kolodin's devoted and exhaustive survey will ever be superseded.

Such being the situation, why another opera book? The answer is that the present volume represents a synthesis. It is not another book of opera synopses, of which delectable sport this editor had more than his share while collaborating with Robert Bagar on *The Victor Book of Operas*. Nor is *The Opera Reader* solely a book of opera backgrounds and analyses, like the excellent *Opera Lover's Companion*, edited by that erudite *aficionada*, Mary Ellis Peltz. I need hardly add that while first Metropolitan casts and performances are uniformly appended, it is by no stretch of the term a guide to Metropolitan history. Yet, while it is none of these things, it is in a limited sense all of them, and something more.

To begin with, although *The Opera Reader* is not primarily a book of opera stories, it is still a story book. These are the stories, sometimes even the plots, behind the operas and often behind the scenes. They are stories that deal with the operas themselves, with singers and conductors and first performances, with episodes in the lives of their composers, with accounts—wherever possible —of how the operas originated in the brains of their makers, grew, took shape, and reached the stage. For each opera a generous background is given that may be regarded as a case history of the work in question: the toil and the tears that went into its making, the hopes, anxieties, trials, setbacks, broken promises and promises fulfilled that were the composer's lot before the fateful day of the "world première."

The Opera Reader is thus a book about the operatic milieu as well. Celebrated prima donnas, great tenors and baritones and singing-actors, illustrious and influential conductors march through its pages as leading figures in a parade of motley glamour and brilliant achievement. They are the dedicated servitors without whom the opera would never have reached the living reality of performance. Woven into most of these essays is a historical background of the comedies and tragedies that have played their part in evolving the personality of each opera through the years. While the object of this aspect of *The Opera Reader* is to provide the average operagoer and nonprofessional music lover with information and entertainment, it also offers students, in convenient form, material that would cost time and effort to dig out of the libraries or to cull from other volumes where the emphasis is on one or another phase of the variegated story of opera.

In compiling these backgrounds the editor drew upon several sources—to name a few, Pitts Sanborn, Dyneley Hussey, Eric Blom, Francis Toye, Ernest Newman, Henry W. Simon, George R. Marek, Herbert F. Peyser, William Foster Apthorp, Olin Downes, Newman Flower, and the brilliant team of Wallace Brockway and Herbert Weinstock. The notes provided by Sanborn, whose assistant I was for many years, first appeared as special articles in the Metropolitan Opera House program book in the late thirties. Much of the research that went into those essays was mine, and I can vouch for every detail of cast and performance having been checked and counterchecked before publication. That does not mean that the virus of error may not have occasionally filtered through. Mr. Newman needs no introduction as the world's foremost musical biographer and conqueror par excellence of that monstrous hybrid of literature—the opera libretto. From both his *Stories of the Great Operas* and *More Stories of Famous Operas,* I have been vouchsafed the eloquent sheaf of backgrounds and biographies that bear his initials. From the Master Musicians Series edited by Mr. Blom I have culled at my pleasure. Of Mr. Peyser I would say that if the bulk of the *Opera Lover's Companion* is his, so is one of its main attractions. Nor should the contributions of the others to that noble repository be underrated. To Henry W. Simon's excellent *Treasury of Grand Opera* and *The Opera* of Messrs. Brockway and Weinstock I owe some of the most illuminating pages found in this compilation. Finally, from the man whose memory I worship as musical scholar, analyst, and historian—William Foster Apthorp—I have borrowed many pages of his *The Opera Past and Present,* published in 1901, but still a model of writing and evaluation for the shorter history of opera.

Such is the chief purpose of this book. Having provided so much material about the machinery behind the opera, the editor thought it unfair to some readers to leave them completely on their own as regards the story—offstage, as it were, but never on. For such readers, as well as for those who might welcome a "refresher," it was deemed best to introduce each "background" with a brief résumé of the plot. These synopses I selected from various sources for their brevity and clarity—such sources being Frederick H. Martens' *A*

Thousand and One Nights of Opera, the *Music Lovers' Encyclopedia* (compiled by Rupert Hughes and completely revised and newly edited by Deems Taylor); Pitts Sanborn's *The Metropolitan Book of the Opera,* to which I gave considerable help; and *The Music Lovers' Almanac,* edited by William Hendelson and Paul Zucker. I have introduced each synopsis with a cast of characters and the voices for which they were written. A few synopses in brackets are from *The Victor Book of Operas* edited and revised by Robert Bagar and myself. Uninitialed synopses are from the *Music Lovers' Encyclopedia.*

To equip the reader with further information that he might absorb at his leisure—and at his pleasure—I also thought it wise to preface each opera or group of operas with a short biography of the composer. For such material I went again to several sources already named, in addition to Oscar Thompson's *Cyclopedia of Music and Musicians,* and one or two other dictionaries and compilations elsewhere named. Here I based my choice on a varying principle. Brevity and pointed detail were again the most desired features of the majority of the biographies. However, in several instances I felt that a slightly longer survey of the composer's career was warranted. Such was the case with Purcell, Gluck, Mozart, Beethoven, Rossini, Meyerbeer, Verdi, Wagner, Tschaikowsky, Puccini, Richard Strauss, Debussy, and Alban Berg. This flexible principle of length was of course also applied to the opera background. While some operas inevitably required more extended treatment, others could do with less. Often I chose an extended essay because it best pictured the particular opera in the step-by-step process of creative evolution.

I believe the presence of a large portion of Edward J. Dent's outline history of opera explains itself. There again it was a matter of offering as succinct a picture as possible of the early genealogy of opera. Several other short histories were considered, all of them good. My choice fell on Dent's because it seemed to fit my pattern best and to duplicate subsequent material least. I have let Mr. Dent take the story down to Gluck. The rest of the book carries it on from there.

This *Opera Reader* would have been incomplete without one other feature—the consistent and uniform inclusion of American premières of great operas and a few Metropolitan facts to round out each background. As the world's leading opera house, as a Mecca for singers of all countries, as the scene of innumerable triumphs, the Metropolitan provides a story inseparable from the story of opera. I owe the paragraphs about outstanding Metropolitan casts and performances in large part to the late Pitts Sanborn and Messrs. Brockway and Weinstock. Added material in brackets is mine. As a rule these details appear after the essays as a factual appendage.

Apart from the work of selection, my job as editor has been to devise and pursue as convenient a formula as possible for the contents of this volume. This formula involves the following sequence:

1. The composer's full name, followed by the place and date of his birth and death
2. The biography of the composer
3. The title of the opera in its original language, followed by an accurate translation of the title, the number of acts, the book on which the opera was based, and the date and place of the opera's first performance
4. The names of the characters and their voices, besides the scene of the action of the opera
5. A short synopsis of the opera
6. A background essay of varying length
7. The American première and first Metropolitan performance with names of earliest singers, etc.

A large proportion of this material is already available in book form. Extracts were made from perhaps fifty books and magazines in all. Whatever novelty exists lies in the arrangement and concentration of this material into one volume. The editor did not have any one kind of opera lover in mind. *The Opera Reader* is intended for all opera lovers, whatever their taste or degree of exposure. There is something here for those who like vital statistics about composers and their operas; something for those who like to snatch up an opera plot and its characters for a hurried consultation; something for those who prefer their history and biography in concise form; and a great deal for those who like to peep behind the dazzling brilliance of an opera in action to the drama, sometimes humdrum and commonplace, sometimes strange and exciting, that went into its making. There is something, too, for those who like to browse in the well-nigh lost corridors that have become the once flourishing operas of Handel.

To all intents and purposes this is a book about European opera—and European opera that stops short of the living composer. After considerable thought and consultation I decided not to include American opera in this volume, not even a brief account of its development. I believe a similar survey should be done, and done soon, in a separate volume. Such a volume should include the so-called "grand" operas that have had their brief glimpses of the Metropolitan moon, but it should include, too, many works on the borderline between the opera and the Broadway musical, scores like George Gershwin's *Porgy and Bess*. It should include works like Virgil Thomson's *Four Saints in Three Acts,* Douglas Moore's *The Devil and Daniel Webster,* and Marc Blitzstein's *The Cradle Will Rock,* and of course the more recent works of the gifted Gian-Carlo Menotti and Leonard Bernstein. These and several other operas of like daring in theme and idiom have hovered on the periphery of the Metropolitan, waiting, perhaps, for the bold stroke of impresarial decision that would one day open its doors to them. The history of American opera is only in part the history of Metropolitan performances of American opera. It may well be, as Aaron Copland points out, that the future of American opera lies outside the opera house. Whatever its home, its past is a lesson, its present a living force, and its future assured.

Louis Biancolli

Key to Contributors

(The following list identifies every set of initials appearing in this volume. In a few instances material by the same author was culled from more than one book. Each such book is named in the key after the author's name, along with the nature of the material reprinted from it. In the case of Pitts Sanborn, whose initials occur more often than any other contributor's, it was thought best to omit them from the short final paragraphs that supply dates and casts of first American and Metropolitan performances. All such *uninitialed* passages are from his *Metropolitan Book of the Opera*. The few opera synopses that appear within brackets are by the editor of *The Opera Reader* and are reprinted from *The Victor Book of Operas*, edited by himself and Robert Bagar. All other material within brackets is also by the editor.)

G.A. Gerald Abraham, editor *The Music of Tchaikovsky,* W. W. Norton, New York, 1946.

W.F.A. William Foster Apthorp, *The Opera Past and Present,* Charles Scribner's Sons, New York, 1905.

W.S.A. William S. Ashbrook, *Opera Lover's Companion,* edited by Mary Ellis Peltz, Ziff-Davis Publishing Company, Chicago, 1948.

M.B. Martin Bernstein, *An Introduction to Music,* Prentice-Hall, Inc., New York, 1937.

E.B. Eric Blom: (a) *Mozart,* J. M. Dent & Sons, Ltd., London, 1935; (b) *Great Modern Composers,* edited by Oscar Thompson, The World Publishing Co., Cleveland, 1943, copyright Dodd, Mead & Company, Inc., New York, 1938.

F.B. Felix Borowski, *Chicago Symphony Program Books.*

W.B., H.W. Wallace Brockway and Herbert Weinstock, *The Opera,* Simon and Schuster, Inc., New York, 1941.

J.N.B. John N. Burk: (a) *The Life and Works of Beethoven,* Random House, New York, 1943; (b) *Boston Symphony Program Book.*

M.D.C. M. D. Calvocoressi, *The International Cyclopedia of Music and Musicians,* edited by Oscar Thompson, Dodd, Mead & Company, Inc., New York, 1952.

G.C. Gilbert Chase, *Great Modern Composers,* edited by Oscar Thompson, The World Publishing Co., Cleveland, 1943, copyright Dodd, Mead & Company, Inc., New York, 1938.

M.C. Martin Cooper, *Gluck,* Chatto & Windus, London, 1935.

E.D. Edward Dickinson, *Opera Lover's Companion,* edited by Mary Ellis Peltz, Ziff-Davis Publishing Company, Chicago, 1948.

E.J.D. Edward J. Dent: (a) *Opera Librettos,* Oxford University Press, London, 1941; (b) *Mozart's "Così Fan Tutte,"* John Lane The Bodley Head Ltd., London, 1946; (c) *Orpheus,* Oxford University Press, London, 1941; (d) *The Musical Companion,* edited by A. L. Bacharach, Victor Gollancz, Ltd., London, 1934.

O.D. Olin Downes, *Ten Operatic Masterpieces,* Broadcast Music Incorporated, G. Ricordi & Company, Charles Scribner's Sons, New York, 1952.

A.E. Alfred Einstein, *Gluck,* translated by Eric Blom, J. M. Dent & Sons, Ltd., London; E. P. Dutton & Co., Inc., New York, 1936.

J.H.E. J. H. Elliot, *Berlioz,* J. M. Dent & Sons, Ltd., London, 1938.

M.F. Maryla Friedlaender, *Opera News,* Jan. 31, 1949.

N.F. Newman Flower, *Handel,* Charles Scribner's Sons, New York, 1948.

W.F. Wolf Franck, *Opera News,* Feb. 18, 1952.

L.G. Lawrence Gilman, *Wagner's Operas,* Farrar & Rinehart, Inc., New York, 1937.

M.G. Madeleine Goss, *Bolero, The Life of Maurice Ravel,* Henry Holt and Company, Inc., New York, 1940.

M.G. Max Graf, *Opera News,* Feb. 10, 1951.

P.H. Philip Hale, *Boston Symphony Program Book.*

W.H., P.Z. William Hendelson and Paul Zucker, *The Music Lovers' Almanac,* Doubleday & Company, Inc., New York, 1947.

R.H. Ralph Hill, *Lives of the Great Composers,* edited by A. L. Bacharach, E. P. Dutton & Co., Inc., New York, 1936.

A.K.H. A. K. Holland, *Purcell,* George Bell & Sons, Ltd., London, 1933.

D.H. Dyneley Hussey: (a) *Some Composers of Opera,* Oxford University Press, London, 1952; (b) *Verdi,* J. M. Dent & Sons, Ltd., London, 1940.

K.O'D.H. Kathleen O'Donnell Hoover, *Opera Lover's Companion,* edited by Mary Ellis Peltz, Ziff-Davis Publishing Company, Chicago, 1948.

E.L. Edward Lockspeiser, *Debussy,* J. M. Dent & Sons, Ltd., London, 1936.

R.A.L. Richard Anthony Leonard, *Music Lovers' Encyclopedia,* compiled by Rupert Hughes, edited by Deems Taylor, Doubleday & Company, New York, 1939.

R.H.L. Robin H. Legge, *Grove's Dictionary of Music and Musicians,* 3d ed., edited by H. C. Colles, The Macmillan Company, New York, 1948.

F.H.M. Frederick H. Martens, *A Thousand and One Nights of Opera,* D. Appleton & Company, Inc., New York, 1926.

G.R.M. George R. Marek, *Puccini,* Simon and Schuster, Inc., New York, 1951.

M.J.M. Mary Jane Matz, *Opera News,* Nov. 28, 1949.

P.N. Paul Nettl, *Opera News,* Jan. 13, 1944, Nov. 28, 1949.

E.N. Ernest Newman: (a) *Stories of the Great Operas,* Alfred A. Knopf, Inc., New York, 1928; (b) *More Stories of Famous Operas,* Alfred A. Knopf, Inc., New York, 1928.

H.F.P.   Herbert F. Peyser, *Opera Lover's Companion,* edited by Mary Ellis Peltz, Ziff-Davis Publishing Company, Chicago, 1948.

W.R.   Willi Reich, *Great Modern Composers,* edited by Oscar Thompson, The World Publishing Co., Cleveland, 1943, copyright Dodd, Mead & Company, Inc., New York, 1938.

C.S.   Cesare Sodero, *Opera Lover's Companion,* edited by Mary Ellis Peltz, Ziff-Davis Publishing Company, Chicago, 1948.

E.J.S.   Edwin J. Stringham, *Listening to Music,* Prentice-Hall, Inc., New York, 1946.

H.W.S.   Henry W. Simon, *A Treasury of Grand Opera,* Simon and Schuster, Inc., New York, 1946.

L.S.   Lisa Sergio, *Opera Lover's Companion,* edited by Mary Ellis Peltz, Ziff-Davis Publishing Company, Chicago, 1948.

P.S.   Pitts Sanborn: (a) opera synopses from *The Metropolitan Book of the Opera,* Simon and Schuster, Inc., New York, 1937; (b) biographies from a formerly published radio magazine; (c) background essays from Metropolitan Opera program books; (d) facts about first American and Metropolitan performances, when not initialled or in brackets, are also by Pitts Sanborn (*The Metropolitan Book of the Opera*).

R.A.S.   R. A. Streatfeild, *Grove's Dictionary of Music and Musicians,* 3d edition, edited by H. C. Colles, The Macmillan Company, New York, 1948.

F.T.   Francis Toye (a) *Giuseppe Verdi,* Alfred A. Knopf, Inc., New York, 1946. (b) *Rossini,* Alfred A. Knopf, Inc., New York, 1934.

O.T.   Oscar Thompson, *The International Cyclopedia of Music and Musicians,* 6th ed., edited by Oscar Thompson, Dodd, Mead & Co., New York, 1952.

H.W.   Herbert Weinstock, *Tchaikovsky,* Alfred A. Knopf, Inc., New York, 1946.

Contents

The Opera Reader

Introduction

THE BEGINNINGS

In the Middle Ages all actors, singers, dancers, acrobats, and minstrels had been regarded as rogues and vagabonds, unless they were in the regular employ of some prince or nobleman and were classed as his servants. The Church had its mystery plays, but they were got up only for certain festivals, and the humbler drama, performed in inn yards or in the open street, was even more irregular in its appearance. It was not until after the beginning of the great social and intellectual change to which we give the general name of the "Renaissance" that drama and music, separately or together, could be organized on something like a regular system.

The Renaissance began in Italy, and for the rest of the world it may be said that the Renaissance meant the discovery of Italy as the source of all intellectual and artistic inspiration. It is only natural, therefore, that Italy should have been the original home of opera. Italy created opera because Italy had no drama—at least, no drama comparable to that of England and Spain. There is nothing in Italian literature corresponding to the plays of our Elizabethan poets or to those of Lope de Vega and Calderón, unless we go back to the "Sacred Representations," as they were called, which in Spain at any rate had a longer life than in other countries and developed more continuously into normal drama. The Italian religious plays were often of high literary value, but just at the moment when they might have followed the example of their Spanish relatives, they were forbidden to be acted. The only drama that the Italians possessed in the sixteenth century was either the old Latin drama of Plautus and Terence, translated into Italian, and certain imitations of Latin drama written by court poets, such as Ariosto, for occasional court performances, or else the Comedy of Masks, which was acted by strolling players, wherever they could find a "pitch," for the amusement of the common people.

The various Italian courts set the example to the rest of Europe in the extravagance of their pageants and masques, as we may call them. There is no need to describe them here, for most readers will have some idea of the masques and other entertainments which were provided on various occasions for Queen Elizabeth and for James I, and it has recently been shown that practically all of these were modelled as closely as possible on the entertainments of the courts of Florence and Mantua in the preceding generation. Music played a large part in them, but it had not yet reached the point of becoming

1

a complete musical setting of a play. None the less, the materials of opera were all ready to hand; the madrigal, which was the main musical form of the century, was gradually leading the way towards musical drama.

It may be well to warn the reader that madrigals in the sixteenth century were not invariably sung by a chorus without accompaniment. There is abundant evidence to show that they were very often accompanied by instruments, and that they were also sung as solos for a single voice, the other parts being played by instruments. At court festivities they were often performed by singers and players in some sort of theatrical costume, with the adjunct of scenery. Another thing to note is that even as early as in the days of Castiglione (about 1520) people used to recite poetry to the accompaniment of a viol, though we have no very definite record of how this was done.

In considering the history of opera we can observe three different ways in which music is employed. First, it is the direct expression of emotion. The ordinary man expresses himself in prose; in a more exalted form of drama the characters speak in verse, because poetry is a vehicle of intensified self-expression; and singing is a still further intensification of poetry. The singer in an opera appears in fact to create out of his own emotions the music that he sings, and even today an opera-singer cannot really convince his audience unless he acts in such a way as to make them believe that it is his emotions, and not the conductor's beat, that causes the orchestra to play the music written by the composer to express them. The second use of music in opera is for the purposes of dancing, and under that head we must include not merely set dances, but all movements such as processions, marches, battles, and in fact any kind of dumb-show action. Thirdly, music can be used for what we may call "background" purposes—music that describes natural phenomena such as storms, or that fulfils any other function which might perhaps equally well be performed by visible scenery. We shall see that these three functions of music have been treated in different ways by different composers at different periods.

The first attempt at what we can really call an opera was made at Florence in 1597 by a group of musicians and men of letters who were in the habit of meeting to discuss artistic matters at the house of Count Bardi. Their idea was to revive the methods that they believed characteristic of classical Greek tragedy, and their first experiment was a drama on the legend of Apollo and Daphne, written by the poet Ottavio Rinuccini and set to music mainly by Jacopo Peri. The words have survived, but none of the music, except two small fragments composed by Jacopo Corsi. *Dafne* was repeated in 1598 and 1599; in 1600 Rinuccini and Peri produced *Euridice,* an opera on the story of Orpheus and Eurydice. The music of this was printed at the time and has been reprinted in modern form; it is the first opera that has survived complete.

To the same year 1600 belongs what has generally been called the first oratorio, *La Rappresentazione dell' Anima e del Corpo* (The Story of the Body and the Soul); the words were put together from older religious plays and the music was by Emilio de' Cavalieri. The work, however, is not an oratorio as we now understand the term, but an opera, although on a religious subject; it is set to music all the way through, and it was intended to be acted in costume. The *Anima e Corpo* was produced at Rome, but the idea of it was no independent discovery of Cavalieri's; he had been working at Florence for some fifteen years as director of the court entertainments and he was a regular member of the Bardi circle.

Another work that ought to be mentioned here is *L'Amfiparnaso* (1597), composed by Orazio Veechi, a canon of the cathedral of Modena. It is a series of fourteen madrigals in five parts set to words representing scenes of the comedy of masks. As the printed part-books have little woodcuts representing the characters, many historians have supposed that this work was intended to be acted, perhaps in dumb show, or by puppets, while a chorus sang the madrigals. This is quite erroneous; the poet (most probably Giulio Cesare Croce of Bologna) says clearly in the prologue that this comedy is to enter by the ear and not by the eye. The *Amfiparnaso* is in no sense an opera; it is merely a musical presentation of the typical comedy of masks, and as such it is both brilliantly amusing and at the same time a most valuable document for the history of the mask plays. It is no more an opera than were the madrigals on street cries written by contemporary English composers.

The creators of these first operas were for the most part men of noble birth. Peri was rather amateurish as a musician; Rinuccini was a poet of real distinction. *Dafne* and *Euridice* were not written for popular audiences, but for the exclusive society of a highly cultivated court. It was only audiences of that calibre who would appreciate the literary quality of these dramas of classical mythology. The next step in the history of opera is the performance of Monteverdi's *Arianna* at Mantua (1607), followed by his *Orfeo* in 1608. Most of the music to *Arianna* has been lost, and the reader must not judge of its quality by the fragment which has been much dressed up for modern concert purposes. *Orfeo* was performed a few years ago at Oxford, and no more appropriate place could have been found for a revival of it, since it was originally written for a society of ardent young intellectuals. To us it is inevitably a "museum piece," but for all that it is a great masterpiece of musical drama, and it ought to be staged periodically in order that all musicians may see it and hear it and learn from it the fundamental principles of dramatic composition. Monteverdi was a much more professional composer than Peri; he had already had considerable experience as a writer of madrigals and of church music. He saw how to utilize simultaneously all the resources available in his day. He collected a large orchestra and had the imagination to employ different instruments to suit different situations. He has been described as the inventor of very daring harmonies; as a matter of fact, most of his devices had been used before, either by himself or by others, but in *Orfeo* he saw how to turn them to account at the appropriate dramatic moments and to do so without destroying the general sense of musical design running all through the opera. *Orfeo* is a great opera, not so much on account of the striking and ingenious effects of detail as because of its broad sense of musical continuity; considering the date at which it was written, it is a wonderful organic whole, whereas many operas of later times that present singular moments of dramatic power have suffered from the defect of patchiness.

An opera in those days was a large undertaking, such as could only be organized by some great prince for some special festivity; architects of the period who write about the building of theatres take it for granted that a theatre was a purely temporary structure put up for a single occasion. The Barberini family at Rome were great patrons of opera. It is interesting to note that quite soon after the success of *Orfeo* a comic element began to make its appearance in opera. In 1637 the first public opera-house was opened at Venice by the composer Cavalli, and Venice developed such a passion for opera that within the next half-century there was not merely one opera-house but half a dozen or more in that city.

As soon as opera was thrown open to the general public on payment it necessarily became standardized. The orchestra was standardized, and it is at this date that the quartet of strings becomes its regular normal basis. Plots were standardized too; Venetian audiences did not want stories from ancient mythology, in which the main interest lay in the beauty of the poetry, but stories about human beings, though they did at least want their human beings to be heroes. The history of ancient Rome, and still more of the later Roman Empire, was the favourite material of the operatic poets; but a love-interest was required too, and gradually a sort of standard form was evolved in which we generally find four princes and three princesses whose love-affairs resemble more or less a game of musical chairs. The comic element became more and more prominent; here we see the influence of the comedy of masks. Still more important was the scenery; it was a great age of engineering, and the transformations and other spectacular effects, if they really answered to the stage directions and the designs that have come down to us, must have been far beyond anything that our most ingenious and ostentatious producers can show us today.

Venice was a city of great wealth and a great international centre of trade; the only places which could attempt to follow its example were Hamburg and London. But the opera spread from Venice to various other cities in Italy and also to Vienna and other German courts. We must cast a brief glance at the beginnings of opera outside Italy.

The imperial court at Vienna was in those days the most magnificent in Europe, and it was always closely in touch with Italy, especially with Venice. Italian operas, chiefly by Cavalli and another Venetian, Cesti, were produced at Vienna on the most sumptuous scale; the designs for scenery by Burnacini, who worked chiefly at Vienna, are among the most beautiful that have ever been made for the stage. Munich, Stuttgart, and other small German courts followed the example of Vienna as lavishly as they were able.

In Paris there had been various performances of a spectacular kind, and some of them served as models for the English masques; the most famous was the *Ballet comique de la Reine,* organized by Balthazar de Beaujoyeulx (who was really an Italian) in 1581. It was more like a masque than an opera, and the music was put together by various composers. From 1643 onwards Cardinal Mazarin made continual attempts to establish Italian opera in Paris, perhaps more from political than from artistic motives, but it was a long time before he had any success. Madame de Motteville was on duty as a lady-in-waiting at an Italian opera in February 1644, and wrote in her memoirs that there were only about twenty people in the room, "and we all thought we should have died of cold and boredom." In 1655 Michel de la Guerre produced an opera to French words, but the French composers achieved nothing of real importance. Cavalli himself was brought over by Mazarin in 1660 and his *Serse* (Xerxes) was given with magnificent scenery by the great Italian engineer Torelli, but there were endless intrigues among the Italians themselves as well as the intrigues of the French musicians, who were always bitterly jealous of the Italians, and Cavalli finally left Paris in disgust. French audiences did not really care for Italian music; they found it too noisy and violent. It is difficult for us who are accustomed to Verdi and Puccini to find passion and violence in the Italian operas of the seventeenth century, but there is definite evidence to prove that the French regarded them as almost an outrage on good taste.

Giovanni Battista Lulli, born of humble parents at Florence in 1639, was discovered by the Chevalier de Guise on his way from Malta to Paris in 1646 and taken by him to France, where he was soon handed over to Mademoiselle de Montpensier as a sort of page boy. His natural gift for singing and dancing attracted attention to him, and so did his talent for making scurrilous songs. He eventually became a sort of companion to the boy King Louis XIV and danced with the King himself in the court ballets. After various collaborations with Molière in plays with ballets, he astutely managed to secure a patent from the King giving him the sole right to produce operas in Paris, and produced the first really notable French opera, *Les Fêtes de l'Amour et de Bacchus,* in 1672.

If ever opera was a court function, it was in the days of Louis XIV. Every opera of Lulli had to begin with a prologue of gods and goddesses in praise of the King, and the whole opera was carried out in a style that reflected the stiffness of court etiquette. To our ears Lulli's music sounds dry and conventional; how much of it was actually Lulli's is very uncertain, for he employed several assistants. But the conception of the whole was his, as was the characteristic style of the recitative, entirely different from that of the Italians, although as a matter of fact Lulli never learned to speak French correctly himself. The declamation is said to have been modelled on the great French actors of the day. To French ears the declamation of verse was more interesting than the singing of airs, and both ballet and chorus played a much larger part than in the Italian operas. Lulli's music has little of the inward beauty that we find in his contemporaries Purcell and Scarlatti, but he had a genius for construction on the grand scale, and there are few to equal him for grandeur and stateliness.

England, as one might expect, treated opera as a field for amateurish experiments. Just at the moment when opera might have had a chance of establishing itself, the Civil War put an end to theatrical enterprise. But the Puritans were at any rate lovers of music, and Sir William D'Avenant, who had been the last writer of masques under Charles I, saw that it might be possible to get opera accepted when plays were forbidden. What he really wanted to do was to produce his own heroic dramas in verse; in 1656 he got his play *The Siege of Rhodes* set to music by various composers in collaboration, and produced it on a diminutive stage such as one might find in a village hall of today. But it excited interest, and more operas were given, the music of which was chiefly by Matthew Locke. These English operas were quite unlike the Italian or French ones in subject and style, for they were conceived as plays with incidental music. After the Restoration the theatres were re-opened, and D'Avenant's operas were succeeded by adaptations of Shakspere, such as *The Tempest,* in which large quantities of music to words by D'Avenant were introduced. The best of these so-called operas on a large scale was *King Arthur* (1691), by Dryden and Purcell; but it is not an opera in the modern understanding of the term, for most of the principal characters do not sing at all.

The music of *The Siege of Rhodes* is lost, but we possess that of *Psyche* (1674), a very curious opera by Shadwell and Matthew Locke, imitated (but not adapted) from the French "Psyche" of Molière and Lulli. It could only be revived now as a "museum piece," if at all, but it is interesting as showing the English feeling for picturesqueness in preference to formality. Blow's *Venus and Adonis* (1685), though called a masque, probably because it was performed quite privately at court, is a true opera, for it is set to music all through; it was revived a few years ago by Mr. Rutland Boughton at Glastonbury. *Venus and Adonis* served as the model for Purcell's *Dido and Æneas,* the earliest opera that, in England, at any rate, can almost be called a repertory work and not a mere museum piece.

Dido and Æneas was composed in 1689 for performance at a school for young ladies in Chelsea. The reader will note that neither of these two genuine English operas was intended for the public stage; the English public of those days would probably have refused to tolerate them. Both of them are isolated and exceptional works; one may say that they had neither ancestors nor progeny. They are both of them chamber works; they stand to the public theatre as a string quartet of Mozart does to the great symphonies, and are too delicate and intimate for anything but a small theatre. But *Dido and Æneas* is none the less one of the great masterpieces of early opera. "It lasted only an hour," said a modern opera-goer once, "but I felt as if I had been through all the emotions of *Götterdämmerung!*". . . .

In Germany native opera took much longer to establish than in England and France. The first attempt was made by Heinrich Schütz, a famous composer of Protestant church music. Schütz had been a pupil of Gabrieli at Venice, and in 1627 he got Rinuccini's *Dafne* translated into German by Martin Opitz, a poet of some distinction. It was performed at Torgau, a small town in Saxony, to celebrate the marriage of a princess of the Electoral house. The music is lost, and we cannot even be certain whether Schütz composed new music to the play himself or whether, as is more probable, he arranged the original music of Peri. But the Thirty Years' War (1618–48) was as disastrous to German opera as the Civil War was to English opera. The great German music of the seventeenth century is mostly sacred, and such attempts at German opera as were made in Nuremberg, Leipzig, and Hamburg were mainly on Biblical subjects. The first permanent opera in Germany was started at Hamburg in 1678.

Hamburg was the Venice of the north in those days, and in some ways the life of Hamburg was very like that of Restoration London. Jeremy Collier's denunciations of the London stage were a mere trifle compared to those of the Hamburg clergy, and although Hamburg had begun with a sort of religious opera in 1678, the public soon preferred the works of Reinhard Keiser, whose first opera at Hamburg in 1701 dealt with the crimes of a notorious local highwayman. The Hamburg opera must have been a very rough-and-tumble affair, depending largely on amateur performers. Keiser was a man of wildly dissipated life, but there was a spark of genius in him, and he exercised a powerful influence on the young Handel, who came to Hamburg in 1703.

If we take a general survey of operatic history in the seventeenth century we see at once that the main line of its development lay in Italy, though we must not neglect the very important branch of French opera. French opera was the creation of an Italian, but we shall see that France in the following century had very notable contributions to make to the musical drama. In Italy we see opera initiated by a small coterie of aristocratic intellectuals at Florence. It gradually becomes more professional in style, but for a long time it remains associated with the courts of princes, except at Venice. Even at Venice it can hardly have been a popular entertainment; it must always have been supported by the wealthy classes, and we know that the Venetian theatres were built mostly by the great noble families such as the Grimani. At Bologna it was the Formagliari family who did most to establish opera; at Naples, where opera began with the visit of a Venetian company in 1671, it was dependent on the court of the Spanish viceroys, or of the Austrian viceroys during the years in which Naples belonged to Austria.

Looking at the music of the operas by itself, we see a gradual transformation of style and method. At all periods composers of opera have had to employ the musical language and the musical forms of their own day. . . . We have at all times to take into account the interaction between the theatre and the concert-room. The concert-room standardizes the regular forms of song, dance, fugue, etc., because they are in constant demand there. We ought perhaps to warn the reader that we are using the word "concert-room" not in its modern sense, but simply as a collective term for all the occasions, not of church or stage, where music is performed and listened to for its own sake.

But the theatre, as soon as it was definitely established, gradually became the supply centre of musical expression, as opposed to musical formalism. Musical form is not the contradiction of musical expression, as some amateurs imagine; it is the shaping of a series of sounds in order to make them expressive. Take any simple piece of music that you feel to be expressive, an ordinary hymn-tune or even a chant; the expressiveness is due not merely to the particular note that excites emotion, but to the particular place in which it occurs; if it was put in a different place, it would lose its significance. But expression becomes conventionalized with repetition and loses its emotional force, and it is then that we need the influence of the theatre to stimulate a keener expression of emotion, which in its turn gets transferred to the concert-room and again becomes standardized.

And it often becomes standardized in the theatre too; when that happens we have a period of operatic decadence. But in listening to old operas, and especially to museum pieces, we must try to put ourselves back into their own period and learn to adjust our minds to their methods of expression; and then the value of emotional expression is settled, not by its violence, but by its being placed exactly in the right situation.

The whole tendency of opera in the seventeenth century was to become more musical and less like an ordinary play in verse; that means that the emotion, instead of being distributed more or less evenly throughout the opera (and therefore never covering a very wide range) became concentrated in the songs, while the recitative (which was necessary to carry on the story) became more and more conventional and dull. We notice this all the more in the Italian operas, because the Italian theatre made hardly any use of "background music." A palace may fall to ruins, or a dragon rise from the sea, but the music takes no notice of it whatever. Music had not yet discovered the technique for that sort of thing, and if it had, it would probably have been impossible to synchronize it with the stage effects—we know how difficult it is to achieve this even nowadays in an opera of Wagner.

We notice more and more the over-elaboration of scenic effects and spectacle; if it were possible to carry out an exact reproduction of an opera by Cavalli today, we should probably think that the music was negligible in relation to the scenery. This passion for "machines" was characteristic of the age; it affected the French and English theatres no less than the Italian. It was a worship of mechanism at which we moderns have no right to scoff, for we moderns are at this moment worshipping mechanism just as foolishly, and with considerably less sense of beauty.

The seventeenth century at any rate realized that opera must deal with subjects remote from common life. Shakspere, though he never adopted an operatic attitude to music itself on the stage, had something of the Italian operatic view of drama, in that he separated the lofty style of his tragic and serious parts from the low comedy of his clowns. The opera never attempted comedy of manners, and such a thing did not exist in Italy, even in the spoken drama. An Italian opera by the end of the century bore a considerable resemblance to a Victorian melodrama, with its chivalrous hero, its villain, its persecuted heroine, often in disguise, and its comic servants, male and female. The reason is that English melodrama is actually descended from the opera, just as Victorian pantomimes were descended from the so-called operas of Purcell. The word "melodrama" means "music-drama," and *melodrama* was for most of the seventeenth century the regular name for an opera; we meet it constantly in the word-books, though sometimes the work is called *dramma per musica*. The name *opera* appears to have been a colloquial expression. It penetrated to French and English fairly early in the century; Evelyn's diary speaks of an "Opera (for so they call shews of that kind)" at Rome in 1644; D'Avenant uses the word in 1656. The word *opera*, it need hardly be said, simply means "a work."

Purcell died in 1695 and it so happened that there was no English composer living who was equal to carrying on his work for the theatre. Early in the following century an attempt was made to introduce Italian opera in London, and though the first efforts were not in themselves very successful, Italian opera soon became so firmly established that it exists there still. There was nothing surprising about this. Paris was the only great city which supported an opera of its own in its own language. The German courts all had their Italian operas, and Hamburg was becoming gradually Italianized; Keiser's operas were often sung in a mixture of Italian and German. Madrid and Lisbon set up their Italian operas in the course of the century; Copenhagen and St. Petersburg did the same. All over Europe Italian was the language of music, except in France, and even France had eventually to yield to the Italian invasion, though it did so by the process of swallowing the Italian composers, as it did Lulli, and doing its best to make Frenchmen of them.

In saying that Italian was the language of music, it is not meant that all musicians habitually talked Italian, or even that they always set Italian words to music; though even in the matter of spoken language Italian was certainly the one in which musicians of different nationalities would most probably converse with each other. When Dr. Burney travelled over most of Europe in 1770–72 in search of materials for his *History of Music,* he seems to have found Italian the most useful language, as he had very little knowledge of German. Germany was overrun with Italian musicians, and German musicians had to Italianize their musical style if they wanted to be anything more distinguished than mere church organists. Ever since about 1600 German musicians, if they could possibly manage it, had gone to Italy to learn composition, and even German church music in the seventeenth century shows the ever increasing influence of Italy. Most of the great palaces and churches of the period were not only designed by Italian architects (or at least by pupils of Italians), but actually built by Italian stonemasons, who travelled everywhere, for no country could produce their equals in skill. Readers who have been to Dresden may remember a restaurant on the river near the opera-house, called the "Italienisches Dörfchen" (Italian village); it derives its name from the fact that there actually was an Italian village there in the eighteenth century, inhabited by the descendants of the masons who came to build the court church.

When Handel went to Italy in 1706 as a young man of twenty-one, the greatest composer living was Alessandro Scarlatti, who divided his career between Rome and Naples. Most of his operas were written for Naples, and he is the creator of what was then the standard Italian opera form and style. Today his operas are not even museum pieces, and the only songs from them that are familiar to the ordinary concert-goer, such as "O cessate di piagarmi," belong to his very early works and are not typical of his maturity. The favourite opera songs of Handel will give the general reader a sufficiently adequate idea of his riper style.

Scarlatti's operas show a gradual reform of operatic method, though those reforms led to conventions that a modern musician finds very hard to appreciate. In the first place, the chaotic libretti of the Venetians were simplified and made more dignified in style; the poets were in all probability influenced by the plays of Racine. We see the comic characters being kept in order and put in their proper place; they gradually sink like a sediment to the ends of the acts—in the third act entering just before the final *dénouement,* which is really an untying of knots. A little later on, the two comic characters drop out of the opera altogether, and their scenes become *intermezzi* which could without trouble be transferred from one opera to another.

In the second place, Scarlatti is responsible for the standardization of the aria in the *da capo* form that is the horror of musicians nowadays. His own audiences would never have felt that there was anything odd about it; it was much clearer and more concise, capable, too, of more intense expression, than the forms it superseded. It could be adapted to any emotion—joy, sorrow, rage, despair. Scarlatti also invented the accompanied recitative, as it is called. Most recitative, the dull parts which had to get on with the story of the play, was accompanied only by the harpsichord in what is called *recitativo secco,* dry recitative, as many writers have with obvious facetiousness observed. To bring in the stringed instruments to accompany recitative created a new emotional atmosphere. Most readers will remember the way in which Bach, in the "St. Matthew Passion," always brings in the string quartet to accompany the words of Jesus. We have been taught to notice this effect in Bach, but we are apt to neglect it in the oratorios of Handel, for few singers and conductors realize that the entry of the strings means a change of mood and a new emotional atmosphere in the character who is singing.

A third and a very important invention of Scarlatti was the "ensemble of perplexity," which is still characteristic of opera and a valuable means of effect that cannot be obtained in a spoken play. A situation arises, affecting perhaps four characters on the stage, each in a different way; they express their feelings simultaneously in a quartet. Sullivan parodied the device in *The Mikado*—"Here's a how-de-do!" Old Scarlatti had parodied himself nearly two centuries before.

It is appropriate at this point to discuss some of the conventions of opera which are apt to irritate unmusical people and those who expect absolute realism in opera. Even in the eighteenth century, as we shall see, some people objected to the action being held up in order that a singer might show off his voice. But the cause for objection lay not in the musical form but in the music with which second-rate composers filled it. Nobody ever complained of the ensembles in *Carmen* or *Die Meistersinger* for holding up the action, simply because the music is so enthralling that we only wish it would go on longer.

Supposing that in some play a messenger comes on and says: "The queen is dead." This is a mere piece of information; it must be made as clear as possible, so that nobody can miss it. In an opera, therefore, it must be stated in recitative. But the queen's death will certainly produce various emotional states in the characters on the stage, possibly in the messenger himself. Any actor knows how difficult it is to express these emotions if he has no words to say. A poet can give him words, though they are not the words he would use in private life; the musician must give him music to sing, and the shape of that music will depend partly on the quality of the emotion and partly on the normal musical style of the period. Handel will have to do it one way, Wagner another; their styles will differ just as Shakspere's will from a modern poet's. The musician, especially in Handel's day, will hold up the action longer than the poet; but it is a curious property of music that it can destroy our sense of time, as long as it really holds our interest. An "ensemble of perplexity," if it were spoken, would probably be unimpressive and possibly ridiculous; even if a great poet achieved it, the actors would find it curiously difficult to speak, for it would have to be timed accurately and very carefully rehearsed, so that the different speeches dovetailed into one another like a piece of music. Like a piece of music—music does this for the singers without their having to think about the technique of it.

Handel's operas are mentioned here in preference to Scarlatti's because most English readers are more or less familiar with the Handelian style of music; moreover since 1920 there has been a great revival of Handel's operas in Germany, although their vogue is now already over and they have returned once more to our category of museum pieces. Between 1711 and 1741 Handel produced nearly forty operas on the London stage. Scarlatti's last opera came out in 1721 and Handel, whose real genius belonged to the theatre, carried the Scarlattian type of opera to its climax; but by force of external circumstances Handel's operatic career was on the whole a failure.

Italian opera now began to be a profitable business, and Italy's chief export. What made the success of Italian opera was not so much the music as the singers, and here we must speak of that curious phenomenon the Italian artificial soprano. It had been discovered more than a hundred years before that a boy's treble voice could be preserved by a barbarous surgical operation, and it was further discovered that in favourable cases such voices could be immensely strengthened in the course of years. This horrible practice did not begin in the theatre, but in the church, owing to the difficulty of obtaining good choirboys in Italy; it was officially condemned, but connived at in practice, and singers of this type were singing in the Papal choir at Rome almost up to the end of the nineteenth century. As far as can be ascertained, the practice was confined exclusively to Italy, with the exception of a small number of Germans; male sopranos dominated the operatic stage in all countries except France, but the singers themselves were Italian. Dr. Burney made great efforts to find out where the operation was generally performed, but there was not unnaturally some mystery about it; he came, however, to the conclusion that Naples, as one might expect, was the chief source of supply.

The first Italian male soprano heard in England was Siface, who came over at the desire of Mary of Modena, wife of James II, about 1687; he had previously been a member of the Pope's chapel. The last who appeared on the English stage was Velluti, who sang in London in 1825; he died in 1861. For practically two centuries all the hero parts in Italian opera were sung by sopranos (or sometimes contraltos) of this kind; at certain periods women were forbidden altogether to sing on the stage in Rome, and male sopranos had to take female parts as well. In the early days of Italian opera in London, on the other hand, the male soprano parts were sometimes sung by women. Nicolini, whose acting was highly praised by Addison, was the first to make a success on the London stage. Out of the thousands who submitted to the operation, only comparatively few attained eminence, but the most famous of them obtained gigantic salaries, especially in London.

The great difficulty of reviving Handelian or even later Italian opera nowadays lies in the fact that the chief male parts were always written for sopranos. If they are sung by women, they lose their dramatic character; we find it difficult today to tolerate even a female Siebel in Gounod's *Faust,* though we still accept Mozart's Cherubino. (The reason is that Siebel is a serious character and Cherubino a comic one.) If we transpose the music for tenors, the music suffers, especially as hardly any modern tenors can sing the florid passages. The singers of the eighteenth century, and especially the male sopranos, cultivated an extraordinary agility in florid passages; audiences of those days delighted in a type of *coloratura* that would have horrified even the age of Patti. The only opera songs approaching that style which are heard now are those of Mozart, and even the songs of Costanza in *Seraglio* and of the Queen of Night in *The Magic Flute* are simple compared with the flourishes every singer was expected to throw off in the days of Handel.

Opera had indeed become no more than a concert in costume, though there were a few composers who maintained a fairly high standard. The curious thing is that just at this very moment there arose the strange case of a librettist who was a real poet—Metastasio. His first drama for music was *Didone,* set to music by Vinci in 1724. Metastasio devoted his life to writing libretti for operas; they have great dramatic force, within their peculiar convention, and they belong to the great things of Italian literature—on this point all Italian critics are agreed. The result was that every composer in Italy, and many outside, set Metastasio's dramas to music over and over again; some composers even set the same play twice, to entirely different music. Audiences of those days must have known the plays by heart, and this tended even more to turn operas into a sort of singing competition.

All this time France remained severely apart. Lulli died in 1681 and his tradition was continued by Campra and Destouches; in 1739 Rameau, then no longer a young man, started on his career as an opera-composer. Rameau's operas, for some of which Voltaire furnished the words, have all the stiff ceremonial of Lulli's, but Rameau was a really great musician and his operas have fairly recently been revived in Paris with no less success than those of Handel in Germany. Rameau's music is little known in England, except a few of his harpsichord pieces; unfortunately the performance of one of his operas would entail enormous labour and expense if it was to be at all adequate. His subjects, like those of Lulli, are chiefly classical, but treated in the manner of Racine, one may say; the declamatory recitative, of which Rameau was a consummate master, was a great attraction for his own audiences. The songs, exquisite as they are, seldom have the passion or grandeur of Handel's; on the other hand, the choruses and ballets are magnificent. The art of Rameau was essentially French, and intimately associated with the French language.

Practically all the operas we have so far considered were composed for court theatres and for audiences of highly cultivated people with a dignified taste both in literature and in music. The modern reader may think it shocking that in those days culture was the privilege of an aristocracy, but it was culture carried to a very high degree. . . .

We must now turn to an altogether different type of musical drama, which from the eighteenth century onwards has acquired increasing importance—comic opera.

Quite early in the seventeenth century there had been attempts at comic opera, especially at Rome, and one or two composers produced some very amusing scenes of popular life, but there was no continuous tradition of comic opera as a genre by itself until 1709, when a little theatre at Naples was opened for operas in the local dialect dealing with everyday characters instead of classical heroes. Even the great Scarlatti himself wrote a comic opera for this theatre, in 1718, when he was nearly sixty, and he seems to have thoroughly enjoyed making fun of his own grand manner. Pergolesi's *La Serva Padrona* (1733) gives some idea of their musical style, but this charming little work is not a real comic opera of its period; it is only a set of comic *intermezzi* intended for performance between the acts of a serious opera. The comic operas were generally in three acts, and sometimes even had their own comic *intermezzi*. They were generally performed by people who regarded themselves as actors; the artificial sopranos never sang in them, although the custom was kept up of giving the chief male parts to high voices, sung by women in male costume. We see here the origin of the "principal boy" of a Victorian pantomime or musical comedy.

A Neapolitan comic-opera company came to London in 1740 and performed *La Serva Padrona* with fair success, but its great reputation was made in 1752, when an Italian company acted it in Paris. The visit of this company was the cause of the famous *guerre des bouffons,* the war of the musicians (and still more of the journalists) over the relative merits of French and Italian music. The ultimate victory was with Italy; French audiences were becoming tired of the grand academic manner of Rameau and could hardly resist the natural spontaneous humour of the Italians and their lively tunefulness. Here it may be mentioned that in those days French opera was unbearable to anyone who was not a Frenchman; both English and Italian travellers give the most ludicrous accounts of it—to their ears it simply was not music at all.

Pergolesi was by no means a great composer; his grand operas are often dull and carelessly written, and Martini, the learned theorist who taught Mozart as a boy, quite rightly said that his famous "Stabat Mater" was in the style of a musical comedy. But he is a historic figure, and he had a certain sentimental charm so attractive that it conquered the whole of musical Europe. . . . [A] complete change of musical language . . . took place at this time in German instrumental music, the change from the suites and concertos of J. S. Bach to the sonatas of his son Emanuel and the symphonies of the men who just preceded Haydn and Mozart. The new style of melody was not their invention; it came from Naples, from the trivial comic operas which everybody wanted to hear. People in provincial towns north of the Alps, who could not go to see an Italian opera, wanted to play the music at home on their own violins and harpsichords; the composers provided them with suitable sonatas. Electors and prince-bishops wanted Italian musical-comedy tunes played during dinner; as their chapel-masters could not obtain the originals (for they were never printed), they composed something that sounded much the same. And they wrote sonatas and symphonies, not because they thought there was anything particularly noble or uplifting about that particular form, but simply because it was the ordinary musical form of the opera songs, whether serious or frivolous.

More Italian comic operas came to Paris; Naples was always the chief source of supply, but Venice contributed a good many. A composer from Parma, Egidio Romualdo Duni, settled in Paris, followed the example of Lulli in writing his name as Duny, and created a prolific school of French comic opera, in which he was followed by Monsigny, Dalayrac, and others. The main difference between the French and Italian comic operas was that the French preferred the connecting dialogue spoken, whereas the Italians always stuck to recitative.

In England there was a similar wave of comic opera; but it had begun much earlier, with a more or less native product. In 1728 there came out *The Beggar's Opera,* a brilliant social and political satire by John Gay; it also satirized the Italian opera in its form, as it contained a large number of amusing songs which Dr. Pepusch, a learned German musical antiquary, adapted to the popular tunes of the day. People sometimes talk of *The Beggar's Opera* as if it was all made up of English folk-songs, but many of them were of French or Italian origin, and there were bits of Purcell and Handel as well. Gay's amusing sequel to this opera, *Polly,* was forbidden performance by the censorship of the government; the enormous crop of English "ballad operas" which delighted popular audiences up to the end of the century gradually drifted more and more into mere namby-pamby sentimentality. Italian influence made itself felt in London, as in Paris; Galuppi of Venice enjoyed an enormous vogue, and his comic operas contributed a good deal towards the formation of the characteristic English style.

England being always closely in touch with Hamburg, the first English ballad operas made their way to Germany, and just as the German theatre owed its rise to the visit of the English actors in the days of Shakspere, so

German comic opera derived its origin from English music. J. A. Hiller and Dittersdorf were the most successful composers in this line. German comic opera, however, was also influenced by the Italians; Galuppi had been fortunate enough to have librettos written for him by the famous playwright Goldoni, and Goldoni's librettos were often adapted by the German composers.

Let us pause for a moment and review the general operatic situation of Europe as it was about 1760. We saw opera start in Florence as the experiment of a few intellectuals. It is taken up as a diversion for princes. Venice commercializes it and to some extent vulgarizes it, but at the same time gives it an impetus that causes it to spread beyond the Alps. Wherever it goes, it requires the patronage of a cultivated court; if it fails to find that soil, it degenerates either artistically, as at Hamburg, or financially, as in London. The small Italian courts lose their political importance, and in the eighteenth century their place (as far as opera is concerned) is taken by Paris and the German courts that are trying to follow the model set up by Louis XIV. In Paris opera is French, but everywhere else it is Italian. Italy makes the operas and exports them, along with composers, singers, players, and scene-painters. For Italy, at any rate, it is a huge commercial business, and as soon as opera becomes commercial, it becomes degraded. French grand opera only survived up to the end of Rameau's days because it was purely French.

Comic opera as a work of art (for we can regard the Neapolitan comedies as artistic) could only come into being after serious opera had established a routine technique of composition. It was a welcome reaction against the overconventionalized form of the grand opera which it often satirized; but comic opera became commercialized even faster than serious opera, because it was cheaper to produce and more lucrative to undertake. When the last performance of Rameau's *Dardanus* took place, in 1760, there was not a single composer in Europe whose operas had the least claim to distinction, except Hasse at Dresden and Jommelli at Stuttgart, the last survivors of the dignified old Italian style.

The moment was right for the historic reforms of Gluck. . . .

E. J. D.

Ludwig van Beethoven

(Bonn, Germany, Dec. 16, 1770–Mar. 26, 1827, Vienna)

Ludwig van Beethoven was, as the prefix *van* indicates, of Flemish ancestry. He was . . . the son of Johann van Beethoven, a tenor in the chapel choir of the Elector of Bonn. His musical gifts made themselves manifest during his early boyhood, and the father, seeing in the lad a second Mozart and hoping to reap financial gain thereby, cruelly forced him to practice an inordinate length of time, much to the neglect of his general education. His musical training was for a time under the supervision of his ne'er-do-well father and later under Tobias Pfeifer, a wandering actor-musician who boarded with the family. These youthful influences were of great significance in the formation of Beethoven's character. Maltreated and abused, with no one in whom he might confide or trust, it is small wonder that he felt himself isolated and excluded from the world. Deprived of the rudiments of a general education, suffering because of the social inferiority of his family and the degradation brought upon it by his drunkard father, Beethoven developed a character and personality for which artistic expression served as the sole means of relief. The few benevolent forces that operated upon Beethoven during his youth in Bonn were the chapel organist, Neefe, who gave him conscientious and sympathetic instruction, and the cultured von Breuning family, at whose home he was a frequent visitor. Eventually he became Neefe's assistant. In 1787 Beethoven journeyed to Vienna. He played before Mozart, who is said to have been impressed by his ability to extemporize, but the illness of his mother brought the youth back to Bonn before anything materialized from this artistic contact.

Two events, both of great importance in Beethoven's artistic development, occurred after his return to Bonn. The first was the beginning of his acquaintanceship with the young Count Ferdinand von Waldstein, the earliest of the many cultured, art-loving members of the nobility who through their interest and magnanimity aided in the unfolding of Beethoven's talents. The second was the formation in 1788 of an opera company at the Electoral Court. Beethoven became a member of the opera orchestra, playing viola. The significance of this activity on his part cannot be overestimated. As a youth in his late 'teens, he was enabled to become intimately acquainted with the mechanism of the orchestra and, through participation in performance, to learn the important works of the time, notably the operas of Mozart. In July 1792 Haydn, returning from the first series of his London concerts, stopped at Bonn. Beethoven was introduced to him and showed him some of his compositions. It has often been surmised that Haydn invited him to be his pupil,

17

although direct evidence is lacking. In November of the same year Beethoven again set out for Vienna, to remain there for the rest of his life.

After his arrival in the Austrian capital Beethoven immediately busied himself with study. His teachers were Haydn, with whom his relations were neither happy nor fruitful; Albrechtsberger, who gave him over two years of instruction in counterpoint; and Salieri, under whom he studied dramatic composition. Mozart had been dead for a year and the stage was now set for the appearance of a pianist of Beethoven's abilities. It was not long before his phenomenal pianistic talents were known to most of the nobility of Vienna. His services were much in demand and so rapidly did his fame increase that he appeared as soloist at several benefit concerts. During these early years he also came in contact with other princely patrons and counselors—Prince Karl Lichnowsky, Baron van Swieten, and Prince Lobkowitz.

For some time Beethoven's proficiency as a pianist obscured public recognition of him as a composer. One of his first public successes was won by his Septet in E-flat Major, Opus 20 (for violin, viola, 'cello, double bass, clarinet, bassoon, and horn), which with its piquant instrumentation and attractive melodies immediately became popular. On the same program in which the Septet was first performed publicly (there had been prior private performances at the Schwarzenberg Palace), the First Symphony also had its première (April 2, 1800). This work was not well received and, like many of the other works which followed, was at first deemed eccentric and perverse by the Viennese. These initial condemnations, however, were almost invariably short-lived and were quickly supplanted by general approbation and enthusiasm.

The period 1799–1814 is an astounding record of artistic creativeness. During this comparatively short time Beethoven composed eight symphonies, three concertos for piano, a concerto for violin, seven sonatas for piano, eleven string quartets, much other chamber music, the opera *Leonore,* and the music for Goethe's "Egmont," as well as many shorter works. The Viennese public quickly came to appreciate the unique genius living in their midst; and at one time (1808–1809), when it seemed as if he might be lost to the city because of an offer of the post of Kapellmeister at the court of Jerome Bonaparte at Cassel, the Archduke Rudolph and the Princes Lobkowitz and Kinsky came forward and guaranteed him an annual income if he would remain. Unfortunately, the intrinsic value of this financial settlement was much reduced afterwards by monetary inflation. Nevertheless this magnanimous act is a clear indication of Beethoven's importance in the musical life of Vienna as well as of the artistic discernment of his patrons.

Beethoven's success, however, was marred by the greatest misfortune that could possibly befall a musician—deafness. The disease had made itself manifest as early as 1799, and in a most moving document, a letter to his brother written in 1802, Beethoven pathetically described his own despair at the life of isolation that lay before him. By 1814 the deafness had become so complete that he was prevented from making any further appearances as a soloist. At the first performance of the great Ninth Symphony in 1824, the composer, who sat on the stage, had to be turned around so that he might see the tumultuous applause which the second movement had brought forth.

Yet another cause for unhappiness was the composer's disappointment in love. Several ladies of the upper classes were the objects of his affection, but his uncouthness and personal unattractiveness coupled with the rigid class distinctions of the period caused his aspirations to end in bitter frustration.

A nephew, the son of his brother Kaspar, became his ward in 1815. Beethoven, seeking some outlet for the abundant store of affection pent up within him, lavished all manner of care and attention upon the unworthy youth. Much to his uncle's dismay he turned out to be a weak individual, unsuccessful even in an attempt to commit suicide (1826).

Because of his deafness, Beethoven became quite detached from the active musical life of Vienna; but so great had his fame become that individuals came from far and wide to see him. Inasmuch as the composer could not hear, remarks had to be addressed to him in writing. Fortunately, these "conversation books" have been preserved. A commission to compose music even came from so distant a point as Boston, Massachusetts. The English piano manufacturer Broadwood presented Beethoven with one of his new grand pianos; another English admirer sent him a forty-volume set of the works of Handel.

All this attention, however, must be regarded as superficial. The last decade of Beethoven's life was spent in complete spiritual isolation. But this isolation bore magnificent artistic fruit—the "Missa Solemnis," the Ninth Symphony, and the last string quartets—works which in their intense subjectivity, vastness of dimensions, and absolute freedom from convention, present serious problems to the listener.

In December 1826 signs of dropsy made themselves manifest, and after much suffering Beethoven died on March 26, 1827.

M. B.

Fidelio

OPERA IN 2 ACTS

Book by JOSEPH SONNLEITHNER and GEORG FRIEDRICH TREITSCHKE after a
drama by JEAN NICOLAS BOUILLY

First performance: Theater an der Wien, Vienna, Nov. 20, 1805

CHARACTERS

Florestan, a Spanish nobleman, TENOR
Leonore, his wife, who disguises herself
and takes the name of *Fidelio,* so-
PRANO
Don Fernando, Prime Minister of Spain
and friend of Florestan, BASS

Pizarro, governor of the prison, and
enemy of Florestan, BASS
Rocco, chief jailer, BASS
Marcellina, Rocco's daughter, SOPRANO
Jacquino, Rocco's assistant, in love with
Marcellina, TENOR

Prisoners, Guards, Soldiers, and People

*The action takes place in the eighteenth century at a fortress used for the confine-
ment of political offenders, near Seville, Spain*

Fidelio is the story of Leonore, faithful wife of Florestan, a Spanish nobleman
unjustly imprisoned by his enemy, the evil Pizarro. Refusing to believe the false
reports of Florestan's death, Leonore disguises herself as a youth, Fidelio, and
obtains employment in the prison under Rocco, the chief jailer. The opera opens
on a scene of traditional comedy between Rocco's daughter, Marcellina, who has
fallen in love with the gentle Fidelio and refuses to marry her former sweetheart,
the turnkey, Jacquino, now unhappy and jealous.

Fidelio prevails upon Rocco to let her accompany him to the more secret portions
of the prison, hoping to see her husband and help him escape. Meanwhile news has
arrived that Don Fernando, Prime Minister of Spain, is expected any moment on a
visit to the jail. Don Fernando is a close friend of Florestan and his coming endangers
Pizarro's hatred and revenge, which he expresses in the passage, "Ha, Welch' ein
Augenblick," a distillation of pure rage. Summoning Rocco, he orders the old man
to kill Florestan, and when Rocco refuses, Pizarro declares he will commit the murder himself, and sends Rocco to dig the grave. Fidelio overhears the plot, singing
her great faith in the power of love, "Abscheulicher, wo eilst du hin?" one of the
high points of the opera. Descending to the dungeon with Rocco, she first fails to
recognize Florestan, so changed is he with suffering. Pizarro enters with a dagger,
and Fidelio throws herself between them and cries out her identity. For a moment
Pizarro is staggered, but he raises the dagger again and is about to strike when
Fidelio draws a pistol and points it at Pizarro's head. Florestan is saved, a flourish
of trumpets is heard, and Don Fernando appears to bring freedom and justice to the
prisoners.   W. H., P. Z.

When Beethoven, in his letter to Wegeler in 1801, spoke of his success in all musical forms except those of "opera and the church," he was revealing an ambition, which, at least so far as the opera was concerned, lay close to his heart. His eagerness when the opportunity came to him in 1804 overrode a certain lack of working experience, for his expertness in theatre craft was necessarily drawn from nothing more substantial than the routine at Bonn, his studies of vocal writing with Salieri, his perusal of available scores by Cherubini, Méhul, or other contemporaries, and his direct observation in the theatres of Vienna, where he was often seen.

The crowded performances were a reminder of the glory which was showering upon talents far less than his own. Cherubini, much applauded in Paris, held his great respect. There was Paisiello in Naples; Päer, lately settled in Dresden. In Vienna Salieri, Vogler, Seyfried, had enjoyed the production of many a stage piece, reaping esteem and reward. Beethoven hoped and strove mightily to do the same. The impresarios of Vienna remembered the success of his Ballet "The Creations of Prometheus." They were aware that his name would arouse anticipation and they were ready to gamble with it.

Since opera was the only form of music in Vienna which coincided with public entertainment, it alone could bring the ducats rolling in. Cherubini afforded an example of a long famous composer discovered overnight in Vienna to be an effective writer of operas. In 1803, when the operas of Cherubini had been given in Italy and Paris for some twenty years, Schikaneder at the Theater-an-der-Wien and Baron Braun at the Burg Theater awoke suddenly to the fact that a golden opportunity was at hand. They fell over each other's heels importing his latest operas from Paris, and even came out simultaneously with the same piece, differently titled. Schikaneder offered to provide Beethoven with an opera libretto which he himself would write, and Beethoven received the idea favorably. He moved into the Theater building where free lodgings were allowed him, according to custom, and is supposed to have made some sketches for an opera of which not even the subject is known. In the following season, Braun bought out the Theater-an-der-Wien. Schikaneder was excluded —so was Beethoven, from his opera project and probably from his lodgings as well. But fortune soon turned his way again. In November, 1804, the Baron put his former rival in charge of the theatre—a tribute to the value of that arch-showman, and presently we find Beethoven back in his lodgings and at work upon another opera. The text was a German adaptation which Sonnleithner, Secretary of the Burg Theater, had made of a French piece then six years old—Bouilly's "Léonore."

There began a struggle intense and prolonged. Beethoven alone with his libretto must subdue to his purpose an adversary far different from the pliant and responsive instruments which had always leapt to serve his greater thoughts. Now there were prosaic stretches of text, stage situations which must become a part of him and would not, the necessity of holding down his beloved orchestra as a background for vocal advantage. To adapt himself to the traditional *Singspiel* of the expired eighteenth century, infusing the stylized airs and ensembles with true and moving dramatic expressiveness, would have required a performer of miracles, a Mozart at the very least. Beethoven sometimes performed miracles, but he was not temperamentally constituted for this one. Mozart had the touch and go of the theatre which could accept an inanity without hesitation and on the instant turn it into music of immortal beauty. Beethoven approached his subject slowly, laboriously, from within. In those parts where the characters and their dilemma took hold of him, the sheer power of his conviction overcame wooden conventions, and the story came to moving life. In none of his works was there a more remarkable manifestation of his will power.

The first libretto proposed to Beethoven (other than what he may have had from Schikaneder, the stage clown who wrote *The Magic Flute* text) was an extraordinarily happy choice. It was not a good piece of literature—no libretto of its day was that. But the subject had sprung from French revolutionary ideals; it played upon the great, all-absorbing motive of liberation from tyranny, and was consequently the one subject that could have set Beethoven on fire. Bouilly, a French lawyer, and the librettist of Cherubini's *The Water Carrier,* had written the original book for Paris in 1798, as "Léonore, ou l'Amour Conjugal," and Gaveaux had set it. Bouilly let it be known in his memoirs that the tale of the imprisonment of Florestan by a political enemy, and the efforts of his wife, Léonore, to liberate him by disguising herself as a jailer at the risk of her life, had a basis of fact in the days of the Terror. He had also intimated that he had set the scene in Spain for discretionary reasons. The book had been popular enough to make its way, in those days of free borrowing, into three languages. Paër had composed a score for an Italian version, *Leonora,* which opened the Dresden season in 1804, just at the time that Beethoven began to compose his German version. Sonnleithner had been called into service for this translation. The title was changed to *Fidelio,* so as to avoid confusion with Paër's opera; Beethoven naturally much preferred the real name to the assumed name of his heroine, and struggled in vain to keep the title. He showed his preference by naming two overtures "Leonore" when they were separately performed and published.

Beethoven could not rise above those scenes in Bouilly's text which were no more than a typical romantic effusion of the time. But the concept of cruel oppression overcome through a conjugal fidelity all-enduring and all-surpassing was to Beethoven more than the current coin of romantic tale-telling. It was a vitalizing impulse transcending pedestrian dialogue and stock situations. The pity of Florestan wasting away his life in a dungeon with no gleam of hope became something for every generation to feel, whatever its fashion in sentiment. The plight of his fellow prisoners, wan shadows of the men they once were—Beethoven lived and suffered in these with a compassion which too has outlasted all fashions. Leonore was to him woman's love at its noblest, deep and quiet, unfaltering and unquestioning.

Beethoven composed the scenes in order, as if to preserve in his own mind the continuity of unfoldment. The many pages of the sketchbooks, an astonishing tangle of notations decipherable only to himself, are proof of his devotion to his task, but proof no less of his labors to subjugate a resistant medium to his expressive intent. He made eighteen beginnings to the famous air "In des Lebens Frühlingstagen" before he found what he was seeking: the full sense of Florestan's hopeless vision of the fair world which has been shut out to him. The jubilant final chorus "O namenlose Freude" was also arrived at by many stages.

Beethoven retired to Hetzendorf for the summer months of 1805 and between June and September made his last rounding out of the score. Returning to Vienna and his quarters in the Theater-an-der-Wien, he was able to hand to Sebastian Meier the complete music in performable shape. The opera was promptly put into rehearsal.

And now began the first episode in the unfortunate early career of *Fidelio*. When the initial performance was announced the attention of all Vienna was distracted by fearful speculations. The armies of France were moving steadily up the Rhine Valley, and across Southern Germany. Austria lay before them, and Austria's capital would be Napoleon's certain objective. Ulm fell on October 20th, and ten days later the news came that the boundary had been crossed. Bernadotte was in occupation of Salzburg. The progress down the Danube continued. Vienna, fair and proud, inviolate through her centuries, lay quite undefended. The nobility packed their jewels in their carriages and joined the trek of refugees which crowded the roads to Brünn or Pressburg. The best male singers were not available for *Fidelio*. Demmer, a tenor successful in light rôles, had little idea of the character of Florestan. The villainous Don Pizzaro fell to Sebastian Meier, who was a better stage manager than baritone. Anna Pauline Milder, the Leonore, had an ample voice; it was when she was only fourteen that Haydn had listened to her and exclaimed: "My dear child, you have a voice like a house!" Milder was to become famous in this part, but only later, with maturity and experience. She was now only twenty. The conscientious Seyfried rehearsed the opera, but the rehearsals were hasty and preoccupied. The tension and uncertainty which gripped Vienna made its way to the stage and orchestra.

On November 13th, just a week before the scheduled first performance, the French battalions marched into Vienna. Napoleon had let it be known through his generals that he was the well-wisher of the Austrians, their protector against Russian barbarism. The Viennese were to be treated with courtesy; even the volunteer guards were to be left unmolested. The citizens did not know how to receive the invaders. The procession was a strange spectacle, and they gazed upon it in curious silence. The invaders were silent too. The emblazoned *grenadiers á cheval* were proud figures in their polished cuirasses, but the horses under them looked dejected. The infantry were mud-splashed and unshaven; here and there one carried a loaf of bread or a ham on the point of his bayonet. They seemed to come without end, day and night, some marching on toward Hungary or northward, some pitching camp in the suburbs, the officers taking occupation of the princely mansions in the town. The reports of distant cannon could be heard; it was said that the French were engaged in a terrific battle with the Russians, that the Austrian army to the south was being annihilated by the Italians. But nothing was known. All communication was suppressed and, with it, all news. What could not be concealed was the presence of French wounded who were being brought in on stretchers from the Russian front. Austrian prisoners, too, were herded in. They could give no clear information except that the country was laid waste, the armies were living on it, and the people were starving.

The magistrates as much as ordered the townspeople to ignore what might be going on about them, and to forget their troubles in the pleasures of their parks. The Court Theatres were commanded to be kept open. *Othello* was acted before an empty house on the night before the occupation. Operas of Cherubini or Zingarelli were to follow *Fidelio* at intervals.

There was no excitement over *Fidelio,* no anticipation. Almost all of Beethoven's friends were away, and those who remained had other things to worry about. The rehearsals were listless. In an over-run Vienna the rigid presence of men at arms seemed to make the private misfortunes of a legendary family in Spain dim and unimportant. Beethoven could gaze from his window in the Pasqualati house on the Mölker Bastei toward Hetzendorf and the Schönbrunn gardens where, in the heat of recent summer days, he had dreamed out his *Fidelio.* Now Schönbrunn was heavily guarded, for the Emperor Napoleon sat in state at the Palace, receiving delegations. Napoleon knew nothing of an opera about to be produced, which had been composed a short while before in the paths beneath the Palace window, where his sentries were now pacing. He did not know that the composer, a fiery little man who had once inscribed "Bonaparte" upon a symphony and then thought better of it, was gazing toward the violated Palace and speculating, quite correctly, that his own kind of power was more far-reaching in time and space, its impress upon mankind far more enduring. This proposition would have interested Napoleon not in the least. Music for him had a single function: to soothe and relax. He considered Cherubini taxing, more learned than tuneful. Finding him by chance in Vienna at the time, he patronized him for reasons of good appearance; it was fitting to surround himself with a retinue of culture. He much preferred Paisiello.

On November 20, 1805, *Fidelio* was first unfolded before a scattered assemblage who were mostly French officers, present because the Theater-an-der-Wien was open under orders and there was nothing else to do. Even if they had been able to follow the German text, these men of action would have preferred a more elegant and sprightly show to this one with its drab prison sets, and its woeful tale of virtue oppressed. On the second night, a young doctor from Edinburgh, Henry P. Reeve, attended *Fidelio* and described what he saw. "Beethoven presided at the pianoforte. He is a small, dark, young-looking man, and wears spectacles." Reeve found the plot "a miserable mixture of low manners and romantic situations," "the music equal to any praise." This would look like musical acumen had not the Scottish doctor attended Zingarelli's *Romeo and Juliet* the following week, and found it likewise "above all praise." He finally reports that "a copy of complimentary verses was showered down from the upper balcony at the end of the piece." This vain attempt to stir acclaim for Beethoven is attributable to the faithful Stephan von Breuning. After three performances the public for *Fidelio* vanished altogether and the opera was dropped. Several critics managed to be there, despite conditions, and delivered their post mortems to the effect that Beethoven had written a dull opera without even the interest of his usual startling "singularities." None seemed to suspect that the opera might contain passages of imperishable beauty.

In December, the immediate emergency having passed, Baron Braun decided to give the opera another try; some of the initial expense might be saved, and there was the chance that, given a proper audience, it would after all prove worthy of its composer's reputation. It was generally agreed between the *régisseur* Meier and a group of Beethoven's friends that the first act moved too slowly. It must be cut. A night session was arranged at the Palace of Lichnowsky, at which the act was to be played and discussed with Beethoven. The imperious composer who never permitted questioning of his artistic judgment was strangely meek. He could not afford to be otherwise, for he knew not how to face the problems of dealing with the limitations and vanities of singers, the insistence of the stage director, the behavior of the crowds before the footlights, with their prejudices and their failure to respond at vital moments. All these people must be mollified if the whole venture were to be saved. Compromise on every side for the obdurate Beethoven! A composer like Gluck, who had the theatre in his blood, could follow through his clear intentions to the bitter end. Beethoven knew how to be adamant; but now his unease and inexperience threw him upon the mercy and advice of others.

Treitschke and Meier of the Theater were at Lichnowsky's, and Clement, the leader of the violins. Von Collin, author of "Coriolan" and the playwright Lange would give literary advice. There was the tenor Röckel, a young man of twenty; there was Karl van Beethoven, interested in the salvation of a possible money-getter. Seyfried, as conductor at the theatre and friend of Beethoven, must surely have been present.

Röckel has described the scene:

Meier had prepared me for the coming storm when Beethoven should be advised to leave out three whole numbers in the first act. . . . I had arrived in Vienna only a short while before, and there met Beethoven for the first time. As the whole opera was to be gone through, we went directly to work. Princess Lichnowsky played on the grand piano from the great score, and Clement, sitting in a corner of the room, accompanied with his violin the whole opera by heart, playing all the solos of the different instruments. The extraordinary memory of Clement having been universally known, nobody was astonished by it except myself. Meier and I made ourselves useful by singing as well as we could, he the lower, I the higher parts. Though the friends of Beethoven were fully prepared for the impending battle, they had never seen him in that excitement before, and without the prayers and entreaties of the Princess, an invalid, who was a second mother to Beethoven and acknowledged by himself as such, his united friends were not likely to have succeeded in an enterprise they had undertaken without confidence.

It must have been doubly hard for Beethoven to throw overboard music written with his heart's blood, some of it incomparably fine, and to yield to the combined pressure of his friends on such a subject. Once reconciled, he fell into a mood of reckless gaiety.

When after their efforts from seven until after one o'clock, the sacrifice of the three numbers was accomplished, and when we, exhausted, hungry and thirsty, went to revive ourselves with a splendid supper—then none was happier and gayer than Beethoven. His fury had been replaced by exhilaration. He saw me, opposite to him, intently occupied with a French dish and asked me what I was eating. I answered: "I don't know," and with his lion's voice he roared out: "He eats like a wolf without knowing what! Ha, ha, ha!"

Stephan von Breuning made the necessary condensations of the text, and Beethoven made the necessary excisions in the score. He reduced the acts from three to two. He was urged to re-write the overture. The one then used, and now known as "No. 2," was too symphonic and involved, said the operatic experts. Undertaking a simplification, he became lost in his subject, and quite forgot the grave admonitions that not otherwise could his beloved *Fidelio* make him the successful operatic composer he longed to be. Without a text to cope with, alone with his beloved orchestra, he spoke in his true strength, producing a concert overture which, before the lowered curtain, told far more powerfully than the cumbrous stage could ever tell of loyalty, ringing conviction, joyous release. The new Overture ("No. 3") lost some of the quasi-theatrical directness and impact of the second, and became more symphonically involved. Instead of aiding the illusion to come, it was destined to crush the opening scene between Marcellina at her ironing board and Jaquino, her loutish lover, into silly puppetry. It was not until he made a fourth attempt at an overture and for a later revival wrote the one which still bears the name *Fidelio* that he found the suitable way lightly to bow in the pleasantly jogging, homely level of the opening scene.

The revised score for the second mounting of *Fidelio* was barely ready for rehearsal. There were signs of a favorable reception at the first performance (March 29th), but things did not go well. Beethoven refused to conduct the second performance, for the orchestra, he complained, paid no attention to the dynamic indications. After two performances, the opera was once more withdrawn. Some remarkable critical statements accompanied the second going down of *Fidelio*—one of which referred to the glorious liberating trumpet call as a "postillion horn solo," and another which waved aside the new overture as "abominable cacophony." Breuning attributed the second failure to cabals against the composer. It is easier to believe that Beethoven, unhappy and angry when he could not bring about an adequate performance with only one full rehearsal, became as usual a disrupting force.

Fidelio was mounted again in the following season; its audience perceptibly grew. But Beethoven now conceived the idea that he was being cheated of his full percentage. He went to the office of the Baron Braun and made his complaint. The Baron, knowing of Beethoven's reputed suspiciousness (Roeckel tells this), protested mildly that his employees were trustworthy, and that if there were any shortage in the accounting he would lose more by it than Beethoven. Very likely the audiences would further increase. Until now they had been pretty well limited to the highest-priced seats—the stalls and first rows of the floor. It was to be hoped that the seats above would later be occupied.

"I don't write for the galleries!" exclaimed Beethoven.

"No?" replied the Baron. "My dear sir, even Mozart did not disdain to write for the galleries."

If the Baron wished to bring to an end his troubles with *Fidelio* and its vexatious composer, he could not have hit upon a surer way to do it.

"My score," Beethoven shouted. "Immediately. There will be no more performances. Give me my score!"

The Baron rang a bell and ordered that the score be returned at once to its author. So Beethoven, closing the door upon the career which had been his fondest ambition, found himself with his much-labored manuscript on his hands. Perhaps what had been most infuriating about the intendant's remark was its entire truth. Beethoven could tell himself proudly that he wrote for those of finer perceptions. So did Mozart, but that pupil of the school of necessity knew that to be a successful operatic composer, one must at the same time write for all and sundry. He had found the way, even before he had begun to grow up. Beethoven had not, so far as his opera was concerned, and nothing could have been more bitter to him than to hear it as a taunt from the lips of the man who controlled its destiny. *Fidelio* was quite without the combination of qualities by which the knowing composer contrives to win the mixed thousands in the dark spaces beyond the footlights—grateful displays of vocal-

ism, incisive declamation, lush melody, spectacle, bright costumes, lively choruses. When Beethoven told Braun that he did not write for the galleries, he
should rather have said that when an idea fully possessed him, he was incapable of courting the galleries with broadly externalized effects. His idea
could grow and expand within him until it became irresistible, but not by
resort to the obvious. The transfiguring power latent in *Fidelio* was so without
ostentation that it could pass unnoticed. Only after the revival seven years
later would it begin to win popular understanding.

Nevertheless, he labored with all that was in him to achieve adequate performance and general acceptance. It became his intermittent problem through
about ten years of his life, from the end of 1803, when he made his first sketches,
until 1814, when he made the second complete revision. They were the years
of his greatest fertility. Into none of his music did he put more affectionate
care. When his last illness was upon him, Beethoven extracted from his confusion of papers the manuscript score of *Fidelio* and presented it to Schindler
with the words: "Of all my children, this is the one that cost me the worst
birth-pangs, the one that brought me the most sorrow; and for that reason it
is the one most dear to me."

J. N. B.

The question of which overture or overtures to use in presenting the opera
is answered at the Metropolitan (following Gustav Mahler's example)
by beginning the performance with the *Fidelio* overture and offering "Leonore"
No. 3 as an intermezzo in the darkened house between the two scenes of the
second act. It is scarcely necessary to add that "Leonore" No. 3, widely regarded as the greatest of all overtures, is continually played in concerts.

Paris heard *Fidelio* in a French version, May 5, 1832; London, in German,
May 18, 1832, and in English, June 12, 1835. In Italian, with recitatives by
Balfe of *Bohemian Girl* fame, pursuant to the Italian prejudice against spoken
dialogue in opera, it was further given in London in 1851. The American
première took place at the Park Theater, New York, in an English version,
Sept. 9, 1839. In German it was presented at the Broadway Theater, Dec. 29,
1856.

[The young Metropolitan Opera Company first staged it on November 19,
1884, with the phenomenal Marianne Brandt making her local debut as Leonora
and Leopold Damrosch conducting.]

Vincenzo Bellini

(Catania, Sicily, Nov. 1, 1801–Sept. 24, 1835, Puteaux, near Paris)

Beside the jocund Rossini with his perpetual flow of good humour and *bons mots;* beside the handsome and gay Donizetti, Bellini presents a pale and somewhat effeminate personality. The son of an organist, he was . . . sent to the Naples Conservatoire by a Sicilian nobleman who perceived some promise of music in the sickly child and paid his fees. . . . From Naples he graduated to Milan, where *Il Pirata* was given in 1827. Its expressive lyrical melodies sung by the tenor, Rubini, aroused great enthusiasm, and the opera was soon given in Rome and Paris. *La Straniera* followed in 1829, and next year at the Fenice in Venice a version of *Romeo and Juliet* in which Pasta appeared as Romeo, yet another survival of the *castrato* tradition. Then came real success with *La Sonnambula,* a tragi-comedy with a tenderness and charm that might well regain its former popularity, and *Norma.*

Norma!—what an array of great singers' names is conjured up by that title! Pasta, Grisi, Tietjens, Lilli Lehmann—every great dramatic soprano down to our own day, when Rosa Ponselle has essayed it, has wished to match her powers against Bellini's melodies. Here was the climax of the old classical opera. For though Spontini might adopt the airs of the late Master of Balliol College and claim that, in this sphere of opera, what he did not know was not knowledge, Bellini in *Norma* contrived to breathe life into the statuesque figures, and Norma lives as assuredly as Galatea and will no doubt return to the stage whenever a singer is born capable, and therefore desirous, of singing her music. For, though Bellini had no great resources as a composer, he had great integrity as an artist and set his face against the abuses of his time. What is more important, he could, when at his best, draw—and I use the word advisedly, for *line* was his strong suit—lyrical melody for the voice, in which an absolute firmness and purity of outline were combined with a most sensuous beauty. I can think of no better parallel for his qualities—dangerous as such comparisons between the arts may be—than the draughtsmanship of his contemporary, Ingres, which shows a similar classical firmness of outline and yet the utmost sensuousness of feeling. So, when first I set eyes on the painter's portrait of Mme Moitessier in the National Gallery, I involuntarily exclaimed "Casta diva!".

Bellini never equalled *Norma. Beatrice di Tenda,* produced in 1833 in Venice, had little success and is now forgotten. He went to London for its performance there and thence to Paris, where Rossini procured him a commission from the Théâtre Italien. *I Puritani di Scozia,* Bellini's sole excursion into the popular field of British history, was composed under the eye of Rossini who took a genuine interest in the sickly young man. The opera was produced in 1835 and had a great success, as well it might with such a quartet as Grisi and Giovanni Rubini, Tamburini and Lablache in the cast. *Puritani,* now hardly possible to revive except on some commemorative occasion, contains perhaps the greatest fund of the characteristic Bellinian cantilena, at once sweet and melancholy, which the musical public today knows only at second hand through the melodies of certain pieces by Chopin and Liszt.

On 24 September 1835, within a few weeks of the production of *Puritani,* Bellini was carried off by the disease that had so long cast its shadow over him, at the house of an English admirer at Puteaux just outside Paris, where he had sought refuge and rest. The melodies of *Puritani* fitted to the Office for the Dead were sung at his funeral by members of the operatic cast. Rossini, himself far from well, attended the interment at the Pére Lachaise cemetery in the pouring rain, and headed the subscriptions raised to pay the expenses. He later spent a good deal of time in putting Bellini's affairs in order and securing to his family the fruits of his success.

D. H.

La Sonnambula

[The Somnambulist]

OPERA IN 3 ACTS

Book by FELICE ROMANI

First performance: Teatro Carcano, Milan, Mar. 6, 1831

CHARACTERS

Amina, fiancée of Elvino, SOPRANO
Elvino, a wealthy peasant, TENOR
Lisa, an innkeeper, in love with Elvino,
  SOPRANO
Teresa, a milleress, MEZZO-SOPRANO

Count Rodolfo, lord of the village, BASS
Alessio, a peasant, in love with Lisa,
  BASS
A Notary, TENOR
Peasants and Peasant Women

The action takes place in a Swiss village in the early nineteenth century

Amina, who will shortly marry Elvino, a wealthy countryman, is addicted to sleepwalking and one night in her sleep walks into the chambers of Rodolfo, who is staying at the inn, and enjoying at the moment Amina arrives the attentions of Lisa, the inn's mistress. Rodolfo, observing Amina's condition, courteously leaves the room to her as she lies down in his bed. Lisa, who has been the loser in the competition for Elvino, spreads the news that Amina has been indiscreet with Rodolfo. A highly curious group, including an incredulous Elvino, come to the inn to see her sleeping in Rodolfo's bed. All is resolved in the end when a handkerchief of Lisa's is found in Rodolfo's room, and when the somnambulism is dramatically proved real as Amina walks a dangerous plank across the mill wheel, and is awakened by Elvino himself as he takes her in his arms.

The frail Bellini was lucky in always having powerful backers. Born of poor parents in a remote Sicilian town, he found a wealthy nobleman to send him through music school in Naples. There the noted Zingarelli, whose pert and lightsome songs are still occasionally heard, guided his talent for easy melody and sentimental phrase. In 1826, when Bellini was twenty-three years old, the same Barbaia who had furthered Rossini's career and had given *Euryanthe* to an ungrateful Vienna heard the young man's first opera (a school exercise), which was produced privately. It was made possible for his first professional opera to be given at the Teatro San Carlo in 1826, and this was sufficiently successful both to stimulate Barbaia into ordering a second work, *Il Pirata,* and to cure at once any feeling of unprofessionalism Bellini might have had. His luck held: the librettist Barbaia found for him was Felice Romani, the best in Italy; the cast for the *première* at La Scala included the golden-voiced Rubini and Henriette-Clémentine Méric-Lalande, a popular French soprano. This was a hit: Bellini's fame spread beyond Italy, and Rossini tendered his compliments. The opera repeated its Milanese success in Vienna three months later, and it went on to become something of a favorite because of the tenor Rubini's partiality for the sentimental "Tu vedrai," in which his much-admired vibrato had full play. But as *Il Pirata* was a weak and poorly constructed score, it disappeared before the middle of the century.

As Bellini's last three operas are the only ones we are ever likely to hear, there is no point wasting time on the preceding ones. Remarkably selected casts gained for most of them a measure of success quite beyond their intrinsic deserts. For instance, when *La Straniera* was first performed at La Scala in 1829, with Caroline Unger, Méric-Lalande, and Tamburini, the composer was called to the stage thirty times—an ovation he never equaled; on the other hand, when *Zaïra* was sung at Parma with a dim galaxy of local stars, it lasted for just one night and was never heard again. This taught Bellini that a man's career cannot be entrusted to incompetent throats: thereafter he stipulated in his contracts the singers to be assigned to various roles—and he never failed again.

This partial usurpation of the manager's prerogatives marks an important development in the production end of opera: the composer has now become so important that the opera house which wants the prestige of a *première* must accede to his demands that full justice be done to his work. And the singer's tyranny has become a legitimate one: he no longer dictates to the composer, but has been moved to his proper place on the auction block—a precious something on whose best efforts the success of an opera is largely dependent.

Late in 1830, it happened that the Teatro Carcano in Milan had a fine troupe of singers at its disposal, and, unwilling to waste their good fortune, the managers commissioned an opera apiece from Bellini and Donizetti. Fatefully for the future of a seventeen-year-old peasant boy by the name of Giuseppe Verdi, the censor stepped in and prevented Bellini from finishing his setting of a Romani libretto based on Hugo's "Hernani." The subject was too hot for a Europe having one of its periodic spasms of revolution. So Romani, who was supplying Donizetti with a safe biography of Anne Boleyn, gave Bellini an even safer one about the tragicomic vicissitudes of a female sleepwalker. Henry VIII's addlepated queen reached the stage, as *Anna Bolena,* three months before *La Sonnambula:* it was Donizetti's thirty-third opera, but the first to give him a Continental reputation. Yet, Bellini scored heavily over his more practiced rival. When Pasta and Rubini got through their performance of *La Sonnambula* on March 6, 1831, they had launched one of the most nearly indestructible masterpieces of the florid school and had been first to sign a register that was to contain the names of the greatest sopranos and tenors of many decades. . . .

The really tremendous vogue once enjoyed by *La Sonnambula*—it was, for example, the first grand opera to be heard in Chicago (1850)—is easily understandable. A brief musical tale, notable for its straightforwardness and unwillingness to spin itself out to irrelevant lengths, this little opera is primarily pleasant entertainment. The well-constructed, uninvolved, if (to the skeptic modern mind) rather silly libretto was exactly right for the effusions of Bellini's fundamentally unpretentious muse: it presented simple situations, obvious emotions, strong but not violent contrasts. Of them Bellini made the most, unless realism be considered a *sine qua non* of "the most." *La Sonnambula* is as romantic as *Der Freischütz,* but its romanticism is Italian, delicately tinted by what was doubtless a superficial acquaintance with the current fashions in European literature. There is an idyllic, a positively sentimental, note here, traceable to that faded chronicler of French Darbys and Joans, Bernardin de Saint-Pierre.

This idyllic note, miscalled "elegiac," was Bellini's peculiar forte, and he illustrated it in *La Sonnambula* with melodies such as had never been heard before—melodies that seem at their most characteristic here, because here in purest form. The line of Amina's song in "Ah! non credea" is impeccable in draftsmanship and is traced in silverpoint. It is utterly irresistible even when sketched out in the piano's faulty legato, and something inexpressibly better when sung by a great soprano. The ending of this aria illustrates one of Bellini's strengths, for when Amina begins to warble whole cascades of sixteenth notes to a syllable, these *fioriture* seem to rise inevitably as the only possible resolution of the built-up emotion. Compare it with the more showy, almost Rossinian air that follows on its heels—the famous "Ah! non giunge," and see what was Bellini's real métier. The second aria is exciting fireworks, but little more.

The *réclame* Bellini reaped because of *La Sonnambula* brought him another commission from La Scala. This time the fecund Romani turned to the Druids of Gaul, and spun a libretto that Schopenhauer, otherwise a man of common sense, exaggeratedly called the best libretto in existence.

As Pasta was not a light soprano, but a dramatic type who excelled in emotion, and never entirely mastered *bel canto,* it is not surprising that a few definitely heavy sopranos have found the role of Amina attractive. Yet, it is primarily a role for coloraturas. Patti liked it so well that she used it for her Paris and London debuts, as well as for her second appearance at the Academy of Music, New York. The great Canadian soprano, Emma Albani, played Amina at her world (Messina, 1870), London, and New York debuts. The famous García sisters, Malibran and Viardot-García, both sang it, though the former was a contralto who had added an effective upper register to her voice by sheer obstinacy. Malibran was also the first to sing *La Sonnambula* in English—a custom that did much to popularize the opera in an England that had hesitated to accept its composer. Jenny Lind was one of the greatest of Aminas, and of her singing of the aria "Ah! non credea" Queen Victoria rhapsodized in her diary: "It was all *piano,* and clear and sweet, and like the sighing of a zephyr; yet all heard. Who could describe those long notes, drawn out till they quite melt away; that shake which becomes softer and softer; those very piano- and flute-like notes, and those round, fresh tones that are so youthful." Minnie Hauk, an Amina of fourteen, first appeared in public at the old Brooklyn Academy of Music. Ilma di Murska and Fanny Persiani were amazingly agile, if less subtle than Lind or Patti, while Etelka Gerster, who made her American bow in *La Sonnambula,* was in some ways the most admired Amina ever to sing in America. More modern interpreters of the role have been Sembrich, Tetrazzini, Galli-Curci, and Pons, the first in a historic performance at the Metropolitan in 1905, when she was supported by Caruso and Pol Plançon. Malibran and Lind had no doubt considered themselves realists in the part, but Elvira de Hidalgo, a Spanish singer of somewhat less than first magnitude, distanced all comers by playing Amina barefooted.

W. B., H. W.

[*La Sonnambula* was first performed in America at the Park Theater, on November 13, 1835, in English. The first American performance in the original Italian occurred at Palmo's Opera House, New York, on May 13, 1844. Four years later, Bellini's sleepwalking opera underwent another change—as *The Room Scrambler,* a burlesque produced at the Olympic Theater of New York. . . . Sembrich sang the part of Amina in the first Metropolitan performance of November 15, 1883.]

Norma

LYRIC TRAGEDY IN 2 ACTS

Book by Giuseppe Felice Romani, based on a story by Alexandre Soumet and Louis Belmontet

First performance: La Scala, Milan, Dec. 26, 1831

CHARACTERS

Pollione (Severus), Roman proconsul in Gaul, TENOR

Flavio, a centurion, TENOR

Oroveso (Orovist), the Archdruid, Norma's father, BASS

Norma, high priestess of the Druid temple of Esus, SOPRANO

Adalgisa, a virgin of the temple of Esus, MEZZO-SOPRANO

Clotilda, confidante of Norma, SOPRANO

Priests and Officers of the Temple, Gallic Warriors, Priestesses and Virgins of the Temple, and the Two Children of Norma and Pollione

The action takes place in Gaul during the Roman occupation, about 50 B.C.

In the sacred grove, Orovist, chief druid, begs the god's aid to overcome the Romans, while Severus, proconsul in Gaul, and his confidant Flavius listen in the shadows. The Gauls go and Severus tells his mad passion for Adalgisa, a young druidess. Norma, chief druidess, Orovist's daughter, has forsworn her vow of chastity to bear Severus two sons, but his new love makes her image pale. As the Romans depart, Norma comes to declare the god's will. Obediently the druids receive her words: Rome shall perish, but the time is not yet ripe! As the grove falls silent Adalgisa seeks in prayer strength to resist her passion, only to promise, once Severus joins her, to flee with him to Rome. Norma, when Adalgisa confesses her sinful secret, gives her the kiss of sisterhood; but when she asks her lover's name Severus appears, and avows his passion. He meets Norma's reproaches with scorn, and Adalgisa rejects him.

Norma, dagger raised to slay her sleeping babes and self, shrinks from the horrid deed. Instead, she bids Adalgisa take the children to Severus and become his wife, but noble-hearted Adalgisa offers to lead recreant Severus back to her. Adalgisa's effort is vain. Severus swears to make her his by force. Then Norma calls the Gauls to arms. As they greet her words with enthusiasm Clothilde enters: a Roman has been seized in the hall where the druid priestesses were at prayer. When Severus, lurking in the priestesses' hall to carry off Adalgisa, is brought in to be slain by Norma's sacrificial knife she promises to save him if he will abandon Adalgisa. The proud Roman prefers death, but when Norma tells him the young priestess also will perish in the flames, Severus begs her to spare the girl. But Norma has summoned the druids. She bids them build a funeral pyre for a Roman and a traitorous priestess. "Who is the priestess?" the druids ask. "I myself," Norma replies. Severus' love is rekindled by Norma's greatness of soul, and the heroic druidess is led to the pyre with her Roman lover, mistress of his heart at the last.

F. H. M.

A role which has made a mighty and constant appeal to great lyric tragedi- ennes is that Celtic sister of Medea, the Druidess Norma. Giuditta Pasta cre- ated it at the historic Teatro alla Scala, Milan, on December 26, 1831, the first in a stately procession of Druid priestesses continuing to our own day. But before considering that renowned singing-actress and some of her distinguished successors, let us glance at the opera itself which has the Druidess for heroine.

Felice Romani supplied Bellini in the case of *Norma* with an exceptionally fine libretto, written in poetic and flowing verse, and the value placed by Ital- ians on Bellini's music may be gathered from the following characteristic opinion expressed many decades after the composer's death:

"Here is the immortal drama which better perhaps than any other is worthy to sum up and represent Italian opera as a type."

Nor has admiration for *Norma* been limited to fellow-countrymen of its com- poser. Though the work of Bellini's that particularly influenced Richard Wag- ner happened to be *I Capuleti ed I Montecchi,* he wrote concerning *Norma:* "This opera among all the creations of Bellini is the one which, with the most profound reality, joins to the richest vein of melody the most intimate passion." The French composer Halévy declared: "I would give all my music to have written 'Casta diva.'" Incidentally, the priestess' prayer to the moon was altered by Bellini eight times before he moulded it into final form.

Bellini himself regarded *Norma* as his masterpiece. When a Parisian lady asked him which one of his operas he preferred, Bellini evaded the question. "But if you were out at sea, and should be shipwrecked?—" she persisted. "Ah!" he cried before she could finish the query, "I would leave all the rest and try to save *Norma.*"

Yet in spite of the signal virtues of libretto and score, *Norma* barely escaped failure on its opening night. It is said that only the genius of Pasta saved it. Up to the duet between Norma and Adalgisa the audience had sat unmoved, and Pasta herself believed the occasion a fiasco. But the duet for the two women broke the ice, and thenceforth the opera proceeded on its course to an obbligato of rapturous applause. In London, too, it was Pasta who through her commanding art overcame an initial apathy, Pasta, whose admittedly im- perfect voice the pianist Moscheles described as at first "veiled," but coming out triumphantly at a later stage "like the sun breaking through the mist."

At La Scala the part of the young priestess Adalgisa (either soprano or mezzo-soprano) had been taken by a youthful member of a prominent oper- atic family, one Giulia Grisi, who was destined to become the most famous

of all Normas. Her study of Pasta in the original cast was reflected in her singing and acting when she gave up Adalgisa in favor of the heroine, and Pasta
generously recognized the young soprano as the inheritor of her mantle.

Of Grisi the eminent English critic Chorley, a witness by ear and eye, says:

Her Norma, doubtless her grandest performance, was modelled on that of Mme.
Pasta—perhaps, in some points, was an improvement on the model, because there
was more of animal passion in it; and this (as in the scene of imperious and abrupt
rage which closes the first act) could be driven to extremity without its becoming
repulsive, owing to the absence of the slightest coarseness in her personal beauty.
There was in it the wild ferocity of the tigress, but a certain frantic charm there-
with which carried away the hearer—nay, which possibly belongs to the true reading of the character of the Druid priestess unfaithful to her vows.

Then, taking up another celebrated singer, Chorley goes on: "I think this
must be so, from recollecting how signally the attempt of a younger Norma to
color the part differently failed; I allude to Mlle. Lind."

The Norma of the "Swedish nightingale" Chorley did not like at all.

That Mlle. Lind made strange mistakes in consulting her own personality rather
than the play [he says] was to be seen in her Norma. I had heard those wondrous
discoverers, the German critical public, delight in her reading as "maidenly"—praise
original, to say the least of it, when the well-known story is remembered. Elaborately wrought as it was, it was pale, weak, as compared with the rendering of the
real Norma. . . . So that Mme. Grisi's reality kept the stage and swept Mlle. Lind's
novelty from it as with a whirlwind of fire.

Maria Malibran, Garcia's brilliant daughter, sang Norma before her untimely
death in 1836, and it was as Norma that the sculptor Geefs portrayed her in
white marble for the chapel erected to her memory at Laaken by her husband,
the violinist de Bériot. From the dome a single beam of light falls upon the
statue amid surrounding shadows, causing it to appear, in the words of the
Countess de Merlin, "like a fantastic thought, the dream of a poet."

Therese Tietiens, a native of Hamburg, was a greatly applauded Norma of
the eighteen-sixties and seventies. One of the sensations of her initial season
in London was her singing of "Casta diva." Her successor as Norma was, in
a sense, the late Lilli Lehmann, the first Norma at the Metropolitan Opera
House on February 27, 1890. The writer of these notes had the privilege of a
little chat with Mme. Lehmann several years ago in Salzburg. She spoke with
a princely scorn of the trivial ways of young singers: "They think they can
motor all the afternoon, then go to the Conditorie and fill up on sweets, and
then throw on something black or something white and skip out on the stage
and be Donna Anna or Norma. But it isn't done that way. And, besides, those
parts take an enormous technic."

At the time Mme. Lehmann was engaged in writing brochures about the
interpretation of certain of her chief rôles. "I am sorry you never heard me as

Norma," she remarked. "I learned the part from my mother, who had learned it from Richard Wagner."

For further testimony to Mme. Lehmann's admiration for *Norma* one has only to turn to her book "My Path through Life." There she goes on record as follows:

This opera, which bears so much love within it, may not be treated indifferently or just killed off. It should be sung and acted with fanatical consecration, rendered by the chorus and orchestra, especially, with artistic reverence; led with authority by the conductor, and to every single eighth note should be given the musical tribute that is its due.

Outstanding Normas of the present century in New York have been Rosa Raisa, appearing with the visiting Chicago company, and Rosa Ponselle at the Metropolitan Opera House. The importance of the other leading rôles should not be overlooked, either. Giulia Grisi has had admirable successors not only as Norma, but as Adalgisa, and Mario, Grisi's husband, was an admired Pollione.

P. S.

London first heard *Norma* in Italian in 1833 and in English, at Drury Lane, in 1837. It was introduced to New York in an English version at the Park Theater, Feb. 25, 1841; in Italian at Niblo's Garden, Sept. 20, 1843.

Alban Berg

(Vienna, Feb. 9, 1885–Dec. 25, 1935, Vienna)

With only brief interruptions, Berg's life was spent almost exclusively in Vienna. With few distractions from outside, Berg developed a rich inner life. The artistic sense of the boy, growing up in the comfortable home of a well-to-do middle-class family, awakened very early. At first, however, he was influenced primarily by literary impressions: Ibsen, Wilde and German literature at the turn of the century stimulated the youth. Self-taught, inspired by the musical studies of his brother, Charley, and his sister, he began to compose at the age of fifteen. His first songs, written in 1900, were "Heiliger Himmel" (Franz Evers), "Herbstgefühl" (Siegfried Fleischer), "Unter der Linden" (Walther von der Vogelweide). From this point on music was the youth's strongest medium of expression. In 1904 the nineteen-year-old youth made the acquaintance of Arnold Schönberg, who was teaching in Vienna at the time. With this, his future was decided: he who had shortly before taken a public office gave up his official career to devote himself exclusively to music.

The influence which his apprenticeship with Schönberg had upon Berg cannot be overestimated. It was a true awakening, which freed all that which was subconsciously slumbering in the sensitive youth. How much Schönberg appreciated Berg's great talent is shown, moreover, in the following words which he dedicated to Berg in 1930: "With pleasure I take this opportunity to pay tribute to the work and products of my pupil and friend, Alban Berg. Were not he and our mutual friend and his fellow-pupil, Anton von Webern, the greatest credit to my influence as a teacher, and were not these two my support in times of great artistic stress; for who could find anything better on this earth than their loyalty, steadfastness, and love?" . . . .

Berg, in turn, always felt indebted to Schönberg's instruction, even when he frequently struck out on a road different from that of his master. For he knew that he owed to him the foundation of his ability and the whole spiritual trend of his creative work. Berg has acknowledged his profound indebtedness to Schönberg in the greater part of his writings on music and also by dedicating to his teacher three of his most important works: the Three Orchestra Pieces, Opus 6, his Chamber Concerto, and the opera *Lulu*.

In March, 1913, in Vienna, under the direction of Schönberg, Alban Berg's first orchestral work was performed: Nos. 2 and 4 of the Altenberg songs, Opus 4. The songs caused one of the worst concert scandals of all time. A riot broke out in the audience and the concert had to be cut short. This first contact with the general public made a deep and lasting impression on Berg.

In May, 1914, Berg saw the dramatic fragment "Wozzeck" by Georg Büchner in a Viennese theatre and immediately resolved to make an opera out of the play. During his military service in the [First] World War he found little time for this work. Nevertheless, the text of *Wozzeck* was finished by 1917, the music by 1920. After three fragments had been performed with great success in Frankfurt-am-Main in 1924, the première of the entire opera took place on Dec. 14, 1925, at the State Opera in Berlin under the direction of Erich Kleiber, which assured Berg his place in the world and made him famous as a composer overnight. The work created a sensation and was repeated several times in Berlin. But the opera also gave rise to violent polemics. Universal-Edition has preserved the most interesting in a special pamphlet "Alban Bergs Wozzeck und die Musikkritik." After the première *Wozzeck* embarked on a triumphant career, unique for such a difficult modern opera. . . .

Immediately after the completion of *Wozzeck,* while writing some chamber music works (Chamber Concerto and Lyric Suite), Berg began looking for the subject for a new opera. The "Wein-Arie" (1929) is to a certain extent a forerunner. After much deliberation and hesitation Berg finally decided in 1928 to compose music to Frank Wedekind's tragedy "Lulu." Thus he returned once again to a play he had seen in his youth (1905). By the spring of 1929 Berg had finished with his adaptation of the text of "Lulu." In 1934 he completed the work in "particel," that is, in a version for which the vocal parts had been completely worked out, whereas the part for orchestra was noted on from two to three staves. Berg worked at the instrumentation up to his death. About one-third of the third act is finished. A musician familiar with Berg's method could complete the rest along Berg's lines on the basis of the particella, but such a task would demand time, self-sacrifice, and devotion.

In the summer of 1934 Berg combined five symphonic excerpts from *Lulu* into a sort of Suite, which was played for the first time in Berlin under Kleiber late in November, 1934, with great success and was immediately repeated a number of times. On December 11, 1935, the suite was played in Vienna. Berg, who was already fatally ill, took part in the preparations for the performance and was able to appear at the concert in person and acknowledge the recognition. It was the first time that he heard an orchestra play any of the music of *Lulu,* as well as the last time that any music reached his ears. The premiere of *Lulu* took place in Zurich after Berg's death. The work was brought to its first stage performance in June, 1937, under Robert Denzler's direction.

In the Spring of 1935 Berg interrupted the instrumentation of *Lulu* and began composing a violin concerto, which was suggested to him by the American violinist, Louis Krasner. Berg hesitated over its execution a long time and was undecided about the form which the work should take. Late in the Spring of 1935 a beloved young friend, Manon Gropius, died. She was the beautiful daughter of Alma Maria Mahler, with whom Berg and his wife were close friends. In a state of feverish activity, at an almost unheard-of pace, he sketched within a few weeks the complete violin concerto, giving it the form of a requiem for Manon Gropius, never suspecting that it was to be his own requiem. On Aug. 11, 1935, the score of the concerto was finished. It was not performed until after Berg's death. Hermann Scherchen conducted it for the first time on April 19, 1936, in Barcelona. The soloist was Krasner, who has since played the concerto many times in many cities of Europe and America.

After completing the violin concerto, Berg wanted to take a brief rest. An abscess, however, forced him to enter a hospital in December. After a short period of intense, but stoical suffering, he died on December 24, 1935. Up to his last breath he occupied himself incessantly in his delirium with his opera *Lulu*.

W. R.

Wozzeck

OPERA IN 3 ACTS (15 SCENES)

Book by the COMPOSER, after GEORG BÜCHNER's drama
of the same name

First performance: Staatsoper, Berlin, Dec. 14, 1925

CHARACTERS

Wozzeck, BARITONE (AND SPEAKING VOICE)
The Drum Major, HEROIC TENOR
Andres, LYRIC TENOR (AND SPEAKING VOICE)

The Captain, BUFFO TENOR
The Doctor, BUFFO BASS
Marie, SOPRANO
Margret, CONTRALTO

Wozzeck, a poor soldier in a small town in Germany, is the plaything of an adverse destiny. He is the symbol incarnate of all that is weak, nondescript, and to be dismissed with contempt. His Captain, through the powers given him by his superior office, practically forces Wozzeck to be the audience for his long, rambling, and ineffectual philosophizings. The regimental Doctor makes Wozzeck the subject of his inconclusive medical experimenting. He is, in short, the composite of the eternal downtrodden.

Marie, Wozzeck's mistress, by whom he has a son, is susceptible to the charms of other males. The first act sees this phase of the subject well established, with Marie launching into an affair with the handsome Drum Major. Wozzeck reproves her unavailingly. The second act develops these matters to a further climax when Wozzeck is thrashed by the Drum Major, and paves the way for the coming events with Wozzeck's mutterings of vengeance.

In the third act Wozzeck stabs Marie to death beside a woodland pond. He himself dies in trying to retrieve the dagger from the waters. It closes with a macabre irony as the curtain comes down upon their orphaned son riding a hobbyhorse.

P. S.

Alban Berg's *Wozzeck* is perhaps the most remarkable opera of the modern age. One says "perhaps," because he would be a bold man indeed who would say what the world of fifty years hence will think of it. Is this weird, sordid, tragical and compassionate creation a last word in musical decadence and ultra-sophistication, or is it a score prophetic of a tonal art subtler, emotionally more sensitive, psychologically more profound, than any other composer has predicated?

It is simple to say that this is a "period piece," the consequence of the despair and decadence of the exhausted Europe of the 1920's, following the first world war; that it represents a mood and an outlook of the past, applicable neither to the present nor the future of our civilization; that therefore it will in due course be out-moded and discarded by future generations. But this does not fit with present indications. *Wozzeck* saw the light in 1925, when it was looked upon as an anarchical offshoot of the Schönberg school of atonality—a first-class aberration, as the Doctor calls Wozzeck's hallucinations in the opera—of a composer of dubious powers. But the opera slowly gained headway, first in Middle Europe and neighboring countries. Then its radius began to widen. At this writing, it is twenty-seven years old. In the past five years alone it has advanced remarkably in the public's interest. It was an attractive feature of the international music festivals of Salzburg in 1951, Florence and Paris of 1952. England heard it for the first time in the previous year. It is scheduled for performance in South American countries in 1953. It was quiet for a long time in the United States, after two pioneer performances under Leopold Stokowski in New York and Philadelphia in 1931. It became a feature of the Spring repertory of the New York City Opera Company in April of 1952. The Western world is more interested in this work in the mid-century than ever before. There is a further fact of great importance: in the year 1952 *Wozzeck* remains, at least so far as musico-dramatic technic is concerned, the most advanced opera of the modern era.

When *Wozzeck* first appeared, it gave the impression of an isolated experiment, an oddity of a certain school and trend of musical thought. It had, certainly, novel features. Its most unusual characteristic was Berg's use of eighteenth-century musical forms, such as the toccata, the fugue, the suite, the passacaglia, as part of its sub-structure; forms which would seem to stiffen and formalize the progress of the action, but which do nothing of the sort as Berg utilizes them. Then there was his use of the *gesangsprache*—the song-speech, which is but a slight variant, if any, of Schönberg's *sprechgesang*—speech-song. The singers employ a vocal production which is between singing and speaking, and which clings closely in rhythm and inflection, but *not* in pitch, to the music. As for the system of "atonality"—non-tonality—Schönberg had fully established that before Berg had come prominently into public view. It is the system which dispenses entirely with the principles of harmonic relations and the gravitation of chords to tonal center which have been in force from the time of J. S. Bach to the present day. Some claim that this is merely twelve intervals of the chromatic scale, arranged in a tonal anarchy, resulting in music, if it can be called music, without form, and void. The atonalists have a remedy for that situation, in their invention of the device of the "tone-row." This is a series of tones made arbitrarily, we might say geometrically, from the fixed order, and serving as a structural basis for the composition; much as the old plain-chant, used as a "cantus firmus," was employed by the mediaeval masters to provide a center of departure for the counterpoint of the voices. Much could be said regarding the validity or non-validity of this theory, which has gained many adherents since Schönberg formulated it. The discussion is not essential here. In all music, particularly in the domain of opera, we are not concerned with the composer's technical methods, but with what he says. And the future will judge Berg by this criterion alone. And the present discovers that he has much to say.

But behind these external novelties of procedure, it is clear that *Wozzeck* has ancestors. Wagner is there, as he is in the whole development of Schönberg and his school. Debussy, also, is there, and the Strauss of *Salome* and *Elektra* and also Puccini, strangely as he may figure in this company. But these are assimilations, not imitations, and only represent the immense· amount of discovery and invention accumulated by great masters of opera music for Berg's employment in his own way. Looked at from this angle, *Wozzeck* is one of the most eclectic scores that have been composed, and one that clings to no single system or method of composition to communicate its contents. Common chords are there, as well as other chords that had not been before on land or sea; and all are potent in original ways. Like it or not, the opera comes over the footlights. It is first class theatre. One may ask whether he is hearing music. It is all organized and integrated, masterfully, towards a dramatic end. The form is perfectly balanced and unified, and worked out in most exquisite and intricate style. The artist is passionately sincere, as well as master of his means. He is a neurasthenic: there is no question about it. He is both realist and psychologist. Fortunately—it is the redemption of his work, if there is redemption for it—he is two things, not one. He is a most sensitive artist, and a humanitarian to the bottom of his soul. This double aspect of his nature is luminous in the score. The story is sordid and tragical to a degree. It is told in terms prevailingly of bitterness and sardonic portrayal, yet also with tenderness and pity. By the side of passages about as dissonant as the human ear, fairly well inured to the ugliness of much contemporaneous art can tolerate, are other passages of a sudden shining beauty, even exaltation, which move us deeply with the thought of the mercy of Him who is not unmindful of the fall of the sparrow. Of such constituent elements, as it appears to the writer, is this opera of Berg's made. It is significant that he, the disciple of Schönberg, had his doubts of the theory of atonality.

Another striking circumstance in the history of this opera, based on the drama by Georg Büchner (1813–1837), is the manner in which the subject of social injustice is treated by Büchner, who died an exile by reason of his democratic political beliefs, and the recurrence of this theme in Berg's consciousness a century later. An actual event in Germany led to Büchner's play, or at least the sketches for it that were found among his papers after he died. This event was the murder in Leipzig, in 1821, by one Johann Christian Woyzeck, an ex-soldier and apoplectically-inclined barber, age 41, of his mistress, a widow of 46, with whom he consorted for two years, but who, at the same time, appears to have had an unfortunate penchant for soldiers. Resentful of her treatment of him, and in a jealous rage at her accessibility to others, Woyzeck one day bought a knife and killed her.

What made the case unusual in view of its tawdry criminal character, was the lawyer's defense of a killer who made no attempt to escape his sentence, appearing to seek the supreme penalty rather than evade it. The trial centered upon the question of whether this man was a deliberate criminal or a maniac. It was shown that he had had hallucinations and a persecution complex, and believed that he was pursued with inimical purpose by Freemasons. For a period of eighteen months, noted psychiatrists and legal lights were engaged to thrash out the question. The presiding judge, Hofrat Clarus, remained convinced of Woyzeck's moral guilt. Finally Woyzeck was executed in the Leipzig market-place, August 27, 1824. But the case did not end there. It was argued publicly and at great length for fourteen years, until in 1838 Hans Meyer published complete documents of the case and supported the Hofrat's decision. A. H. J. Knight, in his book, "Georg Büchner," points out the significance of the long discussion of the affair, which he attributes in large part to the general intellectual attitude of the 1820's—E. T. A. Hoffmann's period, incidentally—towards the visionary mind, "the point being that the decade in question was divided, more than any previous decade, between a materialistic and a romantic explanation of the processes of the human mind and nature in general." This attitude of mind was doubtless Büchner's, whose father was a doctor and a free-thinker, and through whose office Büchner had complete access to the documents of the Woyzeck case.

Georg Büchner, an anatomist, a poet and dramatist who died in his twenty-fourth year, and who promised, had he lived, to become one of the greatest men in German literature, never completed or published the play which inspired Berg's opera the century after. His only publications were a drama, "Danton's Tod," of which an opera has lately been made,* a treatise upon "The Nervous System of the Barbel" † which won him his doctorate at the University of Zürich, and a political pamphlet, "Der Hessische Landbote," which got him into trouble. "Woyzeck," which was the original name of the drama—was found among his papers after he died, as a series of sketched scenes, on partly un-numbered pages, some of them hardly legible, and some representing alternate versions of the same episodes. The confusion and impreciseness of this material were such that Ludwig Büchner,‡ when he published a volume of his brother Georg's posthumous writings in 1850, did not dare include "Woyzeck" among them. But in 1875 the novelist, Karl Emil

* *Danton's Tod*, Gottfried von Einem, 1947.

† Large European fresh-water fish with fleshy filaments hanging from mouth; Büchner was a student of Comparative Anatomy.

‡ Physician and noted philosopher.

Franzos (1848–1904), secured access to this manuscript and published it with his own editing in 1879. It was the Franzos version, presented for the first time that season on the stage, which Berg saw in 1914, and used for his opera. It was not till 1922 that Fritz Bergemann completed his edition of Büchner's "Collected Works and Letters," which exhibited in a glaring light certain of Franzos' errors. The extent of these may be gauged by the fact that Franzos had even misspelled the title of the drama, which was "Woyzeck" and not "Wozzeck." However, "Wozzeck" has remained ever since the title of the opera and various translations of the play. Franzos' own editorial interpolation, in the scene of Wozzeck's self-destruction in the pool of the last act, also remains. "He drowns" is the stage direction of Franzos, not Büchner. But the point need hardly concern us. The episode serves well Berg's purpose—Berg, who said wisely that the composer must be his own stage manager.

And in certain respects the brief, sketchy nature of the scenes of *Wozzeck,* as they fell into Berg's hands, also served his purpose in a way ideal for the composer. . . . Novels have been cut, tightened, altered in sequence to make drama, and dramas have in turn been shortened and condensed to make practicable scenarios for treatment by the composer. Here the material of the various episodes was already present in a highly condensed form, which concentrated action and emotion in a few sentences, and left the composer room to expand these moments freely with his music. Berg, however, used the surgeon's knife with great skill. The twenty-six scenes he cut to fifteen, five each for the three acts, and he connected his scenes, as Debussy does in *Pelléas et Mélisande,* by orchestral interludes between the falling and rising of each curtain. He had commenced work upon the libretto in 1914, when he was called to military duty, for which he was later found unfit. He finished the book in 1917. He finished the composition of the music in 1920, and completed the orchestration in April of 1921. Four years later came the première of the opera.

O. D.

Wozzeck has had a career unique among modernist operas, for in the eleven years following its *première* at the Berlin Staatsoper, on December 14, 1925, it had 166 performances in twenty-nine separate cities. This furore would not have been a too extraordinary greeting to a ripe veristic work like *I Gioielli della Madonna,* for instance, but *Wozzeck,* written in difficult Schönbergian idiom, would not have seemed an easy work to produce or to take—the Berlin *première* required 137 rehearsals, and the score calls for four separate orchestras of widely varying make-up, one of them including the instruments of a military band. Finally, the composer, his own librettist, had, if anything, over-emphasized the psychosexual sordidness of the drama on which it was based, a work of the symbolic naturalist Georg Büchner, who had lived almost a century before Hofmannsthal.

The early performances of *Wozzeck* created such violent partisanship pro and con that the topical literature about it was collected in a sizable volume. Little more than five years after the Berlin *première, Wozzeck* was staged by the Philadelphia Grand Opera Association, at Philadelphia (March 19, 1931), with Stokowski conducting. Anne Roselle was the Marie, Ivan Ivantzoff the Wozzeck. Both this performance and its repetition in New York with the same forces, on November 24 [1931], brought most enthusiastic acclaim from music lovers of every stripe.

W. B., H. W.

Hector Berlioz

(Côte St. André [Isère], France, Dec. 11, 1803–Mar. 8, 1869, Paris)

Berlioz's father, a doctor in good practice, wished his son to follow the same profession, and Hector studied medicine for a time, though he disliked it intensely. He had no early formal musical education, though he studied harmony and counterpoint surreptitiously, but without much real profit until the hearing of a Haydn quartet gave him inspiration and understanding. He was sent to Paris in 1822 to complete his medical studies, and from there he announced his revolt to his father, who cut off supplies and left the young man to fend for himself. Meanwhile he had had some lessons in composition from Lesueur, then a professor at the Paris Conservatoire. He entered himself as a student in 1823, but found the teaching and the atmosphere alien to his rebellious genius. Lesueur seems to have been the only teacher for whom he felt genuine respect.

His life at this period was hard, and he had to support himself by singing in the chorus of the Théâtre Gymnase. He had composed a mass performed at the Church of St. Roch, and now wrote other works including a cantata named "La Mort d'Orphée," the manuscript of which was only discovered in 1923; but none of them had any success. He left the Conservatoire in 1825, to devote himself to a systematic study of the works of Beethoven, Gluck, Weber and other masters. Success came at last with his cantata, "La Mort de Sardanapale" (1830), for which he was awarded the Prix de Rome. The terms of the prize provided for three years' study abroad, the first two to be spent in Italy. There he wrote an overture to "King Lear," "Le Retour à la vie," a continuation of an earlier symphonic work, "Episode de la vie d'un artiste," the lovely song, "La Captive," and other works. Before the two years were up he begged leave to return to Paris.

The reason was partly nostalgia for a city which he always dearly loved, though he found little appreciation there, and partly his passion for the famous Irish actress, Henrietta Smithson, who was then playing Shakespearian parts in Paris. The "Episode de la vie d'un artiste" had been inspired by her, and the performance of this work, with its continuation, at the Paris Conservatoire in 1832 caused her to regard Berlioz more favorably than before. It also won the praise of Paganini, who said to the composer: "Vous commencez par où les autres ont fini." Berlioz married Henrietta in 1833. The union was by no means a happy one, and difficulties were aggravated by poverty. She was compelled by an accident to leave the stage, and no place as professor or conductor was available for Berlioz, in rebellion against the correctness of the

French school and a pioneer of the romantic movement. He was able to support himself and his family by acting as a musical critic, which left him little time for composition. Yet the period between his marriage with Henrietta and their stormy separation in 1840 was rich in production. To these seven years belong the dramatic symphonies, "Harold en Italie," "Symphonie funèbre et triomphale," and "Roméo et Juliette"; the opera *Benvenuto Cellini* (1837); and the Requiem, commissioned by the French Government for performance in memory of those who fell at Constantine, Algeria.

Berlioz was given the Legion of Honor, and began to write (1838) for the *Journal des Débats,* to which he contributed at intervals until 1863. There he conducted his polemic against the conservative critics of the day. But official musical Paris remained obdurate. He was invited to visit Germany, where Robert Schumann, who had analyzed the "Episode" in the *Neue Zeitschrift für Musik,* had prepared the way for him. Henrietta declined to accompany him, and the miserable breach followed. Berlioz supported her until her death in 1854, but there was no renewal of affection. The visit to Germany was delayed until 1842, but was a triumphal success. In all the great musical centers Berlioz was received with enthusiasm. But in Paris he conducted the works of other composers. In 1846 his cantata, "La Damnation de Faust," was played in Paris, but was coldly received. He paid visits to Austria (1845), Russia (1847), and England (four times between 1847 and 1855), but recognition abroad did not compensate him for apathy at home. *Benvenuto Cellini* was played, at the invitation of Liszt, at Weimar in 1852, and in London in 1853; and the oratorio-trilogy, "L'Enfance du Christ," in Weimar in 1855. The "Hymne à la France" was written for an industrial exhibition in 1844; the "Damnation de Faust" in 1845; the "Te Deum" for the Paris exhibition of 1855; the short opera *Béatrice et Bénédict* was produced at Baden in 1862; and *Les Troyens à Carthage* had a short run at the Théâtre Lyrique in Paris in 1863.

After the death of his first wife in 1854, Berlioz married a mediocre singer, Martin [Marie] Recio, who rather hindered than helped him, since she demanded leading parts in his production. But he was inconsolable at her death in 1862. The failure of *Les Troyens* in 1863 was a further blow. He had a great reception in Vienna (1866) and St. Petersburg (1867), but his health was failing and he died in Paris in 1869. He had been admitted to the Académie Française in 1856, and in 1852 had received the one official post of his lifetime —the librarianship of the Conservatoire.*

* Encyclopaedia Britannica.

Benvenuto Cellini

OPERA IN 3 ACTS

Book by DE WAILLY and JULES BARBIER

First performance: Opéra, Paris, Sept. 3, 1838

CHARACTERS

Balducci, Treasurer of the Pope, BASS
Teresa, his daughter, SOPRANO
Benvenuto Cellini, a goldsmith, TENOR

Fieramosco, a sculptor, BARITONE
Pompeo, a bravo, BARITONE
Cardinal Salviati, BASS

The action takes place in Rome in 1532

That famous Roman goldsmith of the Renaissance, Benvenuto Cellini, is represented in this opera as in love with Teresa, daughter of Balducci, the papal treasurer.
Also in love with her is Fieramosco, a rival of Cellini in his art. Cardinal Salviati
decrees that Fieramosco shall cast the statue of Perseus, which Cellini has been slow
about completing. But when Cellini consents to cast it at once, the cardinal promises
him a pardon for having stabbed Fieramosco's friend, Pompeo, and likewise the
hand of Teresa in marriage if the work be finished within an hour. Through miraculous diligence the goal is achieved. When the mold is broken and the statue revealed, Balducci himself bestows his blessing upon the betrothed couple.

P. S.

Berlioz planned the composition of *Benvenuto Cellini* early in 1834. He
wished to write a semi-serious opera, depicting passions; a work abounding in
surprises, contrasts, crowds in action; a work with local color. He chose for
his hero Benvenuto Cellini, "a bandit of genius," as he characterized the Italian artist. Adolphe Boschot thinks that Berlioz found himself in Cellini, a
brother of Childe Harold and of the declaiming artist in Berlioz's "Retour à
la Vie," undisciplined, torn by passions, mocked by the stupid bourgeoisie, a
hero of 1830. The musician saw Rome, its monuments and squares, dagger-
thrusts, open-air harlequinades. Excited by reading Cellini's Memoirs and
E. T. A. Hoffmann's short story "Salvator Rosa," Berlioz wished Alfred de
Vigny to write a libretto, with Cellini as the hero. Vigny, busy, recommended
Wailly, who in turn sought the aid of Barbier; but Vigny criticised and corrected and suggested until nearly the time of performance. The libretto was
read to the management of the Opéra Comique in August, 1834. It was rejected. "They are afraid of me," wrote Berlioz; "they look on me at the Opéra

Comique as a sapper, an upsetter of the national genre: they refuse the libretto, that they will not be obliged to admit the music of a madman."

Berlioz wrote on October 2, 1836, that all he had to do was to orchestrate the work. On April 11, 1837, he wrote, "My opera is finished." The first mention made by Berlioz of the opera was in a letter to Ferrand, the 15th or 16th of May, 1834; on August 31 of that year the libretto was ready and the "Chant des Ciseleurs," which opens the second scene, was composed. This music was performed at concerts given by Berlioz, November 23 and December 7, 1834, and then entitled "Les Ciseleurs de Florence: trio with chorus and orchestra."

In 1837 Heinrich Heine wrote from Paris: "We shall soon have an opera from Berlioz; the subject is an episode from the life of Benvenuto Cellini, the casting of his Perseus. Something extraordinary is expected, for this composer has already achieved the extraordinary." And Heine regretted that Berlioz had cut off his immense antediluvian bush of hair that bristled over his forehead like a forest over a steep precipice.

The letters and memoirs of Berlioz give much information concerning his trials and tribulations in the rehearsal and production of the opera. The music was considered so difficult that there were twenty-nine full rehearsals. According to the rule of the Parisian opera-houses, Berlioz was not allowed to conduct his own work. Habeneck was apparently unfriendly. Some of the orchestral players found the music very original; others were indifferent, bored, hostile; two in place of playing their part were heard by Berlioz playing the old tune "J'ai du bon tabac." On the stage, male dancers would pinch the ballet girls and cry out with them, mingling their cries with the voices of the singers. Duponchel, the director of the opera-house, did not interfere; he did not condescend to attend the rehearsals. When he heard that some of the orchestra admired the music, he remarked: "Did you ever see such a shifting of opinion! Berlioz's music is found to be charming and our idiotic musicians praise it to the skies."

The performance was announced for September 3, 1838, and in several books of reference this date is given as that of the first performance; but Duprez had a sore throat, and the performance was postponed until the 10th. The second and the third were on September 12 and 14, and there were no more that year. There were four in 1839, and at the first, January 10, Alexis Dupont replaced Duprez. Alizard replaced Dériyis after the first, and in 1839 Miss Nau was substituted for Mme. Dorus-Gras.

Meyerbeer, Paganini, and Spontini were present at the first performance. Don François de Paule, brother of the Queen of Spain, sat in the royal box surrounded with princesses. The audience was a brilliant one, but the opera failed dismally, although the music was praised by leading critics, and Théophile Gautier predicted that the opera would influence the future of music for good or evil. Berlioz was caricatured as the composer of "Malvenuto Cellini."

According to Berlioz's account of the performance the overture had "an exaggerated success, and all the rest was hissed with admirable ensemble and energy." Duprez was excellent in the violent scenes, but his voice no longer lent itself easily to gentle passages, to music of revery. Mmes. Dorus-Gras and Stoltz found favor with Berlioz, and of the latter he wrote: "Mme. Stoltz drew such attention in her rondo of the second act, 'Mais qu'ai-je donc?' that this rôle [Ascanio] can be considered as her point of departure toward the extravagant position she acquired later at the Opéra from the height of which she was so brusquely hurled." But Gustave Bord in his "Life of Rosina Stoltz" (Paris, 1909) says that as Ascanio she did not add much to her reputation. "It was only stated that as her legs were well made, the male part was well suited to her."

In the letter to his sister Adèle dated July 12, 1838, Berlioz wrote: "Duprez-Cellini is superb; one can form no idea of the energy and the beauty of his singing." In a letter to his father dated September 20, 1838, that the "gigantic amour-propre" of Duprez might postpone further performances. "The success has not been concentrated on him; the two women singers, on the contrary, have had the honors in singing and acting. Consequently he no longer wishes to take the part, and A. Dupont will replace him; but as he did not any more than I expect this, he is obliged to learn the whole of the music." Duprez in his "Souvenirs d'un chanteur" says: "It is known that the talent of Berlioz, otherwise an excellent musician, was not exactly melodic." To the tenor's "Italianized ears" the music of Berlioz was strange. Furthermore, expecting the birth of a son the night of the third performance, Duprez was not at ease on the stage, and when in the last act he saw the physician radiant behind the scenes, he lost his head through joy and made a mess of the "complicated and learned music." He also wrote, "I acquitted myself badly in this adventure; that is not, however, the cause of the non-success of *Benvenuto Cellini,* though the composer held me responsible and always bore a grudge against me."

The stage settings were mediocre, as though the management had expected a failure and prepared for it. Familiar or trivial expressions in the libretto provoked laughter. The libretto was condemned before the end of the first scene. As for the music, the audience did not hear or care. There was laughter, there was hissing; there were imitations of animals; there was even a ventriloquist. Only the two women on the stage were undisturbed. Boschot says that Duprez sang "in a condescending manner."

The next morning Berlioz made cuts in the score and corrections in the libretto. The second performance was on September 12. A small audience; receipts, 2,733 francs, the half of an average receipt. There was no hissing, but applause in the half-empty hall was pathetic. Third performance on September 14: A small audience; receipts below 3,000 francs.

The majority of the critics were favorable towards Berlioz and the opera.

Perhaps they wished to raise him, a colleague in criticism, from his fall. Théophile Gautier recalled the heroic days of 1830.

After the third performance Duprez wished to give up the rôle; the opera did not draw; Mme. Dorus-Gras's engagement ended the 15th of September, nevertheless the bills for a month or two announced a forthcoming performance, the fourth. Alexis Dupont, the successor of Duprez, was slow in learning his part. Josephina Nau replaced Mme. Dorus-Gras. Rehearsals were held. The date November 21 was definitely appointed, but "on account of the indisposition of an artist" the *Siège de Corinth* was substituted. The fourth performance did not take place until January 11, 1839. The receipts were less than 3,000 francs; while *Robert le Diable* after one hundred and seventy performances was still bringing in more than 6,000 francs. Yet Berlioz wrote to Liszt, who was at Rome, that the opera-house was crowded. The first act was afterwards performed three times.

Not until 1913 was there a revival of *Benvenuto Cellini* in Paris. It was at the Théâtre des Champs-Élysées, on March 31, 1913. . . . Felix Weingartner conducted. There were six performances.

The opera, arranged in four acts, with a libretto translated into German by Riccius, was produced by Liszt at Weimar on March 20, 1852, with Beck as Cellini and Mme. Milde as Teresa. Berlioz was not able to attend the performance. He wrote on February 10 to Morel, before the performance: "They have been at work on it for four months. I cleaned it well, re-sewed and restored it. I had not looked at it for thirteen years; it is devilishly *vivace*." Arranged in three acts and with the text translation into German by Peter Cornelius, the opera was performed at Weimar in February, 1856. The score was published as Op. 23 and dedicated to the Grand Duchess of Weimar.

The opera failed at London on June 25, 1853. Berlioz conducted. Chorley said:

The evening was one of the most melancholy evenings which I ever passed in any theatre. *Benvenuto Cellini* failed more decidedly than any foreign opera I recollect to have seen performed in London. At an early period of the evening the humor of the audience began to show itself, and the painful spectacle had to be endured of seeing the composer conducting his own work through every stage of its condemnation.

Some say there was a cabal led by Costa in the interest of Italian art. The chief singers were Mmes. Julienne-Dejean and Nauier-Didiée; Messrs. Tamberlik, Formes and Tagliafico. There was even an attempt to prevent the performance of "The Roman Carnival," which was played before the second act, although this same overture had been applauded by a London concert audience in 1848. Chorley criticized the music of the opera apparently without prejudice and with keen discrimination. The following quotation from his article bears on the overture:

The ease of the singers is disregarded with a despotism which is virtually another confession of weakness. As music, the scene in the second act, known in another form as its composer's happiest overture, "The Roman Carnival," has the true Italian spirit of the joyous time; but the chorus-singers are so run out of breath, and are so perpetually called on to catch or snatch at some passage, which ought to be struck off with the sharpest decision, that the real spirit instinct in the music is thoroughly driven out of it.

Benvenuto Cellini has been the hero of other operas than that of Berlioz.

Cellini a Parigi, music by Lauro Rossi, produced at Turin in June, 1845. The chief part was composed for Mme. de la Grange.

Benvenuto Cellini, music by Louis Schlosser, produced at Darmstadt about 1845.

Benvenuto Cellini, or *Der Guss des Perseus,* music by Franz Lachner, produced at Munich in 1849.

Benvenuto Cellini, libretto by Prechtler, music by Leo Kern, produced at Budapest in 1854.

Benvenuto Cellini, music by Orsini, produced without success at the Mercadante Theatre, Naples, May 1875.

Benvenuto Cellini, libretto by Perosio, music by E. Bozzano, produced at the Politeama, Genoa, May 20, 1877, without success. The chief singers were Signoretti, Medica, Cherubini, and Mmes. Ollandini and Mestres.

Ascanio, opera in five acts, libretto by Louis Gallet, music by Camille Saint-Saëns, produced at the Opéra, Paris, March 21, 1890.

Benvenuto, lyric drama in four acts, libretto by Gaston Hirsch, music by Eugène Diaz, son of the celebrated painter, produced at the Opéra-Comique, Paris, December 3, 1890. Cellini has forsaken his mistress, Pasilea Guasconti, and she plots to prevent his marriage with Delphe de Montsolm. Pasilea arranges an ambuscade, and the sculptor kills two of his foes. Obliged to run away from Florence, he goes to Rome, where he is imprisoned and sentenced to death. Delphe is badly poisoned by a letter sent by Pasilea, but she recovers. The Ambassador of France succeeds in having Cellini's sentence changed to banishment. Delphe is restored to life, and Pasilea stabs herself to escape the scaffold as a poisoner. The music was characterized as devoid of original ideas and hopelessly old-fashioned. The cast was as follows: Benvenuto, Renaud; Pompeo, brother of Pasilea, Carbonne; Cosme de Médicis, Lonati; Andrea, Clément; Orazio, Bernaest; De Jasi, Maris; De Cagli, Gilibert; Pasilea, Mme. Deschamps-Jehin; Delphe, Miss Yvel. An aria from this opera has been sung in concert more than once in Boston.

Benvenuto Cellini, in three acts, music by Angelo Tubi, produced at Parma, February 20, 1906.

Ballets: "Benvenuto Cellini" by Antonio Buzzi about 1860 and by Luigi Venzano about 1870.

P. H.

Les Troyens

[The Trojans]

LYRIC OPERA IN 6 ACTS (2 PARTS)

Book by the COMPOSER

First performance (second part only): Théâtre Lyrique, Paris, Nov. 4, 1863

CHARACTERS

Cassandra, MEZZO-SOPRANO	*Choroebus*, BARITONE
Dido, MEZZO-SOPRANO	*Iopas*, TENOR
Anna, CONTRALTO	*Narbal*, BASS
Aeneas, TENOR	*Hylas*, TENOR

PART I: THREE ACTS

La Prise de Troie (The Capture of Troy)

The Trojans in the deserted Greek camp talk of the great wooden horse the departed invaders have built in honor of Pallas when Cassandra appears and prophesies Troy's destruction. Her betrothed Choroëbus begs her to leave the doomed city and on her refusal swears to remain with her. The Trojans sacrifice to the gods beneath the walls of Troy (Act II), but while Priam blesses Astyanax, son of dead Hector, brought by his weeping mother Andromache, Cassandra again prophesies Troy's downfall, only to be told by Æneas that the people have dragged the wooden horse into the town.

Hector's ghost appears to Æneas in his tent (Act III), telling him Troy is doomed and bidding him found a new empire in Italy. Then Pantheus rushes in: Troy is aflame; Greek warriors have crept out of the wooden horse; Æneas must lead the Trojans to battle. In the temple of Cybele, Cassandra tells how Æneas, bravely fighting, has escaped, but that her lover Choroëbus has fallen. As the victorious Greeks rush in she plunges the dagger into her heart, an example followed by her priestesses.

PART II: THREE ACTS

Les Troyens à Carthage (The Trojans at Carthage)

Irabas' wooing rejected by Dido (Act I), Æneas, cast ashore at Carthage, reveals himself as King Priam's son, defeats Irabas and his Numidians and wins the heart of the Carthaginian queen. Nymphs bathing in a forest pool hide as Tyrian huntsmen appear (Act II), and when these scatter as the tempest breaks Dido and Æneas take refuge in a grotto. But neither stolen moments of passion nor festivals and dances (Act III) can hold the hero. The shades of Priam, Hector, and Cassandra urge him

56

to set sail for Italy. Deaf to Dido's prayers he boards his ship and when she sees it dwindle on the horizon she mounts the funeral pyre. Prophesying the birth of Hannibal, her avenger, she kills herself with Æneas' sword, and above the sonorous strains of the "Trojan March" echo the curses of the people of Carthage on Æneas and the Roman race, whose founder he is destined to be.

F. H. M.

Early in 1858 Berlioz told Bülow that he was completing *Les Troyens* and added that strange and mingled emotions possessed him during its composition: "At one time it is passion, joy, tenderness worthy of an artist of twenty. Then come disgust, coldness and aversion to work." Berlioz frequently read the libretto to circles of friends, whose applause encouraged him to continue his colossal task. A letter to Louis (February, 1858) contains the confession that Berlioz was more pleased with what he had just written—the fifth act—than with all his former works. The sailor's song had been coupled in Berlioz's mind with thoughts of his beloved son, who was then sailing the Indian Ocean. (In the scores as finally published, this song occurs at the beginning of Act III of *Les Troyens à Carthage*.) In May, Berlioz told his son of a concert which he had conducted in the Conservatoire, with "prodigious success."

The immense opera was now completed and lay ready for performance. Berlioz at once opened negotiations for its production. The emperor (Napoleon III) was interested, but, Berlioz told Ferrand, "not sufficiently fond of music to interfere directly." The composer met with vague promises and evasions when he approached the powers at the Opéra, who had made other commitments for many months ahead. In 1858 he was, however, elected by the French Government—along with Auber, Halévy, Meyerbeer and other famous musicians—as a member of the commission appointed to discuss the elevation of pitch and to prepare a report on the whole question. Berlioz contributed to the Débats an interesting article designed for popular enlightenment. The report of the commission finally appeared in 1859, and the recommendations were officially adopted. It was during 1858 that Berlioz spent an evening with Wagner, who had just arrived in Paris, and read to the German composer the text of *Les Troyens*. Wagner did his best to conceal his misgivings before the author, but his letters show that he clearly foresaw disaster for the opera.

Early in 1859 Berlioz told Morel that he was about to organize a sacred concert during Holy Week: the need for money was urgent. At this function "L'Enfance du Christ" was performed, excellently and with great success. To Ferrand, Berlioz spoke of a projected concert in Bordeaux—it took place in June—and hopefully looked forward to his usual appointment at Baden-Baden in August. Of *Les Troyens* he merely said that he was "cool," owing to the inability of finding suitable singers; he would rather be stabbed with the kitchen knife than hear the monologue of the Queen of Carthage badly sung!

Influential Parisians were, however, already interested in the opera; Léon Carvalho, the famous manager of the Théâtre Lyrique, was among the enthusiasts. It was in October 1859 that Wagner went to call on Berlioz, whom he encountered returning from medical treatment, and was shocked by the feeble state of the elder man's health. In November Berlioz directed the production of Gluck's *Orfeo* at the Théâtre Lyrique.

In 1860 Berlioz began writing *Béatrice et Bénédict,* a comic opera which, he said, rested him after the exertions of *Les Troyens.* He could not write quickly enough, and sometimes actually began one number before its predecessor had been completed. *Les Troyens* still lay waiting.

Berlioz resolved to torment himself no longer; he would not seek Fortune, but wait for her. In the meantime the vocal score would, he hoped, be published. This did not materialize, and in spite of his resolutions the delays and intrigues finally exasperated Berlioz, whose health was now quite shattered. His comments on the Paris performances of *Tannhäuser* in 1861—the most notorious fiasco in Wagner's stormy career—were malicious and unjust; they were obviously the product of a mind poisoned by incessant sickness and embittered by repeated disappointments. Berlioz had, as we have seen, been scrupulously fair to Wagner only a few months before, when the German composer had given miscellaneous concerts in Paris; although Wagner had been moved to observe, as early as 1860, that Berlioz had become "the victim of envy." The two great men seemed fated never to meet on a basis of mutual understanding.

Berlioz was still writing articles, working painfully and laboriously under physical distress. Paris and France continued to afford him small encouragements; early in 1861 he was given an ovation at the Conservatoire after scenes from *Faust* had been performed. He also dined with the emperor; but he found conversation difficult and was "magnificently bored." The libretto of *Les Troyens* was attracting more and more supporters to his cause: Berlioz himself was convinced that he had written a great work.

In the meantime work on *Béatrice et Bénédict,* so joyfully begun, had been suspended. His illness made composition a labour and, moreover, journalism and superintendence of rehearsals of Weber's *Freischütz*—which, after a month, were abandoned—made other claims on his time. However, in June 1861, Berlioz informed Louis that the score of Béatrice was now getting on by degrees, in spite of difficulties.

The extent to which Berlioz was attaching his hopes to *Les Troyens* was disclosed by a statement in a letter to Ferrand that he had declined a lucrative offer to visit the United States: he would not leave Paris while there was a chance of his being asked for the great opera. None the less he risked incurring the displeasure of the Opéra authorities by declining to conduct rehearsals of Gluck's *Alceste:* he refused point-blank to consider transpositions and other alterations required by one of the singers.

Letters to Louis Berlioz were frequent during this period. The young man was captious, disappointed and a little inclined to blame his father for his various misfortunes. The replies of Berlioz were informed by generous good will: no neglect or ingratitude on the part of his boy could goad him into the bitterness with which he sometimes launched against others who injured him less deeply.

At the Baden Festival in 1861 "Harold en Italie" received a performance that fully satisfied Berlioz. The composer now looked forward to the production of *Béatrice et Bénédict* in the following year—also at the festival in Baden —and to the *première* of *Les Troyens,* now definitely fixed for March 1863. Berlioz had, after all, assisted with parts of *Alceste,* and his stock had risen at the Opéra. A new choral work, "Le Temple universel," was written during 1861 and twice performed at Paris in the autumn. *Béatrice et Bénédict* was completed early in the following year.

Berlioz's second wife, Marie, died suddenly in June 1862; her mother henceforward looked after the composer with great care and devotion. In August he travelled to Baden-Baden, where *Béatrice et Bénédict* was produced in the new theatre with success. Berlioz conducted the first performance; but he suffered so violently from neuralgia that he felt no emotion and took no interest. "The result of this eccentric coolness," he told Ferrand, "was that I conducted better than usual." Later in the month, back in Paris, Berlioz was adding to the opera for the purposes of publication. To Ferrand he wrote: "I am in a hurry to untie or cut all the bonds which chain me to art, so that I may be ready at any time to say to death: 'Whenever you please!' "

Early in 1863 Berlioz had cause for optimism. Concerts in Paris, at which extracts from *Béatrice et Bénédict* were performed brought him further tributes. *Les Troyens* was to be produced at the end of the year by Carvalho at the Théâtre Lyrique. Berlioz had finally broken off negotiations with the Opéra. He wrote to Davison that the authorities had played with him for three years and that he was anxious to hear his great opera before he died: hence he had yielded to Carvalho, who was eager to produce the work. *Béatrice* was about to be published; the little opera was due for production at Weimar; and the whole of "L'Enfance" was in preparation for a great festival at Strasbourg.

The German performances of *Béatrice* were brilliantly successful. From Weimar Berlioz travelled to Löwenberg, where he conducted the Prince of Hohenzollern's private orchestra and was overwhelmed with honours. Berlioz's music was being played all over Germany with conspicuous success. These triumphs, coupled with hopes for *Les Troyens,* sustained him throughout dreadful suffering, which increased as time went on. In March he exclaimed to Ferrand: "God, how I suffer! And I have not time even for that." He returned to Paris at the end of April, weary and ill, to find that rehearsals of *Les Troyens* had not been begun. Pecuniary difficulties were holding up progress. Berlioz finally had to consent to the presentation of the last three acts only—the second part, *Les Troyens à Carthage*—with a specially written pro-logue. The first two acts, comprising *La Prise de Troie*, were shelved.

It was about this time that Berlioz had an affair with a young girl referred to by him as Amélie (surname unknown). The records are disjointed and obscure, but there appears to have been more pain than comfort in the rela-tionship between the two. Amélie, it would seem, died in 1864; she was only in her twenties.

During the summer and autumn of 1863 Berlioz received further artistic encouragements. He had an overwhelming success with "L'Enfance du Christ" at Strasbourg in June; and this time he returned to Paris to find that Carvalho had secured from the French Government a large subsidy for *Les Troyens* and was in a position to proceed confidently. Apart from the usual August trip to Baden-Baden, where *Béatrice* was again performed—and whither Louis, home on leave, travelled with his father—the composer concentrated on the prepara-tion of his vast opera and was gratified by its development in rehearsal.

Les Troyens à Carthage was finally produced early in November 1863, and was given twenty-two times. The early performances created a profound im-pression among the musicians assembled; Meyerbeer heard the opera on sev-eral nights, and was deeply moved. The press as a whole was laudatory—"the French papers speak in the highest terms of Berlioz's new opera," noted the British *Musical Times*—and congratulations poured upon Berlioz. The score had been sold to the firm of Choudens for a considerable sum. There were a few malicious commentaries—a cartoon in a comic paper represented a baby labelled *"Tannhäuser"* asking for his little brother (*"Troyens"*) and a gro-tesque parody was later staged at another theatre—but the reception of the work was, on the whole, highly favourable. Berlioz's account of the production in the "Memoirs," to which he added a few chapters later in life, is misleading. The accusations against Carvalho are unjust: the manager took heavy risks and undoubtedly exerted himself to make the performances successful, though numerous modifications had to be made.

The production was, however, only a twenty-two days' wonder. *Les Troyens à Carthage* was never performed again during Berlioz's lifetime; the first part of *Les Troyens, La Prise de Troie*, was not heard at all until twenty-one years after his death, when the whole great opera was produced at Carlsruhe. An-other nine years passed before Paris witnessed a performance of the first two acts.

Berlioz did not tempt Providence again. His career as a composer was ended.

Little remains to be told. He had finally laid down his pen. He was even able to abandon his abhorred journalism; the royalties on the performances of *Les Troyens,* together with receipts from the sale of the score, had at least done that much for him. He finally resigned from the *Journal des Débats* and handed the work over to d'Ortigue, who had previously deputized for him during his absences abroad. It was with gleeful relief that he wrote (early in 1864) that he had not been inside a lyric theatre for two months. With characteristic hyperbole he told Morel that he spent his evenings walking past the theatres simply to enjoy the pleasure of not entering them. In a letter to Davison he addressed the *Times* critic as "poor galley slave!"

In August 1864 Berlioz was gazetted Officer of the Legion of Honour, a distinction announced to him by Marshal Vaillant in what the composer described as "a charming letter." He was fêted at a banquet held at the Ministry. He entertained, however, no illusions concerning the real state of Parisian musical culture. "Everything is dead," he told Morel, "save the authority of fools."

J. H. E.

Georges Bizet

(Paris, Oct 25, 1838–June 3, 1875, Bougival, near Paris)

Bizet's father came of the artisan class and was a teacher of singing. His mother, like Gounod's, was a talented pianist, and from her he received his first music-lessons. He showed a precocious talent and already gave evidence of an exceptional memory for music. So when his parents had imparted to him all that they could teach, they sought to enter him at the Conservatoire at the age of nine. Authority was at first contemptuous, but when the boy showed that he could name and explain all the chords, however unusual, that were played on the pianoforte, contempt gave place to admiration. In 1848 Alexandre César Leopold Georges Bizet entered the Conservatoire before his tenth birthday.

He studied with Guillaume Zimmerman, who had been a pupil of Cherubini's and stood for the conservative traditions in the Conservatoire. Gounod had married Zimmerman's daughter and, as he was old and ailing, often deputized for him in the classroom. So Gounod came to know Bizet at an early age, won the respect of his pupil, and exercised a great influence upon his development. Halévy was still Professor of Composition, and his daughter, Geneviève, was to become Bizet's wife, while his nephew, Ludovic Halévy, was part-author of the libretto of *Le Docteur Miracle* and later of *Carmen*.

More important than the forgotten operetta is Bizet's Symphony in C Major composed in 1855, but never performed in the composer's lifetime and lost to sight until exactly eighty years later it was produced to the admiration of an astonished world by Felix Weingartner. Written in the space of a month, the Symphony bears witness not merely to Bizet's facility in composition, but also to a quite extraordinary precocity in the development of his musical imagination, that puts him in a class with Mozart and Mendelssohn, though not quite on the same level. For Bizet's Symphony, unlike "The Midsummer Night's Dream" Overture, is almost in the nature of a pastiche of the Viennese symphony—a cross between Haydn and early Schubert, though there is little probability that he had any opportunity of hearing much, if any, of Schubert's music.

The Prix de Rome, won in 1857, took Bizet to Italy, for which country he conceived a passionate admiration, though he had nothing but contempt for the Italians, so that at the end of his time at the Villa Medici he applied for leave to remain in Rome for another year instead of proceeding, as Gounod had done, to Germany. At this time his portrait was painted by Giacometti who shows him as a strikingly handsome young man with abundant curly hair and a soft, incipient beard. He wears pince-nez, but his poor vision has not yet produced the rather strained look of his later portraits.

During these years Bizet occupied himself with various operatic projects, most of them abortive. *Don Procopio,* an *opera buffa,* was completed, but not published until 1905 nor performed until the following year. His career as an opera-composer really begins with the production at the Théâtre Lyrique of *Les Pêcheurs de Perles.* The Théâtre Lyrique was the most enterprising of the Paris opera-houses. The Opéra itself was content to repeat the established repertory before an audience which was more interested in being seen than in attending to the performance. The production there of *Tannhäuser* in 1861 would have been an exceptional event, even if there had not been the notorious uproar. Nor need we put all the blame for the scandal upon the bad taste of the Jockey Club, when those who should have known better—writers like Mérimée and even Berlioz—showed themselves completely insensitive to Wagner's originality. If foreign genius was spurned, native talent received little encouragement.

The Opéra Comique, situated now in the Salle Favart, had likewise settled down into a routine, dominated by the octogenarian Auber who was still composing operas exactly like those he had written thirty years before, except that they lacked the old verve and had lost all pretension to individuality.

Only at the Théâtre Lyrique, under the direction of Léon Carvaille or Carvalho, did originality and youth have a chance. It was there, as we have seen, that *Faust* had its first hearing. There, too, Berlioz's *Les Troyens à Carthage* was produced. Bizet was the fortunate beneficiary of a new grant made by the Government to the Théâtre Lyrique on condition that each year a three-act opera by a recent winner of the Grand Prix de Rome was produced. It was in these circumstances that Carvalho offered Bizet the libretto of *Les Pêcheurs de Perles.*

The new opera was produced in September 1863 and achieved a modest success. It was damned by most of the critics, who accused Bizet of scoring noisily, of being wilfully bizarre, and, worst crime of all, of imitating Wagner. This last charge may well have been made against Bizet on account of his known admiration for Wagner, which had occasionally been expressed with some intemperance by the young enthusiast when confronted by stupidity and intolerance. Gounod, whose *Faust* had similarly been criticized for its Wagnerian tendencies (!), sought to restrain Bizet's tendency to outrage conventional opinion with his tongue. The way to kill bad music, he suggested, was to write good music; in twenty years' time Wagner, Berlioz, Schumann would reckon plenty of victims. "Be yourself," he urged, "and though you will be alone to-day, you will have the world at your feet to-morrow." Berlioz, as usual indifferent to current opinion, alone had a good word to say for *Les Pêcheurs de Perles* in the judicious article he wrote for *Le Journal des Débats.*

Having essayed this oriental theme, Bizet, whose taste lay always in the direction of the exotic, next turned to Russian history. His score of *Ivan le Terrible* was lost to view until about twenty-five years ago it came to light among the effects of the composer's widow who died in 1926. It was composed for the Théâtre Lyrique, but withdrawn by Bizet before it was quite finished because he felt that he had fallen too much under the influence of Verdi.

To this period belongs Bizet's friendship with Edmond Galabert, a young musician, whom he accepted as a pupil, and his association with Céleste Mogador, one-time circus-rider and now Comtesse de Chabrillan. From Galabert's memoirs we learn that Bizet insisted on the importance to a musician of a general education, especially in literature. This was a tenet far in advance of the usual opinion of the day. In music he set before his pupil as examples for study the operas of Mozart and Weber, and Bach's Preludes and Fugues. It is also of interest to note, as it is the conspicuous feature of his own orchestration, that he insists on the need for "air" in instrumentation. "Each part," he says, "must have around it room to move."

The Countess, for her part, acted as Egeria—an odd Egeria as she had no taste in music and was almost illiterate. She may, or may not, have been Bizet's mistress, as she had been Alfred de Musset's among a host of others. She set at his disposal a room where he could work and he spent much of his time with her. Despite her illiteracy, she fancied herself as a novelist and produced memoirs in which Bizet figures as an "aristocratic savage" who rarely laughed, watched over by his father, who regarded him with the reverence which "the Holy Virgin must have had for her Son."

Bizet was unhappy and, perhaps, already ill. He had since his student days suffered from an affection of the throat and chest, which he described as "angina"—not the familiar angina pectoris, a heart disease, but more probably quinsy or chronic tonsillitis. In these circumstances he set to work in the summer of 1866 upon the composition of a new opera for Carvalho. *La Jolie Fille de Perth*, based upon Scott's novel, was completed by December, but various difficulties at the Théâtre Lyrique, including the defection of Christine Nilsson who preferred to sing Ophelia in Ambroise Thomas's *Hamlet* at the Opéra, delayed its production until Christmas 1867. In the autumn he wrote to Galabert in high spirits:

I am completely happy! Never did an opera have a better start! The general rehearsal produced a great effect! . . . The director is delighted! The orchestra and singers are full of enthusiasm! And what is more important than all that, my dear friend, the score of *La Jolie Fille* is a good piece of work! . . . Now forward! No more evening parties! No more fits and starts! No more mistresses! All that is finished! I am talking seriously. I have met an adorable girl whom I love. . . .

The adorable girl was Geneviève Halévy, who became his wife two years later. In the meantime, however, there was a rift. Only a few days later Bizet wrote that the family had opposed the match; perhaps they had heard about the mistresses. Nor were fits and starts at an end. *La Jolie Fille* had a good press and eighteen performances, and it brought its composer a fair reward in francs. But it was handicapped by a bad libretto and was succeeded by half a dozen abortive essays all started under the same handicap, until in 1871 the one-act *Djamileh* was completed.

Meanwhile Napoleon III's Empire had crumbled. During the first stages of the catastrophe Bizet enlisted in the National Guard and remained in Paris throughout the siege. When the city fell and the riotings of the Communards made life more unbearable even than the disciplined assaults of the enemy, Bizet, disgusted with the stupidity, cowardice, and inefficiency he saw around him, took his frightened wife away from Paris to a place of safety. He even contemplated going abroad—to Italy, to England, or America.

Auber had died during the Commune, unable to survive the destruction of his world; Carvalho had left the Théâtre Lyrique, which had gone bankrupt but survived under the direction of Jules Pasdeloup; while at the Opéra Comique Adolphe de Leuven had since 1869 shared the management with Camille du Locle. Du Locle was a man of enterprise and immediately set about attracting new talent, to the consternation of his conservative partner. He approached Bizet who enthusiastically agreed to assist him in the reform of *opéra comique*. Young Victorien Sardou was also brought into the scheme. By comparison with de Leuven, the author of a hundred opera-books, he was a radical dramatist. But before the projected three-act opera had proceeded far, war and revolution made its production too costly, and the one-act *Djamileh,* based on Alfred de Musset's "Namouna," was substituted for it, and after long delays was produced in May 1872—a charming lyrical piece with, once more, an oriental setting, but with too little dramatic action to be successful in the theatre. "If only one of the characters would drop a plate!" said old de Leuven, not ungratified at the ill success of his partner's newfangled policy.

Bizet was fated to meet with failure and with lack of understanding from the critics and the public throughout his life. Only after his death did fame come to him, when on the very night of his funeral *Carmen,* hitherto damned by all, was suddenly discovered to be a masterpiece. The astonishing aspect of the criticisms of *Djamileh* is their unanimous insistence on the Wagnerian character of the score. One can only wonder what the critics knew of Wagner when they made this charge against music, which was so utterly un-Germanic and whose faults, whatever they are, could certainly not be attributed to Wagnerian influence. It is as though Poulenc were to be attacked for being unduly influenced by the theories of Schoenberg. In the same spirit Gounod had been attacked for imitating the late Quartets of Beethoven, which he was known to admire, and which his critic regarded as the source of all corruption in contemporary German music!

Although his artistic career brought these disappointments, his life during the short time that remained was ideally happy. At his funeral Gounod, moved to tears, related in the course of his tribute to his friend and pupil, how Geneviève Bizet had told him that there was not one moment in their married life that she would not wish to live again. When his son and only child, Jacques, was born in 1872, he was beside himself with delight.

During these last years he was occupied upon the two masterpieces by which he is most generally known—the music for Alphonse Daudet's tragedy, "L'Arlésienne," and *Carmen*. To these may be added the delightful Suite, "Jeux d'Enfants," originally composed for pianoforte duet, but orchestrated in part by Bizet himself as a "Petite Suite." This was contemporary with *Djamileh* and has become widely known in recent years through its adaptation as a ballet by Massine.

The music for "L'Arlésienne" was commissioned by Carvalho, who, having failed with opera at the Théâtre Lyrique, was now directing drama at the Vaudeville. Bizet was allowed an orchestra of twenty-six and a chorus. But the limitation of his resources only stimulated the composer, who put all his genius into the score which at a stroke raised the status of incidental music in the theatre from its deplorably low level. According to a writer quoted by Mr. Winton Dean, one stock device of the hacks who normally supplied such music was "to accompany every mention of the Virgin Mary with a banal tune on violins, two clarinets and three cornets in unison over a tremolo on violoncello and double bass."

For this reason "L'Arlésienne" brought Bizet little reward. The critics did not think such music worth their attention, and only Reyer, Berlioz's successor on the *Journal des Débats,* spoke up and acclaimed it a masterpiece. "Go and listen to 'L'Arlésienne,' you young musicians," he wrote, "who as yet disappoint your teachers, and perhaps you will be encouraged . . . when you see how much has been achieved by one who, only a few years back, was at school like yourselves."

The music had better success when, shortly after the production of the play, a suite arranged for full orchestra from it was played at one of Pasdeloup's concerts. It is a pity, incidentally, that in concert performances nowadays Guiraud's patchwork arrangement of the "Farandole" has supplanted Bizet's original "Carillon."

"L'Arlésienne" is a drama of real life played out against a Provençal background. As such it struck a new note in the drama of the nineteenth century— a note which was sustained in *Carmen,* likewise a drama of real life whose characters are neither princes nor legendary heroes, but ordinary men and women. The theme of Prosper Mérimée's novel, from which Henri Meilhac and Ludovic Halévy adapted their libretto, was the corruption of an ordinary, decent soldier by the vicious Carmen. The librettists invented Micaela, as a contrast to Carmen and as a symbol of José's origins and character, and produced the best libretto in the history of nineteenth-century French opera. Those who judge *Carmen* from the old stilted English translation—which contained such lines as 'Ha! what a glance! How saucy and audacious!'—should study the original text which is not without considerable literary merit and dramatically is quite first-rate. Bizet himself contributed to this result. His in the main are the words of the "Habanera" and he proposed beginning the "Seguidilla" with the words "Près des remparts de Séville" in place of the librettists' flat "J'irai dimanche en voiture," which for the sake of rhyme involved Carmen in the consumption of *une friture*.

The composition of *Carmen* was begun in the spring of 1873, but was laid aside for a time owing to a disagreement with the Opéra Comique, in favour of a work for the Opéra. This project, like so many in Bizet's career, came to nothing owing to the destruction of the opera-house by fire on 28 October. So work on *Carmen* was resumed, Bizet's differences with du Locle having apparently been overcome. He was seriously ill during the spring with a renewal of his throat-affection, but recovered his health somewhat at Bougival, where he had found a retreat from Paris. There the score was finished during the summer.

The production of *Carmen* was delayed by the opposition of de Leuven, who thought the subject quite outrageous. The Opéra Comique was essentially a "family theatre," where the good bourgeois of Paris took their sons and daughters, expecting blameless entertainment. Even du Locle and Halévy seem to have had their doubts, and when the opera was at last put into rehearsal at the beginning of 1875, they insisted on the action being toned down. There were other difficulties. In particular, the orchestral players, accustomed to the trivial scores of Auber and his like, found Bizet's delicately coloured instrumentation difficult to realize, while the chorus, expected for once in their lives to act, grumbled that some of their music was impossible to sing.

At last on 3 March *Carmen* was produced, and de Leuven's prognostication of its effects on the conventional public proved only too true. Halévy describes how, after a fairly warm reception for the first act, the audience grew more and more frigid, until at the end it was positively glacial. Bizet was disconsolate and wandered about Paris half the night with Guiraud, who after his death did him the disservice of composing the recitatives which have ever since replaced the spoken dialogue in most performances of *Carmen*. It is necessary, therefore, to emphasize the fact that Bizet's last work is in form an *opéra comique*.

It has often been said that the initial failure of *Carmen*, which was damned by the critics with hardly an exception, killed the composer, who died early on the morning of 3 June. It may well be that depression of spirits caused by a bitter disappointment laid him open to a renewal of the old infection of his throat. But the malady had been progressively gaining on him, and, in default of the later discoveries of medical science which would easily have saved his life, there is little reason to suppose that he could have survived another severe attack.

It was a dire calamity. At the age of thirty-five he had at last found himself and created his one masterpiece. Who knows what such a musician might not have achieved had he been allowed the normal span of life! At thirty-seven Verdi had not yet composed *Rigoletto* and Wagner had just finished *Lohengrin*. How small, comparatively speaking, would be their reputations, had they been cut off at that age! Even with the example of Rossini before us, which there is no reason to suppose that the sanguine Bizet would ever have followed, it is impossible not to feel that his early death was a major disaster in the history of music.

D. H.

Carmen

OPÉRA COMIQUE IN 4 ACTS

Book by HENRI MEILHAC and LUDOVIC HALÉVY, based on
PROSPER MÉRIMÉE's Story

First performance: Opéra Comique, Paris, Mar. 3, 1875

CHARACTERS

Don José, a brigadier, TENOR
Escamillo, a toreador, BARITONE
Zuniga, a captain, BASS
Moralès, a brigadier, BARITONE
Le Dancaire, TENOR
Le Remendado, TENOR
Micaëla, a peasant girl, SOPRANO

Frasquita, gypsy friend of Carmen,
  SOPRANO
Mercédès, gypsy friend of Carmen,
  SOPRANO
Carmen, a cigarette girl, and a gypsy,
  MEZZO-SOPRANO

An Innkeeper, Guide, Officer, Dragoons, Cigarette Girls, Gypsies, Smugglers

The action takes place at Seville, Spain, about 1820

Looking for her lover, Micaela, the country maid to whom Don José, corporal of dragoons, is engaged, enters a square in Seville. The relief arrives (military music and "Street Boys' Song") after she has gone, and José is told she has been seeking him. He thinks of her while the cigarette girls—their leader captivating Carmen— pour from the factory opposite. When soldiers, crowding around her, ask her to choose a lover she sings ("Habanera") with the indifferent José in mind: "If you do not love me, I'll love you and if I love you, beware!" and flings the flowers she wears to José with a provocative look and shrug. Micaela next delivers a kiss and letter from his mother (urging him to marry her) to her soldier. But now there is uproar in the factory. Carmen has stabbed another girl; José brings her out a prisoner. Pretending love, she so works on him he loosens the rope tying her hands, and she makes her escape.

In Lillia Pastia's tavern on Seville ramparts are Carmen, Frasquita and Mercedes (gypsy songs and dances). Jealous Morales, angry at Carmen's indifference, taunts her with loving José, sentenced to two months in the guardhouse for her escape. She laughs at the idea, and when the famous bullfighter Escamillo enters, devotes herself to him, enraging Morales, till both men leave. The tavern closed for the night, the innkeeper admits two smugglers. The other girls leave with them, but Carmen remains to meet José, and persuades him to join the lawless band. He comes, confesses his love, and Carmen so bewitches him he ignores the trumpet call to duty. Yet when she asks him to betray his soldier honor and join the smugglers he refuses. Fate then knocks at the door in the shape of Morales. When he orders José to leave, the latter disobeys and draws his sword. Smugglers and gypsies rush in to prevent a fight, but the die is cast. José knows his army days are over and joins the band.

José, on guard in the smugglers' mountain camp, is rallied by Carmen on his gloom. He tells her his thoughts are with an old woman who prays for her son in whom she believes, and the heartless gypsy mocks him, suggesting he abandon his uncongenial life. He protests his passion, then finding her unmoved, threatens to kill her. Death comes as fate decrees, is her answer, and she joins Frasquita and Mercedes, who are telling fortunes. The cards, no matter how she deals, predict she and her lover will die. The girls go to help the smugglers distract the attention of the guards and Micaela comes in. Before she can reveal herself a shot rings out; Escamillo enters seeking the gypsy girl. José (whose shot has not wounded him), wild with jealousy, challenges him. The advent of Carmen prevents a struggle, and Escamillo leaves, offering to meet José anywhere, at any time, and inviting all to the next bullfight in Seville. Micaela now tells José his mother lies on her deathbed and implores him to go to her. Unwilling to leave Carmen, he first refuses, then goes, vowing to return.

Carmen, now his love, beside him, the bullfighter in a gala procession of officials and *toreros,* enters the square where the people await their idol. About to enter the ring, Escamillo bids Carmen farewell, both vowing undying love. She ignores Frasquita and Mercedes, who warn her José may seek her. He appears—the man she has morally and physically destroyed—a dramatic contrast to his triumphant rival. Ruined, cheated, an outcast because of his love, he cannot forget it. He implores Carmen to be kind to him. But Escamillo's name sounds in the arena amid wild applause; Carmen's every thought is there. She repulses José with biting scorn, with such open joy in her passion for the bullfighter that, when Escamillo's name is again thundered forth by the unseen crowd José stabs her to the heart. As the crowd pours from the arena, Escamillo, seeking Carmen, at their head, José flings himself despairingly upon the dead body of the woman he adored.

F. H. M.

While no outstanding success in the beginning, *Carmen* had fifty performances at the Opéra-Comique before it was a year old. Then it was shelved at that house and not revived for seven years, during which time it became so popular in other French cities, as well as in England, Germany, and Italy, that the company was practically forced to revive it. Since then it has been a staple of the repertoire at the Opéra-Comique and in practically every other opera house in the world. After *Faust* it is the most popular French opera in modern history, and today—in the United States, at least—it is rapidly overtaking the prodigious number of performances Gounod's masterpiece has had.

The reason some of its original critics did not take to the work at once was its violence and the unsavory, low-class character of its heroine. Literary critics apparently had stronger stomachs than opera critics in nineteenth-century France, for the original story of *Carmen,* by Prosper Mérimée (who died five years before the *première* of Bizet's opera), was generally regarded as an excellent piece of writing. And Mérimée's Carmen is a much more unsavory and low-class character than the heroine put into the libretto by Henri Meilhac and Ludovic Halévy.*

Meilhac and Halévy knew their business. Their Carmen, unlike Mérimée's, is not married to an unpleasant thug while carrying on with a soldier; she does not go in for picking watches out of strangers' pockets; she does not go in for fighting with knives and conniving at murder; nor does she give up Don José for a mere picador. Mérimée's heroine, they knew, had to be washed—if not scrubbed—before she could be made presentable to the Opéra-Comique. They did their job with consummate skill: *Carmen* has just about as good a libretto as there is. Even so, the management disliked it right from the beginning. One member, Leuven, summarized its point of view like this:

"Isn't she assassinated by her lover?" he asked Halévy. "At the Opéra-Comique! A family theater! A theater for the promotion of marriages! We rent five or six boxes every night for these meetings of young couples. You are going to put our audience to flight. No, it's impossible." He begged Halévy not to let Carmen die. "Death has never been seen on this stage, do you hear, never! Don't let her die, I beg of you, my dear child."

One reason for Leuven's horror, obviously, was that [in Bizet's day] the word *comique* in Opéra-Comique really meant comedy and only operas with happy endings were performed. Since that time, some historians of music claim, the distinction between grand opera and *opéra comique* as given in Paris has come to mean that there are no spoken words in the former, while the latter has an appreciable amount of spoken dialogue. The distinction is almost valueless. For more than a generation the Opéra-Comique in Paris has included such works as *Tosca* and *Tristan et Isolde* in its repertoire, neither of which has spoken dialogue and both of which have very, very sad endings. Yet, with *Carmen* the French maintain this distinction by giving it in its original form—that is, with a good deal of spoken dialogue.

. . . Today both critics and public have hardier moral stomachs, stomachs that calmly digest even such unpleasant concoctions as *Salomé*. The Opéra-Comique has given *Carmen* well over twenty-two hundred times, and in 1940 the Metropolitan Opera Guild chose this tale of illicit love and brutal violence for its special children's matinees. America has also seen a Russian version called *Carmencita and the Soldier,* a Negro version called *Carmen Jones,* three motion-picture versions, and a bilingual performance in which Gertrud Wettergren, assuming the role at the Metropolitan on one day's notice, sang in Swedish while the rest of the cast sang in French.

Various reasons have been given for the enduring popularity of the opera.

---

* This Halévy should not be confused with his uncle, Jacques Halévy, Bizet's father-in-law and the composer of *La Juive*.

One is that it is so very Spanish. Spaniards usually deny this, and the opera has not been particularly popular in Spain. To non-Spanish ears, portions of the music certainly do sound like authentic local color, especially the Prelude to the last act. Yet there are many famous pages—like the "Flower Song" and the first-act duet between Don José and Micaela—that sound no more Spanish than anything in *Faust*.

Another reason given for its popularity is the attraction of the title role for almost any female singer. It may be sung by either soprano or contralto, and some women have essayed it with practically no voice at all. It lends itself to more varieties of stage business than any other role in opera. Every new Carmen is in some ways different from the others, and a great deal of nonsense is issued by press agents about the latest one going back to study the original sources. The ultimate original source is, of course, Mérimée's story, and any singer who tried to be faithful to that would necessarily be unfaithful to the librettists of the opera. The success or lack of it seems to be directly proportional to the success the singer has in projecting across the footlights—both dramatically and musically—a convincing and attractive gypsy. So many early Carmens seem to have been so successful with this role that any contemporary singer has to conquer the conservative and sentimental memories of older operagoers, who will softly murmur about Minnie Hauk, Emma Calvé, Zélie de Lussan, Maria Gay, Olive Fremstad, or any one of half a dozen others. . . .

Still another element contributing to the popularity of the opera is a few of its tunes. The "Habanera" and the "Toreador Song" * are now almost a part of our folk music. Yet one or two popular tunes are not enough to insure comparative immortality for any opera. Who recalls even the plot of Bishop's *Clari, the Maid of Milan,* in which "Home, Sweet Home" is the principal musical fare?

The ultimate cause for *Carmen's* success lies, I think, in the public's excellent taste. *Carmen* is just about as nearly perfect an opera as there is. It has a good, vigorous, believable story; it has at least two three-dimensional characters; even its minor characters are sketched with complete credibility. It is good theater throughout, and the music not only refuses to get in its way, but it helps at every turn. It underlines the dramatic situations; it has tunes that are at once singable, memorable, and in character; it suggests vividly the bright color of the setting; its orchestration is brilliant without ever overshadowing the voices or the action. No other opera in the standard repertoire makes it at once so unmistakably clear what all the shooting and the shouting are about, and in few other operas do the shooting and the shouting seem to matter so much.

H. W. S.

---

* The "Toreador Song" was actually inserted into the opera by Bizet over his own poorer judgment. He had written a more dignified aria for the baritone, which is said to have been out of character. When he turned up with the most popular baritone number in all opera, he remarked, "Ah well, they want filth. Here it is."

The world may thank the Parisian theatrical manager Léon Carvalho for bringing Bizet the first subject matter worthy of his remarkable sense of atmosphere. Demoted from the helm of the Opéra Lyrique to that of the humbler Théâtre du Vaudeville, where opera was unproducible, this intrepid impresario had set out to introduce a Gallic melodrama modeled after Beethoven's "Egmont." For his first venture he chose Daudet's "L'Arlésienne" for theme and entrusted Bizet with the incidental music. Bizet had never set foot in the South of France; yet, the group of numbers he devised convey the tang of Provençal soil and the poetry of Provençal song—from bardic noëls of King René's day to age-old shepherds' lays of Provence. Not even the circumstance that these orchestral pieces and choruses had to be moulded for the Vaudeville's twenty-six-piece orchestra could hamper their imagery. To hear the "L'Arlésienne Suite" in its original form is to know that its brilliance and sonority owe nothing to the arrangement for symphony orchestra made by Ernest Guiraud in which it survives outside of France.

Conscious, at last, of his full powers, Bizet himself chose the subject for his next effort—Mérimée's "Carmen"; and chose it with a conviction so firm that he had no difficulty in persuading the ablest team of theatre poets of the day, Henri Meilhac and Ludovic Halévy, to adapt it for him. The root of this sovereign among short stories had been a meeting between Mérimée, during a visit to Spain in 1830, and the American-born Countess Montijo whose four-year-old daughter was by Bizet's time to be empress of France. From this garrulous matron Mérimée had learned of little-known episodes in the reign of Don Pedro the Cruel, each of which, with one exception, he was later to turn to account for a critical study of that monarch. The omitted episode was such a shattering adventure of jealousy that he preferred to treat it as a separate tale, re-cast in a gypsy setting; and his "Letters to an Unknown" shed light on his change of locale. "You asked me the other day," he reminds his anonymous confidante, "where I obtained my knowledge of gypsy dialect. I had so many things to tell you that I forgot to reply. I acquired it from Mr. Borrow. His book is the most compelling I have ever read." This uniquely compelling book had been "The Zincali," which the Romany-souled George Borrow had woven from his own experiences among brigands and smugglers of the Peninsula. Indeed, without Borrow's remarkable exposé of *gitano* life Mérimée's "Carmen" might never have been written. Countess Montijo's story had quite faded from his mind when the appearance of the French edition of "The Zincali" (Paris, 1842) recalled it and fired him to develop it *à la* Borrow. And if he appropriated countless details of plot and description, he atoned a little for the taking with the sheer perfection of his style.

His "Carmen" first came out in the *Revue des Deux Mondes* of October, 1845, and stunned Paris—still obstinately romanticist—with its amorality. By the time Bizet decided to base an opera upon it literary circles of the capital were beginning to dabble in realism, but the Parisian theatre continued hostile.

To proceed with his idea called, therefore, for courage of a high order, especially since he meant to adhere as closely as possible to Mérimée. The libretto as he first planned it ("Théâtre de Meilhac et Halévy," Vol. VII) abounds in brutal dialogue, little of which remains in Guiraud's adaptation for accompanied recitative in which it has come down. It cites, for instance, Carmen's smuggling of a file and gold piece into José's prison cell and pictures the harsh relief into which the incident throws their two natures when they meet soon afterward at Pastia's tavern. And it treats the duel in the mountain scene as one of the crises of the drama, rather than as a passing episode. Mérimée's own portrait of a bullfighter in his "Les Courses de Taureaux" is no more biting a study of the type than the Escamillo of this scene. Bizet's wish to retain the verity and somber beauty of the tale is everywhere apparent. The Carmen he conceived and urged Meilhac and Halévy to re-create for him was the primitive wanton with a human strain whom Mérimée had brought to life, rather than the French coquette in gypsy trappings whom we know.

Naturally, with transference to another medium, particularly that of nineteenth century opera, certain changes were inevitable. The Basque hero's brutalities had to be toned down to a lover's crime of passion. The lowly picador Lucas had to be reincarnated as a dashing *espada* and made to integrate Carmen's many promiscuities. Her depraved husband, García Le Borgne, had to be banished, together with the thefts and assassinations in which she was his ready accomplice. And in order to provide a foil to so unprincipled a heroine a virtuous Navarraise had to be introduced. These and various smaller changes were routine matters which Bizet could not well protest. But it is gratifying to learn from memoirs of his associates that he detested Micaela's too conscious prudery, that he forbade the injection of a pathetic air in the card scene and in the final act in which Carmen was to have been shown capable of reform; that until the end he hounded his librettists to picture Mérimée's gypsy as Mérimée had conceived her. A sketch of Act I owned by the heirs of Emile Strauss, a cousin of Mme. Bizet, shows that he wrote the verses for the Habanera himself, and that the idea of resorting to Pushkin's "Les Bohémiens" for Carmen's scorching challenge to the authorities, "Coupes-moi, brûles-moi," was neither Meilhac's nor Halévy's, but his own.

"Day before yesterday," wrote Friedrich Nietzsche late in the year 1881 to his sister Elizabeth Förster-Nietzsche, "I heard *Carmen,* an opera by some Frenchman named Bizet. I was thunderstruck! How vital, how impassioned, how Southern!" Five days later, in a note to the composer Peter Gast, he vows to hear it is "worth a whole journey to Spain." In other words, this untraveled and un-erudite Parisian composer who had never so much as glimpsed the Spanish frontier, whose conception of what lay beyond could only have derived from reading Mérimée and perhaps "Don Quixote" or "Gil Blas," whose meagre education would have made research in Spanish music impossible even if resources in that field had been available in his day, had created an example of Spanish music that was to disseminate its spirit throughout the world and incite more eager interest in its development than any aroused by Glinka, Rimsky-Korsakoff, and others of greater learning and of first-hand knowledge of Spain. In point of fact, except for the air to habanera rhythm in Act I, the Prelude to Act IV, and a few scattered phrases, the music of *Carmen* is not really Spanish at all; even in these numbers it is more often the Spain of the music hall than that of the folk that sounds. Bizet's greater achievement was to create a non-existent Spain and suffuse it with an electrifying atmosphere.

Long after his death, his widow (daughter of his old master at the Conservatory, Jacques-François Halévy) expressed the belief that the sole source from which he drew an idea of Spanish form had been the album "Fleurs d'Espagne" (1864) compiled by Sebastian Yradier, a mediocre Spanish singing teacher imported to Paris by the Empress Eugénie. His "Fleurs" seems nevertheless to have filled a certain need in its day. Daudet associated one of its airs with a character in "Fromont jeune et Risler aîné"; the younger Dumas put another air in the mouth of the heroine of "L'Ami de Femmes"; Lenepveu, Philipot, and various other composers of operetta drew upon it for themes; Patti, Malibran, Viardot-Garcia and other current divas dipped into it for repertory. Bizet's acknowledgement to Yradier's publishers in the first edition of *Carmen* shows that he, too, borrowed one number—"El Areglito," a banal ballad to a Cuban tune of Moorish source—for Carmen's entrance air. But there are no documents to support the hardy legend that he had recourse to Yradier only as a last resort after many unsuccessful attempts to please Célestine Galli-Marié, the first interpreter of the title role. The absence of any indications in the autograph that her entrance air was rewritten, and the presence at the close of Act I of a twenty-five-measure orchestral repetition of its theme, showing that it was conceived as an integral part of the music, denote, rather, that he borrowed the air in the very early stages of the composition.

But evidence has come to light that Bizet had recourse to other sources. In *Le Ménestrel* of March, 1925, the French musicologist Julien Tiersot tells of an ex-employee of his acquaintance in the library of the Conservatory who had amassed a collection of valuable autographs by pocketing slips on which famous musicians applied for books. One slip in his collection bore the signature "Bizet" and the words "I request a list of the Spanish songs in the possession of the Library." Tiersot ascertained that the only genuine Spanish music then on the Conservatory shelves had been "Echos d'Espagne" (1872), an anonymous anthology sometimes wrongly attributed to Yradier, whose "Fleurs d'Espagne" the Conservatory did not list. The "Echos" were found to consist of authentic Spanish airs which the preface stated to have been, barring one air by the elder Manuel García, of unknown origin. The preface told, further, that this air by García derived from his own "El Poeta çalculista," an opus which his biographers classify as a "tonadilla," a kind of Spanish intermezzo that seems to have been his favorite vocal form of composition. Tiersot consulted the García manuscripts at the Conservatory and not only found this air in "El Poeta calculista" but recognized it as Bizet's model for his Prelude to the final act of *Carmen*—those one hundred and sixty-four measures of flurrying Moorish figurations that are among the most haunting pages in the opera. In the context of García's air he even spotted the *Carmen* Fate motive—that five-note phrase with the augmented second that sums up, with its sombre inevitability, the entire tragedy.

But García, too, may have borrowed. Around this same time a fragment of his lost tonadilla "Griado fingido" (a discovery of Joaquin Nin's) came to Tiersot's notice; and the striking similarity which it bore to the air from "El Poeta calculista," together with the pungent street flavor of each, convinced him that both were variants of some Spanish street song on which the gypsy-born García had embroidered, much as Bizet, seven decades later, and with infinitely deeper penetration of the folk spirit that begat it, was to embroider.

For the rest of the opera Bizet either relied on his intuition for Spanish atmosphere or made no attempt at local color. For a few themes he even fell back on ideas he had originally conceived for an unfinished setting for Sardou's "Grisélidis." Yet, had he known the proper Spanish forms he could not have bared the soul of each character with greater naturalness or thrust. His essentially French declamation in the final scene is even more searching a delineation of human cruelty and despair than Mérimée's own dénouement.

"Yesterday I heard Bizet's masterpiece for the twentieth time," begins one of the most noted pages in music criticism: "The Case of Wagner" (1896). Here Nietzsche hails Bizet as quite as much of a saviour of art as Wagner.

But with Bizet one may flee the fog-ridden North and the misty Wagnerian esthetic. His music has the tang of sunny climates, their bracing air, their clearness. It voices a sensibility hitherto unknown to us, a gaiety we have never experienced, neither French, nor German, but African; destiny lowers over it; its joy is short-lived, sudden, ruthless. I envy Bizet for having had the courage of this Southern sunburnt sensibility never before voiced in the music of civilized Europe . . . Music must be Mediterraneanized!

True, Nietzsche at the time was in search of a type of opera which he could oppose to the music drama of his dethroned idol Wagner, and *Carmen,* by reason of its extraordinary popularity, offered the needed work. Yet, ulterior motives alone cannot have prompted his rapturous endorsement, for the opera itself would have compelled appreciation from a man of his musical awareness. What might conceivably have intensified his natural enthusiasm is the attraction which the primitive ever holds for the over-civilized man.

In a sense, the music to come after Bizet did capture the Mediterranean tang of *Carmen*. The Italian realists—not only such consummate masters of *verismo* as Puccini and Montemezzi but Grand Guignol verists like Mascagni and Leoncavallo—each echoed the "Southern sun-burnt sensibility" which Bizet had had the courage—and genius—to voice, if none echoed it with his style or his taste. But Bizet's greater contribution to opera was to have created a score in which the rising *opéra lyrique* of France emerged from its prettified framework for a moment of true drama. And though his *Carmen* had no lineal descendant—for French opera either continued the salon lyricism of Gounod or turned to the Wagnerian world—it reaffirmed the essential qualities of French opera with a power that established *opéra lyrique* as a national form and attracted to its orbit the foremost exponents of national and veristic opera of Europe.

K. O'D. H.

The first performance of *Carmen* in the United States took place at the Academy of Music, New York, Oct. 23, 1878, in Italian. Minnie Hauk (Carmen), Mme. Sinico (Micaela), Italo Campanini (Don José), and Giuseppe del Puente (Escamillo) had the chief roles. Though the work has been sung here oftenest in the original French, it has been given in English, in German, and even in Russian (in a much altered version entitled *Carmencita and the Soldier*). Gertrud Wettergren, a Swede, sang Carmen at the Metropolitan Opera House, New York, Jan. 16, 1936, in her native tongue, while the other performers proceeded as usual in official French.

[*Carmen* was performed at the Metropolitan during its opening season, on Jan. 9, 1884. The performance was in Italian, and the cast included Trebelli, Campanini, and del Puente.]

A memorable Metropolitan *Carmen* cast of the 1890's offered Zélie de Lussan, Melba, and the De Reszké brothers in the leading parts. Gay, Farrar, Caruso, and Noté sang them there in 1908, with Arturo Toscanini conducting. The demand for *Carmen* in New York may be gathered from the fact that in one season at the Metropolitan Calvé sang the part as often as fifteen times. At Oscar Hammerstein's Manhattan Opera House during the season of 1906-7 there were nineteen performances of *Carmen,* the first fifteen with Bressler-Gianoli as the heroine, the last four with Calvé. On Dec. 27, 1935, Rosa Ponselle added Carmen to her repertory, likewise at the Metropolitan, with Hilda Burke, Giovanni Martinelli, and Ezio Pinza as her chief associates.

In this country *Carmen* provoked no less discussion than it had done in Paris. *The New York Times* called the plot not only "uninteresting even to dulness," but "almost offensive in its combined puerility and brutality." According to the New York *Tribune,* "To say that Bizet in his music hesitates between *Lohengrin* and *La Belle Hélène* is hardly an exaggerated statement of his odd position." Reviewers in Cincinnati and Cleveland fell foul of the opera on moral grounds.

For the *première* of *Carmen* in Vienna Ernest Guiraud, a native of New Orleans, composed recitatives to take the place of the spoken dialogue. These recitatives are used habitually in this country, though never in France.

                                                                              P. S.

Arrigo Boïto

(Padua, Italy, Feb. 24, 1842–June 10, 1918, Milan)

One of the few musicians altruistic enough to subordinate personal acclaim and public favor to the ideals of music was Arrigo Boïto. . . . Though known in this country principally as the librettist of Verdi's last—and probably greatest—operas, the Shakespearean *Otello* (1887) and *Falstaff* (1893), Boïto is an important composer in his own right. His international reputation in this regard is gradually growing now; in his native Italy his works have always been highly esteemed.

His extensive travels on the continent and in England brought Boïto in closer contact with the general trend of European music than any other contemporary Italian composer save Verdi. His journeys fathered his ardent desire to reform Italian music along the lines of Berlioz and Wagner. He criticized even the works of Verdi, whose best friend he was to become.

Boïto first met Verdi while writing the words for the senior composer's "Hymn of the Nations" in 1862. His unselfish interest in the furtherance of music as an art is best seen in his insistence that Verdi, for fourteen years idle in the field of opera, return to composition for the stage, a return which resulted in *Falstaff* and *Otello*.

Boïto's principal work, the opera *Mefistofele,* was a complete failure at its *première* in Milan in 1868. But, revised and performed again at Bologna in 1875, it gradually became more and more popular everywhere. Its first unfavorable reception is probably explained by the fact that *Mefistofele* was for a while considered a competitor of Gounod's *Faust,* since both librettos had their source in Goethe's masterwork, "Faust." The Boïto score, however, more closely follows the idea of Goethe's work, sometimes even sacrificing dramatic effect in retaining the original's depth and meaning.

The son of an Italian painter and a Polish countess, Arrigo Boïto lived to witness many of the most important events in modern European history, as well as an astounding revolution in style in every field of the arts. Old enough to sense the Romanticism lavished on literature and music in the mid-Nineteenth Century, he was but a boy when Victor Hugo, the French Romanticist, complimented him on his knowledge of the classics. In the course of his lifetime, Boïto was torn between literature and music; his literary and critical works rank him high in Italy.

He studied at the Conservatory of Milan, graduating with the composition of a cantata, "Il 4 Giugno" (1860). It was his cantata, "Le Sorelle d'Italia" (1862), one of his own poems set to music in collaboration with a friend,

Franco Faccio, which brought him a government prize making possible his first sojourns in France and Germany. Visiting now in many countries of Europe, he studied assiduously their literature and music, but it was French and German art in which he was most absorbed. This interest led eventually to his *Mefistofele*. Always his own librettist, Boïto wrote two other operas: *Nerone,* completed by Arturo Toscanini and first performed under the great conductor's baton in Milan in 1924, and *Ero e Leandro,* of which only fragments remain today.

W. H., P. Z.

Mefistofele

OPERA IN A PROLOGUE, 4 ACTS, AND AN EPILOGUE

Book by the COMPOSER, based on GOETHE's *Faust*

First performance: La Scala, Milan, Mar. 5, 1868

CHARACTERS

Faust, TENOR
Mephistopheles, BASS
Wagner, a student, TENOR

Margherita, SOPRANO
Marta, Margherita's mother, CONTRALTO
Helen of Troy, SOPRANO

The action takes place in Frankfurt and in Greece

Mephistopheles appears (Prologue) about to descend to earth to tempt Faust, too wise in his own conceit. Angelic choirs sing in chorus, while cherubim and seraphim cast themselves before the Throne, and the voices of repentant sinners swell heaven's harmonies.

Bells peal gaily in Frankfurt, soldiers and students sing, peasants dance, and cheers ring out as the Elector rides past. To escape a grey friar who clings to him like a shadow, Faust leaves the streets for his study. As he turns from an apostrophe to Nature and opens his Bible, Mephistopheles (the monk) darts from a dark corner with a scream. Dropping his grey gown he stands forth in knightly dress, and promising to do Faust's bidding in exchange for his soul, bears him off on his cloak.

While Mephistopheles dallies with Marta, Margherita's mother, Faust wins the daughter's heart in the garden. After the Evil One and his victim have left (change of scene), they attend the witches' Sabbath on the Brocken. There, on a Grecian river bank Faust meets Helen of Troy, to whom he makes passionate love; and the shade of the World's Desire tells of the fall of Troy while Greek sirens weave voluptuous dances about her fifteenth century lover, picturing Margherita's fate, till Mephistopheles holds up the crystal globe they give him, crying "Behold the earth!" and the fantastic revels end.

Margherita in prison, convicted of the murder of her nameless child, calls on God to forgive her. Insane, she does not understand Faust, who has come to release her, and on the stroke of dawn he leaves at Mephistopheles' summons, as Margherita dies, angelic voices singing her pardon.

Faust (Epilogue), burdened with remorse, refuses Mephistopheles' traveling cloak. In vain the Archfiend surrounds him with voluptuous women in a final assault on his senses. The philosopher opens his Bible: while the lamp holds out to burn, the Scriptures tell him he may be saved. He turns to Heaven, prays and—dies. Celestial roses, covering his body, show that Divine forgiveness has been vouchsafed him. Mephistopheles, foiled, disappears, while angel voices exult in the Archfiend's defeat and Faust's salvation.

F. H. M.

In 1866 the war with Austria put an end to musical business. Boïto, Faccio, and others joined the volunteer corps under Garibaldi, and fought bravely. When the campaign was over, Boïto thought of a literary career in Paris. Victor Hugo urged him to come, and gave him a warm letter of introduction to Émile de Girardin. Boïto arrived at Paris in the spring of 1867, determined to be a journalist; but Girardin was then the hero of a political *cause célèbre,* and, as the introduction led to nothing, Boïto visited a sister in Poland. He sketched there the music for an arrangement of Goethe's whole poem, and completed some of the chief scenes, but without thought of a performance, for he purposed to return to Paris in the fall. Meanwhile the managers of La Scala heard that Boïto was at work on *Faust,* and managed to obtain the opera.

It must be fairly owned [says Mazzucato] that the public was not ready to understand the new language he intended to speak, nor did the poet and composer know clearly what he was going to say to them. There is no denying that the original *Mefistofele,* though poetically and philosophically admirable, was, taken as an opera, both incongruous and amorphous. It was an interminable work, with very deficient and feeble orchestration, no dramatic interest, and composed without the most distant thought of pleasing the taste of opera-goers. The conception was sublime and the outline bold and startling; but it was little more than a sketch, or a cartoon for a fresco, and the real work was absolutely wanting. It would have taken at least a year to get it properly ready, if the author had chosen to follow up the original scheme; but Boïto found himself with very few months before him, barely sufficient to put the materials together.

There were fifty-two rehearsals. The interpreters at last were enthusiastic over the music. All the seats and standing-room were sold weeks before the performance. Boïto was allowed to conduct the opera, and the libretto was published and sold before the opening night,—two breaches of custom.

The Prologue provoked thunders of applause. The first act was received coolly; the Garden Scene displeased the audience. The "Sabba Romantico" was considered irreverent, and the audience hissed and howled, for at the moment of Mephistopheles' coronation the wizards and witches knelt and sang the plain-song of the "Tantum Ergo."

Boïto's partisans stood him in good stead, and kept up to the very end of the opera a strong opposition to the majority, but this of course served only to increase the disturbance. Challenges were exchanged, resulting in duels the next morning. The confusion and clamor in the theatre reached such a pitch that during the fourth and fifth acts it was at times utterly impossible to hear either chorus or orchestra. When the curtain fell for the last time, all the members of the orchestra rose to their feet like one man and enthusiastically cheered the unfortunate composer; a rush was made from the pit into the stalls, and a shrieking and howling crowd hissing and applauding wildly rushed forward toward the orchestra. The house was cleared and the frantic audience fought it out in the streets until the next morning. The performance had lasted nearly six hours.

It is said that the interpreters of the chief characters were wholly inadequate. In the course of the week the Prologue and first, second, and third acts were given at one performance, and on the following night the Prologue, fourth and fifth acts. The conflict still raged, and the chief of police thought it best to interfere. *Mefistofele* was withdrawn *by order.*

Cambiesi, in his History of La Scala, recording the production of *Mefistofele,* adds this critical note: *Cattivo,* which means "miserable."

The score of the original version has not been printed. "The *Mefistofele* in its present form bears the same relation to the original work as W. G. Wills's 'Faust' to Goethe's masterpiece: it is an adaptation for the stage, of more practical use than the original, but of far less artistic import."

In the first version of the opera Faust was a baritone. The scene at Frankfort in the first act and the "Sabba Romantico" were much more freely developed, and each might have been performed as a cantata. The scene at the Emperor's Palace has been cut out. A highly original "Intermezzo sinfonico" stood between the fourth and fifth acts.

It was meant to illustrate the battle of the Emperor against the pseudo-Emperor, supported by the infernal legions led by Faust and Mephistopheles—the incident which in Goethe's poem leads to the last period of Faust's life. The three themes— that is the Fanfare of the Emperor, the Fanfare of the pseudo-Emperor, and the *Fanfare infernale*—were beautiful in conception and interwoven in a masterly manner, and the scene was brought to a close by Mefistofele leading off with "Te Deum Laudamus" after the victory.

P. H.

The achievement of Arrigo Boïto in providing Verdi with two librettos of surpassing excellence would be enough to keep his name fresh in any history of the opera. His selflessness in turning aside from the composition of his own *Nerone* to serve another man has often been pointed out. Yet, an examination of his operas shows that Boïto's choice was a proof of his critical acumen: his literary gifts surpassed his musical. An intellectual of volatile character, sensitive, refined, squeamish, and a touch feminine, Boïto, who had devoured libraries of theory by his early twenties, was wont to ponder and polish a musical phrase until it had lost not only its bloom but also its connection with neighboring phrases on either side. Yet, he managed to write one opera—*Mefistofele* —not too sicklied over with the pale cast of thought. After that, he labored over *Nerone,* his second and last completed opera, for fifty-four years. He did not live to see this unwieldy epic performed: six years after his death, Toscanini conducted its *première* at La Scala on May 1, 1924. Received with riotous enthusiasm by a distinguished audience, *Nerone* nevertheless has not emigrated. The character of the music may be deduced from a single suggestive incident: in 1902, after permitting *Nerone* to be announced for La Scala, this most encyclopedic of closet musicians withdrew it, saying that he did not "know" harmony, and was going to study it in some mountain retreat.

Mefistofele was merely a more youthful example of the hesitant processes of this exacerbated mentality. It was first produced at La Scala on March 5, 1868, and ran six hours, its unqualified failure retiring it for seven years, during which Boïto subjected it to a major overhauling. Faust was changed from a baritone to a tenor, and the opera, much shortened, was presented again at Bologna on October 4, 1875. This time it was successful: it has remained popular in Italy and has had fitful spells of popularity elsewhere. Examination of this version shows that Boïto had studied the techniques of many masters— Beethoven, Berlioz, Verdi, possibly Wagner. It shows him, more ambitious than Messrs. Barbier, Carré, and Gounod, attempting to compass the whole of Goethe's history of man. But it shows him, unfortunately, less musically vital than Gounod, to whom he might well have given some of his sheer power of intellection in exchange for some of the Frenchman's sensuality. The music is clever, but parched and thin. Life of its own it has but little—certain performers, notably Chaliapin, the most famed of its Devils, have been able to galvanize it with their own vitality. That the score of *Mefistofele* was ransacked for ideas by many of Boïto's younger contemporaries, even possibly by Verdi himself, is unquestionable, and Huneker's summing up of the situation is essentially true: "Boïto seems to have been the pivotal point of the neo-Italian school—himself remaining in the background—while the youngsters profited by his many experimentings."

One of the most interesting of the early *Mefistofeles* outside Italy was the London *première,* on July 6, 1880, when the apparently unrivaled quartet of Nilsson (Margherita and Elena), Trebelli (Marta and Pantalis), Italo Campanini (Faust), and Nannetti (Mefistofele) sang it at Her Majesty's. The Academy of Music staged the first American *Mefistofele,* with Valleria, Annie Louise Cary, Campanini, and Novara, on November 24, 1880. Excepting Nannetti, the Her Majesty's group appeared in the first Metropolitan performance, on December 5, 1883, with Mirabella as the Devil. Plançon and Renaud, both singing actors in the best French tradition, also interpreted Mefistofele in New York, but the role is most intimately connected with the name of Fyodor Chaliapin, who used it for his Metropolitan debut, on November 20, 1907. Farrar was the Margherita, Rappold the Elena, and Riccardo Martin, also making his Metropolitan debut, the Faust, in which role Beniamino Gigli also made his bow there, on November 26, 1920. Although the Devil remained one of Chaliapin's most admired roles, *Mefistofele* disappeared from the Metropolitan long before he did and has not been heard there since the season of 1925–26.

                                                                  W. B., H. W.

Alexander Borodin

(St. Petersburg, Nov. 11, 1833–Feb. 27, 1887, St. Petersburg)

Alexander Porphyrievitch Borodin was one of the most distinguished members of the small group of Russian composers (commonly, but misleadingly, called "The great Five," or "The mighty handful") who came after Glinka and, following his lead, aimed at writing thoroughly Russian music. That his musical output should have been of so great a significance is particularly remarkable for the reason that composition was not his profession, but merely a spare time occupation, indulged in obedience to an irresistible impulse. He was a scientist and a doctor, and also devoted a large part of his time to organizing musical education—especially courses for women.

Borodin was born out of wedlock, his father being a Georgian nobleman, Prince Luke Ghedeanoff, and his mother, Eudoxia Kleineke, née Antonova. According to Russian usage in such cases, he was registered as the legitimate son of one of his father's serfs, Porphyry Borodin. His father died in 1840, and he was brought up under his mother's care. He showed an early interest in both music and science. At the age of nine, he composed a little Polka, the manuscript of which is preserved. It shows slight but unmistakable signs of imaginativeness.

From that time on he began to receive music lessons. He also used to play piano duets and chamber music with friends. In 1847 he composed a flute concerto and a string trio (manuscripts lost). In 1850 he matriculated at the Academy of Medicine and Surgery, receiving his degree in 1855. He continued to devote to music all the time he could afford. And throughout his life, his dual activities pursued their course; he made his mark in the field of chemistry as well as in music. Continuing his scientific studies abroad, he met in Heidelberg a young Russian pianist, Catherine Protopopova, who in 1863 became his wife.

During these years he turned out a few compositions, notably piano fugues (1855; lost), a string sextet (1860; lost) and a piano quintet (1862; preserved in manuscript; it shows signs of individuality). But in the matter of composition, he remained entirely self-taught until, in 1862, he met Balakireff, who was already teaching Cui and Mussorgsky, and who persuaded him to take up the study of the craft in earnest, and to start by composing a symphony forthwith.

This task was carried out under Balakireff's strict supervision; it proceeded slowly, and the symphony was finished in 1867 only. It was first performed on Jan. 16, 1869, Balakireff conducting. It was received with favour, although found amateurish in many respects. Borodin revised it later. In its final form, it reveals a measure of inexperience in conception, but a fine sense of technique, and glowing imagination.

In 1866–67, he turned out a farcical opera, *The Bogatyrs* (The Valiant Knights), the score of which consisted partly of original music, partly of parodies of the music of Meyerbeer, Rossini, Seroff and others. This was produced in October, 1867, at Moscow, without its authorship being revealed. It had no success. The score, the manuscript of which was discovered in 1922 (and produced in 1936), is described by Russian critics of today as teeming with wit and humour.

That year was marked by other activities. Borodin started planning a second symphony, composed four of his finest songs ("The Queen of the Sea," "The Song of the Dark Forest," "Dissonance" and "My song is fierce and bitter") and turned his thoughts to composing an opera. He first attempted to set to music a libretto of his own devising, after Mey's play "The Tsar's Bride," but soon gave up the notion. In 1869 Vladimir Stassoff . . . suggested to him the subject of *Prince Igor,* which he took up with enthusiasm. He experienced many difficulties in building up the libretto, composed the music fitfully, at long intervals, and did not succeed in finishing it.

The Second Symphony, in B Minor, was finished in 1877. A good many musical ideas conceived for *Prince Igor* were used in this work, which accounts for its epic character. The first performance took place on March 10, 1877, under unsatisfactory conditions, which rendered failure unavoidable. Both it and the First Symphony were to win appreciation abroad before finding favour in Russia, where the critics, especially, were no less indignant with him on account of his bold innovations than they were with Mussorgsky for the same reason.

In 1877, in the course of a journey abroad for professional purposes, Borodin paid a visit to Liszt in Weimar, and received from him high praise and warm encouragement. In 1880, the performance, upon Liszt's recommendation, of his First Symphony at Baden-Baden opened the long series of successes scored by his music abroad. Upon returning home, he finished the splendid String Quartet in A Major, which he had begun planning in 1875. After that, he strove to concentrate upon making headway with *Igor*. The list of his other compositions during the following years is short: a few songs, a few instrumental pieces, the tone-picture "On the Steppes of Central Asia" (1880, commissioned for a performance of tableaux vivants), a second string quartet (D Major, 1881–85), an orchestral Scherzo (1885). In 1886 he started outlining a Third Symphony, in A Minor, of which two movements were finished in rough draft when death overtook him unexpectedly on Feb. 27, 1887, caused by a heart aneurism.

In 1885 and 1886 Borodin had paid visits to Belgium and witnessed the ever-growing success of his music there. He also had the joy of learning that it enjoyed equally great success in several European countries and in the United States. He was the first Russian composer to achieve an international reputation.

M. D. C.

Prince Igor

OPERA IN A PROLOGUE AND 4 ACTS

Book by the COMPOSER and VLADIMIR STASSOV

First performance: Imperial Opera House, St. Petersburg, Oct. 23, 1890

CHARACTERS

Prince Igor, BARITONE
Jaroslavna, his wife, SOPRANO
Vladimir, their son, TENOR
Prince Galitsky, Igor's brother-in-law, BASS
Khan Kontchak, BASS

Kontchakovna, his daughter, CONTRALTO
Nurse, SOPRANO
Erochka, a warrior, TENOR
Skula, a warrior, BASS
Ovlour, TENOR

Courtiers, Peasants, Soldiers, Citizens, Tartars, Polovtsian Maidens and Warriors

The action takes place in medieval and semilegendary Russia

Prince Igor of Severski, after entrusting his wife Yaroslovna to the care of Prince Galitsky, his brother-in-law, sets out from Poutivle with his army to vanquish the Polovtses, a hostile Oriental tribe encamped near by. Vladimir, his son, accompanies him. In his absence Prince Galitsky secretly plots with two deserters, Eroshka and Skoula, to seize the government. Yaroslovna violently denounces her brother when she gets wind of the conspiracy. To make matters worse, news arrives of Prince Igor's defeat at the hands of the savage Polovtses.

While Prince Galitsky is completing his *coup d'état,* Igor and his son are being lavishly entertained by their hospitable captor, the Khan Konchak. When Ovlour, a Polovtsian convert to Christianity, offers Vladimir a means of escape, the young son of Igor refuses, out of gratitude to his magnanimous foe. Besides, he has fallen in love with Konchakovna, the khan's daughter. He thinks better of the offer later when the Polovtsians return from his father's capital city dragging prisoners and laden with the spoils of war.

Vladimir, Igor, and Ovlour make their escape. Prince Igor and the Polovtsian renegade arrive in Poutivle, where the usurper Galitsky is promptly unseated. Vladimir, however, is captured during their flight and is saved only by the intercession of the khan's daughter.

P. S.

The struggle between Russian and Asiatic nationalities pleased Borodin. He wrote the libretto [of *Prince Igor*] and thoroughly prepared himself: he read old epic poems, "The Battle Beyond the Don," "The Battle of Mamaï"; he read the epics and folk-songs of Little Russia; he collected old folk-tunes and received from the traveler Hunfalvi, songs of Middle Asia; he introduced comic characters for the sake of contrast. Having composed a few pages of music, he was discouraged at the end of the year. Stassov hints that Borodin's discouragement grew from those near him, among them his wife: the time had passed, they said, for writing operas on heroic or legendary subjects; the modern drama was the thing. When any one deplored in his presence the loss of so much material, he replied that it would go into his second symphony.

In 1871 Ghédeunov, the director of the Russian Opera, wished to produce an operatic ballet *Mlada*. The fourth act was intrusted to Borodin. He, Cui, Moussorgsky, and Rimsky-Korsakov were to write the vocal music; Minkus, the ballet music. Borodin read and read books on the religious ceremonies of the Slavs, [and] the treatise by Professor Srezniewski. He worked zealously on the music. The scenery demanded so great an expense that the production was postponed. Borodin turned to his second symphony, but did not forget *Prince Igor*. Encouraged by Dr. Schonorov, who served in the Caucasus, he revised the libretto, introducing material intended for *Mlada*.

He worked under disadvantages. His wife, Catherine Sergeïewna Protopopowa (she died August 9, 1887), an excellent pianist, was an invalid; his own health was wretched. In April, 1875, he wrote a dismal letter to Mme. Karmalina in which he spoke of his professional, academic, and scientific work, his interest in the teaching of women, his embarrassed pecuniary condition. His mind was distracted.

I am like a consumptive who, hardly able to breathe, dreams of taking the goat's-milk cure, of traveling in the Midi, or running over fields studded with flowers. Yet I dream of writing an opera. . . . I have already written a grand Polovtsian march, an air for Jaroslavna, the lament of Jaroslavna in the last act, a little chorus of women in the camp of the Polovtsi, and Oriental dances (for the Polovtsi were Oriental people), I have put together various material, I have completed several numbers. But when shall I be done with it all? I do not know.

Alfred Habet's "Life of Borodin" (Paris, 1893), with a free use of Stassov's biography and the correspondence, contains much of interest about the composition of *Prince Igor* and Borodin's opinions about opera in general. He wrote in 1876:

When I speak of this work, I am obliged to laugh at myself. I am reminded of the sorcerer in *Russlan,* who, while his heart is full of love for Naina, does not perceive that time flies, nor does he prepare himself to solve the question until he is white, as is his betrothed, with age. . . . I compose better in summer, for I am then fully in health. . . . Now that a chorus from *Igor* has been performed, the public knows that I am composing an opera. I find myself in the position of a girl who has lost her innocence and for that very reason acquired a sort of freedom; today, whether I wish it or not, I must complete the work. . . . I have always disagreed with many of my friends about opera. Recitative is not in my nature or

character. I am attracted by melody and cantilena. I am more and more borne towards rounded and concrete forms. In opera as in decorative art, details, minutiæ
are out of place; only grand lines are necessary; everything should be clear, decided,
practicable for voices and instruments, and the voices should take the first place;
the orchestra the second.

Early in 1877 he wrote:

We old sinners, as always, are in the whirlwind of life—professional duty, science,
art. We hurry on and do not reach the goal. Time flies like an express train. The
beard grows gray, wrinkles make deeper hollows. We begin a hundred different
things. Shall we ever finish any of them? I am always a poet in my soul, and I
nourish the hope of leading my opera to the last measure, and yet I often mock
at myself. I advance slowly, and there are great gaps in my work.

[In his autobiography,* Rimsky-Korsakov tells of the ordeal of coaxing and
cajolery to which he subjected his friend late in 1878 to prepare several excerpts from *Prince Igor* for a series of concerts at the Free Music School which
he was sponsoring.]

How much pleading and importuning I had to spend on dear old Borodin to
persuade him to orchestrate several numbers for these concerts. His swarming engagements in connection with his professorship and medical courses for women are
always in the way.

Owing to his infinite kindliness and his entire lack of self-love, these surroundings
made it extremely inconvenient for him to work at composition. One might come
again and again, and keep demanding how much he had written. Net result—a
page or two of score, or else—nothing at all. To the query: "Alexander Porphyrievich, have you done the writing?" he would reply: "I have," and then it would
turn out that the writing he had done was on a batch of letters!

"Alexander Porphyrievich, have—you—finally—transposed such and such a number of the opera score?"

"Yes, I have," he would reply earnestly.

"Well, thank the Lord! at last!"

"I transposed it from the piano to the table," he would continue with the same
earnestness and composure!

A really definite plan and scenario were still non-existent; at times more or less
completed numbers were composed, and again—numbers that were merely sketchy
and chaotic. Still, by this time, the following had been composed: Konchak's aria,
Vladimir Galitzki's song, Jaroslavna's Lament and her arioso, the closing chorus,
the Polovtsian dances, and the chorus at Vladimir Galitzki's feast. I had to beg the
author for these excerpts for performance at the concerts of the School. Konchak's
aria he had orchestrated throughout, but there was no end to the waiting for the
orchestration of the Polovtsian dances and of the closing chorus. And yet these numbers had been announced and rehearsed by me with the chorus. It was high time
to copy out the parts.

---

* "My Musical Life," translated by Judah A. Joffe, Alfred A. Knopf (revised), 1942.

In despair I heaped reproaches on Borodin. He, too, was not over-happy. At last, giving up all hope, I offered to help him with the orchestration. Thereupon he came to my house in the evening, bringing with him the hardly touched score of the Polovtsian dances; and the three of us—he, Liadov, and I—took it apart and began to score it in hot haste. To gain time, we wrote in pencil and not in ink. Thus we sat at work until late at night. Borodin covered the finished sheets of the score with liquid gelatine, to keep our pencil marks intact; and in order to have the sheets dry the sooner, he hung them out like wash on lines in my study. Thus the number was ready and passed on to the copyist. The orchestration of the closing chorus I did almost single-handed, as Liadov was absent for some reason. Thus, thanks to the concerts of the Free Music School, some numbers were finished partly by the composer himself and partly with my help, during that year as well as during the following season of 1879–80. At all events, had there been no concerts of the Free Music School, the fate of the opera, *Prince Igor,* would have been different.

Borodin did not think it possible to produce *Prince Igor* on a foreign stage. "It is essentially," he said, "a national opera, interesting only to us Russians, who love to steep our patriotism in the sources of our history, and to see the origins of our nationality alive again on the stage."

P. H.

"The funny thing about these Russian operas," a man in the audience at Drury Lane was heard to remark during the great Russian season of 1914, "is that they're all written by someone else." That is particularly true of *Prince Igor*. Ostensibly the composer of it was Borodin. But, faithful to the Russian habit, he left a good deal to be done to it by other people after his death, which occurred with tragic suddenness at a musical party he was giving in his own house. Rimsky-Korsakov scored the Prologue (i.e., the opening stage scene), the first, second and fourth acts and the Polovtsian March in the third. Glazounov orchestrated the remainder of the third act as Borodin had left it, and completed the composition of this act from the composer's sketches. The choral accompaniment and the introductory recitative to Kontchakovna's cavatina in the second act were Rimsky-Korsakov's work. The overture and the short chorus of Russian prisoners in this act were given their present form by Glazounov from his recollections of Borodin's playing of them on the piano: the scoring of the overture is Glazounov's. (The feat of putting the overture into shape is not so remarkable a one as would appear at first sight, for there is practically nothing in it that is not in the opera itself.) Finally, we cannot be sure whether some of the melodies in *Prince Igor* that seem to be folk-tunes are really such, or Borodin's own, though influenced by his eager study of Russian and Central Asiatic folk-music.

The length of *Prince Igor* makes a certain amount of cutting inevitable in the theatre, while of course the looseness of its dramatic construction makes it an easy prey for the modern producer, who sometimes makes no bones about omitting certain scenes altogether and re-distributing others to suit his own notions of what is right and proper. But if the construction is technically loose it is not incoherent; and the chief result of the producer's monkeying about with it is generally to confuse the spectator who is doing his best to follow the story by depriving him of some main connecting thread or other. Reduction to the time-limit of an ordinary performance is easily obtainable by declining to follow Borodin slavishly to the end in some of his needless musical repetitions: the score benefits, indeed, by a fairly lavish use of the blue pencil in this respect. But the one thing that should not be interfered with is the ground plan of the work.

                                                                    E. N.

Prince Igor was a success, but the management of the Maryinsky Theatre soon took the precaution of cutting Act III, and finally of dropping it altogether. This left of Glazounov's handiwork only the overture, and even that was omitted when the opera at last reached New York, in Italian, on December 30, 1915. The Metropolitan's decision to produce *Prince Igor* came as a result of the interest in Russian opera aroused by the first American performance of *Boris Godunov* two years earlier. Toscanini had enthusiastically taken it under his wing, intending to conduct it, but left the company in the spring of 1915, when a natural desire to offer his services to Italy, which had just entered the First World War, offered the temperamental conductor an excellent excuse for putting into effect his oft-expressed intention of withdrawing from the annoyances to which, he alleged, he was subjected at the Metropolitan. So it was Giorgio Polacco who conducted this important *première*. The principal roles were taken by Alda, Amato, and Didur. New York was not as responsive as the management had hoped, and after eight repetitions spread over three successive seasons, *Prince Igor* was dropped permanently from the Metropolitan repertoire.

In France, where it had the benefit of a Diaghilev production, with Chaliapin as Prince Galitzky, *Igor* fared better. In London, Sir Thomas Beecham added it to the Covent Garden repertoire in 1912, with Chaliapin again as Galitzky, and there it drew large and warmly appreciative audiences. Its survival, in the United States at least, is limited to the ballet music—the Polovtsian Dances from Act II—that Fokine used for one of his most vivid and popular choreographic creations. . . .

                                                                    W. B., H. W.

Gustave Charpentier

(Dieuze [Meurthe], France, June 25, 1860—lives in Paris)

"Among my pupils," wrote Massenet, "was one whose only aim was to startle with his writing. I advised him to find some pretty young girl and let his heart speak through his music. It was Charpentier." Gustave Charpentier, who was to dedicate his genius to a city—the *ville féerique* that Paris seemed to him on arriving from his native Lorraine—and to a city type—the ever appealing Mimi Pinson of sewing-room dreams and drudgery. De Musset begat her, Murger developed her, Charpentier was to perpetuate her. And thanks to her and to the Paris she symbolizes he was to realize his will to startle; for his one notable opera survives not by virtue of its once daring music or the once daring standards it expounds, but through the fact that the Paris of Mimi Pinson, with all its magic, poetry, and tragedy, has the principal role in the cast of characters.

Charpentier was born in 1860 in the village of Dieuze. His father seems to have been a baker of the Ragueneau order, given to deserting his ovens and flour bins to improvise on the flute or French horn. Thus, the infant Gustave absorbed a smattering of *solfège* at the same time that he learned to walk and talk. In 1871 the entire population of Dieuze fled from the Prussian invasion to Tourcoing, near the Belgian frontier. Here, a local music master primed the eleven-year-old Charpentier boy for a second violin desk in the municipal band, with the result that the lad's introduction to operatic literature began on the handsome scale of selections from *Orfeo, Fidelio, Don Giovanni,* and works of like stature. Often rich industrialists of the district came to the concerts in the public square, and the astute Gustave could note something like envy of his and his fellow-bandmembers' musical talent on their part—an impression later to be recorded in *Louise* (Act II, Scene 3: "Le désir des grands seigneurs . . . d'être artistes!").

His future passion for regimenting the French laboring classes into musical activities also asserted itself at this time. During rest hours, the textile factory where he worked resounded with shaky Serenades which the employees performed under his direction. Not even the proprietor escaped his proselytism, and turned musical with a fervor that impelled him to finance young Charpentier in a course of violin lessons at the conservatory of nearby Lille. But it was the savings of the townspeople of Tourcoing that made up the purse which enabled him to pursue his musical studies in Paris—a fact that left its imprint on him.

During his first year at the Paris Conservatory Charpentier was conspicuous for lack of application. So often he neglected to prepare the work allotted him, or filled his exercises with music-hall tunes and other pranks, that his professors asked that he be dismissed. A tour of the provinces as violinist restored him to his senses and to the good graces of the faculty, and it was at this point that Massenet took him on. After steeping him in the principles of orchestration and vocal writing, he interested him in the form of the cantata. Within a year the now zealous pupil produced an experiment entitled "Didon," based on Augé de Lassus' elegy for Queen Dido, that won him a Prix de Rome. But one circumstance tarnished this golden prospect of three years' study among ideal surroundings and freedom from material cares: Charpentier had fallen in love—with Paris!

From the hour of his arrival from drab Tourcoing he had turned Parisian, or rather *Montmartrois,* to his very soul. The thought of life anywhere but on the *Butte* had become intolerable to him. Three times he made ready to leave for Rome, three times he put off the journey in an agony of nostalgia. In 1887 he finally brought himself to make the break and found to his surprise that his unwanted new environment did not dampen creativeness. During this exile he composed the bulk of his whole output, including sketches that were one day to grow into the "Impressions d'Italie" and the opera *Louise.* And few of his later works have the originality or zest of these Roman efforts. His first offering to the Prix de Rome committee, a brash choral symphony which he called "La Vie du Poète," nearly brought about a feud among the judges. Massenet applauded it with delight. Ambroise Thomas, after listening to a few pages, stalked out of the room in disgust. Gounod remarked: "Here, at last, we have a true musician! He composes in C natural, and no one else but the Almighty could do that!"

The success of *Louise* [in February, 1900] was immediate and complete. During the first season it was given one hundred times. In 1935 it had its thousandth performance in Paris, a record that only three other operas—*La Dame Blanche, Faust,* and *Mignon*—have attained.

Except for his settings for Baudelaire's "Les Fleurs du Mal" and Verlaine's "Impressions Fausses," which have never received the attention they deserve, and an unpublished symphonic poem picturing Munich with the verve of the "Impressions d'Italie" and more sensitive feeling, Charpentier's writing of his post-*Louise* period has little musical significance. During a brief absorption in mysticism he expanded "La Vie du Poète" into the opera *Julien,* but the result was a libretto overloaded with symbolism and unconvincing musical treatment. Soon afterward the rumor spread that he was drafting a scenario on the adventures of Louise's and Julien's daughter, Marie; but nothing seems to have come of the project and we know of no further ventures that he has made in the operatic field. This waning creativeness has been ascribed to privations which he suffered while waiting for the production of *Louise,* and to various other reasons. The basic cause was probably a lack of creative ideas. Not alone his musical genius but his whole philosophy went into the composing of *Louise,* and after he had proclaimed his revolutionary convictions, exalted his own romance, and apotheosized his adored Paris with this one work he had little left to say.

But if opera lost a composer, the midinette gained a patron saint. Charpentier's aim to better her lot gradually became an all-engrossing interest. Thanks to him the countless Mimis, Musettas, and Louises who keep up the age-old prestige of Parisian needlework are now privileged young women. At each revival of *Louise* in Paris special performances are given for them. Unsold seats for the best plays, as well, are available to them. At a popular academy, the Mimi Pinson Conservatory, founded in 1902, they learn French folk songs and folk dances and are trained to sing in opera choruses. In summer they vacation in rural corners of France. And each spring the working classes of the principal French industrial towns gather in a vast festival, usually directed by the composer in person, to crown a seamstress elected by popular vote as their Muse. (The idea originated in a mock ceremony once held in Montmartre which Charpentier had introduced into *Louise,* elaborated into the choreographic scene in Act III, supposing that he was depicting an established custom. A few weeks before the première friends had pointed out one difficulty: the ceremony had never existed as a custom. So he hastily inaugurated the practice by organizing a coronation of a seamstress on the square in front of the Hôtel de Ville.)

For many years Charpentier has ceased to be the Bohemian of popular conception—the *Montmartrois* of long hair, velvet jacket, and baggy trousers whom Steinlen and Willette immortalized with their pencil. The button of a Commander of the Legion of Honor now adorns his lapel, but his appearance is otherwise inconspicuous. He lives in modest quarters in the shadow of the *Sacré Coeur* which he has occupied off and on for the last forty-five years, supervises the courses at his conservatory for midinettes, prepares his annual fetes—a film of these Coronations, taken on his own *ciné-Gaumont,* will one day be released to the public—and aids the French working classes in innumerable smaller ways. The musical world persists in hoping that he will break his long silence, although few other composers of his ripe age have continued to produce until the end. Silence, moreover, is well earned in his case. The muses chose him for the lyric theatre's bard of humble things—a role that required high artistic courage—and like the classic heroine of his Prix de Rome cantata he may say, "I have lived and accomplished the deeds for which destiny made me."

K. O'D. H.

Louise

MUSICAL ROMANCE IN 4 ACTS (5 SCENES)

Book by the COMPOSER

First performance: Opéra Comique, Paris, Feb. 2, 1900

CHARACTERS

Louise, SOPRANO
Her Mother, CONTRALTO
Her Father, BARITONE
Julien, TENOR

Irma, SOPRANO
An Errand Girl, MEZZO-SOPRANO
The King of the Fools, TENOR

Peddlers, Housekeepers, Working People, Grisettes, Street Boys, Bohemians

The action takes place in Paris toward the end of the nineteenth century

Bohemian life in Paris at the turn of the century is placed upon the stage in Charpentier's opera. Louise herself, who is employed at a dressmaker's, is in love with Julien, a painter, who lives close by. But her father, a canny workingman, disapproves of painters and their improvident ways, and will not hear of her marriage. Julien, however, is determined to win her, and even sings to her outside the dressmaker's workroom. Louise, tired of the strict discipline of her father and mother, elopes with Julien, to live with him among painters, students, and other Bohemians on the heights of Montmartre.

In the midst of a Bohemian festivity, when Louise is about to be crowned Queen of Montmartre, her mother appears to tell her her father is dying. He is not quite that, however, and the return of Louise revives him. But when he begs her to remain under the parental roof, she refuses to do so. In his rage the father throws a chair at her, but she dodges and escapes through the door, to return to Julien. The curtain falls on the father shouting, "Oh, Paris!" in the tone of a curse.

P. S.

Before he left Paris [for Rome, in 1887] Charpentier had coaxed the publisher Hartmann into promising him a libretto. As soon as he had adjusted himself to the Villa Médicis he wrote Hartmann to remind him of the agreement. He received no answer and wrote again. This second plea, too, was ignored; so he decided to be his own librettist and set out to find a subject. But his meager education had not equipped him with the necessary literary judgment, and the mass of plays and novels he skimmed through offered no ideas for a plot. Meanwhile it had occurred to him that an episode in his own career could be the basis of an opera. Soon after settling in Paris he had become attached (out of respect, perhaps, for Massenet's advice) to a pretty seamstress employed in a dressmaking shop in the rue Lepic, the still extant *Atelier* Arnoux. Both lovers meant to exalt free love with their romance, but before long they had parted in mutual disillusion and gone their respective ways—Charpentier on the road to fame and fortune, the seamstress, whose name was Louise Jehan, to oblivion. After the rupture she is known to have deserted Montmartre for Montparnasse, and there is a legend that she ended her days as the crusty *concièrge* of a Left Bank building, consoled, let us hope, by the fact that Charpentier at least remained faithful to her type.

During the period of his attachment to Louise Jehan he had frequented the Théâtre Antoine and Lugné Poë's new playhouse as often as his slender means allowed. Each performance had sent him back to his garret room with his head churning with doctrines of Ibsen, Richepin, Zola, or other revolutionary authors who made up the repertory. Conversations over Montmartre *café* tables with the anarchists Sebastien Faure and Jules Matha had forged these impressions into convictions that were thereafter to color everything he wrote. In Rome, as he worked out the plan of his libretto the very slogans that had been blared into his ears found their way into the text: "Tout être a le droit d'être libre" (Act III, Scene 1); "Est-ce que les bons lits, les belles robes, comme le soleil, ne devraient pas être à tout le monde?" (Act II, Scene 2); "Ceux qui ont des rentes aujourd'hui n'en auront peut-être plus demain" (Act I, Scene 4). And the musical setting he sketched sounded strains of the Socialist hymn "Ravachole: Gloire aux anarchistes!" (Act III, Scene 2); "Propos du philosophe" (Act II, Scene 3); "Anathème du père" (Act IV).

On his return to Paris some friend with a literary flair (on whose identity no two Charpentier scholars agree) helped him develop his scenario. In the atmosphere of his beloved Montmartre the music developed itself. But finding a producer was a less simple matter. For ten years no theatrical manager in the capital would give serious consideration to an opera that had Montmartre for a background, female emancipation for a basis, a tenorless last act, and music of more or less shocking dissonance. But Charpentier preferred to starve—and without the credit of a music-loving grocer on the *Butte* would have done so —rather than modify *Louise*. By the time Albert Carré, who wished to inaugurate his management of the Opéra-Comique with a striking novelty, accepted the work its composer had reached middle age.

Yet, during this prolonged delay Charpentier's reputation had not languished. His "Vie du Poète" and "Impressions d'Italie" had been performed at the Colonne concerts and met with a turbulent response. His settings for poems of Verlaine and Baudelaire had had private hearings that left artistic circles buzzing with discussion. And after the production of *Louise* had been announced information that leaked out from backstage whipped public curiosity to a pitch that has been equalled in the history of the French stage only by Rostand's "Chantecler."

Marthe Rioton, a debutante of that season at the Comique, was the first interpreter of the role of Louise. Three months after the première, on February 2, 1900, illness cut short this gifted mezzo's career. Meanwhile Charpentier had coached a young Scotch-American singer, whom Sybil Sanderson had placed on the reserve roster of the Comique, to substitute for Rioton if necessary. The May 24, 1905, issue of *La Liberté* gives her own description of what followed:

"I was moulding away waiting for a chance to sing some secondary role when Manager Carré asked me one day, 'Could you sing Louise, Miss Garden?' 'Certainly,' I answered with the temerity of my twenty-two years; 'tomorrow, if you like.' 'Then come to the performance. We may need you.' Rioton got through the first act, but it was evident that she was straining to keep up. During the intermission an attendant suddenly hissed in my ear, 'Get into your costume. Rioton can't go on.' Ten minutes later I was dressed as Louise and, though I'd not had a single rehearsal, oblivious of all except that my great chance had come. The rumble of the rising curtain and the sight of the dim auditorium brought me to my senses and nearly froze me with fright. But I had to sing, so I sang"—with a grasp of the role that made operatic history.

K. O'D. H.

When Gustave Charpentier peddled *Louise* for ten years from one opera house to another he met the same unsympathetic suggestions which Bizet had suffered with *Carmen* and Wagner with *Tannhäuser*. Various Parisian managers inspected the score, said complimentary things about it and declared themselves ready to produce the work—if the composer would submit to a few operations. One wanted to relegate the period of action from what was then the present to 1830 or even back to the age of Louis XIV. Another took violent exception to the modern dress of the characters and called for period costumes. A third made the most gorgeous suggestion of all—Louise was not to leave the parental roof at the end amid the crash of breaking furniture and with fatherly imprecations ringing in her ears. Instead, when all seemed lost, Julien was to bounce through the window ("bounce" was the word!), press his beloved to his bosom and kneel with her before the raging old *ouvrier,* who would suddenly relent and, with the approved gesture, bless his children!

Charming, no doubt, but it did not happen. Charpentier waited a little longer and in the end *Louise* entered the Opéra-Comique just as he had written it. It has been a classic of a sort ever since. That does not signify a hundred per cent acceptance. *Louise* is one man's meat and another's poison. The great opera-going public has, on the whole, taken it to its heart. On the other hand not all musicians made their peace with it. Debussy, for example, loathed it. He declared that "it supplied only too well the need for that cheap and idiotic art which has such appeal." He called it "more silly than harmful" and said that if this was what was to be called "life" he would prefer to die then and there. The critic, Pierre de Bréville, summarized the matter by remarking that, in spite of all discussions and disagreements, *Louise* is a work that it is necessary to hear. "Sometimes it irritates, sometimes it bores, sometimes it moves, but it never is an indifferent thing."

Those words are as substantially true today as in 1900, when they were written. Yet *Louise* has inevitably lost the timeliness of almost a half-century ago. Except for some enduringly human qualities—love, tenderness, the fierce clash of wills—it is no longer contemporaneous. It seems to have receded a century, and become a romantic social document of an age which now appears immemorially remote. These preachments about free love and the rights of young people to pry themselves loose from their mother's apron strings, this chatter to the effect that "every human being has the right to be free and the duty to love" strike some of us today as preposterously bourgeois and Victorian.

The element which continues to endear *Louise* is probably its evocation of Paris—which remains, even if an abstraction, the principal character of the opera. It is the dazzling, magical, heartless, cruel city that Louise adores, to which she and her lover address their prayers and to whose delirious whirl she surrenders unconditionally at the end of the opera—for, whether Julien is on hand to receive her or not we have no means of knowing. This Paris is more a figment of Charpentier's imagination than a reality. He himself came from the drab, provincial, manufacturing town of Tourcoing. The Paris he worshipped was a Paris he evolved out of his inner consciousness. The Paris of reality was neither so good nor so bad as it seemed to him.

Louise is Charpentier's solitary monument. In the perspective of time whatever else he wrote is unimportant—the orchestral suite "Impressions d'Italie," the so-called symphony-drama, "La Vie du Poète," the clap-trap pageant "Le Couronnement de la Muse," some songs and the appalling opera, *Julien*. Most of these were either preparations for *Louise* or scraps and shavings left over from it. Yet possibly *Louise* is all one had a right to demand of him. In its way it is a monument in operatic history.

It makes a singular impression of unity, on the whole, yet it is not a unified work. The first and the fourth act offer us realism somewhat in the tradition of Zola. The opening scene of the second act is a strange, somewhat long-winded mixture of symbolism, alternating with photography, dabs of local color and some accessories of lyric opera *à la* Puccini's *Bohème*. The dressmaker establishment is out-and-out *opéra-comique,* while the third act, on the hill of Montmartre, is purest spectacular grand opera, barring a brief dip toward music drama at the close. Unquestionably it is this act which caused Debussy to damn the work as "a thousand times more conventional than Meyerbeer's *Huguenots*."

The music of *Louise* is a curious assortment of elements new and old, strong and weak. It is genuinely eloquent at one moment, annoyingly awkward at the next, here dull, there gripping, seldom polished, profoundly original and yet frequently with an accent quite its own. Sentimentality lies heavily over many pages. Yet certain of the more sentimental moments rank among the best. The instrumentation—especially the writing for brass—is sometimes amazingly clumsy. Considering the time it was written—about 1890—the harmony is not without its audacities. At the turn of the century people were probably not so calm in the face of ninth chords as they are today, when children are brought up on the twelve-tone scale.

Charpentier used the leading motive system in *Louise,* though not in the highly developed, symphonic Wagnerian way. His numerous thematic labels seem pasted on the score like so many postage stamps. From time to time you hear several of them simultaneously, in counterpoint, with more or less emotional intent.

H. F. P.

The use to which Charpentier puts Paris street cries is his most individual achievement in *Louise.* Sometime before the year 1545, when his collected vocal works were first published, Jannequin wove a part-song from these plaintive chants that for centuries have touted everything from birdseed to rush chairs through Paris byways. A ballet devised from them is known to have been a favorite with Louis XIV. In 1857 Georges Kastner built a two-hundred-page symphony upon them. In 1899 Delius span them into his Nocturne for Orchestra. But each of these men, in his own way, had treated them merely pictorially. Charpentier sensed drama within them and allotted them specific dramatic functions. In faint antiphonal refrains they usher in, one after another, the dawn of a Montmartre day. A goatherd's piping encourages the lovers to realize their dream of happiness. A birdseed vendor's "Mouron pour les Petits Oiseaux" promises them protection. An artichoke peddler's "A la Tendress', la Verduress'" tells of the joys that await them. A carrot vendor spurs Julien to woo Louise. A ragman and a vendor of green peas, potatoes, and broth hail the midinette's surrender. When the spirit of Paris lures the enamoured pair to the consummation of their love each of these haunting calls becomes a voice in the city's distant *Libres* chorus, a token of her message of freedom. And the orchestration by means of which they all cast their spell over the score is a feat of virtuosity.

K. O'D. H.

It was Mary Garden who introduced *Louise* to America, at the Manhattan Opera House, on January 3, 1908, with Bressler-Gianoli (the Mother), Dalmorès (Julien), and Gilibert (the Father). Farrar was the first Metropolitan Louise (January 15, 1921), and the role has been sung there since by Bori and

Grace Moore. In six scattered seasons, the opera attained little more than two dozen Metropolitan performances, while Garden, besides her stupendous record at the Comique, sang it many times elsewhere, particularly in Chicago. In Paris, where the octogenarian Charpentier still lives as this is written, the popularity of *Louise* has continued unabated. [Its thousandth performance at the Comique is now history.]

W. B., H. W.

Claude Debussy

(St. Germain-en-Laye, France, Aug. 22, 1862–Mar. 25, 1918, Paris)

Achille Claude Debussy has been called the most original talent in music since Mozart, though he liked best the simple title of "musicien français," which he conferred upon himself. In any event, he was the dominating musical influence not only in France, but throughout Europe and in America, from the beginning of the present century until the [First] World War.

There is some mystification about Debussy's early years, due in part to his scarcely ever mentioning his childhood. Nevertheless, certain facts are established. Like Louis XIV, he was born at Saint-Germain-en-Laye, near Paris, the date being August 22, 1862. At the time of his birth, his parents, who were not at all musical, kept a small china shop. They soon removed to Clichy and then to Paris, where Debussy was to spend most of his life. He was the oldest of five children.

Debussy's early education was rudimentary, and up to his twentieth year, at least, traces of illiteracy lingered in his letters. His later intellectual development may be attributed in part to his association with the poet Pierre Louÿs, some of whose poems he set to music. He began to take piano lessons at the age of nine, though without disclosing any particular talent. However, he engaged the attention of a pianist who had been a pupil of Chopin and who had the keenness of perception to discover talent where no one else had done so. It is an interesting coincidence that this lady, Mme. Mauté de Fleurville, was the mother-in-law of Paul Verlaine, between whose poetry and Debussy's music there is an unmistakable affinity.

Teaching him for nothing, she prepared him for the Paris Conservatory, which he entered in October, 1873. His father, who had wished him to become a sailor, now was converted to the idea of a musical career, even in his enthusiasm forcing the boy to work as many as eight hours a day or stand punishment. At the Conservatory Debussy's career was not altogether serene, some of his professors sympathizing little with his unconventional tendencies. A visit to Russia as one of the retinue of Mme. von Meck (Tschaikowsky's patroness) first brought him into touch with Slavic influences, which were eventually to affect his style. As a pianist he won several prizes at the Conservatoires, and his cantata, "L'Enfant Prodigue" (The Prodigal Son), purposely composed in the style of Massenet, achieved its goal of obtaining for him the coveted Prix de Rome.

He now began to reshape his musical idiom, exhibiting more originality in his orchestral suite "Printemps," however, than in his setting of Rossetti's

"Blessed Damozel" ("La Damoiselle Élue"). He also set out deliberately to increase his literary culture, frequenting to that end the society not only of Pierre Louÿs, but of Stephane Mallarmé, Henri de Regnier, and others of the Symbolist and Impressionist poets. Songs and piano pieces exhibiting his musical progress followed, and at length, in 1894, his orchestral "Afternoon of a Faun" (L'Après-midi d'un Faune), inspired by Mallarmé's cryptic eclogue, revealed the matured and highly personal Debussy.

The individuality of his rhythm, his subtle and exquisitely elaborated orchestration, his novel harmonic scheme with its use of old ecclesiastical modes and the whole-tone scale, the finesse and sensitiveness of his writing, its Gallic avoidance of all excess, and at times its kinship in mood with the French composers—especially the harpsichordists—of the seventeenth and early eighteenth centuries combined to give this music a character special and apart. True, after the western world became acquainted with the work of that singular Russian genius, Moussorgsky, the originality of Debussy's style (compare especially "Clouds") suffered a little with respect to authenticity, still it remains sufficiently his own not only to differentiate him but to win a flock of imitators and assimilators.

While at work on "The Afternoon of a Faun" Debussy brought out his admired string quartet (1893). In 1898 he gave the world the orchestral nocturne "Clouds," "Festivals," and "Sirens" (this last with wordless chorus). There were also fine songs, and in 1902 his only opera *Pelléas et Mélisande,* the text taken from Maeterlinck's play of the same name, was produced at the Paris Opéra Comique. This unique work, though received at first with consternation and even jeers, was soon recognized as the one true music drama, the only perfect union of the note and the word. Although within the next ten or eleven years Debussy was to give the world such notable works as his tone poems of the ocean entitled "La Mer," his orchestral tribute to Spain called collectively "Iberia," his incidental music to d'Annunzio's drama "The Martyrdom of St. Sebastian," and the two books of piano preludes, *Pelléas et Mélisande* remains the summit of his achievement.

With the access of fortune Debussy gave rein to his innate love of luxury and he also put away the wife of his youth to contract a second marriage more advantageous from the worldly point of view. He died in Paris on March 25, 1918, after suffering for years from a wasting illness.

The [First] World War had affected him deeply and it was then that he insisted on the appellation "musicien français." During those dark years he composed the "Berceuse héroïque," a tribute to King Albert of the Belgians and his soldiers and the "Noël des enfants qui n'ont plus de maison." At the time of his death Paris was under bombardment from airplanes and the famous "Big Bertha." He was too weak to be carried down to the cellar when warning came of the enemy Gothas and his modest funeral procession crossed Paris to the Père-Lachaise cemetery while guns boomed.

P. S.

Pelléas et Mélisande

LYRIC DRAMA IN 5 ACTS (12 SCENES)

Poem by Maurice Maeterlinck

First performance: Opéra Comique, Paris, Apr. 30, 1902

CHARACTERS

Arkel, King of Allemonde, a fictitious domain, BASS

Geneviève, wife of his son, SOPRANO

Golaud, her elder son, BARITONE

Pelléas, his half brother, TENOR

Mélisande, a mysterious young princess, SOPRANO

Yniold, young son of Golaud through a former marriage, SOPRANO

A Physician, Servants, Blind Beggars, etc.

The action takes place in legendary times

While hunting, Golaud, the widowed grandson of old King Arkel of Allemonde, loses his way in a forest. He comes upon the wraithlike Mélisande weeping over the loss of a crown that has fallen to the bottom of a well. Timorous and aloof, she gives Golaud no inkling of her identity beyond her name. But at length, she consents to go with him. Golaud would now take Mélisande as his bride. He writes to Pelléas, his half-brother, to persuade their mother Geneviève to gain Arkel's approval. Bringing Mélisande, Golaud returns to the castle. Mélisande and Pelléas are drawn to one another. Once, while they are seated together at the edge of a fountain, Mélisande's wedding ring falls into the water. Meanwhile, Golaud has been wounded during a hunt. As Mélisande nurses him, he looks in vain for the ring on her finger. To his anxious questioning Mélisande replies with an untruth: she has lost the ring in a grotto while gathering shells for his son Yniold. Golaud insists that she recover it. Together Pelléas and Mélisande approach the grotto. She must at least see the place before she is forced to another lie. But they are frightened off by the ominous sight of three blind old men sitting motionless at the mouth of the grotto.

Golaud has become suspicious. One evening Mélisande leans out of her tower window to speak with Pelléas on the castle grounds below. Her long tresses are unclasped and fall about Pelléas' face. He caresses them lovingly. Thus together Golaud surprises them. Nervously he laughs at their childish sport and then walks away with Pelléas. Tortured by ever-deepening suspicion, Golaud later questions little Yniold about them. He even lifts the boy up to Mélisande's window to spy on the lovers. Yniold reports to his father that Pelléas and Mélisande are standing apart, silent, gazing at the light. Returning from a hunt, Golaud, now savage with jealousy, rushes murder-bent upon Mélisande while she is talking with Arkel, and only checks himself in the hope that a better opportunity will offer itself. He has not long to wait. At the fountain one night Pelléas and Mélisande are bidding each other good-by. As they cling together, Golaud bursts upon them and runs Pelléas through with his sword. In terror Mélisande escapes. Later, as she lies dying in childbed, Golaud, still rent by his ugly suspicions, demands the truth: has she loved Pelléas guiltily? Mélisande answers feebly that she has committed no wrong in loving Pelléas. She has a glimpse of her child and then she dies.

P. S.

It was decided to give *Pelléas* at the Opéra-Comique in 1902, and rehearsals began on 13th January. But it was only in March that the date of the dress rehearsal was fixed for 27th April and the first public performance for three days later. Debussy was taken by surprise, for during the rehearsals a number of revisions were recommended and orchestral interludes were seen to be necessary to allow time for the scenery to be changed. Many passages were thus not completed until the last moment. Robert Godet mentions that during these months he had "to settle affairs with the legatee of one of his patrons (i.e. Georges Hartmann) and this exposed him to daily summonses for debts he could not repay." To complicate matters still further a quarrel broke out between Debussy and Maeterlinck. For a time it was thought that the whole production would be wrecked.

So much scandal went about as the result of this quarrel that it is difficult to reconstruct the episode truthfully. Here is, I think, the most authoritative version, by Georgette Leblanc, Maeterlinck's wife, around whom the affair centered. The scene is in the Rue Raynouard in Passy at the end of 1901:

Debussy came to play his score. The position of the piano forced him to turn his back to us and permitted Maeterlinck to make desperate signs to me. Not understanding music in the least the time seemed long to him. Several times he wanted to escape, but I held him back. Resigned, he lit his pipe.

At this first hearing of *Pelléas* many of its beauties escaped me, but with the prelude for the death of Mélisande I felt that special, that unique emotion we undergo in the presence of a masterpiece.

. . . It was late. Two candles outlined Debussy's silhouette. Maeterlinck was half asleep in his arm-chair. Before my eyes the high windows framed the soft blue of growing night.

Just before he left we talked of the casting. I longed to play the part. Maeterlinck urged it. Debussy said he would be delighted. It was decided that I should begin to study Mélisande immediately. We arranged for the first rehearsal.

There were two or three rehearsals at my house and two at his, the fifth floor in the Rue Cardinet, where he lived in an extremely modest apartment. . . .

My work with Debussy was progressing, when one day Maeterlinck read in a paper that another artist had been engaged to create Mélisande and that she was rehearsing with him. That Debussy should do such a thing surprised me, as he was not a man to pay meaningless compliments. My enunciation gave him a pleasure that he constantly commented upon. Was it not the poem of *Pelléas* that had inspired him? Had he not followed it word for word as no other composer had ever done before? No, certainly the quarrel was not between him and me. It came from the Opéra-Comique and my disagreeable adventure connected with *Carmen*. . . .

Maeterlinck, thus betrayed by Debussy, referred the case to the Society of Authors, thinking that he was legally within his rights. He was mistaken, first because the law gives precedence to the musician rather than to the author, and furthermore because in his preliminary authorization he had added a gracious clause: "The piece may be played where, how and when you like."

Justly annoyed to find himself stripped before the law, Maeterlinck brandished his cane and announced to me that he was going to "give Debussy a drubbing to teach him what was what."

My love had none of the stoic quality of the heroines of antiquity. This threat of a beating terrified me, and I clung to Maeterlinck, who jumped briskly out of the window. (Our ground-floor flat in the Rue Raynouard was half-way up the slope of the street. We had to go down through the garden in order to reach the *porte-cochère* and then climb the hill. We often went out through the window.) I waited in agony, convinced of disaster. I did not picture Debussy with his tragic mask of a face taking kindly to a reprimand.

I watched the deserted street for Maeterlinck's return. Finally he appeared at the top of the hill, brandishing his cane to heaven with comic gestures.

The story was pitiable. As soon as he entered the *salon* he had threatened Debussy, who dropped into a chair while Mme. Debussy distractedly ran toward her husband with a bottle of smelling salts. She had begged the poet to go away and, my word! there was nothing else to do.

Maeterlinck, who did not like musicians any more than music, kept saying as he laughed: "They're all crazy, all off their heads, these musicians!"

This scarcely reassured me. I thought that after Maeterlinck had left Debussy would arise from his chair in terrible wrath. Perhaps his seconds would call on us the next day.

As for Maeterlinck, he found it only just to attack the management of the Opéra-Comique.*

Whereupon Maeterlinck wrote a letter, dated 14th April 1902, to *Le Figaro,* in which, besides opposing the substitution of another singer for Georgette Leblanc in the part of Mélisande, he says:

> They have managed to exclude me from my work, and from now on it is in the hands of the enemy. Arbitrary and absurd cuts have made it incomprehensible. They have retained passages that I wished to suppress or improve as I did in the libretto which has just appeared and from which it will be seen how far the text adopted by the Opéra-Comique differs from the authentic version. In a word, the

---

* Translation by Janet Flanner.

Pelléas in question is a work which is strange and almost hostile to me; and deprived of all control over my work, I can only wish for its immediate and decided failure.

M. Maeterlinck

The question of a duel did arise, possibly as the result of this letter, and Albert Carré and Robert de Flers both offered to take the place of Debussy. But eventually the affair blew over, although Maeterlinck was for a long time deeply hurt by the way in which he considered his wife had been slighted. He heard only one act of Debussy's work, many years later, in New York.

The part of Mélisande was thus given to Mary Garden, a young Scotch-American girl who, ironically enough, had made a romantic début some years previously in the opera which was an object of Debussy's special hatred—*Louise*. Here is the cast of the first performance:

Mélisande	Mary Garden
Geneviève	J. Gerville-Réache
Pelléas	Jean Périer
Golaud	Hector Dufranne
Arkel	Félix Vieuille
Yniold	Blondin

Scenery painted by Jusseaume and Ronson

Conductor	André Messager

Several things combined to make the dress rehearsal a rather painful experience. At the doors a "Select Programme" was sold, in which the plot was maliciously ridiculed. Maeterlinck's letter had afforded just the opportunity to laugh a new work off that a certain section of the Paris musical public always awaits, and during the performance there was the uproar that, ever since Victor Hugo's "Hernani," traditionally accompanies the first production of a great work in France. The storm broke forth in the second act at the words of Mélisande, "Je ne suis pas heureuse." At mention of the words "petit père," in the scene between Golaud and Yniold, the house set up peals of laughter. At one point in this scene the uproar almost brought the curtain down. "Sont-ils près du lit?" asks Golaud; and with the sweetest innocence Yniold replies: "Je ne vois pas le lit." At the request of a government official this passage, as well as Yniold's scene with the sheep in the same act, was cut at the first public performance and has never been restored.

The reception in the press was divided. Romain Rolland in the Berlin paper, *Morgen,* had no hesitation in proclaiming that *Pelléas* "was one of the three or four outstanding achievements in French musical history." Gaston Carraud in *La Liberté* made a pertinent comparison when he spoke of Debussy taking his place "more definitely even than Wagner among the sensualists in music of whom Mozart was the greatest." Some weeks later he enlarged on the connection with Mozart in the journal, *Minerva:*

M. Debussy is really a classical composer. I am not speaking paradoxically. After the unbridled romanticism to which music has fallen a prey, he has the lucidity, the tact, the restraint and the sense of proportion that characterize the classical composers. He has the same controlled emotion as they; he has their charm and dignity of expression, their scorn of emphasis, exaggeration and mere effect.*

The notice in *Le Journal* was by Catulle Mendès, Debussy's former collaborator in "Rodrigue et Chimène." He wrote:

Every artist has noted the collaboration [of Debussy and Maeterlinck] with great pleasure. By their delicate and subtle sensibility, the similarity of their emotions and dreams, their fraternity, one might say, they seem as well matched as possible. One expected—what is so rare in an opera-house—a really homogeneous work, as if inspired by one man in which the spoken drama would of itself develop into a musical drama.

If our hope was not always deceived, it was too seldom realized. There was often disagreement, sometimes divorcement, just when we expected that perfect concord more indispensable in this work than in any other.

Mendès then goes on to speak of "Debussy's persistence in getting music out of unmusical phrases," and amazingly concludes: "We came away from this performance with two desires—one, to hear the score in the concert-hall without the singers, and the other, to see the play of Maeterlinck without music, on the dramatic stage."

One other criticism may be quoted as expressing a curious view shared by not a few people. It is by Camille Bellaigue and appeared in the *Revue des deux mondes.*

I remember when we were both students at the Conservatoire. When M. Debussy used to play the piano he used to puff on the strong beats of the bar. We used to poke fun at this habit of his. He has certainly got over it. In his rhythm now there are no accents. In his structureless art the abolishment of rhythm goes hand in hand with the abolishment of melody. . . . After hearing the work one feels the uneasiness and agony of the hero who sighs: "Il ne me reste rien si je m'en vais ainsi. Et tous ces souvenirs c'est comme j'emportais un peu d'eau dans un sac de mousseline." But there is something more and something worse. Art such as this is unhealthy and harmful. I know that there are distinguished and pure-minded people who have no use for music and who not only do not like it but are afraid of it, for, as they say, it strikes at their very being, weakens and dissolves their conscience. When it comes to music such as this they are quite right. It dissolves us because it is itself in a state of dissolution. Its hardly perceptible vitality tends to the lowering and the ruin of our existence. It contains germs, not of life and progress, but of decadence and death.

* Translation by Maire and Grace O'Brien.

This reminds one unmistakably of the theories of Max Nordau, who, in his once-famous book, "Degeneration," so bitterly attacked the Impressionists and Symbolists. The director of the Conservatoire, Théodore Dubois, so feared the nefarious influence of *Pelléas* that he forbade students of the composition classes to hear it.

Within a short time *Pelléas* became a great box-office success. But one performance was dissatisfying, and Debussy characteristically wrote to Messager:

I suppose I had to expect the consequences of such excitement—I fell into an awful state of depression. The performance last Saturday didn't go off very well. All sorts of silly little things happened which really had nothing to do with me. There'll be another performance next Thursday unless something unfortunate happens in the meantime. I am quite incapable of putting a good face on things when I am discouraged, as you know.

The following performance was again a success. There was then a question of giving the part of *Pelléas* to a woman.

It may seem strange, but it's not altogether silly [Debussy wrote to Messager]. Pelléas has not the ways of making love of a hussar, and when he finally does resolve upon something his plans are so quickly checked by the sword of Golaud that the idea might be worth considering. I must admit that I would rather like to see. . . . Without speaking of the change in sex there would be a change in the scheme of timbres which worries me rather. Perhaps I am more curious about it than genuinely interested. I will await your advice.

The idea was dropped.

In the course of the year, the musical historian Jules Combarieu, then an official of the Ministry of Education, proposed Debussy for the decoration of the Croix d'Honneur. He accepted it, but only, as he told Louis Laloy, "for the joy it will give my old parents and all those who love me." * He soon found life in the public eye, which the success of his opera had brought him, distasteful. In June, at the end of the Paris season, he wrote to Godet:

It is I, Claude Debussy, and I am none the prouder for being he. You will never know what remorse I feel for this unmentionable behaviour to you—you whom I love with all my heart! Truth to tell, I am tired out. It is like neurasthenia—a fashionable illness to which I thought I was immune. Apparently the mental and nervous strain of these last months have got the better of me, for I couldn't even think of writing to Godet. I have just now a moment when I feel less fagged and I beg you not to think too badly of me and to believe that there's nothing rotten in the state of Denmark. As for your article, I can hardly thank you, it would almost be an insult. Besides, I did not need to be reminded of your sensitive understanding and your scrupulously loyal love of beauty. . . . To come back to the story, I must tell you that the dress rehearsal has given me the most wretched trouble. What I fore-

---

* Paul Valéry's comment in a letter of congratulation was: "Every real artist has the power, some day, to decorate the government."

see is that I shall continually be pushed into public life. I am not really made for that kind of thing and all I shall be is my clumsy self. . . .

Well, I am anxious to see these performances of *Pelléas* over. It's time they were. They are beginning to take it for one of the repertory works. The singers are beginning to improvise and the orchestra are getting heavy. They'll soon be thinking more of *La Dame blanche.* . . . But I think I've got some way of getting the orchestral score published.

I will write to you shortly when I am in less of a hurry. I want this to reach you as soon as possible.

Then he retired for the summer to the home of his parents-in-law at Bichain in Burgundy. *Pelléas* was given in the autumn and again during the following year. The Opéra-Comique, he told Durand in 1903, "is absurdly taking up all my time, and this life of the theatre disgusts me and deadens me."

E. L.

When Oscar Hammerstein introduced *Pelléas et Mélisande* to America at the Manhattan Opera House, Feb. 19, 1908, one local critic objected that Debussy's tone combinations "sting and blister and pain and outrage the ear." From another reviewer the score's seemingly amorphous texture even elicited the word "jellyfish." With the exception of Vittorio Arimondi as Arkel, instead of Félix Vieulle, the principal singing actors were those of the world *première* six years earlier: Mary Garden (Mélisande), Jeanne Gerville-Réache (Geneviève), Jean Périer (Pelléas), and Hector Dufranne (Golaud).

When the Metropolitan staged the work for the first time, March 21, 1925, Lucrezia Bori, Kathleen Howard, Edward Johnson, Clarence Whitehill, and Léon Rothier were the chief artists.

Léo Delibes

(St. Germain-du-Val [Sarthe], France, Feb. 21, 1836–Jan. 16, 1891, Paris)

The composer of four operas, among them the charmingly romantic *Lakmé,* Léo Delibes nevertheless owes his fame perhaps still more to his work in the less pretentious category of ballet. Faithful to tradition, French opera of the Nineteenth Century preserved for ballet its important function as *scènes de ballets* or *divertimenti,* an indispensable part of grand opera. Ballets were rarely independently performed. In composing scores of genuine musical value for ballet alone, Delibes contributed much to the development of this art form.

Following his graduation from the Paris Conservatoire, he became accompanist at the Théâtre Lyrique and organist at the Church of St.-Jean et St.-François (1853). His first work for the stage appeared two years later, a one-act operetta, *Deux sous de charbon.* Within the next ten years, he composed twelve more operettas in much the same style. However, the strong competition in the musical life of Paris at that time made it difficult for Delibes to gain a position of outstanding influence.

His appointment as second chorus master at the Grand Opéra (1865) marked an important point in his career, for it was then that he turned his hand to writing ballet. His first work in this line, "La Source" (1866), first presented at the Opéra, enjoyed a notable reception. Not until four years later, however, did he score a major triumph with "Coppélia, ou la fille aux yeux d'émail," which has been enchanting audiences since the day of its first performance. Following this came "Sylvia" (1876), also a universal favorite.

Delibes retained his chorus master position at the Grand Opéra until 1881, when he resigned to become professor of composition at the Conservatoire. While here, he finished probably his most pretentious work, the opera *Lakmé,* written in the best Romantic tradition, with a melodious, vivacious score following the then popular "exotic" line. This work, set in a wholly imaginary India, was produced almost simultaneously in Paris, London, and New York in 1883. At first only fairly successful in this country, *Lakmé* has in recent years gained a notable popularity with Lily Pons in the title role. Her light but graceful coloratura gives sufficient weight to the famous "Bell Song" from the opera and she has made the part of Lakmé peculiarly her own.

In the field of opera, Delibes' reputation rests on this single work. Other compositions include the comedy-opera, *Le roi l'a dit* (1873), a cantata, "Alger" (1856), and fifteen songs in the German *lied* style. Delibes' influence gave an impetus to the revived popularity of the Romantic ballet at the turn of the last century, leading ultimately to the international acclaim accorded to the Russian ballet.   W. H., P. Z.

Lakmé

OPÉRA COMIQUE IN 3 ACTS

Book by EDMOND GOUDINET and PHILIPPE GILLE, based on
GOUDINET's poem *Le Mariage de Loti*

First performance: Opéra Comique, Paris, Apr. 14, 1883

CHARACTERS

Gerald, a British officer, TENOR
Frédéric, his friend, also a British officer,
  BARITONE
Nilakantha, a Brahman priest, BASS
Hadji, a Hindu slave, TENOR
Lakmé, daughter of Nilakantha,
  SOPRANO
Ellen, daughter of the Governor,
  SOPRANO

Rose, her friend, SOPRANO
Mrs. Benson, governess of the young
  ladies, MEZZO-SOPRANO
Mallika, slave of Lakmé, MEZZO-SOPRANO
A Fortuneteller
A Chinese Merchant
A Sepoy

*Hindus, Men and Women, English Officers and Ladies, Sailors, Bayaderes, China-
men, Musicians, Brahmans, etc.*

The action takes place in India in the middle of the nineteenth century

Lakmé, daughter of Nilakantha, a Hindu priest resentful of all foreigners, particularly Britishers, returns from her flower-gathering to find Gerald, a British soldier, trespassing upon inviolate temple grounds, the penalty for which is death.
Gerald, struck by her beauty, at once forgets his fiancée Ellen and falls in love with
Lakmé. He steals away in time to escape the watchful eye of Nilakantha.

Telltale footprints apprise the embittered priest that an intruder has violated the
sanctity of the temple. Lakmé, pressed by her father, refuses to tell Gerald's name.
To discover the offender's identity Nilakantha resorts to stratagem. Accompanied by
Lakmé, he attends a religious festival held in the public square. Among the onlookers
are Britishers. Commanded by the priest, Lakmé sings the captivating "Bell Song"
and unwittingly causes Gerald to betray himself. As he does so, Nilakantha buries a
knife in his back.

Gerald is hurried off to a retreat in the woods, and there Lakmé, skilled in the
use of healing herbs, nurses him back to health. To seal their pledge of constancy,
Lakmé departs to prepare a love potion. In her absence Gerald's friend, Frederick,
comes to recall the British officer to his duties. Lakmé returns with the potion just
as drums and fifes further remind Gerald that he is a soldier. A conflict rages in his

breast, but the stern voice of duty prevails. Crushed, Lakmé swallows poison, and as she lies dying in Gerald's arms, her father promises that Gerald shall go forth unharmed.

P. S.

Long before anyone had dreamt of such a thing as the motion picture, let alone Hollywood, *Lakmé* demanded type casting. Here was an opera with an exotic heroine. Like Selika, the barbarian queen in *L'Africaine,* the girl Lakmé, to produce her just effect, had to satisfy the eye. The daughter of the fanatical Hindu priest charged her impersonator with a double scenic burden, to look her part and to sing it. And it was easier to find a soprano equipped for the high staccati of the "Bell Song" than to pick one who could issue with verisimilitude from a heathen temple in an East Indian jungle.

Let us now listen to an eminent contemporary and compatriot of Delibes. The month of August, 1879, Massenet and his family spent as guests of Giulio Ricordi, the music publisher, at the Villa d'Este "in that picturesque and marvelous country which is bathed by the Lake of Como." There Massenet saw "a quite adorable young girl, a rose hardly yet in bloom, who at that time was studying singing with a renowned Italian professor."

Arrigo Boito, the celebrated author of *Mefistofele* [Massenet goes on] who was also enjoying country life at the Villa d'Este, had been struck as I had been by the very individual timbre of that voice. That exquisite voice, already prodigiously supple, belonged to the future artist who was to become unforgettable in her creation of *Lakmé* by my glorious and so deeply regretted Léo Delibes. I have named Marie Van Zandt.

Born in New York on October 8, 1861 (according to the books), Marie Van Zandt, a high soprano, made her operatic début at Turin in 1879 as Zerlina in *Don Giovanni.* In 1880 she joined the company at the Paris Opéra Comique, where she created the title rôle in *Lakmé* on April 14, 1883. A peculiar fitness for the part of the Hindu girl has always been dwelt upon. Joseph Loisel, devoted student of *Lakmé,* writes of Van Zandt with special eloquence:

Her unusual type, charming and untamed; her presence at once chaste and provocative, less voluptuous than the Rarahu of Loti, but designed to awaken the same sensations, her childlike graces, her physique, in a word, designated her as the living personification of Lakmé, to such a point that the critic of *Le Figaro* declared that in the future the part could never be played under a different guise.

The same writer remarks that in July, 1905, Henri de Curzon, amid the praise he bestowed upon Sigrid Arnoldson, the famous Swedish soprano, when she appeared as Lakmé, specified her physical resemblance to the creatress of the rôle. It is also noteworthy that when about that time the part was assigned to Angèle Pronot the reviewers objected that her kind of beauty was a little too majestic and her figure too lofty.

Perhaps [admitted a writer in *Comoedia*] we have been wrong to see in Lakmé a slender and delicate apparition. The memory of Van Zandt represents her thus. However, nothing in the work itself stipulates that she should be a thin and small creature.

Gerald [the writer goes on] having as fiancée an English girl of the traditional sort, would not have fallen in love with a young foreigner as ethereally pure in type as the daughter of the Viceroy. It is physical unlikeness which makes men fickle. Therefore, Mlle. Pornot is quite all right as she is, even though Lakmé becomes thus less mysterious.

In spite of the prophecy set down in *Le Figaro, Lakmé* proved stronger than its heroine. A host of sopranos, varying in face and figure, have impersonated Nilakantha's daughter since the time of Marie Van Zandt, and today *Lakmé* stands with *Carmen, Mignon,* and *Werther* among the works most frequently performed at the Opéra Comique. Still we are assured by Henri de Curzon that no successor of Van Zandt has effaced her memory.

"There have been," he says, "and always will be many excellent Lakmés, but few could express so happily the sometimes contrasting traits of the character and her voice."

With respect to the demands made on Van Zandt's voice Loisel declares that the rôle of Lakmé

requires, in fact, almost diametrically opposed qualities, which are seldom united in a single artist; the long phrases charged with feeling, all hot with passion or else delicately shaded with a restrained emotion, demand a lyric soprano; the vocalises, the runs, the staccati, all that is brilliant in the rôle, want the virtuosity of a florid singer.

And Loisel adds this picturesque detail about the American vocalist: "In the 'Legend of the Daughter of the Pariahs' [Bell Song] one observed a certain detached 'E' like the prize at the summit of a greased pole."

Lakmé did not reach New York until the American Opera Company presented it in English at the Academy of Music on March 1, 1886, with Pauline l'Allemand in the name part. We are assured that what pleased the audience most in the lady's performance was her rolling down a flight of steps in the death scene, anticipating rotary achievements in future productions of grand opera.

The first performance of *Lakmé* at the Metropolitan Opera House took place in Italian on April 7, 1890, with Adelina Patti as the heroine. On February 22, 1891, New York was at last to hear the work in the original French and with the original Lakmé, Marie Van Zandt. The Parisian triumph, however, was not duplicated, and there was only one repetition that season. Whereupon, *Lakmé* went into limbo here until it was revived for Marcella Sembrich on

January 28, 1907. But the revival was short-lived. Three performances constituted its record.

The opera was next heard from in New York on March 21, 1910, when Oscar Hammerstein, five days before the close of his last season of grand opera at the Manhattan Opera House, presented it in Italian with Luisa Tetrazzini as Lakmé and John McCormack as Gerald. Mme. Tetrazzini, who had dazzled her hearers with the "Bell Song" as an interpolation in the lesson scene of *The Barber of Seville,* now had a chance to sing the entire rôle, which she did with such brilliant success that Hammerstein announced that he would present *Lakmé* again with Mme. Tetrazzini and Mr. McCormack, but in French, during the following season—a season that never came to pass.

On March 24, 1917, came a revival at the Metropolitan, presenting Maria Barrientos as Lakmé. Again three performances made the record of the revival. Though meanwhile Amelita Galli-Curci, with the visiting Chicago company, appeared in the work in New York, it was not until the Metropolitan revival of February 19, 1932, that *Lakmé* took a firm and lasting hold on the affections of the local public, and this phenomenon was unquestionably due to the special suitability of Mme. Lily Pons for the exotic and ingratiating rôle of the Hindu heroine.

P. S.

Gaetano Donizetti

(Bergamo, Italy, Nov. 29, 1797–Apr. 8, 1848, Bergamo)

Donizetti studied at Naples under Simon Mayr, the operatic composer, and then under Mattei at Bologna. After his return to Bergamo, his father insisted upon his giving lessons in order to earn his living. Donizetti revolted, and enlisted in the army. His regiment was quartered at Venice, and here the young composer's first opera, *Enrico Conte di Borgogna,* saw the light in 1818.

The success of this work, and of a second opera brought out in the following year, established Donizetti's reputation. He obtained his discharge from the army, and henceforth his operas followed each other in rapid and uninterrupted succession at the rate of three or four a year. Although he had to contend successively with two such dangerous rivals as Rossini and Bellini he succeeded in taking firm hold of the public, and the brilliant reception accorded to his *Anna Bolena* at Milan, where Pasta and Rubini appeared in it, carried his name beyond the limits of his own country. In 1835 Donizetti went for the first time to Paris, where, however, his *Marino Faliero* failed to hold its own against Bellini's *Puritani,* then recently produced at the Théâtre Italien. The disappointed composer went to Naples, where the enormous success of his *Lucia di Lammermoor* (1835) consoled him for his failure in Paris. Returning to Paris he produced at the Opéra-Comique what proved eventually his most popular opera, *La Fille du Régiment,* but it was not till after the work had made the round of the theatres of Germany and Italy that it found favor with the French. A revival in Paris of his *Lucrezia Borgia,* produced at Milan in 1833, was interrupted by Victor Hugo's claim for infringement of copyright, and the libretto was altered. *La Favorita,* generally considered Donizetti's masterpiece, was produced in 1840. His next important work, *Linda di Chamounix,* was written for Vienna, where it was received most favorably in 1842, and the same success attended the production of *Don Pasquale* in Paris in 1843. Soon after this event the first signs of a fatal disease, caused to a great extent by overwork, began to show themselves. The utter failure of *Don Sebastian,* a large opera produced soon after *Don Pasquale,* is said to have hastened the catastrophe. A paralytic stroke in 1844 deprived Donizetti of his reason, and for four years he lingered on in a state of mental and physical prostration. A visit to his country was proposed as a last resource, but he reached his native place only to die there on April 8, 1848.

The sum total of his operas amounts to sixty-four [or sixty-five]. The large number of his works accounts for many of their chief defects. His rapidity of working made all revision impossible. It is said that he once wrote the instrumentation of a whole opera within thirty hours. And yet it may be doubted whether more elaboration would have essentially improved his work, for the dramatic last act of *Favorita,* infinitely superior to the preceding ones, is also said to have been the product of a single night.

Without boasting the sweetness of Bellini or the sparkle of Rossini, Donizetti won the popular ear by his flow of melody and by his rare skill in writing for the voice, to which qualities may be added his power of humorous delineation, as evinced in *Don Pasquale* and *L'Elisir d'Amore,* which works will probably last as long as anything he ever wrote.*

* Encyclopaedia Britannica.

L'Elisir d'Amore

[The Elixir of Love]

OPERA BUFFA IN 2 ACTS

Book by Felice Romani

First performance: Teatro della Canobbiana, Milan, May 12, 1832

CHARACTERS

Adina, a wealthy and independent young woman, SOPRANO

Nemorino, a young peasant, in love with Adina, TENOR

Belcore, a sergeant of the village garrison, BASS

Dr. Dulcamara, a traveling quack doctor, BASS

A Landlord, a Notary, Peasants, Soldiers, Villagers

The action takes place in a little Italian village during the nineteenth century

Nemorino, a young farmer, whose wealthy uncle lies near death, is passionately fond of the capricious Adina. Belcore, a sergeant, also loves her. The two suitors are kept in a state of indecision by her changeable disposition. Dr. Dulcamara, an itinerant quack, arrives at the village in great style. In the song, "Udite, udite o rustici," he dwells upon the merits of his medicines.

Buying a bottle of the Elixir of Love—which is really wine—Nemorino, while under its spell, loses favor with Adina. She determines to marry the sergeant in a week. The villages gather in the second act to witness the signing of the marriage contract. Adina, the sergeant, and the notary retire for the ceremony. Nemorino enters, and seeing Dulcamara, entreats him to give him some potion that will win Adina's love. The youth has no money, and the quack refuses him.

In the midst of these discussions, Belcore puts in an appearance. He seems to be downcast, for Adina, with her usual variableness, has decided to put off the ceremony until that evening. Upon learning that Nemorino desires money, the sergeant urges him to enlist, because of the bonus of twenty pounds. Nemorino does so, and buys the second elixir post-haste.

The village girls, discovering that the death of Nemorino's uncle has made the boy rich, vie for his attention. The surprised Nemorino attributes his sudden popularity to the elixir, and decides to arouse his beloved's jealousy. He is so successful that she buys back Nemorino's army contract and joyously embraces her true love.

P. S.

123

DONIZETTI'S EARLY OPERAS

Bellini's death, as well as Rossini's continuing abstention from the stage, left the field of Italian opera to the facile and copious Donizetti, their most considerable rival. Far and away the least interesting of the three, he was, both temporally and stylistically, a link between them and the young but rapidly maturing Verdi of *Ernani* and *Luisa Miller*. With touches of Rossini's verve and pace, Bellini's *bel canto* languid smoothness, and even, at rare moments, Verdi's realism, Donizetti lacks a strong musical personality. As a composer, he was something of a virtuoso, with all the accompanying defects. In the space of twenty-six years he composed sixty-five operas (some of them, it must be admitted, mere one-act operettas). Many of these are but improvised banquets of song, with not a few of the viands warmed over from previous feasts. He composed a one-acter * in nine days, and the last act of *La Favorite,* one of his most popular scores, was spun off in a few hours.

The results of this slapdash haste in composition are what we would expect (Donizetti was not Mozart, and only occasionally was he Rossini) : poor construction, feeble passagework, drearily manufactured accompaniments, acceptance of anything that came along. He had a good-natured contempt for anyone who worked more slowly than he did. Once, when told that Rossini had composed *Il Barbiere di Siviglia* in thirteen days, he replied, "Why not? He's so lazy." In short, Donizetti was the exact opposite of Bellini, who once wrote to Giovanni Ricordi, his publisher, firmly but politely demanding four times the usual fee for an opera, on the grounds that he composed only one opera while other men did four.

Donizetti exaggerated the tendency inaugurated by Rossini to look in almost any direction for a libretto. In Rossini, this freedom of choice had an element of creativeness; Donizetti, inheriting it, construed it as a license to accept any story. Glancing over the titles of his operas, one visualizes him poring over a terrestrial globe, suddenly darting down to fix a pin in some, to him, exotic spot, and thinking triumphantly, "Here I shall erect another opera." In *La Regina di Golconda* he reached India's coral strand, though his nearest approach to Greenland's icy mountains was Liverpool, which he celebrated in a score about some evidently not very fussy girl who dwelt in a hermitage there. From his titles alone comes evidence of an interest in such ill-assorted places as Calais, Chamonix, Saardam, Rome, Granada, and Kenilworth. Was the oddly captioned *Otto mese in due ore* † laid in the United States, then, as now, the

---

* It was called *Il Campanello di notte,* and by a mere chance it has survived. In 1917, The Society of American Singers, having made a hit with two Mozart one-acters, *Bastien und Bastienne* and *Der Schauspieldirektor,* revived it in an English adaptation at the Lyceum Theater, New York. The leading role in this obscene work was sung by David Bispham, the eminent Quaker baritone.
† Eight Months in Two Hours.

home of speed? Did *Il Diluvio universale* * end on Mount Ararat? . . . They are a very far cry from the Greek and Roman myths that constituted the subject matter of the earliest operas, and almost as far from the heroic exploits, historic and pseudo-historic, that had for so long been the whole business of *opera seria*. Rossini had indeed opened a Pandora's box when he turned to Shakespeare and Scott, to actual modern history, for the materials of his musical invention. The last ill lies doubtless in that box, and no man can prophesy what it will be. Since Paul Hindemith dramatized a daily news report in his audacious *Neues vom Tage,* all bets are off.

Donizetti's first thirty-two operas can be dismissed completely without loss to history, and certainly without loss to music. Then, with his thirty-third, exactly at the halfway mark of his output, he rang the bell with *Anna Bolena*. It was a bell that was destined to clang and clamor, tinkle and knell, through thirty-two more operas, and to echo and re-echo through every opera house in the world, dimly and ever more dimly, up to the present time. It was a bell of base alloy, often flat, often murderously shrill, often soporific, yet occasionally emitting a silvery tone, all the more surprising because so rare. Of his second thirty-two, *Lucia di Lammermoor* is still a fixture wherever opera is given, and another, *Don Pasquale,* should be. A scant five rounds out the roster of those Donizetti operas which, for one reason or another, are still presentable. *Anna Bolena* itself is not among the presentable. Its glory departed with the great trio who sang it in its youth—Pasta as Anne Boleyn, Rubini as Percy, and Lablache as Henry VIII.

Yet, a presentation of this faded score would certainly astonish English-speaking audiences, for in Act III occurs a melody they know as "Home, Sweet Home." Will not every loyal Englishman swear that Sir Henry R. Bishop, perpetrator of "Lo, Here the Gentle Lark," was the only fabricator of this most epidemic of heart songs? Where, then, did Donizetti get the tune he used in *Anna Bolena?* Did he borrow it from Bishop himself, who years before applying it to John Howard Payne's verses in his opera *Clari, or The Maid of Milan,* had published it as a Sicilian folk melody? Possibly it was just what Bishop had at first said it was—a Sicilian folk melody—and not his own brain child, as he established in a court of law . . . after it became famous.

Not so exemplary in its sentiments as "Home, Sweet Home," but more attractive musically, was the aria "Una furtiva lagrima" that made the fortune of the sparkling *buffa* score Donizetti wrote two years after *Anna Bolena*. This was *L'Elisir d'amore,* to words by Felice Romani, an opera much inferior to *Don Pasquale,* and scarcely the equal of *La Fille du régiment,* yet witty enough to show the strength of Donizetti's comic talent. Incidentally, it has seemed to be more popular in this century than any opera of Donizetti's

---

* The Universal Deluge.

except *Lucia,* a fact which at the Metropolitan was due to the role of Elvino's being one of Caruso's favorites. Naturally, as the tenor is given "Una furtiva lagrima." Yet, the role proved ultimately thankless to its superb interpreter, for he was singing it at the Brooklyn Academy of Music, on December 11, 1920, when he was stricken with the pleurisy of which he died eight months later. . . .

W. B., H. W.

"You are invited to attend the general rehearsal of a new work by Signor Maestro Donizetti, *L'Elisir d'Amore,* which will take place next Friday, May 11, 1832, at half past eight o'clock at the Canobbiana Theatre."

Such was the invitation of the director of the Milan Opera House to Count Harteg, Governor of Lombardy, on a Spring day over one hundred years ago. The opera had an enthusiastic reception. It held the boards for thirty-two consecutive evenings. The Milanese public refused to tire of applauding the amusing love story.

Every belle in Milan was aware that the opera was dedicated in a sense to her, as is evident from Donizetti's letter to Ricordi: "Since in your goodness you have left to me the choice of the dedication of *L'Elisir d'Amore,* I would be most grateful to have it read, 'To the fair sex of Milan.' Who knows better how to distill it? And who can dispense it better?"

In the composer's jocular tone one senses his pleasure in the success of the work, not to speak of his gallantry toward the ladies. Various amorous adventures fell his way in life, but his soul's depths contained but one name. This was Virginia Vasselli, the beautiful young wife whom a cruel malady snatched from him after a few hours of happiness and whose loss he tried to fill with a variety of other excitements.

As is generally known, *L'Elisir* was composed in a fortnight. The libretto, from Scribe's "Filtro," was the work of Felice Romani. Poet and composer worked in perfect harmony as far as the second act, according to contemporary observers.

Then trouble started. Donizetti absolutely insisted on the introduction of a Romanza. The poet categorically refused. After much discussion and dissension, he yielded. The fruit of his surrender was the most popular number in the entire score—"Una furtiva lagrima."

The new work was interpreted by Sabina Heinefetter, Dabadie, the tenor il Genero and the buffo Frezzolini. It crossed the borders in 1835, when Tadolini and Sante made it wildly popular in Vienna. By 1839 it reached France, where the soprano Fanny Tacchinardi-Persiani interpreted the heroine. A contemporary newspaper reported that Donizetti had composed one aria especially for this Adina, which happily represented the "vivacious poetry of Donizetti." This aria is believed to have been sung in the Naples production, but left no trace.

A charming incident was related of the effect of the comedy on the London public, where a circle of critics were speaking of it with a certain disdain. Felix Mendelssohn alone raised a voice of protest. "I would be happy to have composed *L'Elisir d'Amore,*" he retorted. . . .

M. F.

The American *première* of *L'Elisir d'Amore* took place at the Park Theater, New York, June 18, 1838, in English. It was presented in Italian at Palmo's Opera House, New York, May 22, 1844. [At the first Metropolitan *L'Elisir,* on January 23, 1904, Caruso sang "Una furtiva lagrima" so ravishingly that the performance could only continue after he had repeated it. Sembrich was the Adina.]

Lucia di Lammermoor

OPERA IN 3 ACTS

Book by SALVATORE CAMMARANO, based on WALTER SCOTT's novel
The Bride of Lammermoor

First performance: Teatro San Carlo, Naples, Sept. 26, 1835

CHARACTERS

Lord Enrico (Henry) Ashton, of
Lammermoor, BARITONE
Raimondo (Raymond) Bide-the-bent,
chaplain at Lammermoor, BASS
Edgardo (Edgar), master of
Ravenswood, TENOR

Lord Arturo (Arthur) Bucklaw, Lucia's
prospective husband, TENOR
Lucia (Lucy), his sister, SOPRANO
Alisa (Alice), companion to Lucia,
SOPRANO OR MEZZO-SOPRANO
Normando (Norman), follower of Lord
Ashton, TENOR

Followers of Ashton, Inhabitants of Lammermoor, etc.

The action takes place in Scotland near the close of the seventeenth century

In spite of a feud between their houses, Lucy Ashton (Lucia) and Edgar of Ravenswood (Edgardo) are in love. He is to go to France on a political mission, and beforehand the lovers meet in the park of Lammermoor Castle and in a long and impassioned duet plight their truth anew. Henry Ashton (Enrico), Lucy's brother, persuades her by means of a forged letter that the absent Edgar is untrue to her; whereupon, at her brother's behest, she agrees to marry Arthur Bucklaw (Arturo).

As the marriage contract is signed, the returned Edgar forces his way into the great hall of the castle. Convinced that Lucy has betrayed him, he throws the ring she has given him at her feet, calling down curses on her and her house. In this scene occurs the famous sextet, one of Donizetti's loftiest inspirations.

Lucy, her mind wrecked by the dire happenings, slays Bucklaw in the bridal chamber. In her disarray she bursts upon the lingering guests to sing the world-famous "Mad Scene," to the obbligato of an agile and obedient flute, expiring with her concluding note. Edgar, meanwhile, has repaired to the churchyard where his ancestors lie entombed. After an elaborate scene, which gives a tenor's best abilities full scope, he, on learning of Lucy's death, buries his dagger in his own heart, differing thus from his prototype in the novel, who is engulfed in quicksands.

P. S.

Scott's famous novel "The Bride of Lammermoor" appealed as operatic material to more than one Italian composer of the eighteen-thirties. Donizetti in 1835 was invited to write a new opera by the Society of Industry and Fine Arts of Naples, and the theatre chosen for the production was the historic San Carlo. Thanks to the enterprise of Salvatore Cammarano, he already had in hand the libretto of *Lucia di Lammermoor*.

Bellini had been dead a short time [Florimo tells us]. One day a common friend of those two great geniuses said to Donizetti: "What a pity Bellini is dead! *Lucia* would have been absolutely a subject for his fine musical vein, all passion and melancholy." Donizetti, his pride wounded, replied: "I will torment what little talent I may possess that even I may succeed!"

The opera was brought out (September 26, 1835) and had the enthusiastic success of which everyone knows. Some days later Donizetti saw his friend again and, stopping him, said: "I hope my *Lucia* has pleased you; have I wronged my friend Bellini? I imagined I was invoking his beautiful spirit, and that inspired me with *Lucia!*"

At the San Carlo, Gilbert Duprez, a French tenor, created Edgardo (Scott's Master of Ravenswood) and Fanny Persiani, an Italian soprano, Lucia (Scott's Lucy Ashton). Duprez, the thirteenth of twenty-two children born to a Parisian perfumer, lived to be nearly ninety, dying on September 23, 1896. A book of his last years is entitled "Recréations de mon grand âge." Henry Fothergill Chorley, writing of him in 1845, says: "M. Duprez was here [London] for a second time—the finest dramatic tenor singer I have ever heard and seen on the stage," and again specifies "the incomparable declamation of M. Duprez."

Fanny Persiani (1812–1867) reached London concurrently with *Lucia di Lammermoor* in 1838. Of this "most accomplished singer," who "was always a greater favorite with the artists and the connoisseurs than with the public," Chorley gives one of his most vivid accounts:

Never was there woman less vulgar, in physiognomy or in manner, than she; but never was there one whose appearance on the stage was less distinguished. She was not precisely insignificant to see, so much as pale, plain, and anxious. . . . She was singularly tasteless in her dress. Her one good point was her hair, which was splendidly profuse and of an agreeable color.

So much for the visual. Her voice

was an acute soprano . . . acrid and piercing rather than sweet, penetrating rather than full . . . a voice in the sound of which, considered as sound, no one could by any possibility find pleasure. . . . She had, however, one excellent quality the might and completeness of which made the want of many others forgiven. . . .

She was such a mistress of the art of singing as few women in our, or in any time, have been.

Her voice, we are assured,

was developed to its utmost capacities. Every fibre of her frame seemed to have a part in her singing. . . . She was never careless, never unfinished . . . and occasionally, in the employment of her vast and varied resources, rising to an animation which . . . amounted to that display of conscious power which is resistless. The perfection with which she wrought up certain songs—such as the *Sonnambula* finale, or the mad scene in *Lucia*—if considered in respect to style, and to what style can do, has not in my experience been exceeded, has been very rarely approached.

She had the finest possible sense of accent, giving each phrase its fullest measure. Every group of notes "was divided and expressed by her with as much precision as the best of violinists (who *has* the gift of accent) brings into his bowing. And this was done with that secure musical ease which made her anxious, mournful face and her acute, acid voice forgotten."

Chorley speaks in particular of one evening when she sang in *Tancredi* with Alboni as "a perfect revel of vocal skill, daring, triumphant, perfect, riveting by its display of art." It was with reference to some such performance that Mendelssohn, who worshipped at the shrine of Jenny Lind, said: "Well, I do like Mme. Persiani dearly. She is such a thorough artist and she sings so earnestly, and there is such a pleasant, *bitter* tone in her voice!"

Jenny Lind, by the way, was as a rule no favorite of Chorley's, but concerning her Lammermoor bride he has this high praise:

She was the only Lucia (as was pointed out to me by M. Berlioz) who prepared for the last dismal heartbreak by her agony in the moment when she is impressed with the falsehood of her lover by her haughty and tyrannical brother. Her madness was fearfully touching in proportion as it had been foreseen.

Lucia di Lammermoor, introduced to New York at Niblo's Garden on September 15, 1843, was the second work presented at the Metropolitan Opera House, on October 24, 1883. It then provided an American début for Marcella Sembrich, who was to sing her last Metropolitan Lucia a quarter of a century later. In the same rôle that distinguished soprano had made her London début on June 12, 1880.

The record of *Lucia* in New York alone as a vehicle for débutantes is perhaps unique. It was in the name part that Adelina Patti, then only sixteen, made her initial appearance on any stage at the old Academy of Music on November 24, 1859. Lucia was Nellie Melba's first rôle in America, on December 4, 1893, at the Metropolitan. As Lucia, Maria Barrientos effected at the Metropolitan her North American début on January 30, 1916, and Lily Pons her first appearance on this side of the Atlantic, likewise at the Metropolitan, on January 3, 1931.

Though the opera of Luisa Tetrazzini's New York début, on January 15, 1908, at the Manhattan Opera House, was *La Traviata,* her final appearance in opera here, reversing procedure, took place at the Metropolitan on May 3, 1913, in *Lucia.*

P. S.

Don Pasquale

OPERA BUFFA IN 3 ACTS

Book by the COMPOSER, after CAMMARANO's *Ser Marc' Antonio*

First performance: Théâtre des Italiens, Paris, Jan. 4, 1843

CHARACTERS

Don Pasquale, an old bachelor, BASS   *Dr. Malatesta,* a physician, BARITONE
Ernesto, his nephew, TENOR   *A Notary,* BASS
Norina, a young widow, SOPRANO   *Valets, Chambermaids, Dressmakers, etc.*

The action takes place in Rome, early in the nineteenth century

Don Pasquale, an old bachelor, frowns on the affection of Ernesto, his nephew, for Norina, a charming young widow. Doctor Malatesta, the Don's friend and physician, however, sympathizes with the young lovers, and decides to help them. To the Don he sings the praises of his sister—a fictitious person—and Don Pasquale is all agog with excitement.

Norina is taken into the secret by being made to masquerade as the sister, and the stage is now set for the deception. Magnificently arrayed, Don Pasquale struts about like a peacock. The doctor and Norina arrive presently, and also a false notary. Just before the mock ceremony is performed, Ernesto comes upon the scene and, unaware of the trick, attempts to stop the proceedings. But he is restrained by the doctor.

As soon as Don Pasquale and Norina are "married" she, thoroughly coached by the doctor, makes all sorts of preposterous and expensive pronouncements concerning their future life. The poor Don is practically driven to distraction by her excessively luxurious tastes. To add further to his discomfort, Norina purposely drops an amatory note. Engineered further by the doctor, the plot advances to a meeting between the lovers in Don Pasquale's garden, where Ernesto sings the melodious "Serenade." When the plotters feel that the Don has had enough they reveal to him the true state of things, and so relieved is he to find himself free of this costly young woman that he gives the young lovers his blessing.

P. S.

Historians speak respectfully, as in duty bound, of Paisiello's *The Barber of Seville* (1780); but the fact remains that of the enormous repertory of Italian comic opera in the last quarter of the eighteenth century and the first half of the nineteenth only three works still keep the boards intact, not merely respected as museum pieces but admired as masterpieces that seem, for all the changes that have taken place in music since their day, to be perennially young. These three works are Rossini's *The Barber of Seville* (1816), Donizetti's *L'Elisir d'Amore* (1832), and his *Don Pasquale* (1843), which was nearly the last of its composer's sixty-odd operas. Already in 1843 he showed signs of exhaustion and a tendency to morbid melancholy: he was, in fact, suffering from a cerebro-spinal disease.* In 1845 he became paralysed. Almost the whole of 1846 and the first six months of 1847 he spent in an asylum at Ivry. In October of the latter year he was removed to his native town, Bergamo, where he died on the 8th April 1848.

The libretto of *Don Pasquale* is from Donizetti's own pen. He seems, indeed, to have had a decided gift for this kind of thing: the book of more than one of his early operas is his own work, and one at least of these, *Il Campanello di Notte,* is a little gem of humorous inventiveness, even if, as is probable, he derived the fundamental idea of it from a farce he had seen in Paris. For the general idea of *Don Pasquale* he was indebted to a comic opera produced in Milan in 1810, *Ser Marcantonio,* the composer of which was one Stefano Pavesi and the librettist Angelo Anelli. The plot of this hinges upon two eternally popular themes of the Italian comic theatre, that of the anxiety of the relatives of a rich man as to the dispositions he may have made in his will, and that of an elderly bachelor who suddenly decides to plunge into matrimony, and is given reason to regret it later.† Old Marcantonio perturbs his expectant relations by informing them that he intends to marry and hopes to become a father. The news is particularly unwelcome to his nephew Medoro and his niece Norina: the former is engaged to a milliner named Bettina, the sister of one Tobia, a stockbroker, who, as the laws of theatrical symmetry demand, is in love with Norina. Together they hatch out a plot by which Bettina is passed off on Marcantonio as the very wife for a man like him, she being an exceptionally inexperienced and modest girl: the mock marriage ceremony is performed by Tobia made up as a notary. Bettina, however, quickly reveals a shrewish temper and a passion for domestic extravagance that frighten the old gentleman out of his wits; so that he is easily persuaded to let Medoro take her off his hands in consideration of a handsome annuity, while Tobia, of course, marries Norina.

In construction, as will be seen, the play ran true to a well-established type: there were two hopeful young relatives, two other lovers, and two servants, one attached to Medoro, the other to Norina. Donizetti wisely rid this traditional pattern of its superfluities. He made shift with only one relative—old

* The cause of his malady does not seem to have been determined beyond question. That the seeds of it had been in him since his youth seems to be suggested by the fact that of his three children (born respectively in 1829, 1836 and 1837) the first lived less than a fortnight and the other two were stillborn.

† The latter of these two themes is probably of great antiquity. A variant of it is found in Ben Jonson's comedy "Epicœne," or "The Silent Woman." Richard Strauss's opera *Die schweigsame Frau* (1935) is based on this.

Pasquale's nephew Ernesto—and consequently a single love interest. This left him room to treat more extensively the character who hatches the ingenious plot against the old bachelor; Tobia now becomes Dr. Malatesta, the trusted friend of Don Pasquale. This drastic simplification and condensation of the too crowded canvas of *Ser Marcantonio* gave Donizetti, of course, more opportunity to expand his simple musical forms and to extract the last ounce of humorous expression out of each situation. The chorus is equally skilfully and economically handled: it appears only twice in the three acts, and on each occasion with perfect appropriateness, consisting as it does of Don Pasquale's house servants.

The wit and humour of the music, the composition of which is said to have occupied Donizetti no more than eleven days, ensured popularity for the work from the beginning. It was first performed in Paris on the 4th January 1843, with a cast that sends our thoughts back wistfully to the great days when singing *was* singing: Lablache was the Pasquale, Tamburini the Malatesta, Mario the Ernesto, and Grisi the Norina. Mario must have made a handsome and sympathetic Ernesto; he not only looked but was a gentleman, by birth as well as training—something of a rarity on the Italian operatic stage of that period. The charming Grisi was his wife. Tamburini was a baritone of unique quality, both as a singer and as an actor. As for Lablache, opera has perhaps never seen or heard his like before or since. He was equally great in serious and in comic rôles. Henry Chorley, who knew something about opera singing, and had heard again and again all the finest artists of the first half of the nineteenth century, described him as "taking him all for all the most remarkable man whom I have ever seen in opera. . . . An organ more richly toned or suave than his voice was never given to mortal." He was "gifted with personal beauty to a rare degree. A grander head was never more grandly set on human shoulders." He was of gigantic stature,

yet one never felt on the stage how huge he was. His shoe was as big as a child's boat. One could have clad the child in one of his gloves; and the child could almost have walked on his belt. But every article of his dress was so excellently fitted to its wearer, was worn so unconsciously, and was so thoroughly in agreement with all that it accompanied, that there was neither time nor temptation for comparison. . . . This handsome young French-Neapolitan had got an amount of general and genial and solid musical culture . . . which, for a singer, has been something with too little precedent. . . . Lablache's perfect acquaintance with the great Roman style, his marvellous voice and, little less marvellous, his power of sustaining and animating his comrades without bearing them down, afforded a distinct idea of how such music might be sung, and how, when well sung, it might move, impress and exalt those who heard it as a portion of a rite.

The reader might do worse than to try to picture to himself, the next time he hears some ill-trained, weary, wobbly victim of the modern mania for pushing people on to the stage before they have acquired much more than the rudiments of a technique, how the recitatives and melodies of Don Pasquale used to be *sung* by Lablache. And when, as is more than likely, he sees some lubberly lout of a bass, who has never been taught anything better, laying on the humour in the grossest fashion, the reader should try to visualise Pasquale as Donizetti conceived him and as Lablache represented him—"the farce of fatness," as Chorley says, "trying to make itself seductive," "the dear silly hero of the farce-opera" wearing a coat "which stuck to him with as terrible a closeness as the outside garment of a sausage does to its contents within," yet, for all that, never for a moment angling for the house-laugh of the mob.

Throughout the entire farce of Lablache's performances nothing was more admirable than his entire avoidance of grossness or coarse imitation. There was, with him, that security which belongs only to persons of rare and admirable tact; and, with that security, the highest power of expressing comedy, tragedy or grotesque—because it belongs to one who will risk nothing hazardous, but who is not afraid of daring anything extraordinary. When I hear of this person's style, and that person's high note, and when I think of Lablache, I am tempted to feel as if I had parted company with real comic genius on the musical stage for ever.

The part of Don Pasquale should never be clowned. The work was at first performed in what was then contemporary costume, an innovation in opera which, however, did not appeal to every spectator. But the very fact that Pasquale, as did Norina, Ernesto and Malatesta also, looked precisely like someone in real life is of itself a proof that the part was never intended by Donizetti as a vehicle for conventional clowning. Pasquale, for all his amorous foolishness, was a gentleman in an epoch when good breeding still counted for something.

E. N.

The first performance in New York took place at the Park Theater, March 9, 1846, in English. It was given in Italian at the Astor Place Opera House, Nov. 29, 1849. Marcella Sembrich was the Metropolitan's first Norina. A noteworthy Metropolitan revival occurred, April 5, 1913, when Arturo Toscanini conducted and the officiating quartet comprised Lucrezia Bori, Umberto Macnez, Antonio Scotti, and Antonio Pini-Corsi.

Christoph Willibald von Gluck

(Erasbach [Upper Palatinate], Bavaria, July 2, 1714–Nov. 15, 1787, Vienna)

In the year 1741, when Handel's last opera, *Deidamia,* was given in London, Gluck's first, *Artaserse,* was brought out in Milan; a coincidence to be deemed significant by the superstitious. The grand autocrat of the old régime makes his parting bow just as the herald of the new comes upon the scene; *le Roy est mort! vive le Roy!*

Christoph Willibald Gluck's . . . parents were in the service of Prinz Lobkowitz, and he passed his childhood at the prince's castle of Eisenberg. His education was tolerably well cared for, according to the notions of the day; at twelve he was sent to a Jesuit school at Kommotau in Bohemia; at eighteen, to Prag, where he studied music under Bohuslav Černohorský, and took to practising on the 'cello. In 1736, being then twenty-two, he entered the private band of prince Melzi in Vienna, soon following his patron to Milan, where he finished his professional studies under Sammartini.* After four years' work at counterpoint and other forms of composition, he felt himself ready to face the world as a composer *"en gros,"* as Mendelssohn would have said.†

He had rare good luck: some things he had written for prince Melzi's chamber-music got him the commission to write a grand opera for the court theatre. For his libretto he took Metastasio's "Artaserse." Even in this, his first opera, he determined to cut loose from many of the traditions of the "Oratorio" school, and write music that should be at once more dramatic and more scenic. But he told no one of his intention, and finished his score—all but one aria— to suit himself. With this one aria lacking, the opera was put into rehearsal, and every musical dabster present pooh-poohed the "new style" most contemptuously. This Gluck had counted on; before the final rehearsal he wrote the missing aria wholly in the conventional style, and a still larger gathering of *cognoscenti* than had been at the first rehearsal praised it highly, even suspecting it of coming from the pen of Sammartini himself. The audience on the opening night straightway quashed this verdict, though, crying out that that particular aria was simply insipid and quite unworthy of the rest of the score. Thus did our young Oberpfälzer slyboots score one off his first judges!

So Gluck had from the first this ambition to make the Opera more dramatic than his predecessors and contemporaries had done. But he had as yet no

---

* Giovanni Battista Sammartini, who ran a good third to the tie between Boccherini and Josef Haydn in the legendary race for the "invention" of the string quartet.

† "I am a wholesale pianist (*engros Pianist*); I can't play small things in public!"—Felix Mendelssohn, *reported orally.*

definite formula; his innovations were still evolutionary, rather than revolutionary; he did nothing that could be called radical. Yet what he did was new enough to scare the critics, who, as academic policemen, guarded nothing more carefully than the inviolable sacredness of traditional forms. But, if severely handled at times by the critics, Gluck would now and then get compensating sympathy from others. When a certain passage in the aria "Se mai senti spirarti sul volto," in his *Clemenza di Tito* (Naples, 1751), was scathingly criticised, it was shown to old Durante,* who said: "I do not feel like deciding whether this passage is entirely in accordance with the rules of composition; but this I can tell you, that all of us, myself to begin with, would be very proud of having thought of and written such a passage!"

From 1741 on, Gluck continued writing Italian operas; with enormous success in Italy and Vienna, in spite of the critics, if with no success whatever in England. He travelled a good deal, and the hearing of some Rameau operas in Paris must have given him wholesome food for meditation. From about 1755 to 1761 he showed signs of lapsing into mere conventionalism, and seemed to treat opera-writing as sheer practice-work, to gain technical facility. His mind was really filled with other matters; he had been for some time applying himself with zeal to filling out the gaps in his defective general education, studying æsthetics, languages, and literature, and getting what good he could from frequenting the society of cultivated people. He had plainly become dissatisfied with the scope and efficacy of his dramatic innovations in Opera, and was meditating a more thorough and logically formulated reform.

At last (about 1760) he met the right man to help him: the Italian poet Raniero de' Calzabigi, of Leghorn, editor of Metastasio's works in Paris, Counsellor at the Netherland Chamber of Accounts in Vienna, noted writer on æsthetics, etc., etc. With him he talked the problem over: the defects of the Italian *opera seria,* and how these defects were best to be cured. The two pitched upon the following items as lying at the root of the reigning evil: the irresponsible vanity of the virtuoso singer, and the flaccid conventionality of the Metastasio libretto—full of poetic beauty (of a sort), but almost totally lacking dramatic quality, especially such as could be intensified by music.

The practical upshot was that Calzabigi wrote the text of *Orfeo ed Euridice,* and Gluck set it to music. One can not help smiling at the work's having first to be submitted to Metastasio, to avoid the foregone conclusion of a fiasco; the court poet's influence was not to be trifled with! Still more must one smile at Metastasio's carrying his friendship for Gluck and Calzabigi to the point of "agreeing to offer no active opposition to the new work," sure in his good heart that the public would take the trouble of damning it off his hands; he little dreamt that he was digging his own grave!

---

* Francesco Durante (1684–1755), then, at the age of sixty-seven, the recognized supreme master of Neapolitan church music.

Orfeo, brought out at the Vienna Burgtheater on October 5, 1762, was the first cannon-shot of the new Revolution. It was no *"Veni, vidi, vici,"* being considerably discussed at first; but the public came to it gradually, and Gluck's campaign opened with a very palpable victory. Much the same was true of *Alceste*—the libretto by Calzabigi, after Euripides—given on December 26, 1766. This work fairly separated the sheep from the goats in the Viennese public; the more seriously inclined saw that it was on a still higher plane of tragic grandeur than *Orfeo,* but a large mass of opera-goers found it rather too much of a good thing. "If that is the sort of evening's entertainment the Court Opera is to provide, good bye; we can go to church without paying two Gulden!" Gluck had to find out that fighting long-established convention is no bed of roses, and that impeccably attired patrons of aristocratic Opera are much inclined to resent seriousness that has not been cured of its deformity by sweetly-warbling divinities of the virtuoso species. But unquestionable success came with time, and *Alceste* established Gluck's position even more firmly than *Orfeo* had done.

Passing over *Paride ed Elena*—a strong work, but ill received by the public—and some other minor matters, we come to Gluck's meeting with the second poet who was to have a determining influence upon his destiny: the bailli du Rollet, attaché to the French legation in Vienna. Du Rollet encouraged Gluck's already-formed wish to go to Paris, as the properest field for him. He had become dissatisfied with the executive means he found in Vienna, and longed for the Académie de Musique, where there were "well skilled and intelligent actors, who combined a noble and soulful play of gesture with the art of song." Du Rollet took Racine's *Iphigénie en Aulide* and turned it into a libretto, Gluck setting to work forthwith upon the score; even before it was completed, it was pronounced to be just the thing for Paris.

To wish to go to Paris was one thing; to get officially invited thither, another. It seemed to French chauvinism that Paris had already quite foreigners enough to put up with in resident Italian musicians, and that the prospect of having to do with an admittedly strong German, and an æsthetic revolutionary to boot, was rather appalling. There was plotting and counterplotting galore, letter-writing without end. At last Marie Antoinette's influence carried the day, —she had been Gluck's pupil in Vienna, before her marriage,—and she succeeded in doing more for her former teacher than crowned heads or rich patrons (who have troubles of their own) often do for those who need their help. But Marie Antoinette's getting Gluck his invitation was enough to set madame Dubarry tooth and nail against him—just to show the world that a king's particular Fair Perdition was not to be outdone in court influence by any woman alive, let alone a Dauphine! The Dubarry was really at the bottom of most of the anti-Gluck agitation in Paris.

When Gluck came to Paris in 1773, with his *Iphigénie* all ready for the boards, his expectations of the *personnel* of the Académie de Musique were not wholly fulfilled. He found the acting as good as he had expected, but principals, chorus, and orchestra had fallen into the most deplorable musical habits; it took all his personal force, indomitable Teutonic pertinacity, and skill as a conductor, to whip them up to the mark. He succeeded, though, and *Iphigénie en Aulide* was brought to a satisfactory performance on April 19, 1774. It made a colder impression at first than any of his operas had in Vienna, but, like them, gradually made its way with the public. Then the storm broke loose!

The chief contestants in this famous Gluck controversy were, on Gluck's side, the abbé Arnaud and the *Anonyme de Vaugirard* (really Suard by name); on the opposing side, Marmontel, La Harpe, Guinguené, d'Alembert, the chevalier de Chastilleux, Framéry, and Coqueau. Grimm held a dignifiedly neutral position, or tried to make believe he did; two of the most important of Gluck's favourers were Jean-Jacques [Rousseau] and Voltaire, but neither of the two took any active part in the fight. La Harpe—whose sharp wit fairly took the bit in its teeth, and got beyond his own or any one's control—was the *enfant terrible* of the whole business, and did his own side as much harm as good; the Anonyme de Vaugirard took an especial delight in getting a rise out of him and prodding him to desperation.

Upon the whole, with all the wit, acute thought, and literary ability brought to bear upon the matter, first and last, this once-great controversy is no very edifying reading now; what controversialists on new æsthetic problems most lack is originality, the new problems suggest to them no new arguments, neither does the world's past experience in similar cases stead them a jot. It is always the same old story, over and over again, this organized kicking against the Rising Sun. Read the discussion between Monteverdi and Artusi in the first decade of the seventeenth century, the pen-and-ink tiffs between Wagnerians and anti-Wagnerians in the third quarter of the nineteenth, and you will have read practically all that was urged for and against Gluck in Paris in the 'seventies of the eighteenth. It was, in the last analysis, merely a Wotan and Fricka business, a volcanic conspuation of the New, *des Niedagewesenen,* on the one hand, a firmly convinced championing of it, on the other. The anti-Gluck side of the controversy is well summarized by Schmid: "These criticisms had two different purposes: first, they tried to prove that the Ritter von Gluck lacked all power of song, and next, that he set things to music that were not appropriate to song." And, if the intelligent reader knows of any "new light" in the whole history of Lyric Drama of whom this has not been said, he will confer a favour upon the present author by mentioning his name!

The impression produced by *Iphigénie en Aulide* as the performances wore on was still strengthened by *Orphée et Euridice,* given in August, 1774, in a translation by Moline, with the part of Orphée, originally written for contralto, transposed for Legros's high tenor. Of *l'Arbre enchanté* (Versailles, February 20, 1775) and the three-act ballet "Cythère assiégée" (Académie de

Musique, August 1, 1775), nothing need be said here. Gluck had returned to Vienna for a while, taking with him a remodelled version of the text of his *Alceste* by du Rollet and Quinault's libretto of *Armide et Renaud,* meaning to retouch the former score, and reset the latter text, for Paris. He was at work on both scores in Vienna when he got news of the latest trick of his opponents in Paris: the Italian, Piccinni, had been invited, and was to set Quinault's "Roland" for the Académie de Musique. Gluck's pride was bitten to the quick; a flaming letter of his to du Rollet found its way (without his leave) into the *Année littéraire,* and only served still further to exasperate the opposition. The Italophiles now had a champion of their own, and the Gluck controversy became the Gluck-Piccinni war, compared to which the old Handel-Bononcini business in London was a mere squabble.

In 1776 Gluck came back to Paris, and *Alceste* was given at the Académie de Musique on April 23. It was a bad night for the Gluckists; the opera was roundly hissed, the disappointed composer whimpering out *"Alceste est tom-bée!"* upon a friend's shoulder. *"Oui, tombée du ciel!"* replied the latter, fain to seek consolation in an epigram. But the fiasco was only for a while; *Alceste's* gradual success in Vienna was repeated in Paris, and Gluck once more ended by carrying the day.

On September 23, 1777, *Armide* was brought out; the immediate result was about the same as usual, only that indifference took the place of hissing. For one thing, the anti-Gluckists could not howl at Gluck's "impudence" in daring to reset a text already set by the great Lully, as it had been feared they would; for their own Piccinni had put them in a glass house by setting Quinault's "Roland," of which Lully was also the original composer.* Moreover, Gluck had paid French taste no mean compliment in taking Quinault's "Armide et Renaud" exactly as it stood, without subjecting it to those modifications which he had had made in all his previous classical libretti. But the indifference with which *Armide* was greeted at first soon wore off, and by the time Piccinni was ready with his *Roland* Gluck's position was again very strong indeed. Piccinni, to say the truth, was rather a laggardly champion, taking an infinite time in coming up to the scratch; which is partly to be accounted for by the poor man's not knowing a word of French when he first set to work upon his score. But on January 27, 1778, *Roland* was at last brought out, after endless trouble and squabbling at rehearsals; as a first cannon-shot into the Gluckist camp, it did a certain amount of execution, at least, the controversy became doubly acrid after it. It remained at white heat until the final "duel" settled matters.

It was agreed that both Gluck and Piccinni should write an opera, *Iphigénie en Tauride;* they could thus fight it out between them on the same ground. Gluck took a libretto by Guillard; Piccinni, one by Dubreuil. This "duel," as

---

* Piccinni did not, like Gluck, set Quinault's text as it stood, but in an adaptation by Marmontel.

usual, was rather a long one, Gluck's opera being given on May 18, 1779, Piccinni's not till January 23, 1781—some time after Gluck had left Paris for good. The result, however, was decisive; Gluck's *Iphigénie* capped the climax of his Paris successes, was indeed the first of his Paris operas that won unquestionable public favour on the opening night, whereas Piccinni's had a mere *succès d'estime* even with its own party, the more eager of whom tried to explain its quasi-failure with the general public by the undeniable fact that, on the second night, the beauteous Laguerre (who sang Iphigénie) was hopelessly the worse for strong liquor—*"Iphigénie en Champagne!"* said pert Sophie Arnould, who had sung Gluck's first Iphigénie.

It is quite plain that the success of Gluck's *Iphigénie en Tauride* was thoroughly genuine, based on the quality of the work itself. No less strong an opera could have so utterly routed Piccinni's as it did; especially as Gluck, after his *Iphigénie,* had had a palpable failure with his *Écho et Narcisse* on September 24, 1779, thus leaving Paris with his latest opera on record as a fiasco. Piccinni was, in truth, no weakling at all; he was even something of a dramatic reformer in Opera himself, quite as much as Gluck in his earlier Italian and Viennese days. But Gluck had far outstripped him since then, and had, moreover, as much greater force of innate genius than he as Handel had than Bononcini. Piccinni was swept from the stage into oblivion, not because he was weak, but because Gluck was stronger; also because the Gluck idea was stouter and truer than his. Had he not been inadvisedly brought to Paris to take part in that unequal contest with the doughty Austrian, he might have gone comfortably down in history as a worthy forerunner of the Gluck Reform; but, being thus brought face to face with and in opposition to it, he was crushed.

Écho et Narcisse was Gluck's last work for the stage; with it he leaves the history of Opera.* He died of apoplexy in Vienna on November 15, 1787.

As a reformer, Gluck was but little of a radical, hardly anything of a theorist. The best confession of artistic faith we have from his pen, his preface to *Alceste,* stands in history, with Peri's to *Euridice* and Victor Hugo's to "Cromwell," as one of the most famous of its kind. But there is very little constructive theorizing in it; it is, for the most part, negative in character, pointing out what is most to be avoided in opera-writing. It is a document of sheer sound artistic common sense, not a philosophico-scientific marshalling of principles to a firmly based theory; admirable as far as it goes, but not going far. Had Gluck's Reform rested with this document alone, there would have been little life in it.

---

* *Les Danaïdes* (text by du Rollet and Tschudi), which was brought out at the Académie de Musique on April 26, 1784, was advertised as "by Gluck and Salieri"; but, after the thirteenth performance, Gluck announced that the score was entirely by Salieri. The libretto was sent to Gluck in 1783, with the request to write the score; but he did not feel in condition to undertake the work then, and handed over the text to his pupil—"the foreigner who alone had learnt his manner of him, since no German cared to."

The real essence and mainspring of this much-talked-of Reform was Gluck's own intrinsic dramatic genius; his true strength as a reformer lay in his work, not in his doctrine. In him the old dramatic spirit of Peri, Monteverdi, and Cavalli breathed fresh and strong again; and it was the vigourous expression he gave to this spirit in his music that won him adherents, while his ruthless sacrifice of the time-honoured conventional operatic frippery to this expression made him enemies among those to whom old habits were dear.

What was new in Gluck was his musico-dramatic individuality, his style; for there was little really new in his principles. Not only did these date back, as far as they went, to the earliest days of Opera, but the artistic sins and abuses he stigmatized—the slavish subserviency of composers to the whims of the virtuoso singer, the sacrifice of dramatic interest to irrelevant musical developments—had been pointed out and deplored by more than one musician before him.

Gluck's Reform did not lack precursory heralds; the evils he set himself to cure had long been recognized as such, and he was not the first to attempt to cure them. But he was the first to strike the decisive blow, to go, if not quite to the root of the matter, at least as near to the root as was necessary for his purpose. And, as for his lack of radicalism, note how, in his preface, all even of the negative theses have their conditioning *if* or *when*. He does not oppose vocal ornamentation, for instance, absolutely and along the whole line, but only when it becomes damaging to dramatic common sense. He showed the same lack of uncompromising radicalism in his practice: there is many a vocal show-piece in his operas, but brought in in the right place, not into the midst of an ardent dramatic action.

Gluck is fairly to be regarded as the Father of Modern Opera; a sufficient commentary on this is the very fact that his are the earliest operas that hold the stage to this day. He followed Philipp Emanuel Bach and Haydn in employing a standard composition of the orchestra,* and banished the time-honoured *cembalo* (harpsichord) from it; he was thus the first opera-composer to write out his scores completely, leaving nothing to be added by the cembalist. He was equally great in impassioned or pathetic melody and in every form of recitative; his dramatic use of the chorus can hardly be surpassed in mastery. The opening scenes of the first and second acts of his *Orfeo*—Euridice's funeral rites, and Orfeo's entrance into Hades—are still unsurpassed masterpieces in this last particular.

Like most "new" men, Gluck was terribly fastidious about the style in which his works were to be given. Concerning Orfeo's aria, "Che farò senza Euridice?" he writes to the duke of Braganza: "Were one to make the slightest change in it, in the tempo or the mode of expression, it would become an air for the marionette stage. In a piece of this order, a more or less sustained note, a

---

* Up to, and including, Handel, there had been no standard composition of the orchestra, the aggregations of instruments used by composers being exceedingly various.

forcing of the tone, a neglect of the proper tempo, a trill, roulade, etc., can entirely destroy the effect of a scene." He was an inexorable rehearser, infinitely hard to satisfy.

In a specific sense, Gluck's great achievement was to fix the form of French Grand Opera for nearly a century, taking the form as already established by Lully and Rameau for a basis. What may be called the Gluck formula subsisted with but slight modification in France until Meyerbeer came above the horizon. From *Orfeo ed Euridice* to *Iphigénie en Tauride,* his operas are distinctly *grand* operas; to produce their proper effect, they need not only fine acting and singing and a competent orchestra, but a vast, well equipped stage and the most copious spectacular paraphernalia, especially a superb ballet. They are essentially spectacular operas, and it is the prominence of this feature in them that has most militated against their being adequately given in this country.

Gluck united in an unparalleled degree warmth of temperament with a certain classic reserve in expression; he was at home in classical and mythological subjects, in the stately classic manner; the true "romantic" strenuousness he had not, he would have made but a poor hand at it with a Shaksperian libretto. But it would be a dull ear that could not catch the poignancy that lurks behind his measured dignity of expression, a dull heart that did not beat responsively to the expansive force of his emotional heat. Perhaps he is at his most poignant in his musical pictures of perfect happiness; in grief and pathos he is great, but in serene, unalloyed bliss, greater still. There is a deeper well of tears in the chorus of beatified spirits in his *Orfeo,* than in "Che farò senza Euridice?" or "Malheureuse Iphigénie!" Few men have produced such overwhelming effects on the lyric stage with so beautiful a simplicity of means; let us part from him with his pet maxim (whether wholly true or not, matters little) on his lips: "Simplicity and Truth are the sole right principles of the Beautiful in works of art."

W. F. A.

Orfeo ed Euridice

[Orpheus and Eurydice]

DRAMA FOR MUSIC IN 4 ACTS

Book by RANIERO DE CALZABIGI, based on a Greek legend

First performance: Hofburgtheater, Vienna, Oct. 5, 1762

CHARACTERS

Orpheus, legendary Greek singer and musician, CONTRALTO

Eurydice, his wife, SOPRANO

Amor (Love), SOPRANO

Happy Shade, SOPRANO

Happy Shades, Furies, Shepherds, Shepherdesses, Heroes, and Heroines

The action takes place in legendary Greece

In the opening scene we behold Orpheus mourning beside the tomb of Eurydice. He will descend to the underworld in search of her. But there is a warning he must heed—never to look upon her as he leads her back. After passing through Hades undeterred by Cerberus and the Furies, he finds Eurydice in the Elysian Fields. But while he leads her back to earth, she implores him, if he loves her, not to avert his face.

At last, in sheer weariness, he gazes upon her only to learn the meaning of the warning, for Eurydice, obedient to destiny, leaves him to go back to the Elysian Fields. Thereupon he sings the celebrated aria "Che farò senza Euridice?" known in English as "I Have Lost My Eurydice." But Amor appears to him and tells him that the gods in pity at his despair will give him Eurydice again, and the opera ends in Love's Temple where she rejoins him.

P. S.

Gluck owed the direct impulse towards *Orfeo* to the influence of Ranieri Calzabigi, an Italian poet who was something of an adventurer like Casanova; he had come to Vienna in 1761. Calzabigi had edited the collected works of Metastasio for publication in Paris, but he had no great admiration for him; Gluck and the old poet seem to have been on terms of secret hostility.

A fact about the production of *Orfeo* in 1762 which has not generally been mentioned by historians is that the opera was preceded by a French comedy, not only on the first night, which celebrated the name-day of the Emperor, but at all succeeding performances. This at once accounts for the extreme shortness of *Orfeo,* which although in three acts would not take more than about an hour and a half in performance if given without intervals. This is much the same length as Purcell's *Dido and Aeneas.* It may also account for the fact that *Orfeo* has only three characters instead of the regulation six or seven in all Metastasio's dramas. Gluck's main activity during the previous few years had been the production of French comic operas; it is evident that the court wanted something musical to fill up an evening after a French play, but not too long or too expensive to produce. The occasion provided Gluck and Calzabigi with the opportunity of trying an experiment, provided that it was on a small scale.

The libretto of *Orfeo* reduces the story to the barest minimum (it must be remembered that the Paris version of 1774 is much longer, owing to additional songs and much additional ballet music). The Orpheus operas of Peri and Monteverdi had included more of the original legend—the pursuit of Eurydice by Aristaeus, her wedding, her death by the bite of a snake, the episode of Pluto and Proserpine in Hades, and the final chorus of Maenads. Moreover, Calzabigi and Gluck were not allowed to forget that they were providing a court entertainment; the opera begins with an overture so festive in character as to contrast unpleasantly with the opening scene of the funeral, and it ends with the resurrection of Eurydice and a *vaudeville* in the French comic opera style—a series of solos with a choral refrain, just like the finales of Mozart's *Entführung* and Rossini's *Barber of Seville.* And Cupid is obviously intended to be more or less of a comic character altogether; he is the traditional "god from the machine," but he is very definitely a small boy who knows a great deal more about the "facts of life" than is generally considered suitable at his age in these days.

What Gluck was aiming at, and what has made his opera immortal, was truth of emotion and intensity of feeling. We sometimes are led to think that Gluck's operatic figures all belong to a world of imaginary antiquity, a world of marble statues, rather than of human beings. That certainly was not his own intention. The return to antiquity was intended to be a return to nature. In *Orfeo* the choruses of infernal and happy spirits in Act II serve only as contrasts to the passionate humanity of Orpheus and Eurydice. It is very easy for English audiences, especially when they see *Orpheus* performed in a foreign language, to form a false conception of the opera. We are tempted to concentrate too much attention on the exquisite ballet music, or on the magnificent choruses of the second act, and we may perhaps think that the third act, except for the all-too-famous aria "Che farò senza Euridice," is something of an anticlimax and hardly more than a tedious stretch of unintelligible recitative.

But the third act is the dramatic climax of the whole opera. It introduces us to Eurydice—the real Eurydice, not the faint ghost whom we see in the Elysian Fields. It is a wonderful study of a woman's emotions, her gradual awakening from the condition of a passionless spirit to her consciousness of life and womanhood. She is like the woman ghost in the prologue to that strange opera *Tarare,* written by Beaumarchais and Gluck's pupil Salieri; we see a vision of souls who have not yet been assigned to human bodies—not one knows what he is to become after birth, except the woman, who even in that prehuman stage of existence knows that the one thing she craves is *l'amour.*

Orfeo as produced in Vienna was an Italian opera; the poet, the singers, the arranger of the dances, and the designer of the scenery were all Italians. Gluck himself had been educated entirely as an Italian composer. The idea of chorus and ballet was French, but the melodic line of the music is Italian, and this is true even of Cupid's song, which is the nearest approach to a French comic opera melody. The first song of Orpheus—three similar stanzas separated by recitatives—has been claimed by the German historian, Hermann Abert, as being in the Berlin song style of the period; it is much more like the Venetian popular sentimental songs of the eighteenth century. The metrical scheme of the infernal spirits' chorus—a metre at once familiar to all English hearers, though with very different associations—is one which was always employed for infernal spirits in the operas of Cavalli and Stradella. The rippling accompaniment of Orpheus' monologue in Elysium, which Hermann Abert thinks must have been modelled on Handel's "nature-painting," is to be found in any number of minor Italian opera composers such as Vinci and Rinaldo di Capua.

But Abert, in his preface to the reprint of the score, points out with perfect justice that although isolated scenes of the greatest dramatic intensity may be found in the works of Jommelli, Traetta, Perez, and Majo, it is only Gluck who can sustain this intensity throughout an entire opera.

In 1769 *Orfeo* was given at Parma, the entire opera forming the third act of a miscellaneous gala entertainment. Later on in the same year it was sung in London by the Parma cast (Millico, the famous *castrato,* as Orpheus) but with all sorts of additions by other composers. In 1774 the opera was completely remodelled for Paris, with a French version by P. L. Moline which falls far short of the Italian in literary merit. It has often been asked why Gluck should have composed the part of Orpheus in 1762 for a contralto and had it sung by a *castrato,* Gaetano Guadagni. The only answer is that at that date it was simply unthinkable that the hero of a serious opera should be anything else but a male soprano or contralto. Guadagni was one of the greatest singers of his time; Handel had employed him in London to sing in "Messiah" and "Samson," and he had been coached in those parts by Charles Burney. But Paris never employed *castrati* at the Opera; it was only Italians and a few Germans who submitted to the necessary operation. Gluck was therefore obliged to transpose the part of Orpheus for a tenor, and in the course of doing so remodelled it considerably. The opera was also lengthened by the insertion of some extra vocal numbers and ballet music. For a long time it was believed that the florid *aria* sung by Orpheus at the end of Act I in the French version ("L'espoir renaît dans mon âme," or in some editions "Amour, viens rendre à mon âme") was not by Gluck at all, but by Bertoni, and inserted solely to please the singer Legros; but there is no doubt whatever that it is by Gluck himself, as it came from *Le Feste d'Apollo,* the Parma entertainment of 1769. The trio "Tendre Amour," sung after Eurydice's return to the Temple of Love, comes from *Paride ed Elena* (Vienna, 1770).

Orfeo had six performances at Vienna in 1762 and 1763; in 1781 there was a single French performance there, and a single Italian one. After that the opera was never heard in Vienna again until 1862, and then only in concert form. The first stage revival did not take place until 1882 (in German). The first performance in English was at Dublin in 1784. There were isolated performances in various countries in the eighteenth century, some according to the Italian version, some according to the French, but it was only in Paris that *Orphée* maintained its place steadily in the repertory, of course in the Paris version with a tenor as Orpheus. After 1814 performances became rarer and the opera was almost forgotten. But in 1842 Madame Viardot-Garcia sang some airs from it at a Conservatoire concert, and this was the beginning (under German influences) of the revival of *Orphée* in Paris as a show-piece for a female contralto.

Berlin gave *Orpheus* in German (from the Paris version) with a tenor in 1808; the next German performance was at Dresden in 1838. Spontini revived the Italian version with a female Orpheus at Berlin in 1821. Liszt seems to have inaugurated a more important German revival at Weimar in 1854; on this occasion he composed his own symphonic poem "Orpheus" as a substitute for Gluck's rather trivial overture, and ended the opera with a finale of his own too. During the next few years Wagner's sister Johanna made a great success in Germany as Orpheus; but it may be noted that neither Wagner himself, nor Weber, ever conducted the work.

The most important revival was that of 1859 in Paris at the Théâtre-Lyrique, when Mme Viardot was with some difficulty persuaded to sing the part of Orpheus in a version compiled by Berlioz from both the Vienna and Paris versions. The Berlioz version has since then remained the basis of all standard versions of the opera, although in 1914 an attempt was made in Germany to restore the original Italian version of 1762. Mme Viardot's success came just at the moment of contralto-worship all over Europe. Berlioz had suddenly discovered the romantic character of the contralto voice, up to that time supposed to be absolutely non-existent in France. Miss Dolby had in 1846 created "O rest in the Lord." On the Italian stage there was the incomparable Marietta Alboni. German critics tried to justify the female contralto in *Orpheus* on the grounds of its "elegiac" character and found the male tenor too human for so highly spiritualized a part. An excuse had also to be found for the celebrated air "Che farò," which to many musicians has seemed much too cheerful for its tragic situation. Abert is honest enough to say that here is the one weak moment of the opera. It is in the form of a rondo, most unusual in the operas of that day, and Berlioz tells us how Mme Viardot solved the problem of singing it. The first time she sang it with an air of restrained grief, the second time *pianissimo* and *sotto voce,* the third rather faster, with an expression of utter despair. The plain fact is that "Che farò" is a tune which everybody can remember, and that has caused it to become the central feature of the opera, just as "Batti, batti" became to old-fashioned opera connoisseurs the most important item of *Don Giovanni.* It is interesting to note that Offenbach's operetta *Orphée aux Enfers,* in which the tune is used, came out in 1858, the year *before* Mme Viardot's triumph. And as far back as 1778 Traetta had made fun of it in a comic opera produced at Venice, *Il Cavaliere Errante,* in which a character who has been rendered insane by magical arts thinks he is Orpheus and sings "Che farò" preceded by a grotesque recitative.

Italy had never been much interested in Gluck after he was dead, but in 1889 *Orpheus* was sung at Milan in a translation of the Paris version, the Orpheus being Giulia Ravogli, who with her sister as Eurydice had a notable success in London. London had already shown considerable interest in *Orpheus* in 1860, and some six months before the Ravogli sisters appeared there, Stanford had organized performances of the opera in English at Cambridge (May 1890). In 1892 he gave a performance at the Royal College of Music, in which Clara Butt, then a student, made her first appearance as Orpheus. She sang the part again at Covent Garden in 1920.

E. J. D.

The American *première* took place at the Winter Garden, New York, May 25, 1863, an English translation by Fanny Malone Raymond being used. On Dec. 30, 1891, the original Italian text was employed for a revival at the Metropolitan Opera House, New York, with Giulia Ravogli (Orpheus) and her sister Sofia Ravogli (Eurydice).

Arturo Toscanini conducted the memorable Metropolitan revival of Dec. 23, 1909, when Louise Homer appeared as Orpheus, Johanna Gadski as Eurydice, Alma Gluck as the Happy Spirit, and Bella Alten as Amor. Before Mr. Toscanini's retirement from the Metropolitan five years later, Marie Delna and Margaret Matzenauer were also heard there as Orpheus, Marie Rappold as Eurydice, Anna Case as the Happy Spirit, and Lenora Sparkes as Amor. [Performances recurred till 1913. Gluck's masterpiece was then shelved by the Metropolitan for twenty-two years, returning during the spring season of 1936. For that production a double cast was used, members of the American Ballet Ensemble miming the action on the stage, while the singers held forth from the orchestra pit. On November 26, 1939, Kerstin Thorborg won great acclaim with her performance of the title role.]

Alceste

"TRAGEDIA IN MUSICA" (TRAGEDY IN MUSIC) IN 2 ACTS

Book by Raniero de' Calzabigi, after Euripides

First performance: Vienna, Dec. 16, 1767

First performance in Paris of revised French version by Bailly du Roullet:
Apr. 23, 1776

CHARACTERS

Admetos, King of Pharae, TENOR   *Apollo,* the Greek sun-god, BARITONE
Alceste, his wife, SOPRANO   *Apollo's High Priest,* BASS
Evander, a messenger, TENOR   *Thanatos,* god of death, BASS
Hercules, ancient Greek hero, BASS

Priests, Priestesses, Attendants, and the People of Pharae

The action takes place in legendary Greece

The people of Pharae learn with dismay that their king, Admetos, is dying. Accompanied by her children, Alceste enters the temple of Apollo to entreat the gods to spare her husband's life. The people join their prayers with hers, and suddenly the voice of Apollo is heard: Admetos can be saved, but on one condition—someone must die in his place. All except Alceste draw back in dread, but the Queen offers herself. The priests consult Apollo, who gives his consent. In an outburst of majestic power Alceste invokes the gods of the nether world in the magnificent aria, "Divinités du Styx." Again the people of Pharae are lamenting. Admetos has recovered, but now he has resolved to follow his devoted wife to the next world. At this point the Greek hero Hercules steps into the picture. Fresh from great exploits, Hercules comes to the feast at his friend Admetos' table. When he hears of Alceste's fate, he swears he will snatch her from the very gates of Hades. Alceste, donning a sacrificial veil, prepares to receive death. Admetos appears, determined to stop Alceste or die with her. The pair exchange tender avowals, as Thanatos steps forward to claim his prey. Hercules rushes in and snatches Alceste from Thanatos. The couple are reunited with great rejoicing, and Apollo, moved by such devotion, blesses them.

(a) *ALCESTE* IN VIENNA

To the Grand Duke of Tuscany, Peter Leopold, who later, after the death of Joseph II, was to become emperor under the name of Leopold II, was dedicated the score of *Alceste,* published, like that of *Orfeo,* two years after the first performance, which took place on 16th December 1767 (exactly three years before the birth of Beethoven). It was printed in Vienna (1769), not in Paris. The score of *Orfeo* had contained no dedication or preface, whereas that of *Alceste* bore a dedication in Italian that is at the same time in the nature of a programme and was, of course, written by Calzabigi, the librettist, although it was signed by Gluck. It is the document of the accomplished revolution in operatic history, or rather the reinstatement of opera on the throne of its earlier dignity. The history of opera begins with a kind of artistic conspiracy: the Florentine *camerata* took it into their heads to call antique tragedy back to life again and created the *dramma per musica*. Gluck too called his *Alceste* a *tragedia in musica,* and in his dedication found such flattering words for the illustrious city that had given rise to the musical drama that here again one suspects premeditation. The dedication has been reproduced hundreds of times, generally very faultily, and it is so important that it must not be omitted here:

Your Royal Highness,

When I undertook to write the music for *Alceste,* I resolved to divest it entirely of all those abuses, introduced into it either by the mistaken vanity of singers or by the too great complaisance of composers, which have so long disfigured Italian opera and made of the most splendid and most beautiful of spectacles the most ridiculous and wearisome. I have striven to restrict music to its true office of serving poetry by means of expression and by following the situations of the story, without interrupting the action or stifling it with a useless superfluity of ornaments; and I believed that it should do this in the same way as telling colours affect a correct and well-ordered drawing, by a well-assorted contrast of light and shade, which serves to animate the figures without altering their contours. Thus I did not wish to arrest an actor in the greatest heat of dialogue in order to wait for a tiresome *ritornello,* nor to hold him up in the middle of a word on a vowel favourable to his voice, nor to make display of the agility of his fine voice in some long-drawn passage, nor to wait while the orchestra gives him time to recover his breath for a cadenza. I did not think it my duty to pass quickly over the second section of an aria of which the words are perhaps the most impassioned and important, in order to repeat regularly four times over those of the first part, and to finish the aria where its sense may perhaps not end for the convenience of the singer who wishes to show that he can capriciously vary a passage in a number of guises; in short, I have sought to abolish all the abuses against which good sense and reason have long cried out in vain.

I have felt that the overture ought to apprise the spectators of the nature of the action that is to be represented and to form, so to speak, its argument; that the concerted instruments should be introduced in proportion to the interest and the intensity of the words, and not leave that sharp contrast between the aria and the recitative in the dialogue, so as not to break a period unreasonably nor wantonly disturb the force and heat of the action.

Furthermore, I believed that my greatest labour should be devoted to seeking a beautiful simplicity, and I have avoided making displays of difficulty at the expense of clearness; nor did I judge it desirable to discover novelties if it was not naturally suggested by the situation and the expression; and there is no rule which I have not thought it right to set aside willingly for the sake of an intended effect.

Such are my principles. By good fortune my designs were wonderfully furthered by the librettist, in which the celebrated author, devising a new dramatic scheme, had substituted for florid descriptions, unnatural paragons and sententious, cold morality, heartfelt language, strong passions, interesting situations and an endlessly varied spectacle. The success of the work justified my maxims, and the universal approbation of so enlightened a city has made it clearly evident that simplicity, truth and naturalness are the great principles of beauty in all artistic manifestations. For all that, in spite of repeated urgings on the part of some most eminent persons to decide upon the publication of this opera of mine in print, I was well aware of all the risk run in combating such firmly and profoundly rooted prejudices, and I thus felt the necessity of fortifying myself with the most powerful patronage of YOUR ROYAL HIGHNESS, whose August Name I beg you may have the grace to prefix to this my opera, a name which with so much justice enjoys the suffrages of an enlightened Europe. The great protector of the fine arts, who reigns over a nation that had the glory of making them arise again from universal oppression and which itself has produced the greatest models, in a city that was always the first to shake off the yoke of vulgar prejudices in order to clear a path for perfection, may alone undertake the reform of that noble spectacle in which all the fine arts take so great a share.

If this should succeed, the glory of having moved the first stone will remain for me, and in this public testimonial of Your Highness's furtherance of the same, I have the honour to subscribe myself, with the most humble respect,

Your Royal Highness's

Most humble, most devoted and most obliged

servant,

CHRISTOFORO GLUCK

This was the open declaration of war against the *conventions* of opera, to which all operatic composers other than Gluck paid more or less homage, and had done so in the past. Let it not be believed that the declaration came like a thunderbolt out of the blue. Criticism of opera is nearly as old as opera itself. The species had, at the very beginning, found an ideal aim for itself in the imaginary conception of the antique drama to which it looked up. The more it departed from that conception, the more violent became the assaults of criticism, which took the most manifold forms: parody, satire, aesthetic reasoning and so on. The most fruitful of these forms was the parody, from whose womb the *opera buffa* and the *opéra comique* sprang; and it is difficult to resist the thought that Gluck perhaps became the reformer of the Italian opera seria for the very reason that he had lacked the "safety valve" of a gift to express himself freely, to discharge himself, as it were, in the domain of the Italian *opera buffa*. That is how he was destined to exercise a truly creative criticism on the *opera seria* and to become a critical creator.

What are we to say to these aesthetic controversies, seeing them as we do from a vantage-point almost two centuries distant? We say that they never touched the vital point of the matter. The abolition of the male soprano, the avoidance of inopportune *fioriture* and cadenzas, the destruction of the conventional aria form—all these are mere superficialities. A striving after simplicity, truth and naturalness may be questionable and ambiguous, for might not some new aesthetic Pilate ask: what *is* truth in opera? Is Handel as an opera composer not simple and natural too? In the last resort it is a question of the eternal and for ever undecided *fundamental* conflict between opera and drama. As a great and penetrating critic of Shakespeare has said, opera is the natural enemy of the drama.

That is the heart of the matter. What Gluck did was simply this: he once again shifted the balance between opera and drama, more or less as, before him, the Venetian musicians after Monteverdi had moved the operatic centre of gravity in the direction of music, or as later Hugo Wolf, after Schubert and Schumann, moved the centre of gravity in song towards declamation and the accompaniment. Gluck forced music back in favour of drama; but it was only a question of finding the *balance* between music and drama, a stroke of fortune that has occurred rarely in the history of opera—three or four times at the most. He wrote operas *different* from those of his more ingenuous Italian contemporaries; but it nevertheless remains an open question whether his are better than theirs.

Opera is the drama's natural enemy; but it is also something essentially different from the drama and cannot be said to have merely swallowed it whole, as the wolf swallowed Red-Riding-Hood. The excellence of an opera does not depend on the degree to which it submits to "reform." That an opera cannot do without dramatic content and must not be a bare succession of beautiful musical numbers is certain. But does not the proportion of music and drama often fluctuate within one and the same opera? Is not everything that happens in the second act of *Don Giovanni,* up to the churchyard scene, so much trifling, dramatically speaking? Yet Mozart bridges this dramatic gap by music, music that is doubly enchanting. Does not in the second act of *Tristan* the outward action stand still until the appearance of the king? And yet this colloquy in song is perhaps the peak, or at any rate the deepest, most abysmal depth in Wagnerian music-drama. On the other hand, it is equally certain that opera is incapable of expressing dramatic significance with too small a modicum of music. Gluck once declared he forgot that he was a musician when he composed an opera, a pronouncement which, like the pronouncements of all "reformers," had better be accepted *cum grano salis.* The truth is that he never forgot it and that he merely intended to make it understood, as politely as possible, that the common or operatic musicians of his time too often forgot that they were dramatists. Gluck did not defeat Piccinni by his principles (if indeed he defeated him at all), but by his personality.

Alceste has not the youthfulness and the undying theatrical charm of *Orfeo*, but it was destined to remain Gluck's and Calzabigi's chief work and masterpiece. Let Calzabigi himself relate the plot of Euripides' tragedy:

Admetus, king of Pharae in Thessaly, husband of Alcestis, finding himself about to lose his life, Apollo, who had been received by him on being exiled from heaven, induces the Fates to spare his life on condition that one be found to die in his stead. Alcestis agrees to the exchange and dies; but Hercules, the friend of Admetus, who had come to Pharae at this juncture, recovers Alcestis from Thanatos and restores her to her husband.

Such is the content of the famous tragedy of Euripides entitled "Alcestis"; but in the place of Hercules I have introduced Apollo beholden to Admetus, to work this miracle out of gratitude.

This independence of Euripides on Calzabigi's part proves his dramatic sense. The "Alcestis" of Euripides is not a glorification of conjugal devotion, but of hospitality. Hercules comes by chance into the house of mourning, whence the body of Alcestis is about to be removed; but Admetus, not to offend against the laws of hospitality, tells him that a stranger had died under his roof. Intemperate Hercules eats, drinks and blusters in his quarters until a servant indignantly reproves and enlightens him. Whereupon Hercules lies in wait for Thanatos (Death) at the funeral monument and leads the veiled Alcestis back to her husband.

Only where drama was a cult could such a solution be admitted; only in the Athenian amphitheatre was this Hercules possible. Unfortunately, in the Paris *Alceste* of 1776—if one may anticipate—the reviser, Guillard, reintroduced Hercules, and it is probable that the aria for that character, "C'est en vain que l'Enfer," is not by Gluck at all, but by Gossec, who furbished it up from an old aria from Gluck's *Ezio* ("Ecco alle mie catene"). Hercules enters the sacred grove while Admetus and Alcestis are still engaged in the noble contest for the sacrifice. He scares the divinities of death away with his club, and Apollo appears, promising the athlete immortality and admittance to the assembly of the gods. Alcestis never carries out her sacrifice, so that the unravelling approaches that of the old *festa teatrale*. But again, exactly as in the case of *Orfeo ed Euridice*, we cannot simply decide in favour either of the Italian or the French version of *Alceste*. Gluck made more radical changes in this work for Paris than in any other opera of his, and this cost him more labour than the writing of a new work would have done; his representation of the inward conflict of Alcestis, the wife and mother held to life by so many tender bonds, is much more affecting; he made a broader scene of the incident where the crowd gives vent to joy at the restoration of its ruler; he made the scenes between husband and wife more profound. Thus the ideal form of *Alceste* for present-day use would again be a compromise between two versions.

The earlier *Alceste*, too, has its dramatic faults. Two Metastasian confidants are still retained in it, a relapse on the poet's part to which relapses on Gluck's correspond, such as an occasional use of *recitativo secco* that is hard to explain. Apollo's gratitude for the kindly treatment he received in the disguise of a servant is no *visible*, plastic motive, so that he remains to some extent in the character of a *deus ex machina*. On the other hand the apparition of the spirits in the death scene is perhaps too theatrical, for Hades should not become as palpable here as in *Orfeo*. The greatest weakness lies in the character and the position of Admetus. He should unquestionably grow into the chief figure next to Alcestis, as in *Parsifal* Amfortas is the chief figure next to the hero. A sacrifice such as he accepts should not be acceptable even to the hallowed person of a king whose duty it is to preserve himself for his people. But the conflict in Admetus's soul is but languid, and even during the flattering chorus of the conclusion he remains too much in the background and too inactive. Here none but Beethoven could have given Gluck the lesson he needed, *i.e.* with the finale of *Fidelio*, that cantata-like glorification of the heroine, and Admetus should have taken a share similar to that of Florestan. That, however, would have meant an abandonment to music of which Gluck, the dramatist and anti-musician, was not capable, nor desired to be capable.

Still, what a great artistic feat is here, taken all round, and what an abundance of incidental beauty! The realistic proclamation of the oracle by the herald (*banditore*), the people's scene of lamentation before the palace, with the solos of Ismene and Evander, the mourning dumb-show, the orchestral interjections, Alcestis's resolve to sacrifice herself, her farewell from Admetus and her last request to him, weighed down as she is with the heaviness of death. Beauty enters with the overture, called an *intrada* by Gluck, presumably because it leads without a break into the scene. It is the first truly tragic introduction to an opera. . . .

The outward success of *Alceste* was great. Calzabigi, in a letter to Montefani, speaks of sixty performances in Vienna, and in his "Riposta" even of seventy in two series, of which the second began in 1778. In Italy the work was a complete failure only in Bologna (1778), which ever since 1763 had been unfavourably disposed towards Gluck. In Padua (1777), Naples (1785) and Florence (1786), on the other hand, it was afforded at least respectful attention, although we may be sure that the representations nowhere did justice to Gluck's demands. Calzabigi pointed out that, with the exception of *Orfeo*, which Gluck was able to produce personally at Parma in 1769, none of his works was seen in Italy in the light it required for its effect:

They are pieces for the *theatre* and not for the chamber, rather like the Athena of Pheidias, which at first sight in the studio looked raw, rude and carelessly hewn out; but afterwards, seen on the noble site for which it was predestined, had an effect of the most surprising beauty. . . . The Italian public has as yet little idea of these theatrical optics.

Gluck was certainly dissatisfied. In the dedication of *Paride ed Elena* he (or rather Calzabigi as his spokesman) makes use of the same image:

The only reason that induced me to issue my music of *Alceste* in print was the hope of finding followers who, by way of the paths already opened up and stimulated by the ample suffrages of an enlightened public, would be quickened into abolishing the abuses that have insinuated themselves into the Italian spectacles, and to bring them to the highest possible degree of perfection. I am grieved to say that I have so far tried this in vain. Dilettanti and smatterers, of whom there is an infinite crowd, and who are the greatest of obstacles to the progress of the fine arts, have set themselves against a method which, once it gained a foothold, would destroy at one blow their pretensions to any power of decision and any capacity for action. It has been thought that *Alceste* may be judged after having been rehearsed at haphazard, badly conducted and worse performed; that it is possible to calculate in a chamber the effect it is capable of making in a theatre, which is as wise as it would have been, in a city of Greece in the old days, to attempt to judge at the distance of a few feet the statues intended to be set upon the highest columns.

A. E.

(b) *ALCESTE* IN PARIS

When Gluck returned to Paris in the February of 1776, bearing with him his new French version of *Alceste,* he returned to a public the half of which was frankly hostile, while he had had the misfortune to prejudice against him the other half—his real admirers—by his arrogance and hastiness.

Alceste was performed on April 23. It was not a great success, the third act falling definitely flat. The alterations in the order of the scenes and the introduction of an entirely new character, Hercules, in order to bring about a more convincing *dénouement,* did to a great extent alter the old opera. The whole work was more closely knit together: it moved more quickly and was more suited to the stage, but a certain amount of the slow-moving poetry of the Italian version was lost. Gluck had reversed the opening scenes of Acts II and III. In the Italian version, Act II opens with Alceste and Ismene in the grove of Death, and this, in the French version, is the opening scene of Act III, while the choral scene celebrating Admetus' recovery, which opens Act III in the Italian, is transferred to Act II in the French. The figure of Hercules, who appears, as in the Euripides tragedy, to rescue his wife's friend, is not really a great improvement dramatically. For nothing can alter the fact that *Alceste* is the most monotonous of operas. This was the most striking thing about it to Rousseau, who wrote:

I know of no opera in which the passions are less varied than in *Alceste;* almost everything turns on two sentiments, affliction and terror, and the prolonged employment of these two sentiments must have cost the composer incredible pains to avoid the most lamentable monotony. Generally speaking, the more warmth there is in the situations and expressions, the more prompt and rapid should be their passage;

otherwise the force of the emotion decreases in the hearers; and when the proper limit is passed, the actor strives in vain, for the spectator grows cold and finally impatient.

The composer, however, was of a very different opinion:

Alceste can only displease now when it is new. It has not had time yet; I say that it will please equally in two hundred years, if the French language does not change; and my reason for saying so is that I have built wholly on nature, which is never subject to changes of fashion.

Gluck did not realize that although, as Romain Rolland has pointed out, the principles of dramatic verity may not alter, our conception of them is perpetually changing. This was a point which the eighteenth century, with its carefully finished and polished theories and systems, could not afford to realize. For the moment, the failure of *Alceste* was explained, by some at least, more simply: Gluck had not given the part of Alceste to Sophie Arnould, who had sung both Iphigenie and Eurydice, but to Rosalie Lavasseur, a more robust singer and more suited than the rather frail Sophie Arnould to the part of Alceste. It was common knowledge that Sophie Arnould was furious, and it was generally believed that she did her best to prevent the opera from succeeding. If this was true, she was not successful for long. After a few performances the real worth of *Alceste* was realized by the French public. Gluck was no longer there; for on the 22nd April, the day before the performance of *Alceste* in Paris, his niece Marianne, whom he had left in Vienna with his wife, died of smallpox. Frau Gluck, knowing what a blow this would be to her husband, left Vienna as soon as possible to join him and to do her best to console him for the loss of the "little nightingale," as he had called Marianne. In the early summer Gluck and his wife left Paris to return to Vienna, where he still had his new opera *Armide* to finish.

In the meanwhile Paris did not forget him. For on the 17th July of this year (1776) a number of people—men of letters, artists, amateurs and members of high society—commissioned the sculptor Houdon to make a bust of Gluck: and it was this bust which was exhibited at the Salon of 1777 and then set up, by royal command, in the foyer of the Opera, by the side of Rameau.

M. C.

[Pauline Viardot, who had earlier sung Orpheus with prodigious success, again proved a sensation in the title role of *Alceste* when the Paris Opéra revived the work on October 21, 1861. Unless records to the contrary turn up, the honor of presenting *Alceste* for the first time in America goes to Wellesley College, where Gluck's opera was given twice in March, 1938. The Metropolitan Opera House waited till January 24, 1941, before producing it. A successful earlier revival of Gluck's *Orfeo* had encouraged the management to hazard a production of the 174-year-old novelty. Ettore Panizza conducted, and Marjorie

Lawrence and René Maison headed the cast. In an English version prepared by John Gutman, *Alceste*—or "Alcestis"—returned to the Metropolitan on March 4, 1952. There were five performances in all, the last on April 1. In all five the Alcestis was Kirsten Flagstad, who had chosen it as her farewell role in America, having previously sung it in Zurich in 1943 in a German version. Brian Sullivan was the Admetus and Alberto Erede conducted. In speaking of Mme. Flagstad's interpretation as "an unforgettable revelation of that which is incomparable and immortal in Gluck himself," Olin Downes, the music critic of *The New York Times,* echoed the feelings of thousands who attended the profoundly moving revival.]

Charles Gounod

(Paris, June 17, 1818–Oct. 17, 1893, Paris)

The composer of *Faust* came of an artistic family, his ancestors having been craftsmen in the employment of Louis XVI at the Louvre. His father was a painter sufficiently accomplished to have won a Prix de Rome in 1783. Gounod was educated musically at first by his mother, who was left a widow in 1823, and later, after a normal classical education, at the Conservatoire where he studied under Halévy, author of *La Juive,* Paër, and Lesueur. Like his father he won a second Prix de Rome in 1837, and then achieved the Grand Prix in 1839.

The Grand Prix de Rome was in effect a scholarship whose holder was required to study for two years at the Villa Medici in Rome, after which he might spend a further year abroad, usually in Germany or Austria. Gounod occupied himself at the Villa Medici, where Ingres, the great painter, was at this time Director, with the study of the old Italian masters, especially Palestrina, and with the composition of liturgical music. During his years in Rome he made the acquaintance of Fanny Mendelssohn (Hensel), who was on a visit to Italy. Her diary gives a picture of the young Frenchman as the irresponsible member of a trio of students, who called themselves the three *Caprices en la* [Bousquet] *en mi* [Gounod] and *en si bémolle* [Dugasseau]; who one night had to be put to bed after behaving "almost as if he were intoxicated" and blackguarding Beethoven. But a few weeks later Fanny gives a very different picture of a more sober Gounod joining a religious society of young enthusiasts who, under the influence of the eloquent Père Lacordaire, hoped to apply Christian art to the conversion of the worldly minded. Bousquet even feared that Gounod would abandon music for religion. This Youth Movement, as it would be called nowadays, was a reaction against the materialism and hollow ostentation of Napoleon III's France.

At the end of his term at the Villa Medici, Gounod spent a year in Vienna, Berlin, and Leipzig, where he stayed with Mendelssohn, renewed acquaintance with his sister, and got to know the music of Schumann as well as of Mendelssohn himself.

After his return in 1843 to Paris, where he became a church organist, Gounod actually began to study for the priesthood, but renounced his intention before he had proceeded far. It was during these years that he composed the famous Messe solennelle in G, that typical expression of mid-nineteenth-century religious feeling, not the less sincere for being unctuous and sentimental. Although Gounod remained a devout Christian to the end and occupied his later years in the composition of sacred works, many of them written for the Birmingham Festival and at one time favourites with the British public, it was in the theatre that he won lasting fame. "The Redemption" and "Mors et Vita," those pallid "musical frescoes" (as he designated them), are unlikely to regain their former popularity.

Gounod began his career as an opera-composer in 1851 with *Sapho,* which was produced at the Opéra with Pauline Viardot-Garcia in the principal part. He had met the great singer, Malibran's sister, in Rome, and it was her influence that turned his attention to opera. All that has survived of this work is the air, "O ma lyre immortelle," which sometimes appears in concert programmes. In *Sapho* and in the music for Ponsard's "Ulysse," produced at the Comédie Française in 1852, Gounod sought to produce an antique effect both of rhythm and harmony. Already he seems to have been arriving at a *"musique plane et peinte en fresque,"* which suggests a musical parallel to the contemporary mural paintings of Puvis de Chavannes. But these pale, flat forms, however appropriate to oratorio, were singularly ineffectual in the theatre. Dramatic forcefulness was, indeed, never conspicuous in Gounod's music.

An even less successful essay in Romantic horror-opera, *La Nonne Sanglante,* produced in 1854, with a libretto founded on a story in Matthew Lewis's lurid novel, "The Monk," ended for a time Gounod's connexion with the Opéra. After a nervous breakdown, brought on by the effects of his ill success upon his hypersensitive nature, he proceeded to study in the more modest school of the Théâtre Lyrique, for which he wrote a witty *opéra comique* based on Molière's "Le Medécin malgré lui." The libretto was by MM. Carré and Barbier, whose names are familiar to us as the adaptors of Goethe's "Faust," to the setting of which Gounod now applied himself.

Wisely MM. Carré and Barbier concentrated upon the incident of Gretchen, leaving aside the more philosophical and epic, as well as the more daemonic, aspects of Goethe's drama. The result is a libretto which was admirably suited to Gounod's talent. His ingratiating melody and his fine sense of colour both in harmony and instrumentation had full scope, and he produced, if not a complete realization of Goethe's drama, a lyrical opera of great charm, which has firmly established itself as a popular favourite. The love-music of the Garden Scene beginning with Faust's melodious "Salut demeure" set the standard for such operatic music in France for the rest of the century, though none of Gounod's successors, with one exception, could rival the combination of sweetness and sensibility here displayed. Too often the sensuousness was diluted and became merely sugary. And in the Church Scene he handled most effectively a situation, so popular in nineteenth-century opera, in which liturgical music is used as the contrasting background to a dramatic scene. Here for once Gounod shows something like real power in his music.

Gounod never repeated the success of *Faust. La Reine de Saba* with a libretto by Gérard de Nerval, produced at the Opéra in 1862, and even the fresh and unpretentious *Mireille,* based on a poem by the Provençal Fréderic Mistral and given at the Théâtre Lyrique in 1864, failed to sustain his reputation. Only *Romeo et Juliette,* which followed three years later, came within measurable distance of *Faust,* and it cannot be said to have recaptured the rapture of Shakespeare's young lovers. Juliette is but a pale reflection of Gounod's Marguerite. . . .

Gounod . . . added nothing to his own reputation in his latter years. A sojourn in England during the Franco-Prussian war revived the influence of Mendelssohn upon his mind and turned his thoughts to oratorio. For a while he occupied in English musical life the foremost place which Mendelssohn had held a generation earlier. After his return to Paris he continued for a while to compose operas, none of which survived initial failure, until about ten years before his death he sank into a religious melancholia. There had always been a conflict between his sensual nature and his spiritual ideals, which only once found a satisfactory resolution—in *Faust.* Even Bizet, at first his devoted admirer, found his later music "dreadful." There was, for a time, a coolness between the two on this account, but the breach was happily mended before Bizet's death by the circumstance that the younger man was entrusted with the arrangements for a revival of *Roméo et Juliette* at the Opéra Comique in 1873. His care and enthusiasm in this matter won Gounod's affectionate thanks, and though Bizet no doubt maintained his reservations about Gounod's music, there was certainly nothing of the crocodile in Gounod's tears when he spoke at the funeral in the Père Lachaise cemetery on 5 June 1875.

D. H.

Faust

OPERA IN 5 ACTS

Book by JULES BARBIER and MICHEL CARRÉ, based on GOETHE's *Faust*

First performance: Théâtre Lyrique, Paris, Mar. 19, 1859

CHARACTERS

Faust, TENOR

Mephistopheles, BASS

Valentine, Marguerite's brother, BARITONE

Wagner, a student, BARITONE

Marguerite, SOPRANO

Siebel, a youth, in love with Marguerite, SOPRANO

Martha, friend of Marguerite, MEZZO-SOPRANO

Peasants, Townspeople, Soldiers, Students, Priests, Boys, etc.

The action takes place in Germany in the sixteenth century

Faust, an aged scientist and philosopher, despairing of his futile quest for the secrets of eternal youth, contemplates suicide. Before drinking poison he invokes the powers of darkness. Mephistopheles appears and offers him first gold, then glory, in exchange for his soul. But it is not until he promises him youth and conjures up a vision of a beautiful girl, Marguerite, that Faust is lured into signing the fatal parchment. The bargain is sealed and Faust is transformed into a handsome young man.

At a table in the courtyard of a tavern there are some students, among them Siebel, a young boy who is in love with Marguerite. The group is joined by Valentin, Marguerite's brother, who is about to go off to war and begs Heaven to protect her in his absence. Mephistopheles enters and proceeds to amuse and awe the crowd. His entertainment becomes objectionable when he proposes a toast to Marguerite. Valentin takes exception and defies the sinister intruder. Soon Marguerite appears on her return from church. With Siebel distracted by Mephistopheles, Faust takes the opportunity to offer to escort her home, but she refuses.

Marguerite's garden. Siebel enters and, finding her absent, proceeds to pluck a bouquet for her. Mephistopheles enters with Faust who begs him to leave him there alone, but Mephistopheles returns with a box of jewels which he places at Marguerite's door, assuring Faust it will easily offset Siebel's humble offering. As they leave Marguerite enters, still haunted by the memory of the handsome youth who spoke to her in the street. She discovers the jewels and adorns herself with them. Martha, her old nurse, arrives and tries to convince the conscience-stricken girl that she should keep the jewels since they were surely meant for her. Mephistopheles and Faust re-enter. This time the suitor's wooing is not ignored. While the young people are engrossed in each other, Martha sets her cap for Mephistopheles, who has a difficult time dodging the amorous duenna. As darkness falls, Marguerite begs Faust to leave, promising to see him the next day. On his way out, Faust is intercepted by Mephistopheles, who derides his lack of persistence. Just then, Marguerite opens her window and, thinking herself alone, sings of her love. Faust runs to her arms while Mephistopheles gloats over his triumph.

A street in front of Marguerite's house. Valentin, whose regiment has just returned, hurries to the house anxious to see his sister. Siebel, knowing that Faust has left Marguerite with an illegitimate child, tries unsuccessfully to prevent Valentin's entering. Mephistopheles and Faust enter on the street. Mephistopheles sings a serenade and Valentin, blind with rage, comes out and challenges his sister's seducer. Guided by Mephistopheles, Faust's sword pierces Valentin's heart. Marguerite comes out in time to receive her dying brother's curse.

The Church. Crushed by the succession of tragic events, Marguerite has come to the Church hoping to find comfort in God. But as she begins to pray, she hears the voice of Mephistopheles telling her that she is beyond divine mercy and that eternal flames await her. She collapses in a faint.

The last scene finds Marguerite in prison condemned to die for the murder of her child. Mephistopheles has managed to secure Faust's entrance into the dungeon and hands him a set of keys that will enable him to set Marguerite free. Faust begs Marguerite to follow him but she hardly recognizes him and babbles incoherently about their first meeting. Suddenly she sees Mephistopheles and shrinks from him in horror. She implores God to forgive her and falls dead on her cot as the angels sing of her redemption.*

When the Germans put on Gounod's opera *Faust,* they advertise it as *Margarete.* One reason is that Goethe's play, "Faust," may occupy the same stage another night in the same week. Another reason is the great respect they have for their national poet and their resentment that a Frenchman should have composed the most successful of the many operatic treatments his masterwork has had. The change in title really constitutes a trenchant critical comment on the libretto.

This libretto, written by the successful French dramatist Jules Barbier,† has in it practically none of the philosophical significance of Goethe's poem, which deals with the problems of good and evil and ends, in Part II, with the triumph of good. Barbier's Faust stops being a philosopher promptly after the first ten minutes of singing, and during those first ten minutes he complains more than he philosophizes.

The central figure in the opera is really Marguerite, and Marguerite is a fig-

* From a New York City Center program-book.

† Michel Carré is always given credit for having written the text with Barbier. Though Carré was commissioned to do so, he was unenthusiastic over the idea because he had already written a play on the subject. His contributions to the opera, says Ernest Newman, include only the texts of two numbers—Marguerite's "King of Thule" and Mephisto's "Calf of Gold."

ure invented by Goethe. She does not appear in the sixteenth-century Spiess biography of Dr. Faustus or in Marlowe or in the medieval puppet plays, or in any part of the twenty-eight versions of the story that appeared during the sixty years Goethe was working on his poem. It is therefore unnecessary here to go into a discussion of the literary history of the Faust legend. All we need to do is to see how Carré treated Goethe's "Faust," and the character of Marguerite particularly.

Goethe's "Faust" is, of course, generally acknowledged to be one of the great masterpieces of world literature. Nevertheless, outside of its native country, it is seldom accorded a stage performance, for Goethe's genius was not essentially dramatic. From the point of view of dramatic action—and especially operatic action—Barbier made his version worthy of the literally thousands of performances it has achieved by summarily cutting out all the purely philosophical dialogue, compressing the action, bringing the scenes down to a reasonable number, adding a few original and effective touches, and making of Marguerite an essentially more sympathetic character. This is not to say that it would hold the stage without Gounod's music; but Barbier was writing a libretto for an opera, not a play of spoken verses. As such, it is highly successful.

Marguerite is essentially the figure Goethe created—a peasant girl, simple and direct. The simplicity and directness of the opera's heroine, however, are greater than her originals. She does not pester her lover about his religion. She accepts him as he is. Nor does she descend to giving her mother a sleeping potion so that she and Faust may make love undisturbed. Barbier avoids that unpleasantness by making an orphan of her. Finally, Barbier's Marguerite is not coy. She does not lead Faust on, finally giving in after a long suit. Instead, she succumbs the very first night in a transport of ecstasy, without planning, without misgiving. Berlioz chose that passage ("Il m'aime," at the end of the garden scene) as the finest in the opera.

Faust and Mephistopheles are not improved on in the same way. Rather, they lose in depth—necessarily, because their excuse for being in Goethe lies largely in their philosophical discourses, not in their actions. Faust, particularly, becomes a two-dimensional figure, a conventional operatic tenor. In Goethe, Faust does not gain real moral stature before Part II anyway, and the opera deals only with Part I.

. . . Goethe tells us, as Barbier does not, what book Faust is reading in the first scene—the "Prophecies of Nostradamus." Marguerite's home, too, is specifically Leipzig in Goethe but only "a small German town" in Barbier.

The idea of writing music for Goethe's "Faust" fascinated Gounod many years before he started working on it. It is a theme that has fascinated many musicians—Schumann, Liszt, Wagner, Spohr, Berlioz, Boito, to name the first that come to mind. Beethoven and Meyerbeer both considered it. Gounod, however, took the idea really seriously only after a conversation with Barbier— or maybe it was with Carvalho, director of the Théâtre-Lyrique in Paris. All three men wrote accounts of the genesis of the idea, each claiming credit for himself. It makes little difference who had the idea first: all three collaborated, Barbier by supplying the libretto, Gounod by writing the music, Carvalho by offering to produce it.

Gounod and Barbier began work in 1857, but halfway through the composition news came that the Théâtre Porte Saint-Martin was putting on a "Faust" by one Dennery. As this theater was better equipped for spectacular effects than the Lyrique, Carvalho hesitated to compete and commissioned the disappointed author and composer to write instead a comic opera based on Molière's "Doctor in Spite of Himself."

Dennery's *Faust,* however, was a failure, and on March 19, 1859, the Théâtre-Lyrique produced Gounod's opera, the greatest popular success Gounod or any other French composer ever had. It was given not as we hear it today, but as an *opéra comique*—that is, with spoken dialogue. It was not until 1869 that music was added for the recitatives and the ballet music inserted for the production at the Paris Grand Opéra.

The 1859 *première* had Mme. Carvalho as Marguerite and Balanqué as Mephistopheles, both of whom, Gounod tells us in his "Memoirs," were wonderfully well cast, despite a tendency to overact on the part of the basso. Barbot, a middle-aged tenor, was not quite equal to the demands of the title role, and at one point in the rehearsals Gounod seriously considered taking over the part himself. He liked his own little voice.

It is sometimes said that the opera at first was a failure. The number of recorded performances in the first season belie this statement, but it was only slowly that the work achieved its enormous popularity. The Paris Grand Opéra, since 1869, has given well over two thousand performances; the Metropolitan's score is pushing hard on to three hundred. . . .

In 1863 it was introduced to London in two different theaters, one playing it in English and the other in Italian. The same year New York also heard it for the first time—in German at one theater and in Italian at another. . . . It is now, of course, part of the standard repertoire of every opera company in the Western world.

Gounod wrote the music soon after a severe nervous breakdown. As he tells us in his autobiography (which stops short after the production of *Faust*), it captured the imagination of the public more than anything else he wrote. Whether it is really his best, he is not so sure—but that seems to be the opinion of posterity anyway. Today it is fashionable among musical sophisticates to be condescending about it—not because it is popular (*Carmen,* which is quite as popular today, has earned itself a great deal of respect), but because its music is said to be "perfumed charm," its melodies and harmonic devices obvious.

It did not so strike the critics of the 1860's, who made almost as much fuss about Gounod as they did about Wagner. The much-maligned "Soldiers' Chorus" (originally written, by the way, for an uncompleted opera called *Ivan* *the Terrible*) thrilled that sour Britisher Chorley. "I shall never forget," he wrote, "the riotous enthusiasm which burst out when this magnificent chorus, to which an army of myriads might sweep on its way to victory, electrified the ears of the Théâtre-Lyrique on the night of the first performance of the opera." The love duet, he reported, was something completely new to the operatic world of its day.* But, striking and strikingly popular as many of its individual passages are, they cannot alone account for the enormous popularity of *Faust*. Only a work with something consistently great about it could survive the many thousands of performances this one has had and still sound vital and fresh enough to hold audiences everywhere almost ninety years after its *première*. Many other operas have had as great a success for a few years and then been forgotten.

H. W. S.

No other lyric drama has been quite so closely identified with the Metropolitan Opera House as *Faust*. The association dates from the very beginning. *Faust* was selected to open the first season of opera at the recently completed Metropolitan on October 22, 1883. The performance, in view of the singers participating, must have been brilliant as well as historic. Christine Nilsson, who had been particularly admired as Marguerite, lent the occasion the distinction of her presence. Opposite her was a Faust no less famous, Italo Campanini. Another eminent artist, Giuseppe del Puente, appeared as Valentin, and still another, Sofia Scalchi, as Siebel. An esteemed basso, Francesco Novara, impersonated Mephistopheles. The opera was sung in an Italian translation.

When a year later opera in German began its eight-year occupation of the Metropolitan, *Faust* remained in the repertory. Indeed, Marguerite was one of Lilli Lehmann's parts, and that great artist occasioned comment by speaking instead of singing the short monotone recitative that precedes the "King of Thule" song. Still, it was not during the all-German régime, but when opera in Italian and French succeeded that period (which had been notable in particular for the local premières of several of Wagner's later works) that *Faust* assumed its empire. Looking over the records of nine or ten seasons, no one could wonder that the noted critic, Mr. W. J. Henderson, remembering the Festspielhaus at Bayreuth, should wittily dub the Metropolitan the Faustspielhaus!

The coming to New York from the Paris Opéra of Jean and Edouard de Reszké to sing Faust and Mephistopheles at the Metropolitan, and the appearance in company with those rare singing-actors of a number of unusual sopranos as Marguerite, determined the dominance of Gounod's melodious score. Outstanding at that time among the singers of Marguerite were Emma Eames

---

* Of course, Chorley may be regarded as a prejudiced critic: he supplied the frightful translation used in 1864 and published ever since in the standard Schirmer edition.

(the first to sing the part here with the brothers de Reszké), Nellie Melba, Emma Calvé, and Lillian Nordica.

To go back to the Metropolitan's original Marguerite, Herman Klein, who for a great many years listened to singers and appraised their qualities, has described Christine Nilsson as

a dreamy, poetic, sylphlike creature; tall and graceful; with a marvelous complexion, clear blue-grey eyes and markedly Scandinavian features. . . . Apart from the effect of Nilsson's extraordinary personal beauty and poetic charm, the predominant impression she created both as singer and actress was one of astonishing originality. There was about her singing a quality that suggested the idea of a supernatural musical being of the type of fairies or water-nymphs or Rhinemaidens. It struck one most of all, perhaps, in the curious bell-like ring of a voice that was sweetly metallic and deliciously pure; that had a seductive timbre such as the Loreley might have simulated, only more human and emotional in its appeal and intensely musical throughout.

In *Faust* she

embodied the Nuremberg Gretchen herself in the flesh; a dreamy, poetic, amorous girl, developing by a gradual dramatic evolution into the dolorous, disillusioned, and ultimately distraught creature of the church and prison scenes. With amazing art did she depict this change, so as to make it perceptible not alone by her acting, but in the growing depth and intensity of her vocal coloring. She almost made it hard to realize that the joyous, light-hearted voice warbling the "Jewel Song" came from the same throat as the love-music of the garden scene; or, again, the touching despair of her appeal in the episode of Valentin's death and the final defiance of Mephistopheles in the prison scene. None of Nilsson's many imitators ever succeeded in graduating or bringing out these contrasts with the same striking force.

Those who habitually think of Emma Calvé in terms of Carmen and Santuzza may learn with surprise that in her Metropolitan days she was likewise acclaimed here as Marguerite, both in Gounod's *Faust* and in Boïto's *Mefistofele*. Sir Augustus Harris, the famous London manager, is quoted as saying of Calvé:

A troublesome creature, decidedly, but well worth all the trouble she gives. As a woman she is wilful, capricious, rather bad-tempered. As an artist she always wants her own way; but, once she has got it, you can rely upon her doing the most splendid things imaginable and working her hardest to secure an all-around success.

Though the vocal excellence of Emma Eames, Melba, and Nordica in Gounod's music was unquestioned, dramatically the Marguerite of Calvé stood out as supreme in the de Reszké period. An enthusiast wrote concerning this impersonation:

Marguerite as first and foremost that of a soprano destined by nature and life and by
What an evening of revelation it was to all who have looked upon the part of

all the graces of art for one purpose, to reach with ease and sustain with perfect purity the highest notes in "Jewel Song" or prison scene. Mme. Calvé is a Marguerite of another sort.

The simplicity of her first appearance was dwelt upon.

She is not a prima donna making a grand stage entrance; awaiting the welcoming burst of applause; she is the village girl passing across the square, and it is to Faust himself she sings in telling him she is not a fine lady. Then she hurried away like a young girl, running in the embarrassment of her shyness. . . .

A proof of her genius is shown in the exit after the death of Valentin, when overcome, haggard, beside herself, she slowly quits the body of her brother before going to her home. It is the first manifestation of her madness, and prophecies and explains the killing of her child.

In the prison scene no artist has risen to the height of Mme. Calvé. Neither Miolan-Carvalho, for whom Gounod wrote the role, nor Nilsson, nor Devriès, nor any other has reached such dramatic depth of feeling.

A word is added with regard to the stage presence of "this new and incomparable Marguerite." Calvé was stouter than the romantic Marguerites who had preceded her had been and also a "decided brunette." Nevertheless, "the illusion of the blonde German girl is genuine and veritable. A good deal of white and red is necessary, and one of the thick blonde braids (ingeniously) hangs in front of one shoulder, thus giving Marguerite a chance to braid the end now and then; in another way, most femininely, it adds to her look of girlishness." And the rhapsodizing writer sums it all up in a tribute to the "overwhelmingly delicious crowd of perfections and fascinations of this most human, most tender, most thrilling Marguerite."

Jean de Reszké, handsome of face and figure, knightly of bearing, a singer "about as near perfection as it is given to mortals to hear," was the Metropolitan's ideal Faust.

P. S.

Roméo et Juliette

[Romeo and Juliet]

OPERA IN 5 ACTS

Book by JULES BARBIER and MICHEL CARRÉ, after SHAKESPEARE

First performance: Théâtre Lyrique, Paris, Apr. 27, 1867

CHARACTERS

Juliet, daughter of Capulet, SOPRANO
Stephano, page to Romeo, SOPRANO
Gertrude, Juliet's nurse, MEZZO-SOPRANO
Romeo, a Montague, TENOR
Tybalt, Capulet's nephew, TENOR
Benvolio, friend of Romeo, TENOR
Mercutio, friend of Romeo, BARITONE

Paris, Capulet's kinsman, BARITONE
Gregorio, Capulet's kinsman, BARITONE
Capulet, a Veronese nobleman, BASSO CANTANTE
Friar Laurence, BASS
The Duke of Verona, BASS

Guests, Relatives, and Retainers of the Capulets and Montagues

The action takes place in Verona in the fourteenth century

After a Prologue (introducing the cast in tableaux) Romeo and his friends appear at the gay masquerade in the Capulet mansion. There he sees Juliet and they lose their hearts to each other.

At a pavilion in the Capulet gardens is staged the immortal balcony scene between the lovers (graceful, swaying nocturnal music suggestive of Weber) temporarily interrupted by the appearance of the servants seeking Romeo.

In Friar Laurent's cell, the priest secretly marries the lovers to end the feud between the rival families. Then, in the street before the Capulet house, Tybalt kills Mercutio and Romeo, avenging his friend, slays Tybalt and is banished from Verona.

But Romeo returns from exile and hurries to Juliet's chamber to celebrate their bridal; yet no sooner has he gone than the girl's father tells her she must marry another. It is then the hapless victim of fate takes the sleeping potion from Friar Laurent which casts her into a deathlike trance.

The news of Juliet's death brings Romeo posthaste from Mantua where he had again retired, provided with the poison he has bought, to visit Juliet's tomb. There, convinced he has lost her, he drinks the poison "with a kiss" and Juliet, awakening in time to let him die in her arms, thrusts the dagger into her own heart.

F. H. M.

Gounod composed twelve operas, of which the fourth can probably pass as the most popular in the world. Three others have a vitality of a sort. The remaining eight are as dead as mutton, even if now and then an extract or two finds its way into a concert program. There is perhaps not a person living who ever experienced a performance of *Sapho, La Nonne Sanglante, Philémon et Baucis, La Reine de Saba, La Colombe, Cinq-Mars, Polyeucte* or *Le Tribut de Zamora.* On the other hand, many have heard *Mireille* which, if not universally cherished, like *Faust,* remains a staple of the Paris Opéra-Comique and the provincial French theatre. To some, including the writer of these lines, it is in its unpretentious way the best thing Gounod ever wrote, not even excepting *Faust.* As for the lyric version he made out of Molière's "Le Médecin Malgré Lui" it now and then enjoys a fitful revival by some small opera company or conservatory only to fall asleep again for years.

And what of *Roméo et Juliette?* It ranks in popularity after *Faust*—but a long way after! In earlier days it had its more or less assured place in the conventional repertory. Now it is in and out of the current lists, with ever lengthening intervals of absence. The truth seems to be that the emergence of the piece depends very largely on the two artists available for the name parts. The Paris Opéra still clings to it for its own sake, though even there it disappears for years on end. In Continental opera houses outside of France it had to all intents vanished even before the First World War.

Certain of *Roméo's* organic flaws were recognized by French critics from the first. The work was first performed at the Théâtre Lyrique, Paris, in 1867, eight years after *Faust.* The librettists who operated on Shakespeare, Jules Barbier and Michel Carré, were the same worthies who previously had tailored Goethe to Gounod's measure. But whereas in the first case they contrived to supply the composer with a book shrewdly adapted with chances for theatrical contrasts and musical variety, in the second, they could produce not very much more than a succession of love duets, now tender, now sorrowful. And the scope and character of Gounod's musical inspiration was such that the score in large degree became a series of sentimental numbers couched in a lyric vein which had been worked with much more freshness and originality in *Faust.*

This was not Gounod's notion. When he began work on it at Saint Raphael, on the French Riviera, in 1865, he believed implicitly in the value of that music which flowed without effort from his pen. He wrote to a friend that he felt as if he were twenty rather than fifty and that his characters were so alive to him that they kept him ceaseless company.

Nobody has pointed out the fundamental defect of the work as a whole so acutely as Ernest Newman when he declares that "one of the incurable delusions of the musical world is that *Romeo and Juliet* is ideal material for an opera." Led astray by the sympathetic figures of the young lovers, "both composers and librettists," continues the greatest of English-speaking critics, "have failed to perceive that apart from these two there is very little in the play that lends itself readily to the purposes of opera. Romeo and Juliet themselves have their defects in this regard. For even in opera one looks for some development of character . . . and the lovers of Verona do not develop. It is events that develop, not they. Each of them is good for one aria and together they are good for a love duet and a death duet. That, however, is about as far as the opera composer can profitably go with them. For the rest, there is hardly anyone in the play who is of sufficient importance in himself to be worth wasting much time over in an opera, or with a dramatic physiognomy definite enough to lend itself to musical characterization. Friar Lawrence is not so much a personage as a moral principle. Tybalt, Paris, Mercutio, the Nurse, the old heads of the families, are alive in the play but in opera have to be sketched so cursorily that they necessarily become mere lay figures."

Mr. Newman further calls the efforts of Gounod and his librettists "a gallant attempt to recast Shakespeare's play in terms of musical drama in the sense in which that term was understood in the 1860's." Yet all the gallantry of the endeavor fails to conceal the mistake of trying what is basically impossible. It may be conceded, however, that Messrs. Barbier and Carré adapted Shakespeare conscientiously, according to their lights. They displayed somewhat more re-spect for the poet than French operatic craftsmen have so often done in season-ing a foreign classic to the palates of countrymen. True, they permitted them-selves the privilege of inventing a new character, the page Stephano, whom Shakespeare never knew and who has nothing particular to do with the plot. A trousered soprano, a pale reflection of Siébel, Stephano's chief reason for existence is the operatic need of fortifying the ensemble of women's voices.

It was not the fault of the librettists, of course, that the music which Gounod wrote for the love scenes, though on a much lower plane of invention, is in its general style disturbingly similar to that of *Faust*.

There are numbers in *Roméo* like Juliet's waltz song, Romeo's *cavatina* in the garden scene, the duets of the lovers and the scene in the tomb that are highly effective lyric theatre, contrived with skilled craftsmanship. But even at their best these pages emphasize the composer's weakness rather than his strength—the weakness of a lyricist who had said everything better once before.

H. F. P.

Roméo et Juliette, like *Faust,* is in the standard repertoire of almost all major opera houses. At its world *première* in Paris, on April 27, 1867, with Miolan-Carvalho as the heroine, it was instantly acclaimed, and ran one hundred con-secutive performances at the Lyrique, easily asserting itself as the most popular opera ever written on this Shakespearean theme. It then moved triumphantly to the Comique, and finally ended at the Opéra, where it remained a beloved fixture.

With its New York history dating back to November 15, 1867, when Hauk sang Juliette in Italian at the Academy of Music, *Roméo* was chosen to open the Metropolitan season of 1891–92. This was in some respects a more significant performance than the *Faust* of 1883, for whereas in the earlier performance familiar artists had merely moved uptown, this first Metropolitan *Roméo,* on December 14, 1891, introduced three artists who were to become mainstays of many succeeding seasons—Eames and Jean and Édouard de Reszke in the respective roles of Juliette, Roméo, and Frère Laurent. As the De Reszkes had created these roles at the Opéra *première* of *Roméo,* on November 28, 1888, and as Eames had made her world debut as Juliette at the same institution on March 13, 1889, replacing Patti, they had a thorough understanding of their roles, besides a sense of teamwork that had come from singing them often together. This performance was also the beginning of a—at that time—bold experiment of turning away from giving little but German opera, and most of that little in German. *Roméo* was excellently enough produced to make the Metropolitan patrons breathe more easily. The same trio sang *Roméo* for the opening of the 1894–95 season, and would have done so for that of 1899–1900 but for the absence of Jean: in his place was Alvarez, who had made his world debut at the Opéra as Roméo, and on this occasion made his Metropolitan debut.

On November 23, 1906, Geraldine Farrar made her Metropolitan debut as Juliette, opening that season. But she was not happy in the part, and during the reign of this gifted lyric soprano *Roméo et Juliette* was all but allowed to lapse. On November 25, 1922, with new settings designed by Josef Urban, it was revived for Bori, supported by Gigli (Roméo), De Luca (Mercutio), and Rothier (Frère Laurent). Thereafter it was heard at least once a year until the season of 1935–36, with Grace Moore or Eidé Noréna (*née* Kaja Hansen Eidé), the Norwegian soprano, as Juliette. More recently, the role has been sung by the Brazilian Bidu Sayao, the Flemish Vina Bovy, and the American Helen Jepson.

In Chicago, too, *Roméo* has had an exciting history. Not only did it open the Auditorium, on December 10, 1889, with Patti, but it was also the last opera to be given there—January 26, 1929—before the resident company moved to the luxurious Insull-sponsored skyscraper on the Chicago River. There it was that, with Roméo's sword, Jean de Reszke held at bay a lunatic who had leaped upon the stage, pinning him to a wall until members of the behind-the-scenes crew could come to his assistance, thus permitting the opera to continue. On January 26, 1918, at the Lexington Theater, the Chicago Opera Association gave New Yorkers an excellent *Roméo* with singers almost unknown to the Atlantic seaboard. Lucien Muratore, a second Jean de Reszke in the elegant suavity of his acting and in his glamorous stage presence, sang Roméo. His Juliette was not his songstress wife, the widely advertised "most beautiful woman in the world," the Roman Lina Cavalieri, but the lovely Breton soprano, Geneviève Vix. Others in that interesting cast were Hector Dufranne, Gustave Huberdeau, and Alfred Maguenat.

W. B., H. W.

SHAKESPEARE IN MUSIC

Gounod's *Roméo et Juliette* reminds one of that romantic corner outside the city of Verona, in Northern Italy, where it is believed that Juliet lies buried under a marble slab, screened by trailing ivy and perfumed, in the Springtime, by clusters of pink roses. For many centuries lovers have found their way to the cloistered garden beyond the wrought iron gates and, alone or in pairs, have bowed their heads and silently told their own love-story to the spirit that hovers around the grave. The happy couples, no doubt, have warded off the saddening spell of the nook, in the knowledge that they, in living flesh, bore testimony to the happy ending of many a romance. The lone or sorrowful ones, perhaps, have found comfort in the thought that others before them had paid a dear price for one perfect moment of bliss.

An old peasant from the hills near Verona, where the castles of the Capulets and Montagues still show their heavy frame against the sky, stood gazing at the tomb when I, too, made my pilgrimage there. He brought a smile to my lips as he touched me lightly on the arm and said, in a paternal voice: "Signorina, don't be sad. Love does not always die so young." He had a long white beard and looked old enough to have known the romantic lovers himself. Presently he added: "It was a great love affair, and so beautiful that *un inglese!* (an Englishman), made poetry from it. Il Signor Cecchespi (Mr. Shakespeare). We Italians should make the music, but Verdi is dead." He shrugged his shoulders hopelessly as if music had come to an end with Verdi.

Later, as I walked past the ancient house of the Capulets, where Juliet lived —if she did live at all—I fell to wondering why this tale of love, out of which Shakespeare created the typical love-tragedy of all ages, had not been used by Verdi. *Romeo and Juliet* certainly offered an ideal texture upon which to embroider as inspiring a pattern of music as his vein could produce. The Italian composer *had* drawn inspiration from Shakespeare and the result had been amazing. *Otello* and *Falstaff* from "Othello" and "The Merry Wives of Windsor," were Verdi's last and greatest operatic works. In both he surpassed himself and nothing has been produced since, in Italian opera, that can approach them.

The Italian version of *Otello* is by Arrigo Boïto, a poet and composer himself, who followed the Shakespearean text most faithfully with only such alterations as the operatic setting required. *Falstaff's* libretto was also the work of Boïto, who wove into it several passages from "Henry IV."

A considerable number of operas, great and small, good and bad, have been inspired by Shakespeare. No less than ninety, to take only those which were actually performed. Only a dozen or so of these, however, survive as works of major importance. Twelve is a small figure as compared to ninety, but if we consider that the operagoers' book does not include more than two hundred of the fifteen hundred operas listed in a standard opera dictionary, and that these fifteen hundred, in turn, are selected from a repertory of 50,000 it would seem that Shakespeare's inspiration had been effective.

The sources to which he, himself, turned for material cover a vast range, for of the thirty-five plays we know, no less than sixteen are Italian in setting, origin or character, nine are laid in Great Britain and the rest in Greece, Denmark, France or Ancient Rome. Shakespeare, therefore, had something to suit the taste of almost any composer in search of characters to clothe in music.

"Hamlet" appealed particularly to eighteenth century Italians, several of whom, including the great Scarlatti, set the Shakespearean masterpiece to music. Towards the close of the nineteenth century, Ambroise Thomas, French composer best known through his opera *Mignon,* also wrote a *Hamlet,* based on a French parody of the play, into which he wove Scandinavian folk-music. Not quite forgotten is Nicolai's comic opera drawn from "The Merry Wives of Windsor," produced in 1849, and showing a deep understanding of the play's wit and finesse. Eight other composers, French, German, English and Italian, also handled this subject at that time, but were entirely overshadowed by Verdi's jewel, which seems to have concluded the series so far.

Some twelve years ago, Gustave Holst produced an opera in London, called *At the Boar's Head* drawn from two parts of "Henry IV," for which he revived thirty-five Elizabethan folk themes which made the score racy, effective and true to the spirit of the comedy.

"Twelfth Night," "All's Well That Ends Well," "As You Like It" were set to music before our century, but all of them appear to have been quickly shelved. Rossini wrote a powerful operatic *Otello,* faithful to Shakespeare in all but the episode of the handkerchief which he replaced by a letter, and which held its own until displaced by Verdi's greater work. Bellini, author of the celebrated *Norma,* transplanted the moor to Persia, but even his *Otello* stood little chance of survival when Verdi's appeared.

Richard Wagner's first comic opera in grand style was drawn from Shakespeare. He called it *Love's Veto* or *The Novice of Parma* and the plot and the treatment of the characters are taken from "Measure for Measure."

Wagner's admiration for the English playwright was so intense even in his boyhood that at the age of fourteen he began to write a tragedy which he himself described as a combination of "Hamlet" and "King Lear." Murders and deaths were so numerous in it, that ghosts returned constantly to the stage to save otherwise hopeless situations. *Measure for Measure* or *Love's Veto* was composed and produced at Magdeburg, in a bankrupt theatre, with singers who had only been given twelve days to learn their roles and who forgot them when the curtain rose the first night. The second performance was called off because the husband of the leading lady, in a fit of jealousy, bounced on the second tenor in the wings, beat his own wife and was locked up. After this Wagner did not turn to Shakespeare again, but *Love's Veto* has occasionally been revived in Germany with no small degree of success.

"Macbeth" was first set to music by a Frenchman, Chelard, in 1825 and before him Humperdinck of *Haensel und Gretel* fame, had been successfully inspired by this play. Verdi's attempt at *Macbeth* was a failure. There is a recent *Macbeth* by Ernest Bloch in which the scene of Duncan's murder is particularly gripping both musically and dramatically. Herman Goetz composed a famous *Taming of the Shrew* in four acts given at the Metropolitan in 1916, I believe, for the Shakespeare Commemoration, Artur Bodanzky coming from Mannheim for the performance. In 1924 a Frenchman, Charles Silver, clothed these characters in modern music with amazingly good results.

No less a composer than Debussy wrote incidental music for "King Lear," and "Cymbeline" provided the libretto for Edmond Missa's *Dinah,* a French interpretation of Shakespeare's Imogen. But the most famous reaction to "Cymbeline" is Franz Schubert's delightful serenade, "Hark, Hark the Lark!"

"A Winter's Tale" inspired two outstanding operas, one by the German, Max Bruch, called *Hermione,* rich in melody and well suited to the spirit of the play, and the other the swan song of Karl Goldmark, the Austrian composer, best known through his music for Dickens' "Cricket on the Hearth." The overture from his *Winter's Tale* is often played as a symphonic poem.

Most appealing to the imagination of composers of all lands, has been "The Tempest." Three musical scores by Germans came out in one year, 1798, followed in the nineteenth century by seven more hailing from different countries. At the close of the century Thomas composed a ballet with charming themes such as the well-known "Slumber of Miranda." The plot of "The Tempest" is of particular interest to America, because it seems that Shakespeare drew it from the account of the shipwreck of an English vessel engaged in colonizing Virginia.

"Much Ado About Nothing" was used by the French composer Hector Berlioz, whose operatic fame is due chiefly to his *Damnation of Faust,* but whose Shakespearean opera *Beatrice and Benedict* fully deserves its not infrequent revivals.

Just as popular and beloved as it is great, is Mendelssohn's incidental music for "A Midsummer Night's Dream." So perfect is the score in its interpretation of Shakespeare's unique characters that Thomas' more recent opera on the book was completely cast into oblivion almost as soon as it appeared.

Other operas than Gounod's have been based on "Romeo and Juliet." The first, in order of time, was by Georg Benda in 1772, followed by the successful work of Daniel Steibelt, a famous pianist of the same period, but both were outdone by Zingarelli, whose *Romeo and Juliet* moved Napoleon to tears when he heard it in Milan. The most recent of all is by Riccardo Zandonai, popular in Italy and a good opera as a whole although little known in other countries.

In 1861 Shakespeare himself was the hero of an opera called after him, by the Venetian Tommasso, which has left little trace of its passing.

Great as some of these operas are, it would be difficult to say that they had increased Shakespeare's fame. Shakespeare, too, has given us music: the music of his verse, the musical quality of some of his characters, and, closely akin to an orchestral accompaniment, is the symphony of his lines which keep his personages alive after one dramatic scene has subsided and before another has taken shape. Frequently, also, does he bring in musicians to play for his characters on the stage. His own love of music is best revealed by Lorenzo's words to Jessica, in "The Merchant of Venice":

> "The man that hath no music in himself,
> Nor is not mov'd with concord of sweet sounds,
> Is fit for treasons, stratagems and spoils;
> The motions of his spirit are dull as night,
> And his affections dark as Erebus:
> Let no such man be trusted."

L. S.

Fromental Halévy

(Paris, May 27, 1799–Mar. 17, 1862, Nice, France)

More than one of the Jewish Jacques François Fromental Elias Halévy's relations, by blood or by marriage, achieved distinction in the nineteenth century
world of music, art or letters. First of all there was his brother Léon, archaeologist and dramatist. Heine, who disliked both the Halévys, polished them off together in a single epigram: asked what he thought of Léon he replied: "He's
as dull as if his brother had composed him." Léon's son, Ludovic, produced,
in collaboration with Henry Meilhac, some of the best light-opera and opéra-
comique libretti of his own or any other period, notably those of Offenbach's
La Grande Duchesse de Gérolstein, La Vie Parisienne and *La Belle Hélène;*
while the pair turned Prosper Mérimée's "Carmen" into a "book" for Bizet.
The Meilhac-Halévy comedy "Le Réveillon" was the immediate source of the
libretto of *Die Fledermaus.* Halévy's daughter married Bizet, who completed
two works left unfinished by his father-in-law at his death.

Heine's epigram must not be taken too seriously: Halévy was anything but
a dull composer, though it is true that of his many operas only *La Juive* keeps
the stage today. This, as it happened, was a comparatively early work, produced
in Paris on the 23rd February 1835—that is to say, between *Robert the Devil*
and *The Huguenots.* After the huge success of the latter (1836) Halévy seems
to have succumbed to the temptation to follow to some extent in Meyerbeer's
footsteps; apparently he had not force of character enough to concentrate
doggedly on the development of his own unquestionable individuality. Wagner,
who never showed much appreciation of the French genius in general, and
was never greatly drawn to the Jews, thought really well of Halévy. During
his distressful Paris period of 1839–1842 Wagner did a good deal of "arranging" for the publisher Schlesinger; and one of the newest successes he had to
dish up in this way was Halévy's *La Reine de Chypre* (1841). Close acquaintance with the score of this gave him a higher opinion of contemporary French
opera than certain other works had done; and this favourable opinion was confirmed, in spite of some absurdities in the work, when he saw *La Reine de
Chypre* on the stage. "I sincerely rejoiced," he says in his autobiography, "to
see once more the better side of Halévy, to whom I had taken a great fancy
from the time of his *La Juive,* and of whose vigorous talent I had formed a
very favourable opinion." Wagner made Halévy's personal acquaintance about
that time: he found him a modest, amiable man, devoid of vanity where his
own work was concerned, but at the same time comprehensibly sceptical as to
the worth of contemporary opera in general.

It is never good for an artist to doubt the validity of the genre in which it is his lot to work; and perhaps it was this spirit of critical scepticism, combined with a constitutional tendency to indolence,* that accounted for Halévy's never quite fulfilling in later life the high promise of *La Juive*. Wagner saw him again fairly frequently in Paris in 1860–1: he found, to his regret, that Halévy had given up in discouragement the struggle against the tendencies of the epoch. "From my final visit to him," he says, "I came away grieved at the enervation, moral and aesthetic, of one of the last of the significant French musicians," and with a clearer perception of "the universal hypocrisy or the frankly impudent exploitation of the prevailing degeneracy on the part of all who could be regarded as Halévy's successors." There are plentiful grounds, indeed, for surmising that Halévy had more in him than ever came to full fruition.

E. N.

* He died of consumption.

La Juive

[The Jewess]

OPERA IN 5 ACTS

Book by EUGÈNE SCRIBE

First performance: Opéra, Paris, Feb. 23, 1835

CHARACTERS

Cardinal Brogny, presiding at the Council of Constance, BASS
Leopold, prince of the realm, TENOR
Eudoxie, the emperor's niece, and Leopold's betrothed, SOPRANO
Eléazar, a Jewish goldsmith, TENOR
Rachel (Recha), his daughter, SOPRANO

Ruggiero, chief bailiff of Constance, BARITONE
Albert, an officer of the imperial guard, BASS
Emperor Sigismund, A SILENT ROLE
Courtiers, Priests, Soldiers, Populace

The action takes place in Constance at the time of the historic Council in 1414

In Constance (1414) when the Jew goldsmith Eleazar's irreverent hammering punctuates pious hymns with which the people celebrate Prince Leopold's victory over the Hussites, he and his daughter Recha, torn from their shop and about to be done to death, are saved by Cardinal Brogni. Recha is not Jewish at all. When Brogni burned Eleazar's two boys as heretics, the latter's hideous revenge was to snatch his babe from her father's burning palace and bring it up to worship the God of Isaac under the name of Recha. Is it strange he refuses the hands of friendship offered by Brogni? In knightly armor Leopold has defeated the Hussites. In the smock of the Jewish painter Samuel he has stormed the heart of Recha. After eating Passover bread in her father's home, he leads his sweetheart to the cathedral steps to watch Emperor Sigismund's entry into town. But—Jewish feet on the steps of God's house in the Middle Ages stood in a slippery place. Mobbed, Leopold's whispered word to an officer, however, wins the lovers an instant release.

Yet when Leopold confesses to Eleazar that, though he loves Recha, he cannot marry her, being a Christian, he barely dodges the dagger the Jew hurls and in the town hall where the Emperor Sigismund feasts with Prince Leopold and his bride Eudoxia, abandoned Recha denounces her betrayer. Death is the portion of a Christian who loves a Jewess. Cardinal Brogni excommunicates Leopold, Recha, and Eleazar, and they are led to prison.

In Recha's cell Eudoxia induces Recha to clear Leopold when she testifies, while Brogni vainly pleads with stony-hearted Eleazar to reveal the hiding place of his long-lost daughter.

179

In the cathedral square, oil boils in the cauldrons in which Recha and Eleazar are to cross the great divide. For the last time Brogni implores Eleazar to tell him where his daughter may be. Eleazar turns to Recha. Would she care to live in splendor as a Christian? She prefers to die a Jewess with her father, is the reply. Then the savage Jew, waiting till Recha has been pushed over the cauldron's rim cries exultantly, "There is your child!" and plunges happily to his death.

F. H. M.

The libretto of *La Juive* is one of Scribe's best efforts: this was certainly one of the operas Wagner had in mind when he said that the famous text-manufacturer of that epoch could turn out a really good piece of dramatic carpentry when uncorrupted by Meyerbeer. It is true that both the construction and the diction of *La Juive* are grand-operatic in the manner of the Paris of the first half of the nineteenth century: each of the characters sometimes says and does things which no human being could ever be imagined saying or doing anywhere but in opera. But for all that, the plot bears critical examination, the action is admirably planned for progressive theatrical effect, and the characters in general, and especially the Jew Eleazar and his adopted daughter Rachel, are entirely credible. There is abundant scope not only for fine singing but for intelligent acting in both these rôles.

The scene of the drama was originally laid in the Spain of the Inquisition period, and the part of Eleazar was designed for a high bass. Later it was re-cast for the leading French tenor of the period, Adolphe Nourrit, to whom we owe the present ending of the fourth act. Apparently Scribe had terminated the act with a short chorus following on the scene between Eleazar and Brogni. Nourrit suggested that a monologue was called for here in which the Jew could express to the full the conflict of emotions in his breast,—the struggle between his desire to save Rachel and his thirst for revenge on the persecutors of his race; and Halévy agreed with him. Although the words of this long scene—commencing with the recitative "Va prononcer ma mort" and continuing with the aria "Rachel! quand du Seigneur la grâce tutélaire"—are printed as Scribe's in the complete edition of the latter's plays, they are said to be from Nourrit's pen. They are interesting for the light they throw on the points which an intelligent singer of that epoch regarded as likely to prove especially effective.

The scene of the drama is the Swiss town of Constance in the year 1414, and the main theme of it the eternal antagonism of Christian and Jew. Cardinal de Brogni, by the way, was a historical character: in August 1414 he presided in Constance over a council of princes and ecclesiastics that had been convened to try to establish peace between the various sects within the Church.

E. N.

The only opera that might have come from Meyerbeer's own pen is the passionately written *La Juive*, by Jacques François Fromental Elias Halévy, seven years his junior. And even *La Juive*, composed when only *Il Crociato* and *Robert* existed to show how Meyerbeer was maturing, was less a slavish imitation than a natural expression of a man whose character was much like Meyerbeer's—scholarly, devoted to craftsmanship, eclectic. Halévy, in his best opera, is almost as much Cherubini's pupil as Meyerbeer's friend.

In one respect, *La Juive* is superior to any score of Meyerbeer's: it is more truly felt, establishes an integrity, preserves a unity, with a persistence that would have carried Meyerbeer to the heights of musical greatness. Halévy, unlike Meyerbeer, never allows his flair for experimentation to run away with him: it is almost always religiously controlled. The tragedy of the perfectly schooled Halévy was that he was facile and prolix, and set without enthusiasm almost thirty operas, most often to any catchpenny book that came along. In Scribe's *La Juive*, for all its rant and fustian, he found a dramatic story that set his devoutly Jewish imagination on fire.

The intellectual Nourrit, who had an advisory voice in the shaping of several Meyerbeer scores . . . was, naturally, the Eléazar * of the opening performance, at the Opéra, on February 23, 1835. The Rachel was Cornélie Falcon, the Eudoxie was Dorus-Gras, and the Cardinal was Levasseur. Viardot-García, a little later, was unexcelled as Rachel. Among the tenors of the time who sang Eléazar, Duprez was superb, and Mario was insufferable—possibly because the role gave him no opportunity to look handsome. Marianne Brandt, the future Wagnerian mezzo, made her operatic debut, in Graz, as Rachel.

La Juive, like so many French operas of the period, was first heard in the United States at New Orleans (1844), and the next year reached New York, where it has been sung in French, German, Italian, Russian, and Yiddish. Materna was the Rachel of the first Metropolitan performance, of the season of 1884–85, given in German under Leopold Damrosch. The revival of December 7, 1887, brought together the largely Wagnerian cast of Lilli Lehmann, Schröder-Hanfstängel, Niemann, Fischer, and Alvary. The next season, Paul Kalisch, Lehmann's husband, took Niemann's role. After two more performances in German during the 1889–90 season, *La Juive* was dropped from the Metropolitan repertoire for thirty years. Then, on November 22, 1919, it was revived in French. Caruso, as the Eléazar, was singing his thirty-sixth and last Metropolitan role, with Ponselle and Rothier, besides Orville Harrold, who was making his Metropolitan debut.

Of Caruso's performance, Irving Kolodin, in his informative "The Metropolitan Opera: 1883–1939," wrote: "It was without doubt the most striking

---

* [Great tenors have shown a special fondness for the role of the valiant Jewish goldsmith and have gone to great pains to observe faithfully every aspect of the religious issue involved. In studying the role Caruso consulted rabbinical authorities on the precise detail of dress and gesture. It is said that even the most devout Jew could not detect any lapse from orthodox form in his portrayal.]

artistic triumph of his career. Some quality in the character had inflamed Caruso's imagination; and the impersonation he finally presented was the product of more care and study, especially dramatically, than any of the thirty-five other roles he sang during his career in New York. It was particularly impressive as the accomplishment of a singer whose position in the esteem of the public was inviolate; and spoke more highly for his development as an artist than any verbal tribute could."

A year later, on November 15, *La Juive*, with the same principals, was used to inaugurate the Metropolitan season of 1920–21. It was Caruso's last opening night. On December 24, with Florence Easton replacing Ponselle, he sang *La Juive* once more. It was his farewell to the Metropolitan—and to opera. He was a sick man, and eight months later, after apparent recovery, he died at his native Naples. *La Juive* did not drop from the repertoire with his death: it has been given more than two dozen times since, with Martinelli as Eléazar and Ponselle, Rethberg, and Lawrence as his erring daughter.

Comedy as well as tragedy is connected with the history of *La Juive*. In a Chicago performance, in the early twenties, Rosa Raisa, until then a passionately doleful Rachel, was the innocent victim of a ludicrous anticlimax in the final scene. Thrown into what purported to be a huge caldron of boiling oil, she bounced practically back onto the stage. A too-coddling stage director had over-cushioned her landing by flooring the caldron with some elastic material. In this instance, even those in the pit, who seldom have any fun, could see Raisa's death gymnastics.

W. B., H. W.

George Frideric Handel

(Halle, Germany, Feb. 23, 1685–Apr. 14, 1759, London)

His Majesty's servant Mr. George Frideric Handel has been described as quite the most superb figure in the history of music. He was richly endowed, he acquired great learning, he composed with a prodigal hand, he pursued his career in several countries, he became an important figure in the great world, and he died full of years and honors. Among English-speaking peoples he is universally known through his oratorio "The Messiah" and his miscalled "Largo."

Handel was born on February 23, 1685, at Halle, a Saxon city not so far from Eisenach, where Bach was born on March 21 of the same year. Handel's father, a barber who, in the way of the time also acted as surgeon and so became surgeon and valet to the Prince of Saxe-Magdeburg, at the age of sixty-two married for a second time, the bride being Dorothea Taust, daughter of a neighboring pastor. The future composer was the second son of this marriage. The elder Handel, intending him for the law, frowned upon his taste for music. Nevertheless, the boy secretly taught himself the harpsichord. When he was seven he paid a determining visit to a half-brother who was valet at the court of Saxe-Weissenfels. There the Duke heard him play on the chapel organ and insisted that he be trained in music. Returning to Halle, he became a pupil in theory and composition of the organist of the cathedral, played oboe, harpsichord, and organ, served as assistant organist to his teacher, wrote sonatas, and for three years provided a motet for every Sunday. When his father took him to Berlin in 1696 his skill as organist and harpsichordist and especially his ability to improvise so impressed the Elector Friedrich that he offered to pay the boy's expenses for further study in Italy. The father refused, and took his son back to Halle. The next year the elder Handel died, and the son, after finishing his course at the gymnasium, entered Halle University as a law student, pursuant to the elder's wish. However, he acted at the same time as organist at the Moritzburg Cathedral, receiving as salary about the equivalent of $85 per annum.

In this dual arrangement music got the better of the law, and in 1703 Handel, though only eighteen, took the first step toward an international career by going to Hamburg to play violin and later harpsichord with the German opera company. Here he became friendly with the composers Telemann and Mattheson (later his biographer), and also wrote three operas and his first oratorio, a "Passion According to St. John." By 1706 he had saved 200 ducats, whereupon he proceeded to Italy, where he remained for three years.

These years were of the utmost importance in the enriching and maturing of his style. He was cordially welcomed in Florence, Venice, Rome, and Naples; he met Corelli, Lotti, and the two Scarlattis; he brought out three oratorios and two operas, all to Italian texts, of which the opera *Agrippina* (Venice 1709) had a sensational success, making him famous throughout the peninsula.

From this triumph he reluctantly went back to Germany, where he was appointed Kapellmeister to the Elector of Hanover. In 1710 he visited England for the first time, making such a hit with a new Italian opera, *Rinaldo,* at the Haymarket Theatre, London, that he was urged to stay on in England. But he dutifully went back to Hanover. In 1712, however, he returned to London, with the proviso, though, that he should go back to Hanover "within a reasonable time." An ode for Queen Anne's birthday and a "Te Deum and Jubilate" in celebration of the Peace of Utrecht made him highly popular in England and won him an annuity of 200 pounds from the sovereign, with the result that Hanover faded from his memory. At the same time he seems to have overlooked the fact that queens are not immortal and that on the death of Queen Anne the British throne would pass to the House of Hanover. As a matter of fact, George I, who had become King of England in 1714, did resent Handel's unreasonable absence, but in due course peace was made and the annuity confirmed. In 1716 Handel even accompanied the new sovereign on a visit to Hanover. Thenceforth until 1737 Handel's story is one of prodigious creative activity, various worldly honors, and all the excitement attendant upon the production as well as the composition of operas, despite all which he found time for an occasional trip to the Continent. In 1726 he was naturalized an Englishman, but certain English elements in his music are more influential than citizenship in his being classed as an English composer.

Organist and composer to the Duke of Chandos, music-master to the daughters of the Prince of Wales, he was appointed director of the Royal Academy of Music, founded mainly for the production of Italian opera, and consequently entered upon a new period as an operatic composer. As an impresario he had to endure the rivalry and intrigues of Bononcini, Ariosti, Porpora, and Hasse, as well as to manage capricious and rebellious singers. A man of commanding physique, independent character, hot temper, and utterly fearless, Handel, though witty, humorous, kindly, and charitable, lacked tact. He set the intractable prima donna Cuzzoni in her place by holding her out of a window and threatening to drop her unless she sang what she was told to sing, and he was no less blunt, even if less violent, with rival impresarios. Eventually his opera-giving ended in failure and in 1737 he suffered a stroke, due to his all-but-superhuman labors. A sojourn at Aix-la-Chapelle improved his health and before 1741 he had written several more operas, including his only comic opera, *Xerxes,* which contains the beautiful larghetto aria that has been falsely dubbed "Handel's Largo." In all, between 1705 and 1741, he composed forty-six operas, a treasury of inspired music.

As told above, he had begun as an oratorio-writer with the "St. John Passion" in 1704 and subsequently he had composed such important works . . . as "Acis and Galatea," "Esther," "Deborah," "Alexander's Feast," "Saul," "Israel in Egypt," the "Ode for St. Cecilia's Day," and "L'Allegro, il Pensieroso ed il Moderator," but not until the composition of "The Messiah" did Handel forsake opera entirely for oratorio and become the foremost of all composers of oratorio. In 1741 he was invited by the Viceroy of Ireland to visit Dublin, where "The Messiah" was successfully brought out on April 13, 1742. When he returned to London he found himself again the popular idol that he had been before the failure of his operatic fortunes. Thereupon, at the age of fifty-seven, he began what was virtually a second career.

Oratorio followed oratorio, including such masterpieces as "Samson," "Semele," "Judas Maccabaeus," "Solomon," "Theodora," and "Jephtha." Thus Handel retrieved his fortunes while he added immeasurably to a fame already great. In 1752, while he was at work on "Jephtha" his eyesight began to fail. Three unsuccessful operations resulted in complete loss of sight. So, like Bach, Handel spent the end of his life in blindness. Nevertheless he continued to play in public and to compose. On April 6, 1759, he presided at the organ on the occasion of a performance of "The Messiah" at Covent Garden. Eight days later he died in his own house in Brook Street. On the 20th he was buried in Westminster Abbey.

Handel never married and no love affair of his has been recorded.

This brief account of one of the most prolific of the great composers and one of the world's supreme melodists in dwelling on the forty-six operas and thirty-two oratorios has passed over his many anthems and his instrumental compositions. Yet in quality and quantity they by themselves would secure for any musician the rank of greatness.

P. S.

Giulio Cesare

[Julius Caesar]

OPERA IN 3 ACTS

Book by Nicola Haym

First performance: Royal Academy of Music, London, Feb. 20, 1724

The complicated action of the opera may be summarized as follows: Cleopatra, who feels that her brother Ptolemaeus has wrongfully deprived her of Egypt's throne, finally attains her coveted goal through the good offices of Julius Caesar, whom she has first been at pains to bring under her spell. Ptolemaeus is a fine figure of a villain. There is a nefarious intriguer in his counselor Achillas, and, of course, Pompey's widow, the mourning Cornelia, who is saved from a detested marriage with the infatuated Ptolemaeus, and the vengeful Sextus move in stately lamentation toward the general liberation of the happy ending.   P. S.

(The Italian opera directed by Handel at the Royal Academy of Music, London, was in a bad way at the beginning of the year 1724. The failure of Ariosti's opera *Vespasiano* on January 14 had started the run of ill luck. Handel put his shoulder to the wheel, finished *Giulio Cesare,* and directed its production on Feb. 20. Senesino, a celebrated male soprano, was particularly successful as Julius Caesar. Musically the score is one of Handel's best, and the libretto, in its naïve way, is genuinely and steadily dramatic.—P. S.)

When Handel produced his *Giulio Cesare* in February 1724 he had more or less a clear run before him. Haym had given up his personal tamperings with opera, and had now settled down to provide good libretti. This he certainly did. Handel's next four operas owed their libretti to Haym, but *Giulio Cesare* was the poorest of the set.

Meanwhile, the anti-German element was still strong in London: it derided the claims of Handel as it derided the King. The monarch, with his lamentable South Sea Company speech, had made London lose faith in him, and it had never had much to lose. He was scarcely regarded as a monarch, but as a spectacle—a splendidly clad figure amidst the wax-lights—growing obese, and a little crippled with gout and other pains, surrounded with a miscellaneous collection of fair ladies, many of whom tried to talk broken English because they had been elevated to the rank of English duchesses. The real English aristocracy, regular in its attendance at Court, rather amused—with no more than an inherited respect for royalty—was derisive in its comments, and wondered what or who was going to be the subject of the next quarrel between the King and the Prince of Wales. King George had to a great extent forgotten his interest in the Academy; he had forgotten that he was supposed to love music. The revived French farces amused him. He lounged indolently in the boxes, laughing at the blatant indecencies, and throwing comment to the beauties about him. He became less staid, more urgent in trying to enjoy life, which, with its sought savours, seemed to lack just that which would make him a happy man. He had become a feckless *abandonné,* who had left his soul behind in the secret rooms and the unmeasured profligacy of the *Herrenhaus.*

Giulio Cesare was fine work, but it failed to evoke more than average attention. Never was Senesino heard to greater advantage. Handel had given him songs which would have made fame for a gutter singer with a good voice. The extraordinary performance by Senesino provoked almost more attention than the brilliance of Handel's music. Nevertheless, this great triumph of composer and artist passed in a few performances, because London was wearying of good music.

When, soon afterwards, Senesino made an attack upon Anastasia Robinson, and received a flogging from the Earl of Peterborough . . . interest in him and his work had a swift revival. Forged letters began to fly about, supposed to be written by Anastasia to the Italian. Forged letters from Senesino in return were disseminated like circulars of a modern pill. The town was stirred; the King enjoyed the great joke. These funny little scandals were sufficiently ignoble to be the mainstay of a happy evening in any average Society salon. When, during the singing of his great song "Alma del Gran Pompeo" in *Giulio Cesare,* a piece of scenery fell down with a crash and uprising of dust, the wretched Senesino was so startled out of his wits that he dropped in a flood of frightened tears to the stage and Society's ecstasies rose yet higher.

So the ponderous hero who ramped across the stage and sang with the voice of heaven was only a miserable little coward after all! The mysterious personality which had been created about him by the wonder of his singing slipped away like a vanishing cloak of dreams. His heroism stood revealed as so much make-believe, like the stage castle which he had stormed in an earlier Handel opera, to carry away one wing of it on the point of his sword like a trussed fowl. Only one thing was real—as if it were the gift of God left in the wrong body—the magnificent voice that made even an idling King cease his fooling to listen.

Now, in spite of this exhibition, in spite of the fact that, season by season, Senesino became more apparent as a creature with rather second-rate gutter manners and breeding, women still poured upon him their adoration. When ultimately he left England they wept. They loaded him with presents. They crowded about him to get his wretched insincere smile—or even his scorn. They were ready to bear any hurt for him and worship as fiercely as ever.

Such is the power of the human voice. To these many women from the rich villas of Chelsea, from the grandiose mansions of Piccadilly, Senesino was a lone voice singing in a wilderness. Ultimately they let him go like that, and respectable wives of bankers and rich merchants and peers went down to their graves hugging to themselves secret memories of Senesino—memories of nights at the stage door—a glance—a smile. Most respectable wives, all of them. And their more respectable husbands never discovered anything about it.

The god of the whole adventure in the fullness of time went back to his native town of Siena in Italy, and with a good fortune of £15,000—which he had taken from these admirers for seats—built himself a palace. Here he lived with the habits of a prince who had never been educated, sang duets with royalty in public, and settled down to a life of pompous luxury.

N. F.

The first performance in the United States took place at the Academy of Music, Northampton, Mass., May 14, 1927, under the sponsorship of the department of music of Smith College. A dignified and singable English translation was employed, and the version of the score used was based on the edition made by Dr. Oskar Hagen for production at Göttingen in 1923. The musical director was Werner Josten.

On Jan. 21, 1931, *Giulio Cesare* was staged for the first time in New York at the American Woman's Association Club House, likewise in an English version. Here the sponsor was the Graduate School of the Juilliard School of Music. Albert Stoessel conducted.

Tamerlano

[Tamerlane]

OPERA IN 3 ACTS

Book by Nicola Haym

First performance: Royal Academy of Music, London, Oct. 31, 1724

Tamerlane, the medieval conqueror from central Asia, has taken captive the Turkish sultan, Bajazet, his archenemy. Bajazet's daughter Asteria intercedes with him on behalf of her father, and Tamerlane, becoming enamored of the beautiful girl, yields to her entreaties, hoping thus to win her favor.

It is an awkward situation, however, for Tamerlane is on the point of being affianced to Irene, a princess of Trebizond, with whom he is not yet acquainted, and Asteria is already betrothed to Tamerlane's ally, the Greek prince Andronicus.

Naturally Andronicus turns hostile to Tamerlane, and the latter tries to bring about an exchange by transferring Irene to Andronicus with the help of Bajazet and Asteria. At this breach of honor Bajazet waxes furious, but Asteria, believing herself betrayed by Andronicus, is inclined to join Tamerlane. As a result of the intriguing Andronicus determines to kill both Tamerlane and himself.

The courageous Bajazet calls Tamerlane and Asteria to account and haughtily disowns his daughter, but the latter now deserts Tamerlane for her father. Tamerlane in a rage imprisons them both.

Bajazet makes his daughter a present of poison as a last refuge against shame. Once more Tamerlane tries to win Asteria; Andronicus declares himself Tamerlane's rival and Asteria's lover. Asteria again begs Tamerlane's indulgence for her father, when suddenly Bajazet drinks the poison himself and dies cursing his enemy and inviting his daughter to follow him in death. Thereupon the sobered Tamerlane, recognizing the loftiness of his enemy's soul, gives Asteria to Andronicus, to win Irene for himself.

P. S.

With *Giulio Cesare*, Handel had returned to the opera of romance, of movement, of martial airs, and tense passion. Yet the public seemed to have but little liking for it. Had he been such a student of the public's requirements as he is often stated to have been, he would have changed the style of the next work he put out. Handel knew when his work was good, and also when it was bad. The public apathy had been merely an adverse mood in an excitable age. He would not budge an inch from the attitude that he had assumed—

189

namely that he composed for his art and not for the public. He made Nicolò
Haym write another libretto for him at once, and Haym produced *Tamerlane*.
The opera has a story and a fine one, but Haym certainly did his best to disguise it! He was muddled in his libretto of *Giulio Cesare,* and he was muddled in *Tamerlane*. But Handel's music, and the acting and singing of Cuzzoni and Senesino, smoothed away many difficulties and made *Tamerlane* a
coherent whole.

Handel began to compose *Tamerlane* on 3 July 1724 and completed it in
twenty days. Like all his greatest achievements it was the outcome of concentration when he lived in one room, ate, slept, worked, existed in an atmosphere that breathed the romance of his notes. *Tamerlane* reflects that concentration. The harmony is brilliant, and it carries some of the most passionate
melodies that ever sprang from the master's brain. Cuzzoni's and Senesino's
duet: "I am thine, my only treasure," was one of the greatest triumphs Handel
had known till this moment. The intimate sorrow of it, the yearning, carried
every man and woman who listened into the heart of a great love story. "I
could die with joy to please you, for my life is only thine." As these two wonderful voices stole aloft tears streamed down the faces of the people. The hard-
ened from the salons, blasé to all sentiment, who yet went to the opera because it was the thing to do, and who normally used the time as an excuse
to laugh and joke in an undertone, were softly crying.

The talk about *Tamerlane* had caused the decaying King to take a new
interest in the opera, and the great duet made him cease his idle and dis-
reputable talk to listen. Then the opera had an added interest, because it introduced Handel's new singer Borosini. A curious creature. A man exactly
Handel's own age, who had wandered about southern Europe with a tenor
voice that created enormous interest for a time, till the repetition of it repelled.
Borosini, in the course of these wanderings, had married another singer, Leonore d'Ambreville. When Handel made his contract with Borosini, who was
then singing at Prague, he had to engage his wife also. They were neither of
them great singers, but their advent interested people as another Handel diversion. For two years they sang for Handel, then their vogue waned, and
they disappeared from the country.

Tamerlane had one virtue above most of the Handel operas—it built up
carefully to a tremendous climax. Probably Handel never attained a greater
finale than he did in *Tamerlane* until he left opera for oratorio. The close of
the work, the dramatic pathos he reached in his notes when the broken Emperor Bajazet passes to death, was the triumph of one carried out of himself
by enthusiasm for his task. Bajazet's song, "Dearest daughter, weep no more,"
was a masterpiece of attainment. Such a heart-breaking had never been displayed in music before.

Tamerlane sent its audiences weeping into the street when the curtain fell.
All through that autumn it held the theatre, and it would have been unques-

tionably a great financial success but for the extravagance and loose commercial habits of the Academy directors. It was a paying proposition all the time, but money was being poured down the drain in absurd inconsequent ways, because no one cared very much what happened so long as the Academy's doors were kept open.

Handel was probably the only person who had any thought about this side of the venture. Heidegger * was too busy with his masquerades. The various governing peers, now that the novelty of the Academy had worn off, sought other novelties to divert idle lives. The King had fallen irreparably to the lure of the wax-lights, the powdered ladies and the French farces. The dull old fellow's days were waning. He was pushing away constantly recurring illnesses as nuisances, persuading himself that a life of eternal pleasure was not taking its toll. In a couple of years more he was to die a heavy, bent up, crying figure in a coach outside Osnaburg. Not a bit regal, not a bit the autocratic adventurer, but very humble when Death touched his shoulder.

No sooner had the curtain fallen on the last performance of *Tamerlane* than Handel was ready with a new opera. He was fighting hard for the falling fortunes of the Academy. If it failed he was conscious that there must come a serious blow to his prestige. Bononcini was like some lowing beast, snapping in frantic frenzy at every Handelian move made by the Academy directors. They were going to destruction with Handel. He told them so. In truth they were, but only because they had not enough commercial instinct between them to keep open the doors of an average shop for a month, let alone a great venture like the Academy.

Handel produced his *Rodelinda* on 13 February 1725. He only composed the last notes of it on 20 January. He knew that the Academy was approaching dissolution unless something important happened to stir the town.

In a way, he gave the town all it wanted to talk about with his *Rodelinda*. Haym's Italian libretto, more human than most of his works, and dealing with the emotions of a deserted Lombardian queen, was sufficient excuse for Handel's emotional songs. Although in *Rodelinda* Handel never reached the powers he displayed in *Tamerlane,* he produced a fine work. It was Cuzzoni who provided the diversion. She appeared in a brown silk dress trimmed with silver that caught the town. None of the songs of Handel brought the audiences to *Rodelinda;* they came to see the brown and silver dress, to talk about it, to copy it. Cuzzoni started a fashion which swept through Society like an epidemic. Though the singer appeared very plump and squat in the brown and silver dress, every Society woman in the audience—with that imagination which is truly woman's—foresaw what she herself would look like in such a combination of artistic colour. Handel had made an opera, and Cuzzoni a season's fashion. And the odd thing about *Rodelinda* is that the fashion Cuz-

* [John James Heidegger (1659–1749), opera manager and partner of Handel at the Haymarket Theatre.]

zoni set on that February night in 1725 has lived longer than the beauties Handel put into that work. . . . But Cuzzoni's brown and silver dress has run the gamut of empires, has gone out of fashion and ramped through fashion again, and acquired its place as a delicate thought in colour schemes.

The season ended on 19 May. Then for a while Handel was silent. He produced nothing fresh until he began his new opera *Scipio* on 12 March 1726. *Scipio* had a good average run of thirteen nights, but had only one big Handelian number in it, the march which, later on, was purloined by the promoters of *Polly,* the sequel to the *Beggar's Opera.*

He was now forty-one; he had reached what we moderns know as "midchannel." It had not been difficult going thus far, considering his times and the wild and wonderful temperaments of those with whom he had to deal.

But the world was changing. He was changing. All the melody he had produced in those years was as nothing to what was yet to come. The best of it was to emerge from the vicious and unremitting hurt of the world, driven upon him without flinch or pity. Jealousies, the changing of friends, the foolish quarrels of kings and their spoiled offspring were to bring him wounds which he never sought or deserved. Out of suffering and hidden lament came his sweeter singing. Had it not been for enmities and disappointments he would have been a lesser voice in universal music. Because he was to endure so did he come to discover the world's grief, its tenderness, and by his divine gift change it into a song of hope.

N. F.

Serse

[Xerxes]

OPERA IN 3 ACTS

Librettist unknown

First performance: The King's Theater, London, April 15, 1738

According to the intricate plot, Xerxes, king of Persia, his brother Arsamenes, and two sisters, Romilda and Atalanta, daughters of the general Ariodantes, are very much at cross purposes. Other characters are the Princess Amastris, beloved of Xerxes, and Elvira, the comic servant of Arsamenes.

The complications of the action bring ridicule on royal despotism, which would fain extend its dominion even over love, but which is balked by the wit of a clever woman. The inconstant Xerxes has looked with favor on Romilda, though already his brother Arsamenes is in love with her. To overcome the rival, Xerxes thinks of no better means than the use of the royal prerogative. How the opponents circumvent his brutal orders and bring them to naught provides the substance of the action.

P. S.

(Last but three of Handel's forty-six operas, *Serse* differs from the others in being a comedy, even in some respects a burlesque of opera itself. The observer can only grasp the real quality of the work if he thinks not only of Handel but of Offenbach and his librettists, Meilhac and Halévy, and the English parodists, Gilbert and Sullivan.

Undoubtedly *Serse* is one of the most delectable musical comedies ever contrived. The humorous extravaganza about the Persian potentate and his amorous caprices is excellent theater, comparing favorably with *The Marriage of Figaro* and *The Barber of Seville,* and distinctly clearer to the unaided eye than either *Così fan tutte* or *Gianni Schicchi.*

There is a feast of music, too, from the matchless opening aria, "Ombra mai fu" (miscalled "Handel's Largo") on, compact of beguiling melody and robust comic power. The superb George Frideric in his flower-market scene even deigns to remember the coster tunes of London, as though he were an earlier, and greater, Charpentier depicting Paris!

A paradox not seldom observed is apparent in the fact that Handel's one comic opera belongs to the most trying period of his life, when he was beset by physical and financial ills. Nevertheless, he took only seven weeks to put his new lyric drama together.—P. S.)

Handel was fifty-three, and if his intellect was only just on the threshold of the great maturity which gave his best-remembered works to the world, his physical powers were sinking. Rheumatism, the product of his absurd neglect of his health, had been fought down once, but was beginning to recur. He drew more and more into himself, his pride smitten by his inability to force a way by settlement with those who held him in thrall. His friends suggested that a benefit concert should be given for him. He scouted the idea. He was angry—violently angry. He had not come down to beggary, he declared, and such affairs were the bald admission of a flat purse. This at fifty-three, when he had written more notes—and better notes—than any man for many epochs. He let off salvoes from his mingled English-German vocabulary. He swore. He stormed. Ultimately they made him accept the concert.

It was given on 28 March 1738. Far from being considered in the nature of a charity, Society looked upon it as a special affair that should not be missed. The theatre filled, and still Society poured in. "Over five hundred persons of rank and fashion were discovered on the stage." And the profit to Handel for that one night, when he secretly hugged to himself his pride, was a record figure. Society, all London, told him, in that spontaneous honouring, that if he were in the throes of penury he was still Handel. The concert gave him something over a thousand pounds with which he paid del Pò,* and condemned him to the Shades with all the other creditors to keep him company.

His financial worries at an end for a while, he completed *Serse* and produced it at the King's Theatre on 15 April. It was the second of the two operas for which Heidegger had offered him £1,000. *Serse* is one of the big mysteries in Handel's life. No one knows where he obtained the libretto, or why he should suddenly adopt broad farce and expect to make a success of it. He may have had it in his mind to cut into the success of *The Beggar's Opera,* but *Serse* was about the last work that would do so. Certainly he could have been in no mood for farce after the anxieties on the grounds of health and finance through which he had passed, and from which he had not as yet escaped. In spite of all the incongruity of *Serse,* it produced the air which, through the two centuries that have since elapsed, has been far better known to the public at large, and more frequently played, than anything Handel ever composed— an air about the shadow of a plane-tree, and better known as the famous "Largo." Out of this absurdity, *Serse,* which had no *raison d'être,* no beginning and no end, Handel in a mood conjured a piece of melody which, now, as then, holds a theatre audience when it is played, and remains one of the master melodies of the world. Not that *Serse* could succeed on a single air. Before the season had ended the King's Theatre had closed down, and Heidegger had decided that, for the time at any rate, Handel was an expensive form of speculation.

* [Husband of Anna Strada, an Italian soprano discovered by Handel.]

But one man, at least, had made a lot of money out of Handel whilst the theatres had been losing on him. This was Jonathan Tyers, who ran Vauxhall Gardens as an evening pleasure haunt for the better classes of Society. Tyers was a queer mixture of artistic inclination and hard commercialism. He had opened the Gardens six years before on a stretch of ground he leased from Elizabeth Masters at the cheap rental of £250 a year. It had been a great opening. The Prince of Wales had been present, with a guard of one hundred soldiers with fixed bayonets. Tyers arranged all possible demonstration for the pomp-loving Frederick, and the hundred bayonets was the finishing touch, for only four hundred persons paid for admission! Frederick, with his little army, was disgusted; all this would make him appear a coward to a handful of people. If something had occurred to provide an excuse for the use of this armed might, things would not have been so bad. The ceremony lasted from nine o'clock in the evening until four o'clock in the morning, and the only unexpected incident was that a drunken waiter put on a masquerading dress, and a pickpocket stole fifty guineas from a visitor, and was caught red-handed.

In spite of the fiasco of the opening, the Prince remained a constant visitor to Vauxhall Gardens till his death. Its open immoralities appealed to him. One bought a silver season ticket, a beautiful trifle designed by Hogarth, or paid a guinea to mingle with the select for the evening. Tyers ran the Gardens to pay, and he made them pay by appealing to the passions on the one hand, and the artistic senses on the other. Vauxhall Gardens after dark held the cream of the night life of London. Everybody went there. One dined there, met the ladies of the town, and listened to Handel-music, played by the finest orchestras obtainable, whilst they supped. For Tyers had always run Handel on his bands. He may have had no sense of music, he may have had Handel played just because people were in the habit of going to hear his music. Whatever was at the back of his mind, he was faithful to Handel.

Vauxhall Gardens soon came into high favour. One went there usually by boat, and at Westminster and Whitehall Stairs barges and boats were always in waiting during the evening for the hire of intending visitors. Despite the loose morals of the place, bishops visited it and somehow managed to retain their characters. City men took their families, attended by a footman carrying provisions. The scene at the landing-stage was unlike any other in London, for, although Tyers had beadles placed there to keep order, the commotion was beyond description. All the boats were mixed up in hopeless confusion, there was a mob of people in wonderful dresses shouting and swearing and quarrelling, and a parcel of ugly fellows running out into the water to pull one violently ashore. Then the crowd streamed through a dark passage into the glaring splendour of a thousand lamps.

Tyers, canny fellow, looked after his patrons well. The food was of the best; the wines—there were no wines in proclivities further. He commissioned

Roubillac, the principal sculptor of the time, to cut him a statue of Handel for £300, and Handel actually sat for the purpose. Handel was then put up in marble, a sitting figure playing a lyre, and the queue to the Gardens grew more dense than ever. The fame of the statue passed to the Continent, and Mattheson, Handel's old friend at Hamburg, now possibly a little jealous, wrote a letter pointing out that England had honoured his compatriot by this manœuvre. That it was merely the trick of a glorified restaurant-keeper to pander to the mood of his patrons, did not occur to him. For no one benefited from the statue except Tyers, and, of course, the sculptor, and the former proved once more that fame is a profitable commodity to trade upon.

At no time in his life were the changing moods of Handel so obvious as in this year 1738—moods due, no doubt, to his health and anxieties. The man with strong opinions from which he would never depart, who forced his will on the public and gave them what he wanted whether the public liked it or not, began to hesitate. He seemed uncertain of himself, more uncertain of the public taste. What else could have urged him to waste his energies on such a silly affair as *Serse?* And now, realising when the summer came that he had made another mistake, he switched right over again and composed [the oratorio] *Saul.*

N. F.

The first performance in America seems to have been that of May 13, 1928, given by the music department of Smith College in the Academy of Music, Northampton, Mass. Bayard Quincy Morgan had made a clear and pithy English translation of the text, Werner Josten directed, and the part of Xerxes was entrusted to the young tenor, Charles Kullmann, and that of Romilda to the well-known soprano, Mabel Garrison.

It is worthy of note that in this opera Handel took a leaf from *The Beggar's Opera* of ten years earlier, besides anticipating by many leaves the Sullivan scores of a century and a half later.

Engelbert Humperdinck

(Siegburg, Germany, Sept. 1, 1854–Sept. 27, 1921, Neustrelitz, Germany)

After studying at the Gymnasium at Paderborn he [Humperdinck] entered the Cologne Conservatorium under Ferdinand Hiller in 1872, and while a student there he won (1876) the Frankfort Mozart Stipendium. By the aid of this fund he proceeded to Munich, where he was a pupil at first of Franz Lachner and later of Josef Rheinberger at the Royal Music School (1877–1879). Next Humperdinck won the Mendelssohn Stiftung of Berlin in 1879, and promptly went to Italy, where at Naples he met Richard Wagner. At Wagner's invitation Humperdinck followed him to Bayreuth, and materially assisted him during 1880–81 in the preparation for the production of *Parsifal*. But having won still another prize in the latter year—the Meyerbeer prize of Berlin—he set out south once more, and after travelling again in Italy, France and Spain, he settled for two years at Barcelona, where in 1885–86 he taught theory of music in the Conservatoire. In 1887 he returned to Cologne, and from 1890–96 he was a professor at the Hoch Conservatorium in Frankfort; he was a teacher of harmony in Stockhausen's Vocal School, as well as musical critic for the *Frankfürter Zeitung*. Meanwhile he had not been idle as a composer, for in 1880 he produced a "Humoreske" for orchestra, which enjoyed a vogue in Germany; in 1884 his popular choral work "Das Glück von Edenhall" was first sung, and the choral ballade "Die Wallfahrt nach Kevlaar" in 1887, as well as a large quantity of music in the smaller forms, for male or mixed choirs.

In 1893 his masterpiece, the opera *Hänsel und Gretel* (libretto by his sister A. Wette), was brought to a hearing at Weimar on Dec. 23, and immediately captivated all music-lovers, so that it ran a rapid course the wide world over (London, Apr. 1895), and was warmly welcomed as an antidote to the then prevailing craze for the lurid work of the young Italian school of Mascagni, etc. This he followed up with another opera (originally a play accompanied with music throughout), *Königskinder* in 1896, and *Dornröschen* in 1902, neither of which made any success comparable with that of the first-named work. The full operatic version of *Königskinder* appeared in New York, 1910, Berlin and London, 1911. A "Maurische Rhapsodie" for orchestra was produced in 1898. In 1896 the Kaiser created Humperdinck professor, and in 1897 he went to live at Boppard, but in 1900 he was once again in Berlin, where he had been appointed head of a Meister-Schule for musical composition, and a member of the Senate of the Royal Akademie der Künste. His opera, "Die Heirath wider Willen," was brought out at Berlin, Apr. 14, 1905. Incidental music to a number of plays followed for productions in Berlin, namely "The Merchant of Venice" (1905), "The Winter's Tale" and "The Tempest" (1906), "As You Like It" (1907), "Lysistrata" (Aristophanes) (1908), "The Blue Bird" (Maeterlinck) (1910). That to "The Miracle" (London, 1911) attracted wider attention because of the magnificence of Reinhardt's production both in Europe and in America (1924). Two other operas, *Die Marketenderin* (Cologne, 1914) and *Gaudeamus* (Darmstadt, 1919), must be named.

R. H. L.

Hänsel und Gretel

FAIRY PLAY IN 3 TABLEAUX

Book by ADELHEID WETTE, after a fairy tale by LUDWIG GRIMM

First performance: Hoftheater, Weimar, Germany, Dec. 23, 1893

CHARACTERS

Peter, a poor broommaker, BARITONE
Gertrude, his wife, MEZZO-SOPRANO
Hänsel, their son, MEZZO-SOPRANO
Gretel, their daughter, SOPRANO

The Witch, MEZZO-SOPRANO
The Sandman, SOPRANO
The Dewman, SOPRANO
Angels and Gingerbread Children

The hungry children Hänsel and Gretel, broom making in their hut, find a pot of milk and dance around it, neglecting their work. When their mother comes home and angrily chases them, the milk is upset and she drives the little ones out to the forest to pick berries. Back comes her husband from town. He has sold his brooms to advantage. But where are the children? In the forest? The anxious parents hurry out. Perhaps they have strayed to the Ilsenstein, where the wicked witch lives in the cottage into which she lures innocent children and bakes them into gingerbread in her oven.

In the forest (Orchestral Interlude pictures the "Witch's Ride") Gretel is winding a flower wreath under a tree when Hänsel comes running up, his basket full of strawberries. The children eat them, but when they set out for home twilight shadows fill the woods and will-o'-the-wisps and misty shapes frighten them, till the Sandman comes and lulls them to sleep, and as they drowsily sing their "Evening Hymn" angels descend to watch over them.

The Dewman wakes the little sleepers and as they rub their eyes they see the Witch's gingerbread hut and begin to nibble at it. Up comes the old hag and bans them with her magic word: Hänsel is put in a pen to be fattened with apples and raisins, while Gretel must help the Witch. The oven is red hot and the Witch rides triumphantly around her hut when Gretel, who has overheard the magic spell, repeats it, gets the Witch in front of the oven (she has already released Hänsel) and then she and her brother quickly push her in and close the door. The Witch must burn and that is the end of her. As the children hug each other in their joy, the oven falls apart with a tremendous crash and all the gingerbread boys and girls who make up the palings of the fence around the Witch's cottage turn into living children once more and rejoice in their release. Father and mother appear to embrace their little ones, and the curtain falls on the hymn of praise to the Heavenly Father for His help in time of need, in which all join.

F. H. M.

An opera that has lived two lives in New York is *Hänsel und Gretel*. It had enjoyed great success in Europe. The novelty of an opera about children for children which appealed, nevertheless, to their elders had made it stand out particularly. In due course Sir Augustus Harris, the well-known London manager, who had earned for himself an enviable reputation by presenting opera at Drury Lane and later at Covent Garden, conceived the idea of taking *Hänsel und Gretel* to America. He decided to use an English version and he secured the services of Anton Seidl as musical director. So he gathered together a company of singers and launched his production at Daly's Theatre on October 8, 1895. One singer already well known to New York audiences was in the cast, Louise Meisslinger. Another singer who was to serve the Metropolitan in minor roles, Jacques Bars, appeared as the father Peter. The remaining singers were Marie Elba (Hänsel), Jeanne Douste (Gretel), Alice Gordon (the mother Gertrude), Cécile Brani (the Sandman), and Edith Johnston (the Dewman).

According to the *New York Herald* of the following day:

When Sir Augustus stepped in front of the curtain at Daly's Theatre last evening and in an amusing speech impressed upon his listeners that in *Hänsel und Gretel* he had brought to this country not only a novelty but what was abroad considered the most important lyric work of the last decade, he told the truth if ever a man did.

But telling the truth was not all of Sir Augustus' story. He electrified some of his hearers by referring to the composer as "Mr. Humperdinckel" and the score as some "beautiful music composed for this occasion." For all the gaiety and the satisfactions of the said occasion, it seems to be true that, in spite of the collaboration of Seidl, the production as a whole was below New York's standards, and it was with difficulty that the opera was kept on for a run of six weeks.

Not until November 25, 1906, was it revived in New York. Then there was an authentic performance. Heinrich Conried, the director at the Metropolitan Opera House, put it on there in the original German with a remarkable cast and Alfred Hertz to conduct. Hänsel was allotted to Lina Abarbanell, who later was to add greatly to her fame by appearing in the operetta, *Madame Sherry*. Bella Alten was the Gretel, playing in the right spirit of childish gaiety. Otto Goritz and Marion Weed proved to be excellent as the anxious father and mother of the babes in the woods, and no less an artist than Louise Homer impersonated the Witch. The verdict was that her make-up alone would have assured her success and that most resourcefully she matched her acting with her make-up. There were those, however, who found that her singing could not quite disguise the natural beauty of her voice and that to hear her opulent tones issuing from the toothless mouth of the "Knusperhexe" gave the listener a curious sensation that Witch and singer were not one and the same person.

Humperdinck had had the singular good fortune in the winter of 1880 at Naples to make the acquaintance of Richard Wagner. The manner of the introduction was unique. Humperdinck had no letter or other word of recommendation to Wagner, so he merely called at his house and sent in a card bearing the inscription "Companion of the Order of The Grail." This "Order" consisted of young musicians in Munich who had united in the interest of Wagner's music in general and of the projected *Parsifal* in particular. The inscription amused Wagner, who received Humperdinck cordially. An association resulted which gave Humperdinck real prominence in the preparations for the world première of *Parsifal* at Bayreuth in the summer of 1882. For one thing, he copied a large part of the score as rapidly as Wagner would give him the completed pages, learning, he said later, "more about orchestration in a few weeks than he could have learned at the conservatory in as many years." He also took charge of the Grail choir, selecting the best voices among the schoolboys of Bayreuth.

But the most amazing incident of Humperdinck's collaboration with Wagner had to do with the "Transformation" scene in the first act of *Parsifal*. The revolving scenery did not move fast enough to keep pace with the corresponding music, which came to a halt before the "Transformation" was complete. Repeated efforts failed to remedy the defect, and finally Wagner, exhausted from his work, announced in a rage that he was done forever with the whole thing. If he had stuck by his words, what would have become of *Parsifal* or, at any rate, of the "Transformation" accompanying the promenade of the Guileless Fool and his mentor Gurnemanz? Humperdinck quietly saved the day by writing the few additional measures that were needed. Timidly he took them to the irate Wagner, and Wagner, as it happened, sealed them with his approval! Later, however, means were found to accelerate the "Transformation," and the Humperdinck addition to the score was not needed. The death of Wagner in the winter of 1883 was a personal blow to Humperdinck. We find him by 1890 a resigned and inconspicuous teacher at the Hoch Conservatory at Frankfort-on-the-Main, his days of Wagnerian collaboration only a treasured memory.

But in another year aid came suddenly from his sister, Frau Adelheid Wette. Frau Wette had hit upon the idea of writing a children's play for use by their own family, and she asked her brother to compose a tune for it. What he supplied so delighted her that her mind leapt to the larger idea of a little opera about Hänsel and Gretel that she and her brother should write together for a theatre in the home. Humperdinck applied himself to the task, which interested him more and more as he worked at it, and eventually the score grew to exceed the confines of a production for children. The little piece for the family circle thus assumed the full-grown proportions of an opera. Begun in 1891, the entire score, including the orchestration, was finished before the end of 1892.

Now came the inevitable problem of obtaining a production. Humperdinck with characteristic modesty first sought to place the work at Gotha, but there the management turned it down. Luckily, however, it came to the attention of Hermann Levy, the conductor of *Parsifal* from the beginning, who at that time was musical director in Munich. Levy was so delighted with the score that he decided on it forthwith for production at the Munich Court Opera. Shortly afterwards no less a personage than Richard Strauss also accepted it for Weimar, where he was then chief Kapellmeister. As things turned out, the Weimar production on December 23, 1893, was the first on any stage, since the Munich performance had had to be postponed. We are told, though, that only Strauss of the Weimar organization regarded the work seriously.

Nevertheless and notwithstanding, the success of *Hänsel und Gretel* at Weimar and soon afterwards at Munich was emphatic. Other cities took it up, and so began a vogue that has lasted till this day. The London première on December 26, 1894, prepared the way for its coming to America.

P. S.

Ruggiero Leoncavallo

(Naples, Mar. 8, 1858–Aug. 9, 1919, Montecatini, Italy)

Leoncavallo was the son of a magistrate. His musical studies began with the pianoforte, which he learnt, first, from a musician named Siri, and afterwards from Simonetti, a teacher of some repute at Naples, the author of an "Enciclopedia del pianista." In due course Leoncavallo was admitted to the Neapolitan Conservatoire, where he became the pupil of Beniamino Cesi for the piano, of Michele Ruta for harmony, and of Lauro Rossi for composition.

At the age of 18 he left the Conservatoire with the diploma of "maestro," and set to work upon an opera. His subject was the tragic story of Chatterton, the libretto being an adaptation of Alfred de Vigny's drama. At Bologna, whither he had gone to attend the lectures of the famous poet and littérateur Carducci, he completed the opera and arranged for its production, but at the last moment the impresario decamped, leaving the unfortunate composer almost penniless. In despair Leoncavallo was compelled to undertake any work that would keep him from starvation. He gave lessons in singing and in piano-playing, and played accompaniments at café-concerts. In the latter capacity he travelled far, visiting England, France, Holland and Germany, and going even as far as Cairo. After many years' wandering he returned to Italy, and presented himself to the house of Ricordi, with the scenario of a vast trilogy dealing with the history of the Renaissance in Italy, for which he had already completed the libretto of the first section, *I Medici*. The latter was accepted, and in a year Leoncavallo had finished the music.

For three years he waited vainly in the hope of seeing his opera produced, and then betook himself in despair to the rival house of Sonzogno. Here he was well received, and for this firm he wrote his 2-act opera *Pagliacci,* which was produced at the Teatro dal Verme, Milan, on May 21, 1892, with very great success. Leoncavallo's name soon became famous throughout Italy, and on Nov. 10, 1893, his *Medici,* the first section of his Renaissance trilogy, "Crepusculum," was produced at the Teatro dal Verme. The work, which deals with the Pazzi conspiracy and the murder of Giuliano de' Medici, was a failure; and the composer, discouraged by its unfavourable reception, never completed, or at any rate never published, the remaining sections of the trilogy, "Savonarola" and "Cesare Borgia." Leoncavallo's early opera, *Chatterton,* which was finally given at the Teatro Nazionale, Rome, on Mar. 10, 1896, was no more successful than *I Medici,* but *La Bohème* (Teatro della Fenice, Venice, May 6, 1897), an adaptation of Henri Murger's novel, was far more favourably received, although handicapped by inevitable comparisons with

Puccini's opera on the same subject, which had been produced with overwhelming success a few months earlier, and was actually being played to crowded audiences at another theatre in Venice at the same time.

Leoncavallo's next opera, *Zaza,* an adaptation of the play by Berton and Simon, was produced at the Teatro Lirico, Milan, on Nov. 10, 1900, with fair success, and has subsequently been performed in Germany, Holland and Paris. *Der Roland* was written in response to a commission of the German Emperor, Wilhelm II, who heard *I Medici* in Berlin in 1894, and believed that in the Italian poet and musician he had found a bard worthy of celebrating the glory of the house of Hohenzollern, as in *I Medici* he had celebrated that of the great Florentine family. *Der Roland* is founded upon Willibald Alexis's romance, "Der Roland von Berlin," which deals with the subjugation of Berlin by the Elector Frederick II. Of this work an Italian translation was made for Leoncavallo's benefit by the Emperor's orders, from which he constructed his own libretto. This, after the music was finished, was translated back into German by Georg Droescher, and the opera was produced at the Royal Opera House in Berlin, on Dec. 13, 1904. In spite of the patronage of the Emperor, and the favour of the Court, *Der Roland* attained no permanent success. It was, in fact, in his most ambitious works, such as this and *I Medici,* that Leoncavallo showed to least advantage. In operas of the type of *Zaza* and *Pagliacci,* his strong feeling for theatrical effect served him well, but his musical inspiration was singularly deficient, and his more pretentious works were hardly more than strings of ill-digested reminiscences.

In 1910 two new operas by him were produced in Rome within four days of each other, *Maia* in 3 acts, libretto by Paul de Choudens, at the Costanzi Theatre, Jan. 15, 1910; and *Malbruk,* a comic opera in 3 acts, libretto by Signor Nessi, at the Teatro Nazionale, on Jan. 19.

Later works, several of them no more than operettas of slight quality, were *I Zingari* (London, 1912), *La reginalla delle rose* (Rome, 1912), *Are You There?* (London, 1913), *La Candidata* (Rome, 1915), *Goffredo Mameli* (Genoa, 1916), *Prestami tua moglie* (Montecatini, 1916), *Edipo Re* (Chicago, 1920).

As a librettist Leoncavallo showed uncommon dramatic ability. Not only did he write the libretti for his own operas, but, like Boïto, he occasionally placed his talent at the service of his friends, as in the case, for instance, of *Mario Wetter,* an opera by the Portuguese composer, Augusto Machado. Apart from his operatic works, Leoncavallo was the composer of a symphonic poem, "Serafita," founded upon Balzac's novel, and of a ballet entitled "La Vita d'una Marionetta."

R. A. S.

Pagliacci

[Strolling Clowns]

DRAMA IN 2 ACTS

Book by the COMPOSER

First performance: Teatro dal Verme, Milan, May 21, 1892

CHARACTERS

Canio, master of the troupe of street
  players (Punchinello),* TENOR
Nedda, his wife (Columbine), SOPRANO
Tonio, a clown (Taddeo), BARITONE

Silvio, a villager, BARITONE
Beppe, a clown (Harlequin), TENOR
Villagers and Peasants

The action takes place in the village of Montalto, in Calabria, on the Feast of the Assumption

Before the curtain rises Tonio prepares the audience for the performance to be given with his Prologue song, "A Word," which explains the play is from life, declares actors are human beings with passions like their own, and that the author has tried to express them.

Wandering players enter a Calabrian village to blare of trumpets, cries of children and curiosity seekers, and Canio, manager of the troupe, announces a performance that evening. He descends from the chariot, but when Tonio helps down Nedda, Canio's wife, he gets a box on the ear, to which he replies with a muttered curse. It is not a happy theatrical family. Canio adores his wife (who betrays him with Silvio, a young villager) and is passionately jealous of her. When bystanders, however, who have noticed the incident utter dubious jests, he shows how deeply he resents suspicion of his wife's faithfulness.

While the vesper bells call the villagers to church, Canio and Beppo drink in the tavern, while Nedda ("Bird Song") expresses her yearning for the golden freedom which would let her follow the urge of her heart. Her song lures Tonio, the misshapen clown, to her, and when his impudent suit for favor from his master's wife is chastised by a blow of the whip, he threatens to betray her illicit love affair. Now

---

* The word *pagliaccio* is sometimes translated "Punchinello," sometimes "clown," meaning not clown in the sense of a circus performer, but the buffoon who received all the "hard knocks" in old Italian comedy; the plural, *pagliacci,* refers to the whole group of actors playing such a comedy. Moreover, the final exclamation, *"La commedia e finita!"* (The comedy is ended!"), is said to have been almost the last speech of the dying Beethoven. The tragedy becomes all the more poignant since it strikes Canio, who is compelled to make others laugh even though his heart breaks; an old but ever effective dramatic device. . . . The word *"pagliacci"* means literally "chopped straws," referring to the straws which strolling players wore in their hats.

205

Silvio comes to persuade Nedda to give over the player's chariot and flee with him that night. She agrees. But they have been overheard. Tonio and Canio (whom he has brought along) interrupt the lovers only in time to see an unknown leap the wall. While Tonio boasts his ignoble revenge, Beppo protects Nedda from Canio's dagger. But the villagers are hurrying to the performance. His heart torn with rage and despair Canio must play the buffoon and rouse laughter with tears in his eyes. He is not a man (as he explains in the moving song "Ridi, pagliacci") but a toy to amuse the mob.

Preceded by the Intermezzo which echoes the warning of the Prologue—that the author is telling a true tale—the comedians begin the "Comedy of Columbine" on their strollers' stage. Curiously enough, its incidents parallel the tragedy of the players' real lives. Columbine (Nedda) signs to Harlequin (Beppo) that he may visit her. And Taddeo's clownish advances end in his being driven off by Harlequin. But no sooner do the lovers sit down together than he announces Columbine's husband, the Clown, who has discovered a man in the house. The allusions of the play are bitter realities to Canio, and losing self-control he fills the audience with horror in what they think his superb acting of the injured husband's part. Nedda plays her part in an agony of terror and suddenly—the play passes from comedy to tragedy! Canio demands her lover's name. When she refuses it he stabs her. Calling on Silvio as she dies, he hurries to her aid only to be struck down in turn, while the murderer calls out with sinister calm to the excited auditors: "The play is over!"

F. H. M.

There are some striking parallels in the histories of *Pagliacci* and its perennial teammate, *Cavalleria Rusticana*. Both were the works of young, unknown composers eking out wretched lives with hack work. Each achieved an early reputation and lifelong affluence for its creator. Neither composer was ever again able remotely to equal the initial success. Both operas were published by the firm of Sonzogno. Both operas are, of course, examples par excellence of what is called "verism," and as such both have been repeatedly scorned by critics, particularly German critics and others who look to Germany for critical principles. Despite all the vilification, they have both remained enormously popular, and in Germany itself in the year 1938 . . . *Pagliacci* was performed more often than any other grand opera. There it is called *Bajazzo*.

Pagliacci, as a matter of fact, was directly inspired by the success of *Cavalleria,* which had won a prize from Sonzogno in a competition for one-act operas. Leoncavallo, the son of a circuit judge, had been something of a prodigy. At sixteen he had been graduated from the Naples Conservatory; at twenty he had earned the degree of doctor of letters from the University of Bologna. Like Wagner, he considered himself just as much a man of letters as a musician, and he wrote the librettos for most of his own works. On one occasion he said that he did not see how one could set anyone else's words successfully—a remark aimed, apparently, at his rivals Mascagni and Puccini, for he must have forgotten the example of the revered Verdi when he made it.

Leoncavallo's double talent, however, had not enabled him to make a good living. He had tried his hand at accompanying, at being a pianist in Egypt (where he had had to leave rather hurriedly), at operatic coaching. None afforded him a successful livelihood, and for a time he had even been a café pianist. He had great ambitions, however, and got the publisher Ricordi to listen to him read *I Medici,* the first work in a never-completed trilogy meant to glorify the Italian Renaissance, just as Wagner had glorified Teutonic mythology. Ricordi offered him twenty-four hundred francs to compose the music, which he did within a year; but this opera never saw the stage till after the success of *Pagliacci,* and then it was a failure.

So Leoncavallo went back to coaching opera singers till Mascagni had his great success, when he decided on one more try. He wrote the book and composed the music for *Pagliacci* in the space of five months, and Sonzogno accepted it for both publication and production after reading only the libretto. Maybe the offer of the great baritone Victor Maurel, a friend of Leoncavallo's, to create the role of Tonio had something to do with the speedy acceptance. It was produced first at the Teatro dal Verme in Milan on May 21, 1892, when Leoncavallo was thirty-four, and it was an immediate and enormous success. That was just two years and four days after the *première* of its teammate, *Cavalleria Rusticana,* in Rome.

The central dramatic idea of *Pagliacci*—the play-within-a-play during which a real murder of revenge is committed—is at least as old as Thomas Kyd's sixteenth-century "Spanish Tragedie." As it happens, Leoncavallo's story is, according to his own account, based on an actual case tried before his father in Calabria, where the opera is laid. The Canio of real life (whose name was Alessandro) exclaimed after the trial that he'd do it all over again if he had to. Thereupon he received a prison sentence for his double murder, on the expiration of which he became a domestic in the household of a Baroness Sproniere.

The success of the opera was so great that the French dramatist Catulle Mendès threatened suit for plagiarism because his play, "La Femme de Tabarin," with incidental music by Chabrier, had used a similar dramatic device five years earlier. Leoncavallo pointed to a still older play by the Spanish dramatist Estebanez that had used this device, and then told the story of the genesis of his opera (which is based on a play he had written even earlier). Mendès withdrew.

Given the crude, violent, elemental emotions of this story of peasant love and hate, it is difficult to understand the hoity-toity criticism leveled at the opera. The libretto is a little masterpiece of concise, clear story-telling. With the exception of the "Bell Chorus," there is scarcely a line which does not contribute to the painting of character or the advancement of the plot. Even this chorus may be excused on the ground that it denotes the passing of time, while Leoncavallo used to defend it for being a piece of genuine local color.

The music is vigorous and broadly colored, the use of specific themes for specific emotions transparently obvious (though not so obvious that any commentary I have read has succeeded in pointing out all of them). To tell this sort of tale, this is the right sort of music. What do the critics want? Debussyan pastels? Wagnerian grandeur? Gluck's nobility or Mozart's sweetness? *Pagliacci* is all of a piece, a sure dramatic blow between the eyes. The opera public of every country has found it so and therefore given it the ultimate accolade of paying over and over again to hear it. That, in the last analysis—according to both Verdi and Leoncavallo—is the one true test of the merit of an opera.

H. W. S.

The public is so used to consider the eternal twins of opera as a single evening's entertainment that it often forgets the difference between *Cavalleria Rusticana* and *Pagliacci*.

The Mascagni tragedy, which is usually performed first, saw the footlights two years before Leoncavallo's opera. . . . The composer was teaching a variety of instruments in the little town of Cerignola at the time, with especial emphasis on the brass. Thus it is natural that there is a generous use of brass in the score.

At twenty-seven, Mascagni was not the expert in orchestration he later became, yet never again did he win the popularity he achieved with this early work. Perhaps it was the instinct which led him to place the crisis of his drama off stage, which has proved so effective; perhaps it was the insertion of the *Intermezzo,* at the suggestion of the opera's first conductor, Leopoldo Mugnone. But in my opinion, the success of the opera is largely due to its prodigal display of eloquent arias: the aria, prayer and two duets for the soprano, the "Siciliana," "Brindisi" and two duets for the tenor, the song and duet for the baritone, and the charming, if brief air for the mezzo. The choruses in themselves are as lavish as in many a full length opera.

Pagliacci is even more imperfect than *Cavalleria* from the point of view of orchestration, and yet, as Toscanini once told me, if it were corrected, the public would probably not accept it.

It is appropriately chosen to conclude the evening because of its variety, pace, and comedy. When the curtain rises on *Pagliacci,* one would hardly guess its tragic import, if one had not been warned of it in the Prologue. Even in the last scene, the realistic horror of the murder is tempered with prettiness.

The effectiveness of "Vesti la giubba" is a byword among dramatic tenors, and yet I have always secretly resented it because of the fact that five years earlier Verdi used the same musical phrase to which Leoncavallo set "Ridi Pagliaccio!" in the third act of his masterpiece *Otello* to the phrase "A terra! E piangi" and no one made any fuss about it at all!

Both operas deal with the same passionate people, both demonstrated the school of *verismo* which was relatively unexplored in the 'nineties; both are melodic. There, to my way of thinking, the likeness ceases. *Pagliacci* enjoys a liberal sprinkling of superficial musical virtues, superimposed on an excellent libretto. *Cavalleria Rusticana* is a rough diamond, but a pure one.

C. S.

(The immediate and sensational success of *Pagliacci* was due in no small part to its prologue, which, according to the great baritone, Victor Maurel, who sang it in the first presentation, was an afterthought, hurriedly confected in one night by Leoncavallo at Maurel's suggestion. A young conductor of promise officiated at this *première*, one Arturo Toscanini. The fame of *Pagliacci* spread over the musical world like the proverbial wildfire. The American *première*—a hurriedly prepared performance in English—took place at the Grand Opera House, New York, June 15, 1893. On the following Dec. 11 the work was produced at the Metropolitan Opera House, New York, with Nellie Melba as Nedda, Fernando de Lucia as Canio, and Mario Ancona as Tonio. —P. S.)

Like the earliest Metropolitan *Cavalleria*, *Pagliacci* was on a double bill with Gluck's *Orfeo,* but unlike *Cavalleria,* it was just short of a failure. Not until Caruso's assumption, on December 9, 1903, of the role of Canio, which he sang seventy-six times, could the opera be said really to have won New York. Since that notable performance, when Sembrich was the Nedda and Scotti the Tonio, *Pagliacci* has made up for lost time, and now stands fifth (tied with *Die Walküre*) in popularity in the Metropolitan roster. Jean de Reszke, singing in *Pagliacci* for the first and only time, at the Opéra in the fall of 1902, portrayed Canio in what proved to be his farewell to the stage. On January 13, 1910, Lee De Forest, from the stage of the Metropolitan, broadcast to his co-workers in New Jersey a portion of a Caruso *Pagliacci*. This is one of the earliest opera broadcasts on record.

W. B., H. W.

Pietro Mascagni

(Leghorn, Italy, Dec. 7, 1863–Aug. 2, 1945, Rome)

Mascagni's father, who was a baker, intended his son to be a lawyer, and discouraged his attempts to learn the rudiments of music. The budding composer, compelled to prosecute his musical studies by stealth, entered himself surreptitiously as a pupil at the Istituto Luigi Cherubini, where his principal instructor was Alfredo Soffredini. In due course Mascagni's father found out how his son was spending his leisure time, and the musical career of the future composer of *Cavalleria Rusticana* would therefore have come to an untimely close had it not been for the intervention of an amiable uncle, who came forward and offered to adopt the young musician. Transferred to his uncle's house, Mascagni devoted himself in earnest to music, and the first fruits of his labours appeared in the shape of a symphony in C minor for small orchestra, and a "Kyrie" written to celebrate the birthday of Cherubini, both of which were performed at the Istituto in 1879. These were followed after two years by "In Filanda," a cantata for solo voices and orchestra, which was favourably mentioned in a prize competition instituted by the International Exhibition of Music at Milan. These successes reconciled Mascagni's father to the idea of making his son a musician; and at the death of his uncle in 1881 the boy returned to his father's house, where he was allowed to pursue his musical studies in peace. His next composition was a setting of a translation of Schiller's "Ode to Joy," which was performed at the Teatro degli Avvalorati with so much success that Count Florestano de Larderel, a wealthy amateur, offered on the spot to pay for the composer's education at the Milan Conservatoire. Mascagni's career at Milan was not a success. In spite of the sympathy and encouragement of his teachers, among whom were Amilcare Ponchielli and Michele Saladino, he found the course of regular study insupportable. For some time he chafed silently against the trivial round of counterpoint and fugue, and eventually took French leave of his professors, joined a travelling operatic company in the capacity of conductor, and turned his back upon Milan to seek his fortune elsewhere. For many years he led a life of obscurity and privation, travelling through the length and breadth of Italy with one company after another. He had no spare time for composition, but doubtless gained much valuable experience in practical orchestration. After many wanderings Mascagni married and settled at Cerignola near Foggia, where he managed to make a meagre livelihood by giving pianoforte lessons and managing the municipal school of music.

From this obscurity he was suddenly rescued by the success of his one-act

opera, *Cavalleria Rusticana,* which won the first prize in a competition instituted in 1889 by the publisher Sonzogno, and was produced at the Costanzi
Theatre in Rome, May 17, 1890. The libretto was founded by Signori Menasci
and Targioni-Tozzetti upon a well-known story of Sicilian village life by
Giovanni Verga. The opera was received at its first performance with tumultuous applause, and the next day Mascagni awoke to find himself famous.
Cavalleria at once made the tour of Italy, and speedily crossed the Alps. It was
produced in Berlin in the summer of 1890, and in London, at the Shaftesbury
Theatre, under the management of Signor Lago in Oct. 1891. It was first performed in Paris at the Opéra-Comique, Jan. 19, 1892. Everywhere its success
was unquestionable. The public, tired, perhaps, of imitations of Wagner, welcomed the crisp action and direct emotional appeal of the little work. It became
the fashion, and was responsible for a mushroom crop of one-act melodramas.

Since the days of *Cavalleria* Mascagni's fame has steadily declined. His next
work, *L'amico Fritz* (Teatro Costanzi, Rome, Oct. 31, 1891), an adaptation
of Erckmann-Chatrian's well-known novel, made by Daspuro under the ana-
gram of P. Suardon, had more refinement than *Cavalleria,* and was more carefully written, but the composer scarcely attempted to fit his grandiose manner
to the exigencies of an idyll. *I Rantzau* (Teatro della Pergola, Florence, Nov.
10, 1892), another adaptation from Erckmann-Chatrian, by Menasci and Targioni-Tozzetti, was even less successful than *L'amico Fritz. Guglielmo Ratcliff*
(La Scala, Milan, Feb. 1895) was a work of the composer's student days, subsequently revised and rewritten. Mascagni had conceived the extraordinary
notion of setting to music a literal translation of Heine's gloomy tragedy, which
was alone sufficient to doom the work to failure, and his music did little to
relieve the tedium of the libretto. No less decisive was the failure of *Silvano*
(La Scala, Milan, Mar. 1895), a half-hearted bid for popularity in the composer's most hackneyed manner. Meanwhile (1895) Mascagni had been appointed director of the Conservatoire at Pesaro, where his next opera, *Zanetto,*
was produced, Mar. 2, 1896. *Zanetto* is slight in structure, being scored only
for strings and harp, but has considerably more refinement of thought and expression than is customary in Mascagni's work. *Iris* (Teatro Costanzi, Rome,
Nov. 22, 1898), on a Japanese subject, is handicapped by a singularly unpleasant libretto, but nevertheless has won more favour than any of the composer's
works since *Cavalleria.* It shows much skill in the handling of the orchestra,
but its lack of original invention is conspicuous. Mascagni's idea of producing
his next work, *Le maschere* (Jan. 17, 1901), simultaneously in seven different
cities, was a piece of audacious impertinence; but no amount of advertisement
could galvanise *Le maschere* into a success. At Milan, Venice, Verona, Naples
and Turin it was soundly hissed, while at Genoa the audience would not even
allow the performance to be finished. Only at Rome was it received with any
degree of favour. *Amica* (Monte Carlo, Mar. 1905), though produced in more
modest fashion, shared the fate of its predecessor.

Mascagni wrote a cantata for the Leopardi centenary, which was performed at Recanati in 1898, and incidental music for Hall Caine's play, "The Eternal City," which was produced at His Majesty's Theatre, London, in October 1902. Later operas of Mascagni are: *Isabeau* (libretto by Illica), first performed at Buenos Aires, 1911; *Parisina* (on a text by D'Annunzio), given at Milan, 1913; *Lodoletta* (text by G. Forzano), produced at Rome, 1917, and *Il Piccolo Marat* (text by G. Forzano and Giovanni Targioni-Tozzetti), given at Rome, 1921. The composer has also written an operetta in 3 acts, entitled *Si,* on a book supplied by C. Lombardo and A. Franci, which was first produced at Rome in 1919. A Requiem in memory of King Humbert was performed in the Pantheon at Rome in 1900. There exists also a "Rapsodia satanica," a symphonic poem written for a film.

Mascagni has won some fame as a conductor, chiefly owing to repeated tours with specially chosen orchestras through the cities of Europe and America. A protracted tour in the United States in 1903 cost him his place at Pesaro.

Mascagni's reputation rests almost entirely upon *Cavalleria Rusticana.* It owes much to its direct if somewhat brutal libretto, but the music undeniably shows a natural instinct for theatrical effect, and it boasts plenty of catchy, commonplace tunes. The speedy exhaustion of a shallow vein of musical invention, together with the carelessness engendered by a dangerously sudden success, is in great part responsible for the complete collapse of what at one time seemed a talent of bright promise.

R. A. S.

Cavalleria Rusticana

[Rustic Chivalry]

MELODRAMA IN 1 ACT

Book by G. TARGIONI-TOZZETTI and G. MENASCI, based on a tale
by GIOVANNI VERGA

First performance: Teatro Costanzi, Rome, May 17, 1890

CHARACTERS

Santuzza, a village girl in love with
Turiddu, SOPRANO
Lola, wife of Alfio, MEZZO-SOPRANO
Turiddu, a young soldier, TENOR

Alfio, a teamster, BARITONE
Mamma Lucia, mother of Turiddu,
CONTRALTO
Chorus of Peasants and Villagers

The action takes place in a Sicilian village in the latter part of the nineteenth century

It is Easter morning in a Sicilian village, yet the heart of Santuzza, a young peasant girl, knows no Easter peace, for Turiddu (before the curtain rises his voice is heard serenading handsome Lola, Alfio's wife) has robbed her of her honor. Then the deceiver left her to court coquettish Lola whose lover he had been, but who jilted him to marry the carter. The Easter message sounds from the church door, where Santuzza waits to beg her betrayer to make her an honest woman. He laughs at her passionate prayers and when Lola appears (to the accompaniment of a frivolous waltz tune) flings her aside so brutally that she rolls down the church steps as he follows Lola into church to hear Easter Mass. At that moment unsuspecting Alfio comes by. Santuzza reveals the story of his shame and his vow of vengeance makes her realize too late what she has done. (In effective contrast to the tragic catastrophe brewing, the Intermezzo Sinfonico depicts the idyllic peace of the sunny Easter morning.) Mass is over, gaily the drinking chorus rings out in Mother Lucia's inn. Alfio mingles somberly with the others. When he refuses the wine Turiddu offers, Turiddu senses he knows all. A bite in Alfio's right ear shows the betrayer is ready for the duel with knives. With a tearful farewell from his mother, to whom he commends hapless Santuzza, he rushes off. The tense moments of waiting end when the peasants announce Turiddu's death. Alfio's honor is avenged.

F. H. M.

By an operatic "double bill" one can mean dozens of different combinations. By "The Double Bill" one means *Cavalleria Rusticana* and *Pagliacci* and nothing else. It is perhaps the most conspicuous example in music if not of angelic then certainly of indissoluble wedlock. Countless attempts have been made to divorce the pair but in vain. The two works attract each other like some chemical elements. They are what Goethe would call "elective affinities."

It almost seems strange to us that there could ever have been a time in the history of opera when there was no *Cavalleria* and *Pagliacci*. Or else, that the one could have existed without the other. Yet as popular, let alone immortal operas go, they are not old—just a little over fifty. *Pagliacci* even came into the world something like two years *after* its twin. Actually, it is wrong to think of the clown's tragedy as the brother or even the mate of its partner. In most respects it is the offspring of *Cavalleria*. It is different, yet the same. Mascagni's opera could—and did—materialize without Leoncavallo's. Not so the reverse.

So fixed are the two little dramas in the operatic repertory of the world, so habituated has the public become to every feature of them, that it is difficult to understand and appreciate the sensation they first caused. Their subject matter may have been more or less new, with its emphasis on truthfulness to life and that *verismo* which strangely enough had invariably to be a violent, bloody and unappetizing kind of truth. Their brevity was, indeed, something of a departure, though plenty of short operas had been composed before their day. Concision of a sort they undoubtedly exhibited. But even a superficial scrutiny of both *Cavalleria* and *Pagliacci* will show that their novelty is—and, for that matter, always was—more apparent than real.

Strip *Cavalleria* of its paddings, fillings and purely decorative externals, and little more than a small kernel of drama remains. And even this little measure of drama, in spite of the emotional clash it publishes, develops with little outward show of action. *Pagliacci* is rather fuller, more plastic and visual in this regard, though the constructive formulas it operates turn out to be pretty much the same. Nevertheless, both works are kept alive by their rough vitality, their melodic abundance, their emotional turbulence and a use of contrasts that betrays at almost every turn the practiced craftsmen of the theatre.

Cavalleria is cruder and less sophisticated than *Pagliacci* which discloses, for its part, a smoother musical texture and a less definite originality. Some of *Pagliacci* comes (in disguise, to be sure) from Wagner, some of it from other recognizable sources. *Cavalleria* is much less derivative and its melodic idiom does not perceptibly owe anything to anyone unless it be to Italian folk song. Indeed, if there is such a thing as an Italian folk-opera, *Cavalleria Rusticana* is its very model, Verdi and Rossini notwithstanding!

Possibly even better than Leoncavallo, Mascagni grasped the deep artistic truth that action on the stage is not so important in opera as action in the music. It is the seething action in the score cunningly punctuated with periods of repose or alleviation that resolves whatever problems *Cavalleria* may offer.

H. F. P.

We realize with difficulty today what the emergence of *Cavalleria Rusticana* meant to the world in 1890. It was the sudden blazing of a new star in a murky sky. To understand the full force of the phenomenon we must recall the special conditions prevailing at the time operatically. Germany and Italy, the two chief sources of opera for international consumption, were threatening famine. In Germany Wagner had been dead for more than seven years and Richard Strauss had yet to come along with a revivifying stage work. In Italy the grand old Verdi was approaching the end of his illustrious career and Puccini, still a little-known parochial figure, could point only to a mild success with *Le Villi* and an emphatic failure with *Edgar*.

It is true that Massenet and Saint-Saëns had become vital figures in France, but, with other countries, except Belgium, they were still lingering on the threshold. As for Russia, the opening to the western world of its great treasury of operatic riches had scarcely been adumbrated. England and the United States simply did not count.

Into this stagnant twilight of opera burst *Cavalleria Rusticana,* its one impetuous act aflame with the fierce emotions of rude, passionate peasants and its score a veriable volcano of sun-shot, sultry melody. What mattered it that the composer had been utterly unknown and that his brief "melodramma" had resulted from the offer of a prize for a one-acter by the publishing house of Sonzogno? Almost overnight the name of Pietro Mascagni became a household word, and as *Cavalleria Rusticana* raced over the world like wildfire the peoples of the earth were described as suffering from "an acute attack of Mascagnitis."

The pitch of excitement reached in this country before the opera had crossed the Atlantic may be gathered from a glance at the programs of the time. Such was the curiosity aroused in Boston, for instance, that the Boston Symphony Orchestra went so far as to perform for its patrons the prelude and the intermezzo from the sensational new work. Mme. Lillian Nordica, heading a concert company of her own, put on her programs Santuzza's aria "Voi lo sapete" and the duets for Santuzza and Turiddu and for Santuzza and Alfio. But the tug of war came over the staging of *Cavalleria* in New York.

Rudolph Aronson and Oscar Hammerstein both announced the work for production in the autumn of 1891. Aronson proposed opening the season at the Casino with it, intending thus to alter the character of entertainment with which that house was associated. Hammerstein's difficulty was that he had no theatre in readiness. Nevertheless, the two men fought hard to see which should have the honor of breasting the tape. Both performances took place on October 1. Aronson gave at the Casino in the afternoon what he termed a "dress rehearsal." Nevertheless, the "rehearsal" was a real stage performance, and it is amusing to know that Heinrich Conried, who, after running a German theatre in Irving Place, became general manager of the Metropolitan Opera House, was the stage director. The musical director was Gustav Kerker.

All of the five singing-actors enjoyed more or less prominence in this country at one time or another. They were Laura Bellini (Santuzza), Grace Golden (Lola), Helene von Doenhoff (Mama Lucia), Charles Bassett (Turiddu), and William Pruette (Alfio).

Hammerstein's production, that evening, had to put up with the Lenox Lyceum—a minor and ill-equipped concert hall, having a canvas proscenium and small accommodation for scenery. However, the orchestra, conducted by Adolph Neuendorff, was warmly praised, and at the head of the cast was Neuendorff's wife, Georgine von Januschoffsky, as Santuzza. Neuendorff, pianist, violinist, conductor, composer, was a musician of wide and varied experience. He had conducted the first performances in America of *Lohengrin*, at the Stadt Theatre, New York, in 1871, and of *Die Walküre*, at the Academy of Music, New York, in 1877, and for a time he had conducted the concerts of the New York Philharmonic Society. Mme. von Januschoffsky, who had been a leading singer at the Vienna Court Opera, later was heard at the Metropolitan Opera House as Isolde and Brünnhilde, and later still, under the name of Neuendorff, in minor rôles. The other parts were filled by Mrs. Pemberton Hincks (Lola), Jennie Bohner (Mama Lucia), Payne Clark (Turiddu), and Hermon Gerold (Alfio).

Neither Aronson nor Hammerstein, however, really introduced *Cavalleria Rusticana* to America. The credit for that deed goes to Gustav Hinrichs, who gave it at the Grand Opera House, Philadelphia, on September 9, 1891. Minnie Hauk, supported by her own company, followed suit at Chicago on September 30.

Both Aronson and Hammerstein used English texts for their presentations. The first *Cavalleria Rusticana* at the Metropolitan Opera House, on December 30, 1891, was sung in the original Italian. The beautiful Emma Eames appeared as Santuzza, a rôle for which she was unfitted temperamentally. Fun was made of the accordion-pleated skirt with which she decked out the Sicilian village girl. But more fun was made of the tenor Valero, who impersonated Turiddu. It seems that for the "Siciliano," which Turiddu sings behind the curtain in the midst of the prelude as an unseen serenade to Lola, the curtain was lifted contrary to the intentions of librettists and composer in order to give the tenor's voice a better opportunity to resound throughout the house. The singer, however, was modestly concealed by Lola's dwelling, but not modestly enough to prevent him from stepping out into the open to acknowledge the applause. Then the curtain was lowered and the prelude proceeded.

Inasmuch as *Pagliacci* did not yet exist to share gory brackets with *Cavalleria Rusticana*, no less a classic than Gluck's *Orfeo* preceded *Cavalleria* at its Metropolitan première. Aronson at the Casino had prefaced it with Carl Zeller's two-act comic opera *Der Vogelhändler* under the English title of "The Tyrolean."

As a matter of fact, the great days of *Cavalleria Rusticana* at the Metropolitan did not begin till Emma Calvé assumed the rôle of Santuzza when she made her American début on November 29, 1893. That was a momentous occasion in other respects. Gounod's charming little opera *Philémon et Baucis* preceded the Mascagni thriller in the double bill, providing American débuts for Sigrid Arnoldson, a fine Swedish soprano, as Baucis and for the great French basso, Pol Plançon as Jupiter. (Yet, in spite of the success won by Calvé, it has been rumored that the management would have sent her back to Europe if on the December following she had not triumphed sensationally as Carmen.)

As nearly an ideal production as *Cavalleria Rusticana* is likely ever to enjoy was afforded at the Metropolitan in the season of 1908–09, the first showing occurring on December 17, 1908 (the prefatory work on this occasion being *Le Villi,* an American première). Emmy Destinn sang Santuzza, Maria Gay Lola, Marie Mattfeld Mama Lucia, Enrico Caruso Turiddu, and Pasquale Amato Alfio. And above all, Arturo Toscanini conducted.

P. S.

Jules Massenet

(Montaud [Loire], France, May 12, 1842–Aug. 13, 1912, Paris)

He [Massenet] was the youngest son of a former army officer under the First Empire who had become an ironmaster in the vicinity of Saint-Étienne, an important metallurgical centre of the Loire. Owing to ill-health, the father was obliged to abandon this post and the family moved to Paris when the future composer was six years old. His mother provided the family's meagre income by giving piano lessons, and from her he learned to play this instrument. At the age of eleven he entered the Conservatoire, where his first teachers were Adolphe Laurent for piano and Savard for solfège. In 1860 he joined Reber's harmony class, and then completed his studies in composition under Ambroise Thomas. In 1863, at the age of 21, he obtained the First Prize for Fugue, and then won the Grand Prix de Rome with his cantata "David Rizzio." To help support himself while attending the Conservatoire, he had played the drum in the orchestra of the Théâtre Lyrique three nights a week.

He spent three years at Rome, and before returning to Paris in 1866 he married one of his piano-pupils, Mlle. Sainte-Marie. Through the influence of Thomas he succeeded in having his one-act opera, *La Grand'tante,* produced at the Opéra-Comique in 1867. In the same year the Pasdeloup Orchestra played his First Suite for orchestra at one of the Concerts Populaires. About this time he also composed two song-cycles, "Poème d'Avril" and "Poème du Souvenir," published by Hartmann. Following the Franco-Prussian War (in which he served as a member of the National Guard during the siege of Paris), he composed an opera, *Don César de Bazan,* which was produced at the Opéra-Comique (Nov. 30, 1872) with fair success.

In the meantime, he had taken part in a competition sponsored by the Department of Fine Arts for the best setting of an operatic libretto entitled "La Coupe du Roi de Thulé." He was not awarded the prize, because the jury considered that his music was not suitable to the exigencies of the theatre. Nevertheless, he used some of the music in his next opera, *Le Roi de Lahore* (Opéra, April 27, 1877). Before the production of this work he composed incidental music for Leconte de Lisle's drama, "Les Erinnyes" (1873), two orchestral suites, two overtures, choral works, songs and piano pieces, besides the oratorios or sacred dramas, "Marie-Magdeleine" (1873) and "Ève" (1875), both of which were very successful. A later work in the same style, *La Vierge* (1880), proved a failure.

The first of the operas on which his reputation rests, *Hérodiade,* was produced at Brussels in 1881 and three years later was given at the Italian Opera in Paris with Victor Maurel and the de Reszke brothers in the cast. In 1903 it was revived at the Théâtre Lyrique de la Gaieté with Emma Calvé as Salome, and was subsequently given in London and New York. Not until 1921, however, did it reach the Paris Opéra. Massenet continued to write operas without interruption right up to the time of his death, producing 25 works in this form. Of these, the best-known are *Manon* (1884), *Le Cid* (1885), *Esclarmonde* (1889), *Werther* (1892), *Thaïs* (1894), *Sapho* (1897), *Le Jongleur de Notre-Dame* (1902) and *Don Quichotte* (1910). Most of these have held the stage, at least in France, where Massenet enjoyed tremendous popularity. The work by which he is known to opera-goers throughout the world is *Manon,* based on the famous novel by the Abbé Prévost, "Manon Lescaut." Auber and Puccini also wrote operas based on this novel, while Halévy used the subject for a ballet.

Massenet's *Manon* was produced at the Opéra-Comique, Paris, on Jan. 19, 1884. . . . It was given in English by the Carl Rosa Company at Liverpool on Jan. 17, 1885, and in French at Covent Garden on May 19, 1891. The first American performance took place at the Academy of Music, New York, on Dec. 23, 1885. It is one of the most popular operas ever written, and many famous singers have appeared in its two principal roles, Manon (soprano) and Des Grieux (tenor). An innovation which Massenet introduced into this work was that of replacing the *recitativo secco* by dialogue spoken over a subdued orchestral accompaniment. He borrowed the device of the leitmotiv from Wagner, but used it in a thoroughly French manner that stems from Gounod. *Manon* reveals all the qualities and limitations of Massenet's style: its melodies are agreeable and very singable, but border on the sentimentally trite; the orchestration is varied and effective, but lacking in character and originality; the opera lives less by reason of its dramatic quality than by the atmosphere of discreet voluptuousness in which the composer has enveloped the story of the young lovers. Massenet was not a great composer; but it is likely that *Manon* will outlive many a work of more pretentious nature, because it possesses the potent quality of charm.

From 1878 to 1896 Massenet was professor of advanced composition at the Conservatoire. Among his pupils were Alfred Bruneau, Gustave Charpentier, Gabriel Pierné, Xavier Leroux and Paul Vidal. In 1878, at the age of 36, he was elected to the Académie des Beaux-Arts, being the youngest member ever elected to that body. He was made a Chevalier of the Légion d'Honneur in 1876 and attained the rank of Grand-Officier in 1899. In 1934 a bust of the composer was unveiled in the foyer of the Opéra-Comique. On this occasion, Feodor Chaliapin took part in a performance of *Don Quichotte,* a role which he had created at Monte Carlo in 1910, and which he made famous by his incomparable interpretation, contributing towards making this the most successful of Massenet's later operas. Massenet's memoirs were published in 1912 as "Souvenirs d'un Musicien."

O. T.

Manon

OPÉRA COMIQUE IN 5 ACTS

Book by Henri Meilhac and Philippe Gille

First performance: Opéra Comique, Paris, Jan. 19, 1884

CHARACTERS

Chevalier des Grieux, TENOR
Count des Grieux, his father, BASS
Lescaut, Manon's cousin, one of the
   Royal Guards, BARITONE

Guillot de Morfontaine, a roué,
   Minister of France, BASS
De Brétigny, a nobleman, BARITONE
Manon, an adventuress, SOPRANO

Actresses, Students, Guards, Travelers, etc.

The action takes place in Amiens, Paris, and Le Havre, about the year 1721

In the first act we have the meeting of Manon—on her way to a convent—with the handsome young Chevalier des Grieux; love at first sight—elopement. In the second act we find them living together in Paris. Des Grieux would like his father's consent to their marriage. De Bretigny enters with Lescaut (in this opera Manon's cousin, not her brother). While Lescaut engages the Chevalier's attention, De Bretigny pictures her a life of splendor if she will leave Des Grieux for him, and tells her, furthermore, that Des Grieux will be abducted by his father's agents that very evening. The visitors gone, Des Grieux in the delicate "Rêve" sings to Manon of his dream of their future. He is called to the door. He does not return. His father's agents have done their work.

The third act opens on a festivity in the Cours-la-Reine. Manon, now the pampered mistress of De Bretigny, enters in all her finery, singing a brilliant, florid solo. The Comte des Grieux, father of her former lover, happens to be there. From him she learns that the Chevalier is at the seminary of St. Sulpice about to take holy orders. To St. Sulpice she hastens and in an impassioned duet persuades the Chevalier to forget his vocation and depart with her.

The fourth act shows us the Hôtel de Transylvanie, a luxurious gambling house. Des Grieux is accused of cheating at cards and when the police raid the place Manon is pointed to as his accomplice. The fifth act takes us to the road to Havre at nightfall. Des Grieux, released through the influence of his father, is awaiting Manon, who with other women of her kind is on her way to be deported to America. Des Grieux and Lescaut have arranged to rescue her. But when she appears, broken and ill, it is too late, and as she and Des Grieux recall their days together she dies in his arms.

P. S.

By the merest chance the Abbé Prévost's famous Louis XV romance, "Manon Lescaut," was adopted as an operatic subject by Massenet. *Hérodiade* had been successfully brought out at the Théâtre-de-la-Monnaie in Brussels on December 19, 1881, and already its composer had begun to think of another opera. One morning in the autumn of 1881, Massenet relates in his "Souvenirs," he was feeling upset and anxious. Carvalho, who was then the director of the Paris Opéra-Comique, had entrusted him with a three-act text. It was "Phoebé" by Henry Meilhac. Massenet had read it and reread it without being in the least taken with it. He was dismayed by the prospect of the work to be done. It made him nervous, impatient.

Impulsively he decided he would end all that by going to see Meilhac, and did so forthwith. It was during this interview between librettist and composer that the latter suggested "Manon Lescaut" as a better subject for collaboration than the disputed "Phoebé." Meilhac's reply to this proposal was an invitation to lunch on the following day at Vachette's, for further conference.

In responding to that invitation [Massenet goes on] one can guess whether I had more aroused curiosity in my heart than appetite in my stomach. I accordingly went to Vachette's, and there, ineffable and quite adorable surprise, I found what? Under my napkin the first two acts of *Manon!* The other three acts were to follow in a few days. The idea of doing this work had haunted me for a long time. This was the dream come true.

The summer Meilhac spent in the royal city of St. Germain-en-Laye near Paris, living in the Pavillon Henri IV.

I went there often to surprise him [Massenet says] ordinarily toward five in the afternoon, when I knew his day's work was over. Then while going out walking we would rearrange the poem. It was there that we decided on the act of the Seminary, and in order to provide a greater contrast to follow that I asked for the Transylvanie act. What pleasure I had from this collaboration, from this work where our ideas were exchanged without ever colliding. . . .

Philippe Gille [Meilhac's associate] came to share this useful collaboration from time to time at the dinner hour, and his presence was so dear to me! How many tender and sweet recollections I have preserved from that time of St. Germain, of its magnificent terrace, of the luxuriant leafage of its beautiful forest!

In the spring of 1883 Massenet was back in Paris, his opera finished, and ready to submit it to Carvalho. At the director's house he found also his wife, Mme. Miolan-Carvalho, the celebrated soprano (who had created for Gounod the rôles of Marguerite, Mireille, and Juliette), as well as his librettists Meilhac and Gille. The reading of the score lasted from nine o'clock till midnight. Massenet reports that his friends appeared charmed. Mme. Carvalho embraced him joyously, repeating again and again, "Why am I not twenty years younger?"

"I did my best to console the great artist," he says, "I wanted her name to be on the score, and to her I dedicated it."

It was necessary now to find a heroine. The men had been chosen easily, but at first no decision was reached with regard to Manon. Massenet thought of Mlle. Vaillant (later Mme. Vaillant-Couturier), a young artist whose "qualities of vocal seduction" had persuaded him to entrust to her copies of several parts of the score. She was, he says, his first Manon.

But Mlle. Vaillant was appearing in operetta at the Nouveautés. Massenet went to Brasseur, the director, "that man of frank and open nature, an incomparable artist," and requested him to cede him Mlle. Vaillant for a new opera.

"Cher monsieur, what you desire is impossible; Mlle. Vaillant is necessary to me. I can't hand her over to you."

"Seriously?"

"Absolutely! But I am thinking if you will write a work for my theatre I will give you this artist. Is it agreed, *bibi?*"

There the discussion rested. While this little exchange of words was going on Massenet had noticed that the Marquis de la Valette, who had first drawn Mlle. Vaillant to his attention, was very much absorbed by a pretty gray hat, all abloom with roses, which continually passed and repassed in the theatre lobby. Suddenly Massenet saw this pretty hat making its way toward him.

"Heilbronn!" I cried.

"Herself!"

"You still sing?" I asked her.

"No, I am rich; and yet, shall I say it to you? I miss the theatre; I am haunted by it. Ah, if I found a fine part!"

"I have one: Manon."

"Manon Lescaut?"

"No, Manon—that tells the whole story!"

"Can I hear the music?"

"Whenever you like."

So it was done. At half-past four in the morning Massenet sang to her the last measures of the death of Manon. "Heilbronn," he tells us, "during this audition had been moved to tears. Through them I heard her say: 'It is my life. . . . But it is my life, that!'"

The next day Carvalho signed up Heilbronn.

The following year [says Massenet] after more than eighty performances I learned of the death of Marie Heilbronn. Ah, who will ever tell the artists how faithful we are to their memory, how deeply we are attached to them, the immense grief that the day of everlasting separation brings us! I preferred to stop the performances rather than to see Manon sung by another.

Not long afterwards the Opéra-Comique disappeared in flames.

"*Manon* was held up for ten years. It was the dear and unique Sibyl Sanderson who revived the work at the [new] Opéra-Comique. She played the two hundredth performance. A glory was reserved for me for the five hundredth. That evening Manon was sung by Mme. Marguerite Carré."

Mme. Carré also sang in the 1000th performance of this work now well on its way toward the 2000 mark at the Opéra-Comique.

P. S.

Next to *Faust* and *Carmen*, *Manon* is the most popular of all French operas. It is also the most famous operatic treatment of the once so celebrated "Histoire de Manon Lescaut et du Chevalier des Grieux" by the Abbé Prévost d'Exiles, who died in 1763. And of all Massenet's twenty-five operas it is the most universally loved and the most viable.

Massenet seemed to attach a good deal of importance to the name of his masterpiece—*Manon* as against the *Manon Lescauts* which preceded and followed his. The writer of these lines remembers a visit he paid the aging composer at his home in the *Rue Vaugirard,* Paris, just a fortnight before his death in 1912. The master was charming, but had little of consequence to say. Two things, however, cling to the writer's memory—in the first place the way he assured his guest that his first name was not "Jules" but "Julien" ("Julien Emile Frédéric," he emphasized); and in the second, that when he composed *Manon* he had been prudent enough to copyright the title in such a way that nobody else could ever write a *Manon*. *Manon Lescaut* if one chose, but *Manon* never! One might almost construe the thing symbolically, for Massenet did write the one, the definitive *Manon*. As for the "Jules" or the "Julien," Massenet had an almost pathological horror of his first name. Just why, nobody knows. Pressed for an explanation he would answer mysteriously that "there was another—a terrible fellow, a creature who wrote military marches and all that sort of thing"! When a work of his was produced he thought it quite sufficient that the program should say "music by Massenet," and let it go at that!

In point of fact, "music by Massenet" has a broader meaning than might appear. Romain Rolland, one of the keenest musical minds that France produced, once alluded to "that Massenet who sleeps in every French heart." The *phrase Massenétique,* a melodic idiom at once graceful, suave, warm, elegant and flowing, if rarely deep, is found in all types of French music of the past half century at least. You are as likely to encounter it in the pages of Debussy as in those of Bruneau or Pierné, Leroux or Charpentier. It is part of the French musical heritage. There are other works of Massenet—especially the later ones —where it often became a formula rather than an inspiration. In *Manon* you meet it at its best and freshest and most spontaneous. That is one reason—but only one—why the average operagoer in this country knows less than nothing about operas like *Le Cid, Le Mage, Cherubin, Panurge, Ariane, Thérèse, Roma, Bacchus* and next to nothing about *Esclarmonde, Grisélidis, Cendrillon, Werther* —which is so incredibly popular in France. If Massenet means anything else to us than *Manon* he means *Thaïs* or *Le Jongleur de Notre Dame*—and this, one suspects, in large degree because of the famous singers at one time or another associated with these works.

Manon is an *opéra-comique*—that is to say it contains quantities of spoken dialogue. But the composer and his admirable librettists, Henri Meilhac and Philippe Gille, have handled this feature somewhat differently from the manner it is treated in *Carmen* and scores of other works. Here the spoken lines are not permitted to interrupt the flow of the music. Instead, they are uttered against an orchestral background which is light but which enhances rather than covers them. They are, moreover, so charming in themselves that one feels they would be thoroughly marred by a delivery in recitative or in a broader *arioso*.

Early in his career some wag called Massenet "Mademoiselle Wagner." The idea was obviously that the composer had succumbed to the fascinations and the potent magic of the composer of *Tristan* and the *Ring* to an extent which suffused his own musical speech with the accents and idioms of Bayreuth, but without possessing Wagner's powers of musical logic and construction. To a degree, of course, this is true. Yet Massenet is a good deal more than a lesser Wagner. If he utilized the Wagnerian system of thematic or longer melodic labels he did not, indeed, weave, develop and connect them in Wagner's symphonic manner. And when it suited his purposes, he did not scorn to employ conventional operatic methods and procedures. In *Manon,* for example, we see less an organic structure than a mosaic, in which melodic and thematic fragments appear and reappear in various dispositions and configurations, like bits of colored glass in a kaleidoscope. Again we meet fully developed pieces of wholly traditional cut. The vocal writing, it is proper to add, is at all times singable and idiomatic.

Massenet was confronted with a problem when he composed *Manon*. Was it not obvious that a story so impregnated with the feeling of the eighteenth century, of the elegances, formalisms, and artificialities of the epoch, should be treated in music which should precisely mirror these qualities? He had, on the other hand, a deeply human tale to deal with, a tale demanding a warmly human and sensuous musical style to interpret and communicate it. Massenet was artist and skilled technician enough to find a balance between what might ordinarily have resulted in contradictions of style. He contrived to evoke and sustain the atmosphere of eighteenth century France. And at the same time he managed to bring to his music what is needed in the way of warmth, charm, voluptuousness, passion and even poignant melancholy.

H. F. P.

Manon was introduced to America at the New York Academy of Music, in Italian, Dec. 23, 1885, with Minnie Hauk as Manon, Giannini as Des Grieux, and Giuseppe del Puente as Lescaut. It was sung in French in New Orleans in 1894, but not in New York until it was presented at the Metropolitan Opera House on Jan. 16, 1895, for the American debut of Sibyl Sanderson. Also in the cast were Jean de Reszké, Mario Ancona, and Pol Plançon (Comte des Grieux). On January 23 of the following year Nellie Melba assumed the role of Manon, with the incomparable Victor Maurel, this time as Lescaut.

Frances Saville was a Metropolitan Manon in 1899, with Ernest van Dyck as Des Grieux. There was a Metropolitan revival Feb. 3, 1909, with Geraldine Farrar, Caruso, Antonio Scotti, and Jean Noté. Edmond Clément, the most distinguished Des Grieux of his time, made his first appearance at the Metropolitan Opera House in that role, Dec. 6, 1909. His chief associates were Miss Farrar, Henry Dutilloy, and Andrés de Segurola. Arturo Toscanini conducted the Metropolitan revival of March 30, 1912, with Mme. Farrar, Enrico Caruso, Dinh Gilly, and Léon Rothier in the leading roles.

From 1909 on the Metropolitan management had omitted the Cours-la-Reine scene. It was restored in the revival of 1919–20, but the scene in the Hôtel de Transylvanie was omitted. Later the Cours-la-Reine was again omitted and the Hôtel de Transylvanie restored. On April 3, 1929, *Manon,* unheard at the Metropolitan since April 14, 1923, was revived there under the direction of Louis Hasselmans, with Lucrezia Bori, Beniamino Gigli, Giuseppe de Luca, and Léon Rothier as the principal singers.

P. S.

Thaïs

COMÉDIE LYRIQUE IN 3 ACTS

Book by Louis Gallet, after the novel by Anatole France

First performance: Opéra, Paris, Mar. 16, 1894

CHARACTERS

Thaïs, a courtesan, SOPRANO
Athanaël, a monk of the Cenobite Order, BARITONE
Nicias, a young Sybarite, TENOR

Palemon, an old monk, BASS
Albine, an abbess, MEZZO-SOPRANO
Crobyle, a slave, SOPRANO
Myrtale, a slave, SOPRANO

Monks, Nuns, Citizens, Servants, Dancers, etc.

The action takes place in Egypt in the early Christian era

The libretto, by Louis Gallet, is in prose, and is based on Anatole France's ironic romance of Alexandria in the early Christian era. It has been concisely summed up as the story of the courtesan who becomes a saint and the monk who becomes a man. Athanaël, the young cenobite, in his desert retreat has a vision of the actress Thaïs, the reigning toast of Alexandria's pleasure-loving worldlings, and determines to save her soul. Accordingly he journeys to Alexandria, where he finds her the mistress of his old friend Nicias. She is immediately attracted to the handsome stranger (who has been fitted out in fashionable attire), and when he tells her of his purpose, she replies that love is the only power in which she believes.

In due course the monk succeeds in converting her to his religion (the popular "Meditation," an intermezzo for solo violin and orchestra, signalizes that spiritual transformation), and he leads her away from her carousing friends to the desert where the holy Albine shall add the repentant courtesan to her White Sisterhood. But meanwhile the fires of an earthly love have been lighted in Athanaël for the woman who has turned forever from the ways of the flesh. A vision of her dying calls the tortured monk from his desert retreat to Albine's convent, where he falls beside her in a frenzy of despair as, with her last breath, she declares her eyes behold the Most High.

P. S.

The libretto of *Thaïs* is by Louis Gallet, who prefaces his "book" with an interesting little essay on what he calls "poésie mélique." In the 1890's, we are told, "the question of prose in music" was occupying the serious consideration of French musicians and others. The Press had even asked a number of eminent or notorious French composers, among them Massenet, Gounod, Saint-

Säens, Reyer, Ambroise Thomas and Benjamin Godard, for their opinions on the matter. These opinions differed considerably, though some of the composers—Gounod in particular—were quite in favour of prose texts for operas. As Gallet points out in his preface, composers invariably upset the rhythms and ignore the rhymes of verse for their own purposes: why then, he asks, go on with the ancient farce of casting words intended for music in the stereotyped moulds of verse form? Why not give the composer a simple prose text and be done with it—for inevitably he will turn whatever lines are given to him into prose: as Gallet ironically puts it, "a 'lyrical poem' [i.e., a poem written for the "lyric stage"] is a work in verse that is handed over to a musician so that he may convert it into prose." The footfalls of poetry and of music rarely coincide: "what rhymes poetically does not always rhyme musically."

Yet oddly enough, when Massenet asked for a prose text for *Thaïs*, Gallet pleaded for a compromise that would allow him, as a man of letters, some scope for the classical niceties of French verse. For this compromise he adopted a name that had been suggested some time earlier by the Belgian composer and savant Gevaert—"poème mélique," signifying a form in which music and poetry would each assert its own inalienable rights while at the same time being politely accommodating towards the rights of the other. Gallet's text, while almost entirely avoiding rhyme, affects a kind of free rhythm that differentiates it from out-and-out prose, a rhythm designed to help rather than impede the composer.

In large part, Massenet has been obliging enough to cut his melodic periods to the size and shape of those of his librettist. In the second act, for instance, Gallet writes: "Je suis Athanaël—moine d'Antinoë!—Je viens du saint désert— et je maudis la chair—et je maudis la mort qui te possède!—et me voici devant toi, femme—comme devant un tombeau;—et je te dis: Thaïs, lève-toi, lève-toi!" The dashes represent the natural sense-endings of the irregular phrases, which suffer no constraint of formal rhythm or number of syllables. Massenet makes his musical phrase-divisions, in the main, at the same points. There is, however, one notable departure on the composer's part from the pattern set him by the poet. Finding the word "femme" superfluous, for his particular purpose, in the long declamatory line he has projected for the sentence "Et me voici devant toi, femme, comme devant un tombeau," he calmly omits it, although it is *the* vital word for Gallet! His procedure here is typical: after having asked for a prose—or near-prose—libretto in order that he might not be perpetually succun·bing to the temptation to maltreat a verse-text for the purposes of music, he does not hesitate to behave just as tyrannically as any other composer towards his "melic" librettist whenever it suits his convenience to do so.

Thaïs was produced for the first time at the Paris Opéra on the 16th March 1894, with Sybil Sanderson as Thaïs, Delmas as Athanaël, and Alvarez as Nicias.

E. N.

More than a dozen of Massenet's operas have reached New York and—during Mary Garden's active career there—Chicago, and there is no doubt that they have been as well represented in some European capitals. But outside France, few have managed to maintain themselves on the boards, and in the United States, only *Manon* and *Thaïs,* the latter precariously, can be said to be in the repertoire. Besides these, several—*Werther, La Navarraise, Sapho, Le Jongleur de Notre Dame,* and *Don Quichotte*—invite comment bcause of variation from the mold or because of unusual historic interest.

Thaïs is merely a pattern opera of high quality. It has the "Méditation," and it has a title role that, having been written for Sibyl Sanderson, a dazzling young American singer whom Massenet intensely admired, not unnaturally has continued to captivate ambitious young sopranos, from Mary Garden to Marjorie Lawrence. It has, also, a smoldering book based on Anatole France's suave and superficial re-creation of early Christian Alexandria, and therefore calls for the most sumptuous efforts of a Joseph Urban. It is high entertainment of a kind that demands no collaboration on the part of the audience. The shifting between murky, sensual religiosity and elegant Eastern pornography affords a contrast that is extraordinarily piquant. Thaïs and the easily tempted Athanaël are roles of juicy possibility, and when, on November 25, 1907, *Thaïs* had its first American showing, at the Manhattan Opera House, Garden, most unforgettable of Thaïses, played opposite the equally superb Renaud. It was the propitious beginning of her operatic career in America. Geraldine Farrar was the first Metropolitan Thaïs, on February 16, 1917, Amato being the Athanaël.

W. B., H. W.

Giacomo Meyerbeer

(Berlin, Sept. 5, 1791–May 2, 1864, Paris)

Giacomo Meyerbeer, whose real name was Jakob Liebmann Beer, came of a wealthy banking family. He began the study of the piano early enough to play a Mozart concerto in public at the age of seven. After studying theory with Zelter and Anselm Weber in Berlin, he went, in 1810, to Darmstadt, where for two years he had as master Abt Vogler and as a fellow pupil C. M. von Weber, who became a close friend. In spite of triumphs as a pianist to off-set the failure of three early operas, Meyerbeer persisted in the belief that the theater was his real field.

In Vienna Salieri assured him that as a corrective of his heavy German style he needed to free himself from scholasticism and to acquire a knowledge of the human voice and how to write for it, which could be done only in Italy. So in 1815 he took up his abode in Venice. Imitating the operatic ways of Rossini, who was already enjoying a tremendous vogue, he wrote a number of Italian operas that pleased, especially the last of the series, *Il Crociato in Egitto* (Venice, 1824). But while on a visit to Berlin he again encountered Weber, who accused him of stooping to become an imitator in order to win favor with the crowd.

For six years thereafter Meyerbeer composed no more. To be sure, besides Weber's reproach, there were family reasons for his silence—the death of his father, his marriage, and the death of two of his children. But at the same time he was making a searching study of French opera from Lully on. In 1826 he had gone to Paris to help prepare a production of *Il Crociato* under-taken by Rossini at his Italian opera house, and in Paris he decided to settle. Then ensued his third and French period as a composer, which established his fame.

The first fruit of the change was *Robert le Diable*. That wildly romantic work, produced at the Paris Opéra in 1831, not only created a furore, but served, along with its innovating predecessors, Auber's *Muette de Portici* and Rossini's *Guillaume Tell,* to alter the course of the lyric drama.

In 1836 Meyerbeer triumphed again on the same stage with *Les Huguenots.* He next worked for a time on two operas, *L'Africaine* and *Le Prophète.* After the successful production of *Les Huguenots* in Berlin in 1842, Frederick William IV appointed him *Generalmusikdirektor* at the Prussian capital. Two years later he brought out there a comic opera, *Das Feldlager in Schlesien,* in which Jenny Lind was to shine. Several numbers from this work were later incorporated in *L'Étoile du nord,* presented at the Paris Opéra Comique in 1854.

In 1849, at the Paris Opéra, Meyerbeer at length brought out *Le Prophète,* a spectacular treatment of a historical theme. His incumbency in Berlin was memorable for his favorable attitude toward Wagner, which was answered with gross ingratitude.

In 1859 Meyerbeer gave fresh proof of his versatility in a fantastic and idyllic work for the Paris Opéra Comique, *Le Pardon de Ploërmel,* and then he turned his attention once more to *L'Africaine,* with which he had been occupied sporadically since 1838. His exceeding anxiety over the final polishing of the score and the picking of a satisfactory cast drew him back to Paris in October, 1863, to supervise the promised production at the Opera. But, after unsparing labors, he fell seriously ill the following April and died May 2. *L'Africaine* was produced posthumously in 1865.

Meyerbeer was one of the most painstaking of all composers, a fact which his detractors usually ignore, and he was also an expert man of the theater. If parts of his operas are uninspired and bombastic, grandiose rather than grand, they are always shrewdly planned from the theatrical standpoint, they never lack style, and each of them can boast pages of indisputable genius. Moreover, Meyerbeer has exerted a determining influence on subsequent opera, affecting Wagner and Verdi no less than French composers. Of his purely instrumental compositions, the overture to "Struensee," a tragedy by his brother Michael, is the most important.

P. S.

With all his deplorable elasticity of artistic conscience, his flirting, now with grandeur, now with courtly elegance, and anon with downright vulgarity, Meyerbeer did the Opera no little good technical service. He loosened the bonds of musical form, and, though not quite obliterating the old landmarks, did much to render traditional forms more scenic. What most composers before him had done only in the act-finale he did at any point in an act where he saw a chance of making the music go hand in hand with a continuous dramatic development, no matter how brief. He obtained many of his dramatic and scenic results, to be sure, more by an extension than by a sacrifice of the old forms; but this was, after all, what most of his predecessors had done in the act-finale.

His style, composite as it was, was in the main essentially dramatic; nevertheless he did not discard the Rossini *coloratura,* over which his early Italian studies had given him a certain mastery. He was particularly fond of giving his second soprani—generally queens or princesses, of but secondary dramatic importance—intrinsically florid parts; his dramatic heroines, on the other hand, seldom have anything purely ornamental to sing, save in closing cadenzas; he seems to have felt that he could ill afford to withhold this concession to the vanity of singers.

Meyerbeer also did noteworthy work in *opéra-comique,* though he could never quite rid himself of a certain ponderousness, not wholly in accord with the genre. But nothing he did was in vain; and, if there had been no *Étoile du Nord* (1854) or *Pardon de Ploërmel* (1859), there surely would never have been a Bizet's *Carmen.*

In the last analysis, the Meyerbeer Opera was just as characteristic an expression of the romantic spirit of 1830 as Victor Hugo's and Dumas's dramas, Alfred de Musset's poetry, Delacroix's canvases, Berlioz's symphonies, or Chopin's pianoforte-music. It was virtually the Dumas Drama set to music, and had all the flaunting virtues and unnatural vices of that school. If it was something very different from the Wagnerian Music-Drama, this was simply because nothing like the Wagnerian Music-Drama could possibly have sprung from the order of ideas which formed the point of departure for the 1830 movement in France. The most that can be expected of a tree is to bear its own fruit!

W. F. A.

Robert le Diable

[Robert the Devil]

OPERA IN 5 ACTS

Book by Eugène Scribe and Germain Delavigne

First performance: Opéra, Paris, Nov. 21, 1831

CHARACTERS

Robert, Duke of Normandy, TENOR
Bertram, the evil one in disguise,
  actually Robert's father, BASS
Rambaldo, a minstrel, TENOR

Isabelle, princess of Sicily, SOPRANO
Alice, Robert's foster sister, SOPRANO
King of Sicily, BASS

The action takes place at Palermo during the thirteenth century

The scene of the fantastic plot is Sicily, whither the Duke, Robert of Normandy, has gone to compete for the hand of the Duke of Messina's daughter, Isabelle, in an elaborate tournament. Alice, Robert's foster sister, has followed him, hoping to influence him for his own good. But he is in the power of Bertram, a demon, who, assuming human form, had made a conquest of the Duchess Berthe, Robert's mother.

First Bertram causes him to lose even the horse and armor he was to use in the tournament by reckless gambling. He then tells Robert that he can acquire supernatural power by carrying away a magic branch from the ruined abbey of St. Rosalie. Wealth, happiness, and immortality will then be his. Bertram calls up from their graves the buried nuns who in life had been false to their vows, and in the midst of their ghostly dance Robert makes off with the branch.

He repairs immediately to Isabelle, entering her apartments unseen. Thanks to the branch he renders her attendants motionless and declares that he will abduct her, but her pleadings in the famous aria, "Robert, toi que j'aime," shake his purpose, and he breaks the branch, and thus the spell.

There is a time limit, it seems, on Bertram's influence, and if Robert fails to sign a pact with the fiend within a certain time, he will be free of him forever. He is about to sign when Alice, who has found out Bertram's reason for haste, interferes, bringing up his mother's warning against the wiles of the fiend. While Robert hesitates the clock strikes twelve and Bertram's power is at an end. Bertram vanishes, and there is a quick change to the interior of the cathedral at Palermo, with Isabelle and the redeemed Robert about to be united in matrimony before the altar while the faithful hymn the glory of God.

P. S.

Meyerbeer was one of the spoiled children of music. He was born rich and remained so. He was prodigiously gifted, so gifted, in fact, that he could pick and choose from a number of careers. He could, it is said, have become the foremost piano virtuoso of the period: instead, he turned to opera, and by the age of twenty-one had produced a score so learned and solemn that it sounded like an oratorio. This was written in German, as was his second opera. These were so indifferently received by his countrymen that when Salieri, no doubt previsaging a parallel between Meyerbeer's and Gluck's career, advised him to visit Italy and learn how to write for the voice, he leaped at the idea.

Meyerbeer arrived in Venice in 1815 during the *Tancredi* madness, and at once was converted to Rossini. Three years later came the first of six unadulteratedly Rossinian operas, one of them a setting of Metastasio's *Semiramide*. Several of these were successful and were performed in various parts of Europe, but by the time the last of them was composed (1822), Meyerbeer was becoming dissatisfied with himself. His plumes were borrowed, and the fascination of Italy, if not worn thin, had at least become easier to exorcise. Weber, who had been a fellow student at the curious academy of the arts conducted by that learned charlatan, the Abbé Vogler, staged one of Meyerbeer's Italian operas at Dresden and also, in the hope of calling the expatriate back to his German senses, restaged his second German opera. As Meyerbeer had a high regard for Weber, he tried to write another German opera and failed so miserably that it never reached the stage. This catapulted him back into the arms of the Circe Venice, where, in 1824, his last and most successful Italian opera was performed.

Il Crociato in Egitto is, in many respects, a fascinating score. In this big spectacle opera based on the Crusades, and with a libretto by that same Gaetano Rossi who fabricated the book of Rossini's *Semiramide,* Meyerbeer stands at the parting of the ways. Gone is the obsession with pure lyric melody, gone the easy, undramatic flow of his first Italian efforts. It is the work of a restive Rossinian. In it, a seer might have found signs of Meyerbeer's future: those few but affectionately contrived *coups de théâtre,* those rumblings of a still-muffled orchestra, those moments of eloquent declamation, that all-over pomp and glitter—were not these the very elemental devices of that eclectic style which Meyerbeer was finally to choose as his own?

At the Venice *première* of *Il Crociato,* at the Fenice, Giovanni Battista Velluti, the last of the great *castrati,* took the soprano part of Armando, the Christian knight, and when the opera was given in London in 1825—the first by Meyerbeer to be heard there—with Malibran and Caradori-Allan, he again sang Armando. The Earl of Mount Edgcumbe, a dilettante critic and composer, said of Velluti:

At the moment when he was expected to appear, the most profound silence reigned in one of the most crowded audiences I ever saw, broken on his entering by loud applauses of encouragement. The first note he uttered gave a shock of surprise, almost of disgust, to inexperienced ears; but his performance was listened to with attention and great applause throughout, with but few audible expressions of disapprobation speedily suppressed. . . . To the old he brought back some pleasing recollections; others, to whom his voice was new, became reconciled to it, and sensible of its merits, while many declared that to the last his tones gave them more pain than pleasure. However, either from curiosity or real admiration, he drew crowded audiences, and no opera but the *Crociato* * was performed to the end of the season.

W. B., H. W.

In 1826 Meyerbeer went to Paris. Here he stopped composing for a while, and began to make a careful study of French literature and art, above all, of the French character; these four years, 1826–30, marked the turning-point in his career. He was eminently a man of enterprise, a born eclectic, unsurpassed in his faculty for turning every opportunity to account; Paris gave him food for thought. There were *La muette* and *Guillaume Tell;* there was the new Berlioz orchestration,—vehemently discussed at the time, but descriable by the discerning eye as big with a whole great future for the Art of Music,—not yet applied to the Lyric Drama; there were, in churches and conservatories, endless old contrapuntal subtleties, long neglected by composers for the stage; best of all, there was, as Wagner has said, a new wind blowing, it was good weather for inventive audacity!

Meyerbeer plodded quietly on, catching idea after idea, and silently perfecting a whole new scheme of Opera; he was plainly not satisfied until he had the plan complete in his brain, well thought out in every detail. For, when he took to active composition again, we find his third, or "grand," manner fully formed; he had no transition period.

The work in which he embodied the results of those four years of thinking and study was *Robert le Diable.* . . . The manner was quite new; a most composite style, if you will, a mosaic style, made up of bits taken from about every composer who had anything worth taking, but—and here is the miracle! —thoroughly personal and individual. No matter how great or how small a genius, there was one force which Meyerbeer indisputably possessed: the force of sharply defined individuality; whencever he may have got an idea, once it had passed through his brain, it came out bearing his mark. No musical style was ever more composite than his; none more unmistakably the composer's own.

No doubt, other folk's ideas got more or less distorted in the process, and perverted from their original meaning. Often, what had been an irrepressible expression of a composer's inmost self was turned into a mere bid for effect. Meyerbeer was a man of no artistic conscience, and his artistic honesty was

---

* A performance of the overture to *Il Crociato*, at the Bowery Theater, New York, on May 9, 1833, was advertised as the first music by Meyerbeer to reach America.

more than dubious; take him in the most charitable way, if Effect was really his god, he served that god with perfect single-heartedness.

Few operas have made so strong a first impression upon any public as *Robert le Diable* made in Paris in 1831. Success is not quite the word for it; *cela faisait explosion,* it made a tremendous noise in the world, was discussed, *pro* and *con,* with a vigour that left no one in doubt as to the work's being, at least, something! Whether great or puny, admirable or outrageous, it was clearly no nothing-at-all. The style was so new, and hence so incomprehensible at first, that everyone connected with the rehearsals—singers, players, conductor—predicted a flat failure. But, when the opening night came, the excitement of the audience was so irrepressible and contagious that, after the duet, "Si j'aurai ce courage?" in the third act, Adolphe Nourrit, who sang the part of Robert, lost head completely and, from sheer madness of nervous tension, took a desperate header down a trap-door that was open by mistake— luckily falling upon a mattress, and so saving his neck.

It is difficult for us now to appreciate how new *Robert* was in 1831. It seems old-fashioned enough to-day! But look at the duet between Alice and Bertram, "Mais Alice, qu'as-tu donc?" in the third act, and think of what an audacity of originality it took to offer those suppressed intermittent whisperings, strung on the barest thread of a melodic idea, to a public brought up on Spontini, Cherubini, Auber, and Rossini! It must have seemed the very impudence of crass, unacademic realism. Take the unaccompanied terzet, "Fatal moment, cruel mystère," in the same act, where a parody on the four-voice cadenza in Beethoven's ninth symphony compelled a whole public to applaud to the echo what, in Beethoven, they had scouted as incomprehensible.*

Robert is, after all, Meyerbeer's freshest and most original work. In *Les Huguenots* (1836) the style is more matured, there are moments of deeper inspiration—passages in the duet, "O ciel! où courez-vous?" between Raoul and Valentine, in the fourth act, have won sincere homage even from Wagner— but the first bloom is wiped off. In *Le Prophète* (1849) maturity of style already degenerates into mannerism; it out-Meyerbeers Meyerbeer. All that can be said of *L'Africaine,* his last opera (1864), is that, if no less mannered than the *Prophète,* it shows greater heartiness of inspiration. In *Robert le Diable* there is a superior freshness of melodic invention, more genuine dash and brilliancy.

W. F. A.

While Paris raved indiscriminately about *Robert,* London received it with chill respect until, in 1847, Jenny Lind chose Alice as her debut role there.†

---

* At a rehearsal of the ninth symphony in Boston, in the nineties, a certain musician was overheard muttering, after the famous quartet-cadenza, "There goes one of Meyerbeer's strongest claims to *originality!*"

† Apparently, though not ill supported, Lind was the one ray of light in an otherwise wretched performance. It was so bad that Mendelssohn, who was almost idolatrous in his devotion to Lind, left the theater at the end of the third act.

In it, she became so popular that the opera was cut to reduce the role of the rival soprano—the Isabelle. A great London cast of the fifties brought together Grisi, Tamburini, and Mario, but it was spoiled by the fact that Grisi had attempted an unsuitable role, and the Bertram—Karl Johann Formes—overacted to the point of impeding the performance. Alice was one of Nilsson's most powerful impersonations, and in London she was once supported by Di Murska as Isabelle, the stentorian Mongini as the accursed Duke, and "Signor Foli" (*né* Allan Foley, of Tipperary) as Bertram. In 1869, a popular baritone by the name of Jean de Reszke raised his voice to sing the tenor role of Robert, and never sang low again: his sister Josephine was the Alice, and Madrid the scene, of this historic event. In only three years, *Robert* reached the United States, where it was given in English at the Park Theater, New York, on April 7, 1834, with Mary Anne Paton as Isabelle. Bosio sang the same role in New York in the fifties. On November 19, 1883, less than a month after opening, the Metropolitan staged *Robert* in an Italian version, with Emmy Fursch-Madi, an eccentric but distinguished soprano, as Alice, supported by Alwina Valleria and Roberto Stagno. After two repetitions that season, the opera was retired permanently from the company's repertoire.

W. B., H. W.

Les Huguenots

[The Huguenots]

OPERA IN 5 ACTS

Book by Eugène Scribe and Émile Deschamps

First performance: Opéra, Paris, Feb. 29, 1836

CHARACTERS

Count de St. Bris, Catholic nobleman, BARITONE

Count de Nevers, Catholic nobleman, BARITONE

Marcel, servant to Raoul, BASS

Marguérite de Valois, betrothed to Henry IV of Navarre, SOPRANO

Raoul de Nangis, a Huguenot nobleman, TENOR

Valentine, daughter of St. Bris, SOPRANO

Urbain, page to Marguérite, SOPRANO or MEZZO-SOPRANO

Ladies and Gentlemen of the Court, both Catholic and Huguenot; Pages, Citizens, Soldiers, the Night Watch, Students, Monks, and the People

The action of the opera takes place during 1572, the first two acts in Touraine, the remainder at Paris

In the Count de Nevers' rooms Catholic nobles carouse with their Protestant guest, Raoul de Nangis. Thither comes Valentine St. Bris who loves Raoul, to ask de Nevers to free her from her troth. After he has done so a page gives Raoul a note: it begs him to meet an unknown—his eyes covered with a scarf lest he see her face.

The maids of honor sing sweetly in Marguerite de Valois' garden . . . and she proposes the marriage of Raoul and Valentine to pledge the reconciliation of Catholics and Protestants. But Raoul (he has seen Valentine in Nevers' rooms) thinks her the latter's mistress, refuses her hand, and only the Queen's presence prevents bloodshed.

The drinking chorus of Protestants and Catholics rises before a Paris inn, and gypsies dance away a quarrel. Valentine, rebetrothed by her father to de Nevers, overhears a plot to kill Raoul when he goes to fight a duel in the Pré aux Clercs with the Count. The clash of steel draws gentlemen of both factions to the spot and when Marguerite de Valois' appearance interrupts the struggle Raoul, apprized of Valentine's effort to save him, knows that he has treated her unjustly.

Valentine, wedded to de Nevers, still loves the Huguenot. When he is hidden behind a curtain in her husband's home, he overhears the plan for the St. Bartholomew massacre. When the Catholic nobles leave, after invoking the blessing on their swords, the church bells of St. Germain l'Auxerrois sound the tocsin, and as Valentine swoons, Raoul leaps from the window to alarm his friends.

In the Hôtel de Nesle he bids the Protestants arm. Next he is found in a church-yard by Valentine, who turns Protestant and is married to him by his soldier-servant Marcel only to be separated from her husband in the combat during which the Catholics slaughter the Huguenot women hiding in the church. But soon on a Paris quay, Raoul, mortally wounded, and Valentine supporting him, are united for eternity by a volley from the muskets of soldiers led by her father.

F. H. M.

On the whole, *Les Huguenots* is Meyerbeer's best work. The fourth act is generally admitted to be not only the finest of the five but the best thing Meyerbeer ever achieved. Even Wagner could find in his heart to praise certain features of it, notably the duet between the lovers Raoul and Valentine; and it is ironically characteristic of Meyerbeer that this scene was an after-thought, suggested to him by the tenor Nourrit after the rehearsals had commenced. The "poet" of *Les Huguenots* was Eugène Scribe, the most indefatigable libretto manufacturer of that epoch. Scribe, as an opera "poet," lived in a strange world of his own, in which any situation, any motive, any psychology was valid so long as it avoided too close contact with common sense. He knew all the rules of the game as the composers and audiences of that day had agreed to play it, and he could turn out the appropriate doggerel in any quantity with the utmost facility at the shortest notice. Meyerbeer, of course, co-operated with him in the texts to which he was to supply the music, suggesting an addition here, an omission there, a modification in some other place, all for the sake of greater "effect"; and though the amour-propre of the great Scribe was occasionally wounded, he always found it politic to fall in with the wishes of the recognised dictator of grand opera. Wagner was right, in the main, when he said that Scribe's Meyerbeer libretti are his worst—"the silliest bombast, the lamest galimathias: actions without happenings, situations of the most insane confusion, characters of the most absurd caricature"—all because Meyerbeer had in mind, at this point or that, some effect or other of surprise, of contrast, of rhythm or of colour, for the exploitation of which he demanded the necessary words.

Both Scribe and Meyerbeer were perhaps born a century too soon: in these days they would have found the ideal sphere for the exhibition of their peculiar talents in Hollywood. The films would have been the perfect instrument for the realisation of their sound commercial policy of a bit of everything for everybody, and the more sensational the better. In *Robert the Devil*, Meyerbeer had sent a thrill through his audience by a scene in the third act in which certain nuns who, when they were alive, had forgotten the lessons learned at their mothers' knees, rise from the dead and indulge in a voluptuous ballet. In *Le Prophète* (1849) there is a ballet of skaters. The connection of these people with the world of the Dutch Anabaptists of the mid-sixteenth century is not very obvious, and indeed they did not appear in Meyerbeer's original score, which had been finished about 1843. But not long before the production of the opera the inventor of the roller skate had been delighting the Parisians night after night with a demonstration of the giddy delights to be had from his invention, and Meyerbeer thought the effect too good to be neglected: so in his new opera there had to be inserted a skating ballet.* In *Les Huguenots* he had what in itself was an excellent subject in the conflict of the Catholic and Protestant faiths, a subject, moreover, palpitatingly up to date, for religious controversy had sprung up once more in France in the 1830's. But Meyerbeer seems to have reflected that while not every Frenchman was interested in sects, every Frenchman worthy of the name was sure to be interested in sex; and so he graced the second act of this religious drama of his with a display of bathing belles. The Universal Provider was never at a loss for something that would be sure to pack the house.

The first performance of *Les Huguenots* took place in the Paris Opéra on the 29th February 1836. No money had been spared to make the *mise en scène* as brilliant as any that Paris had yet seen. The Raoul was Adolphe Nourrit, the leading French tenor of the day. Maria Falcon was the Valentine, Mme. Dorus-Gras the Marguerite, and Nicolas Prosper Levasseur . . . the Marcel.

The action of the opera takes place in August 1572. Of the eight civil wars of religion that racked France in the second half of the sixteenth century, the third, which had begun in 1568, had been terminated in 1570 by the Peace of Saint-Germain, under which the French Protestants were assured toleration. In 1572 Marguerite, the sister of King Charles IX of France, married in Paris Henri of Bourbon, son of the Huguenot Queen of Navarre. A number of Protestant notables attended the wedding, among them the Admiral Coligny. A week or so after the ceremony, on the night of St. Bartholomew, the Catholics rose and massacred some thousands of their rival religionists, Coligny among them. It is in this atmosphere of religious fanaticism that the main action of *Les Huguenots* is set.

E. N.

---

* In *L'Étoile du Nord* (1854) Peter the Great of Russia plays the flute—not for any historical reason but because this opera in its first form, as *Ein Feldlager in Schlesien* (1844), had contained a couple of solos "off" for Frederick the Great of Prussia, who, as everyone knows, prided himself on his flute-playing. When the scene of the opera was transferred from Prussia to Finland and Russia, and the German Frederick became metamorphosed into the Tsar Peter, Meyerbeer thought the flute effects too good to be sacrificed, so he blandly had opportunities made for them in his new score.

Edgar Istel, the eminent German musicologist, has justly called Act IV of *Les Huguenots* "a play within a play." Wagner, archenemy of Meyerbeerism, could never deny its power. In 1840, before he turned on his benefactor, Wagner wrote of it in prose strophes of wild rhapsody, and even as late as 1851, after excoriating Meyerbeer in "Oper und Drama," he tempered his words with an admission that beside the love scene "none but the most finished works of musical art are worthy to be set." Even after his own apotheosis at Bayreuth, Wagner was honest enough to admit the strange power of this act. One evening, during a sojourn in Italy, he mentioned having been moved by an opera he had heard the day before. When asked what it was, he answered, after some hesitation: "I will let you know, if you promise me not to speak about it. Now then—yesterday evening I was at *Les Huguenots,* and was positively wrought up by that fourth act. I implore you not to let a soul know about it—otherwise the Wagnerites will flay me alive!" Fortunately, the Princess von Bülow, who was present at this confession, told the story to a recording angel.

W. B., H. W.

For the first performance in Italian in London, July 20, 1848, a still more remarkable cast was assembled, including Pauline Viardot as Valentine, Jeanne Castellan as Marguerite, Mario as Raoul, and Antonio Tamburini as St. Bris. It was for this occasion that Meyerbeer transformed the Page into a contralto in deference to the celebrated Marietta Alboni, and he also wrote for her a florid aria, "No, no, no, no," to follow the bathers' chorus in the Chenonceaux scene. This number is always omitted in French performances and was last sung in New York by Sofia Scalchi.

Most famous of all Meyerbeer's operas, *Les Huguenots* was given at the Théâtre d'Orléans, New Orleans, for the first time in America, April 29, 1839. The first performance in New York occurred at the Park Theater, Aug. 11, 1845, in the original French. It was sung in New York in Italian in 1850, in German in 1866, and in English in 1869. At the Metropolitan Opera House, where it was presented first in the initial season of 1883–4, it has been sung in German, Italian, and French. *Les Huguenots* is a typical, and perhaps the most noteworthy, example of the historical grand opera of the nineteenth century.

In the 1890's *Les Huguenots* at New York's Metropolitan was regarded as a special festivity. A seven-dollar price scale then replaced the ordinary five-dollar scale to match the seven stars of the presentation. Along with Jean de Reszké as Raoul and Édouard de Reszké as Marcel the public could hear Lilli Lehmann, Lillian Nordica, or Félia Litvinne as Valentine; Sigrid Arnoldson, Nellie Melba, or Marcella Sembrich as Marguerite; Sofia Scalchi, Eugenia Mantelli, or Rosa Olitzka as the Page; Jean Lassalle or Pol Plançon as St. Bris, and Victor Maurel or Mario Ancona as De Nevers.

There was a Metropolitan revival Feb. 3, 1905, in which Enrico Caruso appeared as Raoul, along with Marcel Journet, Nordica, Sembrich, Edyth Walker, Antonio Scotti, and Pol Plançon. In the Metropolitan revival of Dec. 7, 1912, the stellar seven were Caruso, Adamo Didur, Emmy Destinn, Frieda Hempel, Bella Alten, Léon Rothier, and Antonio Scotti.

P. S.

Le Prophète

[The Prophet]

OPERA IN 5 ACTS

Book by Eugène Scribe

First performance: Opéra, Paris, Apr. 16, 1849

CHARACTERS

John of Leyden, The Prophet, chosen leader of the Anabaptists, TENOR
Bertha, his fiancée, SOPRANO
Fidès, mother of John of Leyden, MEZZO-SOPRANO

Count Oberthal, ruler of the domain about Dordrecht, BARITONE
Zacharias, BASS; *Jonas,* TENOR; *Mathisen,* BASS; Anabaptist preachers

Nobles, Citizens, Peasants, Soldiers, Prisoners

The action takes place in Holland and Germany at the time of the Anabaptist uprising in 1534

The story follows the historical events of the Anabaptist uprising under John of Leyden. It opens in a suburb of Dordrecht, Holland. John is betrothed to Bertha, who, because she is a vassal of Count Oberthal, ruler of the district, must seek his permission to wed. Fidès, John's mother, urges Bertha to ask the count. The latter, struck by her beauty, refuses the desired permission.

Three Anabaptist preachers, who notice the extraordinary resemblance of John to a portrait of David in the Münster Cathedral, plead with him to become their leader in the revolt. John is deaf to their exhortations, however, and informs them in the aria "Pour Berthe moi, je soupire" that his future life with Bertha is the only longing he possesses. Bertha rushes in seeking concealment from the count. The pursuers arrive, threatening to kill Fidès, their captive, unless Bertha is delivered to them. John yields in order to save his mother's life, and she invokes blessings on him in the celebrated aria, "Ah, mon fils!"

Leaving behind some bloodstained garments as evidence of his death, John joins the revolt as leader. He is now known as the Prophet. The city of Münster is about to be besieged. A ballet of skaters lends color to the scene. John sings the Triumphal Hymn. And the occupation of Münster is effected.

Fidès now is a street beggar. She meets Bertha and tells her that John is dead. Bertha, thinking the Prophet is responsible, swears vengeance.

During the splendid coronation ceremonies of the Prophet (including the Consecrational March), Fidès recognizes her son, but he disavows her for the safety

244

of both. She is imprisoned as an impostor. After the great scene of Fidès, "O prêtres de Baal," there follows the prison duet between mother and son.

Learning that the enemy forces are approaching, the Anabaptist leaders determine to surrender John. Bertha, still bent on revenge, enters the palace through a secret passage. She finally realizes that John and the Prophet are one, and stabs herself. In the last scene the Anabaptists are carousing. John, now resolved to die, orders the doors of the palace closed just as the enemy enter. There is a great explosion and flames envelop the hall. Fidès embraces her son. All perish in the mounting fire.

P. S.

It was said by his enemies that the Jew Meyerbeer made capital out of the wickedness and dissension of Christians: in *Robert le Diable* he introduced a chorus of lascivious nuns; in *Les Huguenots* he aired the bloody feuds of the French Catholics and Protestants, and in his next important opera, *Le Prophète,* he chose a page from the heretical disputes of the Anabaptists. In 1842, Friedrich Wilhelm IV appointed Meyerbeer his general music director at Berlin, and about the same time Scribe handed him the book based on some unpleasant happenings from the life of John of Leyden, the Dutch heresiarch. They were much to Meyerbeer's liking—in fact, years before, he had considered setting such a book for his favorite tenor, the unfortunate Nourrit, who had, however, neurotically abandoned the Opéra in 1837 and committed suicide two years later. Once more he immersed himself in the lore of the period and within a year had completed *Le Prophète.* But his duties in the Prussian capital, including the composition of a German opera, *Der Feldlager in Schlesien,* in which Lind scored one of her early successes (he rewrote it for Paris, as *L'Étoile du nord,* in 1854), and the staging of *Euryanthe* and *Rienzi,* retarded its production, which he would not allow without his supervision.

Unfortunately, by the time Meyerbeer was able to oversee the production, Duprez, Nourrit's successor at the Opéra, had retired to become a singing teacher, and the best of the available tenors in the company were not competent to sing the role of Jean as originally composed. Meyerbeer, therefore, tried a bold experiment. Viardot-García, the greatest contralto of the age, was available: by reducing the roles of Jean and his betrothed, Berthe, and by building up the contralto role of Fidès, Jean's mother, he created the first great mother role in opera. This involved wholesale reconstruction of the score, and so it was not until April 16, 1849, that Paris had its first opportunity to hear and see another of its idol's grand historical spectacles. On that night, the role of Jean was assigned to Hippolyte Roger, a useful but not spectacular tenor. Viardot-García scored one of her remarkable triumphs, but Meyerbeer himself did not receive an ovation. Had he set *Le Prophète* in the style of *Les Huguenots,* he might have conquered at once, but he was too conscientious to copy himself. However, the sequence of *Robert* and *Les Huguenots* was paralleled, and soon Paris was wildly applauding *Le Prophète.*

The fact that *Le Prophète* caught on at all was a victory in itself, for the experiment of making an older woman the real heroine of an opera was revolutionary, and Meyerbeer did anything but soften the blow by making the hero an execrable creature. The success in the beginning, both on the Continent and in England, was largely a personal one for Viardot-García, who was reputed to have suggested many detailed changes to Meyerbeer, and its continuing life depended on finding other singing actresses with the right voice. Fidès is the biggest thing in the opera.

At the time of its composition, it is unfortunate that Meyerbeer, who had by then achieved an indisputable supremacy on the musical stage, did not compose *Le Prophète* on the bold, simple lines of a mother-and-son drama; instead, he crowded his canvas with a multitude of tableaus, some of them theatrically effective if dramatically irrelevant, others mere period scenes smelling of research and uninspired historic conscientiousness. As a result, *Le Prophète* has a hysteric and disheveled quality that is less pertinent to the riot of the times Meyerbeer tried to portray than to the chaos Scribe gave him, and to which the whole musical score is party. The best that can be said of Scribe's book is that it gave Meyerbeer an opportunity to provide for a spoiled public a sample of practically every device in his huge bag of musical tricks. For taking advantage of this opportunity, instead of seizing on the essentials of Scribe's book to make the magnificent drama that was there for the taking, Meyerbeer has been accused of being consciously untrue to himself. But, as Cecil Gray has wisely said, "Meyerbeer has often been wrongly reproached with insincerity; he simply lacked entirely any very strong or definite convictions. He was an artistic opportunist from want of a clear sense of direction rather than from a lack of moral integrity or conscience."

Le Prophète contains many musical numbers of great distinction, several of considerable fame. Most popular of all is the pompous and very circumstantial Coronation March in Act IV, in which Meyerbeer struck the perfect generic note—perhaps it is carping to say that it would serve as well for the enthronement of King Arthur or George V as for that of a false prophet. Meyerbeer never invented a more universally known tune. Not quite in the same category is the Skaters' Quadrille in Act III, an engagingly rhythmic number that Liszt twisted into a satanically clever and difficult encore piece. The same master arranger put his claws into the dour, turbulent chant of the Anabaptists, "Ad nos, ad salutarem undam," which recurs as a sort of musical basting throughout the score, and concocted a muzzy and magniloquent fantasie and fugue for organ. But there are better things in *Le Prophète* than these sops. Two of Fidès' solos stand out: "Ah! mon fils" is a great voicing of consoling motherhood, while "Donnez, donnez" is a tremulously and affectingly scored expression of sorrow. Few airs in contralto literature are finer than these. Quite different is Fidès' scornful and passionate "O prêtres de Baal." Jean's music is, on the whole, much less interesting, while Berthe's is almost always frankly perfunctory.

The preponderance of emphasis on Fidès has naturally made *Le Prophète* a desired vehicle for those successors of Viardot-García who have the requisites. It happened that in London the same great contralto who had established the role in Paris sang it with Mario as Jean, thus creating a memory for opera-loving Londoners that they were loath to see blemished. They refused to tolerate the otherwise idolized Grisi when she foolishly attempted to sing Fidès a few years later. New Orleans had the American *première,* in 1850. Three years later, *Le Prophète* had reached Niblo's Garden, New York. The Metropolitan *première* occurred during the first season, on March 21, 1884. Nine months later, on December 17, Leopold Damrosch conducted a German version of the opera, with Marianne Brandt as Fidès, Anton Schott as Jean, and Marie Schröder-Hanfstängel as Berthe, and the opera became so popular that season as to equal *Tannhäuser* and *Lohengrin.* A particularly brilliant cast of the late nineties found Jean de Reszke, Marie Brema, and Lilli Lehmann in the three star parts, supported by Édouard de Reszke and Plançon. Schumann-Heink numbered Fidès among her richest characterizations. On February 7, 1917, Caruso, Matzenauer, Muzio, Didur, and Mardones sang *Le Prophète,* and for three seasons the opera came close to becoming a favorite at the Metropolitan. The last revival took place during the season of 1927–28, with Matzenauer again as Fidès. The Jean of Martinelli was not one of his most admired performances.

Between *Le Prophète* and [*L'Africaine*]—Meyerbeer's last and, in some ways, most magnificent opera—intervened two scores, both composed for the Opéra-Comique and both designed (even if Meyerbeer did not so intend them) for a featherbrained type of coloratura display. The first of these was the rewritten *Der Feldlager in Schlesien,* given a new libretto by Scribe and christened *L'Étoile du nord.* The impossible hero of this impossibility was Peter the Great, the heroine the peasant girl he was to seat beside him on the throne. *L'Étoile* all but died with Meyerbeer—a brief career for an opera that had its *première* in 1854. In its youth, it was kept alive by the miraculous agility with which Lind coped with two flutes in the mad scene from the last act, and by the intelligence that Lablache, the Chaliapin of the mid-nineteenth century, brought to the role of Peter's boon companion. Today, outside of Germany, *L'Étoile* no longer shines even momentarily on the concert stage, for few contemporary coloraturas can safely try the cruel tessitura of Catherine's mimetic bouts with the flutes in "Là, là, là, air chéri."

The second of these comic operas was *Le Pardon de Ploërmel,* better known under the name of the Italian version, *Dinorah.* For the book of this nonsensical Breton tale, Meyerbeer deserted Scribe for Barbier and Carré, the librettists of Gounod's *Faust*, the *première* of which preceded *Le Pardon's*, on April 4, 1859, by only a month. The music is of the slightest and lightest, and quite apt for the idiotic girl who idiotically wanders through the three acts. Except for the gracious baritone air "Ah! mon remords te venge," the opera is a shameless coloratura vehicle. It contains the most famous single air that Meyerbeer ever composed, the giddy, tripping, trifling waltz song, "Ombre légère," and this alone has kept for the opera its now precarious hold on the boards.

W. B., H. W.

L'Africaine

[The African Woman]

OPERA IN 5 ACTS

Book by Eugène Scribe

First performance: Opéra, Paris, Apr. 28, 1865

CHARACTERS

Vasco da Gama, officer in the Portuguese Navy, TENOR
Don Pedro, King's Councilor, BASS
Don Diego, member of the King's Council, BASS
Don Alvar, member of the King's Council, TENOR

Inez, daughter of Don Diego, SOPRANO
Anna, her attendant, CONTRALTO
Selika, a captive African queen, SOPRANO
Nelusko, a slave, BARITONE
Grand Inquisitor, BASS

Councilors, Priests, Sailors, Soldiers, Attendants, and Captive Slaves

The action occurs at the end of the fifteenth century and the beginning of the sixteenth, during the time of the daring voyages of conquest and exploration made by Portuguese mariners. The scene shifts from Lisbon to Don Pedro's ship at sea and the island of Madagascar.

The opera opens in the council chamber of the King of Portugal. Inez, betrothed of Vasco da Gama, the explorer, is bewailing his absence. Her father, Don Diego, an admiral, wishes her to marry Don Pedro, president of the royal council. Vasco, who has returned, comes in with startling information concerning a new land he has discovered. As proof, he produces two natives, Selika, an Indian queen, and Nelusko, her henchman. At Don Pedro's instigation, Vasco is thrown into jail.

Selika finds him there. She tells him of her love, and he is overjoyed when she reveals the route to the new land, which he had lost. There follows Selika's exotic slumber song as she watches over Vasco, interrupted occasionally by a barcarole that he trolls in his sleep. In the meantime, Nelusko, jealous of the white interloper, steals in to kill Vasco, but Selika protects him.

Don Pedro, consumed with ambition, sets out in search of the strange country, bringing with him Selika and Nelusko as guides, and also Inez. Nelusko sings the impressive invocation to Adamastor. He plans to destroy the ship, but Vasco [released from jail], aware of the danger surrounding the voyagers, overtakes them in another ship, and apprises them of the treachery. Don Pedro, however, disregards Vasco's warnings, and the craft is boarded by barbarians, Nelusko's people. All the Portuguese are either taken captive or killed.

249

Next we behold Selika's kingdom. In order to save the life of Vasco, she announces that she is his wife. The explorer sings of the astonishing beauties of this exotic country in the rhapsodic aria "O Paradis." Another gem of the opera is the duet between Selika and Vasco.

Inez, it comes about, still lives, and Vasco deserts the Indian queen to fly to his beloved. Selika, knowing now that she has lost Vasco forever, commits suicide by inhaling the lethal perfume of the manchineel tree. When Nelusko finds her dying, he too kills himself, in the same manner.

P. S.

Dinorah was the last of his operas that Meyerbeer was destined to hear. Way back in 1838, Scribe had given him a fantastic libretto about an African slave girl. By 1849, the score was finished, but Meyerbeer was satisfied neither with Scribe's work nor with his own. Therefore he asked for a new libretto, and finally, after endless bickering, Scribe, who at one time had angrily withdrawn the libretto altogether, gave him the revision in 1852. This for the first time included the figure of the opera's present hero, Vasco da Gama, after whom it was temporarily named, and who had been suggested to Scribe by the fact that Jessonda, in Spohr's opera of that name, falls in love with another Portuguese navigator, Tristan da Cunha. There was nothing in the life of Vasco da Gama remotely resembling this foolish sequence of events, and the "African slave girl" Selika is obviously an East Indian, but these facts did not deter Meyerbeer from doing his usual research job and worrying the score to completion in eight years. It was ready in 1860, but production was delayed for four years while the finically conscientious composer changed details, even after the opera was in rehearsal. But Meyerbeer was seventy-two years old, and this time procrastination was fatal. On May 1, 1864, the copying of the last corrections was completed at his house in the Rue Montaigne, and the next day he died. Less than a year later, *L'Africaine*—after three friends * of Meyerbeer had shifted many scenes around to produce harmony between the score and the libretto (as they conceived its requirements)—was sung for the first time.

Much of the delay between the finishing of the score in 1860 and the production at the Opéra on April 28, 1865, was caused by casting difficulties, and even the first Selika—Marie Sax, an ex-*variétés* artist—was not of Meyerbeer's choosing. In the same cast, and far outshining his fellows, was the almost mythically famous Jean-Baptiste Faure, who sang the baritone role of Nelusko. Emilio Naudin followed the dictates of Meyerbeer's will by creating the role of Vasco, while Louis-Henri Obin, Levasseur's successor as professor of singing at the Conservatoire, was the High Priest of Brahma.

* One of them, the formidable music critic, François-Joseph Fétis, in some places cruelly maltreated Meyerbeer's ingenious orchestration, ineptly substituting a saxophone for the bass clarinet—out of friendship for Adolphe Sax, a fellow Belgian, who had invented the instrument.

On July 22, Pauline Lucca, the great singing actress whom Meyerbeer himself had coached in the part of Selika, sang it at Covent Garden, in Italian.
Four years later, as *Die Afrikanerin*, at the Imperial Opera House, Vienna, it
served to introduce a popular operetta singer to grand opera. Her name was
Amalie Materna, and she eventually won her greatest fame as Brünnhilde at
Bayreuth in 1876. Hermann Klein called Lucca's impersonation of the passionate slave "a supreme achievement to be mentioned in the same breath with
the Rosina of Adelina Patti and the Marguerite [*Faust*] of Christine Nilsson."
In more recent times, Selika has been the debut role of such disparate types as
the statuesque and thrilling French dramatic soprano, Lucienne Bréval, and
the Spanish coloratura, María Barrientos.

L'Africaine, in the Italian form of *L'Africana*, reached American shores on
December 1, 1865, at the New York Academy of Music, and there Lucca sang
it seven years later. The first Metropolitan performances began in the season
of 1888–89. On January 15, 1892, Lassalle made his New York debut as Nelusko
in a repetition also remarkable for the first American appearance together of
the already famous trio of Lassalle and the two De Reszkes. On February 13,
1895, there was a moment of unexpected drama for a Metropolitan audience
that had come chiefly to hear Nordica as Selika, Tamagno as Vasco, Ancona
as Nelusko, and Édouard de Reszke as Don Pedro. Lucille Hill, singing the
role of Vasco's sweetheart Inès, fainted, and Mathilde Bauermeister, stepping
out of her menial role as Inès' attendant Anna, assumed Miss Hill's for the
rest of the performance. Lilli Lehmann and Félia Litvinne were other Selikas
of the nineties. On January 11, 1907, Olive Fremstad sang Selika to Caruso's
Vasco, with Marie Rappold as Inès and Riccardo Stracciari as Nelusko, and
with Plançon and Journet in lesser roles. After sixteen years, on March 21, 1923,
L'Africaine was revived for Rosa Ponselle, a magnificent Selika. With her were
Queena Mario, Gigli, Giuseppe Danise, Didur, and Rothier. Later, Elisabeth
Rethberg sang the slave girl, but for the last performances, during the 1933–34
season, Ponselle resumed the role, with Martinelli as her Vasco. With the third
of these, Meyerbeer ceased to be heard in New York.

L'Africaine is an ambiguous score: though the most disciplined of all Meyerbeer's operas in its separate numbers, it is a throwback to the hysterical days
of *Robert le diable*, when the composer was just beginning to understand the
importance of integrating his several idioms. Plainly a work pieced together
over a long period, and written from a number of unreconciled points of view,
it is not a successful opera. It is, generally, a gorgeous and somber score, with
longueurs of spotless academic writing. While it is scenically as spectacular as
Les Huguenots, the music is less theatrical. The false touches that blemish the
score of *Le Prophète*, but which can be excused there as results of a misread-
ing of history, are much more egregious in *L'Africaine*, whose fake Orientalism

came from a faulty reading of an alien culture. (Meyerbeer does not seem to have been sure as to which alien culture he was trying to evoke.)

Yet, when Meyerbeer succeeds in *L'Africaine,* it is, perhaps, on the highest musical level he ever attained. "O Paradis," the great tenor air in Act IV, with its continuation, "Conduisez-moi vers ce navire," is so surpassingly lovely and so just as to seem an act of pure serendipity. Quite as dramatic is Nelusko's primitive evocation of Adamastor, deity of sea and storm, in Act III—"Adamastor, roi des vagues." Most effective of the pseudo-Oriental numbers is Selika's lullaby in Act II, "Sur mes genoux, fils du soleil," an air of entrancing tenderness, while in the final duet between Vasco and Selika—"Ô transports, ô douce extase"—Meyerbeer almost reopened the vein of passion he had found in the last duet between Valentine and Raoul in *Les Huguenots.* As in two or three others of his scores, there are enough fine things in *L'Africaine* to make it tragic that Meyerbeer never managed to produce an opera in which he was consistently at his best from beginning to end. Such an opera would unquestionably have been among the finest ever composed.

"*Aïda* is musically little more than a grandiose pendant or sequel to *L'Africaine.*" Thus Cecil Gray. This is a careless exaggeration: *Aïda* grew, not out of the hints Verdi took from Meyerbeer, but from Verdi's searching study of past opera and of his own abilities as they had developed. Meyerbeer, in truth, founded no school, even though his best tricks can be found in the scores of the most unlikely people. He was like a teacher whose influence persists in detail long after his teachings, in the broader aspects, have been repudiated.

W. B., H. W.

Claudio Monteverdi

(Cremona, Italy, May 15, 1567 [baptismal date]–Nov. 29, 1643, Venice)

Monteverdi * studied under Marc' Antonio Ingegnieri, *maestro di cappella* at the cathedral. From 1590 to 1612 he was in the service of Vincenzo Gonzaga, duke of Mantua, at first as singer and violist, then as *maestro di cappella* and court composer; from 1613 to his death he was *maestro di cappella* at St. Mark's in Venice. He was one of the greatest geniuses, probably the very greatest pioneer, in the whole history of Music . . . the discoverer of the modern Tonal System—a discovery which revolutionized the whole Art of Music. He developed the ponderous, unwieldy *stile rappresentativo* of the *Camerata,* with its leaden accompaniment in long-sustained notes, into the more vivacious and passionate *stile concitato* (or "excited style"), letting the accompaniment take its own rhythm and strike as many repeated notes to the measure as he pleased, thus establishing the basis for nearly all modern writing for a voice, or voices, with instrumental accompaniment. This repercussion of notes, pushed to the due degree of speed, became the string *tremolo*—a device against which the players kicked lustily at first, as physically impossible. He also invented the string *pizzicato*. The whole great Art of Instrumentation owes its origin to him. He and da Gagliano carried the Opera one stage farther in its musical development; not a very long stage, perhaps, but none the less an important one. They threw Dramatic Music, already big with Melody, into her travail-throes; the whole dramatic style showed greater freedom and mastery.

[In] 1607, Monteverdi's first opera, *Orfeo* (the libretto by Alessandro Striggio), was given with great success at the Accademia degl' Invaghiti in Mantua. Toward the end of January, 1608, it was followed by da Gagliano's *Dafne* (Rinuccini's old libretto, revamped for the occasion by the author), given in honour of the duke's youngest son, Ferdinando Gonzaga, being made cardinal. On May 28 of the same year came the most overwhelming success of all, Monteverdi's *Arianna* (the text by Rinuccini), given to celebrate the nuptials of Francesco Gonzaga (the eldest son) and Margherita di Savoia.

In Monteverdi's *Orfeo* . . . the monody has more musical independence, a freer dramatic fire; the orchestration begins to assume an importance of its own; the harmony is richer and more appositely expressive; in short, one feels

* The name is spelt *Monteverdo* in the baptismal register. On the title-pages of most of his published works it stands as *Monteverde*; once as *Monte Verde*. But the 113 autograph letters that have come down to us are, without exception, signed *Monteverdi*. This plural termination is undoubtedly the right one.

a stronger hand at the bellows.* All that remains of *Arianna* is one monologue, Arianna's famous lament, "Lasciatemi morire!" after being abandoned by Teseo. No single composition was ever more famous in its day than this "Lamento"; contemporary letters are rich in accounts of its pathetic beauty and of the overwhelming impression it made upon all listeners. Even to-day we can feel its enormous dramatic power, its wondrous truth and depth of pathos.

So far, the Opera had been distinctly aristocratic, a *bonne bouche* for cultivated *cognoscenti;* but a change was soon to come. In 1637 the first public opera-house—Teatro di San Cassiano—was opened in Venice [for which Monteverdi, two years later, wrote an opera *Adone,* one of his numerous lost works]. With it, the Opera was brought for the first time face to face with the great general public. Thenceforth the people—together with, but quite as much as, crowned heads and affluent nobles—were to be arbiters of its destiny. . . . That the Opera must come down from its high perch of pseudo-Hellenic purism, and appeal to a taste quite other than that of a cultivated aristocracy, was evident enough.

W. F. A.

---

* It is rather curious that, of all Monteverdi's opera-scores, only the first and last—*Orfeo* (Mantua, 1607) and *L'Incoronatione di Poppea* (Venice, 1642)—have been preserved.

Orfeo

[Orpheus]

OPERA IN A PROLOGUE AND 5 ACTS

Book by ALESSANDRO STRIGGIO

First performance: Accademia degl' Invaghiti, Mantua, Feb. 24, 1607

CHARACTERS

Goddess of Music, MEZZO-SOPRANO
First Shepherd, TENOR
Orfeo, BARITONE
Eurydice, SOPRANO
Silvia, a messenger, MEZZO-SOPRANO
Goddess of Hope, MEZZO-SOPRANO

Charon, BASS
Proserpina, CONTRALTO
Pluto, BASS
Apollo, TENOR
Nymphs, Shepherds, Spirits

The action takes place in legendary Greece

[Orpheus mourns his lost Eurydice at her tomb, while shepherds and shepherdesses bring flowers and join in a touching lament. Orpheus is inconsolable in his grief, Orpheus the unrivaled musician of antiquity, at whose divine music, legend tells us, trees uprooted themselves and rocks became loosened from their ledges in order to follow the wonderful sounds. For this Orpheus was the son of Apollo, god of music, and Calliope, muse of epic poetry. Amor, the god of love, is so touched by the anguish of Orpheus that he tells him he may descend to the nether world, the dark realm of Pluto, there to seek the shade of Eurydice. One condition, however, is made: if Orpheus would have Eurydice return to earth with him, he must not turn to look at her until he has recrossed the river Styx. In the awesome depths of Tartarus the frightening bark of Cerberus is heard, and Furies join in a grotesque dance. Although they try to frighten him away, these dark spirits are finally moved to pity with the song of Orpheus' grief, and they allow him to continue his quest. In the happy Elysian fields beneath cheerful skies, the Spirits of the Blessed dance to the song of birds and the murmur of brooks. Gluck's music is marvelously descriptive of the chaste beauty and the tranquil felicity of these happy spirits. A flute solo of ravishing sweetness accentuates the mood of classical antiquity. Here Orpheus finds his beloved, clasps her joyfully to his breast, begs her to follow him, but never looks upon her face. As they mount higher and higher Eurydice becomes increasingly downcast because Orpheus seems no longer to love her. Not once have their eyes met. She would rather remain below than return to earth without his love. Orpheus is bound by the agreement not to reveal the cause of his strange behavior. When they are almost in sight of the land of the living, she cries out

255

with such heart-rending pathos that, in a moment of forgetfulness, Orpheus looks back, only to see her sink lifeless to the ground. Now his sorrow is even more profound than before. Utterly disconsolate, he expresses his grief in a melody of sublime pathos, "Che farò senza Euridice?" ("I have lost my Eurydice"). Amor, who has been watching Orpheus, is so deeply moved by this impassioned outcry that he restores Eurydice to life and permits the rejoicing lovers to proceed to the world above.]

L'Orfeo, Favola in Musica was written for the Duke Vincenzo Gonzaga, Mantuan patron of the arts—the music by his chapel master, Claudio Monteverde (or Monteverdi); the text by his secretary Alessandro Striggio. The piece was performed at Mantua in 1607; so well liked that, according to a contemporary letter, "my Lord the Duke, not satisfied with having been present at the performance, has ordered another, which will be given in the presence of all the ladies of the town." The opera, or "musical fable," was played at Turin two years later, and simultaneously printed in Venice. It passed forthwith into a shadowy existence in the musical histories, where it served as an instance of early opera, showing its composer to be a daring innovator in dramatic effects. There have been several restorations of Orfeo upon the stage of the present century.

Vincent d'Indy found Monteverde to be a direct precursor (despite three intervening centuries) of Debussy's Pelléas et Mélisande in the mating of music and the integral character of a spoken language. This zealous scholar adapted and revived Orfeo in Paris, in 1904. . . . Monteverde has had an authoritative and artistically scrupulous modern spokesman in Francesco Malipiero, who has closely studied his dramatic works.

The original editions of 1609 and 1615 (which have been carefully reproduced by Malipiero, with the indications of the figured bass filled in) present a problem doubly baffling to the faithful transcriber. In the first place, the numerous instruments at Monteverde's disposal in the ducal household are now in large part entirely obsolete. In the second place, the notation (and the instrumentation as well) was often dubiously indicated. The all-important harmonies which accompanied the singing voice were often outlined in a figured bass which can (and has been) variously interpreted. The instrumental portions of the original score are usually in five staves, distributed according to clef, the instruments to be used indicated apart from the actual notation. Such lines as "al suono del organo di legno ed un chitarone," or the direction over the introductory "toccata" that it is to be "heard three times with all the instruments before the rising of the curtain" puts an embarrassing latitude of discretion upon a modern arranger.

L'Orfeo, according to the custom of the day, was innocent of the arias and concerted numbers which later came into vogue under pressure of singers more concerned with exhibiting their vocal abilities than co-operating towards dramatic illusion. At this time the text was for the most part in recitative, with strophic choruses at intervals. When a singer had set verses with a repeated melody, the text and spirit of the situation was not forgotten in bursts of florid virtuosity. . . .

The anachronistic strains that have crept into this libretto have bothered the purists of Greek antiquity. J. A. Westrup, who helped prepare the English version for the Oxford performance in 1925, has pointed out: "In Act III we find Hope (personified) leading Orpheus to the banks of the Styx and at the same time quoting the words of Dante, 'All hope abandon, ye who enter here.' And it is not easy to attempt a reconciliation of the descent of Apollo and the ascension of Orpheus to Heaven with the traditions of Greek mythology, which asserts that the singer was torn to pieces by Thracian women." The prologue is delivered by *"La Musica,"* the spirit of music. Five acts follow. The first is largely pastoral, shows nymphs and shepherds gently celebrating the nuptials of Orpheus and Eurydice in the "glades of Thrace." In the second Act (another pastoral scene), Sylvia, messenger of Eurydice, arrives to tell Orpheus of the death of her mistress by the sting of a serpent. Orpheus utters a moving lament, and vows to penetrate the domain of shadows that he may recover his bride. Act III discloses the River Styx, and the ferryman Charon, who refuses a living mortal passage until at length he succumbs to the spell of Orpheus' song. Pluto, in the fourth act, on the suit of Persephone, grants the lovers release, provided that Orpheus lead forth Eurydice without once looking back. Orpheus, alarmed for Eurydice on account of the pursuing furies, disobeys and must return alone to the light of day. The closing act departs from the letter of the ancient legend. Apollo, as *deus ex machina,* descends from a cloud, and transports the bereaved Orpheus to Heaven, there to dwell in eternal consolation. The shepherds sing a chorus in praise of Apollo, and the dénouement is finally blessed with what R. L. Stuart, the English translator, calls "a concluding Morris dance which is intended either to dispel our sadness over the fate of Eurydice, or to amuse us while we don our plumed hats and swords preparatory to leaving the theatre."

J. N. B.

There has been a heroic effort to insinuate *Orfeo* into the modern repertoire. In 1911, it was produced in Italy. A year later, on April 14, a condensed version of it was sung in English, in concert form, on a Sunday evening at the Metropolitan Opera House, New York. Unfortunately, it was preceded by a typical rag-bag recital by two of the Metropolitan's leading stars, Emmy Destinn and Pasquale Amato, so that by the time *Orfeo* was begun the audience had so tired itself by shouts and applause that it had no appetite left for the opera, and therefore Rita Fornia (Eurydice), Anna Case (a Nymph), Hermann Weil (Orpheus), and Herbert Witherspoon (Pluto) sang to little advantage. Cleofonte Campanini, musical director of the Chicago Grand Opera Company, was quite as unfortunate when, on January 4, 1913, he tried to force a concert performance of *Orfeo* on an Auditorium one third full. Mario Sammarco, as Orpheus, gave a noble interpretation for the unenthusiastic Chicagoans. The first American stage performance of *Orfeo* took place at Northampton, Massachusetts, under the auspices of Smith College, on May 12, 1929, when a new edition, by the Italian modernist and Monteverdi scholar, G. Francesco Malipiero, was used. Charles Kullmann was the Orpheus, and Werner Josten conducted. In England, Professor Edward J. Dent revived *Orfeo* at Oxford, and with considerable success.

W. B., H. W.

[Dimitri Mitropoulos introduced *Orfeo* to a New York Philharmonic-Symphony audience in Carnegie Hall on February 21, 1952. The version used the so-called "orchestral realization" of Ottorino Respighi, first produced at La Scala, Milan, on March 16, 1935. Heading the cast in the concert performance were Mack Harrell as Orfeo and Frances Greer as Eurydice.]

Modest Moussorgsky

(Karev, Government of Pskov, Russia, Mar. 28, 1835–Mar. 21, 1881,
St. Petersburg)

Mussorgsky's early years were spent in the country, at Karevo in the Toropets district three hundred miles to the south of Moscow. . . . His father Peter Mussorgsky was a landowner and his mother came of the same prosperous class, but his father's mother had been a peasant-woman and from her, perhaps, the composer inherited that sympathy with the peasants and that love of their native songs which contributed so much to his art. In childhood he learnt from his nurse the old folk-tales and legends, and lay awake at night thinking how to make music of them. He learnt the pianoforte from his mother and at eleven years of age played one of Field's concertos at a party given to local society by his parents. Two years later he entered the Cadet School, and even there he found some intellectual interest in the company of the chaplain, Father Krupsky, who did his best to stay the youth's appetite for music by lending him the motets of Bortnyansky, a pupil of Galuppi. After receiving his commission, Mussorgsky was introduced to Dargomizhsky, at whose house he became acquainted with Balakirev, César Cui, and Vladimir Stassov, the leaders of the nationalist movement in music whose activities were just beginning to bear fruit. Of this group only Balakirev was a composer by profession from the first. Cui, like Mussorgsky, was an army officer, while of the later disciples, Borodin was a research chemist, Rimsky-Korsakov a sailor. Stassov was a journalist and became the chief propagandist of the group.

While it would be far from the truth to suggest that Mussorgsky remained an amateur composer—few musicians have been consumed more wholly by the authentic fire—he never acquired a technical knowledge adequate to the full realization of his ideas. There was, indeed, no one from whom he could obtain the kind of learning he needed. Rimsky-Korsakov himself, when appointed Professor of Composition at St. Petersburg, had to learn as he taught and ended by becoming as academic as the average professor. So Mussorgsky had to proceed by the light of nature—a powerful illumination, in his case, which revealed unsuspected beauty in unexpected places.

He had thrown up his commission in the Guards in 1858 at the age of nineteen and decided to become a composer. At this time he had a mental or nervous breakdown, which Calvocoressi diagnosed as the result of the drinking bouts in the army combined with the disturbances of adolescence. Naturally sensitive and introspective, he fell a prey for a time to morbid imaginings, concerning which he unburdened himself to Balakirev who had become his

259

teacher and mentor. Balakirev, himself strongly imbued with the national spirit, was just the man to guide Mussorgsky's development—if only he had himself possessed the technical knowledge to pass on to his pupil. The best he could do was to set before the youth examples of composition. He directed his attention to Beethoven's last quartets and, among contemporaries, to the works of Liszt.

After a year or so Balakirev came to the conclusion that Mussorgsky had little talent, and Stassov concurred even more forcibly in this opinion. Indeed, at first Mussorgsky's music gave no indication of individual character or originality. He was slow to develop and, after Balakirev who remained on friendly terms with him gave up trying to teach him, he had to proceed empirically, making his material as he went. His mind began to turn towards the realistic representation of life, whose problems were engaging just then the younger Russian authors and painters. The novels of Turgenev, who was among the first to introduce into literature portraits of simple people, peasants, and clerks, were among the works that attracted his attention. It was a time of intellectual and political ferment, one of whose symptoms was the liberation of the serfs in 1861—an act which deprived the Mussorgsky family of a great part of their income, but of which Modeste generously approved. He surrendered his share of what remained of the estate to his elder brother who was married, and in 1863 obtained employment as a clerk in one of the Government offices at a meagre salary in order to maintain himself.

About this time he began to create those songs in which are pictured the joys and sorrows of the Russian peasant. For the songs he evolved a musical style based upon the normal inflexions of speech. It was an unconscious reversion to the principles of the first Italian opera-composers; for there is no reason to suppose that Mussorgsky had ever heard of Peri and Caccini or even Monteverdi, though he was acquainted with some of Gluck's later operas. This recitative-like vocal line, which he yet contrived to make melodically interesting, is supported by an accompaniment full of unorthodox harmonic inventions, some of them boldly imaginative, and some the crudities of a musician who did not quite know what effect he wanted or how to get it. Good and bad were alike emended after his death by Rimsky-Korsakov who edited the bulk of Mussorgsky's compositions.

Such a style proved ideal for opera. The words could be given the utmost dramatic force and significance without regard to conventional ideas of "form," and Mussorgsky's unorthodox harmony more often than not heightened the effect to a degree that makes Rimsky-Korsakov's softening of his abruptness little less than a crime. Unfortunately Mussorgsky managed to complete only one opera, *Boris Godounoff,* with a libretto by himself based on Pushkin's historical drama. It exists in two versions, the first finished in 1869, when the composer was thirty. After its rejection by the Imperial Theatres, he remodelled the opera, adding the Polish scenes to provide the "love-interest" which was considered indispensable, and the final "revolutionary scene," which contains some of the most imaginative, though thoroughly "realistic," music he ever wrote, and emphasizes the importance of the chorus, the people, as the true protagonist, rather even than Boris himself, of the opera. After many delays *Boris* was at last produced, with many cuts, in . . . 1874. It had a fleeting success with the enthusiasts of the new school, but soon disappeared until it was revived in Rimsky-Korsakov's edition by Diaghilev with Chaliapin in the title-part. Since then the original score has been published and performed. It is fashionable to damn Rimsky-Korsakov out of hand for his meddling with a work of genius, but, while he certainly went too far in softening Mussorgsky's bold strokes, it must be conceded that in the matter of instrumentation there is much in the original score that sounds ineffective and even feeble, because Mussorgsky had very little knowledge of orchestration. Some touching-up is needed and at least it may be claimed in Rimsky-Korsakov's favour that, even if his recension went too far, he made the opera a practicable proposition in the first decade of this century, which the original score would hardly have been.

Moreover, it may be suggested that Rimsky-Korsakov, who shared lodgings with Mussorgsky for two years while the revision of *Boris* was in progress, may reasonably be supposed to have had a better knowledge of Mussorgsky's aims than anyone else. In the matter of *Khovanshchina*, the second of Mussorgsky's large-scale essays in Russian historical opera, some form of editorial salvage was really necessary. For the opera was left in a chaotic state, and little of it was actually orchestrated by Mussorgsky. Yet, even in its sadly muddled condition, this is a noble and majestic work, a kind of Russian *Parsifal* without the less pleasant aspects of Wagner's "sacred" drama.

There was much else left unfinished. There was *The Marriage*, Mussorgsky's first essay in "realistic" opera, modelled to some extent on Dargomizhsky's *The Stone Guest*,* but abandoned in favour of *Boris*. And there was, besides other ventures which proceeded even less far, *The Fair at Sorochintsy*, at which he worked, on and off, from 1858 until his final illness. Under various titles and in various forms, including a symphonic poem, *The Fair* was remodelled and altered, but never took final shape. Of all this labour only the symphonic poem, "A Night on the Bare Mountain"—and that in a version constructed from various sketches by Rimsky-Korsakov, though Mussorgsky did complete an orchestral score of it—is generally familiar. Various attempts to complete the opera by patching together the pieces Mussorgsky composed have not been very successful.

So we must be content with *Boris* and the songs, especially the cycles, "Sunless" and "Songs and Dances of Death" with poems by Golenishchev-Kutuzov, with whom for a time he shared lodgings, and the delightful "Nursery" set for which he himself wrote the words. Here his wonderful mastery of declamation

---

* A setting of Pushkin's version of the Don Juan legend almost entirely in declamatory recitative.

as a flexible and seemingly natural covering of the words is seen at its best. Even those who know no Russian can appreciate something of the extraordinary subtlety of Mussorgsky's craftsmanship in this direction.

His failure to achieve more, to complete what he had begun, to come to definite decisions about what he wanted to do—this failure and the obvious decline of his powers as a composer in his last years were due to his addiction to drink. Whenever an emotional crisis occurred in his life—the death of his mother in 1865 and of his much loved friend the painter M. V. Hartmann * in 1873—he sought, as the saying is, to drown his sorrow in drink to the extent of bringing on attacks of *delirium tremens*. The dipsomania got an ever stronger hold on him, and though he made several efforts to overcome the craving—notably during a concert tour in South Russia when he acted as accompanist to the singer, Darya Leonova—he sank gradually into that terrible and pathetic state of fuddled incapacity which it is so painful for the friends of the sufferer to behold and so impossible for them to relieve.

There is nothing more dreadful in the iconography of music than the contrast between the photograph of the handsome young Guardee with a, perhaps, rather weak mouth, and the portrait of the old drunkard with his wild, pale eyes and sodden expression painted by Repin in hospital shortly before the composer died from a stroke on 28 March 1881, just after his forty-second birthday, in celebration of which someone—like Gluck's convivial friends at luncheon—had given him a bottle of brandy.

D. H.

---

* It was a posthumous exhibition of Hartmann's paintings and designs that inspired the pianoforte work, "Pictures from an Exhibition."

Boris Godounoff

OPERA IN 3 ACTS

Book by the COMPOSER, after the play by ALEXANDER PUSHKIN

First performance: Imperial Opera House, St. Petersburg, Jan. 24, 1874

CHARACTERS

Boris Godounoff, BASS
Xenia, his daughter, SOPRANO
Feodor, his son, MEZZO-SOPRANO
Marina, daughter of the Voyevode of Sandomir, MEZZO-SOPRANO
Prince Shuisky, TENOR
Gregory, a novice, afterwards the Pretender Dmitri (or "The False Demetrius"), TENOR

Varlaam and Missail, vagabond monks, BASS AND TENOR
Pimenn, a monk and chronicler, BASS
Stchelkalov, secretary of the Duma, BARITONE
Innkeeper's wife, MEZZO-SOPRANO
Police Official, BASS
Rangoni, a Jesuit monk, BARITONE
A Nurse, MEZZO-SOPRANO
An Idiot, TENOR

Two Jesuits, Chorus of Boyars and People, etc.

The action takes place in Russia and Poland, 1598–1605

In the courtyard of the Novodievitch (Prologue), Boris—Czar Feodor has died—ostensibly refuses the crown the people offer him under the spur of henchmen's whips and pilgrims' venal prophecies. In Tschudov Convent, Pimen the chronicler inflames the novice Gregory (afterward the False Demetrius), with his tale of how Boris has murdered the Czarevitch, and the youth elects to become the instrument of divine retribution on the usurper.

In the Square of the Kremlin Boris' splendid coronation processional passes with bell chime and pageantry to the cathedral, while the populace, encouraged by the boyars, acclaim him. In a Lithuanian inn Gregory, with bibulous, ballad-singing monks, enters to ask the way to the border, leaping from the window when the Czar's spies come to take him.

Xenia, Boris' daughter, in the women's wing of the Kremlin palace, is wailing for her bridegroom who has died (her nurse trying to comfort her with the "Song of the Flea") when Boris enters, devoured with remorse for his murder of Demetrius. When Count Shuisky reports a False Demetrius has risen in Lithuania (though he himself has seen the murdered boy in his coffin) the Czar breaks down. A mechanical clock chimes, one of his own son Feodor's toys, and while the accusing clangor of the coronation bells rings through his brain, Boris' guilty conscience evokes the vision of his hapless victim, till he writhes on the floor in despair. (The scene is the most harrowing in the opera.)

In Sandomir Castle, Polish girls pay homage to lovely Marina, daughter of the Voivode. Her ambition covets the Muscovite crown, and Demetrius shall place it on her white brow! Gladly she promises the Jesuit Rangoni to win the Russian people to the Roman faith through the Czar whose heart she controls. Later in the castle gardens, where a gay Polonaise is danced, Polish magnates interrupt Marina's and Demetrius' passionate love duet, promising to make the adventurer Czar.

In Kromy forest the starving people beat a boyar, torture an idiot, and cheer Demetrius as he rides by in the light of flaring torches on his way to Moscow and the throne. (This scene, voicing the very soul of the Russian people, with the chorus in the rôle of the "star," Moussorgsky planned to make the final one of the opera but the last act, as usually given, ends with Boris' tragic death.) * In the great reception hall of the Kremlin, while assembled boyars condemn the False Demetrius to death Boris, half insane with the torture of his guilty conscience, appears and breaks down with a terrible cry. Pimen's message (a shepherd has miraculously regained his sight after praying on dead Feodor's grave) kills his last hope. He consigns the empire to his son and dies in agony trying to say: "I still am the Czar!" while his soul passes on to the chant of monks and the toll of bells.

F. H. M.

Moussorgsky set to work on *Boris Godunoff* in 1868 and completed it in 1872. The opera is thus older than *Carmen,* older than *Manon,* older than *Otello* or *Falstaff,* older than even the earliest Puccini or than a number of other lyric dramas which we long ago accepted as established landmarks. Nevertheless the explosive force of *Boris* made itself properly felt only in the twentieth century. Even today many of us are not fully aware of the quantities of dynamite it contains nor of the debt certain outstanding composers of the past forty years owe to it. If ever a work was born before its time, if ever a score could qualify as music of the future it is here.

The record of this stark, rugged, tumultuous masterpiece is one of the most singular in operatic history and full of paradoxes, contradictions and embattled tendencies. The changing aesthetics of two generations are writ large upon it.

The story of *Boris* is to a large degree a story of successive transformations, revisions and further revised versions. And the end, apparently, is not yet. Luckily, the originality of Moussorgsky's "national folk drama" is so vast, its inherent power so tremendous that tamperings and editings, however they may have affected details, have not really enfeebled it as a whole.

When the first version, the so-called "original *Boris,*" was completed and fully scored in the summer of 1870, Moussorgsky submitted the "boiling and

---

* [The Metropolitan reversed its traditional order for the first time on March 6, 1953, when it ended the opera with the forest scene.]

bubbling" product to the advisory committee of the Maryinski Theatre (in what was then St. Petersburg . . .). This committee, consisting of the Russian conductor, Napravnik, a French and a German director of plays and an Italian contrabassist, took one look at the work and turned thumbs down. This summary action was rather more than the composer had anticipated, even if previously the director of the Imperial theatres, Gedeonov, had examined the piece and shown himself "severe but just." The committee was less disposed to be "just" in the Moussorgskyan sense. First of all, the boldness and novelty of the music as a whole upset its members mightily. In the second place they objected to the lack of any leading female role. Nor was that by any means the end of their worries—the Italian contrabassist, for instance, lost his temper over the way the composer had written a passage for divided double basses in the accompaniment of one of the monk Varlaam's songs.

Moussorgsky, deeply hurt, withdrew his score. But upon thinking the matter over carefully and noting that his good friend, Vladimir Stassov, shared certain of the committee's views, he applied himself to a thoroughgoing revision of the work. The new version, finished in 1872, differed in many ways from the first. Most important of the alterations were the introduction of the two Polish scenes, the substitution of the revolutionary scene in the Forest of Kromy for a scene in the Red Square and a reversal of the order of the last two scenes, whereby the work closed with the death of Boris instead of in the wintry forest. There was likewise considerable modification of the scene in the Czar's apartments, with a number of significant additions and extensions elsewhere.

From time to time there had been private hearings of the earlier version. Moussorgsky's intimates were, for the most part, delighted. But it was only in 1873 that some scenes from the revised opera were given publicly at the Maryinski Theatre on the occasion of a benefit. They were so well received that it was decided to produce the entire work in the same house. The first complete *Boris* was performed on January 24, 1874, to the delight of the progressive and the intense annoyance of reactionaries and conservatives. On the one hand bands of young enthusiasts left the theatre singing passages from the opera; on the other, the opposition went so far in its spite as to prevent the presentation at the theatre of some wreaths Moussorgsky's admirers had sent him. This opposition, seemingly organized by reactionary critics, furiously charged the composer with "technical ignorance, vulgarity and want of taste." And so well did it conduct its intrigues that after twenty successful hearings *Boris* was put to silence for years. But as the composer had written to Stassov a little earlier: "Our gaze is fixed upon the future and we are not to be deterred by criticism." Prophetic words! The future was to be his bravest avenger.

With the possible exception of Stassov, Moussorgsky had no warmer, more devoted or more well-meaning friend than Nikolai Rimsky-Korsakoff. Yet in the perspective of time Rimsky has come to play a curiously anomalous part in the destiny of Moussorgsky's works. Approved and defended on the one hand he has been viciously berated on the other. Why? Simply because for what he thought the best interests of *Boris* he reorchestrated the entire work and altered rhythmic, harmonic and other features of the original with a view of removing what he considered technical blemishes. "I hated *Boris* and yet I worshipped it," he once said. While idolizing Moussorgsky's native genius, he had alluded to the latter's "obstinate, bumptious amateurishness." And according to his lights he proceeded to make rough places plain in an edition of the score published in 1896. [A revision, issued in 1908, was the basis of Metropolitan productions preceding that of 1952–53, when the original order of scenes was restored.]

The academic streak was bred in Rimsky's bone. The critic Laroche, a close friend of Tchaikovsky, declared that he suffered from a "mania for perfection." We are told, for one thing, by Rimsky's biographer, Yastrebtzev, that he was

abnormally sensitive on the question of musical keys. . . . For instance, E-flat major, for him, was the proper key for "cities and fortresses." In the geography lesson in *Boris* the Czar sings the phrase: "With one glance thou canst survey the whole Empire, its frontiers, rivers, cities." The three last words are accompanied by the chords of F major, G minor and E-flat, respectively. . . . Rimsky explained that Moussorgsky originally put the word cities before rivers. . . . "This irritated me (Rimsky) greatly because the chord of E-flat did not come in its proper place. I begged Moussorgsky to alter the order of the words so that cities came on the last chord; and do you know, I feel absolutely satisfied now whenever I hear that E-flat."

It is not the purpose of the present writer, however, to pass judgment on the various aspects of the long standing and acrimonious controversy and the merits or demerits of the revision as against the originals. In the first place, the average music lover has not been given sufficient chance of studying and hearing Moussorgsky's version to decide. Only a comparatively small handful of specialists have enjoyed this opportunity. In the second, Rimsky explicitly stated that his own editions were not meant to supersede Moussorgsky's; that if ever there was a popular desire to return to the original it could always be satisfied. We know that Rimsky made more or less wilful alterations in Moussorgsky's rhythms, that he shifted certain bar lines and changed certain harmonies which many insist are not crudities but valuable audacities. Further, we know that Rimsky replaced by a rich and brilliant instrumentation Moussorgsky's rather thin scoring with its preponderance of strings and that he concluded the garden scene with a blazing, if wholly operatic, peroration in lieu of the whispered close devised by the composer. One answer to all these matters is that it was in Rimsky's version that the mighty work proceeded to conquer the world. Another is that even in contemporary Russia, some form of revision must appear needful, else why would a modernist like Dmitri Shostakovich have added still another *Boris* version to the existing abundance?

It is one of the extraordinary properties of *Boris* to be at once the supreme specimen of national opera and at the same time to possess a validity and an appeal which are to the last degree universal. There are episodic details about the text which Moussorgsky drew from Pushkin, from the historian Karamzin and from his own stores of invention. Yet the magnificent canvas, with its multiplicity of figures and its seemingly unrelated cross currents of incident, is no more a patchwork than "Macbeth" or "Richard III." A tremendous and awe-inspiring compendium of the soul of the Russian people, it sets against each other two dominating characters: the spiritually tortured Czar and, now oppressed, now seething, the Folk. The music—even denatured by Rimsky-Korsakoff as you may think it—is in almost every page of such transcendent greatness that it is difficult to speak of it with moderation.

Of all nations on earth Russia is probably richest in its marvelous plenitude of folk song. The music of *Boris* is supersaturated with this element. This is not to say that Moussorgsky has filled his score with actual folk tunes. Rather, he has so steeped himself in the spirit of his native folk song that his melodies are sometimes indistinguishable from the genuine wild flowers of native music. The very first phrases of the orchestral introduction to the prologue make this point instantly clear. The choruses of appeal, supplication, wild lament which fill the scene and the solemn canticles of pilgrims that bring down the curtain carry it further.

Let it be noted that thematic labels, or leading motives, are not few in *Boris*. But if they fill a significant dramatic purpose they are not employed in Wagner's symphonic manner and are rarely the subject of expansion or development. What one does repeatedly encounter is that extraordinarily dramatic element of so much Russian music, the *ostinato*—the repetition, usually in the bass, of a rhythm or a figure of piercing emotional effect.

H. F. P.

THE REAL BORIS

When Czar Ivan IV (the Terrible) of Russia died in 1584, he left behind two sons and one friend. The sons were Feodor of enfeebled body and mind, a man in his mid-teens, and Dimitri, a child whose mother was Ivan's seventh wife. The friend was Boris Godunoff, a boyar who had so faithfully served the Czar that the latter had come to confide in him and to consult him in practically every matter, both public and private. Boris Godunoff was named regent for the half-witted Feodor, and at that time had every intention of carrying out his late friend's wishes honestly and to the best of his ability, which was, unquestionably, great.

Boris' sister, Irene, was soon married to the new Czar, who placed his little half-brother in a monastery some distance from Moscow. The child died. Seven years later Feodor died without an heir, which left Russia without a Czar. The country was thus ruled by Boris and his sister.

Boris stood well, everywhere. He was wise, just, and while every inch a barbarian, was so far removed in temper from the Czars that in a very short time the boyars asked him to assume the crown. He refused, time and again. Finally he yielded. A coronation was held.

The new Czar built two monuments to his friend Ivan. One was a 270-foot tower to the Kremlin. The other was serfdom. At that time the Russian peasantry was free. In great droves the peasants worked where they pleased, owned their own tiny cottages, received pay from the boyar or land owner, and served him as long as he served them. If a boyar ill treated his peasants they were free to go to another and work. A boyar could hire the peasants of another if he chose to offer them more wages in a greater share of the crops they raised. This condition led to ill feeling among the boyars, and resulted in many feuds and intrigues. Boris needed the good will of the boyars. He proclaimed a law that the peasants could not leave the estates on which they worked. This law was in effect till the middle eighteen-hundreds.

Suddenly word came to Boris that Dimitri was not dead and was living in Poland. The next news was that he was coming with an army to claim his throne. On he came. Joining his standard were the peasants, angry with Boris for his law keeping them in one place. They were united with those boyars whose peasants could not come back because Boris' law forced them to remain under other nobles. At the gates of Moscow they learned that Boris was dead —either by murder or suicide. After taking the throne and crown of Ivan IV, Dimitri, an absolute adventurer and pretender, put to death the widow and son of Boris.

This is the true story of Boris Godunoff, made into an historical drama by the Russian poet Pushkin and later into what is probably the richest Russian opera by Moussorgsky.

The coronation offers an excuse for spectacular music, like the scene in *Aïda* in which the Egyptian Army returns. For operatic reason Dimitri is given a sweetheart, Marina. In the opera Dimitri's real name is Gregory, a young monk, who hears the tale of Dimitri's disappearance from an older monk. This tale so fires the imagination of Gregory that he leaves the convent and journeys to Poland, there to perfect his plans, meet Marina and taste the pleasures of love. The tale of Dimitri as told by the older monk is to the whole opera what the narrative of Ferrando in the first scene of *Il Trovatore* is to that opera—the facts that account for all that has gone before.

In the opera Boris can be considered the villain and Dimitri the hero; or it is possible to regard them both as villains, and the piece an opera without a hero. Of course, the art of the singer in the role of Boris may so sway the audience's sympathies to Boris that the public will go away thinking him the hero in the popular sense.

Most operas with an historical background detract from the dignity of the people about whom they are written. Think what *Madame Sans Gêne* does to Napoleon! Witness the impossibility we know as Franchetti's *Cristoforo Colombo,* with poor Columbus dying of love on the tomb of Queen Isabella! The music to *Boris Godunoff* does not, however, belittle Boris. Rather it adds to his stature. No matter what view one takes of his monuments to his friend, or whether one looks upon his acquiring the throne as a theft, one has to admit that Boris did a world of good for Russia both as regent, favorite and Czar in his own right. In the richness of Moussorgsky's score one can find the grandeur that was really Boris Godunoff.

E. D.

The first American *Boris* had the advantage of a production brought as near perfection as the circumstances allowed: Toscanini rehearsed it for two months, and so the Metropolitan orchestra and chorus never more gloriously fulfilled themselves than on March 19, 1913, when the opera had its American *première.* But this impeccable conductor could not find sixteen principals, not to speak of an enormous chorus, who sang Russian or could even be imbued with an understanding of Russian ideas of declamation. So this performance, so flawless in many purely musical respects, began with the handicap of slighting many equally important dramatic values. The Polish Adamo Didur was as admirable as any non-Russian-singing Boris can be, but as he and all his colleagues sang in Italian, the force and dramatic stress of Pushkin's Russian words that Mussorgsky had converted into musical sound syllable by syllable were necessarily lost. The *décor,* brought wholesale from Paris, was as atmospherically correct as the presence, in major roles, of such otherwise excellent, but incurably Occidental, artists as Homer, Anna Case, Andrés de Segurola, Rothier, and Althouse (making his debut) was jarring. Yet, despite these disadvantages, *Boris* had a terrific impact, and box-office receipts heartened Gatti-Casazza (ordinarily no friend to innovation), who had said, in a rather *ex cathedra* strain immediately after the *première:* "I consider *Boris* the most important performance artistically that I have given at the Metropolitan."

After Toscanini left the Metropolitan, *Boris* continued in the repertoire, but indifferent performances were reflected in cooling public interest. Chaliapin changed all that: he first sang the role in New York on December 9, 1921, and kept the opera a going concern until he, too, left the Metropolitan, eight seasons later. Singing in Russian, he gave Manhattan its first opportunity to get the full force and flavor of Mussorgsky's projection of the Czar, but the management provided him with Italian-singing confreres even less satisfactory than those who had supported Didur.

W. B., H. W.

[On March 6, 1953, the Metropolitan revived *Boris Godounoff* in an English version prepared by John Gutman, with Moussorgsky's original orchestration (as "restored" by Karol Rathaus), and with George London (later alternating with Cesare Siepi) in the title role. Fritz Stiedry conducted.]

Wolfgang Amadeus Mozart

(Salzburg, Jan. 27, 1756–Dec. 5, 1791, Vienna)

One of the supreme figures in the history of the art of music, Mozart is also one of the most consistently misrepresented. If he had been no more than the polished master of the "Gallant style" of the late eighteenth century, he would have gone the way of dozens of his forgotten contemporaries. It is precisely because what he produced is so distinctive, so completely above the limitations of any one time and place, that he occupies a special niche in the story of music. Mozart expressed the spirit of his age, but in a far greater degree he transcended it. Into the conventional molds of his time, he poured the quintessence of eternal art. One has but to look beneath the outward grace and mannerisms of the period to see revealed in his full stature the luminous inner spirit, the creator of unfading beauty, the artistic companion of Raphael and Keats in many ways.

Like Beethoven, Mozart came between the close of one great epoch and the beginning of another. His works are not only the culmination of what had gone before, but also a harbinger of a new era. There is indeed something strangely prophetic in the music of Mozart. The opening theme of the G Minor Symphony is as romantic as the "Ode to the West Wind"; the serenity and exquisite formalism of the old intermingles with the passionate lyricism of the new. It is this that constitutes the fascinating duality of the Mozartian style. In him, the two elements meet in perfect fusion, strengthening and balancing each other. The classic serenity is humanized by heart-piercing emotion, and this, in turn, is purified by classic repose and restraint. Nothing better illustrates this duality in Mozart than the fascination which this so-called arch-Classicist had upon the most romantic artists. Chopin is reported to have murmured on his death-bed, "Play Mozart in memory of me—and I will hear you." Marie Henri Beyle (Stendhal), who carried the banner of literary Romanticism in "Chartreuse de Parme" and "Rouge et Noir," as well as in a number of works on musical subjects, wrote for the epitaph on his tombstone: "This soul adored Cimarosa, Mozart, and Shakespeare." Tchaikovsky, one of the most romantic of the Romantics, wrote to Mme. von Meck: "I not only like Mozart, I idolize him. To me the most beautiful opera ever written is *Don Giovanni*. No one else has ever known how to interpret so exquisitely in music the sense of resigned and inconsolable sorrow. . . . It is thanks to Mozart that I have devoted my life to music." If one were to choose the five greatest works in almost any form—opera, symphony, string

271

quartet, and so on—a work by Mozart would most certainly be among those five in any or all the forms.

Wolfgang Amadeus Mozart was born in Salzburg, January 27, 1756, the son of Leopold Mozart, a musician who gained more than local fame as a composer, teacher, and vice-Kapellmeister to the Archbishop of Salzburg. Wolfgang's genius manifested itself from earliest childhood: indeed, he is the most extraordinary example of musical precocity in all history. He picked out tunes on the harpsichord at the age of three; and he composed at four. At six he appeared in concerts with his sister, who was some years his senior. Their father took the two prodigies on a tour over Europe; they played at the Austrian, French, English, and Dutch courts, arousing the greatest enthusiasm everywhere. Thus, Mozart's career opened under the most brilliant auspices. By the time he was twelve he had already written his first cantata, ten symphonies, an Italian opera, and the charming German operetta, *Bastien and Bastienne* (1768). The following year, a tour spread his name through Italy, then the world center of music, where he amazed his audiences with his organ playing and his powers of improvisation. At Rome the boy caused a sensation when, after one hearing of Allegri's fairly long and very involved "Miserere" at the Sistine Chapel, he wrote down the entire work, note for note, from memory—an almost incredible feat!

The remainder of his brief career presents a fantastic pattern of ups and downs, of disappointments dotted with flashes of success; through it all he carried on with lightning speed and fluency the creation of his great works. The system of patronage was still all-powerful: a composer, painter, or poet depended for his livelihood not on his earnings but on the whims and vagaries of princely patrons—public concerts and public support through purchase of publications had not yet come into practice. Ironically enough, Mozart, who so often has been held up as the very incarnation of the classical spirit, was the first composer to revolt against the system of patronage; just as, some decades earlier, Dr. Johnson had been the first man of letters to defy it. Mozart refused to put up with the indignities that his patron, the Archbishop of Salzburg, heaped upon him as a matter of course.

Unfortunately, while the old regime with its system of patronage was beginning to crack, it was still too powerful to be defied. Haydn gracefully submitted and got through life peacefully. Beethoven brushed it aside—but that was two decades later. Mozart came a generation too soon—and was crushed.

Having broken with his patron, he decided to try his fortune in Vienna. Everything depended on his obtaining a permanent appointment at the court. Had he been able to find a patron as appreciative of his genius as Prince Esterhazy was of Haydn's, there is no doubt that his life would have taken an altogether different turn. But despite the fact that both the Empress Maria

Theresa and her son, Joseph II, were aware of his gifts, they never gave him more than passing recognition. Why the greatest musician of his time should have had to go begging for a permanent post when all about him mediocrities were established in comfortable sinecures is one of those mysteries that leave one aghast at the caprices of chance. Actually, Mozart had none of the suavity of the courtier when his artistic integrity was at stake. When the Emperor Joseph II remarked to him that his opera *The Abduction from the Seraglio* (1782) seemed to have "much too many notes," the composer replied frankly: "Exactly as many notes as are necessary, Your Majesty." So too, when the King of Prussia, who was very proud of his orchestra, asked him what he thought of it, Mozart answered, "It contains great virtuosi, but if the gentlemen would play together they would make a better effect."

Lacking the mainstay of economic security, Mozart was doubly exposed to all the emotional instabilities of his temperament; one moment he was in high spirits, the next in deepest dejection. Amidst all the worries and distractions of a hectic life, the divine music continued to pour forth, but at an ever greater cost to its creator. His marriage with Constanze Weber, a pretty, thoughtless girl who seemed to combine in herself all the qualities necessary to make for him the least suitable wife, only added to his difficulties. Extravagance, debts, and illness followed in a constant cycle, aggravating the lack of a deep emotional relationship which might have given him the balance and strength he so desperately needed. Most tragic of all was the lack of understanding and appreciation he so often had to face as an artist from those who played the most decisive parts in his life. Against this dismal and discouraging background was produced some of the most consistently pleasant and sunny music the world has known and enjoyed.

The last years of his life were brightened by the enormous success of his comic opera *The Marriage of Figaro* (1786) and of his dramatic masterpiece *Don Giovanni* (1787). In both of these he at last had a librettist worthy of him—the Italian poet-adventurer, Lorenzo da Ponte, a colorful character who ended his checkered career in the United States. Among other things da Ponte was the first Professor of Italian at Columbia College; he lies buried somewhere in downtown New York, like Mozart himself, in an unmarked grave. *Don Giovanni* was written for Prague where Mozart had his greatest triumph and where he spent the happiest weeks of his life. He composed it while sitting among his friends, enjoying the friendly chatter about him, taking his turn at a game of bowls, and then returning to put down another few lines of the matchless score. Like so many of his works, it was written in its finished form at the first attempt without revision or correction, for it had been thoroughly worked out, down to the last detail, in his head.

Within little more than six weeks in 1788, Mozart produced his three last and greatest symphonies, those in E flat, in G minor (the one we shall study presently), and the one in C (the "Jupiter"). During the three years that were left him there flowed from his pen a steady output of great works. But the struggle against discouragement was becoming ever more unequal; he was, as he put it, "always hovering between hope and anxiety." In the final year of his life, despite a continual turn for the worse in his physical and mental condition, he produced a number of his finest concertos, chamber music of all kinds, his greatest choral work, the "Requiem Mass," and the opera *The Magic Flute* (1791). This wonderfully gay fairy opera was written in the spell of dejection when he returned home, empty-handed, from the coronation of the Emperor Leopold II in Prague (his "Coronation Concerto" and the opera *The Clemency of Titus* [1791] were written for this occasion). The opera was written for Schikaneder, the impresario of a little theater on the outskirts of Vienna, who told Mozart that he could, "to a certain point, consult the taste of connoisseurs and your own glory," but must have "a particular regard to that class of persons who are not judges of good music. . . ." In this manner was born one of the first, if not the first, German romantic operas that paved the way for Weber and Wagner.

Mozart survived the première of *The Magic Flute* by only two months, working feverishly all the while on his "Requiem Mass." The writing of this work forms the final and strangest chapter of his career. He had received a visit from a stranger who had commissioned him to write a "Mass for the Dead" for his master who desired to remain unknown. Mozart accepted the order; but the mystery surrounding the whole matter made a strange impression on him. Actually, it was nothing more than a "ghosting" job for a Count Walsegg, who wished to pass himself off as a composer and needed a Mass in memory of his wife. As Mozart was starting out for the coronation in Prague, the mysterious stranger reappeared, asking what had become of the "Requiem Mass." Profoundly disturbed, Mozart promised to have it ready as soon as he returned. In his highly unsettled state of mind, the summons of the stranger gave him the notion, which grew into a fixed idea as he proceeded, that he was writing his own requiem—and that he might not live to finish it. He redoubled his efforts, working against time on what was to remain as his choral masterpiece, and one of the greatest of all requiems—and he did leave it slightly incomplete; it was finished by his pupil, Franz Süssmayer, who also completed the opera *La Clemenza di Tito*.

Now, when it was too late, bright prospects opened before him. He learned that a number of Hungarian nobles had formed a fund to provide him with an annuity and that in Amsterdam a subscription fund had been started to commission new works from him. Night after night, in the illness of the final month, he would follow in his imagination the performance of his *Magic Flute* at Schikaneder's theatre, looking at his watch and going over the arias as the time for them arrived. He died of what is commonly held to have been a malignant typhus fever,* on December 5, 1791, a month before his thirty-sixth birthday.

He was given a pauper's funeral. A violent storm was raging; the half dozen friends who had come to the service followed to the city gates and then forsook him and turned back. No memorial marked his last resting place; the site was soon forgotten and has not since been discovered. But his monument is truly "more lasting than bronze": an art which for sheer refinement of feeling, exquisiteness of line, and transparency of texture has never been equalled. It is a music of pure song, of fresh and sunlit things, of early morning and never-fading youth—a song dedicated to the eternal ideal of pure and perfect beauty in art.

E. J. S.

---

* Some authorities considered his death due to a general collapse from overwork and irregular living. According to Dr. J. Barrant, and quoted by W. J. Turner in his authoritative biography (Knopf, 1938), Mozart died of Bright's disease.

Die Entführung aus dem Serail

[The Abduction from the Seraglio]

COMIC SONG-PLAY (SINGSPIEL) IN 3 ACTS

Book by GOTTLOB STEPHANIE, after the play by CHRISTOPH FRIEDRICH BRETZNER

First performance: National Theater, Vienna, July 12, 1782

CHARACTERS

Selim, Pasha, SPEAKING PART

Constanza (or *Constanze*), beloved of Belmonte, SOPRANO

Blonda (or *Blondchen*), Constanza's maid and beloved of Pedrillo, SOPRANO

Belmonte, a Spanish nobleman, TENOR

Pedrillo, Belmonte's servant, TENOR

Osmin, overseer of the Pasha's country place, BASS

A Mute

Janissaries, Slaves, Guards

The action takes place in Turkey in the sixteenth century

Belmonte seeks everywhere his betrothed, Constanze, who with her attendant Blondchen has fallen into the hands of Selim Pasha. When Osmin, the Pasha's servant, comes to pluck figs in the garden Belmonte retires. Belmonte returns to obtain news of his servant, Pedrillo. Osmin is angry. Belmonte hears news of Pedrillo and resolves to abduct Constanze. Selim presently appears with Constanze, for whose love he strives in vain. Upon the recommendation of Pedrillo, the Pasha engages Belmonte as builder, but Osmin refuses him access to the palace.

Blondchen repulses the rough lovemaking of Osmin. After a duet, Constanze greets Blondchen in distress, informing her that Selim demands her love and threatens to use force. When she has gone, Pedrillo comes to Blondchen, who is his sweetheart, and informs her that Belmonte is near and that all is ready for flight. Blondchen is filled with joy. Pedrillo induces Osmin to drink, hoping that he will become intoxicated. He succeeds in this plan and gets Osmin out of the way so that Belmonte again sees his beloved Constanze.

Belmonte and Pedrillo come to the garden with ladders. Belmonte succeeds in getting Constanze out, but when Pedrillo is about to escape with Blondchen, they are caught by Osmin, and Belmonte and Constanze are also brought back by the guard. Selim Pasha, who recognizes in Belmonte the son of an enemy, seems about to order their death. His heart, however, is touched by their sorrow; he nobly forgives, and all are set at liberty.

O. T.

OPERA "ALLA TURCA"

During the seventeenth and eighteenth centuries the character of the Turk was quite popular in all of Europe. In Vienna little children were frightened by the word Turk. Persons dressed as Turks sold exotic wares. From the seventeenth century onward, principally after the second siege of Vienna by the Turks in 1687, there was in Vienna a real Turkomania. There was a *Türken-café*, Turkish candies were sold, and Turkish instruments were introduced into military music. The Turk was for a long time a popular figure at masked balls and *Wirtschaften*, the ball entertainments of the Baroque age. The old *Moresca*, a Moorish dance which was performed with bells worn on the feet and wild gestures, was connected not only with the Moors and the Arabs, but also with the Turks.

In fact, the music of the *Moresca* shows a certain similarity to Turkish music as it has been known in Europe since the seventeenth century. Sharply dotted rhythms and an accompaniment of castanets, cymbals or bells were typical of the *Moresca,* just as the great drum, cymbals, triangles and the Turkish crescent were characteristics of the janissary music, played by the bodyguards of the Turkish sultans. During the Turkish wars in Europe this music had become familiar and left traces not only in the military music of the different nations of Europe, but also in numerous compositions of the classical masters.

Italian opera felt the Turkish imprint from the days of the Venetian School. Cara Mustapha was a popular subject that appeared also in Hamburg in 1682 in an opera of the same name. In this old opera, just as in the *Seraglio,* the Turk is opposed by two Spanish captives, Don Gasparo and Donna Manuela. Later Paisiello in his *Arabo cortese* and *Dardane,* Grétry in his *Caravane du Caire,* Monsigny in his fantastic opera *Isle sonnanate,* used the Turkish milieu. Gluck in his *Rencontre imprévue* treated the material in a manner similar to that in the *Seraglio* in 1764. As is well known, the German text of Mozart's opera is derived from that of the Leipsic merchant Christoph Fr. Bretzner who in 1781 wrote a comedy with the following title: "Belmont und Konstanze oder die Entführung aus dem Serail." The musical comedy was not set to music by Mozart in its original version, but in an adaptation of the Viennese writer and playwright Stephanie. The arrangement caused Herr Bretzner to write angrily in the *Leipziger Zeitung* in 1782:

A certain person named Mozart has had the impudence in Vienna to misuse my drama "Belmont und Konstanze" for the text of an opera. I hereby protest solemnly against this invasion of my rights and reserve the right to further action.

CHRISTOPH FRIEDRICH BRETZNER,
composer of "A Little Tipsy."

Poor Bretzner! He scarcely imagined that his name would be handed down to posterity not by his "Little Tipsy" but by the impudent misuse of that certain Mozart.

But back to our theme. There was a whole series of Turkish operas in which the subject was handled in almost the same way as in Bretzner's work. The Italian poet Martinelli wrote a semi-serious opera *La schiava liberata* which was composed in 1768 by Jarnelli, and by Josef Schuster in 1777 for Dresden. In this work the two European women are not freed by intrigue and force, but by peaceful arbitration. In Martinelli's version we find two characters, Soliman and Selim, father and son, who in Mozart's opera are combined into one, as Selim, who has Soliman's majesty and dignity and also the hopeless love and magnanimity of Martinelli's Selim.

Bretzner probably saw Schuster's opera in Dresden. Whether he,. also, saw the English Turkish plays "The Sultan or a Peep into the Seraglio" by T. Bickerstaffe and "The Captive" (1769) is doubtful. In the English ballad-opera, similar themes were treated. In 1740 *The Generous Freemason* demonstrates the same material, utilized on a masonic background. Here, too, the generous and noble Turkish prince, who turns out to be a freemason, is introduced. Presumably Bretzner did not know the English works, but did know *Adelheid von Veltheim* by Grossmann, in which an oriental story of abduction is also treated.

In the opera of the seventeenth century and the first half of the eighteenth century the Turk was for the most part a cruel and unsympathetic fellow, since the Turks and Venetians were bitter enemies, who fought each other up and down the whole Mediterranean. So it happens that the comic opera of all countries presents the Turks as blood-dripping Pashas, thorough scoundrels, stupidly arrogant Kadis and lascivious harem guards. Osmin belongs to the genus of malicious but easily duped guards, Monostatos in *The Magic Flute* to the lascivious kind. In the course of the eighteenth century, however, the picture of the Turk changes. Above all, this is true of the Pasha, who becomes more and more noble and generous. The unsympathetic Turk turns into a goodhumored noble and aristocratic oriental. Presumably this change went hand in hand with the disappearance of Turkish political power and the fact that the Sublime Porte was forced to live in harmony with the European powers. Perhaps the ideas of Jean-Jacques Rousseau were also partly responsible in that it was felt that the orientals, untouched by the decadent European culture, would be a model for European peoples. Travelers' reports, which often spoke of the sultans in complimentary words, had a definite effect upon the conception of what was Turkish. Casanova, who had tarried as a young man in Constantinople, had particularly sympathetic things to say about Ismael Pasha—who, to be sure, stemmed from Europe.

In this connection I should like to refer to a figure in the Vienna of Mozart's time, a figure mentioned in the literature of the period again and again. That was Angelo Soliman, a Negro, born in Somaliland or Abyssinia, who had come as a young man to Sicily, had been "bought" by Prince Lobkowitz, and then in Vienna entered the service of Prince Wenzel Liechtenstein. He was a member of the Masonic Lodge *Zur Wahren Eintracht* in which only the elite of the intellectual and social world of Vienna was received. In my book "Mozart und die Königliche Kunst" I have pointed out that Mozart and Angelo Soliman associated together in the lodge, and that in the protocols we often find Angelo's name directly under that of Mozart. Presumably the two entered the lodge arm in arm and there is no doubt that they were close friends. Karoline Pichler, the Viennese writer of memoirs, to whom we owe Angelo's biography, relates how the noble Moor delighted in singing the songs which he had heard in his youth. Angelo was Catholic, but had in his youth been reared as a Mohammedan. I conjecture that even if he didn't know Turkish songs, he at least sang the songs of the Near East, and that Mozart heard such music from him.

Mozart, of course, used oriental coloring in other works. Not only in *Zaide* and *The Magic Flute,* but also in the "Alla Turca" of his A Major Sonata, and in the last phrase of his A Major Violinconcerto in a ballet fragment. There is room for believing that Gluck's *Pilgrime von Mekka* with its oriental coloring had had its influence on him. But back to the *Seraglio.*

Already in the Overture, which from the eighth bar onward has a decided janissary character, we feel that we are in the Orient, the land of contrasting colors and sensual fervor. The minor passages, above all, the long statement expressing in minor the sadness and longing of the harem women languishing in their prison, give oriental flavor. The melody is then taken over in Belmonte's aria in C Major, a mood in the more familiar manner of the west and expressing the optimism of the lovers. Here Mozart characterizes Orient and Occident through minor and major.

Osmin's song as he picks figs is likewise in the minor. Slowly the melody moves on, indicating the phlegmatic character of Osmin, but the upswing of the "Trallalera" excellently characterizes the fanatical tyrant. Likewise the famous "Drum beim Barte des Propheten" has an oriental character, as does, of course, the chorus of Janissaries, which, according to Mozart himself, was everything one can desire for a janissary chorus and "short and merry and written entirely for the Viennese." But with this short description the *orientalia* of this master opera of Mozart have not been exhausted. One can say that every note in some way or other partakes of the flavor of the Orient. This, of course, is not to mean that Mozart deliberately composed oriental sounding phrases, but during the composition of his opera he lived in such a kind of oriental state of imagination that the fairy-tale coloring of the East impregnated the score.

P. N.

Opera-lovers have every reason to thank the shade of Leopold Mozart, father of the immortal Wolfgang, that the old gentleman did not venture to leave his home in Salzburg to attend the première of *The Abduction from the Seraglio* in Vienna. The composer was thus obliged to write his father full accounts of the various stages of the work in progress, a precious heritage for future generations.

The first of Mozart's letters to Leopold on the subject dates from August, 1781, when he first came in contact with the subject of the article. "The day before yesterday," he wrote, "Stephanie Junior gave me a libretto to compose. I must confess that, however badly he may treat other people, about which I know nothing, he is an excellent friend to me. The libretto is quite good. The subject is Turkish and the title is "Belmonte und Konstanze," or "Die Verführung aus dem Serail." For the Overture, the Chorus in Act I and the final chorus I will write Turkish music. Mlle. Cavalieri, Mlle. Tieber, Mr. Fischer, Mr. Adamberger, Mr. Dauer, and Mr. Walter are to sing in it. I am so delighted at having to compose this opera that I have already finished Cavalieri's first aria, Adamberger's and the trio which closes Act I. The time is short, it is true, for it is to be performed in the middle of September, but the circumstances connected with the date of the performance, and all my other prospects, generally excite me to such a degree that I rush to my desk with the greatest eagerness and remain seated there with the greatest delight. The Grand Duke of Russia is coming here, and that is why Stephanie entreated me, if possible, to compose the opera in this short space of time."

A week later, Mozart continued his fervent correspondence.

I must write in haste [he told his father], for I have only this very instant finished the Janissary Chorus and it is past twelve o'clock and I have promised to drive out with the Aurnhammers and Mlle. Cavalieri to Mingendorf near Laxenberg where the camp is. Adamberger, Mlle. Cavalieri and Fischer are exceedingly pleased with their arias. I lunched yesterday with the Countess Thun and am to do so tomorrow. I played what I have finished composing to her and she told me afterwards that she would venture her life that what I have written so far cannot fail to please. But in this matter I pay no attention whatever to anybody's praise or blame, that is until people will have heard the work as a whole. I simply follow my own feelings. All the same you may judge from this how pleased she must have been to express herself so emphatically.

By September Mozart was busied in a hundred fascinating details.

As the original libretto began with a monologue [he wrote his father on the 26th] I asked Herr Stephanie to make a little arietta out of it, and then to put in a duet instead of making the two chatter together after Osmin's short song . . . in the original text Osmin has nothing else to sing except the trio and the finale, so that he will be given an aria in Act I and another in Act II. Osmin's rage becomes comical with its accompaniment of Turkish music. In working out this aria

I have occasionally given full scope to Fischer's deep notes. The passage, "Drum Beim Barte des Propheten" (by the beard of Allah's prophet) is included in the same tempo, but with quick notes; but as Osmin's rage gradually increases, the *Allegro Assai* comes just when the aria seems to be at an end. This is in a totally different measure and in a different key, which is bound to be very effective.

For just as a man in such a towering rage forgets himself, so must the music too forget itself. But as passions, whether violent or not, must never be expressed in such a way as to excite disgust, and as music, even in the most terrible situations, must never offend the ear, but please the hearer, or in other words, must never cease to be music, so I have gone from F, the original key of the aria, not into a remote key, but into a related one, though not into its most clearly related one, D minor, but into the more distant A minor.

Let me now turn to Belmonte's aria in A major, "O wie ängstlich, o wie feurig." Would you like to know how I have expressed it? And even indicated the throbbing of his heart? By the two violins playing octaves . . . you feel the trembling, the faltering, you see how his throbbing heart begins to swell: this I have expressed by a Crescendo. You hear the whispering and the sighing, which I have indicated by the first violins and the mutes playing in unison.

The Janissary Chorus . . . can be described as lively, short and written to please the Viennese. I have sacrificed Constanza's aria a little to the flexible throat of Mlle. Cavalieri.

Now for the Trio at the close of the first act, it opens quite abruptly, and because the words lend themselves to it, I have made it a fairly respectable piece of three-part writing. Then the major key begins at once pianissimo—it must go very quickly —and I wind up with a great deal of noise, which is always appropriate at the end of an act.*

All sorts of procrastinations and intrigues deferred the day of performance again and again, until at last Joseph II commanded that it should be fixed for 16th July 1782. The house was crammed on this first night, and in spite of an opposing faction that did its best to ruin the composer's chances, the opera was received with rapture. There was frantic applause after every number and many pieces had to be repeated. The music was thought very novel and daring, particularly by the emperor, who prided himself on his solidly conservative tastes and told Mozart that the score was too good for Viennese ears and contained too many notes; to which the composer politely but firmly replied that he had put in exactly as many as were required. The opera was repeated many times during the season and always filled the house.

Although the German *Singspiel* that had been established in 1778 was of a comparatively low and light type, the chief singers engaged for it were artists of distinction, and it so happened that Mozart obtained the services of the best of them. Catharina Cavalieri, a young Viennese in spite of her Italian name, was a soprano of exceptional technical powers, and Therese Teyber, a member of a very musical family, was scarcely less accomplished. Valentin

* *Opera News*, Jan. 13, 1947.

Adamberger was a tenor who delighted Mozart by his refined, musicianly style, while Ludwig Fischer was a *buffo* bass of uncommon gifts, among which was an unusual range of low notes. It was of him that the Archbishop of Salzburg had said that he sang "too low for a bass." . . .

In *Die Entführung aus dem Serail* Mozart was at last wholly in his element, not because of any especial liking for the German *Singspiel* or even because he was himself planning an elopement of sorts, but chiefly because by 1782 he was a fully matured master of his craft and had learnt a good deal about life. Not that his engagement to Constanze was entirely without influence, we may be sure. Weber was not far wrong when he suggested that, although Mozart produced greater works later on, he could never recapture that blithe bridal tone that pervades this ever youthful and endearing work. It is impossible for anyone with the least musical sensibility to imagine a happier evening at a theatre than one spent at a good performance of *The Elopement*. . . .

[In *Die Entführung*, Mozart] enjoyed donning again that amusing Turkish fashion he had already worn in the A major piano Sonata and for which he found plenty of opportunity in the overture, the janissaries' choruses and especially the music for that magnificent figure of fun, the amorous, jealous, cunning and yet gullible Osmin, a character that is to opera what Shakespeare's Falstaff—the greater Falstaff of the historical plays (and incidentally of Elgar's symphonic masterpiece)—is to drama. It is Osmin especially who gives that peculiar and unrepeatable flavour of Viennese *turquerie* to this most delectable of operettas—for that is what *The Elopement* really is, with its spoken dialogue, its lack of a finale to the first act and its conclusion with a mere *vaudeville*. Like Sullivan's pieces, which by the way almost match its musicianly refinements at times, we can call it an opera only by a courteous habit.

This is not to say that it is wanting in great music. Indeed one would not have a note different even where it falls a little short of greatness, for it never ceases to be as delicious as it is apt to its type and subject. Constanze's so-called "torture aria," with its brilliant ornamentation fitted to Cavalieri's "glib gullet," may possibly deserve that name; at any rate certain singers could easily make one think so. Her other two songs are heaven-sent things for virtuoso sopranos, one in the finest bravura style of the concert arias, the other that poignant plaint in G minor.

Blonda's songs are as spritely as Belmonte's are tender. She is a second high soprano (top E) with a part almost as difficult as Constanze's. Pedrillo is a second tenor of the comic servant type, and his aria in which he boasts of his bravery while he trembles at the stirring of every leaf is an admirable piece of *buffo* art. The device of writing high parts for both pairs of lovers yields the most enchantingly airy vocal texture for the quartet in the second act, which is quite extended enough to make an adequate finale for so light a musical play. Adequate, did I say? It is a structure and a collection of tunes of such fascinating grace that one would like to call back every phrase of it to hug it over and over again. But it just flows on happily and will not wait to be loved. That is the worst of music—and the best: it will not be possessed. However, to such a score as that of *The Elopement* you can at least go back for another spell of enticement, and you will never fail to find it fresh.

E. B.

There was a performance of *Die Entführung* in Brooklyn in Feb., 1860, in Italian, under the title of *Belmonte e Constanze,* which was perhaps the first in America. It was presented in German at the German Opera House, New York, Oct. 10, 1862. In recent years an English version was heard in New York and other cities offered by Vladimir Rosing's Rochester, later American, Opera Company, which gave all of its performances in English. [The Metropolitan *première* occurred on December 18, 1946, in an English translation by Ruth and Thomas Martin, with a cast including Eleanor Steber as Constanza, Pierrette Alarie as Blonda, Charles Kullman as Belmonte, Deszo Ernster as Osmin, Hugh Thompson as Selim, John Carter as Pedrillo, and Ludwig Burgstaller as the Mute; the conductor was Emil Cooper.]

Le Nozze di Figaro

[The Marriage of Figaro]

OPERA BUFFA IN 2 ACTS

Book by Lorenzo da Ponte, after Beaumarchais' comedy *Le Mariage de Figaro*

First performance: Burgtheater, Vienna, May 1, 1786

CHARACTERS

Count Almaviva, Grand Corregidor of Andalusia, BARITONE
Figaro, his valet and major-domo of the château, BARITONE
Dr. Bartolo, a physician of Seville, BASS
Don Basilio, music master to the Countess, TENOR
Antonio, gardener of the château and Susanna's uncle, BASS
Don Curzio, counselor-at-law, TENOR
Cherubino, head page to the Count, SOPRANO
Countess Almaviva, SOPRANO
Susanna, head waiting woman to the Countess, betrothed to Figaro, SOPRANO
Marcellina, CONTRALTO
Barbarina, Antonio's daughter, SOPRANO

Servants, Officers of the Court, and Peasants

The action takes place at Count Almaviva's château in the country near Seville

Countess Almaviva (Rosina of "The Barber") discusses with Figaro the fact that her maid and Figaro's fiancée, pretty Susanna, has caught the Count's roving eye. The Count already has dismissed page Cherubino for finding him flirting with Barberina, the gardener's daughter, but when peasant lads and lasses come to thank him for resigning his *jus primæ noctis*, he forgives Cherubino and takes him back. When the Countess hears from Susanna that her husband has begged the girl to meet him in the garden they dress blushing Cherubino in girls' clothes to keep the assignation and shame the philanderer; while the Count is delighted to put off Figaro's wedding to Susanna because of the appearance of old Marcellina, from whom Figaro borrowed money, promising to marry her if it were not returned. But Figaro turns out to be Marcellina's illegitimate son and after peasant boys serenade the Countess and peasant girls bring her flowers, the Count invites all to supper (jolly rococo March, Chorus, and Fandango). Figaro, however, has seen his master slip Susanna a note. In the castle garden Figaro, whose jealousy has led him there to spy on Susanna, finds Barberina, whom Cherubino had promised to meet, while Cherubino, thinking the Countess (disguised as her maid) is Susanna, tries to steal a kiss and Almaviva turning up as the page slips away, gets a box on the ears meant for him. He gives his supposed Susanna a ring and Figaro, when

284

the real Susanna calls him, thinks her the Countess, woos her tenderly and is soundly thumped by his fiancée who, however, at once forgives him. The Countess having slipped away, Almaviva thinks Figaro is kneeling at his wife's feet and while Susanna slips into a summerhouse, seizes his valet and calls for servants and lights. But when he discovers Cherubino, Barberina, and Susanna in the Countess's clothes in the summerhouse, he refuses to pardon the lovers till his wife arrives to show him how cleverly he was fooled. Then, like the great gentleman he is, he begs the Countess to forgive him, and the properly assorted pairs move to the château for "The Marriage of Figaro."

F. H. M.

Haydn often came to Mozart's house to play quartets with Dittersdorf as second violinist and Wanhal as cellist, the host playing the viola. It was here that he met Leopold Mozart, who had come to return his son's visit, staying in Vienna from February to April 1785. (Leopold had made the journey alone, for his daughter had been married in 1784 to a nobleman, Berchthold zu Sonnenberg of St. Gilgen, where she lived in the very house where her mother had been born.) Haydn, who was thirteen years younger than Leopold, warmed his fatherly heart by saying to him, after a home performance of the three new quartets: "I tell you before God, and as an honest man, that your son is the greatest composer I know, either personally or by name; he has taste, and apart from that the greatest science in composition." . . .

The quartet playing did not always take place at the Mozarts', but often at the lodging of Stephen Storace, a promising English composer of twenty-two, who had come to Vienna with his sister Ann Selina, better known as Nancy, who at the age of nineteen was already an opera singer with a reputation in Italy and had just been engaged for the new Italian opera establishment which Vienna had substituted for the unsuccessful German venture. There was almost a musical British colony in the capital, for apart from the Storaces, Thomas Attwood, aged twenty, had come to be, like Stephen Storace, a pupil of Mozart. They soon formed a friendly circle round the Mozart household which was completed by the Irishman Michael Kelly, who, four years older than Nancy Storace, had also made his name as a singer in Italy and was engaged as tenor at the opera. Kelly became a particularly close friend. He visited Mozart almost daily, played billiards with him and received his advice about turning a gift for melodic invention unmatched by technical proficiency to the best advantage. It is to Kelly's attractive "Reminiscences" that we owe one of the best contemporary pen-portraits of Mozart that have been preserved:

He favoured the company by performing fantasias and capriccios on the pianoforte. His feeling, the rapidity of his fingers, the great execution and strength of his left hand particularly, and the apparent inspiration of his modulations, astounded me. After this splendid performance we sat down to supper, and I had the pleasure to be placed at table between him and his wife . . . After supper the young branches of our host had a dance, and Mozart joined them. Madame Mozart told me, that great as his genius was, he was an enthusiast in dancing, and often said that his taste lay in that art, rather than in music.

He was a remarkably small man, very thin and pale, with a profusion of fine hair, of which he was rather vain. He gave me a cordial invitation to his house, of which I availed myself, and passed a great part of my time there. He always received me with kindness and hospitality. He was remarkably fond of punch, of which beverage I have seen him take copious draughts. He was also fond of billiards, and had an excellent billiard table in his house. Many and many a game have I played with him, but always came off second best. He gave Sunday concerts, at which I never was missing. He was kind-hearted, and always ready to oblige; but so very particular, when he played, that if the slightest noise were made, he instantly left off.

Before long both Nancy Storace and Kelly, who was also known as O'Kelly and on the Italian stage as Ochelli, were to be artistically associated with Mozart as well as personally. For it was high time for him to tackle another work for the stage, and the German opera having come to grief, he was naturally looking out, without success at first, as we have seen for an Italian book. Beaumarchais, we know, attracted him, and about the middle of 1786 he found the opportunity to embark on an operatic version of the second comedy in the French author's trilogy—"Le Mariage de Figaro." He had met the right librettist in Lorenzo da Ponte—the right one for him, at any rate, for da Ponte had worked with other composers like Salieri, Gazzaniga, Righini and the italianized Spaniard Martín y Solar with varied success. He was a Venetian Jew by birth, Emanuele Conegliano, but had been christened in his fourteenth year by the Bishop of Ceneda, whose name he adopted. He took holy orders, which did not prevent him from being a complete man of both the world and the half-world, a kind of minor Casanova, less abandoned but also less distinguished than that dangerously attractive model. He was no great literary genius, but an adroit craftsman and neat versifier. At any rate the Beaumarchais subject suited him, and he turned it skilfully into what, but for a weakness in the fourth act, has remained one of the world's best operatic librettos, excising the numerous political allusions in the revolutionary comedy, which did not suit the purposes of the musical stage, but leaving the polished intrigue of the original unimpaired. Moreover, he was shrewd enough to recognize a great composer and saw his advantage in being associated with a genius like Mozart, whose suggestions he knew to be sound and accepted without demur. The book was soon ready to Mozart's hand. He set to work on *Le Nozze di Figaro* with avidity and—who can doubt it?—

with none of the misgivings that may have stirred in his breast, almost unknown to himself, at his own wedding.

Joseph II had always, more or less secretly, favoured Italian opera, and when he found that Vienna was not inclined to make a success of the German venture, he was only too glad to convene a new Italian company in 1783, though not disinclined to let the indigenous singers who were conversant with Italian operatic art be transferred to the new enterprise. His favourite composer, Salieri, was given the first chance to appear with a new work, *La Scuola dei gelosi,* and a piece that shared its success was Sarti's *Fra due litiganti il terzo gode,* which we shall meet again in connection with Mozart. By 1786 an excellent company had been assembled. An ideal cast was chosen for *Figaro:* Steffano Mandini, a fine baritone, as Count Almaviva, a soprano named Laschi as the countess, Nancy Storace as Susanna, and a surpassingly good *basso buffo,* Francesco Benucci, as Figaro. It may well have been for the sake of Kelly, who was an accomplished character actor, that Mozart made a tenor part of Basilio.* Aloysia Lange was not in the running, although she had gone over to the Italian opera together with Cavalieri, Teyber and Adamberger; for it was of course for a production of Anfossi's *Il Curioso indiscreto* at the new establishment that her brother-in-law had written the extra arias for her and Adamberger to sing in that work. In 1785 he was asked to contribute a trio and a quartet to Bianchi's *La Villanella rapita,* and only then was he at last invited to supply an Italian opera of his own.

But *Figaro* was not to be produced without trouble. First of all the emperor, who had already forbidden the performance of Beaumarchais's play, would not hear of its presentation as an opera until da Ponte was able to reassure him that all political allusions had been eliminated. Then the court poet, Giovanni Battista Casti, who was not inclined to tolerate another librettist next to him, began to intrigue against Mozart and da Ponte, with the all too generous support of the intendant, Count Rosenberg, who tried to annoy the composer into withdrawing the work by cutting out the dance in the third act. But the emperor, who attended the rehearsal he had himself ordered, noticed the omission and commanded that it should be rectified. Mozart also suspected machinations on the part of other composers, notably Salieri and Righini, and he was fully upheld in his misgivings, as usual, by his father, who had spent a lifetime scenting mischief, real and imaginary. Kelly, however, confirms the Mozarts' suspicions:

Mozart was as touchy as gunpowder, and swore he would put the score of his opera into the fire, if it was not produced first; his claim was backed by a strong

---

* *Figaro* could thus not be performed with the same cast as a sequel to Paisiello's *Barbiere di Siviglia,* where, as in Rossini's later version, Almaviva is a tenor and Basilio a bass.

party: on the contrary Regini [*sic*] was working like a mole in the dark to get precedence. . . . The third candidate was Maestro di Cappella to the Court, a clever shrewd man, possessed of what Bacon called crooked wisdom.

The story that the singers themselves tried to jeopardize the work by deliberately making mistakes seems to be a pure fabrication of over-zealous biographer-partisans; at any rate the whole company, vocalists and orchestra, broke spontaneously into wild acclamations at one of the rehearsals when Benucci sang "Non piu andrai" in the most rousing manner, and the artists did magnificent work on the night of the production of *Le Nozze di Figaro* (The Marriage of Figaro) on 1st May * 1786. Mozart conducted from the keyboard and, of course, accompanied the *secco* recitatives, a task which Joseph Weigl took over after the third performance. The house was crammed on the first night, and so many of the numbers had to be repeated that the opera lasted nearly twice its appointed time.† For all that, the work was withdrawn after the ninth performance on 18th December, the chief cause being Martin's *Una cosa rara,* which proved an immediate and easy success. That Mozart bore the Spanish composer no grudge for this will appear before long.

Figaro did very little to relieve Mozart of the material anxieties that beset him more and more sorely. Only nine performances were given in eight months for which he received nothing, having been paid a lump sum at the beginning. There were debts to settle, and he paid too much rent as it was for the first floor of the comparatively well-set-up house in the Schulerstrasse, and Constanze was once more with child. The third boy, Johann Thomas Leopold, born on 18th October, died on 15th November, so that pecuniary harassments were accompanied by emotional ones. The worried composer worked hard. But then, as soon as he set pen to paper, the usual miracle happened: trouble forsook him, and he turned out one exquisite piece after another. . . .

The perfect *opera buffa.* . . . True, of course; but it is much more than that. Beaumarchais's exposure of a refined but pernicious civilization is here made the pretext for music as sunnily civilized as the world ought to have become if the dreamers of Mozart's age had been right and the French Revo-

---

* Have socialists ever noticed the date on which this class-subversive opera appeared? If not, a present may here be made them of the observation.

† Only those familiar with Gilbert and Sullivan audiences can have some faint conception nowadays of how undisciplined the opera public was in the eighteenth century. Even Mozart, though he wrote the loveliest orchestral perorations to his arias, which must have been ruined again and again by applause, took this insensitive responsiveness calmly for granted, though he did once say that what he liked most of all was approbation by silence. (But he confessed to Jacquin that he could not tell whether Paisiello's *Le Gare generose* had been well performed in Prague or not, because he had been talking too much.) A characteristic decree was issued after the first *Figaro* performances: it was proclaimed by order that no musical number written for more than one voice would be repeated in future—which amounted to an encouragement to insist on repetition of the arias.

lution had not merely replaced one kind of barbarity by another that has not even the merits of elegance and taste. These qualities *Figaro* has to a degree never again attained in music, and it has moreover a profound humanity, a sympathetic penetration into the hearts of men and women—especially women —prompted by the complete artist's understanding of both good and evil, by a kind of sublimated amorality and naïve philosophy based on feelings rather than on principles.

Music dictated by this frame of mind could hardly have been anything but flawless, and the score of *Figaro,* so far as the composer is concerned, really is without a blemish, apart from its pouring forth an incessant stream of the most bewitching and the most perfectly behaved, aristocratic music imaginable. Where there is a fault or so, it is imposed on the music from the outside. The fact that the first and third acts have no finales may pass, for one may regard the work as being conceived in two acts, divided into four scenes, and consider, moreover, that two more such towering structures and incredibly well managed musico-dramatic developments as the two existing finales would have been too much. The serious defect of that set of arias which brings the action of the fourth act to a standstill, and most of which may fortunately be cut without damage to the work, is due partly to the flagging invention of da Ponte and partly to the convention that allowed opera singers to indulge their exhibitionist instincts at some point or other in a comic opera.

Figaro is Italian comic opera in its final stage of perfection. It humanizes and glorifies the traditional figures of the *commedia dell' arte* * which are very clearly the ancestry of Beaumarchais's characters. Susanna is not only the daughter of Pergolesi's Serpina and the sister of all the *cameriere* of the Italian musical stage, she is the type of Columbine grown into a lovable individuality, and after having shown many traits of the operatic *servetta* in the course of the first three acts, she assumes a warm and noble womanliness in her aria, "Deh vieni, non tardar," in the garden scene, where she sounds quite a new note.

Cherubino points two ways. He is at once the adolescent Don Juan and the descendant of Leandro, who in the Italian improvised comedy is the disciple of Lelio and kindred more or less dissolute fine gentlemen, who gave Beaumarchais his model for the Count. At the same time Cherubino, being given a soprano part, is a late survivor of the male soprano, though by no means the last, for all through the nineteenth century and beyond (e.g., Octavian in Strauss's *Rose Cavalier*) this convention lingered on. . . .

Figaro himself is a survival of Harlequin, or more exactly a modern compound of Arlecchino and Brighella, two servant types with different traits. Bartolo, of course, is no other than the Bolognese doctor who took his idiosyn-

* A detained study of the descent of the characters in *Figaro* will be found in my extensive article on the subject in *The Musical Quarterly* (New York) of October 1927.

crasies from Cassandro or Pantalone; Basilio is partly Tartaglia and partly Brighella; Marcellina has the elements of Columbine which are lacking in Susanna; the Countess—the Rosina of *The Barber of Seville*—is the young lady of the Italian comedy, most commonly called Isabella, who is generally the niece or ward, or both, of Pantaloon.

Now all these figures of the *commedia dell' arte* were mere skeletons, as indeed were the plots of their plays, and the actors were expected to improvise on them as the inspiration of the moment dictated. Something of the same kind is done by Mozart with his music. It is true that Beaumarchais had already made these types into personalities, and that da Ponte had by no means spoiled them. But it is Mozart who made them our personal acquaintances, people to be loved or liked or despised, but all of them to be perfectly understood. For he understood them to the last tremor of the heart, the last twinge of conscience. Each is given infallibly the right music, and each keeps to it even when the parts intermingle in those impeccably elegant concerted pieces, of which the two finales and the sextet in the third act are the major miracles, but not one of which can be imagined capable of improvement in the slightest detail. And it is all immaculately beautiful, most of all, perhaps, the wonderful consolatory music lavished on the unhappy Countess, if a choice must be made. But then it should not, for the opera is as great as a whole as it is captivating in detail.

E. B.

With regard to the American *première* of *Le Nozze di Figaro* there is some doubt. Renamed *The Follies of a Day,* it is said to have been presented in New York as early as 1799. Yet a performance of the work at the Park Theater, New York, in English, May 10, 1824, was advertised as a "first time in America." In any event, the opera in English versions was popular in New York throughout the first half of the nineteenth century.

In the original Italian it was produced at the New York Academy of Music Nov. 23, 1858, and in a German translation at the German Opera House, New York, Dec. 18, 1862. It entered the repertory of the Metropolitan Opera House, in Italian, Jan. 31, 1894, with Lillian Nordica as Susanna, Emma Eames as the Countess Almaviva, Sigrid Arnoldson as Cherubino, Mario Ancona as Figaro, and Édouard de Reszké as Count Almaviva. Emilio Bevignani conducted.

Don Giovanni

[Don Juan]

DRAMMA GIOCOSO IN 2 ACTS

Book by Lorenzo da Ponte

First performance: National Theater, Prague, Oct. 29, 1787

CHARACTERS

Don Giovanni, a licentious young
nobleman, BARITONE (OR BASS)
Don Pedro, the Commandant, BASS
Don Ottavio, betrothed to Donna Anna,
TENOR
Leporello, Don Giovanni's servant, BASS

Masetto, a peasant, BASS (OR BARITONE)
Donna Anna, Don Pedro's daughter,
SOPRANO
Donna Elvira, a lady of Burgos, SOPRANO
Zerlina, betrothed to Masetto, SOPRANO
Peasants, Musicians, Dancers, Demons

The action takes place at Seville, in the middle of the seventeenth century

The rakehelly Spanish noble [Don Giovanni] accompanied by his sly and rascally servant, Leporello, invades by night the house of the commandant of Seville, with whose daughter, Donna Anna, he is infatuated. But Donna Anna, betrothed to Don Ottavio, not only repulses his advances, but, crying out for aid, pursues him. Her father answers her call, only to be slain by Don Giovanni. After the Don and his servant have escaped, Don Ottavio arrives on the scene too late to be of help, but in time to assist Donna Anna in her vengeance.

In the street, Donna Elvira, a lady whom the Don has betrayed and abandoned, encounters him and upbraids him for his cruelty. As the Don precipitately departs, Leporello horrifies the sorrowing lady with a catalogue of his master's thousand-and-three conquests.

Presently the Don crosses the path of a peasant wedding party romping into town for the marriage of Zerlina and Masetto. He is so struck with Zerlina's beauty that he is by way of persuading her to run away with him when Donna Elvira unexpectedly appears and thwarts his plan. However, he gives a grand ball in his palace to which peasantry as well as gentry are bidden, and there once more the same trio save Zerlina from seduction.

After this variety of adventures, we find Don Giovanni bent on further exploits. He is still seeking (though without success) to kidnap Zerlina, who is now living in the house of Donna Elvira under her protection, and when this enterprise ends in nothing more serious than a beating for Masetto, the Don diverts his bravado to other matters by appearing in the cemetery where Donna Anna's father, the

Commendatore, is buried, and inviting the stone statue of the worthy he has slain to sup with him.

As Don Giovanni sits late at table feasting with ladies of his choice, Donna Elvira, faithful unto death, rushes in to beg him to make peace with God. He spurns her, but when she hurries back, shrieking, to seek egress by another door, he sends Leporello to see what is up. Leporello, shrieking in his turn, comes back with word that the statue is at the door. Instead of taking flight, Don Giovanni boldly confronts the unwelcome visitor. The statue clasps the Don's hand in a grasp there is no resisting. At his very feet hell opens, and sinful Don Giovanni, struggle though he may, is cast by his victim's image into the fiery pit. Thus the libertine is punished.

P. S.

Mozart had not intended to go [to Prague in January, 1787]; his desire was to revisit England, perhaps to settle there if his prospects proved but a little brighter than those in Vienna, where by this time he despaired of ever making his way. For lessons were irksome as well as insufficiently remunerative, the court continued to be lukewarm, and he had too many enemies, perhaps not altogether without his own fault, for he had a sharp and none too well guarded critical tongue where other people's music was concerned. The English project came to grief because he was apparently unwilling to go without [his wife] Constanze, and they could not take two babies with them. Just before the death of the younger boy * he asked his father if he would take care of the children for him, in which case he would send them to Salzburg with the two servant wenches. Leopold's answer, dated 17th November 1786, must have been categorical, to judge by his account of it given to his daughter on the same day—more so than it would have been had he known that the younger child had just died:

To-day I was obliged to answer a letter from your brother which has cost me much labour in writing. . . . That I had to write a very emphatical letter, you may well imagine, since he proposed to me nothing less than that I should take care of his 2 children, as half-way through the carnival he desired to make a journey through Germany to England, &c. . . . Not bad, to be sure!—They could travel in all tranquillity,—they might die,—might remain in England,—and I could run after them with the children &c.: or after payment for the children which he offers me for sluts and children &c.—*Basta!* my excuses are forcible, and instructive, if he will make use thereof.

That was that. Leopold's letter had clearly been both forcible and instructive enough to keep the still obedient son of thirty at home. On the other hand there was no reason to interfere with a visit to Prague, indeed no want for Wolfgang to write home about it. He took Constanze with him, feeling per-

* [Johann Thomas Leopold Mozart, born Oct. 18, 1786; died Nov. 15, 1786.]

haps that she could do with some agreeable distraction, poor thing. They found Prague seething with enthusiasm over *Figaro*, which had just been produced there with a positively explosive success. It gave them untold satisfaction to find at a ball that the tunes from the opera had been converted into "nothing but *Contredanses* and *Teutsche*," as Mozart wrote to his friend Gottfried von Jacquin in Vienna, and he was elated to discover that "here they talk of nothing but *Figaro;* scrape, blow, sing and whistle nothing but *Figaro;* visit no opera but *Figaro*, and eternally *Figaro*." Not only that, but *The Elopement* had charmed the Bohemians in 1783. When on 17th January they attended a performance of *Figaro*, the rumour of the composer's presence at once went round the house, and after the overture he was accorded a frenzied ovation. On the 20th he conducted the opera himself; but it was the day before, at a concert he gave in the opera house, that the new Symphony, now always called the "Prague" Symphony, received its first performance.

Mozart and Constanze stayed at the house of Count Johann Joseph Thun during their visit [to Prague], but they also saw much of Franz Dušek and his wife Josepha, whom Mozart had already met at Salzburg. Both were influential musicians, and it was largely due to their devoted friendship that Mozart obtained a commission to write a new opera especially for Prague. The impresario who had brought *Figaro* to the Bohemian capital, Pasquale Bondini, was eager to attach so successful a composer to himself, and when the Mozarts left in February Wolfgang had a contract for a hundred ducats in his pocket.

The work was to be produced the following autumn, so that no time was to be lost. Mozart went straight to da Ponte, who suggested, as though a new idea had just struck him, the tremendous subject of Don Juan, probably without in the least realizing its whole import, but taking it merely as an excellent excuse for good comedy, titillating situations and a fine theatrical thrill at the end. How much Mozart himself saw in it just then it is impossible to guess; but if he was unaware that he would make of it one of the few stage works in the world which have a claim to be called the greatest opera ever written, he must at least have felt that the completely new problems raised by this text, so far as he was concerned,* would make an engrossing task for weeks to come.

Da Ponte's "Memoirs" give an amusing and characteristic account of how this poetical busybody and worldling set to work, though he does not say that he modelled his libretto very closely on that used by Gazzaniga. He at least did not shun concentrated labour, while he knew how to make it highly agreeable for himself, if we may believe the glamorous old-age recollections of an

---

* It was not in itself new. Gluck's *Don Juan* ballet had been produced in Vienna in 1761, and Mozart's music at some points very curiously resembles that of Gazzaniga's opera, *Il Convitato di pietra* (The Stone Guest), produced in Venice early in 1787, though it is impossible to say definitely that he knew this work. He must, on the other hand, have been familiar with Righini's of 1777.

adventurer who, not as abandoned as Casanova, may have been no less mendacious:

> I thought it time . . . to exert my poetic powers again. . . . The opportunity was presented to me by the three above-mentioned composers, Martín, Mozart and Salieri, who all came to me at once asking me for a play. . . .
>
> . . . I went to the emperor, put my ideas before him and informed him that I intended to write these three operas contemporaneously.
>
> "You won't succeed," he replied.
>
> "Perhaps not," I answered, "but I shall make the attempt. At night I shall write for Mozart, and I shall regard it as reading Dante's *Inferno;* in the morning I shall write for Martín, and that will be like reading Petrarch; in the evening for Salieri, and that will be my Tasso." He thought my parallel very good.
>
> Directly I reached home I set to work.
>
> I sat down at my writing table and stayed there for twelve hours on end, with a little bottle of Tokay on my right hand, an inkstand in the middle, and a box of Seville tobacco on the left. A beautiful young girl of sixteen was living in my house with her mother, who looked after the household. (I should have wished to love her only as a daughter—but—) She came into my room whenever I rang the bell, which in truth was fairly often, and particularly when my inspiration seemed to begin to cool. She brought me now a biscuit, now a cup of coffee, or again nothing but her own lovely face, always gay, always smiling and made precisely to inspire poetic fancy and brilliant ideas.

Whether these conditions were the ideal ones in which to tackle Salieri's *Assur* it is hard to decide, and they certainly do not seem to fit Martín's *L'Arbore di Diana;* but it can scarcely be questioned that they suited a Don Juan opera to perfection, always provided that the volatile *abbate* wrote the truth.

Be that as it may, he wrote a sprightly libretto full of well-devised situations which make the spectator quite overlook the fact that his Don Juan, although there is much talk of his amorous escapades, is seen throughout the evening to be notoriously unsuccessful in their pursuit. There is, it must be confessed, an extraordinary confusion about half-way through the second act, which no amount of producer's ingenuity ever succeeds in clearing up satisfactorily; but it must be borne in mind that this may have arisen from subsequent manipulations of the text in which quite possibly Mozart had rather more to say than da Ponte may have liked. What is extremely diverting is that old Casanova himself, who was just about that time writing the recollections of his own Don Juanesque career at the castle of Dux in Bohemia, where he had been charitably offered a librarian's post by an old acquaintance, and who was in Prague in the early autumn of 1787, seems himself to have had a hand in revising, and possibly muddling, da Ponte's libretto at that particular juncture, for a sketch in his handwriting has recently been discovered.

In February 1787 Mozart lost his English friends all at once. The Storaces,

Kelly and Attwood returned home, paying a visit to his father at Salzburg on the way, and he had a last flicker of desire to join them and try his luck in London. In the end it was cautiously decided that they should first look round for an opening for him, and that he might follow later. Then *Don Giovanni* intervened. It was not the only important composition of that period, though, for the two glorious string Quintets in C major and G minor the Serenade for strings, "Eine kleine Nachtmusik" and the grand-scale violin Sonata in A Major belong to it. Also, two outward events occurred in May, one calculated to shake Mozart personally to his depths and the other a linking-up of musical history, as he had the foresight to discern. It seemed little enough to begin with: merely the visit of a sullen-faced youth of seventeen with a thick Rhenish accent, who was introduced to him by some acquaintance. But Mozart, after a somewhat frigid reception of the unprepossessing lad, soon pricked up his ears on being played to on the pianoforte with a startling power and originality, and said to some other visitors in the next room that this young man had better be watched, for he would make a noise in the world before long. The young man did: his name was Ludwig van Beethoven.

On 29th May Mozart heard that his father had died the day before, at the age of sixty-eight. He had not been quite unprepared, for on 4th April he had written home to say he knew that Leopold had been ill and to ask anxiously for news about his condition. But it was a blow to be suddenly told that the old man was no more. There had been estrangements between father and son; Leopold had been harsh and peremptory enough to cause bitterness in a young man who, while anxious to remain dutiful, chafed under restrictions; and Leopold's admonitions had been none the less disagreeable for being, as Wolfgang well knew, based on common sense and affection. But now the old filial tenderness welled up, and he was genuinely afflicted by his loss.

About the end of August the Mozarts left for Prague a second time, Constanze once again in an interesting situation. How far *Don Giovanni* was finished before their departure is not known, but it is certain that a good deal still remained to be done. They lodged at the "Three Golden Lions," but were half the time the guests of the Dušeks, who lived at a country house in "Bertramka's vineyard." There they enjoyed good food, cheerful company, games of darts and skittles and what not, and Mozart intermittently worked at his score on a stone table in the garden, surrounded by ripening grapes and facing the view from the slope.

There was a good deal of trouble with the singers, who, Mozart wrote to Jacquin, were not as accomplished as those in Vienna in catching hold of a new work quickly. The young baritone Luigi Bassi, who sang the title part, complained that he was given no great display aria, and it is said that Mozart composed the duet, "Là ci darem la mano" five times before Bassi was kind enough to say it pleased him. Then Caterina Bondini, the wife of the impresario, probably from fear of spoiling her voice, could not be persuaded to make Zerlina's cry behind the scenes sufficiently realistic. Mozart's remedy was simple: at a rehearsal he suddenly assailed her roughly from behind at the given moment, whereupon she gave forth a scream which he declared to be a perfect sample of what he wanted at the performance. To complete the traditional complications of opera rehearsals, gossip had it that Mozart, perhaps with a view to still greater realism, indulged in love affairs not only with his Zerlina, but also with his Donna Anna, whose interpreter was Teresa Saporiti, and with his Donna Elvira, sung by Caterina Micelli. Saporiti, it was said, had expressed surprise at Mozart's insignificant appearance, whereupon he transferred his affections in a pique. Some of this may be true; all of it certainly is not, since tittle-tattle always has a way of inflating the facts, if any; and as nobody does know how much is true, let us leave it at that, with a strong suspicion that these rumours emanated from those who can never believe an artist to be capable of creating a dramatic figure without having personally gone through its experiences.

Another set of stories is current, about the composition of the overture to *Don Giovanni,* which is supposed to have been written only the night before the performance and distributed to the players, with the ink still wet, to get through at sight as best they could. But Constanze told Nissen, her second husband, distinctly that it was on the last night but one before the production that Mozart wrote down the overture while she regaled him with punch and kept him awake with stories, so that the sight-reading can only, at the worst, have happened at the dress rehearsal. That the whole piece was fully composed in Mozart's mind, according to his astonishing habit, and only needed writing down, may be taken for granted.

That the music for Don Juan's dinner entertainment in the second finale cannot have been ready until quite late is shown by the original libretto, which does not contain the words sung by Don Juan and Leporello while these little wind octets are played. It appears that they were at first to be left to the players' choice, but in the end Mozart interpolated favourite melodies from three recent popular operas; Martín's *Una cosa rara,* Sarti's *Fra due litiganti* and his own *Figaro.*

At last, on 29th October 1787, *Il Dissoluto punito, ossia Il Don Giovanni* (The Debauchee Punished, or Don Juan) was produced. Prague went mad with delight over it, in spite of Mozart's fear lest the public should be bewildered by the novelty of the music, which must have astonished even himself as it fell to him with the inevitability that makes genius after its highest flights stand amazed and ask: "How did I do it?" He conducted the first performance himself, and the artists, anxious to do justice to a work and a composer of whose greatness they had been given ample opportunity to become aware, did the utmost in their power to make the production a success. Those not yet named were Antonio Baglioni as Don Ottavio, Felice Ponziani as Leporello and Giuseppe Lolli, who doubled the parts of the Commendatore and Masetto.

The Mozarts were in no hurry to return to Vienna and their everlasting domestic cares. For once they enjoyed themselves, and their hosts were reluctant to let them go. The new baby was not due just yet * and little Carl was no doubt taken care of by his grandmother. On 3rd November Josepha Dušek, who had been promised a concert aria, locked Mozart into a summer-house at Bertramka and declared that she would not let him out until he had written it down. He obeyed, but retaliated by refusing to give up the piece unless she could sing it at sight. It turned out a grand and extremely difficult thing, full of strange intervals and harmonies; but Josepha, who was a bit of a composer herself and a good clavier player, brilliantly acquitted herself of the task imposed on her by the composer, who dedicated this aria, "Bella mia fiamme," to her.

Two German songs were also written during the visit to Prague, but they were less important than one or two of a group composed earlier that year, among which "Abendempfindung" is particularly interesting as a true forerunner of the Schubertian *Lied* and only less so than "Das Veilchen" of two years earlier because that is the one evidence of Mozart's awareness of Goethe, who as a lad had attended his infant-prodigy display at Frankfort.

On 12th November the Mozart couple were back in Vienna. Three days later Gluck died of a stroke at the age of seventy-three, and by 7th December Joseph II, who could not help being rather impressed by Mozart's successes in Prague, appointed him chamber musician to the court in Gluck's place with eight hundred florins a year. The immediate effect seems to have been to drive him to the composition of various dances for the court balls and to inhibit him from writing larger works, the only one being the curiously empty piano Concerto in D Major—the last but one. Still, though the new appointment amounted to little enough, it may have given the Mozarts some hope of being relieved of the nagging worries that seemed to plague them the more relentlessly the more the master's creative power grew and the more his fame spread beyond Vienna.

Some time early in 1788 Vienna decided to hear the Prague opera. *Don Giovanni* was put into rehearsal with a notable cast—so notable that what Mozart had written for what they considered a set of provincial singers was not good enough for those in the capital. They cleverly attributed the failure of the work at its first performance, on 7th May, to the fact that they had not been allowed to shine sufficiently with solo displays. With the honourable exception of Aloysia Lange, who sang Donna Anna, Francesco Bussani, who took the Commendatore and Masetto,† they all insisted on some extra number or another. Caterina Cavalieri was given Elvira's "Mi tradì," much too lovely a piece to be cut, but rather in the concert-aria style and difficult to fit in logi-

---

* It was to be a girl this time, Theresia, born 27th December 1787, died 29th June 1788.

† Masetto's "Ho capito," often indicated as an extra number in old editions, was in the original score; so was Don Juan's "Metà di voi" in the second act, which is too often omitted.

cally anywhere; * Francesco Morella received a second song for Ottavio, the beautiful though static "Dalla sua pace"; while Luisa Mombelli and Benucci, the original Figaro, were fobbed off with a duet for Zerlina and Leporello that continues deservedly to be neglected as the one inferior number in the whole score.

The opera was given a mere fifteen times in the course of the year and did not reappear in 1789—indeed not until after Mozart's death, when it was revived in a lamentable German translation. Joseph II declared, according to da Ponte, that "the opera is divine, perhaps even more beautiful than *Figaro,* but no food for the teeth of my Viennese," on which Mozart's comment seems to have been: "Let us give them time to chew it. . . ."

It is impossible to conceive that any notion as here set down by Mozart could have come from the pen of any other composer, then or later. What is more, not a single number in *Don Giovanni* can be imagined to occur in any other opera by Mozart himself. Everything is in character, everything coloured by the particular mood into which this great tragi-comic subject cast him.

Tragi-comic, yes, so much is certain; but nobody knows exactly where comedy ends and tragedy begins in what is formally an opera in D minor with a cheerful coda in D major. It is all inextricably blended, laughter for some and tears for others, and then again both in succession, indeed almost together, for one and the same person. Donna Elvira rampages up and down the stage furiously at her first entry with her E flat major aria, but Don Juan and Leporello laugh behind her back while the orchestra chuckles with kindly understanding of the whole situation. And when in that miraculous trio near the beginning of the second act the same two men plan a cruel jest at Elvira's expense, we feel inclined to weep at the tender loveliness of the music, such music as only Mozart could pour out to comfort a woman whose loving heart is about to break, be she Ilia or Constanze, the Countess Almaviva or Pamina, or indeed that most ill-used of all—foolish, infatuated Elvira, wavering miserably between vengeance and forgiveness.

It may be a too personal impression, but I have come to feel certain that this close sympathy with his women characters was his compensation for his lack of that complete understanding between him and any real woman that was one of the afflictions of his life. He became its supreme poet because he was deprived of it by fate, not through any fault of his, much less of Constanze's. That communion between two beings that needs no words was never his; but he knew an artistic equivalent, and it needed music—his music.

How sharply all the characters in *Don Giovanni* stand out! They do so even —this is Mozart's great dramatic secret—when they sing in concert and weave

* It is a wrong, post-Wagnerian and anti-musical principle to suggest, as German critics do almost with one accord, that so perfect a piece should be sacrificed because dramatically it is uncalled-for.

a piece the shape of which leaves nothing to be desired in a purely musical way. The stony-hearted and domineering Donna Anna; her almost despicably humble wooer Ottavio, who saves himself from our contempt by his tenderness; the minx Zerlina, made more sympathetic than perhaps she deserves by a touch of peasant common sense and simple affection; honest Masetto, too dense to be quite clear about the causes of his jealousy; the Commandant, equally dignified as a man and as a statue: they are all, like Elvira, outlined indelibly by music one can never forget.

Ah, if only one could! If only one might recapture that thrill of first acquaintance! There are times at which one would gladly give up the understanding of a score of which one need never fear to reach the bottom, an understanding that deepens with each new hearing or reading and reveals new secrets, for that first rapture on coming into touch with the *Don Giovanni* music. Not a careless rapture, though; rather a careworn one. This opera oppresses its lover with its beauty and with that sympathy with all aspects of life which is almost unhuman. For Mozart seems to love all his characters impartially, if one may judge from the fact that he lavishes the most wonderful music on all, though vastly different music on each. His Shakespearian indulgence covers Don Juan's vices as well as the weakness of Donna Elvira or the hardness of Donna Anna. Each is for him simply a phase of life to be transmuted into a value of art as good as any other. They or Leporello's garlicky vulgarity and pandering knavery. Before Mozart's overmastering art they are all equal.

E. B.

Don Giovanni, ossia Il Dissoluto punito (Don Juan, or The Libertine Punished) had its American *première,* in the original Italian, at the Park Theater, New York, May 23, 1826. Manuel Garcia's company presented it, and the cast included Garcia himself (though a tenor) as Don Giovanni, his wife as Donna Elvira, his son, Manuel, Jr., as Leporello, his daughter, Maria Malibran, as Zerlina, Mme. Barbieri as Donna Anna, Milon as Don Ottavio, and Carlo Angrisani as both Don Pedro and Masetto.

Such was the success of the work that an English version was speedily put on at the Chatham Theater, with H. Wallack, an uncle of the famous actor Lester Wallack, in the title role. Later on Malibran took part in some of the English performances, and the English version remained current in New York till Max Maretzek revived the Italian original at the Astor Place Opera House in 1850. On April 23, 1863, *Don Giovanni* was given at the New York Academy of Music in German.

The first *Don Giovanni* at New York's Metropolitan Opera House was presented Nov. 29, 1883, with Emmy Fursch-Madi (Donna Anna), Christine Nilsson (Donna Elvira), Marcella Sembrich (Zerlina), Italo Campanini (Don Ottavio), Giuseppe Kaschmann (Don Giovanni), and Mirabella (Leporello).

A distinguished cast on Dec. 31, 1894, offered Lillian Nordica (Donna Anna), Emma Eames, Zélie de Lussan, Giuseppe Russitano, Victor Maurel, and Édouard de Reszké. A still more distinguished cast on Jan. 2, 1899, was adorned by Lilli Lehmann, Nordica (Donna Elvira), Sembrich, Thomas Salignac, Maurel, and Édouard de Reszké. An incomparable Masetto of about this time was Charles Gilibert, who after singing the part at the Metropolitan, was heard in it at the Manhattan Opera House in the seasons of 1906-7 and 1907-8, together with Maurice Renaud, the most distinguished Don Giovanni New York has had in at least a half century, except only Maurel.

Gustav Mahler conducted a revival of *Don Giovanni* at the Metropolitan on January 23, 1908, with Eames as Donna Anna, Johanna Gadski as Donna Elvira, Sembrich as Zerlina, Alessandro Bonci as Don Ottavio, Feodor Chaliapin as Leporello, and Robert Blass as the Commendatore.

P. S.

Così fan tutte

[Thus Do All Women]

OPERA BUFFA IN 2 ACTS

Book by Lorenzo da Ponte

First performance: Burgtheater, Vienna, Jan. 26, 1790

CHARACTERS

Fiordiligi, a lady of Ferrara, SOPRANO
Dorabella, her sister, SOPRANO OR MEZZO-
  SOPRANO
Despina, their waiting maid, SOPRANO
Ferrando, an officer, in love with
  Dorabella, TENOR

Guglielmo, an officer, in love with
  Fiordiligi, BARITONE
Don Alfonso, a cynical old bachelor,
  BASSO BUFFO

Soldiers, Servants, Musicians, Boatmen, Wedding Guests, etc.

The action takes place in Naples during the eighteenth century

Don Alfonso lays a wager with the officers Ferrando and Guglielmo, by which they are to test the fidelity of their fiancées, Fiordiligi and Dorabella, for the space of a day. The officers seemingly bid farewell to them, but return disguised as rich Albanians. They are unrecognized and make love to each other's ladies. The maid Despina tries to induce her mistresses to give ear to the rich strangers, but the sisters remain steadfast. Alfonso, who does not wish to lose his wager, bribes Despina, and when the Albanians seemingly take poison before the eyes of the ladies, the maid appears disguised as a physician, and pretends to save their lives by the power of magnetism.

Persuaded by Despina, Dorabella is the first of the two to listen to the pleadings of the disguised Guglielmo, to whom she gives the picture of her betrothed Ferrando. In a fury over the success of his friend, Ferrando then wins Fiordiligi. Despina, at the suggestion of Alfonso, now disguises herself as a notary and brings the marriage contracts. At this moment news arrives of the return of the officers. The cowering Albanians, who have been hidden by the sisters, escape in order to reappear in their true characters. They unmask Despina, show the faithless brides their marriage contracts, and finally reveal their true identities, but at the critical moment Alfonso, who has won the bet, explains all and brings about a reconciliation.

O. T.

One might say that *Così fan tutte* has always been the Cinderella of Mozart's three Italian comic operas; though it is hardly fair to call *The Marriage of Figaro* and *Don Giovanni* "ugly sisters." But they made their way throughout the world in the course of time, whereas *Così fan tutte* was almost completely neglected until the great Mozart revival which took place at Munich about 1895. Even then it would hardly have attracted much notice if it had not been enthusiastically encouraged by Richard Strauss, who in those days was a young conductor hardly known at all as a composer.

The three operas really may be said to form a kind of trilogy, for they are all in the same style, composed for a small theatre and a small company—it might almost be said that they were composed for the same singers; and what is more important, they all three had librettos written by the same poet, the Abbé Lorenzo da Ponte. All three are described on the title-pages of their librettos as *dramma giocoso;* the same word is used too in Mozart's own private manuscript catalogue for his own works. Comic opera of this type, written for perhaps six or seven characters with a minimum of chorus, was a flourishing commercial industry, centered mainly on Venice after the rise of the partnership between the Venetian playwright, Goldoni, and the Venetian composer, Galuppi, who might be called the Gilbert and Sullivan of the eighteenth century. Goldoni wrote not only the spoken comedies which have since made him world famous in the history of the theatre, but also some fifty or sixty librettos for comic operas, set by various composers. They are often trivial and foolish in plot—after all, their one and only object is to amuse—but they are never clumsy or awkward in style; they are written in good conversational Italian, neat in versification and rhyme, admirably suited to musical setting and cleverly constructed for the stage, as long as one accepts the conventions of the time. Da Ponte learned a good deal from Goldoni as regards technique, but he struck out new lines as regards subject; his Italian style is always elegant and natural, and he is marvellously skilful at adapting French plays, such as those of Molière and Beaumarchais, to the requirements of the Italian comic opera stage.

The Marriage of Figaro is a landmark in operatic history because of its libretto, a play which combined an unusual amount of vigorous action on the stage with a background of social and political satire. The original play of Beaumarchais had started as a comic opera based on the older traditions of the comedy of masks. Figaro is a sort of Harlequin, the link between the stage and the audience, ready to talk informally to the spectators at any moment, and to be the mouthpiece for the author's opinions on life in general. Compared with many operas, *Figaro* is conspicuously full of action, but it is really a play of talk. Modern critics have sometimes praised Mozart (for all good points Mozart gets the credit, and for all the shortcomings the librettist is invariably blamed) for eliminating all the political satire in the play and converting it into a banquet of pure melody, others have blamed Da Ponte for presenting his audience with nothing but a sordid comedy of illicit love. Beethoven seems to have taken that view, for he said that he himself could never write music for such immoral stories as those of *Figaro* and *Don Giovanni*. But in 1786, when Mozart's *Figaro* first came out, the play was still forbidden in Vienna, although translations of it were on sale in the bookshops. It has been said of Beaumarchais that he taught the aristocrats themselves to scoff at the old *régime,* and even in Vienna, which was always more reactionary (because more devout and less intelligent) than Paris, there must have been intellectuals who, when they went to see Mozart's opera, could easily supply from memory all that Da Ponte had been obliged to remove either from consideration for the censorship, or—what was more important—consideration for the stage.

Don Giovanni can hardly be called a revolutionary opera, but it could be interpreted in a revolutionary sense. We must never forget that both Da Ponte and Mozart were writing for the practical needs of the moment, and a given cast of singers; they were not consciously creating one of the world's masterpieces for the joy and admiration of eternity. *Don Giovanni* was commissioned by Prague because *Figaro* had been a success there; the Czechs were always, as they are still, immeasurably more musical than the Viennese. It was obvious at once that the new opera would have to follow the general lines of its predecessor, all the more as most of the same singers were to take part in it. *Figaro* had been laid out in four acts because the usual three, or even two, of comic opera were not enough to hold all the material which Da Ponte borrowed from Beaumarchais' five. Da Ponte and Mozart therefore planned *Don Giovanni* on the same lines—the same sort of songs, duets, and ensembles, and in four acts. For some unknown reason the opera was given in two, as it is still. The same unknown reason must have dictated the arrangement of *Così fan tutte* in two acts, although they are exceedingly long ones. In every commercial theatre such matters are decided by extraneous authority; we know how in England the hours of beginning and ending, the distribution into acts and the length of the intervals depends on the hours of normal meal-times, the hours of last trains to the suburbs, as well as of those during which chocolates may be sold in the theatre or drinks in the bar. The construction of Mozart's operas was pretty certainly dictated by similar considerations.

Don Giovanni derives a good deal from Molière, a little from Goldoni, and most of all from Giovanni Bertati, a contemporary librettist. But these sources could only supply isolated incidents and phrases of dialogue; for the general plan and the big ensembles Da Ponte had to make use of his own invention and routine. The chief difference between *Figaro* and *Don Giovanni* is that the former is mostly a drama of talk and the latter entirely a drama of action. Social satire is apparent only in Masetto's song, and in the scene where Masetto collects the peasants to murder Don Giovanni; there is also the very important satirical aspect—derived directly from Molière—of Don Giovanni's complete cynicism as regards morality and religion. We can at any rate say that this opera brings us one step nearer tò the revolution year of 1789.

By the time *Così fan tutte* was put on the stage the Revolution had started in Paris, and there could be no more open satire on the operatic stage in Vienna. Yet satire there is, and on the eternal subject of female frailty. To Mozart's own public there could be nothing in the least shocking about that. Both *Figaro* and *Don Giovanni* dealt undisguisedly with seduction and adultery; the libretto of *Così fan tutte* is as chaste as a novel of Miss Yonge. There is in it not the faintest suggestion of "impropriety," except perhaps for Despina's hints at the way in which the military behave on active service. We may perhaps accept the legend that the plot was suggested by an actual fact of recent date, and it is fairly clear that Da Ponte was influenced by the general scheme of *La Grotta di Trofonio,* an opera by Casti and Salieri (1785) in which the characters of two pairs of lovers are completely changed by the spells of a magician. But apart from these sources, Da Ponte's libretto is entirely his own invention, and it is a singularly accomplished piece of formal craftsmanship.

From a realistic standpoint the plot may be absurd; accept its deliberate artificiality, and the factual details do not matter. Was there a war going on in 1789 between Naples and some other maritime power? Ought not Nelson and Lady Hamilton—such admirable operatic figures, too—to have been brought in? They would have been a great nuisance. The imbecility of the two young ladies may indeed astonish us; but all that is quite subsidiary to the real motive of the opera—the mental processes by which they shift their affections from one lover to another. We see in this libretto what we are to see eventually in *The Magic Flute,* and what we did not see at all in either *Figaro* or *Don Giovanni*—psychological development. In *The Magic Flute* we see Tamino and Pamina going through all sorts of experiences and growing up to maturity thereby; and in that opera everything is perfectly serious as far as these two are concerned. In *Così fan tutte* nothing is serious, except perhaps Don Alfonso's hatred of the whole race of women; and it is curious to note that in both two previous operas the women have little claim on our respect. Da Ponte was a Catholic priest, but he had a considerable knowledge of the female sex. He was a great friend of Casanova, and he eventually died in New York as the father of a family.

The musical planning is masterly. Mozart is allowed an unusually large number of ensembles, and some of them are unusually extended; a great deal of the drama really takes place in the course of these "conversation-pieces." It is quite possible that Mozart may have talked the whole problem out with Da Ponte from the first, telling him exactly what he wanted in the way of musical numbers; even so, we must admire the incredible skill with which Da Ponte has constructed and arranged them. *Così fan tutte,* in fact, so far from being what many German and other critics have called it, the worst libretto ever written, is really about the nearest approach to perfection that any musical dramatist has ever achieved. It is fundamentally a comic opera; but Mozart's singers wanted grand arias in which they could show off all their virtuosity. Da Ponte provides them, with recitatives to introduce them too. But as the singers' art is artificial and formal, he makes all these grand arias and recitatives caricatures of the grand arias of the past; and this is all the better for the singers, for it enables them not merely to show off, but to exaggerate their exhibitionism to the very utmost.

Later generations took all these things with a deadly seriousness. Having no acquaintance with genuine *opera seria,* which after all had been dead for some thirty or forty years when *Così fan tutte* first came out, they could not appreciate the caricature for want of knowledge of the thing caricatured. Audiences of to-day are altogether more sophisticated than their grandparents as regards music and drama, and as regards morals and marriage as well. *Così fan tutte* is an opera for highly sophisticated people; it is the last expression of eighteenth-century artificialism.

Così fan tutte did not have much of a success at Vienna; but what could one expect from a city that had failed to appreciate both *Figaro* and *Don Giovanni?* Prague brought it out in Italian in 1791, before Mozart's death; in the same year it was performed in Italian at Leipzig and Dresden, probably by the same singers. After that, its fate depended on its German translations, and as Dr. Loewenberg says, "No other opera, perhaps, has been subjected to so many different versions and attempts to 'improve' the libretto." Needless to say, it had no success in Italy. It was given at a few Italian towns early in the next century, but it never reached Venice—where it ought to have been at home from the first—until 1934, when it was performed in German by the Vienna State Opera Company. Its first German performance in Vienna had been in 1794. In Paris it was first given in Italian, and afterwards, at widely separated dates, in all sorts of new versions, one being an adaptation of "Love's Labour's Lost."

When *Così fan tutte* was performed for the first time in 1790, Italian *opera buffa* was on its last legs. The general repertory at all the musical theatres of Vienna became increasingly French, and the tendency of French Revolution opera was to what we should call melodrama. Melodrama (in the ordinary English sense of the word) did in fact grow out of opera, and started in France before it was imported into England. The Revolution took the theatre, including opera, very seriously, and both melodrama and melodramatic opera were designed to be powerful influences for moral education. Beethoven's *Fidelio* is the nearest thing to it that modern opera-goers are acquainted with. German native opera was modelling itself more and more on the French type, inclining towards either *bourgeois* stories, melodrama, or wild romantic supernaturalism. The ideal German heroine began to appear, the type of Agathe in *Der Freischütz,* the pure-minded and virtuous *Deutsches Mädchen,* with fair hair in two plaits. We know her as Marguerite in *Faust;* her first appearance was as Pamina in *The Magic Flute.* Her characteristics were simplicity and desperate seriousness, unless she was of the light soprano type, like Annette in *Der Freischütz.* Singers of these types had to do their best with *Figaro* and *Don Giovanni* in German translations, but the result was to make these operas much too serious and generally too clumsy, too, in their interpretations. One might just possibly conceive of Zerlina as a *Deutsches Mädchen,* but there is no part for her in *Così fan tutte.* The romantic German stage wanted to take opera seriously, and to take *Così fan tutte* seriously is to misunderstand it from top to bottom.

E. J. D.

After *Don Giovanni* we are magically transported into yet another world: that of *Così fan tutte.* Well, scarcely a world at all; only a show of marionettes. For nothing could be more ridiculous than to pretend that the preposterous people, the still more preposterous situations of this utterly artificial intrigue, were meant to be believed in, and nothing more absurd than to take da Ponte and Mozart to task for believing in them, which of course they never did. The philistinism of the nineteenth century which professed to take umbrage at this story of two girls who become enamoured of each other's lovers disguised as outlandish adventurers (a disguise which could not take in anybody for a moment) and which led either to the banishment of this fascinating work from the stage or to disastrous attempts at providing it with an expurgated libretto of some kind, was due to the confusion of moral and artistic values that was one of the gross immoralities of that century, with Ruskin presiding as high priest over the orgies held by addicts to aesthetic perversion. The supreme joke is that one cannot possibly help seeing the utter harmlessness of this mildly amusing piece, which contains nothing so seriously unpleasant as the Count's pursuit of Susanna in *Figaro.* Nor is it possible to see how any one could fail to be captivated by its deliberately and delectably artificial music. For once again Mozart achieved the miraculous feat of writing a score which, consistent in style from start to finish, could not by any conceivable chance lend a single one of its numbers to any other work of his. The whole perfume and flavour of the music is new and unique.

Artifice is the keynote of it. What else could it have been? But then again, who else could have made it as unfailingly charming as the master who remains the finest artificer as well as the greatest artist whose services music ever enjoyed? At the same time, of course, he infallibly hits upon the truth of his characters—the truth of their stage existences, which is all there is to them. And he does it by means of parody that has both infinite gusto and endless sympathy in it. Laughing at them, he is never cruel, and takes away the sting of his satire by making game, at the same time, of the musical mannerisms of his time, including his own.

E. B.

This brilliant lyric comedy reached America only on March 24, 1922, at the Metropolitan Opera House, New York. So much of an event was the belated *première* that, in the interest of scenic effect, a small revolving stage was superimposed on the actual Metropolitan stage, and, in the interest of musical effect, special care was taken with the casting. Artur Bodanzky, the musical director of the production, deleted from the score, however, the two arias for tenor. The cast included Florence Easton (Fiordiligi), Frances Peralta (Dorabella), Lucrezia Bori (Despina), George Meader (Ferrando), Giuseppe de Luca (Guglielmo), and Adamo Didur (Don Alfonso).

[Alfred Lunt, the noted American actor and stage director, was engaged by the Metropolitan to direct a revival of the Mozart comedy during the season of 1951–52. Ruth and Thomas Martin supplied a new English version for the bright and sumptuous production, which was conducted by Fritz Stiedry.]

Die Zauberflöte

[The Magic Flute]

OPERA IN 2 ACTS

Book by EMANUEL SCHIKANEDER

First performance: Theater auf der Wieden, Vienna, Sept. 30, 1791

CHARACTERS

Sarastro, High Priest of Isis, BASS
Tamino, an Egyptian prince, TENOR
Papageno, a birdcatcher, BARITONE
The Queen of the Night, SOPRANO
Pamina, her daughter, SOPRANO
Monostatos, a Moor, chief of the slaves
of the temple, TENOR
Papagena, SOPRANO

First Lady, SOPRANO; Second Lady,
MEZZO-SOPRANO; Third Lady,
CONTRALTO; attendants of the Queen
of the Night
First Boy, SOPRANO; Second Boy,
MEZZO-SOPRANO; Third Boy,
CONTRALTO; belonging to the Temple
and fulfilling the designs of Sarastro

Priests and Priestesses of the Temple of Isis; Male and Female Slaves, Warriors of
the Temple; Attendants, etc.

The action takes place in the Temple of Isis at Memphis and its vicinity about the
time of Ramses I

Pamina, daughter of the Queen of Night, is in the hands of Sarastro, the High
Priest of Isis, who hopes to rear the Princess away from her dark mother's influence. Tamino, a youth who has fallen in love with Pamina's picture, is persuaded
by the Queen of Night to rescue the Princess from the High Priest. The youth sets
out accompanied by the cheerfully simple clown, Papageno, a bird-catcher. Tamino
has been armed with a magic flute which will save him from mortal dangers and
Papageno carries a set of bells of similar power.

Pamina, in the palace of Sarastro, is being plagued by the attentions of the wicked
Monostatos, head of the High Priest's troop of slaves, when Papageno enters. Frightened, Monostatos leaves and Papageno urges Pamina to come away with him. But
they are captured in their flight and with Tamino, who also has been seized, are
brought before the wise Sarastro. He ordains that Tamino and Pamina shall wed
once Tamino has passed through a novitiate.

Liberated for the first test and warned to ignore the wiles of all women, Tamino
is confronted with the three bewitching attendants of the Queen of Night, but his
faith in Sarastro keeps him steadfast. The unhappy Pamina, meanwhile, is again
being annoyed by Monostatos when the sudden appearance of her mother saves her.
Giving her daughter a knife, the Queen of Night entreats Pamina to plunge it into

Sarastro's heart. But when Sarastro enters, he reassures Pamina and restores her faith in the ultimate success of the trial.

Thwarted, the Queen of Night plots to destroy the temple and with her three attendants and Monostatos, whom she has enlisted to aid her, enters to wreak her revenge. But with the coming of dawn her powers are broken. Tamino, who has passed triumphantly through his initiation, is happily united with Pamina, and Papageno, the clown, has found a love of his own in the bird woman Papagena.

W. H., P. Z.

The libretto of *The Magic Flute* has long been regarded as an achievement in confusion and a handicap to Mozart's magnificent score. The reasons behind the composition of the opera, the choice of subject, are peculiar enough; when to that is added the fact that the motivation of the plot was reversed after the second scene had been completed, it will be seen how inevitable was its complexity.

The original suggestion for the opera came from Mozart's sometime friend, Emanuel Johann Schikaneder (1748–1812), an itinerant producer, singer, actor, and literary hack, who later performed a similar service when he commissioned from Beethoven what was to become *Fidelio*. Schikaneder had known Mozart from his Salzburg days and had even worked with him as early as the late 1770's, when the impresario, having produced Gebler's play, "Thamos, King of Egypt," persuaded Mozart to revise and add to the incidental music he had already composed.

Early in 1789 Schikaneder, in financial straits, came to Vienna where he found his wife, from whom he had been separated, struggling to make a go of the Theater auf der Wieden. Seeing an opportunity to recoup his fortune with a Viennese success, he returned to his wife and became manager of the theater. At that time the public of the Austrian capital was especially partial to fairy tales of Oriental background and comic operas. The chief purveyor of these popular spectacles was a certain Marinelli, Schikaneder's greatest rival. Marinelli's chief stock in trade was a comic character, Kasperl, who appeared in a whole series of farces.

Schikaneder, in his efforts to find sufficiently fantastic vehicles, turned to a popular collection of Oriental tales gathered by Christoph Martin Wieland (1733–1813), entitled "Dschinnistan," containing a story by one Liebeskind called "Lulu," or "The Magic Flute." With his practical experience in the theater, Schikaneder saw in this romance the ingredients for a fairy opera, replete with all the stock characters from the evil magician and the wronged queen to a comic Kasperl-ish role for himself. Since Mozart's sister-in-law, Josefa Hofer, who later created the Queen of the Night, was a member of his troupe, it was natural that Schikaneder should have persuaded his old friend and former colleague Mozart to write the score for his proposed production based upon the "Lulu" tale.

It is almost conclusively evident that Mozart began to set Schikaneder's libretto in May, 1791. Schikaneder probably was supplying his text piecemeal —a scene or a song at a time, and he had no scruples about having lines reset until they satisfied him. By the middle of June they had reached a point in what we know as the second scene just before the "Bei Männern" duet, when an event occurred which drastically affected the Mozart-Schikaneder project. This was the production, by the rival Marinelli, of a work entitled *Kaspar der Fagottist; oder, die Zauberzither* (Kaspar the Bassoonist; or, the Magic Zither) with music by Wenzel Müller and text drawn from the "Lulu" of Liebeskind. To make matters worse, it was a howling success. Schikaneder was keenly aware of the folly of continuing with his original plan and, being a man of resource and ingenuity, he resolved to salvage his work by changing it in such a way that it would not only differ from the Müller opus but would also, if possible, eclipse it.

It is not difficult to estimate how much Schikaneder and Mozart had accomplished when they were forced to change their course. In addition to the first two scenes as they are generally produced today, there exists in the original libretto another episode which precedes the second scene. It notably contains a trio for three slaves wherein they discuss the relationship between Pamina, Monostatos and Sarastro. If Schikaneder had at this time written anything after the dialogue between Pamina and Papageno which precedes "Bei Männern" there is no record of it, because the whole direction of the plot makes a full turn at this point. It is doubtful if Schikaneder had had time to accomplish more with *The Magic Flute* project, for his many other activities as manager and actor kept him continually busy.

Schikaneder and Mozart, in their dilemma to make their opera different from Müller's *Magic Zither,* hit upon the idea of introducing the ideals of Freemasonry into their plot. It should be remembered that the Masonic order in the eighteenth century was colored by controversial political implications which far outran its benevolent functions. The Masonic ideal of the "regeneration of humanity by moral means" appealed strongly to the liberal-minded men of the time. It was opposed, however, by reactionary factions and clerical parties, especially the Jesuits, as being inimical to the well-being of both Church and State. During the long reign of Maria Theresa the Masons had been persistently persecuted, notwithstanding the fact her husband, Francis I, was a member of a lodge. Under her sons, Joseph II and Leopold II, Freemasonry was encouraged, but an active suppression began again in 1792 under Emperor Francis II.

Since Schikaneder and Mozart were both active Masons, they found it both timely and dramatically appropriate to cast Masonic ideals into a quasiallegory. They thereupon proceeded to employ Masonic ritual and symbolism, coupling them with the "Egyptian" mysteries propounded in that extraordinary book "Sethos" by Abbé Terrasson (1670–1750) which was regarded as authentic by eighteenth century Freemasons.

After "Lulu" underwent this transmogrification, it became possible to identify the chief characters of the Schikaneder plot as contemporary figures. In the Liebeskind original, the prototype of the Queen of the Night is a "radiant fairy" called Perifirime. At her first appearance in the completed opera the Queen is still closely allied with that sympathetic character, and it is only when she assumes the personality of Maria Theresa, the bigoted enemy of the Masonic Ideal, that she becomes a maleficent force. Sarastro, the high priest, stems from a wicked magician with the fancy name of Dilsenghuin, but in the altered version he represents either Freemasonry or, according to Ernest Newman, Ignaz von Born, an eminent and enlightened Austrian scientist and Freemason. And thus Tamino, ambiguously described at his first appearance as a Japanese prince, comes to stand for Joseph II instead of the prototype of Prince Lulu, son of the King of Cashmere, while Pamina is no longer merely the fairy's daughter Sidi, but embraces the attributes of the Austrian people.

Considering the mixed sources from which *The Magic Flute* sprang, it is no surprise to learn that some years after Mozart's death a man named Giesecke came forward with the claim that he and not Schikaneder was the author of *The Magic Flute* libretto. Giesecke, whose real name was Johann Georg Metzler (1761–1833), was a member of Schikaneder's company at the time of the opera's first performance, and was entrusted with the minor role of First Slave for the première. Giesecke was a man of unusual parts and it is somewhat surprising to find him in such a relatively unimportant position. He had first studied law, which he gave up for the stage, becoming intimate with Goethe, Schiller and their circle and he is supposed to be the original of Wilhelm Meister. It would seem, however, that his chief interest was mineralogy which took him from the Viennese stage for a seven-year survey of Greenland and then to a professorship in Dublin, a post he held until his death.

It would seem likely that Giesecke's claim to the authorship of the libretto was based on his skill as collaborator. Schikaneder was perfectly competent to arrange Oriental romances and to lace them with comic parts for himself, but it is more than probable that he was not up to coping with the metaphysical implications of the Masonic scenes and, therefore, had recourse to the talents of his bit-part actor. As a friend of Goethe who had translated "Hamlet," it is probable that Giesecke could handle such sequences as the dialogue between Tamino and the aged priest as well as that of the ordeal by fire and water. The hand of Schikaneder is apparent in much of the opera; the characters of Papageno and Papagena are undoubtedly wholly his, and his happily ingenuous couplets are to be found in many scenes.

The unifying influence in this opera of many sources is the music of Mozart.

It is the scope of Mozart's genius, his instinct for form, and his sympathetic grasp of human idealism which makes *The Magic Flute* a great masterwork.

W. S. A.

Legend dies hard, particularly theatrical or musical legend. One of the most pertinacious fables that ever bedevilled the history of an opera has to do with the libretto of *The Magic Flute.* Almost since the day the work was launched this book has been ridiculed and slandered with a devastation of mockery which ought by all rules of the game to have killed it generations ago.

Actually, the libretto of *The Magic Flute* is one of the best ever written. If Mozart harbored some misgivings when his old friend and brother-mason, Emmanuel Schikaneder, first approached him with the project it was much less the absurdities, the illogic, or the complications of the piece which gave him pause than the idea that he might fail in the attempt to write a so-called magic opera—a type of thing he had never undertaken before. As for Schikaneder, whatever else he may have been he was no fool. For years an itinerant barnstormer, singer, playwright, he had the barnstormer's instinct for what will make an effect in the theatre and what will not. He had acted in his time all sorts of things from Shakespeare (he was even famous for his Hamlet) to musical farces and he had the sense of the stage in his blood. If he saw nothing ridiculous in magic operas, magic farces and other magic spectacles of the kind it was for the excellent reason that he knew his audiences and understood their reactions to nonsense however fantastic and extravagant.

For Schikaneder's public was not that of the grandiose opera house. It was the naive public of the suburb, as distinguished from the sophisticated public of the city proper. The fun and tomfoolery which we find in the comic scenes of *The Magic Flute* are substantially duplicates of the sort of entertainment the patrons of the Viennese *Vorstadt,* or suburban theatre, delighted in and accepted as readily as young children do Punch and Judy. There were a number of these suburban places of entertainment and when one of them had a success—whether in the shape of a spectacular magic piece, with comic scenes jostling more serious ones, or some other form of show—the others made haste to produce something of the identical nature, indeed, if possible, carrying those features which exerted a particular appeal to a point beyond their rivals. Nobody in those days worried about plagiarism, either musical or dramatic. Hence the absurdity of some of the tales which have grown up about *The Magic Flute* and the need which its creators are supposed to have felt of altering it in this or that respect when they discovered that another theatre had, with some other magic piece of similar content, stolen a march on them. If Schikaneder was so particular about certain of the comic portions of his role (Papageno) that he required Mozart to rewrite some of his songs several times it was only because he understood what would take best with the audiences to which he catered.

The Magic Flute, it must be remembered, is not an outright opera but a *Singspiel.* The French equivalent of the *Singspiel* is the *opéra-comique.* Neither the one nor the other is necessarily comic, as we may judge from the example of an *opéra-comique* like *Carmen,* with its tragic outcome. *Carmen,* in its original state and as always given in France, has spoken dialogue in place of recitative. This substitution of the spoken word for recitative is the distinguishing feature of both *singspiel* and *opéra-comique.* And it is, of course, a hall mark of *The Magic Flute.*

Beethoven prized *The Magic Flute* above all other operas of Mozart not only because its plot, with its elevated, humanitarian sentiments, appealed to him far more than the morally questionable intrigues of *The Marriage of Figaro* and *Don Giovanni,* but because it contained the greatest variety of music-lofty and noble pages, such as the air of Sarastro, "Within These Hallowed Dwellings," and "O Isis and Osiris"; the uplifting choruses of the priests, tender love songs and duets, like the meltingly sentimental expressions of the lovers, Pamina and Tamino; songs of a popular, almost folk-like character (Papageno's bird-catcher song and the pretty songs with an *obbligato* of tinkling bells); figurated chorale, dramatic bravura and much else. The listener who hears *The Magic Flute* without being an actual spectator at the performance can scarcely fail to be struck by that extraordinary musical copiousness and diversity of content which caused Beethoven to value Mozart's last opera above all his others. Every scene may be said to have its typical frame and background, its characteristic color and matter.

H. F. P.

The music itself is much more diversified than that of any opera of Mozart's; yet unlike other works of the kind—Strauss's *Frau ohne Schatten,* for instance, which is a kind of modern *Magic Flute*—the disparity of its styles miraculously results in one single and wholly new style. The flashy Italian arias of the Queen of Night next to Sarastro's solemn utterances in Mozart's "masonic" manner; the popular ditties of Papageno side by side with the profound humanity of Pamina's tear-compelling G minor lament and the wonderful dramatic truth of her brief mad scene; the noble classical strains expressing Tamino's love and fortitude; the comic melodrama villainy of Monostatos; the lightly touched-in fairy-tale seriousness of the three genii; the high-minded fugal craft displayed in the overture and the fire-and-water scene contrasted with the easy fun of the Viennese suburban theatre in the incidents of the slaves bewitched by Papageno's bells and the latter's light-hearted scene of pretended suicide; the intrigues of the three ladies-in-waiting outlined in two cunningly devised and most beautiful quintets and in their dark conspirators' music with the queen and the blackamoor just before the end; all this and more is by some marvel of genius fashioned into a single gem of many facets—and of inestimable value.

For all that, it is unjustifiable to say that *The Magic Flute* is Mozart's greatest opera, and none the less so because it is one of the commonplaces of German criticism, to which one must ever pay deference for its scholarship and immensely painstaking research, but by which it is not therefore necessary to let oneself be overawed in the matter of aesthetic apprehension. Where Mozart's operas are concerned, at any rate, German critics, who to begin with can seldom quite reconcile themselves to the vexing fact that Mozart could be as much inspired by the Italian language as by their own, have over and over again fallen into the error of the kind of moral judgment which is capable of leading to so serious a blunder as that of imagining that the music of *Così fan tutte* could possibly be vitiated by its libretto, and it is the same attitude which is responsible for the false notion that because *The Magic Flute* contains elements of greater idealistic aspiration than any other stage work of Mozart's, it necessarily also contains his greatest music. Is it not enough that it should be in its own way as great as the other supreme masterpieces?

To Mozart it was all the same: religious aspiration or amorous pursuits—there was no difference between such extremes for him as an artist. And it was as an artist and nothing else that he approached his opera subjects, though we may be sure that he would not have succeeded so wonderfully had he not understood life from top to bottom as a human being. He could not specialize in any one emotion. His artistic intuition had taught him too much about life as a whole, and it was his mission to pour his knowledge into his work, to be the possession neither of ascetics nor of rakes, but of those in whom the multiform phases of existence had found some sort of balance.

This is his title to lasting glory. It was his tragedy too, no doubt, while he lived, for the conviction grows as one studies him that, occupied as he was with all human experience, he was incapable of devoting himself particularly to one. The happiness that passes all understanding did not come anywhere into his short life, so that it is perhaps a consolation to know how short that life was. But he has had his compensation ever since, for although other great composers have been more admired, more exclusively worshipped and during some phases of musical life more assiduously cultivated, none has ever been so adored as Mozart is by those who apprehend his music. Such apprehension is not easy, and the whole mystery of him is never to be grasped, for his art too passes understanding.

E. B.

Mozart died shortly after the production of *The Magic Flute,* in deep distress. This opera, with the music of his Requiem, was in his mind until the final delirium. While the opera was performing he would take his watch from under his pillow and follow the performance in imagination: "We are now at the end of the act," or "Now comes the grand aria for the Queen of Night." The day before he died, he sang with his weak voice the opening measures of

"Der Vogelfänger bin ich ja," and endeavored to beat the time with his hands. The frivolous and audacious Schikaneder, "sensualist, parasite, spendthrift," filled his purse by this opera: in 1798 he built the Theatre an der Wien. On the roof he put his own statue, clothed in the feather costume of Papageno. His luck was not constant; in 1812 he died in poverty.

P. H.

The American *première* of *The Magic Flute* occurred at the Park Theater, New York, April 17, 1833, in an English adaptation. In an Italian version, the work was given at the Academy of Music, New York, Nov. 21, 1859, and in an uncut German version it was brought out at the German Opera House, New York, Nov. 10, 1862. At the New York Academy of Music it was again heard Jan. 27, 1886, in English.

The first performance at the Metropolitan Opera House, in Italian, took place March 30, 1900, with one of the most remarkable casts ever assembled, including Marcella Sembrich (Queen of the Night), Emma Eames (Pamina), Andreas Dippel (Tamino), Giuseppe Campanari (Papageno), Zélie de Lussan (Papagena), and Pol Plançon (Sarastro), besides Milka Ternina, Eugenia Mantelli, Carrie Bridewell, Suzanne Adams, Eleanore Broadfoot, Rosa Olitzka, Antonio Pini-Corsi, and Adolf Mühlmann in less conspicuous roles. Luigi Mancinelli conducted.

Jacques Offenbach

(Cologne, Jan. 20, 1819–Oct. 5, 1880, Paris)

Offenbach was not the actual creator of the modern French operetta. That distinction belongs to one Hervé (1825–92), a composer, conductor, librettist, singer, scene painter, and many other things, whose real name was Florimond Ronger. But it was Offenbach who took up the genre and gave it its enormous vogue during the Second Empire and afterwards.

Jacques Offenbach was by birth a German. He was born in Cologne on the 20th June 1819, his father, whose real name was Juda Eberscht, being a chorister of the local synagogue. His father gave him his first instruction in music. It was the paternal wish that he should specialise in the violin, but Jacques's predilection was for the 'cello, which instrument he cultivated in secret until he attained a certain proficiency on it.

In his fifteenth year he and his brother went to Paris, where Jacques, in spite of the rule that forbade foreign students admission to the Conservatoire, somehow or other managed to enter that august institution by a side-door. At the same time he obtained, at a salary of 83 francs a month, a post among the 'cellos of the orchestra of the Opéra-Comique, where he and a companion, Seligmann, used to amuse themselves during the performances by playing all sorts of pranks with the music, such as stopping when they liked and beginning again when they liked, missing out every other note, or playing their part in another octave than the right one.

In 1838, after about three years' service at the Opéra-Comique, he left the orchestra and supported himself as best he could by doing musical hack-work of every sort. Not making a commercial success of this he took up his 'cello again, and toured as a virtuoso of sorts through Germany and England.

On his return to Paris he married a Spanish girl, Herminie de Alcain, and for a long time was hard put to it to maintain a very modest establishment. When the revolution broke out in Paris in 1848 he retired to Germany, whence he returned in 1849. A friend of his, Arsène Houssaye, had just been appointed Director of the Théâtre-Français. He was ambitious to effect many reforms in the historic theatre, one of them being the maintenance of a better orchestra than had been customary there, and the provision of better music. He engaged Offenbach as his conductor at 6,000 francs a year.

Offenbach remained at the Théâtre-Français several years, attending to the entr'acte music in general and the incidental music to certain plays, and occasionally contributing some little thing of his own; one of these, the "Chanson de Fortunio," became a great favourite.

It was about this time that Hervé began to make Paris talk to him and his sprightly operettas. Offenbach was quick to see the possibilities of the style, and when, in the summer of 1855, a tiny theatre in the Champs-Elysées that had lately been used by the scientist Lacaze became vacant, he managed somehow or other to scrape up enough money to obtain a lease of it. His license from the Government permitted him to produce musical plays with not more than three or four characters at the outside, a limitation which irked him for a considerable time.

He opened the theatre, which he called the Bouffes-Parisiens, with a little piece entitled *Les deux Aveugles* (The Two Blind Men), which was quickly followed by *Le Violoneux*.

The sparkle of Offenbach's music, the wit of the libretti, and the dash of the acting soon made the Bouffes the rage of Paris; *Les deux Aveugles* itself ran for more than four hundred consecutive performances. In *Le Violoneux* Hortense Schneider, the brilliant singer and actress who was the delight of our grandfathers, and whose name is indelibly associated with that of Offenbach, made her first appearance in his music.

In the winter the theatre in the Champs-Elysées was a little too far out of town for convenience or comfort, so Offenbach took a lease of the Salle Choiseul in the city, where he opened in December with *Ba-Ta-Clan*. Thereafter, for many years, he occupied the two theatres alternately; and in twenty-five years he wrote some hundred works, producing most of them himself.

The chief landmarks in the long story are *Orphée aux Enfers* (1858), *Geneviève de Brabant* (1859), *Barbe-Bleue* (1866), *La Grande Duchesse de Gérolstein* (1867), *La Belle Hélène* (1865), *La Périchole* (1868), *Madame l'Archiduc* (1874), *La Fille du Tambour Major* (1879), and *La Vie Parisienne* (1866). Some of these were produced at other theatres than Offenbach's own; and, to the great anger of the highbrows, he even obtained a footing at the Grand Opera with the ballet "Le Papillon" (1860), and at the Opéra-Comique with *Barkouf* (1861) and *Vert-Vert* (1869).

Offenbach gave up management on his own account in 1861, but in 1873 took over the Gaîté Theatre, where he remained as director till 1875.

Success brought him money, but money did not bring with it prudence; and in the early seventies he found himself practically ruined. To retrieve his fortunes he went on a tour in America in 1875, from which he brought back with him a hundred thousand francs and materials for a book—"Notes d'un Musicien en Voyage" (1877). During the Franco-German War an agitation was worked up against him as a German, although he had become a naturalized Frenchman as long ago as 1860. Sanity returned to the French after the conclusion of the war, and Offenbach once more became the prime musical favourite of the Paris population.

His health had never been particularly good, and he had persistently overworked himself for the greater part of his life. In his later years probably the one thing that kept him alive was his desire to write a work that should show the world that he had something more in him than the dashing Offenbach whom they knew only as a composer of operettas. This was *The Tales of Hoffmann,* which was destined for the Opéra-Comique. The work was virtually completed—it required only a slight revision by Ernest Guiraud—but before it could be produced Offenbach died after an attack of rheumatism of the heart on the night of October 4–5, 1880. His last and greatest work was produced posthumously at the Opéra-Comique on the 10th February 1881.

E. N.

Les Contes d'Hoffmann

[The Tales of Hoffmann]

FANTASTIC OPERA IN A PROLOGUE, 3 ACTS, AND AN EPILOGUE

Book by JULES BARBIER and MICHEL CARRÉ

First performance: Opéra Comique, Paris, Feb. 10, 1881

CHARACTERS

Hoffmann, a poet, TENOR
Nicklausse, his friend, CONTRALTO (OR
BARITONE)
Olympia, Giulietta, and Antonia, the
poet's loves, SOPRANOS
Coppélius, Dapertutto, and Miracle, a
magician under various names,
BARITONE

Schlemil, BASS
Spalanzani, TENOR
Crespel, BASS

An invisible chorus of Wine and Beer Spirits precedes the entry of Town Counselor Lindorf into the Luther Wine Cellar in Nuremberg (Prelude) where he bribes
Hoffmann's servant to give him the singer Stella's *billet-doux* addressed to the poet
Hoffmann. It contains the key to her boudoir and promises a meeting after the
opera. Hoffmann and the students who have been listening to Stella in Mozart's
Don Giovanni enter during the intermission after the first act. They sing and drink,
but Hoffmann, over a bowl of fiery punch, watches Lindorf and tells his friends
the tale of his "love madness," three episodes, beginning with that of Olympia, which
takes shape on the stage.

At a soirée in Spallanzani the physicist's home, Hoffmann falls madly in love
with his supposed daughter Olympia, really a mechanical doll who sings and dances
with consummate art. Her automatic acceptance of his love vows fills Hoffmann
with joy, but when, breathless from the mad dance with her, he falls on a sofa and
breaks the "glasses of optimism," gift of Coppelius (Lindorf in diabolic disguise),
he sees her as she is; and Coppelius, raging that the poet has discovered the truth,
smashes the doll despite Spallanzani's outcries, the guests jeering at wretched Hoffmann as he sees his idol lying in fragments.

In the courtesan Giulietta's palace in Venice, Hoffmann has abandoned ideal for
sensual love. Dapertutto (Lindorf in another diabolic incarnation) is the strumpet's
master. He incites her jealous lover Schlemihl to pick a quarrel with Hoffmann,
and guiding the latter's rapier, makes him slay his rival. His useless murder—
Giulietta's tender song ("Barcarole") echoes from Venice waters as another admirer

carries her off in his gondola—shows Hoffmann he has nearly lost his soul to the Devil, after weighing it with blood for a worthless woman's sake.

In Crespel's home his daughter Antonia pours out her heart in a "Love Romance." Her father and her lover Hoffmann have begged her to give over singing, for with a wonderful voice she has inherited her mother's consumption; and after Doctor Miracle (Lindorf in his third demoniac disguise) has treated her with an elixir she promises Hoffmann never to sing again. But her lover and father gone, Doctor Miracle returns as the ghost of her dead mother, and with pleas not to give up her heritage of wealth and fame lures Antonia to sing her love song again and—die. Rushing in, Hoffmann hears her last sigh only to be accused of her murder by Crespel. Hoffmann's tale is done (Postlude). Overcome by wine and emotion, the poet's head drops on the table. The Muse, who has dried the tears born of his wild passions, appears to him in an aura of golden light, and promises his dreams in the future shall be of her alone. And as Stella stands in the doorway—the performance of *Don Giovanni* is over—Hoffmann does not see her. It is Lindorf's hour, yet when he hurries to take the actress to her lodgings her glance clings to Hoffmann.

F. H. M.

Before 1860, when he became a French subject, Offenbach had already won recognition as the great master of opéra bouffe and the most Parisian of composers. Yet the tremendous vogue enjoyed by his brilliant light works failed to satisfy him. Like the proverbial comedian with his desire to play Hamlet, he wanted above all things to compose a serious opera. And here and there in the light works he had given proof of his ability to write a melody which in tender loveliness was almost worthy of Mozart. The result of his aspiration toward the serious is *Les Contes d'Hoffmann*.

When Offenbach visited this country in 1876 an interviewer for a New York publication, *The Spirit of the Times*, asked him how he came to invent opéra bouffe (he did not exactly "invent" the genre; Hervé, though younger in years, had preceded him).

"Mon Dieu!" replied Offenbach, "it was born with me! I have always possessed a keen perception of the absurd, and I thought music could be made just as droll as any of the other arts, and so I set to work to write comic music."

"But you like serious music better?" persisted his questioner.

"Of course I do. I like my own serious music much better than my lighter compositions."

Already, it seems, Offenbach had *Les Contes d'Hoffmann* in mind.

To digress for a moment, in this same interview the New York reporter inquired of the man from Paris whether he intended to "compose us" an American opéra bouffe.

"Why, yes, probably," came the answer, "if I get hold of a good subject."

"And 'Yankee Doodle,' you must assuredly introduce it into the partition."

"Certainly; it is a very lively and bright melody."

The subject of Offenbach's opera is taken from the fantastic stories of the German romanticist E. T. A. Hoffmann. The librettist, Jules Barbier, brought out at the Paris Odéon as early as 1851 a drama in five acts, written in collaboration with Michel Carré, entitled "Les Contes d'Hoffmann." Whence the libretto for Offenbach's opera.

How early did Offenbach begin work on this opera, which he did not live to finish? As early as 1875 there was talk of the opera, but we are ignorant as to how much of the music Offenbach had then composed. In 1877 one Albert Vizentini, who had been director of the Théâtre Lyrique, was obliged to give up his playhouse when he was prepared to produce Les Contes d'Hoffmann. In fact, the previous year it had been said that he was going to bring out four new operas by Offenbach! Be that as it may, when in the autumn of 1879 Offenbach returned to Paris from his holiday at Etretat he was still working at Les Contes d'Hoffmann in a race, as it were, with death. He was suffering from gout at the time, fearful of not recovering, and obsessed with the desire to live long enough to see this serious opera of his presented at the Opéra-Comique.

There had been a private performance the previous May, after which Offenbach decided to make important alterations in the score. For one thing, the title rôle, originally intended for the baritone Bouby, he proposed to rewrite for the tenor Talazac. In due course rehearsals began at the Opéra-Comique. Weak as he was from his illness, Offenbach was taken to the Opéra-Comique to hear Mlle. Isaac sing the romance, to hear also the duet of Hoffmann and Antonia. He was working on the score on October 3, 1880, when he suddenly fainted. Two days later he was dead. The funeral services were held in the great Church of the Madeleine. Talazac sang music adapted from Les Contes d'Hoffmann. On November 18 a concert was given in memory of Offenbach at which Mmes. Isaac and Ugalde and the chorus of the Opéra-Comique sang the Barcarolle, but the accompaniment was only for two harps and piano. Offenbach had not completed the orchestration. That task was accomplished by Ernest Guiraud, who, by the way, had supplied the recitatives for Carmen.

The initial performance took place on February 10, 1881. So signal was the success that the work had 101 performances that year. Mlle. Isaac has been described as inimitable, "an accomplished singer, an actress, a virtuoso of fine taste." Taskin's "sinister, demoniacal" Dr. Miracle has been called the crowning triumph of a most honorable career, and the actor, we are told, was so pleased with his creation, so proud of it, that he had his silhouette in the costume and attitude of Dr. Miracle stamped on his letter paper.

On the eve of the first performance the opera seemed too long and the entire act of the Lost Looking-Glass was deleted. Talazac complained to Carvalho, the director of the Opéra-Comique, that thus some of the most beguiling pages of his part disappeared. Carvalho replied:

"You can lose a beautiful act while I, I, lose three sets and a hundred costumes!"

P. S.

The American *première* took place at the Fifth Avenue Theater, New York, Oct. 16, 1882. It was the revival, however, of Nov. 15, 1907, at Oscar Hammerstein's Manhattan Opera House, which launched the triumphant career of *Les Contes d'Hoffmann* in the United States. On that occasion Maurice Renaud impersonated Coppelius, Dappertutto, and Dr. Miracle; Charles Gilibert was both the Spalanzani and the Crespel, and Charles Dalmorès sang the title role.

The company at the New York Metropolitan first presented the work Jan. 11, 1913, with Umberto Macnez as Hoffmann, Adamo Didur as Coppelius, Dinh Gilly as Dappertutto, Léon Rothier as Dr. Miracle, Frieda Hempel as Olympia, Olive Fremstad as Giulietta, Lucrezia Bori as Antonia, and Jeanne Maubourg as Nicklausse.

On Sept. 30 of the same year a skillful English version by Charles Henry Meltzer was staged at the Century Theater.

Amilcare Ponchielli

(Paderno Fasolaro, near Cremona, Italy, Sept. 1, 1834–Jan. 17, 1886, Milan)

Less interesting than Boïto as a personality and musical thinker, but quite as influential in the course of Italian opera because he taught Mascagni, Puccini, and Franco Leoni, was Amilcare Ponchielli, the composer of *La Gioconda* and several other works whose popularity was confined to Italy. Although Ponchielli began composing operas in his early twenties, he did not achieve a success until he was almost forty. This was a revision of an early effort—*I Promessi sposi,* which was based on Manzoni's famous novel, and which doubtless drew a large measure of its popularity from that fact. Coming in 1872, when Verdi, with the completion of *Aïda,* might have been expected to retire permanently, *I Promessi sposi* indicated Ponchielli as Verdi's successor, and indeed, during the rest of his comparatively brief career—he died in 1886, one year before the production of *Otello*—he enjoyed that position. *La Gioconda* was the first of his four tremendous successes at La Scala. Of the remaining three, *Il Figliuol prodigo* (1880), a Biblical opera of spectacular character, has been called his finest work—an opinion to be taken on trust by Americans, as the opera has never been performed here. For all practical purposes, *La Gioconda* is Ponchielli.

W. B., H. W.

Ponchielli died too early to follow Verdi in his latest direction, as he doubtless would have done; he reflected rather the influence of the works of the master's third period,—*La forza del destino, Don Carlos,*—which influence, in so far as it was specific, was mainly French. His creative power was considerable, he was decidedly a man of genius, if of the second rank; if he lacked Verdi's vigour of temperament, he had a fine dramatic gift, and his technical musicianship was rather in advance of his day in Italy.

W. F. A.

La Gioconda

[The Joyous One]

OPERA IN 4 ACTS

Book by TOBIA GORRIO, after VICTOR HUGO's historical drama,
Angelo, tyran de Padoue

First performance: La Scala, Milan, Apr. 8, 1876

CHARACTERS

La Gioconda, a ballad singer, SOPRANO   *Laura,* his wife, MEZZO-SOPRANO
La Cieca, her blind mother, CONTRALTO   *Enzo Grimaldo,* a Genoese noble, TENOR
Alvise, an official of the State Inquisition,   *Barnaba,* a spy of the Inquisition,
BASS   BARITONE

*A Boatman, a Public Letter Writer, a Pilot, and Chorus of Monks, Senators, Sailors,
Ladies, Gentlemen, Populace, Masquers, etc.*

The action takes place in Venice in the seventeenth century

Enzo Grimaldo, a pirate in the Adriatic, loves Laura Adorno who is married to
Alvise Badoero, an inquisitor. La Gioconda is in love with Enzo even though she
is a street singer, and he of noble birth. She supports her blind mother, La Cieca.
Barnaba, a spy, wants to possess La Gioconda. In a wild scene before the Doges'
Palace in Venice Barnaba arranges for Enzo and Laura to meet on an island. He
advises Alvise that the meeting will take place. La Gioconda also learns of this
rendezvous. Previously, La Cieca has been accused of witchcraft and would have
been killed had it not been for the intervention of Laura to whom La Cieca gave
her rosary. On the island Enzo and Barnaba arrive, as do shortly Laura and, finally,
La Gioconda. The latter is about to stab Laura when she sees her mother's rosary
and desists. Alvise is about to arrive on a vessel when Laura and La Gioconda leave
the island while Enzo burns his ship. Back in Venice Alvise is bent on avenging
his honour and arranges to have Laura drink poison. La Gioconda substitutes a
sleeping potion so that later at a ball when Alvise draws aside a curtain he reveals
a sleeping, though apparently dead, Laura. Enzo is arrested for denouncing Barnaba
and, in the general mêlée, La Cieca is taken off by Barnaba. La Gioconda cries that
she will give herself to Barnaba if he will but spare Enzo's life. In the last act Enzo
comes to La Gioconda and tells her that he only wants to die on Laura's bier. La
Gioconda then tells him that Laura, who has been brought in still apparently dead,
is only sleeping. She awakens and attests her love for Enzo. La Gioconda helps the
two depart in safety to Illyria while she waits to stab herself as Barnaba enters to

collect on the bargain they made to free Enzo. To avenge himself for losing La Gioconda, Barnaba screams that he has killed La Cieca, but La Gioconda does not hear. She is dead.

A special niche in the hall of Metropolitan fame is occupied by *La Gioconda*. It was the first in a proud sequence of novelties to reach the Metropolitan stage. The new opera house was opened on October 22, 1883. On December 20 *La Gioconda,* then in the eighth year of its age, had there an American première. *La Gioconda* is an opera with six stellar rôles, and the names of the artists assembled to sing them make an imposing array. They were Christine Nilsson (La Gioconda), Emmy Fursch-Madi (Laura Adorno), Sofia Scalchi (La Cieca), Roberto Stagno (Enzo Grimaldo), Giuseppe del Puente (Barnaba), and Francesco (or Franco) Novara (Alvise Badoero). Malvina Cavalazzi headed the ballet in the "Dance of the Hours."

This cast was one of the most remarkable that even the Metropolitan, with its extraordinary record of star casts, has offered the public. Christine Nilsson, of course, ranked among the distinguished sopranos of the latter half of the nineteenth century. The favor she enjoyed may be gathered from her sobriquet of "The second Swedish nightingale," Jenny Lind having been the first. Del Puente was a particularly admired baritone of the period. Although Stagno seems to have enjoyed no great success in New York, Mascagni thought well enough of him to entrust him with the creation of Turiddu in *Cavalleria Rusticana* at Rome in 1890. Scalchi, for her part, was recognized as the foremost Italian contralto of her time. Fursch-Madi, a highly esteemed dramatic soprano, and Novara, a basso in excellent standing, were likewise artists of international reputation.

Four times *La Gioconda* was given at the Metropolitan that season. The next season a German régime, which knew not Ponchielli and his works, was initiated, and no more was heard of *La Gioconda* at the big yellow opera house until a new century was under way. Meanwhile, though, that enterprising impresario of opera in English, Colonel Henry W. Savage, remembered it and re-introduced it to New York in the vernacular. With Yvonne de Tréville as the heroine he brought it forward in March, 1899, at the American Theatre, and with Adelaide Norwood in the same rôle in October, 1901, at the Broadway Theatre.

Doubtless these productions reminded the new powers that guided Metropolitan destinies of the existence of *La Gioconda,* and before Maurice Grau relinquished the directorship there was talk of a revival with Milka Ternina, the renowned Wagnerian soprano, in the same part, and Ernestine Schumann-Heink as the blind mother (La Cieca). It was reserved, however, for Grau's successor, Heinrich Conried, actually to revive the work, which he did on November 28, 1904, playing a trump card by assigning the rôle of Enzo Grimaldo to Caruso, then in his second season at the Metropolitan. The constellation included also three American women of eminent rank—Lillian Nordica (La Gioconda), Louise Homer (Laura Adorno), and Edyth Walker (La Cieca)—besides the Italian baritone Eugenio Giraldoni (Barnaba) and the great French basso Pol Plançon (Alvise Badoero).

Giraldoni, by the way, was one of the most accomplished actors on the lyric stage and had been selected by Puccini to create the rôle of Baron Scarpia in *Tosca* when his operatic version of Sardou's melodrama had its world première at Rome in 1900. So to the duties of the villainous spy Barnaba he brought a valuable experience in villainy acquired as Rome's cruel and conscienceless police chief.

This revival fared so well (four performances) that *La Gioconda* was chosen to open the next Metropolitan season on November 20, 1905. Nordica, Homer, Caruso, and Plançon resumed their rôles, but now Josephine Jacoby was La Cieca and Antonio Scotti, Barnaba. Again there were four performances. But after that season *La Gioconda* at the Metropolitan was shelved till November 15, 1909, when it again opened the season. Only Homer and Caruso were carried over from the Conried revival. This time Emmy Destinn had the name part, Anna Meitschik made her New York début as La Cieca, Pasquale Amato was the Barnaba, and Andrés de Segurola, who had appeared here with Oscar Hammerstein's company at the Manhattan Opera House, made as Alvise Badoero his first appearance at the Metropolitan. Giulio Gatti-Casazza had now replaced Conried as manager of the Metropolitan and his musical generalissimo, Arturo Toscanini, presided at the conductor's desk.

Although the Metropolitan had subsequently shelved *La Gioconda* for one long period and one short one, this revival unmistakably established the work among local best-sellers, and the rich opportunities it provides for sumptuous scenery and elaborate pageantry, not to forget the popular "Dance of the Hours," have made it second only to *Aida* as a favorite seasonal opener. Since the two earlier occasions it has figured thus on November 17, 1913, and November 2, 1925. After the Metropolitan cast lost Caruso and Destinn, Beniamino Gigli and Rosa Ponselle enjoyed particular favor as Enzo Grimaldo and La Gioconda as long as they sang those rôles.

The librettist of *La Gioconda* was Arrigo Boito, who both wrote the text and composed the music for his own opera *Mefistofele* and who also furnished Verdi with texts for *Otello* and *Falstaff* that have won fervid praise. However, in this instance Boito used his anagrammatic signature of Tobia Gorrio. The libretto is based on Victor Hugo's prose play "Angelo, Tyran de Padoue" (1835), which also inspired Mercadente, César Cui, and Eugène d'Albert to operatic composition.

The title of Ponchielli's opera, in English "The Joyous One," is paradoxical, for La Gioconda is one of the most distressful heroines in the entire range of the lyric drama. However, Boito evidently saw a happy augury in the name when in sending Ponchielli the text he wrote: "May 'The Joyous One' bring us both joy!" ("Che 'La Gioconda' ci giocondi entrambi!"). His wish turned out a prophecy.

P. S.

Serge Prokofieff

(Estate Sonzovka, Government of Ekaterinoslav, Russia, Apr. 23, 1891–
Mar. 4, 1953, Moscow)

The composer was the only child of the manager of a large estate on the
Ukrainian steppes. He . . . received his first taste for serious music from his
mother, who was an accomplished pianist. His first recorded composition was
"Hindu Galop," which he picked out on the piano at the age of 5. Having
seen some operas in Moscow he began composing operas of his own. When
Alexander Tanieff, the composer, saw parts of one of them, *Desert Island,* he
suggested that the boy start studying with Reinhold Gliere, then 27. Another
opera produced under Gliere's tutelage, *Feast During the Plague,* caught the
attention of Alexander Glazunoff, who urged that the boy be enrolled in what
was then the St. Petersburg Conservatory. He began his studies there in 1904
at the age of 13, and remained at the conservatory for ten years. But he had
already made his mark on the city's musical life before his graduation. His
teachers included Rimsky-Korsakov, Anatol Liadoff and Nicolas Tcherepnin.

By the time World War I started his father had died and Prokofieff was
granted exemption from military service because he was the only son of a
widow. He employed the time profitably while others were fighting, for at
this time he produced two of his most famous works, the "Classical" Symphony and the Scythian Suite.

After the Russian Revolution he made his way to the United States via
Siberia and the Pacific. He had influential friends here, notably Adolph Bolm,
the dancer, an original member of Sergei Diaghileff's Ballet Russe who was
the director of the Metropolitan Opera ballet when Prokofieff reached New
York in 1918. Recitals were arranged and by the end of the 1918–19 season the
27-year-old Russian composer was "the mode." He had given four recitals at
Aeolian Hall. His music had been played by the Russian Symphony Orchestra
under Modest Altschuler. And he had captured a commission to write an
original opera for the Chicago Opera Company.

He did not make his headquarters in New York though. Instead he chose
Paris. But he returned to this country in 1921 to conduct the opera he had
delivered to Chicago. It was *The Love of Three Oranges,* which in recent
years has proved one of the New York City Opera Company's greatest hits.
But it was not a success when it was new, either in Chicago or New York,
where it was led at the Manhattan Opera House by the composer. Incidentally,
the season in which it was produced was Mary Garden's first one as the director of the Chicago company.

In Paris Prokofieff had profitable associations with two other famous Russians—Diaghileff and Serge Koussevitzky. For the ballet impresario he produced "Chout," a new version of the work called "The Buffoon," which he had already begun before leaving Russia. He also contributed the ballet, "Le Pas d'Acier," which showed the new industrial and social growth of Russia. Dr. Koussevitzky began his famous Concerts Koussevitzky in Paris in 1921 and among the Prokofieff works he introduced was the Second Symphony. After the conductor came to this country to head the Boston Symphony he had the composer come here to appear with the orchestra in 1926 and he saw that Prokofieff got the commission to write his Fourth Symphony to mark the Boston Symphony's fiftieth anniversary.

Prokofieff's tours took him back to Russia for the first time in 1927. He was there only as a visitor, but he was cordially received as a leading Soviet composer. He returned to this country in 1933 and within a few days in New York he played his Fifth Piano Concerto with the Boston Symphony, under his old friend, Dr. Koussevitzky, and his Third Piano Concerto with the New York Philharmonic-Symphony, under Bruno Walter. The latter program also included a suite from his opera, *The Gambler,* that had been staged in Brussels and Leningrad.

After returning to live in Russia, Prokofieff made only one subsequent trip to the United States—in February, 1938. He gave interviews telling how Russia provided a livelihood and leisure for its composers and he was the guest of honor at a program of his works presented by the League of Composers. He was scheduled to return in the winter of 1940 to serve as guest conductor of the New York Philharmonic-Symphony, but it was announced that he could not obtain the necessary visas. His concerts were conducted instead by another composer nine years his senior who had never returned to Russia, Igor Stravinsky.

When Hitler's surprise invasion brought Russia into World War II, Prokofieff was completing his opera, *The Duenna* (done here in 1948 by the Lemonade Opera), and the ballet, "Cinderella" (given here by the Sadler's Wells Ballet in 1949). He dropped these lighter works to compose a march, two war songs and the orchestral suite, "1941." As the impact of the war deepened in his mind he embarked on a work that he felt might match it in scale, an opera based on Leo Tolstoy's "War and Peace." He reported that it was finished by Jan. 1, 1943, when he sent New Year's greetings "to our American friends on behalf of all Soviet composers." *War and Peace* proved so long that it could not be presented in a single evening. Performances were promised for it in Moscow in 1943 and for the Metropolitan Opera in 1944–45. But there were delays in both places, its first part finally being given in Moscow in 1946.

Following *War and Peace* the composer wrote the score for the film, "Ivan the Terrible," directed by Sergei Eisenstein, with whom he had collaborated earlier in writing the score for "Alexander Nevsky." In 1945, the fourth year of the war, Prokofieff returned to the symphonic form for the first time since his Fourth Symphony seventeen years earlier. He produced his Fifth Symphony, which many consider his finest piece of absolute music. He himself said it was "the culmination of a large part of my creative life."

After the defeat of Germany Prokofieff wrote an "Ode to the End of the War," which called for eight harps and four pianos. In 1947 he completed his Sixth Symphony. Then, early in 1948, the blow fell. Along with Shostakovich, Khatchaturian and four lesser known composers, Prokofieff was accused of writing music that "smelled strongly of the spirit of the modern bourgeois music of Europe and America." Prokofieff, like the other composers, acknowledged he was in error. But he went on composing in his own way and at the end of the year he received another rebuke. This one came from Tikhon Khrennikov, secretary-general of the Soviet Composers Union.

After hearing excerpts of Prokofieff's "The Tale of a Real Man," Khrennikov said the composer had still failed to eliminate his "bourgeois formalism." Again Prokofieff admitted he was wrong and later official reports stated he was doing better in a ballet based on tales of the Urals. Little news of his works came from Russia during 1950, but he was well represented in the theatres and concert halls of the rest of the world, with *The Love of Three Oranges* proving an especial success in New York. A new 'cello sonata was announced in February, 1951. His recently completed Seventh Symphony, which was well received in Moscow on the occasion of its première last Feb. 5, . . . [was performed in this country shortly after the composer's death in March 1953.]

Prokofieff was twice married. His first wife was Lina Lluberia, a Spanish soprano, whom he met in the United States. They had two sons. His second wife was Myra Mendelssohn, who collaborated with him on the libretto of *War and Peace.**

* From *The New York Times,* March 9, 1953.

The Love of Three Oranges

[L'Amour des trois oranges]

OPERA IN A PROLOGUE AND 4 ACTS

Book by the COMPOSER, after COUNT CARLO GOZZI's *Fiaba dell' amore delle tre melarancie*

First performance: Auditorium, Chicago, Dec. 30, 1921

CHARACTERS

The King of Clubs, ruler of an imaginary kingdom, whose costume is that of the playing card, BASS

The Prince, his son, TENOR

The Princess Clarisse, the King's niece, CONTRALTO

Leander, the King's prime minister, dressed as the King of Spades, BARITONE

Truffaldino, a jester, TENOR

Pantalon, a courtier in the confidence of the King, BARITONE

The Magician Tchelio, who protects the King, BASS

Fata Morgana, a sorceress who protects Leander, SOPRANO

Linette, CONTRALTO | princesses con-
Nicolette, MEZZO-SOPRANO | cealed in the
Ninette, SOPRANO | three oranges

The Cook (woman), HOARSE BASS (Basse enroué)

Farfarello, a demon, BASS

Smeraldine, a Negress, MEZZO-SOPRANO

Master of Ceremonies, TENOR

The Herald, BASS

The Trumpet, BASS-TROMBONE

Joys, Glooms, Emptyheads, Jesters, Demons, Doctors, Courtiers, Monsters, Drunkards, Gluttons, Guards, Servants, Soldiers

The action takes place in an imaginary kingdom in the mythical long ago

[Prologue: An artistic discussion is on among four sets of personages on what kind of play should be enacted on the present occasion. The Glooms, clad in appropriately somber robes, argue for tragedy. The Joys, in costumes befitting their temperament, hold out for romantic comedy. The Emptyheads disagree with both and call for frank farce. At last, the Jesters (also called the Cynics) enter, and succeed in silencing the squabbling groups. Presently a Herald enters to announce that the King of Clubs is grieving because his son never smiles. The various personages now take refuge in balconies at the sides of the stage, and from there make comments on the play that is enacted. But for their lack of poise and dignity, they would remind one of the chorus in Greek drama.

The King of Clubs, in despair over his son's hopeless dejection, has summoned physicians to diagnose the ailment. After elaborate consultation, the doctors inform the King that to be cured the Prince must learn to laugh. The Prince, alas, like most hypochondriacs, has no sense of humor. The King resolves to try the prescribed remedy. Truffaldino, one of the comic figures, is now assigned the task of preparing a gay festival and masquerade to bring cheer into the Prince's smileless life. All signify approval of the plan except the Prime Minister Leander, who is plotting with the King's niece Clarisse to seize the throne after slaying the Prince. In a sudden evocation of fire and smoke, the wicked witch, Fata Morgana, appears, followed by a swarm of little devils. As a fiendish game of cards ensues between the witch, who is aiding Leander's plot, and Tchelio, the court magician, attendant demons burst into a wild dance. This is graphically depicted in the deftly contrived music of an eerie waltz-scherzo. The Fata Morgana wins and, with a peal of diabolical laughter, vanishes. The jester vainly tries to make the lugubrious Prince laugh, and as festival music comes from afar, the two go off in that direction, whereupon the orchestra plays the brilliant and bizarre "March," built around a swaying theme of irresistible charm.

In the grand court of the palace, merrymakers are busy trying to make the Prince laugh, but their efforts are unavailing for two reasons: the Prince's nature is adamant to gaiety and the evil Fata Morgana is among them, spoiling the fun. Recognizing her, guards seize the sorceress and attempt to eject her. In the struggle that ensues she turns an awkward somersault, a sight so ridiculous that even the Prince is forced to laugh out loud. All rejoice, for the Prince, at long last, is cured! In revenge, the Fata Morgana now pronounces a dire curse on the recovered Prince: he shall again be miserable until he has won the "love of the three oranges."

In the desert the magician Tchelio meets the Prince and pronounces an incantation against the cook who guards the three oranges in the near-by castle. As the Prince and his companion, the jester Truffaldino, head for the castle, the orchestra plays a scherzo, fascinating in its ingeniously woven web of fantasy. Arriving at the castle, the Prince and Truffaldino obtain the coveted oranges after overcoming many hazards. Fatigued, the Prince now goes to sleep. A few moments later Truffaldino is seized by thirst and, as he cuts open one of the oranges, a beautiful Princess steps out, begging for water. Since it is decreed that the oranges must be opened at the water's edge, the helpless Princess promptly dies of thirst. Startled, Truffaldino at length works up courage enough to open a second orange, and, lo! another Princess steps out, only to meet the same fate. Truffaldino rushes out. The spectators in the balconies at the sides of the stage argue excitedly over the fate of the Princess in the third orange. When the Prince awakens, he takes the third orange and cautiously proceeds to open it. The Princess Ninette emerges this time, begs for water, and is about to succumb to a deadly thirst, when the Jesters rush to her rescue with a bucket of water.

The Prince and the Princess Ninette are forced to endure many more trials through the evil power of the Fata Morgana. At one juncture the Princess is even changed into a mouse. The couple finally overcome all the hardships the witch has devised, and in the end are happily married. Thus foiled in her wicked sorcery, the Fata

Morgana is captured and led away, leaving traitorous Leander and Clarisse to face the King's ire without the aid of her magic powers.]

Prokofieff's opera, *The Love of Three Oranges,* one of the most witty, exuberant and audacious scores devised for the modern lyric stage, was given its première in America by the Chicago Opera Company, on the 30th of December 1921. The opera was given three performances in that season, two in Chicago, where the composer conducted the first and Alexander Smallens the second, and a third which Prokofieff directed in New York, to general disparagement by press and public.

The opera was ahead of its time. It was shelved and forgotten so far as America was concerned for some twenty-eight years. It was not heard again on this side of the ocean until given an entirely new production by the New York City Opera Company, Laszlo Halasz director, in the season of 1949–50. The Halasz production, November 1, 1949, was an almost startling success. The opera became overnight the talk of the town and took a permanent place in the repertory of the company. This was due in large part to the character of the production itself, which so well became the fantasy and satire of the libretto, and the dynamic power of Prokofieff's score. An additional factor in the success was, without doubt, the development of taste and receptivity to modern music on the part of the public which had taken place in the intervening odd quarter of a century since the opera first saw the light. It must be remembered that Stravinsky's "Sacre du Printemps," heard in Europe in 1913, did not reach this country till 1924. Nor were the scores of the mature Schoenberg, Hindemith and other spirits of the later day yet appreciated. Prokofieff in the 1920's was the bad and unpredictable boy of contemporaneous music. Twenty-eight years later he was to find himself welcomed by audiences with a keen relish in the boldness and freshness, the masterful technic and harmonic tang of his style. *The Love of Three Oranges,* the *jeu d'esprit* of his twenty-eighth year, first shown the public when he was thirty, had at last come into its own, and was thereafter to stand as one of the most striking and original features of the modern repertory.

The idea of this subject as basis for an opera came, apparently, from the editors of a Russian art magazine which called itself by the name of Carlo Gozzi's historically famous comedy, "The Love of Three Oranges" (L'amore delle tre mellarance). Prokofieff, making in 1918 his first tour of the United States, as pianist-composer, was commissioned by Cleofonte Campanini, then director of the Chicago Opera Company, to furnish the organization with a new work for their 1918–1919 season. Prokofieff had with him the piano score of his own opera based upon Dostoyevsky's "The Gambler," but the orchestral parts were in the library of the Marynsky Theatre in Leningrad, and were unobtainable. When he told Campanini of his scenario of "The Love of Three Oranges," which he was then carrying about with him, the director felt the theme ideal for composition by Prokofieff and a highly provocative feature for his next season. A contract was signed with Prokofieff in January of 1919. The composer set to work with such enthusiasm and address that the opera was completed by the following July, and scored and ready for performance as per contract by the following October.

But Campanini died and the presentation of the new work was postponed. Two years later Mary Garden became the director of the company, and immediately set in motion the machinery for the production, which was costly and magnificent, with scenery by Boris Anisfeld, and a cast including Nina Koshetz and the tenor José Mojica. By some of the avant-garde the work was enthusiastically received, but they were a very small minority. The prevalent point of view was no doubt well expressed by the remark of one scribe, who wrote that *The Love of Three Oranges* cost $130,000 to produce, which at approximately $43,000 an orange was rather high! But in the creative world the artist who laughs last often laughs best. *The Love of Three Oranges,* in mid-twentieth century, has more than vindicated the composer's confidence in himself and his music. Asked by the writer in 1918 whom he considered the three greatest living Russian composers, he replied with entire simplicity and lack of affectation, "Myself, Miaskovsky, and Stravinsky." At the time this appeared as a naïve and amusing overstatement. It is no longer astonishing, save for the exaggeration of the value of Miaskovsky!

One thing which strikes the observer hard about this opera is the remarkable way in which, some hundred and fifty years apart from each other, the drama of the Three Oranges and the opera which it inspired have borne the standard of revolt against the smug, the conservative and the conventional. Carlo Gozzi wrote his play for the Italian *commedia dell' arte* company of Antonio Sacchi in Venice. It was the first of ten "fables" in the Italian vernacular that Gozzi wrote on a wager that by means of these popular-idiomed plays he could put to rout the academic and affected lucubrations of his rivals, Goldoni and the Abate Pietro Chiari, who, Gozzi claimed, were distorting and ruining the innocent *commedia dell' arte,* that great popular dramatic form of the Italian people, by "the labored sophisms, rounded periods with nothing in them . . . sentiments inverted and distorted . . . and above all the use of so many French words and phrases that our own Italian dictionaries and grammars seem to have become superfluous." Gozzi styled this product "a fungous growth," and adds in his own memoirs that "It seemed to me (Gozzi) that I could not castigate the arrogance of these self-styled Menanders * better than by taking our old friends Truffaldino, Tartaglia, Brighella, Pantalon, and Smeraldina under my protection." This is Gozzi's reference to the famous traditional characters

---

* Menander (342–290 B.C.), famous Greek author of more than a hundred comedies remarkable by their realism and fine psychological delineation of their characters.

of the Comedy of Masks which he was not to invest with a fresh significance. His farce-comedy, sensationally successful, proved to be a David's sling against the Goliath enemy of the organized clique of writers and pseudo-classicists of Goldoni and his followers.

The story is told that on a certain day Gozzi and Goldoni met in a barber-shop, when a lively argument ensued. Let Gozzi tell of the issue in his own words.

Chiari and Goldoni replied to my attacks by challenging us to produce a comedy. . . . Spurred by this continual appeal to vogue, I uttered the deliberate opinion that crowded theatres proved nothing with regard to the goodness or the badness of the plays the people came to see; and I further staked my reputation on drawing more folk together than he could do with all his scenic tricks, by simply putting the old wives' fairy story of the Love of Three Oranges upon the boards . . .

In this Gozzi sensationally succeeded. The overwhelming success of his "fables" and farces completely defeated Goldoni and Chiari and actually drove them from Venice. Chiari retired to his country estate and wrote no more plays. Goldoni fled to Paris, where the French revolution was disastrous in its effects upon his art and his fortunes. Gozzi's comedies and farces held the ascendancy in the Venetian theatres for many years.

In a wholly modern and mordant manner, in a spirit which unexpectedly blends lyricism, tenderness, operatic exhibitionism and parody in one, Prokofieff has revived for the twentieth century what Gozzi created with such felicity and breath-taking celerity for the eighteenth. The opera is as the fresh burgeoning of an ancient root, in new forms of wit and parable and fantasy. No modern opera perhaps, with such an "advanced" musical idiom, has gone so far and deep to the eternal sources of fresh popular art, as this gay and paradoxical score of Prokofieff's creation.

If one were to go into details of the scoring the examination would yield other fascinating parallels. The orchestration is a tour de force, perpetually astonishing in new and at first glance eccentric, if not unreasonable, employment of the instruments! The results in actual hearing are astonishing and as diverting as the absurd and often farcical situations on the stage, which these surprising sounds reflect with the most diverting suggestiveness. Plenty of instruments are used, but never for mere volume, always for the exact color, the exact nuance of instrumental tone which is desired. Thus in addition to the usual "string quintet," that is, the body of strings customary in the orchestra, we find triple wood-winds, with an added E-flat clarinet, six horns with the usual complement of trumpets, trombones and tuba. To these instruments are added a celesta and two harps.

It looks like a Richard Strauss combination, but is nothing of the kind. For the "black pages"—when all the instruments are used at once—are rare, while the most unorthodox combinations, glints and shadows of tone occur, paralleling the strange twists and turns of the Gozzi story.

And just as Gozzi satirized the decadence of the *commedia dell' arte,* so does Prokofieff "kid" us by quoting and satirizing at different points Debussy, Verdi, Massenet, Moussorgsky, and Wagner. And all this is done with reckless mastery, sureness of touch, vividness of stroke, tongue-in-the-cheek jocosity. A bold, bad young man, with reverence for nobody or anything, save his art, is diverting himself and us in the course of this parody, which nevertheless confesses his secret adoration of the things that he jests about. One could get up a "quiz" on the score of *The Love of Three Oranges,* and see if the quizzes could identify the various masters of dramatic composition who parade in its pages, as the actors appear in *commedia dell' arte* disguises which are fantastic, overdrawn, absurd and delightful.

The original text of the opera was written in Russian by Prokofieff. It was then translated into French by Prokofieff and Vera Janacoupolos for the Chicago première. The New York production was in English, in a version by Victor Seroff, with a spoken prologue written by Theodore Komisarjevsky. As it happens, the trimming of the tableau which has been mentioned from the composer's scenario brings the succession of events nearer to the sequences of Gozzi's play. But the sum of the whole creation must be credited with highest honors to Prokofieff with his keen sense of humor, and theatrical instinct, and the interplay of his music and text in terms of lightning flashes of jest, and poetry too, and inexhaustible laughter.

O. D.

Giacomo Puccini

(Lucca, Italy, Dec. 23, 1858–Nov. 29, 1924, Brussels)

Giacomo Puccini is the most popular operatic composer since Verdi and one of the most individual of all time. His chief operas—notably *La Bohème, Tosca,* and *Madama Butterfly*—have made him famous wherever a lyric theatre exists.

As a musical family the Puccinis are to Italy what the Bachs are to Germany and the Couperins to France. Giacomo Puccini's talent was a direct inheritance, generation by generation, from his great-great-grandfather, the first Giacomo (1712–1781), through Antonio (1747–1832), Domenico (1771–1815), and Michele, who, like Wagner and Verdi, was born in 1813 and who died in 1864, when his son Giacomo . . . was in his sixth year. Michele, excelling as a teacher, rather than as a composer, left seven young children for his widow, who was only thirty-three, to provide for, with a small inheritance from her husband as her sole aid. To this remarkable woman, determined that Giacomo, her fifth child, should carry on the family tradition in music, infinitely patient in dealing with a difficult disposition, we owe the composer.

As a boy he was restless and unpromising, vaguely eager for travel, but little inclined to music and a poor student at school. An uncle thought he might become a singer (an idea not untinged with irony). But that project proved a failure. The undiscourageable mother, however, made the necessary sacrifices and sent him to the Lucca Institute of Music where he had for teacher Carlo Angeloni, who had been a pupil of his father. This man, who was gifted with patience, sympathy, and tact, succeeded in arousing in Giacomo a real interest in his studies. The wayward young fellow made sufficient progress to become organist in two nearby churches and he also disclosed an ambition to compose.

Accordingly he wrote a cantata, which he entitled "Juno," and entered it in a competition that was announced in connection with an exhibition at Lucca. Though it did not win the prize, its composer still thought enough of it to arrange a public performance, and the audience rewarded him by liking the work. When shortly afterwards he heard *Aida* at the local opera house, he suddenly decided that come what would he must compose for the stage.

The rather shiftless boy had now developed an unforeseen firmness of purpose, and nothing would satisfy him but a chance to study in that centre of operatic activity, Milan. His mother, thanks to a friend at Court, brought him to the attention of Queen Margherita, who assumed the expense of one year for him at the Milan Conservatory, and an uncle of his mother's promised to finance the rest. Thus Puccini was enabled to study there from 1880 until 1883.

He was fortunate in his teachers—Bazzini, best known as author of that popular violin piece, "The Witches Dance," and Ponchielli, composer of *La Gioconda,* who influenced him strongly. His graduation piece, an orchestral "Capriccio sinfonico," amply proved that his was a talent to be taken seriously.

Ponchielli, recognizing in him a special gift for the theatre, introduced Ferdinando Fontana to him as a suitable librettist, and the result was a short opera, *Le Villi,* which was entered in a contest sponsored by the publisher Sonzogno. Again there was the failure to win the prize. Still, the work was successfully staged at the Teatro dal Verme, Milan, on May 31, 1884. It brought Puccini about $400, nearly half of which he paid forthwith to the restaurateur who had given him credit! For Puccini's poverty at that time compelled a way of living which later played a part in his opera of striving youth, *La Bohème.* In fact he prophetically kept a diary in 1881, which he called "Bohemian Life" and in which he recorded his modest expenses. The principal items were coffee, milk, bread, and tobacco. Once a herring is mentioned. Of that Puccini later said: "Yes, I remember it well. It was a supper for four!"

At this time Puccini suffered a severe blow in the death of his mother, which he sought to alleviate by work on another opera. *Edgar,* however, though dignified by a première at Italy's foremost opera house, La Scala, Milan (April 21, 1889), achieved little success, largely because of a poor libretto (again by Fontana). But the composer realized four times as much money from it as he had done from *Le Villi.* There was some talk of Puccini's revising *Edgar,* but he never did so, though he always cherished a fondness for the music. Forsaking the unsatisfactory Fontana, he asked Domenico Oliva to provide him with a libretto from the Abbé Prévost's celebrated novel "Manon Lescaut," undaunted by the fact that the Frenchman Massenet had already had a veritable triumph with an opera on the same subject. Puccini, who had now become exceedingly exacting with respect to texts, rewrote the libretto, however, in collaboration with the publisher Ricordi, and Oliva's name disappeared from the score. *Manon Lescaut* was produced at Turin on February 1, 1896, with a success that has turned out to be lasting, and immediately the composer found himself on the highway to fame and fortune.

His good luck was clinched by his next stage work, *La Bohème* (Turin, February 1, 1896), to a text by Illica and Giacosa. Puccini had made haste slowly, but his fourth opera recompensed his deliberation by placing him definitely in the first rank of living composers for the stage and insuring him wealth as well as fame. He could now live as a country gentleman at Torre del Lago, on a lake near Lucca, and indulge his taste for shooting and boating. His next opera, *Tosca* (Rome, January 14, 1900), the libretto adapted by Illica and Giacosa from Sardou's melodrama written for Sarah Bernhardt, was another lasting success. There came, however, a temporary setback with *Madama*

Butterfly, the text by Illica and Giacosa after the play of John Luther Long and David Belasco.

The first-night audience (La Scala, Milan, February 17, 1904) seemed to dislike the work from the beginning and actually hissed and booed it. Undismayed, Puccini walked off with the score at the end of the performance and there was no second night for some time. That eventually took place at Brescia the following May 28 and was a triumph. Puccini had meantime made some revisions, but they consisted mainly in dividing the opera into three acts instead of two by introducing an orchestral intermezzo between what had been the two scenes of act II and in adding a short solo for tenor in act III. On July 10, 1905, it enjoyed a further triumph at Covent Garden, London, and Henry W. Savage organized a special company to tour America with it in an English translation for two seasons beginning at Washington, D.C., on October 15, 1906, thus forestalling the first American performance in Italian at the Metropolitan Opera House, New York, on February 11, 1907, which the composer came over to attend personally.

This visit to the United States bore tangible fruit in Puccini's next opera, *The Girl of the Golden West,* based on David Belasco's play of the same name. Appropriately, it had its world première (December 10, 1910) at the Metropolitan Opera House, New York, a production supervised in detail by Puccini and Belasco, with Arturo Toscanini as conductor and Caruso, Amato, and Emmy Destinn in the leading roles.

Nearly seven years passed before Puccini gave another opera to the world. Meantime he devoted himself to country life,—shooting, motoring, and especially motorboating. He detested society, declared that an invitation to luncheon or dinner made him ill for a week, and once wrote from Paris, where efforts were being made to fete him: "I hate palaces! I hate capitals! I hate style! I hate horses, cats, and pedigree dogs! I hate steamers, tall hats, and evening dress!" Apparently his early desire to travel did not survive, for he never employed his later wealth and leisure to see the world. His visits to America, for example, were strictly business trips. On the other hand, he did regret that critical enthusiasm for his music had not kept pace with its general popularity and its lucrativeness.

During the [First] World War there was some commotion over Puccini's dealings with an Austrian publisher about an opera of a light nature for Vienna, and the composer was accused both at home and abroad of lack of patriotism. The opera, however, he took away from Vienna, and gave to the Italian publisher Sonzogno, and the initial production took place at Monte Carlo on March 27, 1917. This was *La Rondine,* which in theme might be called Puccini's *Traviata.* Though by no means without charm, the score falls below the composer's mature standard.

On December 14, 1918, the Metropolitan Opera House became once more the scene of a Puccinian world première, when his "triptych" of one-act operas was presented. *Il Tabarro,* a brief melodrama of barge life on the Seine, and *Suor Angelica,* a descendant of the old-time miracle play, have disappeared from the stage. But the third member, *Gianni Schicchi,* a farce of mediaeval Florence, Puccini's one essay in comedy, continues to be performed.

Seeking a new subject for a full-length opera, Puccini now came upon Turandot, a riddle-propounding Chinese princess who was renowned for her inexorable cruelty until love subdued her. He had almost finished the score when a mortal illness, from which he had suffered for some time, carried him off on November 29, 1924, in Brussels, whither he had gone for treatment. Franco Alfano completed the opera from Puccini's sketches and it was produced at La Scala, Milan, on April 25, 1926. On that occasion, at the point in the last act where Puccini had laid down his pen, Arturo Toscanini, who was conducting, put aside his baton and turning to the house said in trembling tones: "Here ends the Master's work." Only at the second performance was *Turandot* given with the ending by Alfano.

Puccini was survived by his wife and two children. It is worthy of note that of his twelve operas all but one (*Edgar*) have been staged at the Metropolitan Opera House—a ratio of performance unequalled by either Wagner or Verdi.

P. S.

Manon Lescaut

OPERA IN 4 ACTS

Book by Domenico Oliva, Marco Praga, Giuseppe Giacosa, Luigi Illica,
and Giulio Ricordi, after the Abbé Prévost's romance
L'Histoire de Manon Lescaut

First performance: Teatro Regio, Turin, Feb. 1, 1893

CHARACTERS

Manon Lescaut, a young girl, SOPRANO
Lescaut, her brother, a sergeant of the
  King's Guards, BARITONE
Chevalier des Grieux, TENOR

Géronte de Ravoir, Treasurer General,
  BASS
Edmond, a student, friend of des Grieux,
  TENOR

An Innkeeper, a Dancing Master, a Sergeant, a Captain, Singers, Students, Citizens, Courtesans, Sailors

The action takes place in Amiens, Paris, Le Havre, and Louisiana during the early part of the eighteenth century

Manon, descending from the coach with her brother Lescaut before the inn at Amiens, sets the heart of the student Des Grieux afire. She promises to meet him. Géronte de Ravoir, royal treasurer-general, covets the lovely girl. His coach is in readiness to abduct her while her brother is gambling in the inn, but when Manon appears Des Grieux carries her off in the old *roué's* equipage to Paris.

In Paris, Des Grieux's pockets soon empty, Manon makes no bones about settling down as Géronte's mistress. He is old and tiresome but she revels in gold, jewels and pretty dresses. (A charming rococo bit, light graceful song and dance, is the "Minuet of Manon's friends.") Returning unexpectedly he finds her with Des Grieux (the passionate Love Duet, "Vieni colle tue braccie") and though she regrets her luxuries, she tells him she prefers Des Grieux's companionship. Warned by her brother that the malicious financier (who has pretended approval of their affection) plans revenge, the girl snatches up her jewels, only to be dragged to jail as a thief, though she drops the jewels at Géronte's feet.

On the Havre quay (an orchestral intermezzo depicts the trip to Havre), the *filles de joie,* the loose women of Paris gathered for deportation to Louisiana, are embarked under guard. Des Grieux's and Lescaut's attempt to free poor Manon foiled, rather than be parted from the pale girl who walks to the ship's side amid the jeers of the crowd, Des Grieux begs to be allowed to work his passage to be near her, and the pitying captain grants his plea.

A gray sky above a vast plain near New Orleans is the setting for the tale's tragic end. Drooping with fatigue Manon stops. When Des Grieux hurries off to seek water for her she thinks herself abandoned. He returns and she dies, the pathetic lovers declaring their affection for each other in a masterly duet which strikes the true tragic note. Des Grieux, as Manon's spirit passes in his arms, despite his frantic pleas for her not to leave him, sinks fainting on her dead body.

F. H. M.

The subject Puccini chose was neither contemporary nor violent, but one which would give opportunity to expansive love music and tuneful sadness. It was the romantic novel of the Abbé Prévost entitled "The Story of the Chevalier des Grieux and of Manon Lescaut." It was an old classic, having been published in 1731, a century and a half before. Puccini fell in love with Manon. She is the first of the faulty, simple, but appealing young girls whose sisters are Mimi, Musetta, Tosca, Cio-Cio-San, and Liù. He was undeterred by the fact that she had already served as the heroine of a successful opera. Massenet's *Manon* was first given on January 19, 1884, and was therefore six years old in 1890. Fraccaroli [an Italian biographer] attempts to excuse Puccini's appropriation of the subject by saying that when Puccini chose *Manon* he did not know that Massenet had written such an opera. This is altogether unlikely. Puccini knew contemporary operatic literature well. So renowned an opera could hardly have escaped his attention. Even if by some chance it had, Ricordi [the music publisher] would have known the Massenet work. It is more likely that Puccini was so enthusiastic over the subject that he did not care who had used it before. He might have excused himself, if excuse were necessary, by remembering that not only Massenet had treated the subject but also Auber (*Manon Lescaut,* 1856) and Halévy (for a ballet, 1830).

As *Manon* was the first subject which kindled Puccini's whole enthusiasm, so was the making of its libretto the first of those quarrelsome and complicated labors which were typical of the making of the later librettos. The first person whom Ricordi suggested as the librettist was a young man of exactly the same age as Puccini, who himself was ambitious to become an opera composer. He was by training equipped either to write words or to compose music. He had studied music at the Naples Conservatory. From there he had gone to Bologna to attend the University and to study literature under Carducci, one of the most renowned Italian poets. He had already composed an opera, *Chatterton,* writing both words and music. This young man was Ruggiero Leoncavallo. Leoncavallo was quite willing to handle a libretto assignment from Ricordi. He was poor and needed whatever work he could get. The collaboration, however, was unsuccessful. Puccini declared himself dissatisfied with Leoncavallo's treatment of the subject and they parted, though on friendly terms.

One night in the spring of 1890 Puccini walked into the Café Savini in Milan, where Marco Praga was playing cards. Marco Praga was a well-known playwright. His comedy, *The Ideal Wife,* was a favorite of the Milanese public. Puccini asked Praga to take a walk with him in the Galleria. He told him that he had in his mind a theme "which does not leave me in peace." He wanted Praga to sketch a libretto for him. Puccini argued persuasively. Praga, though he had never written a libretto before, accepted the commission. For the versification of the libretto, Praga chose a poet who was a friend of his, Domenico Oliva. Puccini discussed the subject in detail. He wanted, he told Praga, his own Manon, a girl frivolous, uncertain, but above all ardent and passionate. He talked only of the girl. Des Grieux left him unmoved. He had read the novel in his own way and was unconcerned with Prévost's avowed purpose: to "paint a blind young man who turns his back on happiness to plunge of his own free will into the worst of misfortunes." (From the introduction to the novel.) No, Manon herself was what fascinated him. Within a week Praga had his outline ready. Puccini liked it. He asked for further details. Praga wrote these. The new outline was again reviewed. Puccini approved it. Oliva began the composition of verses and worked with such a will that within a few days the whole libretto was finished. The three men called on Ricordi and read the libretto to him. Ricordi was enthusiastic and wrote a contract for the opera. Puccini, with the libretto in his pocket, and accompanied by Elvira [his wife] and the two children, departed for Chiasso. They arrived at their little chalet and looked out of the window. There, across the street, nailed to the door of another house, they saw a poster. The poster was a drawing of a clown. Puccini at once guessed the message. He knew that Leoncavallo had also rented a house in the neighborhood and that he was at work on an opera the central character of which was to be a clown, a *pagliaccio.* In his turn, he made a poster and acknowledged the greeting. His poster was a large white hand; in Italian the hand is *la mano.* So far, so good.

As Puccini settled down to the work of composition, he realized that he had made a mistake. Praga's and Oliva's treatment would not do. He announced that he was unhappy with the episodes chosen from the novel, that he "did not succeed in feeling himself near to his vision of Manon." He wished for situations more dramatic; he wished to eliminate the second act, which showed Manon and Des Grieux in their modest house; he wanted a new third act, the outlines of which he had vaguely imagined. New meetings, conferences, discussions ensued. Praga, a playwright who could spend his time more profitably, decided to quit the collaboration. Oliva, less successful or perhaps more compliant, was now retained to do the work alone.

The difficulties remained unsolved. Puccini remained dissatisfied. He called for more and more alterations, new and better situations, new verses. Oliva in turn became tired of such exigent demands and gave the thing up as a bad job (though he did remain as a sort of general adviser).

Now Ricordi bethought himself of the poet Giuseppe Giacosa, who had previously done work for Ricordi and who, as a matter of fact, had sketched for Puccini a libretto on "a Russian subject" which Puccini had refused. He too was a man of considerable attainment, a writer for the theater, a successful lecturer, and author of several good short stories. Giacosa knew another writer, a nimble and quick-witted man by the name of Luigi Illica. On Giacosa's recommendation Illica was now called in to collaborate with him. The work of reshaping the libretto began anew. The old third act now disappeared entirely. In its stead there came into being a new act, the scene laid in Le Havre.

In the meantime Puccini had already set to music certain parts of the existing libretto. Illica had to leave these untouched and devote his skill to an attempt to baste together the various pieces left by his predecessors. Long and laborious were the conferences and far into the night lasted the discussions. The situation got so tense that Illica too would have become fed up had not Ricordi, who was at all times both the arbiter and the father confessor, stepped in and saved the situation by soothing words and sensible counsel. The third act was the most difficult. Finally even this difficulty was solved and Puccini declared himself satisfied. The work on the libretto and the work of composition lasted from the beginning of 1890 to the autumn of 1892, almost three years. Again neither Ricordi nor Puccini had foreseen how long the road was to be. . . .

Ricordi was right when he said that it was a miracle that the libretto turned out to be "not bad." Considering that it is a thing of shreds and patches, it is remarkably good. Manon is a character fathered by six authors, Leoncavallo, Praga, Oliva, Giacosa, Illica, and finally Ricordi himself, who contributed a number of verses (especially to the third act). None of these six authors wished to acknowledge paternity. None felt that he had played a sufficiently decisive role to say that the libretto was by him. Therefore the score was published without crediting any of the six librettists and with this title: *Manon Lescaut, lyric drama in four acts by Giacomo Puccini.* Even the Abbé Prévost had disappeared from the title page.

A weakness of the libretto may be due to the fact that Puccini wished to avoid duplication with Massenet's work. Most of the events on the stage are those which occur in Massenet's opera *between* the acts, though this is not true of the first act, which is similar to Massenet's. The interval between Acts I and II may well hold the librettic broad-jump record, the second famous contender for this record being the interval between Acts I and II of *La Traviata.* At the end of the first act of *Traviata,* Alfredo receives merely the promise of Violetta's favor: she will see him again when the flower she has given him has wilted. At the opening of the second act, we find them in their bucolic refuge well established as lovers. In *Manon Lescaut* Manon meets Des Grieux in the first act and runs away with him. At the beginning of the second, Manon has not only been Des Grieux's mistress and has then broken off with him, but is now already weary of being Geronte's mistress!

The first performance was given on February 1, 1893, at the Teatro Regio in Turin. In January, Puccini went to Turin for the rehearsals. From there he wrote Elvira:

. . . Let them say what they want—this time I have a feeling that I have done a successful piece of work. Here everybody is mad about it. Nevertheless the execution will be wretched, because the voices can hardly be heard. Good-by. I'm hurrying to the rehearsal. It is 11:30. Your Topizio.

Puccini's statement that the performance promised to be wretched can be ascribed to apprehension. According to all the critics, the performance was good. Ferrani as Manon was outstanding. Puccini must have been satisfied with her: he chose her to interpret Mimi at the first production of *La Bohème*.

The première was regarded as an important event, the music critics of Milan making a special trip to Turin in order to be present. The house was sold out. The audience was at first cold and a little skeptical: they wanted to be shown. But early in the first act the coldness melted. *Manon* has a short orchestral introduction. Soon after that Des Grieux sings a charming aria ("Tra voi, belle"). At that moment the house burst into applause. The first cries of *bravo, bravissimo, bis* were heard. Puccini had to show himself on the stage. Then, as the evening wore on, as the new Puccinian melodies unfolded themselves, what a triumph it turned into! The people were enchanted. The excitement, the warmth, the enthusiasm mounted from act to act. Puccini had to appear twenty-five times *during* the acts. The performance ended in a general feast of love and jubilation. Again and again Puccini had to acknowledge the applause, along with Ferrani, the tenor Cremonini, and the conductor Pomé. Ferrani wept with emotion. Puccini bit his nails with nervousness, but smiled and bowed. Then, after more than thirty final calls, the audience reluctantly went home. . . .

The critics spoke of "the impetuous artistic vigor of youth" and of the "young Italian maestro." Puccini was in truth no longer quite so young a man: he was just past thirty-four. But his real age does not matter. *Manon* is a youthful work. And a special charm invests the first sure work, the first unacademic and free-striding accomplishment of a new talent. *Manon* possesses that charm to a high degree. It is fresh and fragrant. It is impulsive and ardent. Neither time nor the advancing sophistication of music has taken from the opera its piquancy. . . .

Yes, it had come, the solid, resounding success! Here was an end to penury! While working on *Manon,* Puccini had written to a friend, "Last night I worked until three A.M. Then I supped on a bunch of onions. . . . I am weary of fighting against misery." Now, when he was almost thirty-five years old, misery was about to end. Now the leading theaters of Italy clamored for the work, and Giulio Ricordi was able to make prudent and profitable arrangements. He had wished that Puccini might climb artistically—"and materially." Now his wish was coming true. Soon Ricordi reported that *Manon* "was marching forth in a forest of laurels." On October 12, 1893, eight months after the première, he writes:

I have seen the latest number of the *Gazzetta,* which is completely given over to *Manon.* It is superfluous to tell you how much I am pleased with this series of triumphant successes. I hope they will continue indefinitely. . . .

Manon was the first opera which extended Puccini's reputation beyond Italy. *Le Villi* and *Edgar* had been given a few performances in Germany (*Edgar* also in Madrid) with indifferent success. Now *Manon* was taken up by a number of the leading European theaters. It reached London's Covent Garden the year after its Turin première. George Bernard Shaw, writing as the music critic of the *World,* hailed the new work:

And when you come to Puccini, the composer of the latest *Manon Lescaut,* then indeed the ground is so transformed that you could almost think yourself in a new country.

Puccini, at least, shows no signs of atrophy of the melodic faculty: he breaks out into catching melodies quite in the vein of Verdi: for example, "Tra voi, belle," in the first act of *Manon,* has all the charm of the tunes beloved by the old operatic guard.

On that and other accounts, Puccini looks to me more like the heir of Verdi than any of his rivals.

G. R. M.

Like Verdi, Puccini reached his first maturity in his middle thirties: *Manon Lescaut* was his *Rigoletto.* In it are, though not frequently in final form, the elements of his musical individuality. Sweet, pungent, and diverse harmonies, lush romantic melodies, calculated contrasts, schooled effects carried out with pared means—such are the qualities of *Manon Lescaut,* and such, often in more exaggerated guises, are those of *La Bohème, La Tosca,* and *Madama Butterfly,* and, to a somewhat lesser extent, of the later operas. From Des Grieux' aria, "Donna non vidi mai," in Act I, descended the many throbbing love songs that can be depended upon to stop the show. Even the Intermezzo, "La Prigionia," which is a small tone poem, has the harmonic tang, feminine charm, and intimate flavor that were to remain the characteristics of Puccini's instrumental interludes. Thus he early established the hallmarks of his manner and told his admirers what to look for. He did not often disappoint them thereafter by departing flagrantly from these stylistic norms. This is not to say that he had a static talent: he improved upon what he had, without adding much that was new. The point is that, except for one period of fumbling, he did improve, and consistently. *Manon Lescaut* set the pattern, too, by having a thoroughly credible libretto, but it was far more disjointed than an experienced and self-confident Puccini would ever again allow collaborators to devise for him. . . .

When Puccini set the same subject matter almost ten years after the *première* of the Massenet *Manon,* many wondered at the boldness of the junior who had dared invite comparison with a work to which a large section of the European public was almost idolatrously attached. But it is now plain that Puccini had only its popularity to fear. His *Manon Lescaut* is, in most musical respects, a far more interesting score than *Manon,* which is its superior only in dramatic unity and impact. When he composed *Manon Lescaut,* Puccini was not yet the master of dramatic craft he grew into only a few years later, and he was not equipped to set his libretto with the theatrical sophistication that Massenet had acquired in large measure. A few years later, Puccini might have insisted on changes in the libretto that would have made it as good a thing as Meilhac and Gille's.

Although *Manon Lescaut* had been presented at the Grand Opera House, Philadelphia, as early as 1894, and in New York, at Wallack's Theater, in 1898, it had to wait for Metropolitan performance until two of its successors, *La Bohème* and *La Tosca,* had been established in the repertoire of that house. The first cast there included, on January 18, 1907, Lina Cavalieri (Manon), Caruso (Des Grieux), and Scotti (Lescaut). After two seasons, *Manon Lescaut* was dropped until November 12, 1912, when it opened the season. Giorgio Polacco, the conductor, and Lucrezia Bori, the triumphant Manon, were making Metropolitan debuts that night; Caruso and Scotti resumed their former roles. Seventeen seasons later, on October 28, 1929, another Bori *Manon Lescaut* was the inaugural offering, with Gigli as Des Grieux and De Luca as Lescaut. On December 28, 1929, Alda, who had recently been divorced from Manager Gatti-Casazza, made her farewell, after twenty-one years at the Metropolitan, in the role of Manon.

W. B., H. W.

La Bohème

OPERA IN 4 ACTS

Book by Giuseppe Giacosa and Luigi Illica, after Henri Murger's novel
Scènes de la Vie de Bohème

First performance: Teatro Regio, Turin, Feb. 1, 1896

CHARACTERS

Rodolfo, a poet, TENOR
Schaunard, a musician, BARITONE
Marcello, a painter, BARITONE
Colline, a philosopher, BASS
Parpignol, a toy vendor, TENOR
Benoit, a landlord, BASS

Mimi, a maker of artificial flowers,
SOPRANO
Alcindoro, a state councilor, BASS
Musetta, SOPRANO
A Custom-house Sergeant, BASS

Students, Working Girls, Citizens, Shopkeepers, Street Vendors, Soldiers, Restaurant Waiters, Boys, Girls, etc.

The action takes place in Paris in the mid-nineteenth century

In his Latin Quarter studio Marcel paints at "The Passage of the Red Sea," while Rudolph kindles a fire with a rejected MS. Colline, who enters, could not pawn his books; but Schaunard has secured a three-day musical engagement from an eccentric Englishman. Two boys bring in food and fuel, purchased with his advance, and the landlord is fobbed off with a drink of wine. After the feast, Rudolph, staying to finish his writing before he meets them at the Café Momus, hears Mimi [a pretty neighbor afflicted with consumption] knock. She faints at the threshold. Rudolph, moved by her beauty, frailty, and little white hands, gropes for the key she has dropped, and finds and hides it in his pocket, to have an excuse to keep her. They tell each other of their life (the melting Love Duet) while moonlight silvers the garret floor and his impatient friends hail the poet from the street.

Christmas Eve in the Café Momus. Rudolph has bought Mimi a bonnet (gay scene with students, work girls, street vendors, a holiday crowd out for a good time) and together with Colline, Schaunard, and Marcel they sit at a table before the Café. Musetta, Rudolph's old flame, comes in with de Mittoneaux, old but rich. Rudolph when Musetta gets rid of Alcindoro becomes reconciled to her. In the artless Latin Quarter way the entire party then leaves both Café and bill—the latter settled by Alcindoro when he returns from the cobbler shop where Musetta had sent him.

Rudolph and Mimi, living together, know the happiness and the wretchedness of more regular unions. One February morning Mimi, her tubercular cough worse, calls Marcel from his tavern lodging, tells him of Rudolph's jealousy, and Rudolph, in turn, explains what torture their life in common is to them; that he loves Mimi, but thinks she is marked for the grave. They agree to part, without rancor. Marcel and Musetta, who have pooled their emotional resources, also quarrel and dissolve partnership.

Rudolph and Marcel are writing, painting and frolicking in their attic studio, when Musetta comes in to say that Mimi, weak and ill, is outside, unable to walk further. She has asked to be allowed to die in the attic where she has been happy. A couch is prepared and Mimi embraces Rudolph tenderly and begs him not to leave her. While the others hurry out they recall their dream of love together; but Mimi soon falls back fainting. As Musetta and the other Bohemians return with medicine, she once more whispers her love for Rudolph and dies, while he flings himself sobbing on her lifeless form.

F. H. M.

Few operas have drawn so clearly on the actual circumstances of its composer's life as *La Bohème* has done, especially in its first act. Rodolfo, Marcello, Schaunard, and Colline in the chill poverty of their Parisian garret reflect the more or less miserable existence led by Puccini when he was a struggling music student in Milan. Both instinct and reflection had told him that his native Lucca could not supply the instruction, the encouragement, the friendships, the artistic atmosphere which would nourish and ripen his talent. So to Milan, that musical centre of northern Italy, he went and when he was just short of twenty-two gained admission to its famous conservatory.

Which was all very well except for the money. Of that necessity there was precious little in the Puccini household at Lucca, where Giacomo's widowed mother had six other children to think about. However, through the kindly offices of a friend of the mother at court, the Marchesa Viola-Marina, Queen Margherita became interested in the aspiring musician and gave him an allowance of one hundred lire a month for a year. An uncle of the mother defrayed the expenses for the two remaining years of the conservatory course.

The sum of one hundred lire a month (then about twenty dollars), though by no means a vast fortune, sufficed to gladden the heart of the young Puccini. Yet the inevitable cloud was there to cast a shadow on the noonday of his good luck, for there were two others to share the penury of his attic room, his brother Michele and an equally impecunious cousin. To add to the embarrassment, the postal official delegated to pay Puccini his allowance was the landlord of the house and that cautious citizen regularly took out the rent of thirty lire (six dollars) before handing over any money to his lodger. The three boys who divided the residue with one another had pretty plain living as a result, whatever the altitude of their thinking.

In the enthusiasm of the first week at the conservatory Puccini wrote to his mother:

My daily life is very simple. I get up at 8:30 and when I do not go to the school I stay indoors and play the piano. . . . At 10:30 I have my lunch and a short walk afterwards. At one I return home and study Bazzini's lesson for a couple of hours; after that from three to five I go to the piano again and play some classic. . . . Oh, how I wish I had money enough to buy all the music I want to get! Five is dinner time, and it is a very frugal meal—soup, cheese, and half a litre of wine. As soon as it is over I go out for a walk and stroll up and down the Galleria. Now comes the end of the chapter—bed!

The landlady, it seems, was as rigorous in her way as her husband. Cooking in the Puccini room she strictly forbade lest it injure the polish on her furniture. Wood and coal had to be smuggled into the house in a handbag, and supplies that required cooking, in coat pockets. While stove or spirit lamp was doing the forbidden service, Puccini would cover the various incidental sounds by seating himself at the piano and reeling off, fortissimo, anything that came into his head. It is said that the landlady who set such store by her furniture dissolved in tears at the touching thought of this most diligent student who would rather grind away at his music than eat.

During the time of exceeding poverty Puccini had to swallow so much thin soup in which floated pieces of vegetable and strips of paste that in later life, so he declared, he felt "violently sick" if confronted with a dish of minestrone or a plate of beans. Once, pathetically enough, he wrote to his mother, to whom his letters as a rule were full of comfort and good cheer, that he would like her to send him a "cassetina" of olive oil. In the big city that luxury cost too much, and he just couldn't stand linseed oil to cook beans in any longer!

Puccini's librettists, Giacosa and Illica, of course based their book on that celebrated "idyl of brick and mortar," Murger's "Scènes de la Vie de Bohème." For dramatic purposes they have not hesitated, and quite rightly, to treat Murger's text with a free hand, though preserving its spirit even when departing from its letter. Thus the four episodes of the opera faithfully mirror bohemian life on the left bank of the Seine a century ago.

P. S.

The idea of extracting an opera from Murger's rich, episodic, and autobiographical novel may have been Illica's. But that is not certain. It could well have been Puccini himself who made the choice. In either case, the choice was not a recondite one. Murger's novel had first appeared serially (in the journal *Le Corsair,* 1847–49), had at the time not received much acclaim, but had then been produced as a play which proved to be so successful that the novel also became a favorite. Some forty years after, the fame of the novel had not died. On the contrary, it received new impetus when the young Italian artists and writers now took it up as their model.

After the success of *Manon,* it was logical that Giacosa and Illica should be chosen as the librettists of the new work. The two men complemented each other. Illica, the quick-tempered, was also the quick-witted one. His imagination was Protean and could dart from one corner of the novel to the next, bobbing up with new episodes and new ideas for dramatic situations. He was impatient of detail. He cared very little about the exact word. This he left to Giacosa, the better, certainly the more careful writer. Giacosa pondered each verse he wrote down. He worked slowly and thoughtfully. He filed and corrected.

The work on the libretto began even before the première of *Manon,* though for a while Puccini was not exclusively occupied with the *Bohème* subject. He considered an opera based on the life of Buddha, a curious choice for him. The exotic setting may have attracted him. Much more seriously he considered "La Lupa," a play by Verga. Ricordi had the play turned into a libretto and submitted it to Puccini. Puccini at first liked it and even began the composition of the music. In the spring of 1894, he went to Sicily in order to confer with Verga and to absorb local color, observe the life of the Sicilian peasants and hear their music. Ricordi asked him to buy Sicilian costumes and shoes which might be used in the performance of the opera. On the steamer on the way back, Puccini met Countess Blandine Gravina, Cosima Wagner's daughter. She questioned him about his plans. He told her the plot of "La Lupa." She very much disapproved of it. "Don't think of it, Maestro," she pleaded. "Don't have anything to do with this drama of sensuality and crime linked to a religious episode. It will bring you bad luck." Puccini was easy to convince. He had already doubted that this veristic subject with the unsympathetic heroine was right for him.

On July 13, 1894, he wrote to Ricordi renouncing the libretto. Henceforth his thoughts belonged to Mimi. . . .

The choice of *La Bohème* led to a break with Leoncavallo. The two men were sitting in a café in Milan when Puccini said, "I have found a libretto of which I am absolutely enamored."

"Which one?" asked Leoncavallo.

"It is based on a French novel, 'La Vie de Bohème.'"

Leoncavallo bounded from his seat. "What! Don't you remember," he cried, "that I suggested 'Bohème' to you, that you told me you had no interest in it? When you didn't want it, I decided to use it for myself. Yes, I am going to set it to music, not you."

"Then," said Puccini, "there will be two 'Bohèmes.'"

Leoncavallo immediately ran to the editor of the *Secolo* to announce his plans and to attempt to forestall Puccini. On the morning after, this newspaper informed its readers that Maestro Leoncavallo was at work on an opera taken from Murger's novel. The afternoon paper of the same day, the *Corriere della*

Sera, carried the notice that Puccini was at work on a new opera to be called *La Bohème.**

Leoncavallo's opera appeared the year after Puccini's opera. It was first given on May 6, 1897, at the Fenice Theater in Venice. Though it is a work of some quality, it never became popular. It was immediately overshadowed by Puccini's masterpiece. It has some slight historic interest because Caruso scored his first success in the Leoncavallo work.

Puccini has been severely blamed for his action. Is the blame justified? Was this an outright appropriation? I do not think so. There is little reason to doubt Puccini's statement that he had forgotten his friend's proposal. He seems to have acted in good faith. The subject was, as I have said, one of general popularity. It is quite probable that he honestly thought the choice unencumbered. Had he been generous, he might have ceded the opera to Leoncavallo—as Offenbach's friend Hector Salomon ceded *The Tales of Hoffmann* to Offenbach, though Salomon had nearly finished the entire score of an opera on the same subject—but this was not Puccini's way.

Though we may absolve Puccini in this case, we must observe a trait in him which is psychologically significant: a subject became more valuable to him the moment he knew that somebody else wanted it—or when somebody else had first used it. There was in him a lack of confidence which rendered an artistic property more desirable once it was stamped with another's approval. That lack of confidence seems to contradict the sureness of judgment that he usually evinced. Yet it was there, arising from time to time to make him needful of precedent. He embarked on *Manon* knowing that Massenet was an immediate predecessor. He was all the more determined to have *Bohème* once he knew that Leoncavallo was working on the same subject. He used an out-and-out subterfuge to wrest *La Tosca* from another composer's hands. And at the end of his life he chose *Turandot,* a subject set to music by his teacher, Bazzini.

Leoncavallo never forgave Puccini. From now on he hated him. As late as 1913—that is, seventeen years after the première of Puccini's opera—his hatred had not died. In October of that year, Leoncavallo was on one of his trips to the United States. Herbert Peyser interviewed him for *Musical America.* Leoncavallo told Peyser: "Is it not a pity that there are opera houses over which a publisher exercises so powerful an influence that the operas of one particular composer are constantly exploited and those of another are barred? Mr. Puccini's works are always heard."

It is to be expected that Ricordi completely took Puccini's side. Ricordi used the fact that "the notorious Leoncavallo," "that grand Kaiser Leoncavallo," was working on the same subject as a means to exhort Puccini to work faster. But Puccini took his time!

* Publication of one's plans in a newspaper was the customary method of staking an artistic claim.

The novel is brimful of incident. Illica's choice was a difficult one. Which episodes were to be used, which of the adventures of the Bohemians were suitable for the play? Illica's first distillation from the novel ran to no fewer than twenty acts. Before these twenty were reduced to four, and before they were set to satisfactory verses, three years were to elapse. Three years awful for the librettists, joyful for Puccini in spite of his frequent resentment against his collaborators, who, he felt, did not give him what he wanted just to spite him. The three men, Illica, Giacosa, and Ricordi, must have known at the beginning what was in store for them. Had they not suffered through the *Manon* labor? With the optimism of artists they perhaps did not want to foresee the extent of the difficulties. After it was over, Giacosa said, "I used up more paper for a few scenes of *Bohème* than for the whole of any of my dramatic works."

Those conferences for *Bohème!* [Illica told Fraccaroli] They were slaughters in which entire acts were cut to pieces, scene after scene sacrificed, ideas judged beautiful and brilliant one moment banished the next, setting at naught in one minute the long, heavy labor of months.

Giacosa, Puccini, Giulio Ricordi, and I. A foursome! A foursome in which Giulio Ricordi was the guiding spirit . . . inserting into our debate Solomonic judgments and violent as well as prophetic encouragements. . . . Giacosa was the equilibrium. In dark moments he was the sun. During the thunderstorm the rainbow. . . . And Puccini? After each session Puccini had to run to the manicurist in order to have his nails attended to. He bit his nails one by one right to the skin. . . .

G. R. M.

The world première of *La Bohème* took place at the Teatro Reggio, Turin, on February 1, 1896, under the direction of Arturo Toscanini. Only a "success of esteem" was the general verdict. Of the Italian reviewers Pozza alone prophesied a triumphant career for the new work, declaring that connoisseurs would find it well written while the general public would find it beautiful. One Bersezio, blaming the score for being hurriedly put together, with little care for selection and polishing, predicted that it would have small influence on the history of opera and might well be dismissed by its composer as a momentary mistake. Villani, another critic, refused to regard the music as more than a passing diversion.

In New York there was similar scepticism. On the day after the first performance at the Metropolitan, given on December 26, 1900, a review in the *Tribune* contained the following:

La Bohème is foul in subject and fulminant and futile in its music. Its heroine is a twin sister of the Woman of the Camellias. . . . But Mimi is fouler than Camille, alias Violetta, for Puccini has not been able to adminster the palliative that lies in Verdi's music. . . .

Silly and inconsequential incidents and dialogues designed to show the devil-may-care life of artistic Bohemia . . . are daubed over with splotches of instrumental color without reason and without effect, except the creation of a sense of boisterous excitement and confusion.

Melba (Mimi) and Saléza (Rodolfo) headed that cast. Later they were succeeded by Sembrich and Caruso. It is scarcely necessary to add that in spite of critical disapproval at the outset, *La Bohème* promptly became a favorite and a best-seller in every country.

P. S.

La Bohème had been sung in Mexico City and Buenos Aires before it reached the United States. The *première* in this country took place at the Los Angeles Theater, Los Angeles, in the original Italian, Oct. 14, 1897. On May 16, 1898, it was introduced to New York at Wallack's Theater in Italian, and on May 28 was presented at the American Theater in English. It was more than four years old when it reached the Metropolitan Opera House.

Tosca

OPERA IN 3 ACTS

Book by GIUSEPPE GIACOSA and LUIGI ILLICA, after VICTORIEN SARDOU's play
La Tosca

First performance: Teatro Costanzi, Rome, Jan. 14, 1900

CHARACTERS

Floria Tosca, a celebrated singer, SOPRANO

Mario Cavaradossi, a painter, TENOR

Baron Scarpia, chief of police, BARITONE

Cesare Angelotti, a political plotter, BASS

A Sacristan, BARITONE OR BASS

Spoletta, a police agent, TENOR

Sciarrone, a gendarme, BASS

A Jailer, a Shepherd Boy, an Executioner, etc.

The action takes place in Rome, in 1800, during a particularly seething period of political intrigue

The painter, Mario Cavaradossi, who loves the singer, Floria Tosca, meets the fugitive, Angelotti, in church and promises to help him escape. Then he sings to a miniature of Tosca the tender aria "Recondita Armonia." Tosca arrives, jealous, but Mario quiets her fears. As he leaves, the Baron Scarpia, chief of police, enters to look for Angelotti, and finds a fan which belongs to the fugitive's costume of disguise. Tosca, returning, is confronted with the fan by Scarpia, and when she leaves again, the Baron sends three agents to follow her. The news of Napoleon's defeat at this time brings the Cardinal and the choir to the celebration of the event, and the scene closes with a splendid "Te Deum."

At the Royal Palace, the Baron orders his men to torture the captured Mario, who knows the whereabouts of Angelotti. Tosca, brought hither by a message from Scarpia, is forced to witness the torture, and finally reveals the hiding place to release her lover from the rack. When it becomes known that Napoleon has really triumphed, Mario cries out in joy and is ordered to execution by the angry Scarpia. Tosca, overwhelmed, makes her impassioned plea, "Vissi d'arte," imploring clemency of Scarpia. Be mine, says the Baron, and Mario shall go free. Tosca consents, and Scarpia writes orders for a mock execution of Mario. When he tries to approach Tosca, she stabs him.

Mario awaits death in prison. "E lucevan le stelle," he sings, in one of the most famous of Puccini's arias. Tosca arrives to tell him the Baron is dead and that the mock execution and passport will free him forever. The soldiers enter; the execution is carried out, but the shots are real, and Mario dies. Tosca, horrified at Scarpia's final treachery, evades the soldiers and flings herself to death from the battlement of the castle.

W. H., P. Z.

From *Bohème* to *Tosca*. At once. Without intermission. Without sense of
fatigue. Without doubt or hesitancy, and feeling nothing but exhilaration at
having solved the question of a new subject. Work, new textual problems to
be grappled with, new music to be composed—what a pleasure! Such was
Puccini's state of mind in the spring of 1896. He was at peace with the world
—or as near to peace as he could ever manage to come. He had struck no reefs
of inactivity.

During the spring he did play a little. He turned his attention to "Mimi I,"
a motorboat he had bought with money earned from *Manon*. He glided out
on the lake in the stillness of the early morning, shattering that stillness and
no doubt annoying the sleeping inhabitants of Torre. The bicycle now stood in
the shed; the new toy was more attractive. "Mimi I" was the first of a succession of boats, each one bigger and more elaborate than its predecessor, until
they were no longer motorboats but yachts.

After a few weeks, even "Mimi I" could not compete in fascination with
the new task. Again and again he returned to his desk to reflect on the Sardou
play, Illica's adaptation of which he had in his hand. Presently he no longer
lived in the Paris of Louis Philippe. He was now an inhabitant of Rome, the
Napoleonic Rome of 1800.

Italy was in the midst of war, though that war took place far away, in
Abyssinia. The Italians were defeated (on March 1, 1896), the Ministry re-
signed, the Socialists published a manifesto against the government, unrest
and discontent were once more bubbling through the country. But at tranquil
Torre these percolations reached only the outer horizon of Puccini's existence.
He was a century removed.

The acquisition of the *Tosca* libretto represents one of the few dishonorable
episodes in the life of a man who was certainly not dishonorable. The Puccini
biographers have attempted to slide over or around the episode with the fewest
possible words. They have laid stress on the fact that Puccini had considered
the *Tosca* subject many years previously—Specht and Fraccaroli say "after
finishing *Edgar*," and Adami, "while he was working on *Manon*." They imply
that this early consideration gave Puccini some sort of right to the libretto. This
is patent nonsense. If a man wants an artistic property but does not acquire it,
and then somebody else does acquire it, the property plainly belongs to the man
who acted. It makes no difference who first had the idea.

Puccini did desire *Tosca* right after he had finished *Edgar*. I am able to prove
this and thus confirm the statements made by other biographers, because I have
come across a letter of his which leaves no doubt on the matter. The letter is
dated May 7, 1889 (by luck one of Puccini's letters is dated clearly!). He wrote
it therefore some two weeks after *Edgar* had had its première.

Dearest Signor Giulio:

After two or three days of bucolic idleness, so that I might rest from all the exertions I have undergone, I realize that my desire for work, instead of diminishing, has returned more strongly than ever. I am thinking of *Tosca*. I implore you to take the necessary steps in order to obtain Sardou's permission. If we had to abandon this idea, it would grieve me exceedingly. In this *Tosca* I see the opera which exactly suits me, one without excessive proportions, one which is a decorative spectacle, and one which gives opportunity for an abundance of music. . . .*

We do not know when or why Puccini abandoned the idea. Perhaps Sardou would not at the time consent to having his profitable play—which was then less than two years old and which Sarah Bernhardt was taking on tour—turned into an operatic libretto, particularly into one to be used by an unknown composer. Perhaps, on the other hand, Puccini simply came to like *Manon* better. Whatever the circumstances, *Tosca* disappears from the correspondence until it turns up in a letter from Ricordi in the summer of 1895. . . .

But if in the intervening years Puccini had forgotten about *Tosca*, Ricordi had not. Ever on the alert for suitable operatic subjects, he had commissioned Illica to turn the play into a libretto, to be used by another composer whose works Ricordi published, Alberto Franchetti. Franchetti was a rich man—he used some of his wealth to give his own operas lavish productions—but he was not a mere dilettante. He had been, by the way, a pupil of Puccini's father. His opera, *Asrael,* written when he was twenty-two, enjoyed a considerable success. In 1892 his best-known opera, *Cristoforo Colombo,* had been produced, and this was followed in 1894 by *Fior d'Alpe,* a less successful effort. Now, in 1894 or 1895, Franchetti was ready for a new libretto. *Tosca* was the subject for which he had signed a contract with Ricordi. Illica had completed the libretto and, very likely, mentioned this, his latest piece of work, to Puccini, in the way of conversation. *Tosca?* Puccini at once remembered his own enthusiasm for *Tosca,* six years before. *Tosca?* But of course that was exactly the subject he needed. All his early interest returned, redoubled now that *Bohème* was half finished and he had no other plans for the future. But somebody else owned the libretto. What difference? That merely made the subject more desirable to him, that merely spurred his ambition. No question about it, he wanted *Tosca,* he *had* to have it. Ricordi *had* to obtain it for him.

Ricordi was now faced with a pretty problem. One of his most promising and famous composers, who was in addition one of his close personal friends, wanted a property pre-empted by another composer who also was his client and to whom he owed allegiance. We do not know what pangs of conscience may have assailed Ricordi or whether he came to his decision with much misgiving. We know only that he decided *Tosca* should be taken away from

* The original letter is owned by S. N. Gallini.

Franchetti and given to Puccini. He rallied Illica to his support—nothing more natural than that Illica also should wish his work to be set to music by Puccini, after the stupendous success of *Manon*—and the two of them called Franchetti to a conference. (Puccini knew about this meeting.) They pointed out to Franchetti that in their late but considered opinion—second thoughts being sometimes better thoughts—they had made a mistake in recommending *Tosca* to him: the subject was much too brutal and bloody. The audience would be repelled by seeing torture on the stage. The scene between Scarpia and Tosca bordered on the lascivious, and the subsequent knifing of Scarpia was bound to place the heroine in an unsympathetic light. Moreover, the political implications of the play were incomprehensible to modern operatic audiences. Franchetti went home and reflected. He came to the conclusion that Ricordi and Illica were right. He relinquished his contractual right to the libretto. The very next day, Puccini signed a contract for it. The crow let go of the bit of cheese. The fox snapped it up.

Approval of the libretto came from high authority, from Verdi himself. According to the critic Gino Monaldi, Verdi, who some years previously had thought of setting Sardou's "Patrie!" to music, said: "There *is* a drama of Sardou's which, had I still time, I would gladly set to music: that is *Tosca*. Provided, however, that Sardou would permit me to change the last act." We need not take this too seriously. It does not seem probable to me that the same Verdi who was occupying himself with Shakespeare's "Othello" would at that stage of his life have really deemed so unsubtle a melodrama as *Tosca* the right material for his music. It is further reported that when Franchetti and Illica went to Paris to read the *Tosca* libretto to Sardou, Verdi was present at the meeting. Illica had written a long speech for Cavaradossi in the third act. The speech voiced the thoughts of a man who is about to die, thoughts about life and art. Verdi, hearing Illica read this speech, was much moved. He took the manuscript from Illica's hands and himself began to read aloud what was written there. There was a tremor in his voice. Whatever be the truth of these anecdotes, it is certain that Verdi admired the libretto. Ricordi said so to Puccini:

October 14, 1896

With Illica I paid a short visit of three hours to Verdi. He had informed himself of what new works were in process, and he told me, "Puccini has a good libretto! Fortunate composer who has that work in his hands!" Our Verdi is a good prophet!! Therefore *laboremus!!*

Puccini knew that the finished libretto not only had to satisfy him but had also to be approved by the original author, the famous and then sixty-five-year-old panjandrum of the Parisian theater, Victorien Sardou. Sardou has long disappeared from the stage. The plays in which Sarah Bernhardt, Coquelin, and other stellar French actors triumphed are no longer given, not even in

France. He is now only a name. Those of us who have a particular interest in the theater can cite in addition to "La Tosca" the titles of one or two of his other plays: "Madame Sans-Gêne" or "Fedora" (both of which were set to music by Giordano), "Cléopâtre" or "Robespierre." It is difficult now to appreciate the extent of his reputation or the magnitude of his sway over the theater of the last decade of the nineteenth century. Puccini knew that it would be necessary to humor this mighty man.

In the meantime, he proceeded with his own plans and laid down the law. He wanted, he said to Illica and Giacosa, a simplification of the original play, retaining only what was bold and dramatic in the drama and eliminating all superfluous episodes, all political by-play, and all long speeches, be they ever so worthy, in the cause of liberty.

The collaboration of the three men was less stormy than it had been for *La Bohème*. Most of the troubles which did occur were due to two causes. Illica was in love with his own work and was not easily persuaded to shorten any of it. In his original sketch, Cavaradossi is made to sing a full aria while he is being tortured, with the voices of Tosca, the judge, and Spoletta taking up his plaint in a formal quartet. Puccini would not tolerate this throwback to an older form of operatic libretto. Illica lost his temper. Then, he absolutely refused to relinquish the long speech planned for Cavaradossi before he dies. This "Latin hymn," which Verdi had praised, Illica loved above all speeches. In vain did Puccini protest that there was no room for philosophy in a melodrama, and particularly not at this point of the action. It was only after many discussions and considerable hard feeling that Puccini was able to reduce the speech to the brief apostrophe, "E lucevan le stelle" ("The stars are shining"). The simple words "Muoio disperato!" ("I die despairing") were written by Puccini.

The second difficulty was due to Giacosa. He disliked *Tosca*. Honest poet that he was, he could not get himself to write the verses. "On first reading," he said, "yes, the rapidity and the variety of the dramatic action appear good, particularly when one peruses for the first time the clever synthesis which Illica has fashioned. But the more one studies the interior of the action, penetrates each scene, and tries to extract lyric and poetic moments from them, the more one becomes persuaded of the absolute inadaptability of the libretto to the lyric theater," etc., etc. *Tosca*, to him, was a drama which had a plot but no poetry, as against *Bohème*, which had poetry but no plot. He protested that he was unable to create real characters out of these puppets. Cavaradossi was nothing but a *Signor Tenore*. Would Puccini be satisfied with a *Signor Tenore?*

Nevertheless, he and Illica finally gave Puccini what he wanted. A comparison of the five-act play with the three-act libretto shows that the play, based on history and describing the efforts of the partisans of Napoleon to rid themselves of the oppression of the government of Naples (yes, Napoleon here is the champion of liberty!), has now become a melodramatic love story pure and simple, or rather a melodramatic love story not so pure and still quite simple. The fight for freedom has become a secondary ingredient of the plot. Few operagoers familiar with *Tosca* have the vaguest notion on whose authority Scarpia is acting; what it is that Angelotti and Cavaradossi are plotting so surreptitiously; over whose victory Cavaradossi exults in the second act; in short, of anything that does not directly concern Tosca herself. Along with an entire act—Act III at Cavaradossi's villa, where Scarpia's police trap Angelotti, and Cavaradossi and Tosca are arrested—many of the original and historic characters have disappeared, including Marie-Caroline, Queen of Naples; the Marquis Attavanti; and the composer Paisiello, who appears in one delightful scene in the Sardou play. Sardou's play has twenty-three characters, Puccini's opera nine. Puccini at first meant to give Tosca some music by Paisiello to sing. He later changed his mind. In the play Paisiello officiates at a gala concert for the Queen at which Tosca is the star. Just as she is ready to sing, a dispatch is brought in announcing the defeat of the royal army. The Queen faints, the soiree is at once terminated—and thus Sarah Bernhardt never needed to sing.

The "big" scenes were preserved. These include the first act in the church, the last act, and the Scarpia-Tosca scene in the Palazzo Farnese. The torture of Cavaradossi and Tosca's betrayal, originally a part of the third act, are now added to this scene; but otherwise it follows the original almost word for word. This was the climax of the play, as it is for many the climax of the opera. Tosca's famous closing line, "E avanti a lui tremava tutta Roma" ("Before him all Rome trembled"), occurs in the original play in what seems to me a slightly less effective version: "Et c'est devant ça que tremblait toute une ville" ("And it is before this that a whole city trembled"). Puccini himself changed the wording. It is curious that in one of the sketches Giacosa eliminated this last line. Puccini immediately complained to Ricordi, "Why has the last line been cut? . . . I put it in and it serves my purpose. It had better be kept in."

What an effect this scene must have made when Sarah Bernhardt played Tosca! We get some inkling of the fascination of this performance when we read one of her biographers, Reynaldo Hahn. He tells us how she was able to summon extraordinary dramatic tenseness in the twinkling of an eye. During the intermission she would sit in her dressing room, laughing and making flippant jokes. When the time for the last act came, she would leave her dressing room at the last possible moment, exclaiming lightheartedly, *"Allons tuer Coq"* (Coquelin, the famous Cyrano, was then playing Scarpia), and rush on the stage. And once on the stage she immediately transformed herself:

What a feeling for effect and what technique in the way in which, after the murder of Scarpia, she wets the napkin to wash away the blood she has on her hands, in which she examines her dress to make sure that she had not stained it, with which she looks out of the window by raising herself lightly on tiptoe! . . . The exit is a miracle of execution. Sarah half opens the door, puts her head out to peer into the corridor, then her shoulders, then her whole body, with the undulating movement of a reptile; the door closes softly, very softly, while the train of her dress disappears. . . . And while the curtains are lowered, we imagine that Tosca, furtive, palpitating, slinks off against the walls, silent as a shadow.

Puccini was certain that by personal conference he could convince Sardou that his precious brain-child might safely be entrusted to him. He was going to Paris, anyway, to stage *La Bohème*. Ricordi reminded him to be *sure* to call on Sardou:

> March 5, 1898
>
> . . . Before you leave Paris, it will be most useful that you have a full meeting with Sardou, who will be *flatté!!* . . . Proceed, *Imperator,* with patience and constancy. . . .

Puccini had quite a time with Sardou, then and later. The playwright, full of years, wealth, and glory, considered himself the last authority on all subjects theatrical, with or without music, the court of ultimate sagacity. He was the autocrat at the apéritif table. He expected everybody, including this anxious composer, to show him deference. Even the divine Sarah never addressed him except as "Maître Chéri." Puccini made a good impression. After discussing the subject for some hours at dinner (half in French, half in Italian), Sardou asked Puccini to play a little of the music for the proposed opera. Puccini had as yet composed almost none of the music. This did not faze him. He sat down at the piano and played for a long time, weaving together a medley of melodies from *Bohème, Manon,* and *Edgar*. Sardou liked what he heard. He declared himself satisfied to leave his play in the hands of the Italian, provided of course his financial terms could be met. These were exorbitant. Sardou wanted fifty thousand francs. They eventually settled on fifteen per cent of the royalties of the opera, for a period of years. (I am not sure of how many years.) It is indicative of the strength of Puccini's desire for *Tosca* that he was willing to forgo fifteen per cent of his income.

Puccini wrote to Ricordi the results of his discussions. Sardou had made innumerable suggestions for the opera. On April 29, 1898, Ricordi acknowledges a letter which must also have contained one of the composer's usual litanies. Ricordi sympathizes with him because he has so much trouble with the cast of *Bohème*. He reminds him of what *"salami"* (hams) even first-class Rodolfos are wont to become after a few performances. Constant vigilance, along with a great quantity of philosophy, is indispensable when one has to deal with singers. (Verdi had said that, also.) Under the circumstances, he understands that Puccini isn't getting much work done on *Tosca*. As to Sardou:

> April 29, 1898
>
> . . . The suggestions of Sardou will certainly have to be reckoned with, partly because he has a great talent for the theater, and partly because we want to interest

him in the work!! But don't forget, my two fine friends, that we are dealing with
an opera and not with a play.

Puccini described Sardou as a "prodigious man." He menaced the composer
with his passion for detail and with his inexhaustible loquacity.

He talked [Puccini said] hours on end without ever being fatigued or fatiguing.
When he set out to tell stories, he was a torrent, a fountain: the anecdotes spouted
from him limpidly and continuously. Many of our conferences turned out to be
simply monologues by Sardou. Very pleasant, to be sure, but hardly useful to the
progress of our *Tosca*. Nonetheless, he showed himself reasonable, and became
reconciled to the necessity of suppressing an entire act. . . .

Early the following year, Puccini again went to Paris, and reported to Ricordi
as follows:

Paris, January 13, 1899

This morning I was at Sardou's for one hour. He told me that he did not like
certain details of the finale. He wants Floria Tosca dead at all costs [on the stage],
poor woman! Now that the sun of the executioner Deibler [the head executioner of
France, who had just died] has set, the Magician [Sardou] wants to be his successor. But I certainly do not agree with him. He admits that Tosca is overwhelmed
by madness [in the final moment] yet he would like her to swoon and expire like
a bird. Then, in the revival which Sarah Bernhardt will play in a few days, Sardou
has introduced a huge flag, fluttering and flashing from the top of the Castello,
which, according to him, will make a wonderful effect. He is so taken up with
that flag that he is more interested in it than in the play itself. But I am still holding
out for my finale with the cry, "Scarpia before God!" [the closing words of the
opera] and the jump from the parapet. Speaking of the parapet, Sardou sketched
the scenery [a sketch which Puccini kept and treasured], and in this sketch Sardou
wants the course of the Tiber to be visible, passing between St. Peter's and the
Castello. I pointed out to him that the *flumen* flowed on the other side, but he, calm
as a fish, replied: "That's of no importance." A nice fellow, all life and fire, but
full of historic-topographical-panoramic inexactitudes. . . . On Saturday morning I
have to go and see Sardou again—so the Magician has decreed. Perhaps he will
insist on killing Spoletta! We shall see.

Puccini had his way. There is no Tiber in the scenery, Tosca jumps from the
parapet uttering the cry Puccini had intended for her, and Spoletta lives,
though to be sure nobody cares whether he lives or dies.

As usual, Puccini had his moments of doubt. Once Sardou consented and
the play belonged to him, Puccini was assailed by misgivings. Was *Tosca,* so
different a subject from his previous texts, really suitable to his talent? Could
he bring it off? Was the drama too violent for his soft music? Puccini carried
his scruples to Sardou himself, and it was Sardou who talked him out of such
nonsense. The conversation, according to Puccini, ran something like this:[*]

* As told by Lucio D'Ambra in his "Lives of Italian Musicians."

PUCCINI: Perhaps it would be better if a Frenchman were to set your play to music.

SARDOU: No, better an Italian. *Tosca* is a Roman work. It needs your Italian song.

PUCCINI: Verdi, our great Verdi, once thought of *Tosca* and gave it up, a sign that the subject intimidated him. Do you wonder, M. Sardou, that *I* am afraid?

SARDOU: Verdi wasn't intimidated, but Verdi is old, Verdi is tired. You ought to be encouraged by the fact that a great composer for the theater such as he had confidence in *Tosca* and recognized in it the opera, the good opera, which it is.

PUCCINI: Alberto Franchetti, also, considered *Tosca* and gave it up in his turn.

SARDOU: That, my dear Maestro, certainly means nothing. Two men considered it: well, that is the best guarantee of *Tosca's* vitality.

PUCCINI: But my music is tenuous, it is delicate, it is written in a different register.

SARDOU [shouting]: There are no registers, M. Puccini; there's only talent!

PUCCINI: My previous heroines, Manon and Mimi, are different from Tosca.

SARDOU: Manon, Mimi, Tosca, it is all the same thing! . . . Women in love all belong to the same family. I have created Marcella and Fernanda, I have created Fedora, Theodora, and Cleopatra. They are all the same woman.

Before the sanguine Sardou disappears from our history, it should be stated that in later years Sardou claimed most of the credit for having persuaded Puccini to compose *Tosca*. When in the fall of 1903 Puccini was once again in Paris to stage the French première of *Tosca* (October 13th), Sardou lorded it over everybody at the rehearsals. He behaved as if he were not only the author of the play but stage manager and composer of the music as well. Puccini said that he expected Sardou any moment to push the conductor out of his place and swing the baton himself. He assured anybody who would listen that the libretto was now superior to his play. When a critic attacked the libretto, finding the subject wrong for musical expression, Sardou replied, "A play which has been given three thousand times is always right."

Puccini composed most of the music in his new villa in Chiatri. He felt that even the inaccessible Torre was not inaccessible enough. He had to bury himself in mountain fastnesses. Only there, he persuaded himself, could he summon the necessary concentration. So his family packed up and went up the mountain.

We must now transport ourselves to the theatrical world of Rome, as of January, 1900, if we are to understand the strange occurrences at the première. A world première in Rome was a very different matter from a world première in Turin or in any of the other small cities. The Roman public considered all other audiences—even those of Milan, though they admitted the eminence of La Scala—provincial. They were not going to be taken in by the glamour of the new première. The new work by the man from the North was to be examined coolly; no mercy was to be shown. And didn't this opera have its locale in Rome itself? And was it not based on history? A Roman is every inch a historian. He is a self-appointed curator of Rome's past. Yes, this opera needed to be carefully appraised.

Tito's * peremptory action of excluding critics and relatives of the singers from the rehearsals, the contretemps with Franchetti, rumors of which had reached the metropolis, and Puccini's own continued "easy" success did not serve to endear the composer, at least to that part of the public which had some professional connection with musical matters. Moreover, Tito had "imported" a stranger, Hohenstein, from La Scala to design the scenery.

All in all, the atmosphere was hardly friendly. Puccini was more than usually nervous. D'Ambra † met Puccini a few hours before the première in a café. The composer was surrounded by his "guard from Lucca," his friends who were smoking fearsome pipes and were equipped with knotty sticks with which, D'Ambra supposed, they would have belabored the shoulders of anybody who did not like the new opera. The gentlemen were talking of a triumph for Lucca. But Puccini himself, sitting there in the back of the café, was melancholy. He sat as always with his hat on his head, the collar of his overcoat raised, the cigarette hanging from his lips, his face clouded. "It will be a triumph," shouted the friends. But Puccini shrugged his shoulders: "You can say that easily, you can talk of a triumph. Don't you know that since *Bohème* all the guns are aimed at me? And if, God forbid, I have made a mistake, all those guns are going to shoot."

Just before the beginning of the performance, a delegate from the prefecture called on Mugnone [the conductor] in his dressing room. "Maestro," he said to him, "don't worry and do not be afraid. But in case there should be some disturbance, kindly bid the orchestra to strike up the national anthem."

Mugnone could hardly take this news calmly. What, he wanted to know, was going to happen? What were the police afraid of? Nothing much. Just that they had received information that at tonight's performance a rival faction was going to explode a bomb in the theater. As the Queen of Italy and most of the aristocracy were expected, precautions had to be taken.

Mugnone kept the news from Puccini. At approximately the time that the opera was supposed to start—Toscanini always started on time, so why not he? —he braced himself and, looking neither to the right nor to the left, went into the pit. He raised the baton, and the harsh chords of the prelude sounded in the theater. The curtain rose, and Angelotti [the escaped prisoner in *Tosca*] entered. At this moment, Mugnone, intent though he was on the music, could not help noticing that there was indeed a disturbance going on behind him. He heard a general murmur of displeasure, a sound that snaps the nerves of a theater man. At the same time, a few members of the claque were applauding loudly when there was obviously nothing to applaud. The sounds grew louder. Mugnone could now hear shouts of "Stop!" "Lower the curtain!" No longer master of himself, he stopped conducting; the curtain was lowered. He rushed backstage, tears in his eyes, to be met by Puccini.

* [Tito Ricordi, the music publisher.]
† [Lucio d'Ambra, an old friend of Puccini, author of "Vite di Musicisti Italiani."]

What had happened? At first nobody knew. Mugnone wept. Puccini paced up and down. But after a few minutes, the attendants reassured them. The disturbance, it turned out, was nothing serious. It was caused by the attempt to start on time. Many of the spectators had not arrived at their seats. The entrances to the orchestra floor were choked with people demanding access. The resulting noise infuriated the standees and others, and they in turn began to shout. Some of the standees had been standing on line since eleven o'clock that morning and, tired and on edge, they now grumbled at the late-comers.

But then the crowd calmed itself. They were, after all, Romans. Moreover, the Queen was expected momentarily—she did in fact not arrive until the first intermission—and it was incumbent upon them to behave representatively. Mugnone sensibly reasoned that after the initial disturbance a rival faction, if indeed there was one in the house, would not attempt a new disturbance. Once more he took heart, re-entered the orchestra pit, and began the opera anew. It is understandable, however, that both he and the singers continued to be nervous.

Because of the circumstances, and probably also because the performance could hardly have been very good, the reception of the opera was something short of triumphal. The people applauded: they could not help being charmed by the melodies and interested in the drama; yet their enthusiasm lacked that boisterous, boiling tumult which the Italians (even the Romans) pour on something they really like. Still, Puccini was called out twenty-two times.

The critics—oh, the critics trotted out their academic purity. They rapped the composer over the knuckles for his choice of the subject. The *Corriere d'Italia,* published in Rome, gave over its entire front page (issue of January 16, 1900) to a discussion of *Tosca,* a sign of the news value of a Puccini première. (It was a news-worthy event not for the Italian press alone. The correspondents of the foreign press—including those of the *New York Times* and the *Chicago Tribune* —were present. A special telegraph service had been set up in the manager's office.) The critic of the *Corriere* believed that the music did not prove equal to the violence of the melodrama. It did not express the action. It seemed to be "tacked on." "While the torture scene of the second act, the murder of Scarpia, and other events equally bloody arrested the attention of the spectators, one could not say that the music of these scenes gripped the souls of the audience." The critic admitted the "abundance of ideas, richness of inspiration, security of design, and the enviable ability to space the music within the drama, an ability shared by few composers." "But," asked he, "is *Tosca* the opera which will carry the name of the Maestro toward immortality? Frankly, I do not think so." What particularly riled the critic was the fact that Puccini had attempted to reconstruct in his music the atmosphere of the Rome of 1800. (He had attempted no such thing, of course.) Could not Puccini see that the cantata (backstage) in the Palazzo Farnese was an anachronism? *"Aïda's* trumpets are

Egyptian as much as I am Chinese, and when I see on the stage historic pageantry accompanied by music which is essentially modern, I have the impression of seeing Dante take a walk dressed in the clothes of the latest mode."
As to Rome itself: "Dawn in Rome is an occurrence so solemn that it can hardly
be expressed within the limits of a symphonic prelude" (in the third act).

Il Nuovo Fanfulla blamed the libretto: "Puccini was seduced by the potent
drama of the French author, but along with seduction came tyranny. In certain
moments the libretto suffocates the composer." (Mascagni was of the same
opinion. He told a reporter: "I have been victimized by poor librettos. Puccini
is the victim of a libretto that is too good." Hardly a friendly thing to say, but
quite in line with the other public pronouncements of that peacock.)

Other critics, however, acknowledged the worth of the opera. Opinions
differed so much that one critic added a footnote to his report: "Idea for a prize
contest: Find two critics who agree on *Tosca*."

There is no point in going on to more quotations. It is easy enough to scoff
at contemporary criticism from the vantage point gained by the passage of
years. It *is* discouraging, however, to realize that in the business of musical
criticism one can be wrong most of the time and succeed.

It all made precious little difference. What happened with *Bohème* happened here again. *Tosca* became popular almost immediately, and in that very
season at the Costanzi twenty performances were given to sold-out houses.
Exactly like *Bohème, Tosca* became an international as well as a national success. In June of 1900—six months after the Rome première—it reached Covent
Garden, where Milka Ternina played Tosca magnificently and Antonio Scotti
made his first appearance as Scarpia. Some eight months after that, *Tosca* was
given at the Metropolitan (February 4, 1901), also with Ternina and Scotti.

The opera has always, of course, been a singer's favorite. Some of the famous
Toscas in our country were, after Ternina, Emma Eames, Claudia Muzio,
Geraldine Farrar, and Maria Jeritza. Puccini particularly admired Jeritza in
the part. Her picture as Tosca hung over his desk at Torre del Lago. Her
famous stunt of singing "Vissi d'arte" while lying prone on the floor came
about accidentally. Jeritza was rehearsing *Tosca* in Vienna under Puccini's
supervision. Being rather too violently carried away by her own emotions, she
slipped from the couch and fell to the floor. Before she could recover herself,
she heard the cue for her aria. She began to sing where she was. Puccini—who,
by the way, had no great love for "Vissi d'arte," believing that the aria held
up the action—approved with enthusiasm. "That is good," he said; "it gives
the aria some life."

The role of Cavaradossi, less grateful than either Tosca's or Scarpia's part,
nonetheless attracted the stellar tenors. . . . Caruso excelled in the part. He
was sent to Puccini as a substitute when it appeared that De Marchi, who had
sung the part in Rome, was unable to fulfill an engagement in Livorno. Puccini

was anxious to obtain a first-class performance in this, Mascagni's home town. Ricordi wrote to Puccini, saying that he had come across a young Neapolitan tenor with a voice of gold. Much as Puccini trusted Ricordi, he still wanted to hear this voice of gold for himself, and so he asked Ricordi to send the man to him. Caruso presented himself at Torre del Lago, and Puccini suggested, after the preliminary amenities, that he sing a little of the music; he was going to accompany him. Caruso sang "Recondita armonia." At the closing note Puccini turned to Caruso and said, "Who sent you to me? God?"

What attracted Puccini to Sardou's play? It is not difficult to guess that the attraction was a twofold one, consisting in equal parts of something old and something new.

As to the old—Floria Tosca was the kind of heroine Puccini could cherish. Not a heroic heroine, but a charming creature, light-hearted by nature, perplexed in the extreme by the infamy of the world. Tosca, like Puccini's previous heroines, "lived for love." If she also "lived for art," so much the better. Love and art were the two things Puccini understood.

G. R. M.

Like *Bohème, Tosca* was introduced to Latin America before it reached New York, the New World *première* being at the Teatro Colón, Buenos Aires, on June 16, 1900. Almost eight months later, Ternina (Tosca) and Scotti (Scarpia), who had already sung the roles at Covent Garden, headed the first Metropolitan cast, on February 4, 1901; Cremonini was the Cavaradossi, Dufriche the Angelotti, and Gilibert the Sacristan. The popularity of the opera was immediate and lasting, and in thirty-six seasons it rolled up a total of 174 performances. As Tosca, Eames made her farewell to the Metropolitan on February 15, 1909, and the same role introduced Muzio to that house on December 4, 1916, with Caruso and Scotti. Tosca was one of Farrar's most admired roles, and even after Jeritza's spectacular interpretation of the tragic Roman singer had become a Metropolitan drawing card, Farrar was urged, when she announced her forthcoming retirement, to sing *Tosca* at her farewell. But the management chose *Zaza* for her valedictory.

Jeritza's first Metropolitan Tosca occurred on December 1, 1921, opposite Scotti and a most unobtrusive Cavaradossi, Aureliano Pertile. She wore no wig to cover her luxuriant blonde hair, though the text explicitly mentions her as brunette. . . . Scotti's Scarpia was rivaled, perhaps excelled, by that of Renaud, who, however, did not sing the role at the Metropolitan. But even he never received the access of adulation that greeted the production of *Tosca* to mark Scotti's twenty-fifth anniversary at the Metropolitan. Opposite him was Jeritza, his thirteenth Metropolitan Tosca. The role of Cavaradossi, obviously so much less dramatic than Scarpia's, nevertheless has attracted many famous tenors. Caruso, to Ternina's Tosca, made his first big Metropolitan hit in this role, and it was one of the three McCormack sang as a regular member of the Metropolitan company—the other two were Rodolfo (*La Bohème*) and Pinkerton (*Madama Butterfly*). It was also chosen by Richard Crooks for his operatic debut, which occurred at Hamburg in 1927.

W. B., H. W.

Madama Butterfly

OPERA IN 3 ACTS

Book by GIUSEPPE GIACOSA and LUIGI ILLICA, after the play by DAVID BELASCO and JOHN LUTHER LONG (based on LONG's story *Madam Butterfly*)

First performance: La Scala, Milan, Feb. 17, 1904

CHARACTERS

Cio-Cio-San (Madama Butterfly), SOPRANO

Suzuki, Cio-Cio-San's servant, MEZZO-SOPRANO

B. F. Pinkerton, Lieutenant in the United States Navy, TENOR

Kate Pinkerton, his American wife, MEZZO-SOPRANO

Sharpless, United States Consul at Nagasaki, BARITONE

Goro, a marriage broker, TENOR

Prince Yamadori, suitor for Cio-Cio-San, BARITONE

The Bonze, Cio-Cio-San's uncle, BASS

Cio-Cio-San's Relations and Friends; Servants

The action takes place in the early 1900's at Nagasaki, Japan

Pinkerton, an officer on a visiting American warship, decides to take a young Japanese girl (Cio-Cio-San) as his "port wife." The first act is taken up with the negotiations and the wedding festivities and ends with an ecstatic duet for bride and bridegroom.

In the second act we see the interior of Cio-Cio-San's house, where, with the child she has borne him in his absence, she is awaiting the return of Pinkerton. The American consul Sharpless proves a sympathetic friend and her maid Suzuki, a devoted attendant.

In the last act Pinkerton's ship has arrived at Nagasaki, and Pinkerton lands, but with him now is the legitimate wife he has married in America. Sharpless has informed him of the existence of the child. The generous Mrs. Pinkerton would like to adopt it. When Cio-Cio-San realizes the true state of affairs, with all its implications, she consents to the adoption for the child's good, bids Pinkerton return in half an hour to fetch it, blindfolds her son and places in his hand a little American flag, and then kills herself with her father's hara-kiri knife.

P. S.

On February 17, 1904, at the celebrated Teatro alla Scala, Milan, *Madama Butterfly* was produced for the first time on any stage. The immediate result was a fiasco. Puccini at the time had already won recognition as the foremost

373

of living Italian composers, thanks to *Manon Lescaut, La Bohème,* and *Tosca.* Distinguished artists had been allotted to his new opera—Rosina Storchio (destined to be particularly famous in her rôle) for Cio-Cio-San, Giovanni Zenatello for Pinkerton, Giuseppe De Luca for Sharpless, Cleofonte Campanini to conduct. Nevertheless and notwithstanding, a fiasco!

Opposition began, we are told, at the entrance of Cio-Cio-San. When after the first act Puccini, who was recovering from a motor accident, limped on the stage supported by his stick, a barrage of hissing interposed between the composer and his applauding friends, chief among them no less a personage than Mascagni. Naturally Puccini refused to go out before the curtain again, but remained sitting in the wings as the disorderly evening proceeded, his mounting anger venting itself in such exclamations as "Louder, you beasts! Shriek at me, yell! But you shall see who is right! That is the best opera I have ever written!"

To preclude the possibility of a second performance at La Scala at that time, with a probable repetition of the rioting, Puccini, when the bitter end had been reached, quietly thanked Campanini for his pains and as quietly picked up the score and walked away with it.

An amusing incident that followed this initial failure has been recounted by Puccini himself. It seems he had a devoted admirer in a bookkeeper at Genoa, who was quite infuriated by the scandalous reception accorded *Madama Butterfly* at Milan. Having the birth of a daughter to register at the City Hall, the bookkeeper answered the clerk's question by giving the name of the child as Butterfly. The astonished functionary asked him whether he wanted his daughter to be burdened for life with the name of a fiasco. But the father persisted.

When Puccini heard of the occurrence, he was sufficiently affected to invite the parents to call on him, bringing the child. Not only they arrived, but the entire clan, quite "Butterfly"-wise, and the composer averred that this visitation, with the sisters and the cousins and the aunts and so forth and so on, constituted the largest reception at which he had ever played host. And Puccini further confessed himself as really somewhat cheered by the numerous proof of confidence.

Just why the première at Milan was a fiasco has never been satisfactorily explained. In the case of the initial *La Traviata* the mistake of casting an obese prima donna as a woman dying of consumption accounted for the work being laughed off the stage. In the case of *Tannhäuser* in Paris the rage of the Jockey Club over a ballet impudently placed at the very beginning of an opera left no room for doubt. But what about *Madama Butterfly?* There has been vague gossip of a cabal. The absence in the original version of a solo for the tenor, or of any tenor at all during what is now the second act, has been blamed. So has the length of the original second act (running more than an hour and a half), which had not yet been divided into two acts.

In any event, whatever the reason, Puccini did not lose faith, despite the behavior of the public and of all the critics save one. Ten days after the disastrous première he wrote to a friend in Rome: "You may well have taken fright at the vile words of the envious press. Have no fear! *Butterfly* is alive, is true, and will shortly rise again. I say it and I maintain it with resolute faith—you shall see—and it will be within a couple of months; I cannot tell you where, for the moment."

As a matter of fact, Brescia was the place, though not till May 28. Meanwhile Puccini had made some revisions in the score, the chief being the elevation of the concluding scene to the dignity of an act, now provided, furthermore, with an arioso for tenor and separated from the preceding act by an intermezzo. At Brescia Campanini was again the conductor and Zenatello the Pinkerton, but Salomea Krusceniska sang Cio-Cio-San and Bellatti Sharpless. The second première proved emphatically successful, starting *Madama Butterfly* off on a triumphant tour of the world.

The planning and writing of *Madama Butterfly* belong to the years 1902 and 1903 (the latter the year of the aforesaid motor accident). Puccini consulted the wife of the Japanese ambassador with respect to many details, and one of her friends in Paris furnished him with some Japanese tunes. The subject, by the way, is supposed to have been suggested to him while on a visit to London by Frank Neilson, then stage manager of Covent Garden.

The play "Madam Butterfly," which David Belasco and John Luther Long had dramatized from a magazine story by Long, was running at the Duke of York's Theatre, and Neilson induced Puccini to see it. At once its operatic possibilities appealed to him, though he was entirely unacquainted with English and had to divine the plot from the remarkably vivid acting of Evelyn Millard and her associates.

P. S.

FIASCO AT LA SCALA

. . . The curtain rose. The beginning of the opera, up to the entrance of Butterfly, was heard in silence. An ominous sign, for Italian audiences do not listen in silence when they like what they are hearing. Just before the entrance of Butterfly—Storchio was standing in the wings with Puccini, her hands cold as ice—a super came by mumbling, "What is the matter with the public?" Storchio broke out into a cold sweat. The assistant conductor pointed: it was her cue. She sang backstage the first phrase of Cio-Cio-San's, that enchanting phrase, "One more step and we have arrived." She was on the stage. Silence. No applause. She continued to sing. And suddenly there was a shout from the balcony. "That is *Bohème*." Immediately the cry was echoed by other voices: "*Bohème! Bohème!* We've heard that already. Give us something new!" Then all was quiet again. Quiet during the wedding ceremony.

Quiet during the long love duet. At the climax of the duet a few handclaps; so sparse were they that in the darkness of the theater they sounded like an emphasis on silence. The curtain fell. Again a little applause—very little— mixed with hisses. There were three curtain calls, in two of which the re- luctant Puccini, leaning on his cane, participated.

During the first intermission, no one came backstage, not a friend, not a journalist. An actor once told me that failure could always be recognized after the first act. If no one appeared to make a fuss over you, you were ready to look for another job. There were two hectic spots on Puccini's face as he walked up and down, smoking one cigarette after another, unmindful of the two firemen stationed backstage. Tito was cold and composed. He went over to Storchio and said, "At the second act the reaction will set in. I swear to you that it will be a success."

The second act began. At one moment Storchio turned around quickly. A draft caught her kimono and it ballooned up. At that a hoarse voice in the audience shouted, "Butterfly is pregnant." Storchio began to weep. She fin- ished "Un bel di" in a voice thickened by tears. There was again scattered applause. But when she introduced the child to Sharpless, pandemonium broke loose. Grunts, growls, groans, laughter, ironic cries of *"Bis!,"* obscene remarks, hisses hailed down on the performers. From then on hardly a note was heard in silence. The derogatory noises reached their climax during the Intermezzo. (We must remember that *Butterfly* in the original version was given in two acts, the Intermezzo connecting Scenes 1 and 2 of Act II.) Tito had had the unfortunate idea of reinforcing the effect of the music by pro- ducing from hidden parts of the auditorium itself the gentle chirping of birds. As the sky darkened and night fell, as Butterfly, Suzuki, and the child stood looking out over the landscape, these aviary twitterings were to be heard. A tasteless bit of realism, which gave a cue to the audience. They answered: they barked like dogs, burst into cock-a-doodle-doos of roosters, brayed like asses, and mooed like cows as if—Storchio said—dawn in Japan were taking place in Noah's Ark. Nothing after that failed to strike the audience as funny. The final scene, the preparation for the suicide and the suicide itself, was heard in comparative quiet, but when the curtain fell, *Butterfly* ended amidst laughter and derogatory shouts. There were no curtain calls, not a single one.

Long before the opera ended, Tonio had come backstage. The boy hurled himself into the arms of Puccini, crying, "Oh, Father! Father!" Puccini hid in one of the dressing rooms, but the furor and the noise reached him there also. He heard "those whistles, those terrible whistles, which humiliate you, which slap you down, which tear your heart into pieces. . . . How is it possible that the public, even if the work be a mistake, can be so ferocious; how is it possible that it cannot pity, that it cannot consider that behind the scenery on that stage there stands an artist who has attemped to create something, a father who loves his work and who suffers to see it tortured, offended, abused?

Good people, one by one, the spectators. But together, once out for evil, they are rabble." *

Puccini slunk home. He had not far to go: his apartment in the Via Verdi was across the street from the Scala. Even these few steps were painful: he hid himself against the walls as if—he said—he had been a man who had committed a dirty crime. He could not understand. As he sat with Elvira, Tito, and Giulio through a sleepless night, he demanded to know how it could have happened that he, who thought himself loved, if not by all, certainly by many, could now be "one against the crowd, defenseless, at the mercy of a furious audience who turned into ridicule the opera born in the deepest recesses of my heart. . . . My whole life passed before me. There were some things beyond the ken of the public's judgment of one night. . . . And I determined that *Madama Butterfly*, however miserably it might have fallen when it took the first step, should not stop here at the Scala of Milan, but would continue its way in the world. . . . I thought of Bellini, remembering the enormous fiasco at the Scala [of *Norma*]; I thought of the cries which met Rossini at the first performance of *The Barber;* I thought of Wagner and the sounds of the hunting horns blown by the Parisian aristocrats who drowned his *Tannhäuser* in ridicule. . . ."

Then other friends came in and Puccini turned to them in a burst of unjust anger: "Have you too whistled at my opera? Did you too shout? Do as you like. I know what I have accomplished, even if the others do not. *Butterfly* is my best opera." After this he became calmer.

His humiliation was not over. Morning came and with it the cries of the newsboys. In his apartment he could not shut out the sounds of those headlines. Of all of them—"Butterfly a Failure," "Puccini Hissed," "Fiasco at the Scala," etc.—the one which hurt him most was, "Butterfly Diabetic Opera, Result of Automobile Accident."

G. R. M.

Puccini's opera reached London on July 10, 1905. Emmy Destinn, Caruso, and Scotti appeared in it, as they were to do later in New York, and Campanini conducted. Henry W. Savage brought it to the United States in the autumn of 1906 in an English version, presenting it first in Washington, on October 15, and in New York, at the Garden Theatre, on November 12.

The first performance in this country in the original Italian took place at the Metropolitan Opera House, in the presence of the composer, on February 11, 1907. An extraordinary quartet filled the leading rôles—Geraldine Farrar as Cio-Cio-San, Louise Homer as Suzuki, Caruso as Pinkerton, and Scotti as Sharpless.

P. S.

---

* As reported by D'Ambra.

La Fanciulla del West

[The Girl of the Golden West]

OPERA IN 3 ACTS

Book by GUELFO CIVINI and CARLO ZANGARINI, after DAVID BELASCO's Play
The Girl of the Golden West

First performance: Metropolitan Opera House, New York, Dec. 10, 1910

CHARACTERS

Minnie, owner of the Polka bar, SOPRANO

Jack Rance, sheriff, BARITONE

Dick Johnson (Ramerrez), TENOR

Nick, bartender at the Polka, TENOR

Ashby, Wells-Fargo agent, BASS

Billy Jackrabbit, an Indian, BASS

Wowkle, his squaw, MEZZO-SOPRANO

Jake Wallace, a traveling camp minstrel, BARITONE

Sonora, BARITONE; *Trin,* TENOR; *Sid,* BARITONE; *Handsome,* BARITONE; *Harry,* TENOR; *Joe,* TENOR; *Happy,* BARITONE; *Larken,* BASS

Jose Castro, member of Ramerrez's gang, BASS

A Postilion, BASS

Men of the Camp

The action takes place at the foot of Cloudy Mountain, in California, during the days of the gold fever, about 1849–50

The action opens in a saloon owned by Minnie in a California mining camp in 1849. We learn shortly that Sheriff Rance wishes to marry Minnie. She will have naught of him, but when presently Dick Johnson enters she feels strongly attracted toward the newcomer. The men in the saloon disperse to join a posse to pursue a bandit, Ramerrez, and Minnie asks Johnson to visit her in her cabin where they may talk undisturbed.

Act II shows the interior of the cabin, whither Johnson comes through snow and storm. A love scene follows, interrupted by the sheriff knocking at the door. Hurriedly Minnie conceals Johnson in the loft and admits Rance, who tells her he is closing in on the outlaw. When Rance has gone, Johnson confesses to Minnie that he is Ramerrez. Minnie upbraids him and sends him out into the blizzard. Shot by Rance, he staggers back to the cabin wounded. Minnie pityingly hides him in the loft again and almost persuades Rance, who returns full of suspicion, that his quarry is not there, when a telltale drop of blood falls through the ceiling boards on Rance's hand. He demands Johnson, but Minnie proposes they play poker for him. If Minnie wins, Johnson goes free; if she loses, she marries Rance. They play; Minnie cheats and wins.

The last act takes place in a forest where Johnson, who has been captured, is about to be strung up on a tree. Minnie saves him by her pleas to the posse, and together they ride away to begin a new life together in some other place.

P. S.

"When that man gets a score in his hands, he burrows in it like a miner, he penetrates all of it, he uncovers all its gold. When he finds the gold—and occasionally even if he does not find it—he brings every last flake of it to the surface." Puccini said this about Toscanini.* To Toscanini was entrusted the task of preparing the world première of *The Girl of the Golden West* at the Metropolitan. He assumed the task in a season in which he also conducted at the Metropolitan incomparable performances of *Armide, Aïda, Madama Butterfly, Bohème, Gioconda, Orfeo, Tristan, Die Meistersinger, Tosca,* and *Otello.* Puccini had finished the score of *The Girl* at the end of July, 1910. Gatti-Casazza, the new, adroit, and enterprising manager of the Metropolitan, had gone to visit the composer at Torre del Lago and had obtained the new opera for his house. Gatti was able to speak persuasively: not only were the directors of the Metropolitan willing to pay handsomely for the privilege of the première, but he could put at Puccini's disposal the best artistic forces, including Toscanini. Furthermore, wasn't it fitting that this "American opera" should first be heard in America? Gatti knew that a new opera by Puccini was now an event of paramount international importance. Obtaining the production was a feat that would bring him glory, particularly if the composer himself was to be present. It was agreed that Puccini would come to New York to supervise the production.

The excitement over this event was slowly heated to the boiling point in the American way—that is, by planned publicity, bits of which were dropped into the public prints as early as May, 1910, and which continued with increasing frequency to bob up right to the day of the première. The New York public was told, for example, that "Puccini is the most successful of all modern composers from a box-office point of view. His income averages $15,000 a week during the season, for not less than one hundred performances of his operas are given throughout the world at a royalty of $150 each." Caruso stated that the new opera was Puccini's best. Clara Louise Kellogg, the American soprano, said, on the other hand, that "no Italian composer had a right to compose a subject requiring the use of American color," for the Italian composer had absolutely no feeling for atmosphere. . . . Puccini was going to conduct the opera himself. No, he was not, said another story, he was going to stage it. In the meantime, Toscanini had brought Puccini and Mascagni together and the two estranged composers had kissed and made up "and should now collaborate on

* Quoted by Fraccaroli in "La Vita di Puccini."

an ode to macaroni" (*New York World*). Puccini owned "three automobiles, three motorboats, and a well-stocked game preserve." Mme. Nordica said, "Mme. Emmy Destinn, who will sing the title role, is a wonderful artist. . . . I cannot but regret, however, that the artist selected is not an American." It was also predicted that "New Yorkers will see a very much older-looking man than he was when he visited that city in 1906 [*sic*]."

Puccini arrived on November 17th accompanied by his son Tonio and by Tito Ricordi. Having given his usual brilliant shipboard interview (what he said was precisely this: "Thank you, thank you! Much pleased! Long live Italy!"), he went that night to hear Toscanini conduct *Aïda*. Caruso, Destinn, and Amato sang. In later interviews he spoke more fluently. He declared that "the music cannot really be called American, for music has no nationality—it is either music or nothing." Contradicting himself, he then said, "For this drama I have composed music that, I feel sure, reflects the spirit of the American people and particularly the strong, vigorous nature of the West. I have never been West, but I have read so much about it that I know it thoroughly." Asked about his next opera, he said that he wanted a good, lusty comedy, that he was tired of tragic subjects. " 'Like Wagner's *Meistersinger?*' someone asked. Mr. Puccini assumed a reverential air. 'No,' he said, 'there is only one *Meistersinger*'" (*New York Herald*).

As Gatti had promised, the cast represented the best that the Metropolitan could offer, which meant that it was the best that the world could offer. Emmy Destinn was Minnie, Caruso was Dick Johnson, Amato was the Sheriff Rance. Belasco took an active part in the rehearsals, intent, he said, "to make the artists act as well as sing." He was much flattered to participate in the production of a grand opera and Puccini was "frankly demonstrative in his delight."

In contrast to [his wife] Elvira's letters to him, his letters to her abound with excitement:

December 7th

The rehearsals are going very well. I believe it will be a success and let's hope it will be a big one. Tomorrow is the dress rehearsal. After the première there will be a supper and reception at the Vanderbilts' and perhaps others to follow—what a pleasure! . . . Tonio is well but I believe he is enamored of a ballerina. It is certain that whenever he can he runs off and I find myself alone. However, he is a good boy and one ought to let him live a little. Fosca has written me a charming letter. . . . And you? How are you? I hope you are better. . . . The opera emerges splendidly, the first act a little long, but the second act magnificent and the third grandiose. Belasco has attended all the rehearsals with great love and interest. Caruso is magnificent in his part, Destinn not bad but she needs more energy. Toscanini, the *zenith!—kind, good, adorable*—in short, I am content with my work and I hope for the best. But how tremendously difficult it is, this music and the staging! . . . I can't wait for the hour to see my little nuisance of a wife again (I am one too, don't get offended). . . .

On December 10, 1910, the opera was performed for the first time. The première was probably the most spectacular and bejeweled event that had ever taken place at the Metropolitan. All of the artistic and social world of New York attempted to be present. The demand for tickets was frantic. Subscribers to the Metropolitan had first choice of seats, at doubled prices. In order to buy a seat, one had to sign the ticket stub; before entering the theater, one had to countersign the ticket. The two signatures were then compared by the doormen at the entrance. If they tallied, you were allowed to enter the sacred precincts. This measure was to prevent ticket speculators from getting hold of the tickets. It was only partially successful; nothing invented by man can stump a ticket speculator. They asked—and received—incredible sums for tickets (as high as thirty times the box-office price) and a brisk business was done in forged signatures. The delay necessitated by countersigning the tickets clogged the lobby of the Metropolitan and in turn created such a traffic jam outside the lobby that all traffic in the vicinity of the opera house came to a standstill. Special police were called out to push back the mob of curious sightseers. The opera could not start on time, though the first automobiles and carriages had drawn up to the opera house as early as seven o'clock.

The performance, led by Toscanini, was resplendent and fiery to the last degree. Here he brought to the surface every last flake of a gold—that wasn't there. The staging also was splendid, thanks to Belasco's master touches. Certainly no trouble had been spared: eight horses galloped onstage during the last act. The elegant audience forgot to be elegant and shouted its pleasure with a will that would have done credit to the audience of a provincial Italian theater. When Puccini appeared for the first time before the curtain, a silver crown was placed on his brow by Gatti-Casazza. Bouquets of flowers were hurled onto the stage. There were fifty-two curtain calls in all, twenty of them after the end of the opera.

When the curtain was lowered for the last time, everyone congratulated everyone else, and Puccini was kissed by one and all. He said to Toscanini and the singers, "My heart is beating like the double-basses in the card scene. I am tremendously pleased with this reception. I couldn't have had better interpreters for my work." He believed, as did everyone else connected with the production, that the new opera was destined for a long and healthy life.

The critics praised the work, though Richard Aldrich of *The New York Times,* who was one of New York's rational and fair-minded music critics, reserved judgment. Unable to praise and unwilling to condemn the opera at short notice, he spoke of its novel features and observed that "there is much that is significant and interesting to be noted in the score," and that Puccini "has now gone still further into this field of augmented intervals and chords of the higher dissonances. He has made much use of the so-called 'whole-tone' scale and the harmonies that associate themselves with it. In a word, there is a marked predilection for the idiom that is coupled particularly with the name of Debussy. . . ."

Puccini was very grateful to Toscanini. Homeward-bound on board the *Lusitania,* he wrote to Elvira:

December 29, 1910

. . . The Toscaninis were very good to me. Carla [Mrs. Toscanini] came to help me pack. I made him a present of a silver table candelabrum which cost $300. . . .*

He had no reason to be pessimistic of his work subsequently. In Rome, Berlin, Vienna, and other cities, at each première, the opera was greeted with immense enthusiasm. At the Metropolitan it was repeated no fewer than eight times in the same season. Only gradually did it become apparent that the new work was a satellite revolving around the sun of Puccini's earlier music and possessing little warmth and light of its own. At the Metropolitan *The Girl* was given thirteen times during the next three years, then fell out of the repertory for fifteen years, to be revived in 1929, when Jeritza appeared as Minnie and in the last act leapt stunningly onto her horse. After the next two seasons, it vanished altogether. In Italy it has fared a little better, though even there it is hardly popular. Occasionally one hears it in an outdoor performance; it can serve as a good spectacle.

I believe *The Girl* to be a remarkably poor opera, all the poorer considering that it followed *Butterfly.* Its first weakness lies in the libretto. We can understand how Puccini may have been led astray by the fascination of Belasco's production of the play. William Winter, in "The Life of David Belasco," writes: "Nothing of the kind which I have ever seen in the Theater has fully equaled in verisimilitude the blizzard on Cloudy Mountain as depicted by Belasco in the Second Act of this fine melodrama—such a bitter and cruel storm of wind-driven snow and ice as he had often suffered under in the strolling days of his nomadic youth." In order to produce this snowstorm and the accompanying moaning of the gale, Belasco employed no fewer than thirty-two assistants, a symphonic band of stagehands, so to speak, who were directed by a centrally located "conductor" and who operated wind and snow machines with the precision of an orchestra, underscoring the lines and helping to give the scene its sense of desolation. In addition, Belasco used a moving panorama which disclosed to the audience first a view of Cloudy Mountain in all its majesty, then seemed to wander down a winding path until it stopped at a settlement where Minnie's saloon, the Polka, was found. The lights were then dimmed for an instant and the scene changed to the interior of the saloon. The action was accompanied by the music of minstrel instruments playing Western and Stephen Foster melodies. No doubt extraordinarily effective! But once

* Toscanini still has the candelabrum. It was bought at Tiffany's.

Puccini had returned home and had sat down to a perusal of the script, he may well have discovered how childish the play really was.

G. R. M.

Even if the music of *La Fanciulla* were good (which it is not), the libretto would prove an all but insuperable bar to sincere appreciation. Singers dressed up as frontiersmen and shouting Italian in a Wild West saloon (the Polkadot) cannot be regarded, particularly by Americans, as the vessels of serious opera. If this obstacle deprived us of the ability to listen properly to some of Puccini's best music, rewriting the book might be worth the trouble. But *La Fanciulla* is as hopeless musically as it is theatrically. The shadows on Puccini's life do not show in it, but the lack of inspiration that visited him because of them is only too evident. Technical care is in the score, the attempt to capture the American flavor by use of native tunes, the gestures of a master craftsman— all are there, and yet fail utterly to animate this musical cadaver. In fact, *La Fanciulla* must have made some of Puccini's warmest admirers fear that the comet-like ascent had ended. *La Rondine,* which issued still-born from his pen in 1917, after seven long years of waiting, was a poor Viennese-waltz operetta —which, nevertheless, Bori used, on March 21, 1936, as her farewell to opera. It must have made them shudder for his future. At fifty-nine, it is not easy to make a comeback.

W. B., H. W.

Gianni Schicchi

OPERA IN 1 ACT

Book by GIOACCHINO FORZANO

First performance: Metropolitan Opera House, New York, Dec. 14, 1918

CHARACTERS

Gianni Schicchi, BARITONE	*Rinuccio,* TENOR
Lauretta, SOPRANO	*La Ciesca,* MEZZO-SOPRANO
Zita, CONTRALTO	*Nella,* MEZZO-SOPRANO

The action takes place in Dante's Florence

In the Florence of Dante's time Buoso Donati, recently deceased, has left all his property to charity. His thunderstruck relatives, gathered in the death chamber, rack their brains for a plan to circumvent this diversion. On the insistence of young Rinuccio they decide to call in Gianni Schicchi, a local character of great wit and resourcefulness, whose daughter Lauretta happens to be Rinuccio's beloved.

When Gianni Schicchi arrives, he quickly conceives a scheme that seems to be the only solution of the problem. Whereupon it is immediately put into action. Donati's body is removed, and Schicchi gets into the bed to impersonate the dead man, of whose demise no one with the exception of the relatives knows. Consequently, when the doctor calls on a visit, he is fooled completely. Seeing now that the plan will work, Gianni Schicchi sends for a notary and witnesses for the drawing up of a new will.

Instead of distributing the Donati possessions to the anxious kinsfolk, however, the masquerader wills the bulk of the estate to Gianni Schicchi! And there is nothing the distracted relatives can do about it because of their part in the deception.

P. S.

La Rondine [his previous opera] finished, Puccini turned again to the project of three one-act operas. He took up *Il Tabarro,* which he had begun in 1913, and completed it late in 1916. Now a new young playwright, Giovacchino Forzano, brought him two ideas. One was a mystic play, its scene set in a convent, its cast entirely made up of nuns. The other was a comic plot, taking as its hero a Florentine miscreant who appears briefly in Dante's *Divine Comedy.* Puccini was delighted with both ideas. His reaction was immediate. He felt such a lift of spirit, such certainty of being right, as he had not experienced in years. Here was the possibility for three-branched entertainment of varied hues, of contrasting moods. Here also was the opportunity of entering two fields unexplored by him: the mystic and the comic.

Puccini bade Forzano to proceed with both librettos, *Suor Angelica* (Sister Angelica) and *Gianni Schicchi*. While the playwright was at work, Puccini kept thinking about the comic subject. He had for so long wished to write a comic opera, so long indeed that he now could not wait any longer. He *had* to compose a comic opera before he did anything else. He asked Forzano to stop work on *Suor Angelica* and write the libretto of *Gianni Schicchi* first. He couched his request in four lines of doggerel:

> *Dopo il Tabarro di tinta nera*
> *sento la voglia di buffeggiare.*
> *Lei non si picchi*
> *se faccio prima quel Gianni Schicchi.**

> (After Tabarro's black tint
> I feel the need to jest.
> Don't be annoyed
> If I first do that Gianni Schicchi.)

First that *Gianni Schicchi*—and it proved to be an altogether delightful libretto. It was easy to see that Forzano was an experienced librettist who knew his business.† Puccini asked for very few changes; there were no such troubles as had beset him with his two preceding operas. There was no need now for the stumbling and retracing of steps, for the weary redoing of lines and situations. The two plays were original subjects. Because Forzano did not have to translate an existing book or play into operatic verses, his task was freer and easier than those of his predecessors. And Puccini could save his energy for the music. He seemed to be young again and to work with the enthusiasm that he had commanded in his best days. The enterprising energy of Gianni Schicchi himself passed into Puccini, buoyed him up, and carried him on to the final opera of the three. Possessing librettos in which he believed with heart and soul, he was able to compose the music joyfully and quickly. He finished both works in a few months.

When Puccini had finished the score of *Suor Angelica,* he submitted the music to a curious audition. He took the manuscript to the nunnery where his sister Iginia lived and played the music to the assembled nuns. He wished to know if they found it in their hearts to forgive Suor Angelica, who had sinfully borne a child. He explained the story to them and then played parts of the

---

* Quoted by Fraccaroli in "La Vita di Puccini."

† Forzano had provided Mascagni with the good libretto of *Lodoletta,* an opera given for the first time in Rome in the same spring in which *La Rondine* was performed in Monte Carlo. *Lodoletta* was an adaptation of Ouida's novel "Two Little Wooden Shoes," which Puccini had considered setting to music.

music. The nuns found it beautiful—Puccini saw tears in their eyes—and at the end, when Angelica pleads, "Madonna, Madonna, save me for the sake of my son!" they absolved their fictional sister.

Once again the Metropolitan carried off the prize of the première. The Tryptich (*Il Trittico*), as the three one-acters were awkwardly named, was given for the first time in New York on December 14, 1918. . . .

Puccini did not journey to New York for this première. It was but a month after the armistice, and travel conditions were as yet uncertain. Nor was Toscanini present. The three operas were conducted by Moranzoni. Again the cast was an illustrious one. Claudia Muzio sang Giorgetta, the heroine of *Il Tabarro*, Geraldine Farrar was Suor Angelica, and De Luca was Gianni Schicchi. Florence Easton played the part of Lauretta, his daughter, and therefore has the distinction of having first sung that ubiquitous aria, "Oh mio babbino caro!" ("Oh my darling daddy!"). Despite this excellent cast, the first two of the three operas did not meet with much favor. That lack of initial success presaged the fate of *Il Tabarro* and *Suor Angelica,* two operas which have never been popular, either in our country or abroad. But *Gianni Schicchi* was a different story. It was an immediate success. Henry Krehbiel, writing in the *New York Tribune,* reported:

> An invigorating breeze blew through the theater when the curtain rose on *Gianni Schicchi.* . . . This comedy is so uproariously funny, the music so full of life, humor, and ingenious devices, that though there is less singing than in the preceding pieces, it was received with uproarious delight. . . .

The news that he had succeeded with his comic opera, that *Gianni Schicchi* had been welcomed with "uproarious delight," was but a mitigated joy to the composer. Two-thirds of the *Trittico* had *not* pleased. He considered this defeat and determined that the Rome première would have to be an especially fine performance. *Suor Angelica* was particularly dear to his heart, according to Gilda Della Rizza, who played the part in Rome. He felt for this music "a special predilection." Della Rizza worked long hours, day and night, under Puccini's direction to perfect the role. Puccini was, as always, terribly nervous. He supervised all rehearsals himself and frequently resorted to camphor injections to keep up his energy.

But at the Costanzi Theater it was also *Gianni Schicchi* which elicited the most enthusiastic approval, though the entire evening was a festive one at which members of the royal family, including the King and the Queen, were present. Aside from Gilda Della Rizza, the cast included Carlo Galeffi as Gianni Schicchi and Maria Labia as the heroine of *Il Tabarro.* The tenor parts in *Gianni Schicchi* and in *Il Tabarro* were sung by one Eduardo Di Giovanni, who evidenced, according to the *Corriere d'Italia,* "uncommon acting and vocal ability," and sang the hymn to Florence "in a magic manner." This tenor is better known to us as Edward Johnson. . . .

It is easy to understand why *Gianni Schicchi* should have outshone its companions and why the people, when they left the theater, should have remembered little else but the final act. *Gianni Schicchi* is bright and brilliant. The plot is entertaining, the central character being one of those rotund rogues that never fail to please us because they are so much cleverer than we are. . . .

Dante entirely disapproved of Gianni Schicchi. Dante meets the shade of Gianni Schicchi in the company of "flagitious Myrrha, who loved her father with more than rightful love" (Canto XXX of "Inferno"). Was Dante particularly severe on Gianni because Dante's wife was a member of the Donati family? Or did the poet have no use for humor?

Though Dante discussed Schicchi with quick scorn, Puccini treated him with very loving care. He is perhaps the only completely successful male character the composer put on the stage, and in writing music for him, he summoned a fresh, free vigor. The music is packed with sunshine and is pleasantly melodious in the moments when comedy stops and sentiment begins, such as when Lauretta makes an appeal to her father or Rinuccio sings of the beauties of Florence. Here again we have the Puccini who is able to create a convincing atmosphere, who invents a style that is indigenous to the work, who produces an entity, a little world that seems to exist. It has been said that the music expresses the beauty of Florence. I doubt if we would say so did we not see, through the open windows, the outlines of Arnolfo's Tower. But even if the geography of the opera were indeterminate, we would feel that the music belongs in a sunny city. The musical style of *Gianni Schicchi* represents a departure from Puccini's previous style, is exactly right for comedy, and is abetted by ingenious orchestration. Occasionally Puccini pokes fun at himself and parodies his own sentimental melodies. The blending of sentiment and sarcasm is an especially ingratiating feature. In music it is possible to mix oil and cold water. Puccini mixes short, mordant phrases with long, leisurely melodies, giving the opera a fine variety. The lights go on and off, though it never gets dark. Altogether, this is a real comedy and possesses that special brand of Mediterranean merriment which is half good-nature and half spite. . . .

G. R. M.

Turandot

OPERA IN 3 ACTS

Book by Giuseppe Adami and Renato Simoni

First performance: La Scala, Milan, Apr. 25, 1926

CHARACTERS

Princess Turandot, SOPRANO
The Emperor Altoum, her father, TENOR
Timur, dethroned Tatar King, BASS
Prince Calaf, the Unknown Prince,
   Timur's son, TENOR
Liù, a young slave girl, SOPRANO

Ping, the Grand Chancellor, BARITONE
Pang, the General Purveyor, TENOR
Pong, the Chief Cook, TENOR
A Mandarin, BARITONE
The Prince of Persia, BARITONE
The Executioner, BARITONE

The action takes place in Peking during legendary times

Amid the confusion of the listening crowd that has gathered at the Imperial Palace, an old man makes his way, supported and guided by a young slave girl, Liù. Suddenly a youth hurries toward them from the crowd. Their whispered conversation reveals that the old man is the dethroned Timur, King of the Tatars, the youth, his son, Calaf, called the "Unknown Prince." Soon there is a movement of agitation in the crowd, because the Prince of Persia, attempting to solve Turandot's riddles, and failing, as all others have done, is now being led to execution. For the Princess Turandot, as a mandarin has previously announced, has decreed that whosoever would win her hand must solve three riddles, and, failing, suffer death. The people, moved by the youthfulness of the Persian prince, cry for mercy. But Turandot, when she appears upon the balcony, silences them by the mere sight of her matchless beauty. The thud of the executioner's ax is heard, then the head of the Persian prince is seen, raised on a pike over the city gates.

The Unknown Prince is greatly thrilled by the beauty of Turandot. Forgetting her cruelty and heedless of the prayers of his father and Liù, and of the warnings of the ghosts of Turandot's executed lovers, and unmindful of the counsels of the three court officials, Ping, Pang, and Pong, he determines to brave the Princess' enigmas. In token of which he sounds the great gong that hangs at the palace gate three times, calling out the name of the Princess.

Accordingly there assembles a multitude of great personages on the staircase that leads to the Imperial Palace. Turandot, coming before them, tells of her grandmother, the chaste Princess Lo-u-ling, who, ravished by the invading Tatars, died most unhappy. To avenge her ancestor's wrongs, Turandot has meted out a cruel fate to all who would be her suitors. She turns to the Unknown Prince, and propounds her direful enigmas. One by one the Unknown Prince answers them, boldly and correctly; he is greeted by shouts of joy from all except Turandot. The Princess, dismayed, begs to be saved from the stranger; but her father, Emperor and guardian of the law, decrees that her word must be held sacred. Turandot therefore pleads with the conqueror for her freedom, and he, answering, says that he will indeed release her from her vow and give up his life even as though he had failed in the trial, should she be able to learn his name ere the morrow.

Thus it comes about that during the entire night heralds search through all the city, but none they find who can rightly name the Unknown Prince. Someone then whispers that an old man and the girl Liù had been seen with him. They are brought to the palace, but Liù cries out that she alone knows the Prince's name, and then, fearing she may reveal the secret during the tortures to which she will be subjected, she quickly seizes a dagger from one of the soldiers and plunges it into her heart. Turandot is troubled—what moved the girl to such self-sacrifice? The Prince, reproaching Turandot, clasps her passionately. Thus is the Princess vanquished, and she confesses that she loves the Unknown Prince. He likewise says that such is his love that he would be happy to die for her, and reveals his name. Knowing him to be the enemy Tatar prince, Turandot again becomes proud and unattainable. Dawn now approaching, she leads him to the palace to announce her victory and his doom. At the throne of the great Emperor she cries out that she has learned the stranger's name; then looking at Calaf, she is shaken by a strange emotion, and murmurs, "His name is Love!" And the multitude that has assembled sings for joy.*

Gozzi was a Venetian playwright of the eighteenth century whose plays were a blend of the fabulous and the comic. It was this blend which at once appealed to Puccini. In the one-acters, he had tried his hand at the mystic and the comic, as separate ingredients. Could he now combine them in one work? Could he combine, as Gozzi had done, serious drama with *commedia dell' arte*? "Yes," said Puccini, and his eyes shone. "Perhaps Gozzi is what we need. *Turandot*. I have seen the play done by Reinhardt in Germany." While Puccini was packing his valise, Simoni telephoned home and had a copy of "Turandot" sent over. It was, however, not the play by Gozzi which he handed to Puccini but, as it turned out, an Italian translation of the German play by Friedrich Schiller, a play based on Gozzi's original "fable" in which Schiller had ennobled Gozzi's work, furnishing it not only with resounding verse but also with Schillerian philosophy. This was the "Turandot" which Puccini read on the train home. Arrived home, he immediately sent a letter to his two friends asking them to go ahead.

This was in the summer of 1920. Here began the longest and most agonizing wrestling with a subject, the most minute examination of word and syllable, the most insistent pleadings, recriminations, encouragements, reproaches,

---

* From "The Victor Book of Operas."

praises, and condemnations, the most arduous redoing and rewriting that any of Puccini's librettists had to suffer.

Though he could not have known that he was never to complete the task, he may have felt that this was the last music he was to write. Thus he became, not only with his librettists but above all with himself, a frightening task-master. He was bent on doing something new, determined to write music of much larger scope, of legendary stature and philosophic implication. *Turandot* was to be his "most important" work. He wished his music to take place in an Oriental, stately pleasure dome, a very different abode from the little house on the hill which had been leased for ninety-nine years. . . .

By the spring of 1921, he began the composition [of *Turandot*], though he was not as yet in possession of the entire libretto. In the late summer, Puccini moved from the house at which he had spent the major part of his life. A peat factory had been erected near his villa at Torre del Lago. The noise and the smell bothered him, the bustle encroached on his privacy. He chose as his next dwelling Viareggio, not far from Torre. He knew the resort well: he had visited it often; his yacht was anchored there. Viareggio was then a quiet seaside resort with a quiet white beach. Today it is a commercial resort, not quite so crowded as Asbury Park but almost as garish. The villa that Puccini built for himself still stands. Most of its furnishings are gone, destroyed by the billeting army or taken away by souvenir hunters. The house is large and is situated some distance from the sea, near the beginning of a pine forest. It is on low-lying ground and is surrounded by pine trees. A forbidding fence separates it from the adjoining properties. It is solid but gloomy and looks, in contrast to the bright little villas, as withdrawn as were its occupants. In constructing this villa, Puccini indulged his fancy for gadgets. The main gate contained a brass plaque. It looked like an ordinary plaque, but if you touched it on a certain spot the gate would open. Puccini's friends knew the combination. His studio was connected by a private staircase to his bedroom, so that at night he could go down to his piano without disturbing the family, who slept upstairs. All kinds of electric bells were installed in the house. The pines around the house concealed water spouts within their branches. By turning a faucet, Puccini could command an artificial rain which spouted from the trees onto the roof of the house. He bought a radio, complete with headphones, and became an avid fan, searching for the signals of faraway stations. He once heard an act of *Bohème* broadcast from London.

Ensconced in his new and spacious villa, he continued to worry over *Turandot*. Sometimes "the sun shines for me," which meant that he was satisfied with his work; at other times he did not know "whether it is work to tear up or to keep." The second-act libretto and music gave him great difficulty, and toward the autumn of 1921 the work languished and he contemplated the possibility of throwing it on the scrap heap. Then, of course, he was "very nearly fed up with my life—and old age is knocking at the door." He became intimidated by the magnitude of the task. The usual doubts came to the fore. He made renewed overtures to Forzano; wished that instead of this formidable fairy tale he could now find "a charming, light, sentimental subject"; still made efforts to save *La Rondine* by again changing the music; and then once more returned to Turandot, the Princess who, though she had "ice in her veins," held him enthralled. It was a constant seesaw of elation and despondency, certainty and doubt, of feeling young and feeling old. He had "such a horror of old age" that he wanted to go to Vienna to have a rejuvenating operation performed on himself. He wrote to Sybil [Seligman]:

January 26, 1923

. . . I think in March I shall go to Vienna to see that doctor! I've met a South American gentleman here, sixty-seven years old, who tells me that the operation is nothing at all and that the benefits are extraordinary—he says he feels as though he were twenty-five again, and that it no longer tires him to walk and his mind is fresh and agile, etc., etc.—why shouldn't I do it too? My dear, my life is my own and means the whole world to me—so why not?

He never went. The only discovery in medicine from which in his last year he benefited was insulin.

Puccini toiled on, drove himself, raced against time, composed quickly—then tore up what he had composed, went back to the libretto to change it, then restarted and recorrected the music. From his letters we may glimpse his struggle:

Turandot gives me no peace. . . . I am in black despair about *Turandot.* . . . We shall win. . . . I have been passing through a crisis with regard to my music. . . . I am in a fever to have some work to do. . . . I have tried again and again to write the music for the introductory scene of Act II and cannot. . . . No! No! No! *Turandot* no! I have received Act III. It is quite impossible. Perhaps—and maybe there's no perhaps—*I* am no longer possible. . . . I stick to my table all day and every day. I am orchestrating. . . . I can assure you that it is going to be beautiful. Shall I be proved wrong, I wonder? You never know nowadays. . . . Hour by hour and minute by minute I think of *Turandot,* and all the music I have written up to now seems a jest in comparison and pleases me no more. . . .

Finally he wrote to Gilda Della Rizza [the soprano]:

Viareggio, February 25, 1924

. . . I am a hermit here. I work from morning to night. I am well advanced, almost at the end. I am satisfied with my work. We shall see how the cruel Princess, once she will show herself at the big show-window [La Scala], will be welcomed. But I'm not thinking about that! I have done as well as I could and am pleased. I don't believe that the part of Turandot is anything for you, but assuredly Liù (the slave), a first-class part as good as the other, is made to order for Gilda. . . .

Of late he had been plagued by a pain in his throat, a pain similar to but now more severe than those he had felt in times past. He wrote to Adami on September 1, 1924: "The trouble in my throat that has been worrying me since March was beginning to appear serious. I am feeling better now, and have, moreover, the assurance that it is rheumatic in origin and that with treatment I shall be cured. But I have had some very black days." He announced in the same letter that Carlo Clausetti [of Ricordi's] had called on him yesterday, and that on his advice he had promised the opera for the Scala. He added, "I wonder if I was wise." The score was finished up to about the middle of the third act. . . . On the sixth of September, Arturo Toscanini—now since his angry departure from the Metropolitan active as the leading conductor of La Scala—called on Puccini in Viareggio. The following day, Puccini joyfully wrote to Adami: "Toscanini has just gone. We are in perfect agreement, and I breathe at last. So the weight is lifted which has oppressed me since April." The end of the troublesome Princess was in sight. He added a postscript: "The little that I played to Toscanini seemed to make a good impression." A fuller audition of the opera was held toward the end of September in one of the small rooms of the Scala Opera House. Renato Simoni was present at this audition. He recalls that Puccini played the music and sang in a hoarse, small voice. As the audition went on, dusk fell and the light faded, but Puccini did not notice. He was pale, his face was gray, he was utterly absorbed in his playing—his body hunched over the score. Toscanini sat next to him and turned the pages. He said little but every so often he patted Puccini on the back. When Puccini had finished, Toscanini expressed himself quietly but decisively. He did not break out into wild enthusiasm; he turned to the exhausted composer with simple solicitude and said, "This is a fine work."

The opera was still unfinished and the problem of the final duet remained unsolved. Puccini wrote to Adami: "It must be a great duet. These two almost superhuman beings descend through love to the level of mankind, and this love must at the end take possession of the whole stage in a great orchestral peroration." Orchestral peroration? Did Puccini mean to close the opera with the orchestra playing the leading part? In the meantime, preparations for the performance were going ahead at La Scala. The painter Galileo Chini was commissioned to design scenery and costumes. . . .

[The condition in Puccini's throat was ultimately diagnosed as cancer. An operation was performed in Brussels on November 24. Four days later he died of a heart attack, almost his last thought being the opera he was working on.]

Puccini had left *Turandot* unfinished. He had planned the final duet and the last scene and left behind him a few sketches. Franco Alfano, a friend of Puccini's and of Toscanini's and a respected opera composer known in Italy for his operas *Sakuntala, Resurrection,* and *The Shade of Don Giovanni,* was entrusted with the task of completing the work. He executed the difficult as-signment as well as he could, as a labor of love, knowing that no matter how he did it he was likely to be criticized. He wrote, he says, a great deal of music which was "willfully" cut. There is no question that had Puccini lived to finish his work, the last duet between Turandot and Calaf—and indeed the entire opera—would have emerged as finer and greater music. Puccini considered this final duet of the greatest importance. From it was to emerge a new Turandot, human, womanly, passionate. In other respects also Puccini would no doubt have improved the work. *Turandot* suffers occasionally from dramatic vague-ness and in certain spots—particularly the first scene of the second act, which presents Ping, Pang, and Pong in philosophic ruminations—from undue length. It is quite likely that Puccini's theatrical instinct would have righted these wrongs had he had time. . . .

Why should this libretto have caused so many difficulties? There were sev-eral causes. The first was a practical one. Adami had become, by the time *Turandot* was commissioned, a successful playwright who could by no means give all of his time to one libretto. Puccini told him that he was happy when he saw that Adami's current play was a success; as long as it drew full houses, Adami would work for him. But the playwright had to worry about his next play, and we can understand that, with all his devotion to Puccini, Adami was more important to Adami. In the second place, it can be said of this libretto, more than of any other, that Puccini wrote it himself and that it would have been easier had he actually written it himself. As it was, he sent off detailed prose versions to Adami—Calaf is to cry thus and thus, the scene is to proceed at once to the torture of Liù, we must have the following soliloquy here, etc., etc.—and left it to the poets to put Puccini's prose into verse. Then, when Puccini received the verses, he was not satisfied or had changed his mind about the particular dramatic fragment. Frequently he suggested two or three dif-ferent versions, adding to Adami's and Simoni's bewilderment. Third and most important, the composer was attempting to preserve something of the spirit of the old play and at the same time he was attempting to add to it the softness and mysticism which he needed for his music. A difficult business! He took over from Gozzi's play the clownish figures, familiar in the *commedia dell' arte*, who weave their path through the action, comment on it, but take no part in it. In *Turandot* Gozzi uses four of them, Pantalone, Tartaglia, Brighella, and Truffaldino. The company of actors for which Gozzi wrote in-cluded four famous actors who specialized in these parts and who were mas-ters at improvisation. These types have an ancient lineage. They had served innumerable playwrights before Gozzi. Puccini reduced the four figures to three and made Ping the Grand Chancellor, Pang the General Purveyor, and Pong the Chief Court Cook. They are not individuals; they sing and act as a trinity. But now they are no longer figures of mere comedy; they are sad

as often as they are merry and in their main scene (Act II, Scene 1) they appear as faded philosophers longing to get away from this bloody and unrestful
court, lamenting that love and quietude have vanished from the world, wishing that they could forget human folly in the peace of the country. They possess
more than a measure of modern melancholy. When Puccini did allow them
to be humorous, he wished their humor to be in the grand or Shakespearean
manner. He instructed Adami: "Do a little of what Shakespeare often does,
when he brings in three or four extraneous types who drink, use bad language,
and speak ill of the King. I have seen this done in 'The Tempest,' among the
Elves and Ariel and Caliban." All this is foreign to Gozzi's fable. "Leave Gozzi
alone for a bit," he demanded, "and work with your own logic and imagination," meaning work with *my* logic and imagination. . . .

   The first performance of *Turandot* was given at La Scala on the twenty-fifth
of April, 1926, a year and four months after the composer's death. It took that
long a time for the completion of the opera, the construction of the scenery,
and the rehearsing of the cast under Toscanini. Rosa Raisa was Turandot,
Maria Zamboni was Liù, Michele Fleta sang Calaf. Some days before his death,
Puccini had realized that he was never going to finish the work. He had said,
"The opera will be given incomplete and somebody will come forward and
say: 'At this point the composer died.'" At the première, at the point halfway
through the third act, Toscanini turned to the audience and said, "Here the
Maestro laid down his pen." These were probably the only public words ever
spoken by Toscanini in a theater. The curtain fell slowly.

G. R. M.

   Turandot is interesting chiefly because in it post-Verdian Italian operatic
music, veristic and romantic, meets, and momentarily merges with, the surge
of influences from northern and eastern Europe—the post-Wagnerism of
Strauss, the atonality of Schönberg, and the polyrhythms and savage colors of
Stravinsky. Whereas in *Madama Butterfly* Puccini had imported Japanese
gramophone records for his exotic *appliqué* work, in *Turandot* he made a profound study of Chinese music and emerged with results reminiscent of Debussy's dilettante reactions to Javanese and Annamese music. In this complex
score, Puccini never forgets that he is creating a musicodramatic work, and is
almost always master of his materials. Yet it is Puccini all the way through,
with a new genius for tragic utterance that reaches its height in the music he
gave to the pitiable Liù. At its worst, where the ultramodern elements do not
mix with the indigenous musical speech, *Turandot* may sound like *Butterfly*
with wrong notes. Flawed though it is, and lacking the final polish that Puccini
might have given it, *Turandot* is a worthy crown to his career of ever-increasing
knowledge. With something slightly less than genius to work with, he might
have gone on because of his insatiable intellect, his unimpaired melodic gift,

and his technical mastery, to produce works in his old age as far ahead of *Manon Lescaut* as *Falstaff* was of *Ernani*. At sixty-six, he died too young.

W. B., H. W.

[The American première of *Turandot* occurred at the Metropolitan Opera House on November 16, 1926, with Maria Jeritza in the title role and Martha Attwood, Giacomo Lauri-Volpi, and Giuseppe de Luca among the other singers. It is widely believed that Puccini designed the part of Turandot with Mme. Jeritza, whom he greatly admired, in mind.]

Henry Purcell

(London, 1658 (or 1659)–Nov. 20, 1695, London)

On 3rd September 1658, Oliver Cromwell anticipated Beethoven by dying during a terrific storm. The Commonwealth was ended and the power of the Puritans broken. In 1660 Charles II succeeded to the throne and there came about an inevitable reaction against the rigours of the Puritan mode of life. Cynicism and profligacy became fashionable; Charles and his Court emulated the luxurious living of the French king, Louis XIV. Evelyn [the diarist] describes how he saw in the royal palace "the new fabric of French tapestry, for design, tenderness of work, and incomparable imitation of the best paintings beyond anything I had ever beheld. Some pieces had Versailles, St. Germain's, and other palaces of the French king, with huntings, figures and landscapes, exotic fowls, and all to the life rarely done. Then for Japan cabinets, screens, pendule clocks, great vases of wrought plate, table-stands, chimney furniture, sconces, branches, brasenas, etc., all of massy silver, and out of number, besides some of her majesty's best paintings." Evelyn gives a picture of the scene at Court six days before Charles's death:

I can never forget the inexpressible luxury, and profaneness, gaming, and all dissoluteness, and, as it were, total forgetfulness of God (it being Sunday evening), which this day se'nnight I was witness of: the king sitting and toying with his concubines, Portsmouth, Cleveland, and Mazarine, etc.; a French boy singing love-songs in that glorious gallery, whilst about twenty of the great courtiers and other dissolute persons were at basset round a large table, a bank of at least £2,000 in gold before them; upon which two gentlemen who were with me made reflections with astonishment.

In 1662 a theatre in Lincoln's Inn Fields was opened, and in the following year another appeared in Drury Lane. In 1671 there was built in Dorset Gardens, near the Temple, another, which specialised in elaborate and spectacular musical productions, such as a version of Shakespeare's "Macbeth" with appropriate incidental music. But in the name of "entertainment" many liberties were taken with Shakespeare, or whoever the author happened to be. New characters were introduced, cuts were made in order to make way for remarkable transformation scenes that smacked of magic and mystery, and songs and dances were added to increase the appeal. In Shakespearian productions a tradition was begun that found its apotheosis in Sir H. Beerbohm Tree's productions at His Majesty's Theatre before the last war.

Among such conditions Henry Purcell, one of England's greatest composers, was born, it is said, in 1658, at a house in St. Anne's Lane, Old Pye Street,

Westminster. Little is known about the origin of his family and hardly more about his life, which is wrapped in obscurity. Purcell's father, also named Henry, held several important posts as a professional musician. He was a Gentleman of the Chapel Royal and sang in the choir at Charles II's coronation. He was also a member of the Royal Band and sang at Westminster Abbey, where he was choirmaster and music copyist, the latter an important position in view of the fairly wholesale destruction of church music during the Puritan regime. Pepys records in his diary on 21st February 1659, that, "after dinner, I went back to Westminster Hall with him [Mr. Crewe] in his coach. Here I met with Mr. Lock and Pursell, Masters of Musique, and went with them to the Coffee House, into a room next the water, by ourselves, where we spent an hour or two. . . . Here we had a variety of brave Italian and Spanish songs, and a canon for eight voices, which Mr. Lock had lately made. . . ."

Purcell appears to have received his first musical instruction from his father at about the tender age of four or five, but on 11th August 1664, Purcell's father died, leaving his son to the care of his brother, Thomas Purcell. Two years previously Thomas Purcell had succeeded Henry Lawes as Musician in Ordinary "for the lute and voyce," for which services he was allowed "the wages and living of six-and-thirty pounds two shillings and sixpence by the year during his life." No doubt through his uncle's influence Purcell now became a chorister in the Chapel Royal, where he remained until his voice broke in his 15th year. Purcell studied under Matthew Locke and Captain Henry Cooke, who was Master of the Children. According to Pepys, Cooke was a vain coxcomb who sang uncommonly well. In 1672 Cooke resigned "by reason of sicknesse" and Pelham Humfrey took his place.

Humfrey at the age of seventeen had been sent to Paris by Charles II to learn the French style of composition from the famous composer Lully. Pepys describes him as follows: "Little Pelham Humphreys lately returned from France, and is an absolute Monsieur, as full of form and confidence and vanity, and disparages everything and everybody's skill but his own. But to hear how he laughs at all the King's musick here, at Blagrave and others, that they cannot keep time or tune, nor understand anything: and at Grebus, the Frenchman, the King's Master of Musick, how he understands nothing, nor can play any instrument, and so cannot compose: and that he will give him a lift out of his place, and that he and the King are mighty great." Purcell does not appear to have been influenced by Humfrey's French predilections. In 1673 Purcell, the "late child of his Majesty's Chapell Royal, whose voice is changed, and gon from the Chapell" was given £30 a year together with fine holland, handkerchiefs, a felt hat and (later) "one and twenty ells, three quarters of holland, and four whole shirts, four half shirts and four bands and cuffs" in return for duties as "keeper, maker, mender, repayrer and tuner of the regalls, organs, virginalls, flutes and recorders and all other kind of wind instruments whatsoever, in ordinary, without fee, to his Majesty, and assistant to John Hingston, and upon the death or other avoydance of the latter, to come in ordinary with fee." In the following year Humfrey died and his post was taken by Dr. John Blow, whose pupil Purcell became.

Two years later Purcell was appointed music copyist at Westminster Abbey, which duties he carried out until 1678. Meanwhile he had already several compositions to his credit, among which was an ode for the King's birthday— "The Address of the Children of the Chapel Royal to the King, and their Master, Captain Cooke, on his Majesties Birthday, A.D. 1670, composed by Master Purcell, one of the Children of the said Chapel." In 1676 Purcell composed music for three plays, Shadwell's "Epsom-Wells" and "Libertine" and Dryden's "Aurenge-Zebe."

In 1677, Matthew Locke, one of the great founders of English opera, died and Purcell was made Composer in Ordinary for the Violin. He also composed an "Elegy" in memory of Locke. In 1680 Dr. Blow resigned so that, it is believed, Purcell could succeed to his post as organist of Westminster Abbey. During the same year Purcell composed his famous opera *Dido and Æneas* for a girls' school in Chelsea. The original copy of the libretto bears the following inscription: "An Opera performed at Mr. Josias Priest's Boarding-school at Chelsey, by young gentlewomen, the words made by Mr. Nat. Tate. The Musick composed by Mr. Henry Purcell." This opera is one of the landmarks of English music and is generally considered to be one of the composer's outstanding achievements. Purcell now appears to have been making a good enough living to get married, for about this time he married Frances Peters, who belonged to a well-known family in the parish of St. Margaret's, Westminster.

The year 1682 was eventful. Purcell was appointed organist of the Chapel Royal, his uncle Thomas, who had done so much for him, died, and his first son, John Baptista, was born; three more sons and a daughter followed at intervals. Furthermore, he composed the music for "The inauguration of the truly loyal and right honourable Sir William Pritchard, Knight, lord Mayor of the City of London, president of the honourable Artillery Company, and a member of the worshipful company of Merchant-Taylors. Performed on Monday, September XXX. 1682." The next year saw Purcell as one of the King's Composers, and as a direct consequence he published a set of "Sonnatas in III Parts" for two violins and bass and bearing a dedication to the King. An advertisement appeared in the *London Gazette* pointing out that

These are to give Notice to all Gentlemen that have subscribed to the Proposals Published by Mr. Henry Purcell for the Printing his Sonatas of three Parts for two Violins and Base to the Harpsecord or Organ, that the said Books are now completely finished, and shall be delivered to them upon the 11th June next: and if any who have not yet Subscribed, shall before that time Subscribe, according to the said Proposals (which is Ten Shillings the whole Sett), which are at Mr. Hall's house in Norfolk-street, or at Mr. Playford's and Mr. Carr's shop in the Temple; for the said Books will not after that time be Sold under 15s. the Sett.

Playford was the leading publisher of the time. In one of his publications there appeared a delightful advertisement concerning his business activities:

At Mr. Playford's shop is sold all sorts of ruled paper for musick and books of all sizes ready bound for musick. Also the excellent cordial called "Elixir Proprietatis," a few drops of which drank in a glass of sack or other liquors is admirable for all coughs, consumption of the lungs, and inward distempers of the body; a book of the manner of taking it is given to all those who buy same. Also if a person desires to be furnished with good new Virginals and Harpsicons, if they send to Mr. Playford's shop they may be furnished at reasonable rates to their content.

Characteristic of Purcell's modesty and an interesting insight to his attitude towards French and Italian music is the preface to the set of "Sonnatas in III Parts," which runs:

Ingenious Reader. Instead of an elaborate harangue on the beauty and the charms of Musick which (after all the learned Encomions that words can contrive) commends itself best by the performances of a skilful hand, and an angelical voice: I shall say but a very few things by way of Preface, concerning the following Book, and its Author: for its Author, he has faithfully endeavoured a just imitation of the most fam'd Italian Masters; principally, to bring the Seriousness and gravity of that sort of Musick into vogue and reputation among our Country-men, whose humour, 'tis time now, should begin to loath the levity and balladry of our neighbours. The attempt he confesses to be bold and daring, there being Pens and Artists of more eminent abilities, much better qualified for the imployment than his, or himself, which he well hopes these his weak endeavours, will in due time provoke, and enflame to a more accurate undertaking. He is not asham'd to own his unskilfulness in Italian Language; but that the unhappiness of his Education, which cannot justly be accounted his fault, however he thinks he may warrantably affirm, that he is not mistaken in the power of the Italian Notes, or elegency of their Compositions, which he would recommend to the English Artists. There has been neither care, nor industry wanting, as well in contriving, as revising the whole Work; which had been abroad in the world much sooner, but that he has now thought fit to cause the whole Thorough Bass to be Engraven, which was a thing quite beside his first Resolutions. It remains only that the English Practitioner be enform'd, that he will find a few terms of Art perhaps unusual to him, the chief of which are these following: *Adagio* and *Grave* which imports nothing but a very slow movement: *Presto*, *Largo* and *Vivace*, a very brisk, swift, or fast movement: *Piano*, soft. The Author has no more to add, but his hearty wishes, that his Book may fall into no other hands but theirs who carry Musical Souls about them; for he is willing to flatter himself into a belief, that with Such his labours will seem neither unpleasant, nor unprofitable. Vale.

At the end of the year 1683 Purcell was appointed "keeper, maker, repairer and mender and tuner of all and every his Majesty's musicall wind instruments; that is to say all regalls, virginalls, organs, flutes, recorders and all other kind of wind instruments whatsoever, in the place of John Hingston, deceased." His salary was £60 in addition to any expenses incurred in the execution of his duties.

In 1685 Charles II died and James II ascended the throne, but three years later James fled and in the following year William and Mary were crowned at Westminster Abbey to the strains of Purcell's organ. Apart from his executive work Purcell was turning out a great deal of composition, much of which was connected with the theatre, such as the music for "The Tempest," "The Massacre of Paris," "The Prophetess or the History of Dioclesian" (Beaumont and Fletcher), and Dryden's "Amphitryon." Dryden's interest in Purcell was awakened when he heard the music for "Dioclesian"; in consequence they became great friends and collaborated in several dramatic works. In his dedication to "Amphitryon" Dryden says: "What has been wanting on my part has been abundantly supplied by the Excellent Composition of Mr. *Purcell;* in whose Person we have at length found an *Englishman* equal with the best abroad. At least my Opinion of him has been such, since his happy and judicious Performances in the late Opera, and the Experiences I have had of him, in the setting of my three Songs for this 'Amphitryon': To all which, and particularly to the Composition of the *Pastoral Dialogue,* the numerous Quire of Fair Ladies gave just an Applause on the Third Day."

Purcell followed this up with the music to Dryden's "King Arthur," which is one of Purcell's most ambitious dramatic works. Dryden prefixed to the text a note in which he said that

There is nothing better, than what I intended, than the Musick; which has since arriv'd to a greater perfection in England, than ever formerly; especially passing through the artful hands of Mr. *Purcell,* who has compos'd it with so great a genius, that he has nothing to fear but an ignorant, ill-judging audience. But the numbers of poetry and vocal musick are sometimes so contrary, that in many places I have been oblig'd to cramp my verses and make them rugged to the hearer: of which I have no reason to repent me, because these sorts of Entertainments are principally design'd for the ear and the eye; and therefore, in reason, my art on this occasion ought to be subservient to his.

In a house on the west side of Dean's Yard, Westminster, Purcell died in the presence of his wife and family on November 20th, 1695. On the same morning Purcell had made his Will, which ran: "I Henry Purcell of the Citty of Westminster gent., being dangerously ill as to the constitution of my body but in good and perfect mind and memory (thanks be to God) doe by these presents publish and declare this to be my last Will and Testament And I doe hereby give and bequeath unto my loveing wife ffrances Purcell all my Estate both reall and personall of what nature & kind soever to her and to her Assignes for ever And I doe hereby constitute and appoint my said loveing wife my sole Executrix of this my last Will and Testament revokeing all former Will or Wills." Purcell was buried in the north aisle of Westminster Abbey "in a magnificent manner." The chief cause of his death was undoubtedly consumption, but Sir John Hawkins, the old historian, gives credence to the story that circulated during the eighteenth century to the effect that Purcell died "by a cold which he caught in the night waiting for admittance to his own house." It is said that he was in the habit of keeping late hours and merry company and on one night, "heated with wine from the tavern at an hour later than prescribed him," his wife had the doors bolted against him. Whatever the reason, England lost one of her greatest musicians, who promised even more than he had achieved.

R. H.

Dido and Aeneas

OPERA IN 3 ACTS

Book by NAHUM TATE, after VIRGIL's *Aeneid*

First performance: About 1689 at Josiah Priest's Boarding School at Chelsea

CHARACTERS

(as the parts are assigned in modern productions)

Dido, Queen of Carthage, CONTRALTO
Belinda, a lady in waiting, SOPRANO
Attendant, MEZZO-SOPRANO
Sorceress, CONTRALTO

Aeneas, prominent in the defense
of Troy and legendary founder
of Rome, BARITONE

Spirit, First Witch, Second Witch, Courtiers, Sailors

The action takes place in ancient Carthage

[The tragic story of the Queen of Carthage is drawn from the fourth book of Virgil's "Aeneid." Tate, of course, made some necessary modifications. Since the opera was intended for performance at a girls' school, Dido's death had to be altered. Instead of committing suicide, the queen is made to die of a broken heart. Anna—Dido's confidante and sister—becomes Belinda. And Tate, following a common practice of the London stage, introduced witches as a set of malign, fateful symbols. Having fled devastated Troy, Aeneas is bound for Latium, where the gods are preparing an empire for him. A storm overtakes Aeneas' fleet, forcing him ashore at Carthage. There he and his men are feted by the widowed queen, Dido, who promptly falls in love with him. Though Aeneas returns her love, the gods frown on this union. Reminding Aeneas of his destiny to found a new nation in Italy, they order his departure from Carthage. With a heavy heart Aeneas sails away. Dido utters her great "Lament" and dies.]

Purcell's introduction to the stage dates from the production of Nat Lee's "Theodosius" in 1680. He was twenty-one. It was a momentous year which saw also the production of his first welcome song, his appointment as organist of Westminster Abbey and the composition of his earliest string fantasies. Hitherto, apart from some juvenile anthems, a few single songs, and the Matthew Locke elegy, he had written little, but he had been busy perfecting his technique, copying and studying the methods of his seniors. Suddenly he emerges as a fully fledged composer. "Theodosius" is a work of little practical importance. The music is not even especially characteristic but it contains the seeds of several of the dramatic forms which Purcell used later in his stage music. The only instruments available for the performance seem to have been a harpsichord and two recorders. For this reason the usual overture and act tunes are wanting, the latter being replaced by songs and duets of a formal nature, having no direct bearing on the action but being in the nature of a general commentary on the situation and sung between the scenes. The songs are indeed in a graceful vein and being no doubt sung in a static position, they have little dramatic significance, but "Hail to the myrtle shade" is interesting as a prototype of the triple-time measures with their changing accents . . . while another, sung after the fourth act, has a lovely flowing movement within a perfectly balanced metrical scheme that Purcell rarely attempted. It is a glorious tune, of a type and shape that do not often occur in Purcell, but quite out of keeping with the gory sentiments of the words. For the rest there is a virginal freshness about the whole score, a directness in the word setting and a completely unforced expression.

The scene which gives the play its musical importance in Purcell's development is the opening Temple scene which is the forerunner of the many scenes of ceremonial in his later works. The taste for ritualistic episodes was probably derived immediately from the librettos of Quinault and the French opera of Lully. Such episodes provided the most obvious chance for the introduction of music, with recitatives and choral movements. Purcell opens with a bass solo, "Prepare, prepare, the rites begin," cast in a melodious declamatory vein which shows already his instinct for dramatic invocation. The solo is echoed by a trio of voices, built on the same bass part. Purcell's sense of stage-atmosphere declares itself at once in the brief ensembles with their dramatic use of rests. The initiatory songs are unhappily marred by the rather mincing nature of the words, but there is one exquisite little movement in which Purcell makes the best use of his scanty instruments as an accompaniment to the bass-solo "Hark, behold the heavenly choir," the flutes playing high up in thirds while the voice is kept in unison with the harpsichord bass. The music is all through touched with a naïve and unaffected simplicity. Almost all the words are set syllabically and there is practically no repetition of phrases. The same key prevails throughout except for an occasional song.

For D'Urfey's "Sir Barnaby Whigg" in the following year Purcell wrote one song, "Blow, Boreas, Blow," which Burney declared to be more "super-annuated" in his day than any of Purcell's songs. It is a blustering nautical scena for tenor and bass, which probably was very amusing in the play. In tone it foreshadows many of Purcell's bravura songs, especially those for the bass voice. "Circe," in 1685, was a notable step forward. Purcell was now in the full maturity of his technical powers. Here again he is faced with a long, sacrificial scene. The play, which need not detain us, as Purcell's aid was apparently sought only in this one scene, deals somewhat freely with the Greek legend of Iphigenia in Tauris. The scene is introduced by a brief instrumental prelude leading straight into the priest's invocation (bass solo) which is then taken up by the chorus and developed at length. The measured tread of the instruments, the impressive repetitions of the words "we must, we must" (sacrifice) divided by echoing phrases on the strings, are very similar in style to the sacrificial scene at the opening of *King Arthur*. But the recitative is much more stolid and indeed if it is rightly attributed to Purcell, as it no doubt must be, is rather dull work for him. The choruses are more vital and are effectively repeated. Then comes a passage for two women soloists, the first part of which, with its declamatory introduction, followed by a splendidly vigorous movement on a running bass, is more characteristically Purcellian. There are frequent changes of tempo, an alternation of solo passages and chorus, a dance of magicians and a final invocation, "Pluto, arise," very powerfully set for bass solo and unmistakably touched by a master-hand. This, although somewhat unsatisfactory from an operatic standpoint, concludes the music on a dramatic note and the scene ends with spoken dialogue. "Circe" and "Theodosius," totally impracticable as they are to-day, are nevertheless of interest as stages in Purcell's development. "Circe" shows a much surer grasp of the constructive values of key-contrast and restatement. The choruses are worked out at greater length and with a finer sense of climax, while the instruments are definitely absorbed into the dramatic scheme. The ritualistic element which is to recur in several of Purcell's later works is the basis of his extended choral movements. It is inevitably static in principle but it has not ceased to be theatrically effective from that day to this.

During the next few years, Purcell wrote little for the theatre except incidental songs and the only play in which he was concerned that calls for notice is D'Urfey's comedy "A Fool's Preferment," a version of Fletcher's "Noble Gentleman," which has half a dozen songs of a kind that was very popular in the 17th century. These are the so-called mad songs.* They are of two kinds—one in which the subject is represented as genuinely distracted by grief or disappointed love (such as the well-known "Bess o' Bedlam," Purcell's finest song in the scena form) and the other in which, for dramatic or comic purposes, the subject performs "all the degrees of madness"—such is the "whimsical variety" with which Altisidora teases the grotesque Knight in "Don Quixote." †

In D'Urfey's comedy the songs are sung by a character who is discovered "crown'd with flowers and antickly drest." They are all apparently self-contained

---

* "The English have more songs on the subject of madness than any of their neighbours" (Bishop Percy). Feigned madness was a common form of begging in the earlier times.

† This is the well known song "From Rosy Bow'rs," the "last song that Mr. Purcell sett, it being in his sickness." D'Urfey himself characterises the various moods as "sullenly mad, mirthfully mad —a swift movement—melancholy madness, fantastically mad, and stark mad." Compare also the powerful bass song "Let the dreadful Engines" in the first part of "Don Quixote" sung by Cardenio "in a wild posture."

songs instead of being welded into one continuous scena but they exhibit various degrees of melancholy madness, from the touching "Fled is my love" and " 'Tis Death alone," in a declamatory style, to the lilting three-four measures of "There's nothing so fatal as woman," one of Purcell's most delightful colloquial songs, and the fantastically worded "I'll sail upon the Dog-star," which is a brilliant bravura effort. They are all for tenor voice and are eminently detachable. In a later scene there is a "Dialogue between Jockey and Jenny," a wooing duet of the usual suggestive Restoration type, which is described as a "Scotch Song" on the strength of its slight excursion into dialect. These imitation dialect songs became very fashionable during the reign of Charles II. There are not necessarily any marked Scottish characteristics in the music. This one is set in a lively six-four movement without breaks between the lines.

Such was the comparatively limited experience of the stage with which Purcell embarked, round about the end of his thirtieth year, on the composition of his first and only complete opera. It has been said that for *Dido and Aeneas* there were no precedents, and that its composition at that moment was a freak of nature or at least an experiment. Masterpiece as *Dido* is, it is the genius of the man and not the uniqueness of the form that is surprising. Purcell had already shown his ability to organise a sequence of movements into one continuous whole in his Odes, anthems and dramatic scenes and the composition of this little work for Mr. Priest's Academy at Chelsea could have given him no trouble from the purely formal point of view once the character of the libretto was settled. In fact, it may be said that it was the very nature of the performance which gave to the opera many of the qualities for which it has been most praised, its concentration, its directness, its swift and vivid presentment of the drama. Not less than any of Purcell's works *Dido and Aeneas* was an occasional piece; written for schoolgirls, so that the chief parts are for soprano; designed for amateurs, so that the music is fairly simple in range and style; adapted to limited resources so that the instrumentation and stage-requirements are kept within modest limits; and since Mr. Priest was a successful teacher of dancing, freely interspersed with dances. In it Purcell invents no new form. The overture, the recitatives, ariosos, songs on a ground bass, choruses and instrumental interludes, had all been attempted before. We cannot trace anything tentative or experimental in the whole work. On the contrary it is the sureness of the strokes that constitutes its chief pride. For the echo chorus there were many precedents * and for the continuous form Blow's "Venus and Adonis" a few years earlier supplied the model. The scenes are all very short and the whole work plays for something like an hour and

---

* A "Fantasia in Echo" quoted by Parry ("Oxford History of Music," Vol. 3, p. 312) published in 1603 by Banchieri contains an anticipation of the typical Purcell echo effect. Banister wrote an Echo song in Shadwell's version of "The Tempest" which Pepys found ' mighty pretty." The introduction of the Echo organ after the Restoration would explain Purcell's frequent adoption of the device.

a quarter. The style is variegated, like all Purcell's work, but that does not prevent it from having a dramatic consistency. It is full of personal mannerisms, yet nowhere did Purcell write with more spontaneous feeling. It is at once simple, sincere, unaffected, technically sophisticated and intensely human.

A fortunate conjunction of circumstances brought the work into being. The librettist was Nahum Tate, shortly afterwards to become Poet Laureate. He was a poor and inept poet, as many grotesque lines in this opera prove. But in adapting, possibly with Purcell's aid, his earlier drama "Brutus of Alba," he proves himself to have had a considerable sense of the stage. *Dido and Aeneas* is, indeed, a very skilful piece of dramatic work on a small scale. If it were not, even Purcell's genius would have failed to overcome the verbal insipidity of many of the individual passages. It is direct and there is scarcely a line of padding, no redundancy. Pitiful as poetry, it is quite excellent as a "book" and why should it be judged on any other grounds? In the second place, there was the factor of the ballet-master, Josiah Priest. Priest was attached to the Dorset Gardens Theatre. He had been associated with Davenant's version of "Macbeth" and he was later to be connected with the productions of *King Arthur,* "Dioclesian" and *The Fairy Queen.* There is no doubt that he was the foremost English exponent of dancing of the day. Purcell's later works were deeply indebted to the introduction of stage-dancing in *Dido and Aeneas.* The music of no composer has a finer quality of movement. Indeed it is tempting to claim for Purcell the title of the greatest master of musical gesture that has ever lived. To Priest Purcell's music must have owed a great deal, besides the chance that his invitation gave him to write an entirely operatic work. In *Dido and Aeneas* he becomes aware for the first time of the full dramatic possibilities of self-contained instrumental music. Opera and ballet are closely allied, the more closely allied the better, for opera is drama in terms of music and music is in the final resort movement. The sacrificial scenes of Purcell's earlier stage efforts, useful enough as points of repose in the action and as excuses for extended choral developments, have the fatal defect as a basis of music-drama that they are static and impede the dramatic movement of the work. In such a school Purcell could never have learned to write a continuous opera and when he reverted to the professional stage, hidebound to the tradition that music should be invoked only for the purposes of pageantry, the outlandish or the supernatural, he had no chance to prove that music was capable of carrying through the whole of the dramatic action. But he had learned his lesson. He had learned how to write characteristic instrumental music and also vocal music, which, as we shall see, conjures up visions of stage-action.

The third factor in *Dido and Aeneas,* and the supreme one, is Purcell's own uncanny sense of dramatic characterisation. This is the clue, it need hardly be said, to the whole of his music, whether he is writing for a church, the platform or the stage. Under this aspect, and in the psychological truth of his music, there are only two other masters that can be placed in the same rank—Mozart and Wagner. It is absurd to represent Purcell as a pleasant little fresh-air composer. His music has the very odour of the theatre. It is immensely artificial; in other words, full of artifice. *Dido* could not remain, what it undoubtedly is, the earliest example of a completely satisfying and dramatic opera, upon whose conventions time has had not the smallest effect, if it were not that it is conceived so intensely in terms of the stage, unhampered by literary or musical theories, devoted quite simply to the practical purpose, and undeviating in its regard for the immediate effect. It came about almost by accident—the English have no talent for working to an artistic theory. It probably seemed quite unimportant at the time and there is no evidence that, after its single performance, it was ever staged for the next two hundred years. Purcell seems to have had no idea that he was making any contribution to that problematical hypothesis, the future of English opera. He simply made a little work for an end-of-term function, and as the young ladies were more gifted in singing, deportment and dancing than in dramatic interpretation, he and his collaborators cast the whole thing in the form of an opera which allowed for plenty of opportunities for the display of their special talents. The story was familiar; the text was simple and easily followed. The drama, with its motive of tragic love, was of the kind that might be expected to appeal to school-girls. Yet in a sense it was universal and it is the human qualities of *Dido* that have kept it alive.

Dido and Aeneas has been so often discussed that there is little need to deal with it in detail here. The songs on ground basses are unforgettable. The vivid dialogue, the swift and dramatic recitatives, the lovely echo chorus "In our deep vaulted cell," the raciness of the sailors' scene, the weird atmosphere of the witches' episodes, the touching emotion of Dido's death song, so much enriched by the final chorus "With drooping wings"—all is conceived with a perfect sense of dramatic fitness. Professor Dent has said that "it conforms to no tradition; it has no sense of style," whereas Mr. Gustav Holst has recognised in it the supreme essential of a unity of style. Style is a difficult matter and may be differently interpreted.* That it is a matter of mere thematic consistency or technical procedure pure and simple is a heresy derived from the modern use of leading themes. We can best define it in connection with dramatic works as the adoption of a fundamental tone which in spite of deviations for particular illustrative purposes yet governs the whole mood of the work. And such fundamental tone Purcell's *Dido and Aeneas* has. It is swift, concise, vital and realistic, despite its romantic subject. There are no trimmings.

---

* Parry defines it as "the consistent adaptation of the materials to the conditions of presentment." Form, he says, is based on the same influences. Parry's criterion is that art must be above all efficient, well-organised—it is the English ethical view. But English art has rarely conformed to English prejudices and has often become highly efficient and at the same time tremendously disorganised. Witness the semi-operas of Purcell's day and the revues of our own.

Every stroke tells. And at the end there is a feeling of complete fulfilment. What more can we ask of a dramatic work?

Yet *Dido and Aeneas* remains outside the category of Purcell's normal theatrical work. His excursion into the field of amateur opera was an isolated event. His main energies were devoted to a professional theatre with quite different ideals. It seems strange that his work in the latter field should be judged by its failure to conform with the example set by his single experiment in writing what is technically a perfect opera, but an opera for amateurs. There is no sign that he was aware of compromising his art in any way by associating it with the current English compromise of the semi-opera. He was sufficiently the man of the hour to have insisted on his method, had he possessed any theories as to the nature of opera. But when it is regretted that Purcell never followed up the precedent of *Dido and Aeneas*, it remains to be proved that he had the smallest perception of the fact that he had done anything out of the way, or that the particular form he adopted was superior to the type of work to which he devoted his main energies during the brief years to come.

A. N. H.

[The revival of Purcell's *Dido and Aneas* in the Mermaid Theatre—a "portable Elizabethan playing place" constructed in St. John's Wood, London, by Bernard Miles—on September 9, 1951, proved an historic occasion. The Dido was Kirsten Flagstad, and the Belinda, Maggie Teyte. So phenomenal was its success that there followed some one hundred performances with the Norwegian soprano in the role of the Queen. Twenty-seven of those performances were mounted at the Royal Exchange as part of the Coronation festivities of the summer of 1953, and thirty-four on a specially built replica of the Mermaid stage in the Nye Teater of Oslo, Norway. Mme. Flagstad, who bade farewell to opera as Dido, was acclaimed for "a poignant and revealing achievement" that combined "magnificent vocal control, beauty of tone, and expressive color of sovereign interpretive power."]

Maurice Ravel

(Ciboure [Basses-Pyrénées] France, Mar. 7, 1875–Dec. 28, 1937, Paris)

His [Ravel's] father's family was French-Swiss; his mother was of Basque descent. A few weeks after his birth, his parents moved to Paris, where Maurice was educated. His father, an engineer, was a musical amateur, and though Maurice showed no overwhelming inclination towards music, he was encouraged to take lessons in piano and harmony from about the age of twelve. His first piano teacher was Henri Ghis, and he took lessons in harmony from Charles-René, who recognized the musical individuality of his young pupil. In 1889 he was admitted to Anthiome's preparatory piano class at the Conservatoire, and two years later passed into Charles de Bériot's class. He also studied harmony under Émile Pessard, and (from 1897) counterpoint under André Gédalge and composition under Gabriel Fauré.

Gédalge has testified that Ravel was a brilliant student of counterpoint. But from the first he showed a penchant for unorthodox harmonic combinations, and he delighted in playing the unconventional pieces of Chabrier and Satie. Though these composers exerted a certain influence upon him, at the age of twenty he already possessed a highly personal and novel style, as shown by the "Menuet Antique" for piano of 1895, followed in 1895–96 by the "Sites Auriculaires" for two pianos, containing the Habanera which was later incorporated into the "Rapsodie Espagnole."

Under the enlightened guidance of Fauré, whose character was free from academic rigidity, Ravel's artistic personality was able to develop spontaneously and to achieve that synthesis of classical balance and daring innovation which was to remain a basic feature of his music. Nevertheless, he had to contend against academic opposition, critical injustice and public indifference before attaining his undisputed place in the foremost rank of French composers. He made his public debut as a composer in 1898, when the "Sites Auriculaires" were performed at a concert of the Société Nationale de Musique, and the following year the same organization gave his "Ouverture de Shéhérazade" for orchestra and the "Pavane pour une Infante défunte" for piano. One critic described the Overture as "some Rimsky-Korsakoff rehashed by a Debussyist who is eager to equal Erik Satie."

During the next few years he composed three striking masterpieces, the "Jeux d'Eau" for piano (1901), the String Quartet in F (1902–03) and the song-cycle "Shéhérazade" (1903). Yet during this period he was to feel the sting of academic hostility. In 1901 he competed for the Prix de Rome, but received only the second prize. He competed for the famous prize again in

1902, and in 1903, both times without success. Finally, in 1905, when for the fourth time he presented himself as a candidate for the award, he was not even passed at the preliminary test, intended only to eliminate incompetent contestants. And this in spite of the fact that he was nearing the age-limit and had a right to expect the customary leniency under such circumstances. This high-handed procedure aroused a storm of protest in French musical circles, leading to a change in the directorship of the Conservatoire.

Though the gates of official success were closed to him, Ravel now produced an unbroken succession of works marked by such originality and perfection that his unmistakable genius had perforce to be acknowledged. The "Miroirs" for piano (1905) showed that he was exploring, technically and poetically, a new world of keyboard music. And the pianistic horizon was further enlarged by the three pieces comprising "Gaspard de la Nuit" (1908). In the field of vocal music, he developed a distinctly personal style of lyrical declamation in the "Histoires Naturelles" (1906)—a style tinged with malicious irony and dry humour. This type of vocal declamation, supported by a very subtle and piquant orchestration, was given a more extensive development in the one-act comic opera *L'Heure Espagnole* (1907), produced at the Opéra-Comique on May 19, 1911. In spite of its witty and vivacious quality, this work did not enjoy an immediate success; but after its revival at La Monnaie, Brussels, in 1921, and at the Paris Opéra in 1922, it was more warmly received. It was given at Covent Garden, London, in 1919; in Chicago and at the Lexington Theatre, New York, in 1920, and at the Metropolitan Opera House, 1925.

Another work of Hispanic inspiration composed in 1907 was the pungently evocative "Rapsodie Espagnole" for orchestra. To this period belongs also the work which is regarded as Ravel's masterpiece, the ballet "Daphnis et Chloé," composed in 1909–11 on a commission from Serge Diaghileff, who produced it with his Russian Ballet at the Châtelet, Paris, on June 8, 1912. . . .

During the World War of 1914–18, Ravel, though of frail physique, served as an ambulance driver at the front until his health gave out and he was obliged to undertake a rest cure. In 1920 he composed one of his very few works written directly for the orchestra, "La Valse," a somewhat cruel evocation of a vanished era, musically very effective. In 1920–22 came the compact Sonata for violin and cello, and then Ravel turned again to the stage with the opera-ballet *L'Enfant et les Sortilèges* (1924–25), produced at Monte Carlo in 1925 and at the Opéra-Comique in 1926.

In 1928 he was commissioned to write a ballet for Ida Rubinstein. As he had produced his most artistic composition on a commission from Diaghileff some twenty years before, so he now produced his most popular composition on a similar commission from Mlle. Rubinstein. This was the famous "Boléro," given at the Paris Opéra in November, 1928. This extraordinary orchestral tour de force is based simply on the repetition of a single theme, in unvarying rhythm, remaining in the key of C Major almost to the very end, and continuing throughout in a gradual crescendo. It took the world by storm, and was heard in every variety of instrumental arrangement, including versions for jazz band, making Ravel's name known even to the masses who cared little about "serious" music.

Though greatly esteemed in the musical world, Ravel up to this time had not been a really popular figure. Since the war he had lived and worked in seclusion at his villa in Monfort l'Amaury, about 40 miles from Paris, avoiding public activity of any kind. After the success of "Boléro," however, he became the most popular musical figure in France. He was repeatedly invited to appear as guest-conductor of his own works, and on every such occasion was enthusiastically acclaimed, though he was not a skilful or effective conductor. He was slight in build, and his movements were angular and precise. His features were sharp and intelligent, the lips thin, with a hint of irony in the set of the mouth.

From 1930, the composition of two piano concertos occupied Ravel simultaneously. One of these was the Concerto in G Major, a scintillating work full of novel effects, first performed at Paris on Jan. 14, 1932; and the other was the Concerto for the Left Hand, written for the one-armed pianist Paul Wittgenstein, by whom it was played for the first time in Vienna on Nov. 27, 1931, Ravel conducting. These two works, so widely dissimilar, illustrate Ravel's capacity for creative renewal. But his creative career came to an end with the three songs for baritone and orchestra entitled "Don Quichotte à Dulcinée," composed in 1932. After this he was stricken with a brain ailment which eventually caused his death. He died in a Paris clinic, following an operation, on Dec. 28, 1937, at the age of 62.

It may be truly said of Ravel that his art was his life. He never married. He shunned the outward signs of fame: twice he refused membership in the Legion of Honour. He visited the United States in 1928, made several trips to England, and toured Europe as guest-conductor of his own works in 1932; but he did not travel extensively. His chief hobby was the collecting of curios and bibelots, of which his house was full. He had a keen sense of humour and enjoyed playing practical jokes upon his friends. He did not care for teaching, but gave lessons to a few pupils, of whom the most distinguished was the English composer, Ralph Vaughan Williams.

G. C.

L'Heure Espagnole

[The Spanish Hour or Spanish Time]

OPERA IN 1 ACT

Book by FRANC NOHAIN

First performance: Opéra Comique, Paris, May 19, 1911

CHARACTERS

Torquemada, a clockmaker,
TENOR-TRIAL *
Concepcion, his young wife, SOPRANO
Ramiro, a muleteer, BARITONE-MARTIN †

Gonzalve, admirer of Concepcion, TENOR
Don Inigo Gomez, admirer of
Concepcion, BUFFO-BASS

The action takes place in the shop of Torquemada, a clockmaker of Toledo, Spain, in the eighteenth century

The naughty adventure of Concepcion, the youthful wife of one Torquemada, an elderly clockmaker in eighteenth-century Toledo, takes place in her husband's shop while the latter is away regulating the town clock. The problem of receiving more than one beau at the same hour Concepcion solves by hiding them from one another in grandfather's-clock cases, which Ramiro, a Herculean muleteer, moves around according to the lady's whim and even, without seeming effort, carries up and downstairs. Frank in her admiration of his muscles and his spryness, she invites him into a room where there are no grandfather's clocks to shift. The returning Torquemada releases the poet-beau and the banker-beau from their gerontic imprisonment and (waste no tears on him!) induces each to buy a clock. Then before the curtain falls, they join with Concepcion and Ramiro in the wicked pastime of singing a quintet.

P. S.

* Antoine Trial was a very popular operatic tenor in Paris in the eighteenth century. "Trial" is now a term used to denote the high, somewhat thin and nasal tenor voice peculiarly fitted for certain comic parts in opera.

† Jean Blaise Martin (1769–1837) was a French baritone famous in his day less for the quality of his acting than for a voice which was almost a tenor in its upper range and a bass in its lower.

It was the custom in the French provincial theatres of that epoch to define a rôle by the name of the actor or singer who had made a reputation for himself in it in Paris; each company had to have its own "Trial," its own "Martin," etc., or as near thereto as it could get. Some of these names are still in use in France as an epitome of the qualities of voice, appearance, style and so on required of a singer of a particular part. Thus Ellen, in *Lakmé,* figures in the list of *dramatis personae* not as a soprano but as a "dugazon." This name comes from a certain Louise Rosalie Dugazon (1735–1821). A "dugazon" part may be either a "jeune dugazon" or a "mère dugazon." It calls mostly for intelligent acting of the soubrette order rather than for brilliant singing.

E. N.

414

Spain, with its wealth of dance and folk music, was very close to the heart of Maurice Ravel. His earliest recollections were centered about the melodies of the Basque coast, and Spanish rhythms were a part of his natural heritage. He was, said Manuel de Falla, "more Spanish than the Spanish themselves"; André Suarèz called him "un Grec d'Espagne."

I recognize Spain all through Ravel, in what he is as well as in what he does. This little man so quaint, nervous, slender, yet unyielding; that cajoling rigidity with the suppleness of laminated steel; that great nose, those sunken cheeks, that angular, slim form; his manner a little distant but so courteous; refined in appearance, abrupt in behavior, yet without incivility; restricted gestures; warmth of embers which forbid themselves to flare up—this is the Spanish *grillon* [cricket].

The music of Spain has always held a great fascination for French composers. Bizet's *Carmen,* Chabrier's "España" (admiration of Ravel's youth), and Debussy's "Ibéria" all bear witness to the close affinity between the French and the Spanish temperaments. Now Ravel, in 1907, was to add two more important compositions to this list: "Rapsodie espagnole" and "L'Heure espagnole."

He had always wished to compose an orchestral work based on the folk themes of Spain. One of his first compositions, the "Habanera," was written in typical Spanish idiom, and since it had never been published he decided to orchestrate and include it in a suite to be called "Rapsodie espagnole." . . .

After the move to Levallois-Perret,* Joseph Ravel [Ravel's father] began to fail in health. He complained of serious headaches and lost all his earlier enthusiasm and energy.† Maurice, whose family meant more to him than anything else in life, was seriously concerned over his father's condition; in order to please him, and to distract him from his ill health, he now decided to compose an opera. Joseph Ravel adored the theater, and it would have meant much to him to see a work of his own son presented on the stage. He took the greatest pride in Maurice's achievements, and had always hoped that one day he would write an opera.

Ravel's first project was based on Gerhard Hauptmann's famous legend-drama, "The Sunken Bell." All legend and poetry appealed to the young French composer, but when these included a mechanical setting (such as the foundry in Hauptmann's tale) they proved irresistibly attractive. Ferdinand Hérold, who translated "Die versunkene Glocke" into French and who collaborated with Ravel in cutting and simplifying the cumbersome German text, wrote: "Ravel did not see [in this scene of the foundry] the small workshop of a craftsman; he dreamed of a vast factory, equipped in elaborate fash-

* [An industrial center on the outskirts of Paris to which Ravel's family had moved in 1905.]
† Some who knew Joseph Ravel believe that he may have suffered from the same disease of the brain which later took the life of his illustrious son.

ion like those of today, and he would have used [i.e., set to music] the innumerable sounds of hammers, saws, files, and sirens."

During an unusually hot June at Levallois-Perret, Ravel worked strenuously at the new project. "For two weeks now I haven't left the grind. Never have I worked with such frenzy. Yes—in Compiègne, but there it was less amusing. It is thrilling to do work for the theater. I won't say it comes all by itself, but that's exactly the best part of it. . . ."

In August of the same summer Maurice finally decided to take his father to Switzerland, hoping that the cooler climate and familiar scenes of Joseph's youth would restore him to better health and spirits. From Switzerland Ravel wrote to his friend Delage:

Hermance, 20 August 1906

So here I am installed in Switzerland, old man, and I no longer regret the ocean so much. . . . It is especially this bland climate, of a surprising purity. My father finds himself rejuvenated, and claims he has hardly any more headaches.

The inhabitants are very curious too. A cousin whom I left a clockmaker is now first violin at the theater in Geneva.

I am awaiting a piano to get back to "The Bell," momentarily interrupted. . . . Just think, there is already—in addition to what you know of the first act—a large part of the second.

But "The Sunken Bell" was destined never to be completed, for the following spring Ravel discovered a curious one-act play by the French poet Franc-Nohain, and was so captivated by the clocks and the music-boxes of "L'Heure espagnole" that he laid aside the former work and never took it up again (though some of its themes were later used in *L'Enfant et les sortilèges*).

When Ravel had finished "L'Heure espagnole" he took it to Franc-Nohain in order to play the score through, as is customary, for the author's approval, himself humming the vocal parts in the usual inadequate composer's voice. After he had finished playing he waited hopefully for Franc-Nohain's comments. But the latter was not gifted with musical imagination; there was only silence.

. . . Finally Franc-Nohain pulled his watch from his pocket: "Fifty-six minutes," he said politely.

Albert Carré, director of the Opéra-Comique, agreed to produce Ravel's opera. But there were difficulties and delays, and although *L'Heure espagnole* was completed in four months' time, it was not until years later—in 1911— that it was given its first performance.

Meanwhile Joseph Ravel's condition grew steadily worse, and on October 13, 1908, he passed away at Levallois-Perret. Maurice was inconsolable, and for many months he could not resume his work. During the year following his father's death he wrote only one composition: "Menuet sur le nom d'Haydn" (for piano).

Ravel called *L'Heure espagnole* a "conversation in music." It is completely different in form from the classical opera, containing few if any of the traditional arias, choruses, and orchestral interludes, and recalling rather the old Italian *opera-buffa*—comedy which is close to farce and at times approaches caricature. It is really an opera in miniature, where the characters resemble marionettes, and everything is compressed into the smallest possible space. The orchestra remains in the background throughout the opera, and the vocal parts are written in such a way that they seem to be spoken rather than sung—*récitatif quasi parlando*. The resulting effect is as natural and unforced as that of an ordinary play or drama, yet more vivid and colorful because of the musical accompaniment which enhances the general effect without ever obtruding. . . .

On May 19, 1911, *L'Heure espagnole* was presented at the Opéra-Comique along with a little-known opera of Massenet's called *Thérèse*. Again the critics were divided in their opinions. Some could see only the risqué side of the work. They called it a "miniature pornographic vaudeville" and regretted that Ravel should have wasted his talents on such an unworthy subject. They said that he was more interested in imitating the mechanism of clocks than in interpreting his characters' emotions; that the people of the play were like the automatic dolls of a musical clock—without soul or life; that the music "made one think of *Pelléas*, but a *Pelléas* reproduced on a gramophone in very slow motion."

All the critics, however, agreed that the orchestration was delightful and without equal in the art of contemporary music. Lalo compared it to the "orchestral imagination of a Richard Strauss; but of a miniature Strauss, a Strauss who works in the infinitely small . . . An orchestration charming, brilliant, unusual, diverse, full of subtle values and rare sonorities." Vuillermoz wrote: "Ravel creates colors. He is painter, goldsmith, and jeweler."

After the first presentation of *L'Heure espagnole* at the Opéra-Comique, Ravel's friends waited anxiously to hear what his reaction would be to the performance. But Ravel—who, as we have seen, was extremely fastidious in his dress—proved to have but one thing on his mind.

"Did you notice that all the *grand monde* is wearing midnight-blue evening clothes?" he exclaimed. "And to think that after I especially ordered a new blue suit for tonight, that stupid tailor of mine forgot to deliver it!"

M. G.

L'Heure Espagnole is perhaps not everyone's opera. It is impossible in any language but French. It is better suited to a small, intimate theatre than to the large opera houses of our capital cities. It has to be taken imaginatively rather than realistically, for even the human characters have about them a touch of the charming unreality of the marionette milieu in which they are set, and which Ravel has described so enchantingly in his orchestra. He never overstresses a point; indeed, for many spectators he perhaps under-stresses some of them. In an age that takes its pleasures heartily, if not, indeed, a trifle vulgarly, Ravel seems a reversion to the better-bred eighteenth century, when the aristocracy in every European country set the tone of social life. Lord Chesterfield impressed it on his son that a gentleman, however vastly he may be amused, never permits himself to do more than smile: he himself, he said, had never been seen to laugh since he came to years of discretion. Ravel never laughs; nor does he wish the spectator to do more than smile at these puppets of his— a smile as thin-lipped and as discreet, if possible, as the composer's own.

The only real singing character in the opera is Gonzalve, who occasionally becomes almost lyrical. For the others, Ravel, in a prefatory note to his score, prescribes a speaking rather than a singing style—what he calls the quasi-parlando of Italian buffo recitative. The final quintet, of course, is in a different category.

E. N.

The American *première* of *L'Heure espagnole* took place at the Chicago Auditorium Jan. 5, 1920, with Yvonne Gall as Concepcion, Alfred Maguenat as Ramiro, and Louis Hasselmans to conduct. The same artists participated in the New York *première,* given by the visiting Chicago company at the Lexington Theater, Jan. 28, 1920. The work was added to the repertory of the Metropolitan Opera House Nov. 7, 1925. Once more Mr. Hasselmans conducted. Lucrezia Bori appeared as Concepcion, Lawrence Tibbett as Ramiro.

Nikolai Rimsky-Korsakoff

(Tikhvin [Government of Novgorod], Russia, Mar. 18, 1844–June 21, 1908,
Estate Lubensk, near St. Petersburg)

Of the original "Five" who created the Russian school of music in the nineteenth century, four were essentially amateurs. Balakireff was looked upon by
his fellows as a professional musician; but Cui was an army officer, an engineer
of fortifications; Borodin was a doctor and a teacher of chemistry; Moussorgsky,
after his retirement from the army, spent his life as a government clerk. Rimsky-
Korsakoff was a naval officer. As a young midshipman he had fallen under the
spell of the fascinating Balakireff, and wrote his first symphony before he
was twenty-one years old. At that time he was so ignorant of music theory
(Balakireff having scorned the necessity for academic training in harmony,
counterpoint, form, etc.) that he did not even know the names of the common
chords.

But Rimsky-Korsakoff was the one member of the famous group who refused to remain an amateur. In fact, he became one of the most skilful musicians of his time, and a consummate master of many aspects of musical technique. He accomplished this through years of unceasing industry. Harmony
and counterpoint he learned only after he had accepted a professorship at the
St. Petersburg Conservatory! He taught simply by teaching himself first and
keeping one jump ahead of his pupils. To understand orchestration more fully
he bought many of the instruments and learned how to play them. He succeeded so well that he was later able to write a manual of orchestration which
remains a classic to this day.

Rimsky-Korsakoff's life was a steady progression, a carefully planned development of a great natural talent. He was a perfectionist, who never ceased
polishing not only the brilliant facets of his music but the very tools of his trade
as well. He seemed never to be idle; and when he was not adding to his own
immense output he was spurring on his friends Borodin and Moussorgsky to
similar achievement—helping them with their orchestrating, even completing
and editing their works after their deaths.

It is curious that for all his methodical mind and well-ordered habits Rimsky-
Korsakoff's music is the most fanciful, picturesque, and charmingly extravagant of all the nineteenth-century Russians. It offers a contrast with the music
of Moussorgsky, for example, that is almost as great as the gulf between the
temperaments of the two men. Moussorgsky's art was that of the natural
dramatist, the realistic interpreter of the hearts of men. His music is often
shaggy and unkempt; it reeks continually of the Russian soil. Rimsky-Korsa-

koff's is melodic, lyrical, and essentially pictorial. It is Russian, but with a blend of the exotic East; and its polished technique often covers melodic ideas that are commonplace. There is no doubt now that Moussorgsky was the more powerful and original genius, for his music has grown steadily with the years and a whole generation of modern composers have fed upon it. Rimsky-Korsakoff's, on the other hand, has declined.

Though he composed in many forms, Rimsky-Korsakoff's operas constitute the great bulk of his works. He wrote fifteen, nearly all of them based on Russian stories, legends, or dramas. For a time they were so important a part of the operatic repertoire in Russia that he seemed destined to become the equivalent in his native country of Wagner in Germany and Verdi in Italy. But in recent years many of these works have faded and now suffer neglect. Outside of Russia one hears only the exquisite *Le Coq d'Or,* and occasionally *Sadko* and *Snyegoorochka.*

Far more popular are the purely orchestral works: the "Capriccio Espagnol," the Russian Easter overture, the "Antar" Suite, and—inevitably—"Scheherezade." There is still great vitality in these pieces, and they are likely to represent their composer on symphonic programmes for many years. They will live because, for one thing, Rimsky-Korsakoff had the gift of lyricism, and his melodies (though often somewhat obvious) nearly always have charm. He knew, too, how to hide their defects by his expert use of colourful harmonies. He was also a past-master of orchestration, by which he gave his music a marvellous clarity of expression, a richness of texture, and a brilliance that is almost Oriental in its opulent splendour. For his discoveries in the science of instrumentation, a host of modern composers—Stravinsky, Ravel, Falla, Respighi, Prokofieff, etc.—owe him a great debt.

Russia owes him a great debt, too. For at a time when nationalism in music was still on trial in western Europe, he was her most ardent and successful propagandist. He proved by his own technical mastery that nationalism need not be synonymous with amateurism. He made it plain that the literature, legend, folk, and church music of a single nation might be made the basis for a treasury of musical inspiration.

R. A. L.

Le Coq d'Or

[The Golden Cock]

OPERA IN 3 ACTS

Book by Vladimir Bielsky, after a poem by Alexander Pushkin

First performance: Zimin's Private Theater, Moscow, May, 1910

CHARACTERS

King Dodon, BASS
Prince Guidon, his son, TENOR
Prince Aphron, his son, BARITONE
General Polkan, BASS

Amelfa, CONTRALTO
The Astrologer, TENOR
The Queen of Shemakha, SOPRANO
The Golden Cockerel, SOPRANO

The action takes place in a mythical land

A mythical king Dodon, presiding in his council chamber, is greeted by such a conflict of ideas on the part of his councilors that the session breaks up in hopeless confusion; whereupon an astrologer arrives on the scene with a Golden Cock, a very accomplished bird that has the gift of prophecy. It is installed on a lofty perch, whence its cries shall warn of threatening danger.

Feeling that all is now well, the King orders his feather bed and goes to sleep, but his slumbers are disturbed by the frantic shrieks of the Golden Cock. The King's sons with their army make a start for a hostile country. Later on the King follows them.

In Act II he finds them slain, but he has comfort when from a tent where he supposed the hostile commander was hidden the lovely Queen of Shemaka steps forth. With song and dance she conquers the foolish old fellow and even consents to become his bride.

In the third act the King and his lovely Queen make their triumphal entry into the capital city. But there is a quick ending to the royal merriment. The Astrologer arrives on the scene and demands in payment for the Golden Cock nothing less than the Queen herself. The King in his fury brandishes his scepter and strikes the Astrologer dead, but the Golden Cock avenges his master straightway by crushing the King's skull with his beak.

As the King falls lifeless, darkness encompasses the scene, and the ironic laughter of the Queen of Shemaka is heard through the ensuing storm. When the darkness passes the Queen and the bird have vanished and the docile people are bewailing the loss of good King Dodon, their wise and peerless monarch, though he had treated them like dogs! As a parting injunction the resurrected Astrologer exhorts the audience to spare their tears, since the Queen and he were the only two live ones in all Dodon's kingdom.   P. S.

Rimsky-Korsakoff did not live to see *Le Coq d'Or* produced. He began the opera in the autumn of 1906 (he was then sixty-two) and worked on it eagerly until it was completed. Trouble followed with the Russian censorship. In December 1907 the composer became seriously ill and the following June he died. It has been said that his death was hastened by his chagrin over the failure to get his work presented. The first performance, at Zimin's Private Theatre in Moscow, did not take place till May 1910.

The difficulty about *Le Coq d'Or* was two-fold. First, there was the element of caricature in the work itself—the humorous portrayal of King Dodon as a doddering old imbecile. Secondly, there was Rimsky-Korsakoff's own behavior.

Today we are a little slow to remember the revolutionary movement of 1905 in Russia, which, though it failed of its complete objective, resulted in certain liberal reforms, among them the establishment of the Duma. In March of that year Rimsky-Korsakoff in an open letter published in the *Russ* not only came out for the freeing of the St. Petersburg Conservatory, where he had been professor of composition and instrumentation since 1871, from the domination of the Imperial Russian Musical Society, but spoke emphatically against the excessive police supervision of the students.

As a consequence he was removed from his professorship. True, his colleagues, including Glazounoff and Liadoff, resigned in protest, and after the Conservatory had obtained a measure of autonomy and Glazounoff had been named director Rimsky-Korsakoff was reinstated.

Yet this experience doubtless gave a sharper edge to the satire expressed in the laughable figure of King Dodon, and the thwarted authorities found their opportunity to get back at the victorious musician by preventing the staging of *Le Coq d'Or* as long as he lived, in spite of the distinguished position held by Rimsky-Korsakoff as a composer of Russian operas and the further fact that the libretto was derived from a narrative poem by the great national poet Pushkin.

When Michel Fokine staged *Le Coq d'Or* for the Diaghileff Ballets Russes, he had the novel idea of putting it on with a double cast. Members of the ballet company mimed the characters and danced in the centre of the stage while the singers, chorus and soloists alike, made their contribution from the side lines. That is to say, they were placed in jury boxes, one on either side, where they devoted themselves exclusively to the business of singing. The Paris Opéra was the scene of the initial representation.

On March 6, 1918, the Metropolitan Opera House afforded its patrons the first performance of *Le Coq d'Or* in America, using a French translation by M. D. Calvocoressi. This production was based on Fokine's choreography, though Adolph Bolm, the King Dodon, who had mimed the same part for Diaghileff, modified the procedure somewhat according to ideas of his own.

The singers in the jury boxes were dressed in collegiate caps and gowns of maroon. For the Ballets Russes the role of the Princess was mimed by Tamara Karsavina, who has called the part perhaps the "most wonderful" of all she ever had. At the Metropolitan Rosina Galli appeared as the Princess. The chief singers of the Metropolitan première were Maria Barrientos (the Princess), Adamo Didur (King Dodon), Rafaelo Diaz (the Astrologer), Sophie Braslau (Amelfa), and Marie Sundelius (the voice of the Cockerel).

Fokine's manner of staging Le Coq d'Or incurred the displeasure of the composer's widow and son. In a letter dated St. Petersburg June 2, 1914, Mme. Rimsky-Korsakoff wrote to the Paris Figaro:

> Information that has arrived from Paris convinces me that M. Diaghileff's *mise-en-scène* is of a character contrary to the author's intention. The opera scenario is now coupled with a ballet scenario; the work written for singing and for dramatic action has been transformed into a kind of semi-ballet, semi-oratorio. . . . Under these conditions, my strictest duty was to use my right to put an end to the exhibitions of what was rather a parody of my husband's work.

The French courts granted the widow the injunction she sought, but the English courts did not, so, though Le Coq d'Or had to be withdrawn forthwith in Paris, it was freely performed in London. Diaghileff justified his course by pointing out that whereas Le Coq d'Or in its original form had not succeeded with the public, his production had been acclaimed.

It has been contended that Rimsky-Korsakoff's own plan for staging the work (abandoned as impracticable) had provided for a double cast in which the singers behind screens should move about synchronously with the visible actors. If that contention be true, the objection made by Mme. Rimsky-Korsakoff seems uncalled for.

In recent years Le Coq d'Or done with a single cast has been highly successful at the Paris Opéra.

P. S.

Gioacchino Rossini

(Pesaro, Italy, Feb. 29, 1792–Nov. 13, 1868, Passy, near Paris)

Rossini was born at Pesaro on the last day of February in 1792, a Leap Year. His father was the functionary we call "town-crier," but with a trumpet in place of a bell. This instrument, and also the horn, he played in the local theatre orchestra, and with these duties combined the inspectorate of public slaughterhouses. Giuseppe Rossini was himself what is called a "character." Of a gay and lively disposition he was nicknamed "Vivazza," and his natural enthusiasm inevitably made him a victim of Revolutionary ardour, when in 1797 Napoleon began his "liberation" (as it would be called nowadays) of Italy. He even composed a Republican hymn, which, he claimed, was inspired by Liberty rather than the Muses.

Like father, like son. The boy was high-spirited and undisciplined. Only his mother, whom he adored, could do anything with him. His education was at first rudimentary, but he acquired some elements of musical taste from a priest, who was an admirer of Mozart and Haydn. Then in 1804 the family moved to Bologna, whose Conservatoire, the Liceo Musicale, was the most famous in Italy. Under competent teachers the boy soon showed an extraordinary ability, and at fourteen he began to get engagements as chorus master and accompanist at the smaller theatres. His voice was of great beauty and he sang frequently in the churches. Indeed, he wished at this time to make a career as a singer.

In 1806, at the same age as Mozart, he received the honour of election to the Accademia Filharmonica, but, in view of his youth, without a vote in council. Like Mozart, too, he had an extremely retentive musical memory. After hearing an air, of which he had been unable to procure a copy by other means, he wrote the whole thing out from memory. In the learning of counterpoint the boy was unfortunate in his teacher, the dull and uncommunicative Padre Mattei. So in later years he came to declare that all he knew in that sphere he had learnt from the works of Haydn and, above all, Mozart whom he loved above all other composers.

During his later years at the Liceo Rossini found himself obliged to absent himself more and more in order to take engagements which would bring in enough money to support his parents, now fallen into destitution. Then in 1810, when he was a young man of eighteen, extremely handsome and already a great favourite with women, he received a commission to compose an opera for the Teatro San Mosé in Venice. This theatre was managed by the Marquis Cavalli, who ran it with a company consisting, as was the custom, of *ma femme et cinq poupées,* and playing in a repertory of one-act farces. Rossini hastened to Venice and was given the libretto of *Un Cambiale di Matrimonio.* This was produced with some success, though not without complaints from the singers about the elaboration of the orchestral accompaniment. . . .

Tancredi, an *opera seria* based on a tragedy by Voltaire who in turn derived his subject from Tasso, was produced at the Fenice Theatre, which still remains an unspoilt monument of eighteenth-century elegance. At first its success was only moderate, and it was not until the opera had been acclaimed elsewhere that it became the rage in Venice, and everyone, from prince to gondolier, suddenly burst out singing "Di tanti palpiti." The general public were ravished by the wealth of charming melody, while the connoisseurs marvelled at the richness and originality of the orchestration. Here was a new vitality agitating the fossilized bones of *opera seria,* to whose conventions Rossini so far subscribed as to cast his hero for a contralto, so that the part was actually sung subsequently by Velluti, the last survivor of the dying tribe of *castrati.* And it is worth remarking that, later in life, Rossini attributed the decadence of the art of singing—then, as now and in every other period, deplored by the elderly—to the disappearance of these highly accomplished singers who also taught their art to others.

Not that approval of Rossini was unanimous. Conservative opinion, embodied in the person of the Earl of Mount Edgecumbe, did not approve of the new ease of movement which Rossini gave to serious opera by using in it some of the more elastic conventions of *opera buffa.* In his "Musical Reminiscences" the Earl complained that "Di tanti palpiti" was capable of being converted into a quadrille; he could not foresee that the themes of Wagner's *Ring of the Nibelung* would be put to the same use by so serious a composer as Fauré! Moreover, both singers and the old-fashioned members of the audience complained of the complexity and noisiness of Rossini's orchestration. Even now a certain touch of blatancy in his music is apt to offend the nicer spirits.

Just three months after *Tancredi,* on 22 May 1813, on which day Richard Wagner was born at Leipzig amid the turmoil of the Napoleonic war, Rossini's next opera, *L'Italiana in Algeri,* was produced in Venice and won immediate favour. The composer's name was becoming known in other cities. First Milan, then Naples claimed his attention. At the Scala Theatre was produced a serious opera, *Aureliano in Palmyra,* about (in Mr. Toye's words) "Romans and Persians of incredible high-mindedness and an exotic Queen Zenobia, of irresistible charm." This forgotten piece must be mentioned because its overture, tacked on to Rossini's comic masterpiece, is familiar to us all. This transfer of an overture from a serious opera to a comedy, and its complete appropriateness to the latter purpose, is a commentary on the taste of the time and, to some extent, a justification of Lord Mount Edgecumbe's strictures.

It was Barbaja, now the prosperous director of the San Carlo Theatre, who summoned Rossini to Naples. Barbaja's company was headed by his mistress, Isabella Colbran, a handsome Spaniard with black hair, dark eyes, and a fine voice of exceptional range. For her Rossini composed *Elisabetta, Regina d'Inghilterra,* to a libretto dealing with the story of Queen Elizabeth and Leicester in a quite apocryphal manner. In this opera Rossini not only provided the recitatives with an orchestral accompaniment throughout, doing away with the *recitativo secco* accompanied by a harpsichord or pianoforte; he also wrote out in full the embellishments of the vocal parts, instead of leaving them to the taste of the singers. This was a real and necessary reform, for the virtuoso singers of the day so larded the airs with *fioriture* and *roulades* of every kind that the composer's melodic ideas were apt to be submerged under the excess of ornament. That Rossini managed to carry through this revolution in operatic practice at a time when the power of the *prima donna* was paramount, argues considerable force of character on his part and an unusual degree of compliance on the part of Mme. Colbran. Perhaps already they were lovers, for such they certainly became later on, and on 16 March 1822 Rossini imprudently married her at Bologna. They both remained, however, on good terms with Barbaja who was possibly tired of the whims and extravagance of this capricious lady. Poor Rossini, who was seven years her junior, was to find her sorely exasperating to his easily fretted nerves.

Meantime in 1816 he had composed for Isabella his best tragedy, *Otello,* which held the stage until it was eclipsed just seventy years later by Verdi's masterpiece. How deeply the younger man revered Rossini and his opera is evident from the fact that he hesitated for a long time before venturing upon the composition of a new *Otello.* Rossini felt a similar respect for Paisiello, now living in retirement at Naples. At least he had the good manners to ask the old composer of a *Barber of Seville* if he had any objection to a new operatic version of Beaumarchais's comedy being made. Though Paisiello raised no objection, his partisans were less obliging and the first performance of Rossini's *Barber,* given in Rome on 20 February 1816, was accompanied by an almost continuous uproar. However, the new work soon established itself in popular favour, once the prejudiced first-night audience had had its fling, and remains to this day one of the most popular operas in the repertory.

The original Rosina of *The Barber of Seville* was Signora Giorgi-Righetti, a contralto for whom a year later Rossini composed *La Cenerentola,* a sophisticated version of the Cinderella story, which deserves more frequent revival than it gets. It is sometimes forgotten that these parts were written for a low voice, the soprano version of Rosina being an arrangement. A famous mezzo-soprano was recently criticized for not choosing something more suitable to her voice than Rosina's "Una voce poco fa." In Rossini's day all singers—even the basses, as Basilio's "Calumny" air bears witness—were expected to be able to sing *coloratura,* and the tradition persisted at least in Verdi's early operas such as *Nabucco* and the first version of *Macbeth.*

Like the rings on the surface of water started by a dropped stone, Rossini's fame now spread wider and wider. First to Vienna whither Barbaja invited him to the Kärnthnerthor Theatre in March 1822 immediately after his marriage to Isabella. Here he won the hearts of the Viennese, exercised an important influence on Schubert, and paid his respects to Beethoven, whose tragic condition of sickness, deafness, and squalor so moved Rossini that he sought to raise funds to relieve the great man's need. From Beethoven, at parting, he received the famous injunction, "Give us more Barbers." Only Weber, jealous for his new-born German opera, stood aloof amid the plaudits. Next, after a month in Paris *en route,* London was visited and conquered, at the cost of a bad Channel crossing which for a while prostrated the timorous Rossini, who once later in life—but only once—ventured on a short journey by the newly invented steam-railway with disastrous results to his nervous system!

When he was sufficiently recovered he was received by King George IV beneath the new-built pleasure-domes of Brighton, and later in London sang tenor in duets from his own operas to His Majesty's bass—a spectacle which was unkindly imaged by the caricaturists of the day. Under the aegis of royal patronage and condescension, Rossini became the lion of society, an expensive lion at from £50 to £100 an evening. His operas, including *The Barber* and *Semiramide* (composed for Venice in 1823), were acclaimed, and society paid two guineas, when guineas were golden, for tickets for two concerts at Almack's, at which Rossini commemorated Byron's death with a cantata, in which he appeared in person as Apollo. He left England with a net profit of £7,000 and a contract, negotiated through the French Ambassador in London, to direct the Théâtre Italien in Paris for a year at a salary of 20,000 francs.

The most important event of his directorate of this theatre—important both in its ultimate consequences and in its illumination of Rossini's character—was his production of Meyerbeer's *Crocciato in Egitto,* which set the young unknown German's feet firmly upon the road to Parisian success. Rossini could bring a caustic wit to bear upon music and persons he disliked, but towards his rivals, and especially towards his juniors, he always showed a generosity and an absence of jealousy which make him one of the most likeable characters in our gallery. Towards Meyerbeer, no less than towards the hardly less generous Donizetti and towards Bellini, who was not so free from the taint of suspicion and jealousy, Rossini was both cordially friendly and helpful. Suffering though he was at the time from illness, he took the greatest pains to ensure the success of Meyerbeer's opera, which indeed paid him the sincerest compliment in the way of imitation. Meyerbeer's goal was achieved and he proceeded to establish himself, by dint of hard work, as the most popular opera-composer in Paris. He never wavered in his admiration for Rossini or in his gratitude for his unselfish help, and, though Rossini came to disapprove certain aspects of

Meyerbeer's later works, which were certainly no models of reticent good taste, there was more than a touch of waggishness in his comment upon the funeral march composed by a nephew of Meyerbeer at the time of his uncle's death: "Don't you think it would have been better if you had died and your uncle had written the funeral march?" He himself did compose an ode to the memory of the man who had ousted him from the favour of the public.

Rossini contributed nothing new to the repertory of the Théâtre Italien, except a cantata hurriedly composed for the coronation festivities of Charles X. He was engaged, apart from the business of supervising the performances including those of his own operas, in perfecting his French and studying Parisian taste, which set a greater store than the Italian upon literary and dramatic excellence, and less upon vocal fireworks, which are, indeed, unsuited to the genius of the French language. The result of these studies, in which he surpassed Meyerbeer who never overcame a certain clumsiness in the setting of French, was the production of French versions, considerably rewritten, of two of his Neapolitan operas under the titles of *Le Siège de Corinthe* (originally *Maometto II*) and *Moïse*. These were but essays towards Rossini's objective— the creation of a French grand opera that would continue the line laid down by Gluck and proceeding through Cherubini and Spontini.

Inevitably the new project would be tinged by the prevailing taste of the day, that is to say it would be romantic rather than classical in its choice of subject. In the world of 1828 the spectacle of resurgent nations struggling to assert their individuality and independence suggested a patriotic theme. Schiller's drama of *William Tell* was accordingly chosen for transformation into a grand opera, the unheroic character of the central episode, at least as a stage spectacle, being overlooked. Indeed, it was rather underlined by the name chosen for the son of William Tell who repeatedly addresses him at the emotional climax of the opera before shooting the apple from his head, as "Jemmy."

Rossini took the composition of *William Tell* with intense seriousness. He studied, in particular, the symphonies of Beethoven with a view to enlarging his emotional range of expression and his command of picturesque orchestration. The most obvious fruit of this study is the storm in the well-known overture, which owes a good deal to the example set by the "Pastoral" Symphony. But altogether *William Tell* was quite the grandest, the most elevated, as well as the longest, opera that had been produced to date. It won, at once, the respect of the musicians—excepting, at first, Berlioz who five years later became its fervent admirer—but it never won real popularity, on account of the very qualities that commended it to the musicians, and also because of its inordinate length.

This comparative failure, to which he was not blinded by the award of the Legion of Honour, wounded Rossini deeply. Always extremely sensitive, he had now become positively morbid in his reaction to popular disapproval. He found himself, moreover, soon outshone, at least in the favour of opera-goers, by Meyerbeer, whose *Robert le Diable* made its sensational appearance in 1831, two years after *William Tell*.

Rossini's material position, too, suddenly collapsed. After his year at the Théâtre Italien, he had entered into a contract with the French Court by which he was to receive a salary of 6,000 francs a year in perpetuity. For this he engaged to compose five grand operas during the next ten years, receiving in addition 15,000 francs for each opera and the proceeds of a benefit performance. It was under this arrangement that *William Tell* was given at the Opéra on 3 August 1829.

Soon after the first performance Rossini left Paris to pay a visit to his parents at Bologna, and remained there for a year. The next opera was not due until 1831 and he could start work on it in Italy. The libretto, which was to have been based on *Faust,* failed to arrive, despite his protests. And then on 30 July 1830 Charles X, his patron who had personally signed his contract, was ignominiously smuggled out of the country, making way for Louis-Philippe. On his return to Paris in September Rossini found his contract cancelled, and it took six years of litigation to compel the new régime to honour the ex-king's signature.

All these circumstances combined with his growing ill health to inhibit Rossini from the further composition of opera. Had he been of a less indolent temperament, had he possessed something of Gluck's ambition or of Wagner's burning zeal to express himself, the Great Renunciation, as it has been called —though it was not a conscious act so much as an indolent neglect to take action—might never have been made. As it was, at the age of thirty-seven the most celebrated opera-composer of his day laid down his pen and during the remaining thirty-nine years of his life contributed nothing more to the theatre.

The latter years were spent mostly in Paris, and at Passy just outside the city. . . . He had the devoted care of Olympe—Olympe Pélissier, ex-mistress of Vernet, the painter, and of several wealthy men, one of whom left her well endowed. He had met her in 1832 at Aix-les-Bains, when Isabella was living in disgrace with her parrots and her dogs near Bologna—"Duchess of Castelnaso," as old Vivazza contemptuously dubbed her. Ever since, she had been his companion, and, when Isabella died, she married him. . . . He was the doyen of European composers, and every musician who visited Paris sought admittance to his famous *soirées,* for which he still condescended to compose the delicious trifles, some of which were rediscovered for our delight in the ballet, "La Boutique Fantasque." Verdi regarded him with veneration and called him "Jupiter"—though he disapproved of Olympe. Wagner, revisiting Paris for the production of *Tannhäuser,* waited upon him, and was moved by his account of that meeting with Beethoven long years before, and astonished, as Mendelssohn had been, to find that his host was a devotee of Bach, who looked forward, more than anything, to the arrival of the latest volume of the great Gesellschaft Edition. This was not the shallow, cynical jester of common gossip, but a real musician and a man of feeling. Wagner retired with a better opinion of Rossini.

Rossini died on Friday, 13 November 1868. He was spared the horrors of war and revolution, and one shudders to think what effect they would have had on the man who fled from Bologna before the first breath of the troubles of '48. He was buried, like Bellini, in Père Lachaise cemetery, and, like Bellini, was later reinterred in his native land—Bellini at Catania, Rossini in Santa Croce at Florence, Italy's Westminster Abbey.

D. H.

Il Barbiere di Siviglia

[The Barber of Seville]

OPERA BUFFA IN 2 ACTS

Book by CESARE STERBINI, after BEAUMARCHAIS' comedy, *Le Barbier de Seville*

First performance: Teatro di Torre Argentina, Rome, Feb. 20, 1816

CHARACTERS

Count Almaviva, TENOR

Bartolo, a physician, BASS

Rosina, his ward, SOPRANO

Basilio, a music teacher, BASS

Figaro, a barber, BARITONE

Berta, a maid, MEZZO-SOPRANO

The action takes place at Seville, during the seventeenth century

Dr. Bartolo, a substantial but elderly citizen, wants to marry his ward, the beautiful Rosina, who lives in his house. Count Almaviva, whom Rosina knows only as Lindoro, is likewise in love with her. The versatile Figaro, barber and factotum, is induced by the count to help him in his predicament.

Though Dr. Bartolo and his ally, the scheming music teacher, Don Basilio, are always on the lookout, Rosina, thanks to Figaro, sends a note to the count, telling him that his love is requited. Next, Almaviva gains admission to Dr. Bartolo's house by posing as a drunken soldier billeted upon the doctor. But the arrival of the guard to arrest the impostor interferes with his plan to see Rosina alone.

Once more he gets into the house, this time pretending to be a music teacher sent in place of Don Basilio, who, he says, is ill. At first this stratagem prospers, for he wins the doctor's favor by showing him Rosina's note and promising to make her think he has had it from a mistress of the count, thus inducing her to drop him. Figaro assists by coming in with his basin under his arm and announcing that he must shave Dr. Bartolo at once. Incidentally, he finds the means to purloin the key of the balcony.

All would be set for an elopement were it not that the supposedly ailing Don Basilio appears on the scene The plotters get rid of him through the count's slyly handing him a purse, and he, assenting to their diagnosis of serious indisposition, retires to go home. While Figaro is shaving Dr. Bartolo, the lovers plan a midnight elopement, but the doctor overhears and sends them all away.

Don Basilio comes back to tell the doctor of the music-teacher ruse. Thereupon Dr. Bartolo decides on quick action and sends Basilio to fetch a notary. He also summons Rosina, shows her her own letter as proof that the count has a mistress, and by arousing her jealousy and anger wins her consent to marry him at once. She even tells him of the projected midnight elopement. Whereupon Dr. Bartolo orders her to her room, locks the door, and runs out to find the police.

432

When, after an orchestral interlude depicting a storm, the count and Figaro step in from the balcony, cloaked and hatted for flight, Rosina receives her suitor with scornful reproaches. Then the count, throwing off his cloak, stands forth dressed as a nobleman and tells her that he is Almaviva, not Lindoro. The truth is now clear to Rosina, and all would be well if the ladder on which the men had climbed to the balcony had not disappeared. While they stand there bewildered, Basilio enters with the notary.

Figaro seizes the opportunity. He instructs the notary to draw up the desired marriage contract. Don Basilio would interfere, but the count, pulling him aside, bribes him with a ring and the promise of a pair of bullets in his head if he makes trouble. Basilio, of course, complies, and the marriage proceeds. Too late to stop the wedding, Dr. Bartolo returns, bringing along an officer and soldiers, whom he bids arrest Almaviva and Figaro as robbers.

When the count reveals who he is and presents Rosina as his wife, affairs take another turn, and all except Dr. Bartolo congratulate the bride and bridegroom. The doctor is furious because by getting rid of the ladder he has made the marriage possible. However, the count wins him over by renouncing Rosina's dowry in his favor. So all ends happily.

P. S.

Some biographers have written as if Rossini had gone to Rome with a definite contract to write two new operas, of which the immortal *Barber of Seville* was the second. This is not the case. The contract for what was eventually to be *The Barber of Seville* was signed by the composer and the Duke Francesco Sforza-Cesarini, the impresario of the Argentina Theater, on the 15th of December, while *Torvaldo* was actually in rehearsal at the Valle. So many inaccurate statements have been made about the production of *The Barber of Seville* that one of such comparatively minor importance seems of little moment. . . .

First, then, it is not true that the Papal censorship had anything whatever to do with the choice of subject. Sforza-Cesarini had originally ordered for Rossini's use an *opera buffa* libretto to contain an important part for the Spanish tenor Garcia. When it arrived, he thought the plot too vulgar and refused it. It was Rossini himself who suggested to the author of the ill-starred *Torvaldo* that he should prepare in its stead a libretto from Beaumarchais's famous play. So far from this being identical with that which Paisiello had so successfully set to music more than thirty years before, both Rossini and Sterbini took great trouble to produce a new libretto thoroughly up to date, the active collaboration of Rossini himself in the matter remaining beyond question.

Second, it is not true that Rossini wrote to Paisiello to ask if he had any objection to *The Barber of Seville* being set once more to music. There was not the slightest reason why he should have done so. It was customary in those days for various composers to set the same libretto over and over again,

Metastasio being the most favored source on which to draw. As a matter of fact, *The Barber of Seville* had been used for musical purposes on two occasions before Paisiello's version in 1782; three Germans and a Frenchman had tackled it between that date and Rossini's production in Rome, while, by a curious coincidence, Morlacchi produced another *Barber of Seville* in Dresden at almost exactly the same time.* What Rossini and his librettist in fact did is this: they called their opera in the first instance *Almaviva* or *L'Inutile Precauzione,* informing the public in a preface to the libretto that the change of title was due to their respect for the previous achievement of Paisiello and explaining various departures from Beaumarchais's original text. In view of Paisiello's well-known attitude towards all other composers, it seems possible that the eminently practical Rossini was making an attempt to prevent any definite act of hostility on the part of the old Neapolitan composer. He might have saved himself the trouble.

Third, it is not true to say, as a distinguished French biographer has done, that Rossini made no use of music from his previous operas in *The Barber.* As we have already seen, he took one phrase and a chorus from *Sigismondo,* making use further of ideas (not whole numbers) from *Aureliano, Signor Bruschino,* and *La Cambiale,* as well as the storm music from *La Pietra del Paragone.* But the suggestion in the opposite sense, frequently made, that he handed over certain numbers to other composers, is equally untrue. It is a fact that he allowed the tenor, Garcia, to serenade Rosina with some arrangements of his own of Spanish popular tunes, but he himself had already written music for the purpose, and in fact insisted on its being restored after the first night. Nor is it a fact that a composer called Romani wrote at Rossini's request one of Bartolo's numbers. This number, "Manca un foglio," was written by Romani when *The Barber* was produced at Florence nine months later. Unfortunately, though Rossini's original number, "A un dottor," is infinitely superior in every respect, the Italians (not the French) have as a rule sung Romani's ever since, presumably because it is much easier. It has, however, been left in the main to foreigners to substitute for the charming music provided for Rosina's singing lesson a succession of imported show pieces, one more inept than the other. Possibly the reason is that the part is usually sung nowadays by a soprano, not a mezzo-soprano.

Lastly, *The Barber* was not produced, as Stendhal says, on the 26th of December 1816; nor on the 16th, the 6th or the 5th of February, as stated by other biographers, including the writer of the article on Rossini in Grove's "Diction-

* To round off the story, the curious may like to know that in the last year of his life Rossini accepted the dedication of yet another version, writing to the composer, a young man called Dall'Argine, a charming letter full of the praises of "Papa Paisiello" and good wishes for his success. Moreover, as recently as 1929 a final attempt, wholly unsuccessful, was made to supersede Rossini's *Barber,* which has now remained for nearly a hundred and twenty years in secure possession of the field—the best possible tribute to its merits.

ary." It is now established from documents recently published that *The Barber of Seville* was first performed on the 20th of February 1816.

The ground having been cleared of definite inaccuracies, a moment's consideration may be given to the vexed question of exactly how long Rossini took to write his masterpiece. He himself specified thirteen days to Wagner, but on other occasions he said twelve. According to Garcia, he wrote it in eight days, and various other periods have been given. What is certain is that Sterbini did not even begin to work on the libretto before the 16th of January. Thus, if we allow a week for final rehearsals and presume that Rossini started on the music a few days after the libretto was actually begun, he could not in any case have taken more than three weeks. Besides we do, in fact, know that the first act was delivered to the theater on the 5th of February, so that a fortnight seems a more probable period of time.

It is, of course, a miracle. The mere writing down of the notes would seem to be an impossibility, quite apart from any consideration of their quality. The reader must also remember, though the overture now associated with *The Barber* was imported from *Aureliano* by way of *Elisabetta,* that Rossini originally wrote an entirely new overture on Spanish popular themes, which has since been lost.* He may, however, have done this during rehearsals. So far as any explanation of the phenomenon is possible, that suggested by Verdi, who insisted that Rossini must have had the music of *The Barber* in his head for some time before he actually began writing it down, seems the most plausible, especially when we remember that it was he himself who pressed the subject on Sterbini.

Everybody knows that the first performance of *The Barber of Seville* was a spectacular failure. The partisans of Paisiello, not improbably at the instigation of the old man himself, turned out in force to jeer and hiss, but this was not the chief trouble. Apparently the management of the Argentina Theater was unpopular in Rome, a fact which the rival management of the Valle was not slow to exploit to its own advantage. How strong the feeling was may be gathered by the fact that, during the famous unison passage in the ensemble at the end of the first act, somebody shouted out: "Here we are at D. C.'s funeral," the allusion, with its scarcely credible bad taste, being to the fact that Duke Cesarini had died during rehearsals only a fortnight before. The account of the evening left by the original Rosina, the mezzo-soprano Signora Giorgi-Righetti, leaves no doubt of the determination of an organized opposition to ruin the opera. They roared with laughter when the tenor began tuning the guitar for his serenade to Rosina. They whistled and shouted during the entire first act. Some say that Don Basilio falling through a trapdoor inad-

---

* The score would seem, however, to have been in existence in 1865, when Arditi announced in the prospectus of his promenade concerts at Her Majesty's Theatre an "overture in B flat, originally written for *Il Barbiere di Siviglia* (first performance in England)." Unless, of course, Arditi was the victim, conscious or unconscious, of a hoax.

vertently left open, and a cat wandering across the stage during the first finale, completed the disaster. When Rossini rose from his seat at the piano to applaud the singers who had made such a brave fight against hopeless odds, he was roundly hissed for what was judged to be his insulting indifference to the verdict of the public. The second act was scarcely listened to at all; irretrievable ruin seemed assured. At the end he just slipped out of the theater and went home.

Signora Giorgi-Righetti says that, wishing to show her sympathy, she later went round to his house and found him sound asleep, but Giulio Fara, who has made a penetrating study of Rossini's psychology, justly doubts the truth of this. From what we know of Rossini's sensitiveness and nervousness, it is extremely unlikely that he met such an ordeal with the indifference implied.* Giorgi-Righetti may well have thought she was telling the truth, and it would have been typical of Rossini, both at the time and later, to corroborate her story. After all, who is to know whether his sleep was not, in fact, a pretense? Just as he pretended at the second performance to be ill, so that he should not have to appear at the piano and expose himself once more to the hostility of the public. It seems far more likely that we have here the first instance of that nervous shrinking from public criticism which was later to play such an important part in Rossini's life. As we shall see, he was discovered on several occasions in ruses of a similar nature. But this was the first of them, and more likely, therefore, to win credence.

His extreme discomfiture did not, however, last long. After the second performance friends hurried to his supposed sickbed to assure him that the evening had been as successful as the first had been disastrous. The Romans, left to themselves and allowed to listen to the music in peace, were not slow in taking The Barber to their hearts, though the fact that the season came to an end a week later prevented there being a great number of further performances. Even then, however, Rossini's adversaries do not seem to have thrown up the sponge, for it is not without significance that five years were to elapse before The Barber, after a triumphal tour through the rest of Italy, was again produced in Rome.

Nor must it be imagined that The Barber won immediate and universal approval elsewhere. The English press dismissed the music as light and careless, and prophesied a short life for the opera. A well-known German musical critic, comparing it unfavorably with Paisiello's Barber, found the music too heavy and confused, notably devoid of the spark of genius so evident in L'Italiana in Algerì. Some of the French critics also professed their preference for Paisiello; others found the first finale painfully noisy and the opera as a whole lacking in cantabile tunes. Nevertheless, it did not take long for The Barber to win the

---

* In later life, by way of comforting the young composer Catelani, who suffered from nerves, Rossini admitted that when he was young he often had to assume a mask of gaiety to hide his nervous terror.

position which it has ever since retained. The musicians, headed by Beethoven, Berlioz, Wagner, and Brahms, though they might disapprove of Rossini in general, always kept a particularly warm place in their hearts for *The Barber* in particular. The public in all countries have never shown any sign of wavering in their allegiance. For more than a hundred years *The Barber,* enjoying as much esteem as popularity, has occupied a unique position in musical literature. . . .

Beyond question, it was the most satisfactory, perhaps the only completely satisfactory, libretto that Rossini ever set to music. True, Sterbini, whom there is no reason to suspect of any particular talent, could not go far wrong. It is often forgotten that Beaumarchais's original "Le Barbier de Séville" was interspersed with songs; all he had to do was to follow the main outlines of the original as faithfully as he could. He must have the credit, however, for having performed his task with intelligence, and for having displayed ingenuity in turning some of Beaumarchais's best ideas, not to say actual lines, into quite tolerable verse, the Calumny Song being a notable instance.

In practice, however, the glory of *The Barber* remains Rossini's alone, quite apart from any share he may have had in the construction of the libretto. Every situation, almost every idea, seems to have suggested to him one musical train of thought after another, nearly all equally felicitous. Indeed, the spontaneity of the score is such that one has an impression of music spouting from his pen, as it were, under high pressure. There are one or two defects in the second act, notably as regards excessive ornamentation, but the first act is sheer perfection, alike in the quality and the differentiation of the various numbers. One has only to think of the dramatic imagination of "La calunnia," the sparkling bustle of "Largo al factotum," the sophisticated ingenuousness of "Una voce," all household words even today. Then there are the deft orchestral touches and, above all, the ingenuity and the mastery displayed in the handling of the various movements of the finale. No comic opera can show anything better.

Some comparison with Mozart's *Marriage of Figaro* is perhaps inevitable. In the matter of recitative and, especially, of the tenderness and the melancholy with which Mozart, reflecting his own personality, invested the characters of Cherubino and the Countess, *Figaro* possesses an undoubted superiority. But it may be doubted whether, as a setting pure and simple of Beaumarchais's text, *The Barber* is not in reality more successful. There is no real passion, much less love, in either of Beaumarchais's plays; there is gallantry, irony, wit— precisely the qualities that Rossini was able to turn into music better than any other man who ever lived. In a sense he was built on very much the same lines as Beaumarchais, both having a good deal in common with the character of Figaro, so that it is not surprising if we get the impression of Figaro's vital, mocking personality dominating everything and everybody in the opera. The naughty Rosina, the dashing Count, the repulsive Bartolo, the unspeakable

Basilio, all really move and have their being in the sprightly intrigues of Figaro, who was something of a literary man before he became a barber. Anyone who has seen Beaumarchais's plays on the stage knows that this is precisely the impression conveyed by them. It was Rossini's great achievement and good fortune to have been able, apparently without effort, to convey the same idea from the beginning to the end of his opera.*

F. T.

To Rossini's *Il Barbiere di Siviglia* belongs the honor of being the first opera sung in New York in Italian. On Nov. 29, 1825, it opened, at the Park Theater, the season of Manuel Garcia's company, which had been imported by Dominick Lynch, a rich wine dealer and amateur of music, and Stephen Price, manager of the theater. An extraordinary cast included the seventeen-year-old Maria Felicita Garcia (subsequently Mme. Malibran) as Rosina; her father, Manuel Garcia, Sr., as Almaviva; her brother, Manuel Garcia, Jr., as Figaro; her mother, Signora Garcia, as Berta; Rosich as Dr. Bartolo, and Angrisani as Don Basilio. The conductor was Nathaniel de Luce.

As a matter of fact, an abridged English version of the work had been presented at the same theater on May 17, 1819, only a little more than three years after the world *première* in Rome (Feb. 20, according to Radiciotti's investigations), in which Garcia the father was the Almaviva, Luigi Zamboni the Figaro, Bartolomeo Botticelli the Dr. Bartolo, Zenobio Vitarelli the Don Basilio, and Gertrude Righetti-Giorgi the Rosina.

Il Barbiere entered the repertory of New York's Metropolitan Opera House Dec. 15, 1883, with Marcella Sembrich as Rosina, Roberto Stagno as Almaviva, Giuseppe del Puente as Figaro, Corsini as Dr. Bartolo, and Mirabella as Don Basilio. Vianesi conducted.

The role of Rosina from the beginning appealed so strongly to singers that soon sopranos had it arranged to suit their voices, almost to the exclusion of the contraltos for whom it had been designed. Thus Adelina Patti became perhaps the most famous of all Rosinas.

P. S.

* As an indication of the scale on which composers were paid in those days the reader may be interested to know what Rossini received for *The Barber of Seville*. There were no royalties, of course, and no publication rights. According to his own account, his remuneration consisted of twelve hundred francs and a nut-brown suit with gilt buttons presented to him by the impresario so that he should look well in the orchestra pit! In his famous interview with Wagner, Rossini amusingly analyzed this payment as working out at a hundred francs a day for each of the thirteen days employed in writing the opera, the suit being taken as worth a hundred francs. It made him, he said, feel very proud, for two and a half francs a day was all that his father had ever been able to earn by playing the trumpet.

As a matter of fact, the accounts of the Argentina Theater show that Rossini received four hundred, not three hundred, scudi as he imagined. But whether the sum total was some sixty or some eighty pounds, it does not seem an excessive price for the world to have paid for a *Barber of Seville*.

La Cenerentola

[Cinderella]

DRAMMA GIOCOSO (JOCOSE DRAMA) IN 2 ACTS

Book by Giacomo Ferretti

First performance: Teatro Valle, Rome, Jan. 25, 1817

CHARACTERS

Cenerentola, CONTRALTO
Clorinda, her step-sister, SOPRANO
Tisbe, her step-sister, CONTRALTO
Don Magnifico, her step-father,
BUFFO-BASS

The Prince (Don Ramiro), TENOR
Alidoro, his friend, BASS
Dandini, the Prince's valet, BARITONE

Ferretti's version of the famous Cinderella story is practically a translation of Étienne's *Cendrillon* with music by Nicoló Isouard. The supernatural element is lacking altogether. The fairy godmother is replaced by Alidoro, a philosopher in the service of the prince. Cinderella is in this version a young woman browbeaten by her two stepsisters, Clorinda and Tisbe, and her stepfather, Don Magnifico.

One day Alidoro, disguised as a beggar, comes to the home of Don Magnifico, seeking alms. The two stepsisters drive him away, but Cinderella gives him her own meal. The "beggar" makes a mental note of this kindness, having already observed the girl's beauty.

Don Ramiro, prince of Salerno, according to the will of his father, must take unto himself a bride by a certain date. He is anxious that some eligible young woman shall marry him for love, not because he is a prince. Changing places with his valet Dandini, the prince pays Don Magnifico a visit. He too is struck with Cinderella's charm.

At a ball in the prince's palace, to which Cinderella goes, after being fashionably fitted out by Alidoro, Dandini, still masquerading as the prince, tells her he loves her. But she informs him that she loves only his squire—really the prince. During the evening Cinderella gives the "squire" one of two matched bracelets she is wearing and then departs.

Some days later the real prince, seeking shelter from a storm, comes to the house of Don Magnifico, and while there sees the other bracelet on the wrist of Cinderella. Straightway the two lovers embrace, and all ends happily.

P. S.

[After the production of *The Barber of Seville* in Rome early in 1816, Rossini made his headquarters in Naples. There he remained for five and a half years on a contract with Domenico Barbaia, the impresario of the historic San Carlo theatre. Rossini was required to write two operas a year. But that was by no means all. There were supervisory tasks to carry out, singers to audition and engage, and several other chores, depending on the whim of Barbaia, a former bottlewasher who had advanced himself to the most coveted position in theatrical Naples. Rossini is understood to have remarked in later years: "Had he been able, Barbaia would have made me run his kitchen." The pay, however, was good, considering that it included, beside the stipend for each opera, a liberal cut of Barbaia's revenue from the gambling tables that were a frequent feature of the Italian opera houses of the time. Rossini was also given free board in Barbaia's house, and, what concerns us here, permission to produce operas in some other Italian city after he had furnished Barbaia with his annual quota of two. During his first year in Naples Rossini composed *La Gazzetta* (produced on September 26, 1816) and "Otello" (produced on December 4, 1816). He was now free to take advantage of the last-mentioned clause of his contract with Barbaia.]

With the completion of the two operas due under his contract, Rossini was now at liberty again to go away from Naples. As a matter of fact, before leaving Rome he had already promised the management of the Valle Theater to return in the autumn to write an opera for production on the 26th of December. For various reasons neither side was able to observe the times stipulated in the contract, and Rossini did not actually arrive in Rome until the middle of December. He found even then that no libretto had been definitely selected, the Papal censorship having objected, apparently with some reason, to the subject originally suggested.

As often happened, Rossini received board and lodging from his impresario as part of his remuneration,* so he and the theater librettist, Ferretti, spent the second night before Christmas drinking tea in the impresario's house and discussing possible subjects. Rossini had retired to bed, and Ferretti, who has left a vivid account of the incident, was sitting by his side, half overcome with sleep, when somehow the idea of Cinderella occurred to both of them.

"Would you write me a libretto?" said Rossini.

"Would you really put it to music?" replied Ferretti, in whom the remembrance of being passed over in favor of Sterbini a year before seems still to have rankled.

"When can I have the scenario?"

---

* In this case the board does not seem to have been satisfactory. The Valle impresario liked food very highly seasoned, which was not at all to Rossini's taste. It is characteristic of him that he almost immediately decided to eat out at his own expense.

"Tomorrow morning if I can keep awake."

"All right. Good night."

Whereupon Rossini turned over and immediately went to sleep. Nothing could better illustrate the happy-go-lucky methods of operatic manufacture in those days.

Ferretti kept his word. By Christmas Day Rossini had received the first installment of the libretto known as *La Cenerentola* (Cinderella), the others arriving at regular intervals during the next three weeks. Rossini seems to have set them to music as they came, and in twenty-four days completed the entire opera, a feat all the more remarkable because, except for the overture, which he borrowed from *La Gazzetta,* and the two *arie del sorbetto,* "Vasto teatro è il mondo" and "Sventurata! Mi credea," which he handed over to a composer called Agolini, all the music was entirely new.*

When *La Cenerentola* was produced on the 25th of January 1817, it met with a reception only less hostile than that given to *The Barber.* But, according to Ferretti, Rossini, though pained and a little stunned by the apparent failure, never doubted for one moment the eventual success of the opera. "It will be very popular in Rome before the end of the season; in the whole of Italy at the end of a year, and in France and England within two years. Impresarios and, still more, prima donnas will end by fighting for it," he assured the disconsolate Ferretti. His prophecy showed remarkable acumen, because *La Cenerentola* over a long period rivaled *The Barber* itself in popularity, and shows signs of returning to favor even at the present time. Deservedly so, for it is a delightful opera.

The libretto has been abused by several biographers, including Radiciotti, but by no means with justice. It is true that Ferretti's version of Cinderella has nothing except its bare bones in common with the story as we know it. The fairy element is dispensed with altogether, partly, no doubt, as a concession to Rossini's well-known dislike of the fantastic, the place of the fairy godmother being taken by an eminently practical philosopher in the service of the Prince. Cinderella herself, with her talk of Paris and Vienna fashions, becomes something very like a poor little débutante bullied by two stepsisters, who in modern parlance would certainly be termed "gold-diggers," and a rascally stepfather who has embezzled her fortune. In short, nothing could be more mundane, prosaic if you will, alike in action and dialogue. But, with this reservation, Ferretti's libretto, following in its main lines Étienne's *Cendrillon,* an operatic version of the story which had met with great favor in Paris, is efficient, even at times ingenious. The action moves well and quickly; the situations are ef-

---

* Radiciotti is not wholly correct in identifying the last allegro with the Count's "Ah, il più lieto" in the finale of *The Barber.* The main ideas are the same, but they are treated differently, the very characteristic and delightful run down from top A to low G sharp, for instance, being in fact peculiar to *Cinderella.* De Curzon and others who have stated that *La Cenerentola* is characterized by many instances of self-borrowing are, it would seem, mistaken.

fective and often, like some of the dialogue, really funny; the characterization is excellent, especially in the cases of the stepfather, Don Magnifico, Dandini, and Cinderella herself. If *La Cenerentola* has failed to maintain a position corresponding to its merits, the responsibility cannot justly be laid upon Ferretti.

Still less can the failure be ascribed to any inferior quality in Rossini's music. For fun, sparkle, and elegance, for almost everything, indeed, except profundity of feeling, the score of *La Cenerentola* could scarcely be improved upon. There is even some genuine pathos in the little song Cinderella sings to herself, and especially in the charming scene where she asks to be allowed to go to the ball. But apart from the excellent workmanship of the concerted music, notably the very typical and original sextet in the second act and the finale of the first, perhaps the most delightful characteristics of the opera are its thoroughgoing, unabashed lightheartedness and its astonishing wealth of musical ideas. It is impossible to particularize the excellent things, so many are they; but, as an example of gaiety, all Dandini's music must be mentioned, to say nothing of the splendid scene when Don Magnifico, half intoxicated, boasts of what he proposes to do when he is made superintendent of the princely cellars. Then there is the delicacy of the overture alike in subject and treatment, the vivacity of the opening scene, not to mention the galaxy of "patter" songs and the thunderstorm, happily conventionalized in music that remains suggestive without ever being out of character with the delicious frivolity of the opera as a whole.

In view of all these charming qualities it does seem odd that *La Cenerentola* should not have survived in the repertory. True, the recitatives are rather commonplace; but then, the recitatives of *The Barber* are in no way remarkable. True, *La Cenerentola,* with its comparatively frequent changes of scene, has not quite the direct appeal of its predecessor, apart from the latter's inestimable advantage in the matter of Beaumarchais's wit, still partly enshrined in the opera. In all probability, however, the main reason for the decline of *La Cenerentola* should be sought in the increasing difficulty of finding a cast of singers adequate to deal with it. Doubtless, the elaborate vocal ornamentation must become a trifle monotonous in any case, though there are several passages in the opera, notably where Cinderella makes her brilliant entry to the ball, where it can be justified on strictly æsthetic grounds. Whether justifiable or unjustifiable, however, the fact remains that singers of sufficient competence have during the last fifty years become increasingly rare. It is not merely a question of finding an adequate Cinderella, though, in view of the fact that she is a mezzo-soprano, this is difficult enough. Practically the whole cast must be possessed of consummate vocal technique if anything like justice is to be done to the music, which is far more exacting in this respect than that of *The Barber of Seville*. Nevertheless, as a work of art the score of *La Cenerentola* must be rated exceedingly high; it is undoubtedly one of the most happy products of the school of Cimarosa, to which it so emphatically belongs.

F. T.

Of the musical numbers the introduction, the duet between Don Magnifico and Dandini, "Un segreto d'importanza"; the *buffo* cavatina of Don Magnifico; and the florid rondo of Cinderella, "Non più mesta accanto al fuoco," which closes the opera, stand out especially in a score which, for melodic invention and comic verve, is scarcely second to *Il Barbiere di Siviglia* itself.

La Cenerentola, ossia La Bontà in trionfo was introduced to America, in the original Italian, at the Park Theater, New York, June 27, 1826, by Manuel Garcia's company, with his daughter Maria (Mme. Malibran) in the name part. For several decades it remained popular in New York, especially in English adaptations.

With the decline of florid singing and, in particular, the scarcity of competent contraltos for the title role, *La Cenerentola* fell into neglect. At Booth's Theater, some of Rossini's music, as arranged by Max Maretzek, was used for a production called *Cinderella,* brought out Oct. 12, 1880. . . . In Italy it entered a period of disuse after a revival at the Teatro dal Verme, Milan, in 1892, in which Guerrina Fabbri sang the name part.

A few years ago *La Cenerentola* was successfully revived in Europe for the late Conchita Supervia, a Spanish contralto of uncommon charm and accomplishment. In Germany and Austria, too, a new edition of the work called *Angelina,* in which the title role is revised to suit a soprano voice, has also been staged.

P. S.

[It was not till 1953, or more than three-quarters of a century after its last performance in New York, that *La Cenerentola* returned to circulation in America. On March 26 of that year it enjoyed a spectacular success with both the press and the public as one of the most brilliant and entertaining novelties of the New York City Opera regime at the City Center. Frances Bible sang the title role, and Joseph Rosenstock, general director of the company (succeeding Laszlo Halasz), conducted. The Rossini opera, long thought dead and beyond feasible resuscitation in this country, had evidently sprung back to renewed and enduring life.]

Semiramide

[Semiramis]

MELODRAMMA TRAGICO (TRAGIC MELODRAMA) IN 2 ACTS

Book by GAETANO ROSSI, after VOLTAIRE's tragedy *Sémiramis*

First performance: Teatro Fenice, Venice, Feb. 3, 1823

CHARACTERS

Semiramide, Queen of Babylon, widow of King Ninus, SOPRANO

Arsaces, Commander of the Army, CONTRALTO

Ghost of Ninus, BASSO

Oroe, chief of the Magi, BASSO

Assur, a prince of the royal blood, BARITONE

Azema, a princess, SOPRANO

The action takes place in ancient Babylon

Semiramis and her lover, Prince Assurus, to employ the more familiar English names, have murdered her husband, Ninus, king of Babylon, and Semiramis has taken possession of the vacant throne. The warrior Arsaces, who is really the queen's son, though she does not know it, returns from a campaign to receive official honors. Semiramis falls in love with the youthful captain, who himself is in love with Princess Azema. During the triumphal festivities the tomb of Ninus suddenly opens and his ghost emerges to declare that Arsaces will one day be king. Semiramis and Arsaces discover their relationship, but the joy of recognition is brief, for Assurus kills Semiramis with a dagger stroke meant for Arsaces. He in turn kills Assurus. Thus both throne and Azema become his.

P. S.

By the middle of December [1822] the Rossinis were in Venice, where he had been offered the then unprecedented sum of five thousand francs to write an opera for the Fenice. Before the new opera, however, he was under contract to produce *Maometto* suitably adapted to the characteristics of the Venetian company. To put it bluntly, *Maometto* was a disastrous failure. Owing to his unexpected activities at Verona, as well as the obligation to direct two court concerts at Venice, when the Czar of Russia and the Emperor of Austria passed through the city on their way back from the Congress, Rossini had not the time to carry out the promised alterations. The tenor, a young Englishman called Sinclair, was handicapped by insufficient familiarity with the

Italian language; Colbran, who seems to have been having continual trouble with her throat about this time, had the unwonted experience of being soundly hissed. All this unfavorably predisposed the public towards the composer, and his enemies in the press openly hinted that he could not possibly find the time to write an important new opera before the end of the season. Rossini, thoroughly on his mettle, confounded all prognostications by composing in thirty-three days an extremely long and complicated opera which the whole of Europe during the next six years agreed in regarding as his masterpiece—a feat as incredible in its way as the composition of *The Barber* itself.*

The opera was the famous *Semiramide,* produced on the 3rd of February 1823, with a libretto adapted from Voltaire's well-known tragedy of the same name by Gaetano Rossi, the author of *Cambiale di Matrimonio* and *Tancredi.* The story is in essence that of Hamlet and Orestes, with the additional complication that the guilty Queen-mother falls in love with her avenging son before she discovers his identity, and that he kills her in mistake for her lover. It is exceedingly ponderous, but possesses at least the unaccustomed merits of intelligibility and sufficiency of action. The music alternately rises to the heights and descends to the depths. Nothing, for instance, could be better than the overture, which, when properly played, sounds as effective today as ever it did. Unlike most of Rossini's overtures, it is mainly built on themes from the opera itself; the andantino is the tune to which an oath of loyalty is taken to Queen Semiramis, and the first theme of the allegro is associated with the awe that invests King Ninus's mausoleum—which, in view of the charming naïveté of the music, might, with greater appropriateness on this occasion, be designated "Ninny's tomb." It is a splendid composition alike as regards thematic material, form, treatment, and scoring, but there are at least two important scenes in the opera worthy to stand beside it. For instance, the whole of the very lengthy finale of Act I is excellent from every point of view. This contains the famous "Qual mesto gemito" ensemble, from which Verdi undoubtedly derived the idea of the "Miserere" in *Trovatore,* both the tune itself and its treatment in canon being wholly admirable. But there is more than this. The utterances of the regal ghost are most impressive in what may be termed the *Don Giovanni* "Commendatore" convention, and as for the final vivace, it provides about the best example extant of the Rossini crescendo, for the effect of excitement produced by the rushing three-four rhythm could not well be surpassed.

The scene towards the end of the second act, where the Queen's lover lies in wait to kill her son, is also of the first order. Here is a most effective and

---

* Radiciotti thinks that he used some of his leisure at Castenaso to sketch out a preliminary plan of the opera, apparently basing his statement on the fact that Rossini subsequently guaranteed to a purchaser the piano at Castenaso as being the one used in the composition of *Semiramide*. Radiciotti may be right, but the evidence is not conclusive. The piano might have been moved from Venice to Castenaso later. And why, if the opera had already been put on the stocks, should Rossini have made such a point of telling Michotte, as he did, that he had written it in thirty-three days?

appropriate orchestral introduction, succeeded by a splendid male chorus and one of the most beautiful and expressive arias for solo bass that Rossini ever wrote. Nor do the merits of *Semiramide* end here. There is a duet between the Queen and her son in the second act that could scarcely be more effective, introduced, too, by some orchestral writing that seems to suggest that Rossini had by no means forgotten his visit to Beethoven. At least two of the arias are very pretty; several choruses are fine, and the recitatives show real power.

On the other hand, much of the music is exceedingly poor, typical instances being the opening and final choruses. In the former the entrance of the "Babylonians and strangers of both sexes" into the Temple of Baal suggests that the cult of that god was a far more frivolous and syncopated affair than is usually supposed. As for the last chorus, it is frankly absurd in its summary cheerfulness, as if intended to suggest to the audience that the gloomy end of the opera is not really a matter for them to worry about. Generally speaking, moreover, the music is too often inappropriate to the situation, the "horror" and "terror" in which the libretto abounds being frequently associated with the most trivial musical phrases. The elaboration of the vocal writing, too, is excessive throughout the opera.

Inevitably, the defects of *Semiramide* were less obvious to a public that troubled little about dramatic verities than they are to us, who have come to take a certain measure of such verities for granted. Indeed, it looks very much as if what are in fact the best portions of *Semiramide* were those that appealed least to the first-night audience, at any rate. It is not true, as has often been stated, that the opera was unfavorably received. But the audience, though they went into raptures over the overture, did not like the first act, which, as a whole, is undoubtedly superior to the second, and contains, moreover, the magnificent finale already alluded to. The opera was redeemed for them in all probability by the prettiness of the tunes and the showy brilliance of all the vocal writing—not to mention the presence of a military band on the stage, a Rossinian innovation much discussed at the time. It is only fair to add that contemporary criticism, though exaggerated in its enthusiasm, did not fail to emphasize the best features of the work, while after the first few performances the public also began to appreciate the superior beauties of the first act. *Semiramide* ran for twenty-eight consecutive nights—in fact, to the end of the season—and Rossini was once more the hero of the hour. Illuminated gondolas, with an Austrian military band playing a selection of tunes from his most popular operas, accompanied him to his house. Nor was his success confined to Venice. During the next few years *Semiramide* was destined to arouse the enthusiasm not only of Italy but of France, England, and Germany. Already the popularity of Rossini's music was unparalleled. In this year, 1823, Radiciotti tells us, at least twenty-three of his operas were being performed in various countries. In Spain and Portugal people would scarcely listen to any other music. In Russia, South America, and Mexico he was easily the favorite composer of the day. Even the Sultan of Turkey liked his military band to play marches and arias from Rossini's operas.

And now *Semiramide* came to sum up and crown the galaxy of successes, being in fact to Rossini very much what Austerlitz had been to Napoleon. The comparison is not merely fanciful. With *Semiramide* Rossini had definitely ceased to be an Italian composer and became a world figure. His astonishing and rapid triumphs in that role can only be compared with those of the great Emperor. There has never been anything quite like them in the history of music. Stendhal, writing in this very year, summarized the facts accurately enough when he said of Rossini: "The glory of this man is only limited by the limits of civilization itself; and he is not yet thirty-two."

F. T.

Venice heard the world *première* of *Semiramide* on February 2, 1823, and gave it a rousing send-off. There is some mystery about its arrival in America: there is a now discredited legend that the Garcías produced it on April 25, 1826, in New York; actually, New Orleans may have been the first American city to hear it, on May 1, 1837. If this latter is so, the first New York performance may not have been until January 3, 1845, at Palmo's Opera House, on Chambers Street, west of Broadway. Melba, Sofia Scalchi, and Édouard de Reszke were the principals in the only Metropolitan performances of *Semiramide,* which occurred during the seasons of 1893–94 and 1894–95. From the very beginning, the opera attracted brilliant casts, starting with Pasta, Malibran, and Antonio Tamburini as Semiramis, Arsaces, and Assur respectively, though the great Spanish mezzo occasionally attempted the name role. The delightful Angiolina Bosio, called by Chorley "next to Mme. Sontag . . . the most lady-like person whom I have seen on the stage of the Italian opera," and who died prematurely, was a widely acclaimed Semiramis. Giulia Grisi and Marietta Alboni, Therese Tietjens and Zelia Trebelli, and Patti and Scalchi made singing history in the duets between the imperious Babylonian queen and her son Arsaces. Sontag was Rossini's favorite Semiramis. In 1868, when at his suggestion Patti first considered playing the part, Rossini composed special cadenzas for her, though before she could use them she was singing at his funeral in Père-Lachaise.

W. B., H. W.

Guillaume Tell

[William Tell]

OPERA IN 4 ACTS

Book by Étienne de Jouy and Hippolyte Bis, after Schiller's play

First performance: Opéra, Paris, Aug. 3, 1829

CHARACTERS

William Tell, BASS ⎫
Arnold, TENOR ⎬ Swiss patriots
Walter Fürst, BASS ⎭
Melcthal, Arnold's father, BASS
Gessler, Governor of Schwitz and Uri, BASS
Rudolph, captain of Gessler's bodyguard, TENOR

Ruodi, a fisherman, TENOR
Leuthold, a shepherd, BASS
Jemmy, William Tell's son, SOPRANO
Hedwig, Tell's wife, SOPRANO
Mathilde, Gessler's daughter and a princess of the House of Hapsburg, SOPRANO

Peasants, Knights, Pages, Ladies of the Train of Mathilde, Three Brides and Their Bridegrooms, Hunters, Soldiers, and Guards

The action takes place in Switzerland during the fourteenth century

The Swiss people are rebellious because of the tyranny of the governor, Gessler. Their disaffection is aggravated in particular by the slaying of Melchtal, the patriarch of the village, accused of fomenting a revolt after the herdsman Leuthold has killed one of Gessler's train for attempting to outrage his daughter. Tell aids Leuthold to escape, and Arnold, Gessler's son, joins the conspirators against the tyrant, though he happens to be in love with Mathilde, a princess of the house of Austria, who may one day rule over them. The men of the conspiring cantons, under the leadership of Tell, meet in the forest at night and swear death to Gessler.

In order to discover the guilty, Gessler has a pole set up in the square at Altdorf, places a hat on it, and orders one and all in token of their loyalty to salute the hat as though it were the governor. Tell refuses thus to degrade himself, and, recognized also as the man who helped Leuthold to get away, he is condemned to prove his rumored skill in archery by shooting an apple from the head of his son, Jemmy. Tell succeeds in doing so, to the exceeding annoyance of the tyrant. But when a second arrow falls from Tell's clothing and, questioned by Gessler, he admits it was intended for the tyrant had the other arrow killed Jemmy, Gessler orders both Tell and the boy to be thrown into a dungeon infested with reptiles. Mathilde, however, protects Jemmy.

Tell eventually escapes and over the stormy lake fares homeward. The Swiss rise and capture the castle; not, however, before Tell himself shoots Gessler. The region wins its liberty, and Mathilde, loyal to the cause of Tell, is united to Arnold.

P. S.

Paris was all agog for the new opera, the first, be it remembered, that Rossini had written wholly and exclusively for the French stage. Every month, beginning in the summer of 1828, the newspapers gave more or less accurate accounts of its progress and of the movements of its distinguished composer. It was in rehearsal; it was not in rehearsal but soon would be. It was to be produced at the end of the year, in the spring or summer of 1829. For each successive postponement various reasons were found, notably the interesting but exasperating condition of the leading lady, who had, most inconsiderately, got married. Her substitute, specially imported from Germany, had proved a failure; later, when she herself had recovered from the effects of matrimony, an attack of hoarseness unfortunately prevented her singing.

There was a certain amount of truth in some of these stories, but the real reason for the repeated postponement of *William Tell* was quite different. It may be summarized as more or less legitimate blackmail on Rossini's part. For some time past he had been engaged in negotiations with La Rochefoucauld [the director] as regards his position in France. When, just before the production of *Moïse,* his Théâtre Italien contract had come to an end, a special post had been invented for him: Composer to His Majesty and Inspector General of Singing, at a yearly salary of twenty thousand francs. Inevitably this strange appointment, which was in reality only an excuse to keep Rossini in touch with the Opéra and secure the benefit of his advice, gave rise to a good deal of ill-natured comment. Rossini, first and foremost, saw the humor of it, and on occasions, after listening with the utmost gravity to the performances of street singers on the boulevards, informed inquiring friends that he was merely carrying out his official duties. As a matter of fact, the money was not ill spent or the post ill named, for everyone was agreed that Rossini did more than any other man to raise the standard of singing in France.

Nevertheless, from an official point of view the position was not satisfactory. To begin with, he did not wish to be tied in perpetuity to residence in Paris; like Verdi later, he sometimes sighed for the comparative tranquillity of Italian life, and as early as 1827 he was asking a friend in Bologna to have his house put in order, because "I shall be back there sooner than you think." Secondly, he felt that his appointment was too dependent on the goodwill of the minister who happened to be responsible for the civil list; not to mention, perhaps, the permanence of the monarchy itself. For some years he had been trying to get the whole matter regularized in a proper contract. At last, in February 1829, he decided to bring matters to a head, writing in this sense to both

La Rochefoucauld and the Minister. He wanted a yearly salary in perpetuity of six thousand francs, in exchange for which he promised to write five operas during the next ten years, *William Tell* ranking as the first, and to remain in Paris for nine months each year; for every opera he was to receive fifteen thousand francs and a benefit performance.

It was not, he wrote, a mere question of self-interest; as La Rochefoucauld knew, he had had better offers from England, Germany, Austria. Did he not desire to show his gratitude to a sovereign who had treated him with such marked consideration, and to work for a theater that was admittedly the best in the world, he would prefer to go home to enjoy a nice long rest; and so on. In all of which there was some truth and a considerable amount of diplomacy. Charles X considered Rossini to be one of the principal ornaments of his court and capital; both La Rochefoucauld and the Minister, La Bouillerie, were well disposed. Nevertheless, the desired contract failed to materialize. So, in March, Rossini let the director of the Opéra understand that, unless it did, he might have to suspend the rehearsals of *William Tell* and refuse permission for the last two acts to be copied. A little later he put his threat into execution, bringing everything at the Opéra to a standstill for a fortnight. The director wrote despairing letters to La Rochefoucauld. Scenery and costumes, all were ready; only Rossini refused to move and would quite possibly withdraw the opera altogether unless his demands were satisfied; it might be unreasonable of him, but there it was. Even then, despite the insistence of La Rochefoucauld, certain influences at court hostile to Rossini delayed matters till April 18, when he finally received the contract. It bore the signature of the King himself, a point which may or may not have seemed of importance to Rossini at the time. Rehearsals began again and *William Tell* was saved for Paris.

On August 3, 1829, it was finally produced before an audience bursting with curiosity. Every seat had been sold for a long time past; boxes were said to have changed hands for as much as five hundred francs. The interest of both the public and the press had been stimulated by rumors about the opera. Rossini, they whispered, had sworn not to indulge in a single crescendo, in any of the familiar devices associated with his name; this was to be an entirely new kind of music. And so it was, a great deal of it, but by no means entirely to their liking. Though *William Tell* was hailed with a salvo of applause by every musician and critic of note, the public remained comparatively indifferent, judging the opera as a whole to be long, cold, and boring. . . .

The importance of *William Tell* is best attested by the enthusiasm of contemporary musicians. Fétis wrote that Rossini had achieved the apparently impossible in registering a further advance on what was best in his previous operas; the most hostile of French critics, Ortigue, added a postscript to his book on Rossini and French opera, emphasizing the unexpected beauties and originality of "this sublime music"; the German critics pointed out the veritable revolution that had taken place in Rossini's conception of dramatic writing. Nor did the composers lag behind the critics. Mendelssohn expressed to Chorley his unstinted admiration; Bellini said that *William Tell* made all contemporary music, including his own, seem like the work of pygmies; Verdi railed against the mutilations subsequently inflicted on such a great masterpiece, and soundly rated the Paris public for gaping at Meyerbeer before they had begun even to understand *William Tell;* Wagner, in his famous interview, told Rossini that, doubtless unwittingly, he had in the best moments of *William Tell* anticipated his own theories.

Most significant of all, however, was the attitude of Berlioz, who had little love for Rossini's music in general and, even after the first performance of *William Tell,* refused to believe that the enthusiasm of the musicians and the critics was really justifiable. But five years later he changed his mind, writing a detailed analysis of the opera that amounts, a few minor criticisms apart, to a veritable pæan of praise. . . .

The inclusion of *William Tell* in the repertory of the leading European opera houses followed as a matter of course during the next few years. Needless to say, in Italy there was trouble with the Austrian censorship, which, in Milan, insisted on the hero becoming William Wallace, the Swiss the Scotch, and the Austrians the English. All references to patriotism, liberty, or tyranny were suppressed, and the scene of the apple was omitted altogether. In Rome the Papal censorship discovered another innocuous patriot for the title role in the person of Rudolf of Sterling; they also thought it well to sprinkle the opera with pious references to God, heaven, and the saints. In Prussia William Tell was replaced by Andreas Hofer; in Russia by Charles the Bold. In Vienna, of all unlikely places, the libretto was allowed to stand, but the public took care to shout: "Long live the Habsburgs" at the end of every performance, lest the authorities should think their loyalty had been undermined!

None of this would have been of vital importance had the opera achieved anywhere a really popular success. But it did not. The Italians are said, for many years, to have preferred *Semiramide,* and the receipts of the first twelve performances at the Paris Opéra, so notably inferior to those for a similar number of performances of *Les Huguenots* and *Robert le Diable,* or even of *La Juive* and *I Vespri Siciliani,* provide the best possible evidence of its comparatively small hold on the public. Doubtless the excessive length was largely responsible. Rossini himself made some drastic cuts almost at once, and three years later authorized a version in three acts that was produced at Bordeaux and Prague. Even such drastic operations failed to save the life of *William Tell* as an entity; the Opéra began giving performances of isolated acts; finally of the second act alone. Years later the director, meeting Rossini in the street, thought to please him by relating that the second act was being given on that night at the Opéra. "What! the whole of it?" came the caustic reply. He had a bitter tongue when the occasion so demanded.

Ten days after the production of *William Tell,* Rossini, accompanied by his wife, set out for Bologna, whither old Vivazza, who seems soon to have had enough of Paris life, had preceded him. On the day of his departure he wrote a "Song of Farewell" to the Parisians. He was grateful to Paris, as well he might be, with its plaudits ringing in his ears and Charles X's contract in his pocket; but he was delighted to be going home. He undoubtedly felt tired, for him exceptionally tired, and he had been suffering from insomnia; a few months' rest would put all that right. No one would have been more surprised than he if he had been told that he would never again write an opera.

F. T.

The remarkable cast of the world *première* included Dabadie in the name part, Laure Cinti-Damoreau as Mathilde, Adolphe Nourrit as Arnold, Levasseur as Walter, and Prévost as Gessler.

One of the longest operas ever written, *Guillaume Tell* is habitually much cut down for the stage. However, an uncut performance was tried in Paris in 1856 and it lasted from 7 P.M. till 1 A.M. Yet the first New York presentation recorded—at the Park Theater, in English, Sept. 19, 1831—sandwiched *Tell* between "the opera *Cinderella*" and a farce *'Twas I!* . . . The sensational success of the tenor Duprez at his debut at the Opéra as Arnold on Aug. 17, 1837, gave *Tell* a new vogue in Paris. Still, the difficulty of finding tenors possessed at once of the strength, the height, and the brilliance of voice demanded by this inexorable role has interfered with the currency of *Tell* in the theater.

The first performance of the opera in New York in French took place at the Park Theater June 16, 1845. It was produced in Italian at the New York Academy of Music April 9, 1855, and at the same house in German April 18, 1866. German was the language of the initial performance at the Metropolitan Opera House, New York, Nov. 28, 1884, with Adolf Robinson in the title role, Udvardi as Arnold, Josef Kögel as Walter, Josef Staudigl as Gessler, Marie Schröder-Hanfstängel as Mathilde, and Marianne Brandt in the small part of Hedwig, Tell's wife.

Francesco Tamagno sang Arnold in an Italian *Tell* presented at the Metropolitan in the course of a supplementary season given by a visiting company in the spring of 1890, and Italian has been the language of all subsequent performances there of *Tell*. The later Arnolds have been Giovanni Martinelli and Giacomo Lauri-Volpi. Mario Ancona and Giuseppe Danise have sung Tell; Édouard de Reszké, José Mardones, Ezio Pinza, and Léon Rothier, Walter;

Pol Plançon, Adamo Didur, and Pavel Ludikar, Gessler. Libia Drog, on Nov. 21, 1894, attempting at her American debut to sing Mathilde after only two days' study, forgot her part in the first measure, broke down, and fled from the stage, leaving the opera to proceed without a prima donna. In the further performances that season Lucille Hill sang the part. The Mathildes of recent years have been Rosa Ponselle, Elisabeth Rethberg, and Editha Fleischer. Orville Harrold distinguished himself as Arnold in an English production of *Tell* at the Century Theater in the autumn of 1914.

P. S.

Camille Saint-Saëns

(Paris, Oct. 9, 1835–Dec. 16, 1921, Algiers)

Saint-Saëns was not satisfied with the making of music or the career of a virtuoso. Organist, pianist, caricaturist, dabbler in science, enamoured of mathematics and astronomy, amateur comedian, feuilletonist, critic, traveller, archæologist—he was a restless man.

He was of less than average height, thin, nervous, sick-faced; with great and exposed forehead, hair habitually short, beard frosted. His eyes were almost level with his face. His eagle-beak would have excited the admiration of Sir Charles Napier, who once exclaimed: "Give me a man with plenty of nose." Irritable, whimsical, ironical, paradoxical, indulging in sudden changes of opinion, he was faithful to friends, appreciative of certain rivals, kindly disposed toward young composers, zealous in practical assistance as well as in verbal encouragement. A man that knew the world and sparkled in conversation; fond of society; at ease and on equal terms with leaders in art, literature, fashion. A man whose Monday receptions were long famous in Paris, eagerly anticipated by *Tout Paris;* yet never so happy as when acting Calchas to Bizet's or Regnault's Helen in Offenbach's delightful *La Belle Hélène,* or impersonating in an extraordinary costume Gounod's Marguerite surprised by the casket of jewels. An indefatigable student of Bach, he parodied the Italian opera of the 30's, 40's, 50's, in *"Gabriella di Vergi,* drama lirico, pochade carnavalesque en parodie d'un opéra italien composé (paroles et musique) par un ancien organiste (œuvre de jeunesse)."

Then there is his amusing "Carnival des Animaux," which was written, as his *Gabriella di Vergi,* without intention of publication. A Parisian from crown of head to sole of foot; yet a nomad.

In 1867 Berlioz called Saint-Saëns "one of the greatest musicians of our epoch." In 1878 Bülow lamented in a letter to Hans von Bronsart that there was no musician in Germany like Saint-Saëns "except you and me." Liszt's admiration for Saint-Saëns is well known. In 1918 there were some, even in this country, who applauded him as the greatest living composer. On the other hand, there have been critics who said that he was too much of a musician to be a great composer or creator. The praise of Gounod—"Saint-Saëns will write at will a work à la Rossini, à la Verdi, à la Schumann, à la Wagner"— was counted by them a reproach; it was regarded as a courteous manner of saying, "Saint-Saëns has the unfortunate faculty of assimilation." Hugues Imbert, discussing him, admitted that there is no graver censure than to say of an artist, "He is incapable of being himself."

So far as an intimate knowledge of music as a science is concerned, so far as fluency and ease of expression are concerned, Saint-Saëns was beyond doubt a remarkable musician.

The ambition of the French composer has long been, first of all, the stage. To achieve glory in the opera house is his dream, his struggle. For this he bends every energy. At a time when his colleagues were looking toward the stage, Saint-Saëns hankered after a more solid and durable reputation. His first work of any length was not an opera, not even an operetta; it was a symphony; his second important work was also a symphony; then followed church music, a third symphony, chamber music, concertos, etc. Not till 1868 did he begin work on his *Samson et Dalila,* which was not completed before 1877. His first opera performed in Paris, *Le Timbre d'Argent* (Théâtre Lyrique, February 23, 1877), was not begun until 1875.

Although he wrote over a dozen operas, only one, *Samson et Dalila,* has true life in the theatre, and there are some who maintain that it should be performed only as an oratorio, though the scene of Samson's undoing in the second act has a passionate expression rarely found in Saint-Saën's other music. *Henry VIII,* praised enthusiastically in 1883, is revived occasionally in Paris.

Saint-Saëns was mightily influenced in thought and expression by predecessors and contemporaries. First of all by Bach, whose influence is felt in unexpected moments: his wig is seen even among the Grecian scenic accessories of *Phryné.* There is no servile imitation, no deliberate attempt to ape the style of the old master. Saint-Saëns had studied Bach so deeply and persistently that it was natural for him to use the same language, to mould his sentences in the same fashion. Then there is the influence of Beethoven, Schumann, Berlioz, Liszt, Wagner.

The symphonic poems, perhaps his masterpieces, were inspired by Saint-Saëns' admiration for Liszt, his close friendship and example. Years ago there were Frenchmen that this music perplexed. Gustave Kahn found little in "Le Rouet d'Omphale," but "singular music, a sort of protest against ordinary evening music, mixed with protests of the double-bass unkindly received by the cymbals—but why insist on the mistake of a musician who has had so many fine hours?" One critic of repute insisted that the popularity of "Danse Macabre" rests entirely on its waltz rhythm.

The charge that his vein of melody is thin and poor is in a way unjust. There are abundant instances of sharply defined melody, unmistakable, original; melody that is drawn rather than colored; as a rule, without perfume, without blood, without emotion. Sometimes it is like an opening at chess: valuable for the contrapuntal complications that may result therefrom. His technical skill is so great that too often he takes thematic material of little worth and develops it in scholastic, arid fashion. There are pages, as in the Septet, where counterpoint is lugged in by the heels and is only pretentious padding. There is mere play of abstract intellect, a solving of problems that interest only the propounder. The element of surprise is only in the work-manship. The progamme might state: "M. Saint-Saëns will now work out his exercise in the sight of the audience." The dryness is not the dryness of third-rate makers of music; it is the dryness of one whose wit and intelligence are known, who insists on abstruse thought, on self-absorption.

His vacillating judgments . . . his shifting opinions . . . are not peculiar to him; nearly every musician or thoughtful amateur has gone through like experiences.

He wrote copiously for the press, books, pamphlets, prefaces, feuilletons, poems, plays. His comedy, "La Crampe des Ecrivains," was produced at Algiers in 1892; the comedy, "Le Roi Apépi," at Béziers in 1903; "Botruocépale," Béziers, 1908. He discussed the phenomena of mirage, the relationship of plants with animals, materialism and music, hypnotism, lyres and citharas, child prodigies, hissing at concerts. The list is very long. The chief works are "Harmonie et Mélodie" (1885); "Notes sur les décors de théâtre dans l'antiquité (1886); "Rimes Familières" (1890); "Gounod et le 'Don Juan' de Mozart" (1893); "Problèmes et Mystères" (1894); "Portraits et Souvenirs" (1899); "École Buissonnière" (same year). The essays on music abound in noble sentiments, shrewd reflections, startling paradoxes, delightful malice.

An extraordinary man and musician. Possessing an uncommon technical equipment as composer, pianist, organist; French in clearness of expression, logic, exquisite taste; a master of rhythm, with a clear appreciation of tonal color and the value of simplicity in orchestration, he is seldom warm and tender; seldom does he indulge himself in sentiment, passion, imagination. With him orthodox form must always be kept in mind, nor could he understand the saying of Plotinus: "Fire surpasses other bodies in beauty, because, compared with the other elements, it obtains the order of form; for it is more eminent than the rest, and is the most subtle of all, bordering as it were on an incorporeal nature." Hence perhaps the reactionary attitude of his later years; his sharp criticism of the more modern school of French composers, including César Franck. His wit and brilliancy are indisputable. He seldom touches the heart or sweeps away the judgment. He was not a great creator, yet his name is ever to be mentioned with respect.

Without consideration of his many admirable compositions, one should bear this in mind: In the face of difficulties, discouragement, misunderstanding, sneers, he worked steadily from his youth up and always to the best of his ability, for righteousness in absolute music; he endeavored to introduce into French music thoughtfulness and sincerity for the advantage and the glory of the country that he dearly loved.

P. H.

Samson et Dalila

[Samson and Delilah]

Book by Ferdinand Lemaire

First performance: Hoftheater, Weimar, Dec. 2, 1877

CHARACTERS

Samson, a Hebrew leader, TENOR
Delilah, a Philistine temptress,
  MEZZO-SOPRANO
High Priest of Dagon, BARITONE

Abimelech, Satrap of Gaza, BASS
An Old Hebrew, BASS
Messenger of the Philistines, TENOR
Chorus of Hebrews and Philistines

The action takes place in Gaza, in Palestine, about 1150 B.C.

When Abimelech boasts that Dagon, god of the Philistines, has overcome Jehovah, Samson gives the signal for revolt by slaying the boaster with his own sword. Israel conquers in battle, hymns of praise fill the air, and the loveliest maids of Philistia, among them bewitching Delilah, appear to move the victor's heart with song and dance. An old Hebrew warns Samson—but when have the young heeded the old? The Hebrew strong man falls a ready victim to Delilah's charms.

Delilah's hatred for Samson—she knows he really does not love her, and that he has a wife at home—is fanned by the high priest of Dagon. He bids her discover the secret of Samson's superhuman strength, so Delilah coaxes, and caresses. At first Samson resists but finally, like many another man, tells her his secret against his better judgment. Then the seductress draws him into her chamber, uses her shears, and appears at the window, the shorn locks in her hand, to signal the Philistines that they may safely seize the hairless hero.

Samson, erstwhile pride of his people and terror of his foes, blinded, an object of derision, turns a treadmill in his dungeon prison. His bitter self-reproaches are too late. Finally, his enemies lead him to Dagon's feast of triumph, there to make a mock of him and his God, but seizing the mighty pillars that support the roof, Samson brings them crashing down on himself and his foes, sharing the death he visits upon them.

F. H. M.

Today *Samson et Dalila* as an opera is as securely established as *Lohengrin* or *Aida*. But such has not been the case always. Particularly in the United States and Great Britain the work long figured as an oratorio, sung in English and under the English title of "Samson and Delilah." Of course, the biblical subject and the importance of the chorus in acts I and III fell right in with the oratorio traditions of the English-speaking countries. In Britain, moreover, a rule of the censorship that remained in force well into the present century forbade the appearance on the stage of any character whatsoever from Holy Writ. Consequently, if the strong man of Israel and the Philistine temptress were to emerge in a public entertainment, they had no choice but to present themselves on the concert platform and in ordinary evening or afternoon attire, a state of affairs obviously inimical to the tragic effect of the shaving off of the seven locks of so puissant a hero's head.

As an oratorio *Samson* was eagerly hailed by a host of choral societies seeking to vary the time-honored round of Handel, Haydn, and Mendelssohn. The first performance in this country was given by the Oratorio Society of New York in Carnegie Hall on March 25, 1892, under the direction of Walter Damrosch. Though naturally the work was presented "in concert form," English was not the only language employed, for Montariol and Marie Ritter-Goetze sang the name parts in French. The Oratorio Society did not tacitly shelve *Samson* till after a performance on April 3, 1906. And meanwhile it had been staged over here, first in New Orleans, then in New York.

New Orleans, with its theatrical heritage from France, could boast a production at its French Opera House on January 4, 1893, only six weeks after the Paris Opéra had first given *Samson*. But what went on in New Orleans had no influence on the course of oratorio in other communities without a French inheritance, nor did the first, and for a score of years only, performance at the Metropolitan Opera House, on February 8, 1895, in spite of New York's influential position and the extraordinary cast participating—Francesco Tamagno as Samson, Eugenia Mantelli as Delilah, Giuseppe Campanari as the High Priest, and Pol Plançon as both Abimelech and an Old Hebrew. *Samson* remained what contemporary wisecrackers had dubbed it, an "operatorio!"

The late Oscar Hammerstein, who made a specialty of French opera, revived *Samson* as a stage work at the Manhattan Opera House on November 13, 1908. Charles Dalmorès sang Samson and Jeanne Gerville-Réache Dalila. Cleofonte Campanini conducted. In the temple scene Odette Valéry caused a sensation by dancing with a living serpent, some four or five feet long, wound about her neck and arms. So emphatic was the success of this production that thenceforth there was no more question in New York of *Samson* as an oratorio, and operatically it was even more firmly grounded by the Metropolitan's taking it up again to open the season of 1915–16. An elaborate production—like Hammerstein's, in the original French—offered Enrico Caruso and Margaret Matzenauer in the roles of the strong man and the temptress, besides Pasquale Amato to sing the High Priest, Carl Schlegel Abimilech, and Léon Rothier an Old Hebrew. So kindly did Giulio Gatti-Casazza's public take to *Samson* that in the twelve seasons between the autumn of 1915 and the spring of 1927 it enjoyed forty-two representations at the Metropolitan. It was then retired till the present season. Not once, but twice, however, *Samson* has served as seasonal opener—for the second time on November 11, 1918, the day of the signing of the Armistice.

On that occasion the curtains parted again after the close of act I to reveal the great square at Gaza thronged with flag-wavers. The choristers were shaking little American banners and before that faithful fellowship Louise Homer (the Dalila) was bearing on high an American flag of stately proportions, while in the same front line Robert Couzinou (the new High Priest) and Léon Rothier vied with each other in clinging to the French tri-color. Caruso held aloft the green, white, and red of Italy; Maria Savage of the chorus lifted the Belgian banner, and the honor of waving the Union Jack fell to Paul Ananian, doubtless because as an Armenian he was the nearest the cast offered to a British subject.

The stage forces and the orchestra made the house resound with "The Star-Spangled Banner," the "Inno di Garibaldi," and "God Save the King." There were cries for something Belgian, but the curtains closed inexorably on the tableau. Before the second act the orchestra played the Italian "Marcia reale" and the Belgian "Brabançonne." From the balcony someone cried "Vive la Belgique." A voice shouted, "Rule, Britannia!" and still another "Vive la France!" Each successive outcry was applauded to the echo. Then the second act went on.

What perhaps none of those who called *Samson* an "operatorio" knew is that it actually was Saint-Saëns's original idea to write an oratorio based on the story related in the sixteenth chapter of Judges. But when he asked the young poet Ferdinand Lemaire to supply the verses, the latter replied: "An oratorio! Why, no, let's do an opera!" That was in 1867. Saint-Saëns went to work with enthusiasm. Yet his friends did their best to dissuade him. "A biblical opera! What madness! No manager would dare put it on!" And this was not Britain but France! Nevertheless Saint-Saëns went on with the work.

While taking part in the celebration of the Beethoven Centenary at Weimar in June, 1870, Saint-Saëns talked with Liszt about *Samson*. Liszt, without knowing a note of the score, said: "Finish your piece; I will have it given at Weimar."

Consequently, despite Saint-Saëns's ever-increasing prestige as a composer, his *Samson et Dalila* had its world première not in France, but, thanks to Liszt, at the Weimar Hoftheater—on December 2, 1877, in a German translation by Richard Pohl. The French première occurred only on March 3, 1890, at the Théâtre des Arts in Rouen. Verdhurt, the producer, took it on to Paris, where he presented it at the little Eden-Théâtre, a stone's throw from the Opéra, on October 31, 1890. Result, a triumph.

The disdainful directors of the Opéra, who had found Rouen too distant to visit, did condescend to step over to the Eden. "Ah, if we had only known!" was their comment. Soon afterwards the Opéra was entrusted to a new management, which finally staged *Samson et Dalila* at their august house on November 23, 1892, before a distinguished and delighted audience that included Sadi Carnot, President of the Republic, and many more notables. Another President of the Republic, Alexandre Millerand, witnessed the Opéra's 500th performance of *Samson* on June 28, 1922. Thus the once scorned biblical piece has taken its place among the most popular works in the repertory of the Paris Opéra, where for many years scarcely a month has gone by without its being given two or three performances.

P. S.

Bedřich Smetana

(Leitomischl, Bohemia, Mar. 2, 1824–May 12, 1884, Prague)

The works of Bedřich Smetana, . . . the founder of modern Czech music, do not merely comprise restyled folk motifs of his people, but ingeniously combine national themes with the spirit and forms of international music of the Nineteenth Century. His opera, *The Bartered Bride,* and his symphonic poem, "Má Vlast" (My Country), dedicated to the city of Prague, clearly demonstrate that the basis of his work is the . . . inborn love of music so typical of his countrymen. It was he and not his pupil, Antonin Dvořák—although the latter is today more popular—who revealed a language new to the musical world.

In the tradition of all parents of potential musicians, Smetana's father was wholeheartedly opposed to a musical career for his son. The boy's first conceptions of theory, therefore, and his early mastery of the piano were largely self-taught. Though the parental objections were withdrawn theoretically when Smetana was nineteen, financial support ceased at the same time and he found himself penniless.

Introduced to the instructor Proksch, by Katherine Kolař, who was to become not only a well-known pianist, but also his wife, he began four years of serious study, during which he earned his livelihood by teaching. Eager to forge ahead in his chosen profession, he gave up his lessons at twenty-three, undertaking an ill-advised concert tour which left him destitute again. But Franz Liszt befriended him, and helped him in establishing a music school of his own.

Though Smetana's first published works were coolly received, his reputation as a performer became international, and in 1856 he became conductor of the Philharmonic Orchestra of Göteborg, Sweden.

During his years in Sweden, agitation for a national school of music was rapidly gaining ground in his native country, a cultural development which reflected the struggle for independence from Austria. In 1861 he left Göteborg to become a leader of this movement in Prague. Though the opening of the national opera house there in 1862 was a definite step toward this goal, the few existing Bohemian operas were not sufficient to maintain a steady repertoire. To fill this gap, Smetana turned his hand to opera composing. His first attempt, *The Brandenburgers in Bohemia* (1863), received only a lukewarm welcome, but his second, the lively and everlastingly lovely *The Bartered Bride,* was greeted with cheers. This work met with considerable success abroad, too, and was presented in this country in 1909, under the baton of Gustav

463

Mahler. A charge of "Wagnerizing" the national opera because of his elaborate orchestration and habit of employing *leitmotivs* was lodged against Smetana with the production of his next opera, *Dalibor* (1868), bringing on a bitter, ten-year war of words.

This hostility toward Smetana preyed on his mind. In 1874, he was forced to resign his conductorship at the opera house because of partial deafness. Within six months of his retirement, he became totally deaf, but like Beethoven he continued to compose. Turning to the symphonic poem, he created his impressive cycle of six works collectively titled "Má Vlast" (My Country), of which the second, "Vltava" (The Moldau), is the most often performed. Here, too, he drew his inspiration from national themes, weaving them together with singularly colorful melodies and orchestration.

In the last years of his life, Smetana suffered excruciating mental agonies. His last works, never completed, did not at all measure up to his earlier compositions. Shortly before his death, he was confined to an asylum, and it was there that he died.

Truly the father of Bohemian music, Smetana wrote the first operas to display definitely Czech characteristics. Far beyond being merely nationalistic, *The Bartered Bride* conquered the stage of the world with its genuine musical qualities. Smetana's work was not confined to symphonic and operatic music. He also wrote chamber music, of which the string quartet "Aus meinen Leben" (From My Life) is of outstanding importance.

                                                            W. H., P. Z.

The Bartered Bride

[Prodaná nevěsta]

COMIC OPERA IN 3 ACTS

Book by KAREL SABINA

First performance: National Theater, Prague, May 30, 1866

CHARACTERS

Kruschina, a peasant, BARITONE
Kathinka, his wife, SOPRANO
Marie, their daughter, SOPRANO
Micha, a landowner, BASS
Agnes, his wife, MEZZO-SOPRANO
Wenzel, their son, TENOR
Hans, Micha's son by a first marriage, TENOR

Kezal, a marriage broker, BASS
Springer, manager of a theatrical troupe, BASS
Esmeralda, a dancer, SOPRANO
Muff, a comedian, TENOR
Comedians, Circus Performers, Villagers

The action takes place in Bohemia, in the nineteenth century

Marie, daughter of Kruschina and Kathinka, rich peasants, is in love with Hans, a mysterious newcomer to the village. The lovers are facing despair because Marie's parents want her to marry Wenzel, the semi-idiotic son of Micha and Agnes, wealthy landowners.

The girl obstinately refuses, however, to consider marriage to Wenzel. So the marriage broker Kezal—the opera's comic lead—goes to work on Hans. He reasons with him; he threatens, he cajoles, entreats, and finally offers a sum of money, if Hans will renounce Marie. The youth is indignant at first, but later he tells Kezal that he will accept three hundred crowns provided that a certain clause be included in the contract. The clause is "Marie shall marry only Micha's son."

Elated with his progress, Kezal agrees to the amendment. And in a little while the whole village witnesses the signing of the agreement.

Heartbroken at the turn of events, Marie is extremely puzzled by Hans' peculiar behavior. He says he still loves her, and while she is inclined to believe him, she cannot correlate that declaration with the selling out to Kezal.

The mystery is cleared up to her—and the audience's—satisfaction when it develops that Hans is Micha's long-lost son by a former marriage. Everything now works perfectly in accordance with the pact between Hans and Kezal. Hans can marry the girl, and he can also keep the three hundred crowns. The only loser is the marriage broker, but, in the joyousness that follows, nobody minds that—save,

465

of course, Kezal. Wenzel, who never cared about Marie anyway, grows rapturous over Esmeralda, a performer with a traveling circus which happens into town.

P. S.

Bedrich Smetana composed a total of nine operas, including the unfinished *Viola*. Yet only one of them so far seems to have taken root outside of Central Europe—*Prodana Nevesta,* known in German as "Die verkaufte Braut," in English as "The Bartered Bride." Though the names of two or three others are more or less familiar to students and travelers—*Dalibor, Libusa,* and *Hubicka* (The Kiss), for instance—the privilege of carrying the fame of Smetana as a composer of opera to the world in general has so far been reserved to *The Bartered Bride.* Smetana, a native of Litomysl in Bohemia, has been described as the founder of the national school of modern Czech music. *The Bartered Bride* is national opera, folk opera, even more redolent of Bohemia's fields and groves than *Der Freischütz* is of German forests.

Nevertheless *The Bartered Bride* is by no means folk opera in a cramping sense. While distinctly of its native soil, it also possesses the universal qualities necessary to give it a world-wide currency. We of other countries delight in its Czech rhythms, its national dances, the characteristic contour of many of its melodies, but we find also in the music more than local color and exotic charm; the flowing humanity is there that transcends limits and boundaries. An eminent Czech musicologist, Professor Zdenek Nejedly of Prague University, has written eloquently, if with a tinge of understandable exaggeration, concerning this work:

"Since Mozart's time there has not been a composer who, with such refined art, and such alluring freshness, could delight the world with such warm, frank, and genial humor as the author of *The Bartered Bride."*

It was in 1859, when Austria had been humiliated by Italy, that the Vienna government modified somewhat the severity of its rule in Bohemia. There followed an immediate impulse toward national expression in the arts, which envisaged, for one thing, the establishment of a theatre where both plays and operas should be performed in the vernacular. In 1862 a Provisional Theatre was opened at Prague as a result of a public subscription. Meanwhile there was pronounced activity in the realms of orchestral and choral music, Smetana being always in the van.

With the Provisional Opera House a reality, the need of furnishing it with a national repertory became urgent. Smetana's first opera, *The Brandenburgers in Bohemia* (Branbori u Cechach), which had been written in 1863, was accordingly brought out there on January 5, 1866. It is an historical and patriotic opera which in its general design has been likened to Moussorgsky's *Boris Godounoff.* Though the reception was enthusiastic, the really great success followed on May 30 when *The Bartered Bride* was produced.

This inspired comedy, by the way, was not in 1866 just as we know it today. It was then divided into two acts comprising twenty numbers, and the dialogue was spoken. When there was question of the work's entering the repertory of the Paris Opéra Comique, Smetana subdivided the first act into two scenes and composed for it a male chorus. To the second act he added the "Spring Dance" and Marie's aria. And the same year he added also the Polka and the Furiant. In this second version *The Bartered Bride* was presented at the Provisional Theatre on January 29, 1869.

But only after further revision for St. Petersburg did the opera emerge as we know it now, in three acts and with the dialogue set as recitative. In this definitive form Smetana himself conducted it at the Provisional Theatre on September 25, 1870. In spite of the fact that the worth of the opera was increased by all this editing and amplifying, Smetana's enemies charged him with ceasing to compose in the national style and desiring to spoil what he had written previously.

It is interesting to learn that the universal favor accorded *The Bartered Bride* aroused a sort of resentment in Smetana much as had happened in the case of *Der Freischütz* and Weber. At a banquet after the hundredth performance of *The Bartered Bride* Smetana gave a humorous account of how the work originated.

Actually a mere trifle [he called it]. I composed it not from ambition, but from defiance, because after *The Brandenburgers* people declared I was a Wagnerite and couldn't do anything in the lighter national style. Consequently, I ran straight to Sabina and so wrote *The Bartered Bride* that according to my then notion even Offenbach could not equal it. And behold, it becomes the occasion for me of this festive day!

The Bartered Bride was a long time in reaching this country, but at last, on February 19, 1909, it was produced at the Metropolitan Opera House. Though Emmy Destinn, who appeared as Marie, was a Czech, there could be no question with the company as constituted of using the original text. Accordingly the German translation was employed. Besides Destinn, who was at her best as Marie, acting, we are informed, with delightful spirit and singing gloriously, the cast boasted a capital Hans in Carl Jörn and a droll Wenzel in Albert Reiss, whose irruption into the circus disguised as a dancing bear occasioned as much excitement among the audience as it did consternation on the stage. Adamo Didur embodied the marriage broker, Kezal. The national dances, arranged by Ottakar Bartik (like Destinn, a Czech), were praised as most picturesque, and it was reported of the circus that "the Hippodrome need not have been ashamed to own it."

The conductor was Gustav Mahler, and the overture, for which he always obtained a whirlwind performance, was played as an introduction to the second act instead of the first lest late arrivals should miss it. That bit of benevolent paternalism had had a local precedent in the case of the overture to *Dinorah* at the Manhattan Opera House.

For four seasons *The Bartered Bride* was on the Metropolitan's active list before the management retired it, to be revived on January 28, 1926, with Maria Müller as Marie, Rudolf Laubenthal as Hans, George Meader as Wenzel, and Michael Bohnen as Kezal. Artur Bodanzky conducted. Three seasons made the span of this revival. The next one occurred on February 4, 1933. Only two performances were given. Again Mr. Bodanzky conducted and Mr. Laubenthal appeared as Hans, but now Marie went to Elisabeth Rethberg, Wenzel to Marek Windheim, and Kezal to Ludwig Hofmann.

Still it remained for the revival of May 16, 1936, in the Metropolitan's "popular" spring season, to turn *The Bartered Bride* into the "hit" it deserves to be here. The previous performances had all been in German. This one was in English. And undoubtedly the well-devised translation, which permitted all the little intricacies of the plot to become clear, was responsible for turning the trick.

P. S.

Richard Strauss

(Munich, June 11, 1864–Sept. 9, 1949, Garmisch-Partenkirchen, Germany)

Richard Strauss was the son of Franz Strauss, first horn player at the Munich court opera, who had married into the wealthy brewers' family of Pschorr, citizens of the Bavarian capital who had won distinction not only by their commercial enterprise, but also by their patronage of the arts. At the age of five, even before he entered the elementary school, the boy began to show great aptitude for music, and at six he composed a "Schneiderpolka" for piano as well as a Christmas song. By the time he was ten and left his first school for the Gymnasium, he had already accumulated a variety of immature but highly promising works. Two of these, the "Festival March" (Op. 1) and the Serenade for wind instruments (Op. 7), were published; the rest have been either destroyed or left in manuscript. In 1880 he finished a Symphony in D Minor, and the following year the first important public performance of a work of his was given by a quartet led by his violin master, Benno Walter. This was the third of the published works—the second according to opus numbers—the String Quartet in A Major. At the age of eighteen he left school for the University and had the thrilling experience of hearing his Symphony conducted in public by Hermann Levi. It was never published, however.

The next year (1883) the young genius decided to give up his university studies and to devote himself to a musical career. He went to Berlin in the winter, but was soon called to Meiningen by Hans von Bülow, who performed the Wind Serenade with the excellent ducal court orchestra there and invited the young composer to become his assistant conductor. Strauss gladly seized the opportunity and struck up a friendship with a member of the orchestra, Alexander Ritter, a man more than 30 years older and an enthusiast for the new school of which Strauss as yet knew very little. It was Ritter who persuaded him to abandon his classical leanings and to take Berlioz, Wagner and Liszt as his models.

So far, the young composer had been working along traditional lines. The two Quartets, the Cello Sonata, the only piano pieces of his which are published and the two Concertos follow the Schumann-Brahms direction of romantic lyricism and classical workmanship; we must be careful nowadays to draw the distinction between them and the works that followed, which was much greater than it appears now that the whole of Strauss's work, in comparison with much that came later, seems romantic and classicist in its tendencies. The choral and orchestral Goethe setting, "Wanderers Sturmlied,"

469

written about the time that Bülow resigned the Meiningen conductorship and handed it on to Strauss (1885), the "Burleske" for piano and orchestra and the symphonic fantasy, "Aus Italien," which was the outcome of a visit to Italy in the Spring of the following year, struck their contemporaries—not all of whom were converted to Wagnerism, much less to the subversive school of Liszt—as new departures of almost shocking audacity, especially the orchestral work, in which Strauss had not hesitated to commit what was considered the vulgarity of introducing the popular song of "Funiculì, funiculà"—on the mistaken assumption, it may be mentioned incidentally, that Denza's frivolous ditty was a genuine Neapolitan folksong.

"Aus Italien" was produced in the Spring of 1887 at Munich, where Strauss had returned after his Italian tour as sub-conductor at the Opera. Several works in the new manner now came from his pen in rapid succession: the Violin Sonata which, compared with that for cello, shows many signs of the acquisition of a more personal style, and the first three of the symphonic poems which are Strauss's most distinctive if not always most successful contribution to music, "Don Juan," "Macbeth" and "Tod und Verklärung." The first of these was produced at Weimar in 1889, the last at Eisenach in 1890. "Macbeth," which in spite of a misleading opus number is the earliest work in the form Strauss had by no means invented, but expanded from Liszt's program works and made more musically significant, has never had the same success as its companions; but although less characteristic, it is remarkable as a first essay and by no means deserves the almost complete neglect into which it has fallen.

In 1889 Strauss resigned his Munich appointment and went to Weimar as assistant conductor to Lassen at the Court Opera, a theatre to which Liszt had lent a special distinction by his pioneer productions of works by Berlioz, Wagner and other composers needing the support of artists who did not look for mere easy popularity. He did well there, so well that in the Summer of 1891 he was invited by Cosima Wagner to conduct *Tannhäuser* at Bayreuth.

At that time people who were not violently against Wagner were as a matter of course as ardently for him. That Strauss was then an out-and-out Wagnerian may be judged from his first opera, *Guntram,* for which he had himself written the libretto. He was seriously ill in 1892 and, as permanent lung trouble was feared, he went on a prolonged tour of the Mediterranean, visiting Sicily, Greece and Egypt, The greater part of *Guntram* was written during this voyage, and he completed it the following year at Weimar, where it was produced on May 10, 1894, with Pauline de Ahna, his future wife, in the part of the heroine. He married in June and resigned his appointment in favour of one in Berlin as conductor of the Philharmonic Orchestra in succession to Bülow, who had died at Cairo in February. Before he left Weimar, however, he took charge of the Tonkünstlerfest there, though he shared the conducting with Mahler, whom he had invited to take part.

Each of the next four years (1895–98) brought forth one of Strauss's tone poems, "Till Eulenspiegels lustige Streiche," based on a folk legend, "Also sprach Zarathustra," derived from Nietzsche, "Don Quixote," whose provenance is obvious, and "Ein Heldenleben," an autobiographical work. These mark his highest development as a purely orchestral composer, though they may be said to contain some of the seeds of decadence, always excepting "Till Eulenspiegel," which has proved, not the most elaborate and masterly of the symphonic poems, but the freshest, most spontaneous and therefore most lasting of them all. The other three caused much offence in some quarters, for various reasons. To base a musical work on Nietzsche was regarded as almost anarchically subversive, the realism of the bleating sheep and the wind machine in "Don Quixote" was considered anti-musical, and for a composer to extol himself as a hero, as Strauss had quite unabashedly done in "Ein Heldenleben," was thought to be a monstrous piece of bad taste. Some of these criticisms were, of course, amply justified. The wind machine is a mere subterfuge and the self-glorification in the last work is unpleasant because it is made too lavishly and luxuriously. But the mastery of Strauss's invention and manipulation of striking thematic material remains remarkable, and whereas such episodes as the "Tanzlied" in "Zarathustra," which is merely a corruption of the Viennese waltz, or the frightful and prolonged noise of the battle section in "Heldenleben," show a surprising lack of discrimination, the touching death scene in "Don Quixote," to mention only one great incident, as well as the whole of "Eulenspiegel," remain permanent musical treasures immune from the changes of fashion. That the fashions have changed cannot be denied. The "adversaries" section in "Heldenleben," which was once regarded as the most savage and vitriolic indictment of the whole tribe of music critics, now sounds almost pretty; but it is still good—better, in fact, than some of the more bombastic music in the work.

The "Sinfonia domestica" of 1903, which continues the autobiography from a more intimate and homely point of view, marked a decline in Strauss's symphonic art, not in mastery, but in felicity of invention, and—if one may anticipate so far for the sake of closing the discussion of one particular phase of his work—the "Alpensinfonie" of 1915 showed complete exhaustion. Strauss had not lost his skill, for the long and complex work was written in the space of a hundred days, but that skill was now applied merely mechanically to the elaboration of material woefully deficient in new ideas. There was scarcely anything in this work he had not said much better before.

Returning to the period during which his genius was unimpaired and still developing, we come upon the second of his operas, *Feuersnot*, which was produced at Dresden on Nov. 21, 1901. It is in a way a retrogression from the symphonic poems that immediately preceded it, more lyrical and romantic, and less prodigal of contrapuntal ingenuity. But this was no doubt due to the nature of Ernst von Wolzogen's libretto, which dealt with an old popular German tale, and to the fact that an opera demands a less elaborate treatment of the orchestral texture if its interest is to remain concentrated on the stage—a principle to which Strauss has, it is true, not always adhered, either in this or in later works, and to which he was at last forced to pay deference in *Ariadne auf Naxos,* which is scored for a small orchestra, and in the domestic opera, *Intermezzo,* where he laid much stress upon clear articulation of the words.

The libretto of *Feuersnot* caused a good deal of moral indignation, and when next Strauss set a German translation of Oscar Wilde's "Salome" as a luxuriously decadent one-act opera, it began to be taken for granted that he liked to treat and was particularly good at treating subjects of a scabrous nature. *Salome* was begun in 1903, before the "Sinfonia domestica" was quite finished. The latter was produced in New York, under the composer's direction,* on March 21, 1904, and the first European performance took place at a festival of the Tonkünstlerverein at Frankfurt-am-Main on June 1. A performance in London followed on Nov. 6. The impression everywhere was that as a symphonist Strauss had declined.

As an operatic composer, however, he went from strength to strength at that period. Not long after *Salome* had been produced at Dresden on Dec. 9, 1905, he began the composition of *Elektra,* the first opera in which he had the collaboration of Hugo von Hofmannsthal, a librettist who was to prove inexhaustibly fertile in new and tempting ideas. The six libretti he wrote for Strauss, not counting the scenario of the ballet, "Josephs Legende" (which was produced by Diaghileff's Russian Ballet in Paris and London just before the outbreak of war in 1914), are not in the least alike. In *Elektra* Hofmannsthal brought modern psychology to bear on the old Greek legend of the return of Orestes to avenge Agamemnon, and Strauss, who had very cunningly conveyed a mixture of sumptuousness and horror in *Salome,* was now called upon to do the same with horror upon horror set in an atmosphere of utter gloom. He succeeded in making the hearer's flesh creep by giving his score the appearance of a kind of musical disease, though the specimen is far from perfect, for it shows some remarkably healthy patches of diatonic beauty that will not fit in with the rest. At the time, however, the work made a sensation as the last word in musical perversity; nowadays it has ceased to shock, though not to impress, and is felt to be excessive only in its ceaseless orchestral welter that will not let the words and the happenings on the stage become sufficiently clear and demands efforts of the performers which are distractingly disproportionate to the effect they are able to make on the hearer.

Elektra was produced at Dresden, on Jan. 25, 1909. In September, 1910, Strauss finished the second Hofmannsthal opera, *Der Rosenkavalier,* which

---

* Strauss has visited America twice: in 1904 when he conducted the first performance of the "Sinfonia domestica" with Wetzler's orchestra and again in 1922 when he conducted the New York Philharmonic and the Philadelphia Orchestra as guest leader among the activities of a successful tour.

was as different as possible from anything he had treated before, except that it still gave the public some excuse for attributing a liking for scandalous subjects to him. But this eighteenth-century Viennese tragi-comedy, with its fine period feeling and its attractive blend of artificiality and humanity, must be one of the six best operatic libretti in the world, and although Strauss's setting is too heavy and highly-wrought, his music has a glamour and pointed allusiveness and mastery that make *Der Rosenkavalier* one of the most fascinating operas, the best by far he ever wrote and, unfortunately, his last consistently great work. Even its uncertainty of style is redeemed by its glowing beauty and sincerity of feeling. It was first heard at Dresden on Jan. 26, 1911.

Ariadne auf Naxos, produced at Stuttgart on Oct. 25, 1912, the third work written with Hofmannsthal and the second composed at the country house Strauss had built for himself at Garmisch, revived some of the minor charms of the previous opera and contains some first-rate music in Ariadne's monologue at the beginning; but it is even more undecided in style and the new first act Strauss wrote for it four years later is exceedingly barren. The incidental music to Molière's "Bourgeois gentilhomme," a shortened German translation of which had been the original prologue to the one-act opera, was delightful, however, and it is now preserved in the form of an orchestral suite. The original form of the work was abandoned, it is said, because it was impossible in the ordinary repertory of German theatres to let actors and opera singers appear on one and the same evening.

At the setting of his own libretto of *Intermezzo* Strauss began to work about 1917, but it was not produced until 1925, in Vienna, where in the meantime the next opera on a large scale, *Die Frau ohne Schatten,* was first heard on Oct. 10, 1919. Here Hofmannsthal had provided Strauss with an elaborate spectacular allegory, a kind of modern and sophisticated *Magic Flute,* which lured some fine music from the composer, but not a consistently great score. A decline of inventive powers is evident and where the music is impressive it is not without its echoes from earlier works that amount at times almost to self-plagiarism. The Viennese ballet-pantomime "Schlagobers" (the Austrian word for whipped cream), produced in Vienna on May 9, 1924, was negligible, and *Intermezzo,* first staged there the following year, contained nothing new apart from the transparency of its texture and an endeavour to revert to a "bel canto" style of singing in order to focus the musical interest primarily upon the stage.

The last but one of Hofmannsthal's libretti, *Die aegyptische Helena,* returned to the psychological subtilization of a classical subject, but overdid it, and the score shows that musical bankruptcy was staring in Strauss's face. The production took place at Dresden on June 6 and Vienna on June 11, 1928, after some wrangling over the rights of priority which seemed in the end hardly worth while. But Hofmannsthal, who died in 1929, had left Strauss yet another work, *Arabella,* a slight but charming and poetical story of mid-nineteenth-century

Vienna, and a subject quite new to Strauss. This work, which appeared at Dresden on July 1, 1933, turned out to be the most refined thing the composer had ever written for the orchestra, exquisite in sound from beginning to end; but unfortunately the beauty of the music was only for the ear; the mind found it almost completely empty of significance, though now and again it touched the heart for a fleeting moment.

Arabella is very unlikely to last, much less ever to recapture the exciting success of the *Rosenkavalier*. Nor is the following opera likely to do so, though it is interesting as Strauss's first trial of a new librettist. This was a man no less distinguished than Hofmannsthal: Stefan Zweig, who provided him with *Die schweigsame Frau,* based on Ben Jonson's "Epicœne," or "The Silent Woman." It was produced at Dresden on June 24, 1935, and proved to be, especially by contrast with *Arabella,* excessively noisy. This, no doubt, was to some extent justified by the nature of the subject of the fanatical hater of all sound, musical and otherwise; but unfortunately Strauss's noise proved to be mostly mere sound and fury, signifying nothing. There is, however, a most welcome and beautiful quiet ending to this opera, as lovely and moving almost as the close of *Don Quixote.*

A few words must be said about Strauss's songs for voice and piano, which . . . are extremely numerous. The very limited choice made from this vast number by all but the most enterprising singers—and very few singers are enterprising—is perhaps a criticism of his work in that line, and it is true that a good many of the songs lack distinction, while some that deserve attention merely duplicate qualities of a high order found in the few examples that have become widely familiar. The singers, after all, must not be blamed overmuch if they keep to the half-dozen of the Strauss songs that have proved permanently attractive, and the most they can be reproached with is that they have not extended their selection to a dozen.

That, it must be admitted, is not enough in so vast a quantity as Strauss wrote to make him a great all-round composer of song: he is merely a composer who happens to have written a few great songs. The rest suffer from various faults: formlessness, pretentiousness of emotional expression or technical elaboration, heavy facetiousness, an ill-judged balance between the voice-part and the instrument, and often a questionable taste in the choice of poetry. It is true that he shares this last defect with even the greatest composers of German Lieder, except Hugo Wolf, and it disfigures even some of those of his songs whose music carries them triumphantly to success. Mackay's poem of "Heimliche Aufforderung," for instance, is grotesquely bombastic and gross in feeling, but the ecstatic, soaring music saves the song nevertheless; and Schack's skittish words in the famous "Ständchen," which accord so ill with the passionate close, are made tolerable by the grace of the music and the delightfully pointed musical declamation. The quality of ecstasy is undoubtedly what has distinguished the best of Strauss's songs most markedly from those of any other composer. The gushing outburst of "Cäcilie" is as truly thrilling in its way as the quieter felicity of "Morgen," and much the same feeling is beautifully expressed in a more subdued manner in "Traum durch die Dämmerung," which seems to be Strauss's own favourite song, since he quotes it in the "hero's works" section of "Ein Heldenleben." It will be noticed that all these songs, as well as the few others which can be said to be popular ("Zueignung," "Allerseelen," "Ruhe, meine Seele," "Schlagende Herzen," "Ich schwebe"), have all very much the same character either of fervour or of charming lightness. The truth is that Strauss's art of song-writing is exceedingly limited, and, moreover, that if it changed at all during the years of his long career, it did so for the worse. But ten or twelve of his best songs will certainly remain among the classics of the German Lied.

E. B.

Salome

DRAMA IN 1 ACT

Poem by Oscar Wilde (German version by Hedwig Lachmann)

First performance: Hofoper, Dresden, Dec. 9, 1905

CHARACTERS

Herod, TENOR

Herodias, MEZZO-SOPRANO

Salome, SOPRANO

Jokanaan, BARITONE

Narraboth, TENOR

The Page of Herodias, MEZZO-SOPRANO

Five Jews, FOUR TENORS, ONE BASS

Two Nazarenes, TENOR, BASS

Two Soldiers, BASSES

A Cappadocian, BASS

A Slave, MUTE PART

The action takes place on a terrace of the palace of Herod, about A.D. *30*

The scene is outside the banquet hall of the palace of the Tetrarch, Herod Antipas. The captain of the guard, Narraboth, watches Salome with fascination as she sits in the great hall. In a cistern can be heard the voice of Jokanaan (John the Baptist) prophesying the coming of the Lord. Salome comes out of the banquet hall and, on hearing Jokanaan's voice, asks that he be brought up so that she can speak to him. When he emerges, tawny and strong, he denounces Herodias, wife of Herod and mother of Salome. Salome, fascinated by this strange man, wants to kiss him. Narraboth, horrified, stabs himself. Jokanaan, uttering a curse, returns to the cistern. Herod and Herodias come into the court from the banquet hall and are annoyed by the presence of the blood of Narraboth. Herod, restless, finally asks Salome to dance for him. She won't until Herod promises to give her what she asks. He promises, and she dances the dance of the seven veils at the conclusion of which she asks for Jokanaan's head on a silver plate. Herod pleads for anything else, but finally consents as Herodias approves the girl's request. When the head is brought from the cistern, Salome takes the plate, and kisses the mouth of Jokanaan. Herod, revolted, orders his soldiers to kill her.

Little is said about Salome or her dance in the New Testament. Matthew wrote: "But when Herod's birthday was kept, the daughter of Herodias danced before them and pleased Herod." She was "instructed of her mother" to ask as a reward "John Baptist's head in a charger." And the king was sorry. The account in Mark's gospel is a little longer, but we learn nothing more about the dance: "And when the daughter of the said Herodias came in and danced, and pleased Herod and them that sat with him, the king said unto the damsel, Ask of me whatsoever thou wilt, and I will give it thee." Then the daughter went forth and said unto her mother, "What shall I ask?" Herodias was wroth with John on account of his public denunciation of her behavior: "For John had said unto Herod, It is not lawful for thee to have thy brother's wife. Therefore Herodias had a quarrel against him, and would have killed him; but she could not. For Herod feared John, knowing that he was a just man and an holy, and observed him; and when he heard him, he did many things, and heard him gladly." Yet Herodias persuaded him to jail John, and Salome danced off the head of the Forerunner.

Nowhere in the New Testament is the daughter of Herodias called by name Salome. She was not killed by order of Herod: she lived and was married twice,—first to Philip, tetrarch of Trachonitus, her uncle on her father's side (she was the daughter of Herod Philip); afterward to her cousin, Aristobulus, son of Herod, the king of Calchas. According to Josephus she had three sons by Aristobulus.

Fantastical legends took their rise from this simple story. According to one, Salome went with her mother and Herod when they were banished from Judæa. They crossed a frozen river, and the ice broke under Salome's feet. She sank in up to her neck; the ice united and she remained suspended by it.

According to others, Herodias was in love with John the Baptist. Spurned by him, she demanded his head,—Josephus assigns, however, a political motive for the execution of the Baptist,—and stabbed with a bodkin the tongue that had railed against her. Or she was condemned to wander till the Last Day, because she laughed at the Saviour on his way to Calvary. Another legend tells us that Herodias attempted to kiss the head of John, but the head blew upon her a terrible blast and sent her flying into space, where she still revolves. Mr. W. J. Henderson, in his lecture on Strauss's *Salome,* quoted from the Homilies of Ælfric the Saxon, who died in 1006: "Some heretics have said that the head blew the king's wife Herodias, for whom he had been slain, so that she went with the winds all over the world; but they erred in that saying, for she lived to the end of her life after the slaying of John." According to some the head was buried at Edessa; some say it was buried in St. Peter's at Rome; others insist that it was buried in the cathedral of Amiens.

In other legends, Herodias rides in the chase of the Wild Hunter, or she is the Wild Huntress. She figures in Heine's "Atta Troll" (1841–42). The poet, looking out of the window of the witch Uraka's hut on the Eve of John the Baptist and in the time of full moon, saw the Wild Hunt hurry through a hollow. Three women were conspicuous in the pageant, Diana, Abunda, and Herodias.

Jacob N. Beam, in an article published in "Modern Language Notes" (January, 1907), says of the story of Salome and the Baptist that this love element is probably wholly of nineteenth-century romantic origin. "It does not seem to have existed in the older authorities on the legends of the martyrs and saints." Eusebius Emesenus spoke of Salome playing with the head as with an apple, but he said nothing of Salome's passion for John. Mr. Beam adds: "In view of the well-known fertility and perversity of Heine's imagination, it is likely that he invented the *Sage,* pure and simple, and assigned a fictitious source."

Wilde no doubt based his story of Salome's passion on the passage in "Atta Troll." He borrowed from Flaubert's story the stage setting, the banquet, the cistern, the voice of the Baptist, the Roman visitors, the desire of Herod for Salome, who in Flaubert's tale is an innocent and charming young girl, hardly knowing John's name.

Percival Pollard translated into English an essay on Salome by a Spaniard, Gomez Carillo, who had talked with Wilde about portraits of Herodias' daughter. This translation was published in an issue of *Papyrus* (1906), edited by Mr. Michael Monahan. Wilde said to Carillo: "I have always longed to go to Spain, that I might see in the Prado Titian's Salome, of which Tintoretto once exclaimed: 'Here at last is a man who paints the quivering flesh!' " And Wilde asked him if Carillo knew the Salome of Stranzioni and that of Alessandro Veronese.

According to Carillo, the dramatist dreamed constantly of Salome and her dance. At times he saw her chaste, and he spoke of her as "a gentle princess, who danced before Herod as if by a call from Heaven." He then saw her quivering body lily tall and pale. "Veils woven by angels conceal her slenderness, her blonde hair flows like molten gold over her shoulders."

And once, seeing the picture of a woman's pale head, severed from her body, Wilde exclaimed: "Why, that is Salome," and he told a story found in a Nubian gospel. A Jewish princess made a present of an apostle's head to a young philosopher. The youth smiled and said unto her: "I should rather have your own head, my dear." The princess went away all pale. That night a slave visited the philosopher, and he bore with him on a golden plate the head of the woman. The scholar looked up and said: "Why all this blood?" and he turned a leaf in Plato. Wilde believed this Jewish princess was Salome.

Picture after picture did not satisfy his ideal. The Salome of Leonardo was too cold in its dignity. He did not tarry before the Salome of Dürer, of Ghirlandajo, of Leclerc, of Van Thulden. The Salome of Regnault was a gypsy with an English complexion. Moreau's revealed to him "the soul of the dancing princess of his dreams," and thinking of this picture, he would quote Huysman's words: "She is nearly naked. In the whirl of the dance the veils are unloosed, the shawls are fallen to the ground, and only jewels clothe her body. The tiniest of girdles spans her hips; a costly jewel glows like a star between her breasts; a chain of garnets fades into the glow of her hair." A woman whom Wilde met by chance in the street set him a-dreaming of Salome; before a jeweller's window he would plan combinations of gems to deck his idol. Sometimes he thought she must have been resplendent in nudity, but

strewn with jewels, all ringing and tinkling in her hair, on her ankles, her wrists, her throat, enclosing her hips and heightening with their myriad glittering reflections the unchastity of that unchaste amber flesh. For of an unknowing Salôme, who is a mere tool, I refuse to hear a word. In Leonardo's painting, her lips disclose the boundless cruelty of her heart. Her splendor must be an abyss; her desire an ocean; . . . that the pearls on her breast die of love; that the bloom of her maidenhood pales the opals and fires the rubies, while even the sapphires on this feverish skin lose the purity of their lustre.

The painters of long ago clothed her in the costume of their own period, and she danced as the noble dames of their day would have minced it, strutted it, or lolled and languished at the court. The dance might have been at a Dutch, Italian, or German ball. See the picture by Israel von Menecken or the one by Karel von Mander. In the latter, Herod is clothed as a deep-thinking philosopher; Salome is sumptuously dressed, with a long flowing train, a high-cut bodice, a jewelled velvet head-dress, and she is attended by a handsome sprig of nobility. In a corner, far in the background, the sworder is already at work on the kneeling John.

In illuminated manuscripts of the fourteenth century and in windows of stained glass, Salome walks on her hands before Herod, to his great delight and to the amazement of his guests, who uplift hands. For in an old version of the New Testament it is said that Salome "vaulted" before Herod. The pictorial representations of this performance are disappointing. The daughter of Herodias is clad as in a meal-sack, and not even her feet are visible. Furthermore, she is sour-visaged.

The early fathers of the church insisted that the dance was suggestive, provocative, wanton. Saint Gregory reproached the Emperor Julian for his misuse of dancing, saying: "If it pleases you to dance, if your inclination drags you to these festivities, of which you seem to be passionately fond, dance as much as you like; but why renew before our eyes the dissolute dances of the barbarous Herodias and the pagans? Perform, rather, the dance of King David before the ark; dance to honor God. These exercises of peace and piety are worthy of an emperor and a Christian."

Poor Salome! The Breton folk-song reminds a maiden whose feet itch of the daughter of Herodias. "When thou seest dancing, think of the bloody head of John the Baptist on the charger, and hellish longing will not fill thy soul."

P. H.

In *Salome,* Strauss let himself go, arriving in one bound at an operatic position as advanced as that which he had attained, years earlier, in his purely instrumental work. Rather as a *coup,* he had managed to secure Oscar Wilde's notorious play, which in the Germany of that day was considered only less lofty than Shakespeare or Goethe. Except for a few brief excisions, Strauss accepted the play, in Hedwig Lachmann's faithful German version, just as it was—a self-contained work of art, and a work of art so jeweled, so static, so immalleable, that it did not require music, and would not have mixed well with it.

Strauss did not attempt to mix the two: he wrote a tone poem with human voices as added instruments in the orchestra, the whole designed to be accompanied by a stage spectacle of an aggressively sense-stimulating nature. For the suggestive, heavily perfumed, and rigidly mannered text, he wrote music that exaggerated each of its qualities. The music tells more than it has to say, is downright aphrodisiac, and ends in tetanic catalepsy. Throughout, the music so overshadows the stage action as to reduce it to mime, and even the greatest of dramatic singers cannot utterly overcome the posed, almost hieratic quality of the drama. Strauss' *Salome* is more decadent than Wilde's play simply because it takes itself more seriously. Or, perhaps, only seems to—with Strauss one is never sure, though now that its magnificent tissue has begun to wear thin and reveal the cotton body to which the brocade is stitched, it is tempting to write *Salome* off as the cold-blooded fabrication of a supercraftsman. And even in the tissue, which used to look so golden and cunningly patterned, it now seems that there are patches of the carelessly commonplace. But what remains of *Salome* is enough, when a powerful singing actress is found for the title role, to provide a good evening in the opera house.

Salome dazzled the world with its piled-up brilliance, its quenchless energy, its battery of shattering effects. It was a magnificent envelope containing little, and musically it was bound to fade. It was a symptom of the bustling imperial Germany of the early twentieth century, with its boasts, its strutting muscularity, its sumptuary excesses, and its glee in the superficials of progress. *Salome* was another course in the continuous champagne banquet of expanding Germany, and it was, though not in the old sense, a national opera. Those who were able to see through the dazzle, being neither too shocked nor too carried away, saw through to the synthetic core and said that Strauss lacked conviction. They said that *Salome* had no inwardness, and it was even whispered that Strauss' creative peak was passed. In 1908, Ernest Newman ended his monograph on Strauss, one of the first in English, on an ominous note: "His new opera, which is to be produced early next year, will probably show whether he is going to realize our best hopes or our worst fears."

Dresden, at whose Königliches Opernhaus *Salome* was first produced on December 9, 1905, accepted it enthusiastically and without hesitation. Soon, despite the ban laid upon it in Berlin by Wilhelm II, patron of Leoncavallo, it was given in many German cities. It was shocking, but the audiences that thronged to see it in Germany left their hypocrisy at home. *Salome's* troubles with Anglo-Saxon morality began in New York, at the Metropolitan, on January 22, 1907.* Conried staged it, at doubled prices, as his annual benefit. Olive Fremstad was the Salome, Marion Weed the Herodias, Karl Burrian (as at Dresden) the Herod, and Karl Perron the Jokanaan. The next morning, a journalistic tempest broke over the heads of the Metropolitan management: the newspapers' morals had been outraged, and they demanded that the opera be dropped. The management could have weathered that, especially as audiences would no doubt have been capacity, but when the directors of the Metropolitan Opera and Real Estate Company threatened to cancel his lease, Conried withdrew the opera. It was seven years before any Strauss opera was heard at the Metropolitan, and twenty-seven years before *Salome* attained another performance there.

Meanwhile, Hammerstein had taken up arms against the freedom of the press to stifle progress in America, and, on January 28, 1909, produced *Salome* in French, at the Manhattan Opera House, with Garden rivaling Fremstad's realistic portrayal, yet failing to get Hammerstein into trouble. The following year, however, when she sang it first in Chicago, with De Cisneros (Herodias), Dalmorès (Herod), and Dufranne (Jokanaan), the most flattering vituperation came her way, and the opera was withdrawn after a single repetition. That same year, after the censor had been placated by changing the names of the Biblical characters, Aïno Ackté, the Finnish soprano, sang the title role at Sir Thomas Beecham's Covent Garden staging of the first *Salome* in England.

W. B., H. W.

* A Tuesday, this performance followed the semipublic dress rehearsal of the preceding Sunday morning, when one thousand guests had a first clandestine glance. Although a Sabbath, the day brought no outbreaks.

Elektra

[Electra]

TRAGEDY IN 1 ACT

Book by HUGO VON HOFMANNSTHAL, "after SOPHOCLES"

First performance: Hofoper, Dresden, Jan. 25, 1909

CHARACTERS

Klytemnestra, Queen, widow of Agamemnon, MEZZO-SOPRANO

Aegisthus, her lover, TENOR

Orestes, her son, BARITONE

Elektra, her daughter, SOPRANO

Chrysothemis, her daughter, SOPRANO

The action takes place in ancient Mycenae

The single set shows the rear of the palace at Mycenae, with the adjacent servants' quarters. This back yard contains the grave of King Agamemnon, who has been murdered in the palace by his wife Clytemnestra and her paramour Aegisthus. Here we find Electra, daughter of Agamemnon, who, together with her sister Chrysothemis, has been ill-treated by their brutish mother and the tyrannical Aegisthus and degraded to the status of servant. Electra's brother, Orestes, has made his escape from Mycenae under menace of death.

Electra, obsessed with revenge, invokes the spirit of her father and promises that one day his children shall dance in triumph on his grave, but how is she to take vengeance upon her mother and Aegisthus? Her own hands are too weak to strike the blow.

Laden with talismans Clytemnestra appears. Debased, a prey to superstition, in mortal terror of the return of her absent son Orestes, Clytemnestra would know from Electra, whom she pronounces "wise," what blood sacrifice can avail to bring her tranquillity and sleep; but Electra only mocks her mother, till in a surge of denunciation she predicts the terrible fate that awaits her. In an agony of horror Clytemnestra is cowering before her daughter, when her confidante comes running up and whispers in her ear. For a moment she is nonplussed. Then she comes to, calls for lights, and in an access of joy lifts her hands threateningly toward Electra and then hastens into the palace. Electra is mystified. Suddenly Chrysothemis rushes into the yard, howling like a wounded animal, "Orestes, Orestes is dead!" Electra refuses to believe. She tries to work her younger and healthier sister up to the point of committing the retributive murder, but all she can win from Chrysothemis, whose obsession is wifehood and motherhood before it shall be too late, is a reiterated "I cannot!" And then the girl escapes through the palace door.

A young stranger is standing in the shadow of the gate. He is Orestes, though at first he will not tell his sister, whom he takes for a servant, who he is. But at length comes recognition. Him she has not to beg. "I shall do it," he says; "I shall do it." Orestes with his old tutor enters the palace. The cries of Clytemnestra as she is struck down are heard from within. Aegisthus comes into the yard through the gate. With mock obsequiousness Electra greets him, detaining him a while until he, too, enters the palace to meet his doom. Women rush into the yard, among them Chrysothemis. Electra seizes her sister, and in a frenzied duet they chant their liberation. Electra, her revenge complete, now dances the promised dance of triumph above her father's grave until she falls. Chrysothemis hurls herself at the door of the palace and beats upon it. "Orestes!" she cries. "Orestes!" There is a silence. The curtain falls.

P. S.

"Elektra" was the first of three plays by Hofmannsthal based on the great heritage of Greek drama in the fifth century B.C. While his "Alcestis" (1911) was written after Euripides' play of the same name, Hofmannsthal's other "Greek" dramas are all connected with Sophocles. The third play "Oedipus the King" by Sophocles which Hofmannsthal translated and adapted for the modern stage in 1910. "Elektra" is an adaptation of Sophocles' drama with the same title; the poet did not take into consideration Euripides' "Elektra." These three Electras are the only ones which are still read today, and Hofmannsthal's is so closely linked to Strauss' opera that only the future holds the answer to the question whether his tragedy will survive on its own merits or as the libretto of Strauss' opera.

We know that the mythical and poetical heritage of classic antiquity has played an immense role in the occidental world. But it is rare that a new version of an old masterpiece conveys a message of its own and therefore survives the test of time like Goethe's "Iphigenia in Tauris." The reason why the heritage of the Greeks is so rarely matched must be sought in their unsurpassable genius, whose wonderful strength Goethe so strikingly described after he had received his friend Humboldt's translation of Aeschylus' "Agamemnon": "Even if one keeps himself occupied sympathetically with everything praiseworthy and good of the oldest and most recent times, such an arch old giant surprises us by its appearance, like a monster, and we have to pull ourselves together in order to meet it in a somewhat dignified manner . . . I admire now more than ever the weaving of this primeval tapestry; the past, the present, and the future are so happily intertwined in their unity that one becomes a seer, i.e., similar to a god, and this is the end the triumph of all poetry, the greatest and the smallest."

It is almost impossible to survey all the attempts to adapt the Elektra of antiquity, but a few examples from the 18th century may suffice to illustrate the many failures. The French dramatist Crébillon (1674–1762), fond of mixing his horror plays with ridiculous love stories, was successful enough to provoke the jealousy of his contemporary Voltaire, who found it necessary to deal with some of the same subjects. This was not the case, however, with Crébillon's "Elektre," which is easily understandable if we read in the preface to this tragedy that Crébillon was criticized for introducing into the action a love story between Elektra and a son of Aegisthus, "but," as he underlines in the list of characters, "from another mother than Klytemnestra." And he summarizes the reply to his critics in the following way: "According to the system of my censors Elektra should be shown completely pitiable: I think I have succeeded better than Sophocles, Euripides, Aeschylus and all those who have dealt with the same subject." In 1714 the writer, translator and Shakespearean commentator, Lewis Theobald (1688–1744), published a translation of Sophocles' "Elektra." Its only retrospective interest lies in its Shakespearean design with five acts. Then there is the "Elektra," which is a "musical declamation" by the director of the Mannheim National Theater, Wolfgang Heribert von Dalberg (1750–1806), who staged Schiller's first three dramas, among them "Kabale und Liebe" on which Verdi's *Luisa Miller* is based. Dalberg's "Elektra," performed in 1781, had only a short life; it was "declaimed" to the music of Cannabich, conductor of the famous electoral orchestra at Mannheim and Munich. In the next year the French composer Lemoyne (1751–1796) had some success with an opera *Elektra* but it seems that this success was due to the musical conditions in Paris where the quarrel between Gluckists and Piccinnists was flourishing. Lemoyne represented himself as a pupil of Gluck but the latter had disavowed him and from this moment on Lemoyne composed exclusively in the style of Piccinni. His only claim to fame came a few years later when he was the first to appear on the Paris stage to acknowledge the applause of the public. The same libretto used by Lemoyne was also set to music by Häffner (1759–1833), later court conductor in Stockholm, who wrote his *Elektra* in the style of Gluck!

This was in 1787, which brings us back to Goethe; for in the same year his "Iphigenia" was published. It was the fourth and final version, a classic in world literature, inspired by Sophocles' "Elektra." Only a few days before his "flight" to Italy Goethe read the Greek tragedy and under its impact the verses of his own play appeared to be "completely bumpy, bad sounding and unreadable. I started at once to change the first scene."

W. F.

News that Strauss was at work on *Elektra* had begun to circulate in September, 1906. Actually, the composer would have preferred to write a comic opera after *Salome,* but his biographer, Max Steinitzer, claims that the difficulty of finding a suitable libretto thwarted the plan. On the advice of a friend, Strauss went to see Max Reinhardt's production of Hugo von Hofmannsthal's one act tragedy, "Elektra" (based on Sophocles), in which Gertrud Eysolt was acting the name part. He felt certain that a musical setting would greatly increase the impact of the drama, and that, in episodes like the recognition of Elektra by Orestes and Elektra's deadly triumph, where the poet had reduced the quantity of text to a minimum, the composer could invest the scenes with atmospheric and emotional values otherwise no more than partially suggested.

Elektra is the first work Strauss wrote in collaboration with Hofmannsthal, though there had been some talk between them previously of basing a work on Calderon's "Daughter of the Air." The correspondence between the two shows that, in planning the operatic transformation of *Elektra,* the composer's suggestions were, in the main, promptly accepted by the dramatist. Indeed, the letters reveal again and again how little friction there was in the atmosphere of the creative workshop. Time and again Hofmannsthal fell in with Strauss' wishes, and was almost instantly rewarded with a grateful missive from the composer. . . .

On the occasion of the Dresden première of *Elektra,* the English critic and Strauss specialist, Alfred Kalisch (who among other things translated the text of that work as well as of the subsequent *Rosenkavalier* and *Ariadne auf Naxos*) contributed to the *Zeitschrift der Internationalen Musikgesellschaft* an article entitled "Impressions of Elektra." Kalisch, originally a barrister, became a music critic in 1894, and was at various times music chronicler for the London *Star,* the *Daily News,* the *World,* and the *Morning Leader.* From the essay which he wrote for the now long-vanished *Zeitschrift,* in which he recounted not only some of the circumstances of the original performance but also various musical and dramatic details of the work itself, the present annotator takes leave to quote. . . .

The air was naturally full of rumors concerning the new work, from which it was not possible to distinguish much that was useful. Most of the sensational reports which were circulated about it were profoundly untrue; such as that story that the farmyards and slaughterhouses of the neighborhood had been ransacked for live stock to figure in the sacrificial procession. As a matter of fact, nothing appeared except a few harmless, necessary sheep. Apart from the stories, when one arrived in Dresden one met *Elektra* everywhere. The shop windows were full of *Elektra* boots, spoons, and beer mugs. Even *Elektra* costumes for skiing occupied the center of one of the windows, and on the day of the first performance we were made to eat *Elektra* ices. . . .

When *Elektra* was first given in New York the late American composer and critic, Arthur Farwell, called it "the marriage of horror and beauty." The "horror" is still there, unmitigated by the passing of more than forty years. The "beauty" is another story. The intervening decades have enhanced and illuminated it from an architectural and a lyrical standpoint that lend a rather absurd sound to all the earlier talk about cacophony, orchestral bewilderments, noise and similar *clichés* of that remote and innocent period.

I even question if the late Ernestine Schumann-Heink, the original Klytemnestra, whose impersonation Strauss was afterwards to criticize adversely,
would venture today to speak of the music as *"ein furchtbares Gebrüll"*—"a
frightful bellowing." I wonder, for that matter, if anyone would dare to do so
in public, though the *Elektra* orchestra, 112 men strong, scarcely leads the
hearer to the arms of Morpheus!

One quality *Elektra* has indisputably preserved for well over a generation
—its monumentality. The tragedy of Sophocles, as Hugo von Hofmannsthal
remodeled it, is dramatically monumental, and monumental, no less, is the
score of Strauss. Like it or reject it as you will, the whole product, for all its
apparent complexity, has the hard simplicity of prehistoric Mykenean architecture, Strauss' biographer, Richard Specht, compared *Elektra* to Rodin, "but
a Rodin who models in gold and ivory." The *Elektra* music should *not* be
compared with that of *Salome* which is rather subtler and aims at something
like the effects of changeable silk. There are few subtleties in the score of
Elektra, which is bigger and vastly more terrible in its impact, more sombre
in its dark ecstasies, more grandiose and immense, so that even its essentially
lyrical quality is shaped on a larger and bolder scale. The strangest paradox
of *Elektra* is that it *became* the vast, elemental phenomenon it did—for Strauss
originally wished to make the creation which followed *Salome* a comic work.
The "comic work" was, indeed, to come a short time later; but in the *Elektra*
tragedy he had to reveal an aspect of his creative heritage. He had to do so
because, as Specht remarked, he was "an evolutionist, not a revolutionist."

When *Elektra* was new, one used to hear no end of twaddle about the
impossibility of catching the words of the text because of the loudness of the
orchestra and one particularly silly joke was current in which the composer
was quoted as exclaiming at a rehearsal: "Louder, louder, I can still hear the
singers!" The truth is Strauss could not find higher praise for a conductor than
to say that the greater percentage of the words was intelligible (it is known
that he himself used to claim that, at the average opera performance, irre-
spective of the language used, he accounted himself more than lucky if he
understood *forty percent* of the text!). And, like Wagner before him, Strauss
was careful that conductors should avoid such dynamic excesses as might
jeopardize the clarity of a singer's text projection. Those who had the opportunity to hear him conduct his own works could notice how restrained the
orchestral dynamic scheme could be without depriving the instrumental tex-
tures of their power.

H. F. P.

For many, *Elektra* confirmed their worst fears. It was louder, more cacoph-
onous, more unrelievedly psychopathic. *Salome* had emitted a mingled odor of
perfume and decay; *Elektra* omitted the perfume, and the decay had become
decomposition. Here was stench in terms of music. Hugo von Hofmannsthal,

they said, had distorted Sophocles and made him hideous, and Strauss had further uglified the result. It was the end, they said, and Strauss, besides being degenerate, was certainly insane. There could be no doubt that so foul a betrayal of art would soon shrivel up and disappear.

But *Elektra* has done nothing of the sort: recent performances have tended to confirm the opinion, at first expressed cautiously, and then with ever-growing conviction, that *Elektra* is a tragic masterpiece of the very first order. It has not faded: it is as shattering, as moving, as profound in terror, as on the night of its *première*. What we can now hear that many of its first baffled listeners could not, because of their consuming interest in its more obvious, less significant aspects, is the abiding conviction that holds *Elektra* together. The noise, the cacophony, even the reek of twisted neuroses and unleashed passion —all have integral functions. In short, *Elektra* is not a deliberate shocker—it merely, since it deals with the naked psyche, has no reticences. Within the limits imposed by the climactic character of the situations, the characters achieve a wholeness that is the best proof of Strauss' searching care in projecting personalities. So intense was that care that the tender lyricism of certain scenes escapes that banality which is all too often Strauss' only counterpoise to the horrible and the grotesque.

Elektra is formally and technically more satisfactory than *Salome*. Little in the libretto or the music is extraneous to the establishment of the atmosphere of tragedy and, in the largest sense, the display of Electra's struggle with fate. To these great issues Strauss' sure-fire theatrical devices—his pictorialism, his automatic program-making, his underlining of each situation—are tributary. In *Elektra*, he kept his unstanchable cleverness in its place. The extreme chromaticism and discord, which sometimes seem willful in *Salome*, are always relevant in *Elektra*, in which they are much more abundantly used. *Elektra*, too, is more singable than *Salome*. The voice parts, instead of doubling instruments in the orchestra, are throughout the note of color that sustains the balance of the palette. In *Salome*, the tone-poem base and the stage action practically dispossess the voice; in *Elektra*, Strauss, become a master of vocal declamation, establishes the parity of the vocal line without sacrificing the equilibrium of the whole structure. He did not damp down the orchestra, the result being that the singers have to work hard. But they work to effect.

At the world *première* of *Elektra* in Dresden, on January 25, 1909, Anna Krull (Electra), Margarete Siems (Chrysothemis), and Perron (Orestes) were less famous than the Clytemnestra—Ernestine Schumann-Heink, who never sang this role after the first performance. "It was frightful," she said. "We were a set of mad women. There is nothing beyond *Elektra*. We have lived to reach the farthest boundary in dramatic writing for the voice with Wagner. But Strauss goes beyond him. His singing voices are lost. We have come to a full stop. I believe Strauss himself sees it."

A year and a week after the *première,* Hammerstein, using a French version, by Henri Gauthier-Villars, of Hofmannsthal's text, presented *Elektra* at the Manhattan Opera House, with Mariette Mazarin (Electra), Gerville-Réache (Clytemnestra), and Gustave Huberdeau (Orestes). Again the Clytemnestra renounced the role as too taxing. Mazarin, though she fainted after the performance, was evidently made of sterner stuff, for she recovered to sing it again six days later, while five days after that she sang Electra in the afternoon and Salomé, in Massenet's *Hérodiade,* in the evening. The holy band of Manhattan critics were almost unanimous in denigrating *Elektra,* but the public hurried to see Mazarin's surpassing interpretation, which was along truly Sophoclean lines.

The first Metropolitan *Elektra* did not occur until December 3, 1932, when Bodanzky conducted a beautifully integrated performance, with Gertrude Kappel (Electra), Ljungberg (Chrysothemis), Branzell (Clytemnestra), and Schorr (Orestes). Ljungberg was later promoted to the name role, while Branzell vacated that of Clytemnestra for Maria Olszewska. An Electra comparable to Mazarin reached the Metropolitan in 1938: Rose Pauly, a Hungarian soprano of marked dramatic gifts, who had previously astounded New York in a concert version of the opera. At the Metropolitan, Thorborg's Clytemnestra was scarcely less remarkable than the Electra.

Schumann-Heink's feeling that Strauss would, in some measure, recant was justified by his next stage work, which was quite different from anything he had done before. "This time I shall write a Mozart opera," he said—and *Der Rosenkavalier* was the result.

W. B., H. W.

[Dimitri Mitropoulos conducted a complete concert version of *Elektra* on the N.Y. Philharmonic-Symphony program of Dec. 22, 1949, in Carnegie Hall. Astrid Varnay sang the title role.]

The natural sequel to an Elektra drama in antiquity was one in which Orestes, in his turn, was shown paying the penalty for his offence against the moral law in the murder of his mother. It is interesting to learn that in 1912 Hofmannsthal expressed the hope that Strauss would now write a symphonic poem on the subject of Orestes and the Furies. Apparently the music was to accompany a ballet, the scenario of which Hofmannsthal enclosed with his letter. "Think of Orestes as represented by Nijinsky, the greatest genius among mimes today!" Strauss's reply has not been published; but no doubt he was too full just then of his *Ariadne auf Naxos* to feel much interest in the world of Orestes and the Furies. When, a year or two later, he began to coquet with ballet, it was in connection with the less exacting subject of Joseph and Potiphar's wife.

E. N.

Der Rosenkavalier

[The Knight of the Rose]

COMEDY FOR MUSIC IN 3 ACTS

Book by HUGO VON HOFMANNSTHAL

First performance: Hofoper, Dresden, Jan. 26, 1911

CHARACTERS

Princess von Werdenberg (The Feldmarschallin), SOPRANO

Octavian, a young boy, scion of a noble family, MEZZO-SOPRANO

Herr von Faninal, a parvenu, BARITONE

Sophie, his daughter, SOPRANO

Baron Ochs auf Lerchenau, her cousin, BASS

Marianne, Faninal's housekeeper, SOPRANO

Valzacchi, an intrigant, TENOR

Annina, his accomplice, CONTRALTO

A Singer, a Flute Player, a Notary, Commissary of Police, Lackeys of Faninal, a Master of Ceremonies, an Innkeeper, a Milliner, a Noble Widow and Three Noble Orphans, a Hairdresser and his Assistants, Waiters, Musicians, Guests, Two Watchmen, Kitchen Servants, and Several Suspicious Apparitions

The action takes place in Vienna, during the early part of the reign of Maria Theresa

Octavian, a seventeen-year-old Austrian youth of noble birth, after a night spent with the Princess von Werdenberg, is breakfasting with her in her bedroom. The Field Marshal Prince von Werdenberg is hunting in Croatia. When the Princess's rustic cousin, Ochs von Lerchenau, is announced, Octavian slips into a soubrette's dress and becomes Mariandl, a waiting-maid. A country Don Juan, Von Lerchenau has come to his betrothal to Sofie, daughter of newly ennobled von Faninal. His cousin the Princess must find him a "Cavalier of the Rose," a gentleman who, according to custom, will present the silver betrothal rose to his fiancée as his proxy. She suggests young Lord Octavian—with whom, in the rôle of Mariandl, the old satyr has begun a flirtation—and then those waiting in the antechamber for an audience with the Princess are admitted. In a burlesque interlude a notary, the Princess *chef*, a dressmaker, a scholar, an animal-merchant, three orphan girls of noble family, a flute player, and an Italian singer crowd about the great lady while the hairdresser attends to her coiffure and an Italian adventurer, Valzacchi and his companion Annina, present their budget of gossip. Then all retire and the Princess is left to her melancholy thoughts. She is growing older. How long before boys of good family will stop coming to her home when the Field Marshal is hunting in Croatia? Octavian, who has returned in cavalry uniform, cannot cheer her up. When

489

she tells him he soon will leave her for some fresh young beauty, he hurries away in a pet, and she sends her negro page after him with the silver rose.

When Octavian enters the Faninal home with the silver rose, Sofie's beauty robs him of speech. After Von Lerchenau's lascivious advances to the convent-bred innocent, and a repulsive Intermezzo in which the Von Lerchenau lackeys attack the Faninal female servants, the two young things, left alone—it is a case of love at sight—cling together in a kiss, interrupted by Valzacchi and Annina who have been spying and whose shouts bring back Von Lerchenau. Octavian wounds the Baron, trying to force a duel, while Faninal curses and servants scream; but the country lover forgets his troubles when Annina slips him a note from the supposed Mariandl and he hurries off to meet her.

In a private chamber in an inn Mariandl (Octavian) drives the amorous Baron mad with rage and fear with a series of practical jokes (carried out by Valzacchi and Annina, now in his employ) and climaxing with Annina's rushing in with ten children, claiming Von Lerchenau is the husband who abandoned her. When the police commissioner arrives Von Lerchenau says Mariandl is Sofie, his bride, and refuses to recognize Faninal (secretly sent for) who is shocked at the lie and the scandal. As the Princess von Werdenberg enters, Octavian, who has dropped his disguise, appears, and resigned to the fact that youth will be served, she drives off Von Lerchenau. Faninal conducts the Princess to her coach and Sofie and Octavian fly into each other's arms. The curtain falls on a little negro page, who trips in after the lovers have gone, looking for the handkerchief the happy young girl has dropped in the ecstasy of her bliss.

F. H. M.

HUGO VON HOFMANNSTHAL

"You are the born librettist," Richard Strauss once wrote to Hugo von Hofmannsthal, "and that is, in my opinion, the supreme praise." *Der Rosenkavalier, Ariadne, Elektra* and others of the first rank of the so-called "modern" operas resulted from the collaboration of these two men; and so much attention has been called to the intimate relationship between them that anyone who reads the material available today would be inclined to forget the vibrant personality and tremendous artistic and intellectual stature of Hofmannsthal, who was a poet, philosopher, dramatist, essayist, conversationalist and man-of-letters long before his first meeting with Richard Strauss.

Hofmannsthal gave signs of genius even during his childhood, and at 17 had achieved no little fame as a lyrical poet. At this time, as in later years, the inevitable passing of life and of time preoccupied him; and we find that he asks the same questions in *Der Rosenkavalier* that he had asked time and time again in the great poems of his youth. Why is it that things change? Why must the Marschallin, the beautiful young Therese, become old? Why can we not stop the clocks? How can we hold to life, when it slips away so quickly?

In his youth, too, he was filled with the same fire and richness of spirit which is found in his work up to the year of his death. Part Austrian, part

Jewish, part Italian, Hofmannsthal was heir to that warm-blooded Southern European, Mediterranean tradition which tolerates and enjoys the little faults, mistakes and immoralities of life, and greets them with a serene smile. There is nothing of the Prussian here, nothing of the Protestant. The cold North, with its strict morality, its myths, and the twilight of its tragic gods is as far removed from the boudoir of the Marschallin as Siegfried is removed from Octavian Rofrano; it is no mere coincidence that *Der Rosenkavalier* is diametrically and absolutely opposed to the works of Wagner; there is a good measure of conscious rebellion involved.

In spirit and in execution *Der Rosenkavalier* looks back to the older operas, to the pre-Wagner, pre-Verdi traditions of *opera buffa,* mimes, and even to the comedies of Shakespeare. If it has ancestors, they are *The Marriage of Figaro, Falstaff, Twelfth Night* and the Restoration comedies. Hofmannsthal had wanted, long before *Der Rosenkavalier* was begun, to turn away from the sombre tone of *Elektra* and work on a comedy, preferably a German comedy. But what to choose for a subject, an era?

Hofmannsthal was never the starving poet, confined to a dingy garret. He was an elegant man, a member of the high ranks of Austrian society, who loved the incomparable richness, the warmth, the brilliance and the eighteenth century. Moreover, he loved Vienna, which was painted lavishly with all the colors and tints of that society. He believed that an author, to write well, must choose something which must satisfy his imagination completely, draw him to it, and inflame him with enthusiasm. And thus *Der Rosenkavalier* was conceived, planned and proposed to Richard Strauss.

"Go right home and send me the first act at once!" Strauss commanded when Hofmannsthal described the play to him, on the last day of March, 1909.

When *Der Rosenkavalier* was completed it proved itself a masterpiece, a drama which shows Hofmannsthal at his best: master of staging and theatre, king among playwrights, great poet, and possessor of an unbounded and sympathetic understanding of humanity.

At the time of its première *Der Rosenkavalier* was severely criticized, just as Strauss had predicted it would be. And the brunt of the criticism was borne by Hofmannsthal. "How could such a great artist lower himself to work on a play of such poor quality?" "How could Hofmannsthal be associated with an immoral work like that?" "It won't last five years," the critics said.

We, in 1949, know how long it has lasted. It has received performances by every major opera company in the United States in the last year-and-a-half. And Hofmannsthal himself is not forgotten. Our debt to him is large. Through him we know the eighteenth-century Austrian language which is long-dead; yet in *Der Rosenkavalier* it seems like an old friend. Because of him, the German-speaking peoples know "Everyman," one of the earliest English dramas. To him we owe the Salzburg Festivals, which he originated to help his country recover after the First World War. And to him we owe the creation of *Der Rosenkavalier,* its merriment, its warmth, its reassurance in difficult times.

M. J. M.

Before *Elektra* was finished the two men, who often were at odds in their dramatic ideas, but who admirably offset each other, were considering various subjects for their next collaboration. Their correspondence of the *Elektra* and *Rosenkavalier* period is extremely revealing of their respective personalities. The more sensitive and perceptive of fine shades of thought and character is Hofmannsthal; the more practical man of the theatre is Strauss.

In 1909 they are talking over a new opera, which Strauss wants to be as scenic and monumental as possible, on the subject of Semiramis, after a play of Calderon. And why? Because Verdi's *Aida* has been playing twice a week, to sold-out houses, says Strauss, "with Wagner and the rest nowhere, simply because of the new Egyptian setting. So I beg that in the case of Semiramis, in the matter of splendid *mise-en-scène* and handsome properties, you will see that neither expense nor trouble are spared." And: "One thing I beg of you; when writing your libretto, give no thought whatever to the music—that is purely my concern. Give me a good plot with plenty of action and incident— few massed scenes—just two or three good, 'fat' parts."

Hofmannsthal answered him rather tartly: "Have no fear, my dear Dr. Strauss; in writing this poem I intend to rely on myself and not at all on the music; this is the only way in which you and I can work together."

This idea, however, was abandoned. The next one was concerned with Hofmannsthal's comedy on the subject of Casanova, which Strauss wanted very much. But Hofmannsthal decided to give this work, which he had conceived for the spoken theatre, to Max Reinhardt. Hofmannsthal explains to Strauss that as the play stands it would not make good opera. "Just as it would have been impossible for Mozart, or any other composer, to have set Beaumarchais' comedy "Le Mariage de Figaro" exactly as he wrote it. . . . I firmly believe that we should never arrive at that really serviceable libretto which I hope we may yet achieve, had I not first got the substance of it written down in the form which suits me best, that of a psychological comedy in prose. . . ."

The "psychological comedy" which took the form of *The Knight of the Rose* suddenly bursts upon us in a letter Hofmannsthal writes Strauss February 11th, 1909, in which he happily informs the composer that in a single flash of inspiration, in the course of three peaceful afternoons, he had produced "an absolutely new and original libretto. The situations are broadly comic, the action is varied and almost as obvious as a pantomime—they are opportunities for lyric passages, fun, humor, even for a short ballet. There are two big roles, one for a baritone, the other for a shapely wench in man's clothes—à la Farrar or Mary Garden. The place and period, Vienna in the time of Maria Theresa."

Hofmannsthal adds that this comedy will be "just half as long as *Die Meistersinger.*" Actually, the same thing happened with *Rosenkavalier* as with *Meistersinger. Rosenkavalier,* given without cuts, is a very long opera.

Nor was the libretto complete as Hofmannsthal first planned it. The first version appears to have lacked its most important character, the Princess Von Werdenberg, wife of the Field Marshal Von Werdenberg—the Princess, noble sacrificial and sadly experienced, who surrenders her last love, the boy Octavian, to a younger, lovelier and more innocent rival, the girl Sophie. It is the Princess who lifts the whole comedy to a level far above the merry farce which Hofmannsthal first described in outline to Strauss. There is a curious hiatus in the published correspondence. She has evidently crept into the plot by the time Strauss receives Hofmannsthal's first act on July 4th of 1909, only five months after he had endorsed the opera's project.

It is noteworthy that Strauss finds this first act, doubtless in the person of the carefully and sensitively drawn portrait of the introspective Princess, "a little too subtle, perhaps, for the general public, but that doesn't matter." Hofmannsthal comes back at him on that point: "Your fear lest the work should prove too subtle does not disturb me. The progress of the action is simple and intelligible enough for even the most unsophisticated public: a fat, elderly, sophisticated suitor, favored by the lady's father, is supplanted by a handsome young fellow—surely simplicity could go no further."

Strauss was delighted with the chance to use his virtuosity as a composer in underscoring the scene of the Princess' levee of the first act. But he shocked Hofmannsthal by bestowing a *fortissimo* upon a word which the writer intended as a detail of Baron Ochs' conversation with the Princess, when he jovially refers to certain antics with the girls at reaping-time in the hay. The word must be whispered, says Hofmannsthal, "slyly, with the hand before the mouth, not bawled, for heaven's sake. It gave me quite a shock to find the word 'Heu' shouted *fortissimo.* Let me earnestly entreat you to alter this—not merely to please me, but for the sake of the opera." Strauss's ideas are more concrete, and he does not intend that the audience shall miss the point of the remark. So he sustains the "Heu," although more softly and "slyly" than apparently he had first intended. The point is not lost when the listener understands the reference.

Hofmannsthal writes of the end of the second act that "I have now made it lively, part vaudeville, part ballet in character. I have purposely avoided a choral climax for this finale so that there may be no comparison with the second finale of *Meistersinger.*"

But Strauss has his own important and excellent ideas, especially in the second act. He has also a phrase that occurs to him, a comical refrain for the Baron. It is "the luck of all the Lerchenaus." Strauss wants broader comedy than Hofmannsthal feels to be desirable. The composer insists on laughs, not merely smiles. He says that so far the work is gay, but not comic. It is to be feared that Hofmannsthal yielded to him too much in this respect. But he saves the situation and gives Strauss the opportunity for some of the loveliest music in the score, in pages which "enable the character of the Princess to soar into the higher realms of pathos." These pages provide a "happy ending" for the young couple, and in the final pages, invoke the loveliness and radiance of the spirit of Mozart.

O. D.

VIENNA BAROQUE

I well remember the surprise in musical circles when, in 1911 Richard Strauss, after completing *Elektra,* brought forth a "comedy for music," *Der Rosenkavalier*. From a composer whose colossal tone poems and operas had repeatedly caused a sensation and aroused both admiration and opposition, everybody expected more of the same bristling dissonances, more of the complicated orchestral masses, more nervous tonal coloring; more music which aroused and shocked the senses—such abominations as Salome's lust, such horrors as the murders in *Elektra*. Instead, he presented us with a musical comedy which adhered to established forms, contained melodies, ensembles, even waltzes! Everyone was dumbfounded. Newspapers began to rattle like windmills. The opera was frequently denounced as a bluff, a giant artificial bubble which soon would burst. In 1904, James Huneker had written to Krehbiel, "Richard Strauss Esq. is a damned big man, judging from the dust he has raised." With *Rosenkavalier* Strauss again proved an expert in the art of "dust raising."

The Viennese, sceptical, suspicious towards innovations, did not at once accord recognition to the work. I was present at its first performance in the capital. The audience remained cool and hardly applauded after the second act, even though Ochs was sung by Richard Mayr who later became the most famous interpreter of the role. The Viennese were strangely affronted by the waltz rhythms which they did not deem worthy to be included in an opera. When I accompanied Strauss to the train afterwards, he was deeply depressed. Finally he broke his long silence with, "if people only knew how difficult it is to write such waltzes!"

Few realized then that this masterpiece would soon enjoy the greatest popularity throughout the world. The poet Hugo von Hofmannsthal had prophesied it in a letter to Strauss (May 12, 1909) when he wrote that the opera would remain for "years, perhaps decades in the repertory." It was he, too, who gave Strauss the idea of including waltzes in the score to suggest the sensuality of the Viennese. While creating the text, he wrote to him, "let yourself be inspired to compose a waltz for the last act, an old-fashioned, sweet, pert Viennese waltz which must pervade the whole act." Strauss wove waltzes throughout the entire score to accent the local color. In accordance with Hofmannsthal's intentions, the opera would become truly Viennese. It would revive the times when Empress Maria Theresa reigned with feminine charm at the Hofburg and at Schönbrunn. Maria Theresa was typically Viennese; she had the statuesque, full-blown, voluptuous figure so highly esteemed in Viennese women. The famous writer of *feuilletons,* Friedrich Uhl, once felt compelled to write, "Paris is ruled by the grace of the Thin, Vienna by the allure of the Stout." It is the Empress Maria Theresa whom Hofmannsthal has characterized in the Marschallin; she has the imposing appearance, the compelling femininity, the commanding personality of the Empress who, however, was a faithful wife and not the mistress of aristocratic youths. Around the Marschallin, Hofmannsthal placed a group of characteristic Viennese types. The dialect which they speak is genuine and gives them a reality; for up to Franz Joseph's time, the nobility and even the Emperor himself used the vigorous, colorful language of the people. Maria Theresa, too, spoke as idiomatic a tongue as any little washerwoman from the suburbs whose dialect was rooted in the soil like the old trees in its numerous gardens.

The Venetian Canaletto has painted the Vienna of Maria Theresa and Charles VI—spacious squares over which aristocrats are carried in chaises; elegant officers on horseback; the new churches of the baroque era; splendid parks and palaces, like those of Prince Eugen who owned three, magnificent with terraces, ponds, sphinxes and fountains. It was Austria's proudest time. Austrian armies were victoriously engaged in combat against Spaniards, Turks, Frenchmen and Bavarians; Austrian governors resided in Brussels and Naples. After the Turks had been defeated and driven out of the Vienna woods and vineyards, there arose in the liberated city the grand palaces of the courtiers, the churches and monasteries which gave Vienna the baroque appearance it still bears today. The emperors added new buildings to their residence, the *Hofburg,* where many of the political and economic affairs of Europe were transacted; they built summer-palaces in Schönbrunn, in Hetzendorf and in the Augarten, where they revelled in festivities and listened to Italian Opera. They also built churches for the new religious orders which revived Catholicism with ostentatious services, sermons and processions; inspired by the enthusiasm of the holy Ignatius Loyola, Filippo Neri and François de Sales, these orders controlled the entire spiritual life of the times.

The aristocrats built in the new Italian style; their palaces had spacious gates, staircases adorned with statues and frescoes; halls, whose ceilings offered painted glimpses of Mount Olympus; balconies on which genii played; roofs, where Greek gods and nude goddesses posed; winter-palaces and summer-palaces surrounded by parks whose ponds were filled with gold-fish, whose hedges hid mythological figures.

The accelerated *joie de vivre* of the times asserted itself in demonstrations of festive splendor heretofore unknown to the world. Enormous equestrian ballets were performed, at which the emperor and his Court rode bejewelled steeds to the strains of operatic arias and choral music. Emperor Charles VI conducted opera in his palace; archdukes and duchesses sang arias and cantatas; aristocrats played instruments in the orchestra. The most famous singers, the most celebrated virtuosi performed for the aristocracy, who flocked to each other's palaces for these events. In lush gilded carriages they arrived, attended by liveried servants. Bewigged gentlemen in silken coats and kneebreeches, a sword dangling at the side, and ladies in enormous crinolines with high-piled coiffures presented a glittering spectacle as they slowly ascended the curving staircase in the flickering light of wax candles held by rows of motionless lackeys. The same pompous society gathered with the same *élan* in church to listen to the sermon, or to participate in a lavish procession which the Emperor himself graced by his presence, marching slowly, candle in hand, behind the Archbishop who carried the monstrance. Almost all young men of nobility were reared in schools supervised by convents, like those of Melk, Kremsmünster and St. Florian—old fortresses of faith which had been rebuilt in the flourishing style of the Italian baroque; courtyard opened into courtyard, wide hallways led from one frescoed room to another, marble saints stood guard over golden altars, plump angels of stone romped through the organ loft. It was a colorful, sumptuous, sensual world, this era of the baroque, which began in Italy but soon swept northward, carried along by the anti-reformation movement, until it encompassed all of southern Germany and reached a peak in the imperial Vienna. There, its peculiar architecture, its new manner of composing opera and church music, its picturesque parades and spectacles took on its most opulent forms.

A very important constituent of this new style of the seventeenth century was the Italian melody. Vienna became entirely a city of Italian music. All composers who wrote operas, ballets, masses, cantatas for the Court were Italians. Music in the Italian style resounded on the royal opera and concert stage, it emanated from the halls of the great aristocratic palaces, from the schools of the convents, from the choirs of the church. To the strains of Italian music emperors were crowned, weddings celebrated, royal offspring welcomed, important visitors received. The world of the baroque was a world filled with Italian melodies.

Hugo von Hofmannsthal had led Richard Strauss into this world. Strauss responded and began to feel more and more at home in it. He grew so fond of this period that the work following *Rosenkavalier* was a recreation of baroque opera. *Ariadne auf Naxos* (1912) is a mixture of Greek mythology and Italian *Commedia dell'arte,* richly endowed with melodious sensuality and intricate ensembles. Strauss' *Josefslegende* (1914) resembles the great ornamental ballets given during the reign of Leopold I, and Charles VI, a truly baroque compound of colorful scenes from the Renaissance, the Orient and the Bible. And lastly, in *Frau ohne Schatten,* he gave modern form to the baroque fairy-tale opera. It is no wonder that Strauss took up residence in Vienna during that time; it had long been his spiritual home.

With *Rosenkavalier*, Strauss had taken the turn towards melody which in its color and sensuality is still the melody of the Italian baroque. This melody found in Mozart the highest perfection and in Strauss a glorious conclusion. The brilliance of *Rosenkavalier* reminds us that at sunset all colors take on added lustre . . . we are permitted a last glance at the lovely melody which was born of the baroque era.

M. G.

The most famous of all the Barons von Ochs von Lerchenau was Richard Mayr, who sang the role about one hundred and fifty times on the stage of the Vienna State Opera and eight times at the Metropolitan in the late twenties. Mayr was a jovial man who could, upon the consumption of several bottles of wine, divulge many interesting experiences concerning Strauss and himself. After such fashion the following dialogue was elucidated: "When I worked on my Baron Ochs, I always thought of you, Mr. Mayr." Asked Mayr, "Am I to take that as a compliment or as an insult?" "Decide for yourself," proffered Strauss, but we may rest assured that the compliment was sincere, for no one was ever able to express better than Mayr the attitude of Ochs, the provincial aristocrat of the eighteenth century.

Another famous singer was Pavel Ludikar, the Czech bass, who sang at the Metropolitan from 1926 to 1932. As Ochs he was not so boisterous as Mayr, but concentrated on the humorous end of the role. Of an inherent scholarly nature, he is highly educated, has good command of several languages. At the first performance of the *Rosenkavalier* at the Milan Scala, Ludikar was asked to interpret the wishes of the composer for the conductor Serafin and other assisting artists.

Mr. Ludikar [suggested Strauss] you will have to explain to the lady that we are not doing *Les Huguenots* or *The Masked Ball,* and that she shouldn't transform the Marschallin into Amelia or Valentine. The princess is a lady of the world, has had several love affairs before Octavian, and will probably have several amorous adventures afterwards. What we want is only the nostalgia of a beautiful lady who notices that her blossom time is past . . . there is no need for her to commit suicide.

In a letter to the Munich publisher, Eugene Spitzweg, Hans von Buelow humorously labeled Richard Strauss "Johann Wagner" (a combination of Richard Wagner and Johann Strauss). Since that time, the name of Richard Strauss has been subjected rather frequently to epigrammatical confusion, particularly in Vienna, where the name Strauss was forever linked with the unforgettable waltz king. A typically acrid Viennese critic once wrote: "If Strauss, then Johann; if Richard, then rather Wagner."

P. N.

Response to Strauss' pleasant change of period, locale, and atmosphere was immediate and warm. After the Dresden *première* of January 26, 1911, *Der Rosenkavalier* was soon heard outside Germany, reaching London on New Year's, 1913. The following December 9, Frieda Hempel was the peerless Marschallin of the first Metropolitan cast, her chief colleagues being Margarete Ober (Octavian), Anna Case (Sophie), Otto Goritz (Baron Ochs), and Hermann Weil (Faninal). Alfred Hertz, who conducted, later (April 24, 1915) bade farewell to the Metropolitan with the same opera. As Sophie, Elisabeth Schumann first appeared at the Metropolitan, on November 20, 1914, while, at the first Bodanzky *Rosenkavalier* there, Edith Mason, also as Sophie, made her Metropolitan debut exactly one year later.

When the United States entered the First World War, and almost the entire German repertoire was dropped from the Metropolitan, *Der Rosenkavalier,* which in four seasons had attained twenty-two performances, vanished until November 17, 1922, when the following cast revived it: Easton (the Marschallin), Jeritza (Octavian), Sundelius (Sophie), Paul Bender, in his debut (Baron Ochs), and Gustav Schützendorf, also in his debut (Faninal). Later that season, Rethberg sang Sophie. Lotte Lehmann, most admired of Marschallins since Hempel, gave her first Metropolitan characterization on January 4, 1935, when her associates were Olszewska, Fleischer, Emanuel List, and Schützendorf.

W. B., H. W.

Ambroise Thomas

(Metz [Moselle], France, Aug. 5, 1811–Feb. 12, 1896, Paris)

Charles Louis Ambroise Thomas, one of the masters of French operetta, and with a certain gift for bigger things, was born at Metz on the 5th August 1811.

His father and mother, both of whom were musical, kept a school of music, and it was from them that he received his first instruction in the art, commencing at the age of four; at seven he took up the violin and the piano. In 1828 he entered the Paris Conservatoire, his master for the piano being Zimmermann, the father-in-law of Gounod. He won the first piano prize in 1829, the first harmony prize in 1830, and the Prix de Rome in 1832. Among the compositions he sent to the Conservatoire from Rome, in accordance with the conditions of the prize, was a duet that earned the praise of Berlioz in one of his *Gazette Musicale* articles.

In Rome, and during the years immediately following his return to Paris, he composed a quantity of chamber music, some songs, a Requiem Mass, and other works; but, as with all French composers until comparatively recently, the only road to fame and fortune for him lay through the theatre.

Influence obtained for him in 1834 an introduction to the Opéra-Comique, where he made his début with the one-act operetta *La Double Échelle*. This was successful, and between that year and 1860 he produced a large number of operas, operettas, and ballets at both the Opéra-Comique and the Opéra.

The most successful of these works were *Mina* (1843), *Le Caïd* (1849), and *Le Songe d'une Nuit d'Été* (1850). In the first of these there were no choruses and no bass or baritone soloist, the three men's parts being all written for tenors. *Le Caïd,* a sprightly and musicianly work, had a great vogue for more than thirty years: a critic of the time aptly characterised Thomas's muse as "a well-brought-up young lady who elects to play the *cocotte.*" In *Le Songe d'une Nuit d'Été,* Queen Elizabeth was presented as in love with Shakespeare. *Raymond* (1851) ran for only thirty-four performances, the opera being dragged down by its libretto, which was an absurd version of the story of the Man in the Iron Mask.

Thomas may have been partly consoled for the failure of *Raymond* by the fact that a few months previously he had been elected to the Institut in the place of Spontini, who had died in January of that year. Among the other ten candidates for the vacant seat was Berlioz. Thomas received thirty votes, Niedermayer five, Batton three, and Berlioz not a single one.

From 1837 to 1851 Thomas had produced a new stage work practically each year. Others followed in 1853, 1855, and 1857, and then, perhaps feeling a little tired and discouraged, he was silent for nearly six years. He had no great hopes of the success of his next work, *Mignon* (17th November 1866). . . . *Mignon* turned out to be one of those works that make the fortune both of the author and of the theatre.

Thomas never quite managed to repeat this colossal success, though *Hamlet* (1868) became very popular also. The part of Ophelia in this was created by Christine Nilsson. Hamlet, in the original version, was a tenor; but the chief tenor at the Opéra-Comique—Gueymard—proving unequal to the rôle, Thomas turned the part into one for a baritone, to be played by the celebrated Faure, who achieved a triumph in it.

Auber died in 1871, and Thomas, thanks to the success of *Mignon* and *Hamlet,* was elected to succeed him as Director of the Paris Conservatoire. His administrative duties seem to have taken up an undue proportion both of his time and his energy, and after *Hamlet* he did little creative work of any importance. Partly by reason of the inane treatment of Dante's famous story by the librettists, partly because of the weakness of the music, *Françoise de Rimini* (1882) was a complete failure; the Prologue to the opera alone had a touch of the old quality about it. Thomas had no better luck with the ballet "La Tempête" (1889), which soon disappeared from the stage.

He was the first composer to live to see the thousandth performance of one of his works. As an old man of eighty-three he was present on the 13th May 1894, at the thousandth performance of *Mignon* at the Opéra-Comique, when he was given an ovation by a distinguished audience. The grand cordon of the Legion of Honour was conferred on him by the President of the Republic, he being the first musician to receive that high dignity. A medal, reproducing the famous Mignon of the painter Ary Scheffer, was struck in commemoration of the celebration.

On the evening following the thousandth performance of *Mignon* there was a gala performance at the Opéra-Comique. The programme, apart from the "Marseillaise," consisted entirely of Ambroise Thomas's works, including the *Raymond* overture, a duet, and a chorus from the *Songe d'une Nuit d'Été* (sung by the soloists and chorus of the Opéra-Comique and a number of Conservatoire pupils), a cavatina from *Raymond* (sung by the tenor Clément), the always popular Gavotte and some vocal numbers from *Mignon*, two arias and a chorus from *Psyché,* and a ballet and a scena from *Hamlet*.

In the last twenty-five years of his life Ambroise Thomas became very serious and self-centred and very much of a solitary: one of his contemporaries described him at this time as a "Verdi solennel." His mind ran a good deal on the idea of death, and a quarter of a century before the end came he had prepared a granite tomb for himself on a storm-swept island off the Breton coast that he had bought. He died in Paris on the 12th February 1896, and was given a public funeral at Montmartre, an eloquent funeral oration being pronounced by Massenet.   E. N.

Mignon

OPÉRA COMIQUE IN 3 ACTS

Book by Michel Carré and Jules Barbier, after Goethe's novel
Wilhelm Meister

First performance: Opéra Comique, Paris, Nov. 17, 1866

CHARACTERS

Mignon, a young girl stolen by gypsies, MEZZO-SOPRANO

Philine, an actress, SOPRANO

Frederick, a young nobleman, BUFFO TENOR or CONTRALTO

Wilhelm Meister, a student on his travels, TENOR

Laertes, an actor, TENOR

Lothario, an Italian nobleman, BASSO CANTANTE

Giarno, a gypsy, BASS

Townsfolk, Peasants, Gypsies, Actors, and Actresses

The action takes place in Germany (Acts I and II) and Italy (Act III) in the late eighteenth century

Lothario, a mad singer seeking a long-lost daughter, enters a German tavern courtyard. There gypsies spread a rug but Giarno, their chief, cannot make seventeen-year-old Mignon dance the egg dance. His whip is raised when Wilhelm Meister, a student, draws pistol and purse and buys the waif. Loving Wilhelm with a love he never suspects Mignon (modestly attired as a page, lest she awaken injurious suspicions) follows her rescuer when he departs with Filena, the actress, and other members of a traveling troupe, to fill an engagement as the company "poet" in the castle of Frederick's uncle (Frederick is one of Filena's admirers).

In the castle Mignon soon realizes Wilhelm loves Filena. Slipping into her old gypsy skirt she goes out to drown herself in the park lake and there meets Lothario. When she tells him her sad tale and in a flash of rage at Filena, asks why heaven does not destroy the castle with lightning, the amiable mad man hurries off to make good heaven's omission. Soon the castle is in flames, the inmates hasten out. Filena, seeing Mignon, says a bouquet Wilhelm has given her is still in the conservatory. Blossoms touched by Wilhelm's hand to perish in the flames? Unthinkable!—to Mignon, at any rate. She rushes into the burning building to rescue them, and is herself rescued by Wilhelm, who rests her on a mossy bank, the withered flowers clutched in her hand.

In Italy—where Lothario, Mignon, and Wilhelm Meister are occupying the Cipriani castle—old Lothario suddenly regains his reason. He remembers the castle is his, that he is Count Cipriani, and identifies Mignon as his little Sperata, whose loss drove him insane. While father and daughter are clasped in each other's arms Wilhelm hastens up (he has heard Filena, whom he now loathes, is on her way to him) and makes the embrace a triple one, pending the chiming of wedding bells for Mignon and himself.

F. H. M.

Ambroise Thomas, who was born in 1811, two and a half months before Liszt and nearly two years before Wagner, did not bring out *Mignon,* the opera on which his chief fame rests, till 1866. On November 17 of that year *Mignon* was produced at the Paris Opéra Comique, though not without misgivings on the part of its author. We are told that at the dress rehearsal he said to a friend he would hesitate to predict for it even fifty performances.

At the première, however, it triumphed so signally that when on the following evening Thomas appeared at a concert in the Cirque des Champs-Elysées the audience stood up and acclaimed him. The public of Paris, not the composer, turned out to be the true prophet, for on May 16, 1894, the venerable gentleman, less than two years before his death, had the unique experience of being present at the 1000th performance of "Mignon" at the Opéra Comique, where now scarcely a month passes—except when for one reason or another the house is dark—without the work being billed at least once.

The original Mignon was Célestine Galli-Marié, who in March, 1875, was likewise to create Carmen. The limited compass of Galli-Marié's voice is reflected in both rôles. Any woman, be she soprano or contralto, possessed of a serviceable medium range, can sing either part in its original state. It was when Christine Nilsson decided to take up Mignon that Thomas revised his heroine's music in the interest of a higher voice.

As composed for the Opéra Comique, *Mignon* exemplifies the style of lyric drama which gives that theatre its name; that is to say, in spite of the non-comic story, the dialogue is not sung but spoken. Moreover, there is something in the nature of the music itself which Camille Bellaigue has pointed out:

> Hanslick [the famous Viennese critic] would not admit that in a work as French in spirit and feeling as *Mignon* the heroine could die. He was right. Among all these melodies is there even one that announces or only permits a tragic ending? . . . As a matter of fact, *Mignon* . . . will be the last example of our opéra comique, the touching relic of a lovable species and a happy art.

On July 5, 1870, *Mignon* was introduced to London at the Drury Lane Theatre in an Italian translation. Since spoken dialogue was foreign to Italian opera, Thomas composed for this occasion the recitatives that are in general use except on the French stage. He also added the graceful rondo-gavotte sung by Frederick in Act II, using the melody of the orchestral gavotte that serves as an introduction to the act. This addition was a tribute to the great contralto

Zelia Trebelli for her willingness to give prominence to what had been a minor part.

In the Italian version arranged for London *Mignon* reached this country, at New York's old Academy of Music, on November 22, 1871. Christine Nilsson sang Mignon and Victor Capoul Wilhelm Meister. The late Victor Maurel told the writer that Nilsson when she emerged from the gypsies' wagon was the most beautiful creature he had ever beheld. Capoul was long regarded as the ideal operatic lover.

Mignon happens to have been the fifth opera presented at the Metropolitan, on October 31, 1883, nine days after the opening. Again Italian was the language and the version that of London, and again Nilsson and Capoul headed the cast. Their principal associates were of corresponding fame—the American soprano Alwina Valleria for the florid rôle of Philine, Sofia Scalchi for Frederick, and Giuseppe del Puente for Lothario.

Although Nilsson long seemed the perfect Mignon to English and American audiences, Galli-Marié was peculiarly identified with the part in Paris. Henri de Curzon declared in 1898 that of all the Mignons that had followed Galli-Marié not one, with the exception of Marie Van Zandt, had "stamped the rôle with a real personality, much less equalled the creatrice." "Mme. Galli-Marié," to quote him further, "had given that complex figure, compact of reverie and passion, of prankishness and anger, of naïveté and poetry, a definitive imprint: it was useless to look further. Such was the character."

Nevertheless, the same authority had warm praise for Marie Van Zandt when as Mignon that American soprano made her début in Paris on March 18, 1880, at the Opéra Comique: "It was like a revelation," his words run. There had been no heralding, scarcely an announcement. All the well-informed knew was that this young girl of seventeen had appeared with success in London in *La Sonnambula* and *Don Giovanni* (Zerlina). To the Parisian public she was introduced in a dangerous rôle, for pronounced originality and genuine talent were necessary to insure success where rivalry had become so keen and Galli-Marié herself was still to be reckoned with.

Marie Van Zandt [according to de Curzon] succeeded completely. Though she was very different from the unequalled creatrice of the rôle, her qualities, thoroughly her own, agreed marvellously with what one expects of Goethe's enigmatic personage, with her sudden contrasts of gentleness and violence, of savagery and profound delicacy, with her appealing charm in spite of everything. And she has remained, all things considered, one of the best Mignons we have ever seen.

As it happens, Marie Van Zandt was the Metropolitan's second Mignon, on February 5, 1892 (still the language was Italian). Scalchi again sang Frederick, and the cast had the further distinction of presenting as Philine the mighty Lilli Lehmann, who had been our first Isolde and our first Brünnhilde in *Siegfried* and *Götterdämmerung*.

Lillian Nordica, who was to be an Isolde the following season, sang Philine's florid measures on December 10, 1894, the Mignon being Mira Heller, the Frederick once more Scalchi.

Boston, in the great days of the Boston Opera House, heard in 1911 one of the extraordinary *Mignon* casts of all time. Luisa Tetrazzini was the Philine and the distinguished French tenor, Edmond Clément, the Wilhelm Meister. With them were Fély Dereyne as Mignon, Jeska Swartz as Frederick, and Léon Rothier as Lothario.

P. S.

[*Mignon* was revived at the Metropolitan on March 6, 1908, in Italian, with Geraldine Farrar (Mignon), Bessie Abott (Filina), Josephine Jacoby (Frederick), Alessandro Bonci (Wilhelm Meister), and Plançon (Lothario). At the next Metropolitan revival, on March 10, 1927, the original French text was used. Lucrezia Bori, Marion Talley, Ellen Dalossy, Beniamino Gigli, and Clarence Whitehill were heard in the chief roles. *Mignon,* which never before had figured in two consecutive Metropolitan seasons, now became one of that theater's perennials.]

Peter Iljitsch Tschaikowsky

(Votinsk [Government of Viatka], Russia, May 7, 1840–Nov. 6, 1893, St. Petersburg)

Peter Iljitsch Tschaikowsky, endowed with a strikingly individual talent and composer of the universally known "Pathetic" symphony, was the first Russian musician to win a secure place for his compositions in other countries. As a symphonist he has proved to be, with the possible exception of Brahms, the most popular since Beethoven, and his fluent vein of melody likewise runs through an impressive number of tone poems and other orchestral pieces, concertos for piano or violin, chamber compositions, operas, ballets, and songs. He also wrote choral music for the Russian Orthodox Church, and it is a noteworthy fact that in nearly every form he attempted he achieved at least one work which has enjoyed conspicuous and lasting favor.

Tschaikowsky was not born into a musical family, nor did he give early signs of special musical gifts himself, though he began to take piano lessons at the age of seven. He was a precocious child, intelligent and amiable, and devoted to his mother. He was also sensitive and shy, and remained so throughout his life. His father, who when Peter was born . . . had been director of a foundry at Votinsk, removed with the family in 1850 to St. Petersburg, where Peter continued his piano lessons, now with first-rate teachers. Still, there was no thought of his making music a career. He took up law and upon graduation in 1859 entered the Ministry of Justice as a clerk. Meanwhile he had kept up his piano lessons and sung in a choral society, but without giving evidences of genius.

At twenty Tschaikowsky was a rather commonplace and frivolous young man, who could improvise agreeably on the piano, but without any idea of writing down his improvisations. Then came a change. His life seemed to him superficial and savorless and the law a mistake. So late in 1861 he turned from dilettantism and began seriously the study of musical theory. However, he stuck to his clerkship until convinced he was "no longer a clerk but a musician." That time came in 1863, when he resigned and faced poverty (his father was dead and his father's fortunes had declined) for the sake of music.

Entering the classes of the Russian Musical Society (which later developed into the St. Petersburg Conservatory), he met the brothers Rubinstein, whose influence was determining. Anton, the celebrated pianist and composer, taught him composition and orchestration, and in spite of Rubinstein's apparent harshness, Tschaikowsky's feeling for him bordered on adoration. Peter proved an able student, so in 1866 the younger Rubinstein, Nicholas, offered him the chair of harmony in the Moscow Conservatory, which he was then organizing. Tschaikowsky accepted and held the post for eleven years.

Though the salary was small, the change was advantageous, for Moscow received him cordially, he made valuable friends, and Nicholas Rubinstein, who took him to live in his house, proved a solicitous and devoted counselor and brought out his compositions. In token of this friendship, interrupted by Rubinstein's untimely death in 1881, Tschaikowsky dedicated the A Minor Piano Trio to his memory.

In 1868 the distinguished French soprano Désirée Artôt, on a professorial visit to Russia, became interested in Tschaikowsky's music and sent for him. He succumbed to the fascination of this brilliant and sympathetic woman and marriage was contemplated. Yet Tschaikowsky hesitated because of his own career. Mlle. Artôt put an end to his indecision by abruptly marrying the Spanish baritone Padilla. While smarting from this experience Tschaikowsky wrote the first of his greater compositions, the overture-fantasy "Romeo and Juliet."

Thenceforth Tschaikowsky's creative activity was extraordinary. Nevertheless he was continually tormented with doubts of his ability, and his nervousness, diffidence, and fits of black melancholy repeatedly brought him to a pass where he had to retire to the country or go to Switzerland or Italy to recover. Nor was his path to glory without thorns. St. Petersburg lagged behind Moscow in recognizing his genius. The operas *Eugene Onegin* and *The Queen of Spades,* which were both to become popular, were failures when first produced. "Romeo and Juliet," received coldly in Paris, was hissed in Vienna. Leopold Auer pronounced the violin concerto too difficult for performance. Indeed, England and America were the only countries in which Tschaikowsky's music won immediate and unequivocal success. Eventually deserved honors came, as the invitation to conduct at the opening of Carnegie Hall, New York, which brought Tschaikowsky here in 1891, and a doctor's degree from Cambridge, England, in 1893.

In 1877 he impulsively entered into an unsuitable marriage, which ended shortly in a separation. And the same year began the historic and singular friendship with Nadejda von Meck. This rich and musical widow, learning of his poverty and uncertain health, settled an annuity of 6000 rubles (about $3000) on him in 1877 and continued to pay it for thirteen years. But with the gift was a stipulation that they should never meet. However, Tschaikowsky's many letters to Mme. von Meck (to whom he dedicated his Fourth Symphony) are of the utmost importance with respect to his life and work. Eventually he was aided also by a bounty from the Czar.

Tschaikowsky regarded the "Pathetic" symphony as his masterpiece. Yet it fell flat when he conducted its première at St. Petersburg on October 28, 1893. A few weeks later, conducted by Napravnik, it made a sensation. But meantime Tschaikowsky had died. Cholera was prevalent in St. Petersburg and people were warned against drinking water that had not been boiled. Tschai-kowsky is said to have disregarded this precaution and on November 2 to have drunk a glass of unboiled water. Cholera developed and he died on the 6th. His brother Modeste gives a detailed account of his last illness. Nonetheless, the story has persisted that he deliberately drank the cholera-infected water or else took some other poison, a theory to which the peculiar melancholy of the "Pathetic" symphony, rising at times to a savage despair, lends color. It is just as well, though, to be skeptical about such stories. Mozart, dying of typhus, moaned in his delirium that he had been poisoned by the jealous Salieri.

P. S.

Eugene Onegin

OPERA IN 3 ACTS

Book by the Composer and K. S. Shilovsky, after the verse romance
by Pushkin

First performance: Small Theater, Moscow, Mar. 17, 1879

CHARACTERS

Mme. *Larina*, a landowner,
MEZZO-SOPRANO
Tatiana, her daughter, SOPRANO
Olga, her daughter, CONTRALTO
Eugene Onegin, a young dandy,
BARITONE

Lensky, his friend, TENOR
Prince Gremin, BASS
Triquet, a Frenchman, TENOR
Filipievna, a nurse, MEZZO-SOPRANO

The action takes place on an estate near the city of St. Petersburg, and also in it, during the nineteenth century

Eugene Onegin, who gives his name to the opera, is a rather Byronic and world-weary gentleman, endowed with a fatal fascination for women, which he exerts without any compunctions as to the pain he may give. Thus he kindles love for himself in the young and unsophisticated Tatiana, a country girl of gentle birth and breeding. She is so indiscreet as to write him a letter avowing her feeling. Onegin in person tells her the love is not reciprocated. Then, having wantonly aroused the jealousy of her sister's suitor Lensky, Onegin fights a duel with that young man and kills him.

In the end the boomerang visits Onegin. Unexpectedly he meets Tatiana herself years afterward at a ball in St. Petersburg. She is now the wife of Prince Gremin, a great noble. As a resplendent woman of the world in the stately setting of the capital Tatiana now fires the passion that the simple country girl had failed to stir. Onegin finds himself desperately in love with her.

He seeks an introduction and gains from her the admission that she loves him still. But that is the end. Nothing will move her from her iron resolve to be faithful to Prince Gremin. So they part, Onegin hopelessly and helplessly enamored of the woman he once had rejected with a gentle scorn.

P. S.

It would certainly be inaccurate to speak of Tchaikovsky * as an operatic composer who wrote symphonies and other instrumental music in his spare

* So spelled by the author.

time. Yet that view of his work as a whole would be no more badly out of focus than the popular one: that he was an instrumental composer who wrote an opera or two. Tchaikovsky wrote six symphonies—seven if you count "Manfred"—but ten operas, and if the non-symphonic instrumental works are thrown into one of the scales we can still put the incidental music for Ostrovsky's "Snow Maiden" and for "Hamlet" (to say nothing of the three ballets) into the other. Even some of the instrumental works, e.g. "Francesca da Rimini," originated in opera-projects. "To refrain from writing operas is, in its way, heroism," wrote Tchaikovsky in 1885. "I don't possess this heroism, and the stage with all its tawdry brilliance none the less attracts me." From July 1854, when, barely fourteen, he wrote to the now almost forgotten poet, V. I. Olkhovsky, about a libretto for a one-act comic-lyric opera, *Hyperbole*—a work which he was certainly quite incapable of composing at that age—to his death nearly forty years later, when he was considering the operatic possibilities of one of George Eliot's "Scenes of Clerical Life" ("The Sad Fortunes of the Rev. Amos Barton"), the spell of the stage was never broken, the longing to succeed on it never stilled. In addition to the ten libretti which he actually set, he began or at least considered no fewer than twenty others. And although of the ten operas he completed some failed to satisfy even himself and only two have won much success in the world, they embody an enormous mass of music far too beautiful and too interesting to be passed heedlessly by. Moreover, Tchaikovsky's search for subjects, his views on their nature and treatment, his work on libretti, throw penetrating light on his creative personality.

The early fascination of the stage is easily accounted for. In the years of Tchaikovsky's impressionable boyhood opera—and Italian opera at that—was the only kind of music that flourished in St. Petersburg. The sole chance of hearing symphonic music was at the Sunday afternoon University concerts, where a mainly amateur band sight-read its way through classical scores. Even the Russian Opera was in a poor state, and the boy went there only to hear his favourite *Life for the Tsar*, itself more Italian than some of our history-book accounts would lead us to believe. But it was the Italian Opera that fascinated him; it was only there, his brother Modest tells us, that he could hear "a good orchestra, good choral singing and first-rate soloists"; it was there that he deepened his early love for *Don Giovanni* and *Der Freischütz* and made the exciting acquaintance of Meyerbeer, Rossini, Donizetti, Bellini and Verdi. And these Italian sympathies were considerably strengthened by the influence of the Neapolitan singing-master Piccioli, who acknowledged no music but that of the last four of those masters and held Beethoven and Glinka in equal contempt. Modest does his best to minimise Piccioli's influence but has to admit it as one of the reasons why "Peter Ilyich at that time preferred operatic music to symphonic and not only took little interest in the latter but even regarded it somewhat disdainfully." In considering Tchaikovsky's career as an opera-composer all this must be kept well in mind.

He began it—and ended it—as a follower of the traditions of Verdi and Meyer-beer and Glinka. Though more than a quarter of a century younger than Wagner, he was—apart from his general dislike of Wagner's music—not interested in "music drama" or operatic reform. Though a contemporary and companion of Dargomizhsky and Mussorgsky, he had no use for operatic realism: "If the quest for realism in opera is carried to its ultimate conclusion, then you will inevitably arrive at a complete negation of opera," he said, apropos of Dargomizhsky's *Stone Guest.* He was content to take, and leave, the conventions of Victorian opera as he found them.

He once stated his very simple aesthetics of opera to Nadezhda von Meck (letter of November 27, 1879):

In composing an opera, the author must constantly think of the stage, i.e., not forget that the theatre needs not only melodies and harmonies but action to hold the attention of the theatre-goer who has come to hear *and see*—finally, that the style of theatre music must correspond to the style of scene-painting: simple, clear and colourful. Just as a picture by Meissonier would lose all its charm if it were put on the stage, so would rich music, full of harmonic subtleties, lose a great deal in the theatre, for there the listener needs sharply drawn melodies against a transparent harmonic background. In my *Voevoda,* however, I was mainly concerned with filigree-work and quite forgot the stage.

And he went on to state yet another reason for his persistent pursuit of operatic success:

The stage often paralyses the composer's musical inspiration, so that symphonic and chamber music stand far higher than operatic music. A symphony or sonata imposes on me no limitations; on the other hand opera possesses the advantage that it gives the possibility to speak in the musical language of the masses. An opera may be given forty times in one season, a symphony perhaps once in ten years.

At the same time, "despite the seductions of opera, I write a symphony, sonata or quartet with infinitely greater pleasure." Again, writing on the same theme to the same correspondent six years later (letter of September 27, 1885), he says:

I am *pleased* by your supercilious attitude to opera. You are right in disapproving this really *false type of art.* But there is something irrepressible that attracts all composers to opera: it is that it alone gives you the means to communicate with the *masses* of the public. My "Manfred" will be played once or twice, then laid aside for Heaven knows how long, and no one but the handful of connoisseurs who go to symphony concerts will know it. Opera, and opera alone, makes you friends with people, makes your music familiar to the real public, makes you the property not merely of separate little circles but—with luck—of the whole nation. I don't think there is anything reprehensible in striving for this, i.e., it wasn't vanity that guided Schumann when he wrote *Genoveva* or Beethoven when he composed his *Fidelio,* but a natural impulse to broaden the circle of their hearers, to act on the hearts of the greatest possible number of people. It isn't just a matter of pursuing external effects, but of choosing subjects of artistic value, interesting, and touching the quick.

"Touching the quick": that was Tchaikovsky's vital test for an opera subject. It must be concerned with strong human emotions. . . .

In May 1877 his brother Modest sent him the scenario of an opera based on Charles Nodier's "Ines de Las-Sierras," but in the very letter in which the composer rejects "Ines" as "too episodic and too little poetic" he tells the story of Elizaveta Lavrovskaya's suggestion that he should compose a "Eugene Onegin." On the face of it, it seems rather a crazy idea; Pushkin's poem is a "novel in verse," not a drama, and it lacks most of the elements of drama; most of its charm lies in the tone and the poetry of the narrative.* "It struck me as wild, and I made no reply," says Tchaikovsky himself. But after a time he thought it "possible"; bought a Pushkin with some difficulty—it was Vol. 1 of the 1838 edition, for the copy has been preserved—spent a sleepless night and produced a scenario corresponding very closely to the action of the opera as we know it and which I quote in place of a synopsis:

First Act. Scene I: Mme. Larina and the nurse are sitting in the garden, making preserves. Duet. A song is heard from the house: Tatyana and Olga sing a duet with harp-accompaniment. Enter reapers (with the last sheaf); they sing and dance. Suddenly the servant announces guests. Enter Eugene and Lensky. Ceremony of introduction and entertainment (bilberry wine). Eugene exchanges impressions with Lensky and Tatyana with Olga: quintet *à la Mozart*. The older women go away to prepare dinner. The young people stay and walk in the garden in pairs (as in Faust). Tatyana is reserved at first, then falls in love.
Scene II: Tatyana's letter.
Scene III: Scene between Onegin and Tatyana.
Second Act. Scene I: Tatyana's name-day. Ball. Lensky's jealousy. He insults Onegin and challenges him. General confusion.
Scene II: Lensky's aria and the duel.
Third Act. Scene I: Moscow. Ball in the Nobles' Hall. Tatyana meets a whole string of aunts and cousins. They sing a chorus. Appearance of the general. He falls in love with Tatyana. She tells him her story and agrees to marry him.
Scene II: Petersburg. Tatyana awaits Onegin. He appears. Big duet. Tatyana still loves him and fights a hard inner battle with herself. Her husband comes. Duty triumphs. Onegin rushes off in despair.

In the definitive form of the opera the principal changes were these:

In Act I, scene 1, there is no "ceremony of entertainment" and no "quintet à la Mozart"; the nurse Filipyevna disappears before the young men enter and Mme.

---

* The English or American reader is referred to Professor Oliver Elton's translation (Pushkin Press, 1943), or that by Babette Deutsch in a volume of Pushkin translations edited by A. Yarmolinsky (Nonesuch Press, 1940).

Larina leaves her daughters alone with the visitors almost immediately. Then follows a *quartet* which might be charitably regarded as *à la Mozart*.

Act III, scene 1, was entirely abandoned in favor of a different ball scene, in Petersburg. Instead of a shy debutante, Tatyana is already a polished woman of the world and already married to "the general," now christened "Prince Gremin." Onegin sees her at this ball.

The very end of the opera gave Tchaikovsky considerable trouble. Tatyana repulses the man who had once repulsed her ("But now, today, my turn has come"). And in Pushkin the scene ends with her quiet, firm avowal (I quote from Professor Elton's admirable version):

> I love you (why sophisticate it?),
> But am another's, pledged; and I
> To him stay constant, till I die.
>
> .   .   .   .
>
> So she departed: and Evgeny
> Like a man thunderstricken stood

Till the sound of the husband's approach breaks the spell. In his own copy of the poem Tchaikovsky first of all underlined the words "So she departed," as if he had intended to follow the poet closely, then crossed out the underlining, allowed Tatyana "overcome with emotion" to "sink on Onegin's breast" and added six pages (in vocal score) of passionate love-duet before she finally nerves herself to dismiss her lover. (There is no final appearance of the husband, as in the poem and the first draft of the scenario.) Even so, the definitive version of the end (made before the first professional performance of the opera at the Bolshoy Theatre, Moscow, on January 11/23, 1881) is said to be closer to Pushkin than the version given at the actual first performance (by students of the Moscow Conservatoire in the Maly Theatre on March 17/29, 1879). One curious point: in the original libretto Onegin's final words were "O death, O death, I go to seek thee!"; according to N. Rukavishnikov "the composer apparently did not care much for this phrase and made no protest when it was changed." But no one knows who was responsible for the substituted line, "Anguish! Dishonour! How pitiful my fate!"

But, broadly speaking, the libretto is Tchaikovsky's own. He preserved Pushkin's own verses wherever possible and imitated his style to the best of his ability in the necessarily numerous interpolations, though these changes and interpolations in a passionately loved classic—almost as much as the lack of conventional drama and the not so very long out-of-date costume of the 1830's—were probably a principal cause of *Onegin's* slow success in its early days.* Thanks to the preservation of Tchaikovsky's own copy of the poem,

---

* Having seen a vocal score of the opera, Turgenev wrote to Leo Tolstoy (November 15/27, 1878): "Undoubtedly notable music. The lyrical, melodic passages are particularly good. But what a libretto!"

we can even trace in his underlinings and crossings-out, not only his shaping of the libretto from most unpromising material, but (as Rukavishnikov says) his "deep sympathy for Tatyana and Lensky and a certain coldness towards Onegin." For instance, in the margin of stanza xxiii of Chapter I, describing Onegin's fashionable room, the composer has scribbled: "unpleasant." . . .

But the majority of Tchaikovsky's marginal markings, and the majority of his more wholesale borrowings from the original text, relate to Tatyana, with whom he was from the first "absolutely in love." It was Tatyana who aroused that "love and pity, as for a real person" which he needed if he was to be genuinely inspired. He told Kashkin many years afterwards: "I had so familiarized myself with the figure of Tatyana that she had become for me a living person in living surroundings. I loved Tatyana and was terribly indignant with Onegin, who seemed to me a cold, heartless coxcomb. He began to set Tatyana's famous letter even before he prepared his libretto. Indeed, two-thirds of the whole opera was written or at least roughed out in short score, by June 23/July 5, 1877—that is, in little more than five weeks after Mme. Lavrovskaya's suggestion; the non-completion of the score till January of the following year was due partly to work on the Fourth Symphony, another favorite work which was composed side by side with *Onegin,* but mainly to the composer's catastrophic marriage and the illness that followed it. . . .

Tchaikovsky himself feared that even *Onegin* would be ineffective. On August 30/September 11, 1877, "when the first fire had passed off" and he could "consider the composition objectively," he confided to Nadezhda von Meck his fear that it was "condemned to fail and to be ignored by the mass of the public. Its content is very unsophisticated, there are no scenic effects, the music lacks brilliance and rhetorical effectiveness." It is true there may be some chosen spirits who "hearing this music, will be touched by those emotions which agitated me when I wrote it." But "on the stage *Onegin* won't be *interesting.* For it won't satisfy the first requirement of opera—*scenic movement.*" His only hope is that it will please those who are capable of appreciating in opera "the simple, everyday feelings common to all mankind." Later, writing to Taneev [the composer] in more pugnacious mood, he could "spit on all stage effect." But he was always sure that *Onegin* could have no future in the theatre. And he almost rejoiced in the fact, for he dreaded to see these ideal characters reduced to the painful realities of the opera stage.

In a letter to Nadezhda von Meck of December 16/28, 1877, he writes:

Where shall I find the *Tatyana* whom Pushkin imagined and whom I've tried to illustrate musically? * Where is the artist who can even approach the ideal Onegin,

* Tschaikowsky's picture of the heroine is best expressed in another letter to his devoted friend and benefactress: "Tatiana is not merely a provincial 'Miss,' who falls in love with a dandy from

that cold dandy penetrated to the marrow with worldly *bon ton?* Where is there
a Lensky, an eighteen-year-old youth with the thick curls and the impetuous and
original ways of a young poet *à la* Schiller? How Pushkin's charming picture will
be vulgarised when it's transferred to the stage with its routine, its senseless traditions, its veterans of both sexes who—like Alexandrova and Kommisarzhevsky
i tutti quanti—shamelessly take on the rôles of sixteen-year-old girls and beardless
youths!

The whole thing was not so much an opera as "lyrical scenes" conceived for
"limited resources and a small stage." It is very odd that, having found the subject which perfectly satisfied his demands for real and sympathetic characters,
for strong, simple human emotions, Tchaikovsky should ever have felt so
doubtful about it—after the first overpowering burst of enthusiasm—and that
he should never have returned to anything like it, except partially in *The
Queen of Spades.*

                                                                    G. A.

The important place which the writings of Pushkin have occupied in the
consciousness of the Russian people for a century past is well indicated by the
number of operas which Russian composers have based upon his works.
Glinka's opera, *Russlan and Ludmilla,* written just after the poet's death, was
the first of them. This opera, together with Dargomijsky's setting of "The
Stone Guest," became models for the nationalist school at St. Petersburg.
Rimsky-Korsakov contrived operas out of three of Pushkin's poems: "Mozart
and Salieri," the "Tsar Saltan," and "The Golden Cock." Moussorgsky turned
to Pushkin for his *Boris Godounov* and César Cui made a setting of "The
Captain's Daughter." In Moscow, Tchaikovsky found subjects for four operas
in the texts of Pushkin: *Eugene Onegin, Pique Dame* (from the short story
in prose), *Mazeppa* (based on Pushkin's "Poltava"), and *Voyevode.* Rach-
maninoff made an opera from "The Covetous Knight," and another, *Aleko,*
from the poem "The Gypsies." Stravinsky's opera-bouffe *Mavra* is derived
from Pushkin's novel in verse, "Kolumna's Little House."

                                                                    J. N. B.

A concert performance in English at Carnegie Hall on Feb. 1, 1908, given
by the Symphony Society, with Walter Damrosch as conductor and Emilio

---

the capital. She is a young and virginal being, untouched as yet by the realities of life, a creature
of pure feminine beauty, a dreamy nature, ever seeking some vague ideal, and striving passionately
to grasp it. So long as she finds nothing that resembles an ideal, she remains unsatisfied but tranquil. It needs only the appearance of a man who—at least externally—stands out from the commonplace surroundings in which he lives, and at once she imagines her ideal has come, and in
her passion becomes oblivious of self. Pushkin has portrayed the power of this virginal love with
such genius that—even in my childhood—it touched me to the quick. If the fire of inspiration
really burned within me when I composed the 'Letter Scene,' it was Pushkin who kindled it."

de Gogorza to sing the title role, introduced *Eugene Onegin* to America. It was staged at the Metropolitan Opera House in an Italian version March 24, 1920. Artur Bodanzky conducted, and the singers included Claudia Muzio (Tatiana), Giovanni Martinelli (Lensky), Giuseppe de Luca (Onegin), and Adamo Didur (Prince Gremin).

Pique Dame

[The Queen of Spades]

TRAGIC OPERA IN 3 ACTS

Book by Modest Tschaikowsky, after a story by Pushkin

First performance: Imperial Opera House, St. Petersburg, Dec. 19, 1890

CHARACTERS

Hermann, officer of the hussars, TENOR
Count Tomsky, his friend, BARITONE
Prince Jeletsky, betrothed to Lisa, BASS
Czekalinsky, TENOR; *Ssurin,* BASS;
  Tschaplitzky, TENOR; *Narumov,* BASS;
  Russian officers and noblemen

The Countess, MEZZO-SOPRANO
Lisa, her granddaughter, SOPRANO
Pauline, her friend, SOPRANO
The Governess, MEZZO-SOPRANO
Mascha, a chambermaid, SOPRANO

Guests, Soldiers, Officers, Promenaders, Masqueraders, etc.

The action takes place in St. Petersburg toward the end of the eighteenth century

Hermann, a poor young officer of the hussars, is an inveterate gambler. He meets Lisa and falls in love with her. Now Lisa is the granddaughter of a sinister old Countess who had once been the belle of St. Petersburg, but who lives now only to play cards. Her astonishing success at this sport has resulted in her being dubbed the Queen of Spades.

Hermann, learning that her luck is due to a secret combination of three cards, determines to obtain it and thus acquire the money needed for him to marry Lisa. From Lisa he obtains the key to the Countess' apartment, where he plans to force the old lady to tell him the secret. But his sudden appearance in her bedroom causes her to die of fright.

However, the ghost of the Countess insists on haunting him, and the ghost is kind enough to reveal the names of the three cards. Lisa endeavors to persuade him not to make use of this spectral knowledge, and when he persists in doing so she drowns herself in the Neva.

At the gambling rooms he plays against a Prince Yeletsky, who has also been bent on marrying Lisa. With the first two cards he wins, piling up the gold before him. But when the third time he stakes it all, instead of an ace he turns up the Queen of Spades. Now the Countess' ghost stands before him grinning in derision. Crazed with fear and his losses, he kills himself.

P. S.

On January 26 [1890] Piotr Ilyich departed for western Europe with no definite destination in mind. . . . In Berlin he hit upon the idea of going to Florence, where he arrived on January 30. The very next day he began to compose *The Queen of Spades*. He had not begun with enthusiasm for the idea, but the libretto Modest [Tchaikovsky] had made for Klenovsky from Pushkin's tale had been approved by the theatrical authorities. He completed the first scene in nine days. On January 31, just having begun work, he wrote in his diary: "Not bad. (The beginning is stolen from Napravnik.)" With few interruptions, he worked at the first sketch until March 15, writing Modest on that date that he had completed the opera three hours before. He set to work the following day on the piano score, finishing that on April 5. The orchestration was begun within about four days, and was finished at Frolovskoye on June 5, the entire task having occupied one hundred and twenty-six days.

From Florence, on February 4, Piotr Ilyich wrote Modest that he found the libretto of *The Queen of Spades* very good, but somewhat wordy. In completing and revising it, he suggested, Modest should be as brief and succinct as possible. He added that he was omitting a few details. All was going with reasonable smoothness when, on February 11, Piotr Ilyich received a letter from Jürgenson [the publisher]. It contained news of Antonina Ivanovna * that, he wrote in his diary, "upset me terribly. . . . Was like a maniac the whole day long. . . . Could not work." No further reference to this news, no clue to its import can be found. Possibly Piotr Ilyich's wife was showing clear signs of the insanity that was to land her in an asylum six years later. Possibly she had been gossiping about her husband, or merely threatening to gossip. He raged over this for one day—and then turned back to *The Queen of Spades*. This was almost the last reference he made, at least in writings that survive, to poor, nymphomaniac, self-deluded Antonina Ivanovna.

In the fourth scene of *The Queen of Spades* the hero, Hermann, appears before the old Countess in her bedroom. As she falls asleep, he begs her to tell him the secret of the three mysterious cards that enabled her always to win. When she refuses—she has been warned that to reveal the secret again will cause her death—Hermann points a pistol at her. She dies of fright, having failed to name the cards. This scene deeply impressed Piotr Ilyich, and he wrote . . . that while composing it he was terrified. Days after, he added: "I am still under the impress of this terror." In his diary he wrote: "Have been very nervous from working. . . . Curious that I should be both so madly inspired and yet find the work so full of difficulties." On February 23, having completed this fourth scene, Piotr Ilyich turned back to the third. Composing the pastiche intermezzo that accompanied an eighteenth-century ballet-divertissement at a ball, he noted in his diary: "At times it seemed to me as

* [Tschaikowsky's wife of a tragic mésalliance that had almost prompted his suicide.]

though I were living in the eighteenth century, and that after Mozart there was nothing."

The most renowned single number in *The Queen of Spades,* Liza's ever popular third-act arioso: "It is near to midnight," was written, both words and music, on March 7. Piotr Ilyich remarked that he agonized while writing the words. "Definitely, I am no poet." The following day he received word from [his manservant] Alexey Sofronov, who had just carried out his wish by renting the Frolovskoye house so that he might be free to lease a place more to his liking. Alexey's wife had died. "Wept," says Piotr Ilyich's diary. He wept again a few days later while composing Hermann's final aria. "Caused by weariness," he guessed, "but maybe because it is really good." Time had done nothing to toughen the light skin that overlay his emotions. Individual suffering, whether real or fictional, could always draw out his easy, sincere, and unashamed tears.

On March 13, having considered his relation to the Moscow Russian Musical Society from all sides, and having discussed the matter by letter, he wrote officially to the Society resigning from its directorate and declining to conduct six concerts during its coming season. He had decided to free himself from all outside duties except those involved in foreign tours, and to use his time as he pleased—which meant in composition. He had learned that his musical friends in Russia were planning to make a jubilee celebration of the twenty-fifth anniversary of his debut—at the Moscow Conservatory, in 1865—as a professional musician. "Of course," he wrote [his brother] Anatoly, "I shall decline all celebrations."

With the piano score of Act II of *The Queen of Spades* all but complete, Piotr Ilyich on March 31 gave his opinion of the opera as a whole in a letter to Modest. "Either I am terribly and inexcusably mistaken, or *The Queen of Spades* is really my chef-d'œuvre. Some of the passages in the fourth scene, for example, on the arrangement of which I was working today, fill me with so much fear, terror, and emotion that *it is impossible* that listeners should not feel at least part of this. . . . I wrote the opera with complete forgetfulness of self and with delight; the orchestration will undoubtedly give me pleasure." On April 8, having completed the piano score, he added: "It seems to me now that the history of the world is divided into two periods: the first consists of everything that has happened since the creation of the world up to the composition of *The Queen of Spades.* The second began a month ago."

Before leaving Florence on April 7, Piotr Ilyich paid a duty call on the Uffizi Gallery. "I must confess," he wrote Modest, "that painting, particularly the old masters, is in general beyond my comprehension and leaves me cold." Some days later, in Rome, he turned to orchestration—an art that left him far from cold—and began to clothe his sketch of *The Queen of Spades.* "I find this work easy . . . and very pleasant," he wrote Anatoly. He had orchestrated the entire first act by April 19. That morning he was guest of honour at a musical held in Sgambati's home. He wrote Nadezhda Filaretovna about it the same day: "Sgambati, the first musician of Rome, learned that I was in Rome, and therefore added my first quartet to his program, and asked me to be present at his morning musicale . . . and so I was forced to spend my working hours in a stuffy hall, to listen to a mediocre performance of my quartet, and to be the subject of the audience's attention and curiosity." He wrote Anatoly that the quartet had been a signal success, and that the newspapers had praised him most warmly. That his mind, as always, turned to Russia was proved by his remarking to Nadezhda Filaretovna that times were bad: "The spirit of reaction has reached such limits that Tolstoy's works are hounded as if they were revolutionary proclamations." He was himself no revolutionary, either political or artistic, but there cannot be doubt that his works, too, would have been hounded were the ideational processes behind music as plain to the average and official mind as are those of literature.

By May 4 Piotr Ilyich was in St. Petersburg. While there, he went to Pavlovsk, where the Waltz from "Sleeping Beauty" was played. He stopped in Moscow for a brief business conference with Jürgenson, after which he continued on to Frolovskoye. Three days later, writing to Anatoly, he said: "I am now going through a period of special love for life. I am full of the awareness of a successfully accomplished tremendous task . . . it seems to me . . . that *The Queen of Spades* is a successful opera . . . for the time being, I am certain of its brilliant future. In Rome I succeeded in orchestrating the first half of the score, and I have begun the second here. Then I want to draft a sextet for stringed instruments." This last was his first mention of what became the "Souvenir of Florence," opus 70, scored for two violins, two violas, cello, and double bass. . . .

Piotr Ilyich wrote "End of opera" on the manuscript orchestra score of *The Queen of Spades* at Frolovskoye on June 5. He looked into *A Dream on the Volga,* Arensky's opera to a libretto by Modest, and wrote Ippolitov-Ivanov that he found in it a great deal to like. On June 25 he set to work on the sextet. "Am writing under unusual strain," he told Modest. "Am embarrassed not by any lack of ideas, but by the novelty of the form. I need six independent and at the same time similar voices. This is incredibly difficult. Haydn could never conquer this difficulty, and never composed any but quartet chamber music." Two remarks are necessary here: Piotr Ilyich himself notably failed to conquer the six difficult voices in "Souvenir of Florence," and he was misinformed about Haydn, who wrote several quintets and at least one sextet.

At the end of June there were guests in Piotr Ilyich's house at Frolovskoye: Jürgenson and Kashkin [the critic and teacher] were there, eager to hear him play over the score of *The Queen of Spades.* "Complete approval," he reported to Modest by letter on July 3. "Do you know, it must really be good, for there are several passages I am completely unable to play; I want to cry each time I come to them, so filled am I with emotion." Soon after that, he was writing

Nadezhda Filaretovna that he was becoming more and more interested in raising flowers, and that he was pleased with his sextet. On July 16, four days after writing Modest that he had completed the rough draft of the sextet, he added: "What a sextet—and what a fugue at the end—it's a pleasure! Awful, how pleased I am with myself. . . . I am becoming more and more fascinated by it, and have cooled off considerably toward *The Queen of Spades*." New love was always best love with Piotr Ilyich, and he was, in all faith, momentarily unable to discern that *The Queen of Spades* was an exceedingly good opera, "Souvenir of Florence" an exceedingly bad sextet.

In response to an invitation from Piotr Ilyich, Arensky [the composer] visited Frolovskoye on July 13 to discuss *A Dream on the Volga*. His host wrote Nadezhda Filaretovna that he found this opera greatly to his liking, and described Arensky as a strange, sickly, and nervous man for whose future he had the gravest fear. After Arensky's visit Piotr Ilyich went to Moscow, where Kashkin joined him for a trip to Lobinskoye, the estate of Nikolay N. Figner, for whom he had designed the role of Hermann in *The Queen of Spades*. On July 19 the three of them read the score, and Piotr Ilyich wrote Modest that the singer was ecstatic about it. "He speaks of it with tears in his eyes—a good sign! . . . All his intentions correspond wholly to my wishes. I am worried about one thing: he asks for a transposition of the brindisi a whole tone down, telling me with good reason that he cannot, for fear of croaking like a frog, sing these really difficult high notes at the end of the opera." He learned, too, that Figner's wife, Medea, was enthusiastic about the role of Liza. This was important, for while there is reason to believe that Vsevolozhsky [the director of the opera house] had asked for *The Queen of Spades* with the Figners in mind, they were sufficiently popular and well established to have refused to appear in it had they not liked their roles. Their presence in the cast would guarantee a measure of temporary popularity for any opera. . . .

On December 6 Piotr Ilyich attended a concert of the St. Petersburg Russian Musical Society. Leopold Auer conducted the rarely played "Manfred." Reporting on this occasion, *Moskovskiye Vyedomosty* noted that "The symphony's composer, so beloved of the public, was called to the platform thrice." In his own St. Petersburg quarters Piotr Ilyich had "Souvenir of Florence" played for a group of friends including Laroche, Glazunov, and Lyadov. He could not entirely escape his twenty-fifth anniversary as a professional musician: the St. Petersburg Conservatory held a celebration of that event on December 15, and he was forced to attend. He was in St. Petersburg for the final rehearsals of *The Queen of Spades*. The dress rehearsal occurred in the presence of Alexander III and Marya Fyodorovna on December 17, the first public performance on the 19th. Napravnik conducted. The singers, some of them artists of the first rank, were at their best. "Throughout the whole evening," Modest says, "artists and audience alike experienced a sense of complete satisfaction rarely felt during any operatic performance." The audience was cumulatively enthusiastic. *The Queen of Spades* was an established, an immediately and permanently established, success.

H. W.

The Metropolitan Opera House, New York, was the scene of the initial American performance, in a German version, March 5, 1910. On May 10, 1922, *Pique Dame* was presented at the New Amsterdam Theater, New York, in the original Russian. The Metropolitan cast included Emmy Destinn as Lisa, Anna Meitschik as the Countess, Leo Slezak as Hermann, and Adamo Didur as Tomsky.

Giuseppe Verdi

(Roncole [Parma], Italy, Oct. 10, 1813–Jan. 27, 1901, Milan)

Verdi's life presents a study in success, artistic and worldly. Except in his early years he prospered. He was born . . . at Le Roncole, a hamlet about three miles from Busseto in the old Duchy of Parma, where his father kept a little inn. The serious, offish child has been described as both "shy and fierce." But he responded to music, following itinerant players and standing transfixed by the tones of the organ in the village church. His father was impressed enough to buy him a spinet when he was seven and to send him for music lessons to the village organist. At ten the child was appointed organist himself. Thereupon his father decided he should go to school at Busseto, though he retained his post at Le Roncole, trudging the distance every Sunday.

In the new surroundings his talent produced a marked impression, especially upon Antonio Barezzi, a well-to-do grocer. He gave the boy employment, introduced him to Ferdinando Provesi, organist of the cathedral and director of the Philharmonic Society, who took him as pupil, and eventually, with the aid of the Monte di Pieta, provided the money for him to continue his studies in Milan. Verdi did so to such good effect that his first opera, *Oberto,* was produced at Milan's famous lyric theatre, La Scala, in November, 1839, stamping him as a rising composer and winning an urgent demand for a second opera. Meanwhile, in 1836, he had married Barezzi's daughter Margherita.

Just when all was going so well calamity smote Verdi—perhaps the more harshly because it was never to smite him again. He had begun work on a comic opera early in 1840, *Il finto Stanislao* (called also "Un giorno di regno") when he was stricken with quinsy. Then, in April, his two young children fell ill and died within two days of each other. In June his wife, whom he loved devotedly, died after a brief illness. And he had a comic opera to complete! It is said that Verdi, saturnine by nature, was permanently affected in his outlook on life and art by this series of blows. The comic opera, composed under such conditions, failed miserably when produced at La Scala in September. Verdi, vowing never to write music again, resolved to support himself by teaching. And, as a matter of fact, he never wrote another comic opera until *Falstaff,* his last work for the stage, fifty-three years later.

Verdi's muse, however, refused to be dismissed. A persuasive libretto on the biblical subject of Nebuchadnezzar got him to composing again. The 9th of March, 1842, *Nabucco* was a triumph at La Scala. Verdi went home that night a made man. And he was only twenty-eight. The following February his *I Lombardi,* also at La Scala, was a second triumph. The 9th of March, 1844,

Ernani, this time in Venice, was a third triumph. Within nine months it was staged in fifteen different theatres!

During this period Verdi found a wise and devoted friend in Giuseppina Strepponi, an eminent soprano, who was the prima donna of *Nabucco* and who he eventually took as his second wife. He also strengthened his relations with Giovanni Riccordi, founder of a famous publishing house which owes much of its prosperity and prestige to his early faith in Verdi.

The operas of the next seven years, though including both *Macbeth* (first version) and *Luisa Miller,* added less to their composer's fame and fortune. However, the very name of Verdi had become a watchword with Italian patriots bent on throwing off the Austrian yoke and uniting all Italy under one king. "Viva V-E-R-D-I!" shouted in an opera house was interpreted as "Viva Vittorio Emmanuele Re d'Italia" from the initial letters of the Sardinian king's name and the hope that one day he would become in reality Re d'Italia (King of Italy).

Incidentally, Verdi himself, a staunch patriot and devotee of Cavour, took a sufficient part in public affairs to act as deputy and later as senator and also to serve on a commission for the reform of the Italian conservatories. Nevertheless, aside from the cares and pleasures of country life at St. Agata, the farm he acquired near Busseto, he remained before all else the composer.

On March 11, 1851, Verdi's fortunes received a fresh impulse when *Rigoletto* was acclaimed in Venice. Two of his major successes followed—*Il Trovatore* (Rome, 1853) and *La Traviata* (Venice, 1853). True, *La Traviata* was a fiasco at its première because the soprano who interpreted the consumptive heroine was so incongruously robust that her death scene provoked ribald laughter. With a different heroine, however, it triumphed. Verdi's operas during the next fourteen years included conspicuously *Les Vêpres Siciliennes* (for the Paris Opera), *Simon Boccanegra* (first version), *Un Ballo in Maschera, La Forza del Destino* (for St. Petersburg), a revision of *Macbeth* (for the Theatre Lyrique, Paris), and *Don Carlos* (for the Paris Opera). Then came a request from the Khedive that he write an opera on an Egyptian subject to be presented in the new opera house at Cairo in honor of the opening of the Suez Canal. The result was *Aida* (December 24, 1871), which in a sense marked the culmination of Verdi's career as a composer for the stage.

A year and a half later Manzoni died. Verdi, who had been an ardent admirer of the great poet and novelist, was moved to compose a Requiem in his memory. It was performed on the first anniversary of his death, May 22, 1874, in St. Mark's Church, Milan, attracting visitors from all over Europe. Verdi now felt that after this achievement in liturgical music he might well lay down his pen. Still, he largely rewrote *Simon Boccanegra* for a revival at La Scala in 1881 and in 1884 revised *Don Carlo* for the Italian stage. Yet it was largely through the influence of Arrigo Boito, a composer and poet of rare culture, that he resumed creative work. *Otello* (Milan, 1887) and *Falstaff*

(Milan, 1893), composed to admirable librettos by Boito, based on Shakespeare's "Othello" and "Merry Wives of Windsor," proved to be two of his greatest works. It has been held little short of miraculous that Verdi, who had not attempted a comic subject since the ill-fated *Finto Stanislao,* should at last at the age of fourscore laugh his great laugh in music.

The laughter was brief. Gloom closed in on the old man. In 1897 his wife died. The following year his final act as a musician was to bring out four short choral works—the "Quattro pezzi sacri," definitely closing his career, though he lingered on till January 27, 1901. This favorite of fortune, who had known fame, wealth, honor, still summed it all up tersely in one of his last letters: "Life is suffering." Thus spake the artist.

P. S.

Ernani

OPERA IN 4 ACTS

Book by Francesco Piave, after Victor Hugo's play *Hernani*

First performance: Teatro la Fenice, Venice, Mar. 9, 1844

CHARACTERS

Don Carlos, King of Castile, BARITONE *Elvira,* betrothed to Don Silva, SOPRANO
Don Ruy Gomez de Silva, a grandee of *Juana,* her nurse, MEZZO-SOPRANO
Spain, BASS
Ernani, a bandit chief, TENOR

Esquires, Attendants, Mountaineers, Bandits, Followers of Don Silva, Followers of the King, Spanish and German Nobles and Ladies, Electors, and Pages

The action takes place in Aragon, Aix-la-Chapelle, and Saragossa, in 1519

Ernani is a typical romantic hero of the time. An outlaw nobleman has turned bandit. He is in dejection because Elvira, whom he loves, is about to marry her guardian, the elderly grandee Don Ruy Gomez de Silva. Elvira is also loved by the King, Don Carlos (Charles V), who, in disguise, enters Don Ruy's castle where preparations are under way for the wedding. The imperial suitor is resorting to force, when Ernani emerges from a secret panel ready to fight both the monarch and Don Ruy (who also has made his appearance) and abduct Elvira.

Once more Ernani succeeds in entering Don Ruy's castle, this time in the garb of a pilgrim. Surprised by the Don, he refuses a duel with him until Elvira is freed from the menace of the King. So bandit and grandee together conspire for her safety, and Ernani answers Don Ruy's graciousness by promising with equal graciousness to kill himself whenever the older man sounds his hunting horn as a signal.

At Charlemagne's tomb at Aix-la-Chapelle the conspirators meet to capture the King, but Don Carlos, who has been meditating within the tomb, overhears them and when he strikes on the bronze door his soldiers gather to seize the plotters. The King condemns them to die, but heedful of Elvira's plea, he turns compassionate and even arranges the betrothal of Elvira and the one-time bandit.

The wedding takes place, and bride and bridegroom are hymning their love when the fatal horn call resounds. Don Ruy appears bearing a dagger and a cup of poison. Ernani, true to his oath, plunges his dagger in his heart and dies in Elvira's arms.

P. S.

The success of *I Lombardi* was not repeated when it was given at Venice in December 1843. Writing to the Countess Giuseppina Appiani, the wife of a Milanese painter and a devoted admirer of Verdi, as she had been of Bellini and Donizetti, he announces *"un gran fiasco,* one of those fiascos that may truly be called classic. They disapproved of or merely tolerated everything, except the *cabaletta* of the 'vision.' That is the whole truth of it, which I tell you without pleasure and without grief." However, though the Venetian public was not pleased, the director of the Fenice Theatre commissioned Verdi to compose a new opera, which was produced in March the following year. After toying with the idea of a *King Lear,* a subject which tempted Verdi over a period of many years, and after rejecting or having rejected other suggestions, Verdi accepted the director's proposal to turn Victor Hugo's "Hernani" into an opera. Francesco Piave, who combined stage-managing at the Fenice Theatre with the composition of librettos, was to provide the text.

Verdi was delighted with the subject, rather less pleased with his librettist, whom he compared unfavourably with Solera, and frankly doubtful about the police. His fears were well grounded, for Hugo's reputation as a prominent liberal and the stage representation of a plot against a crowned head were sufficient to arouse the suspicions of the authorities. However, these suspicions were once more allayed by a few alterations in the text. Verdi then found himself faced with obstacles of another kind, which were only surmounted by an exercise of his extraordinarily strong will-power. He had to fight the director over the question of a horn player appearing on the stage—"A horn player in the Fenice," exclaimed the director, "I never heard of such a thing"—and the *prima donna,* who had taken upon herself to demand of Piave the alteration of the final trio into a solo for herself, over the relative importance of composer and singer. In the event he won, but at the cost of antagonizing the *prima donna,* who, however, in the light of the opera's subsequent success, confessed herself mistaken.

It is hardly surprising that on the first night *Ernani* did not go too well. Mme. Loewe, still aggrieved, sang out of tune and the tenor, Guasco, was in poor voice, suffering from "a hoarseness that made one shudder." However, Verdi continues in his account of the performance to the Countess Appiani: "More or less every piece was applauded, except Guasco's cavatina. . . . There were three calls after the first act, one after the second, three after the third and three or four at the end of the opera. That is the true story."

Ernani has been summed up as showing "three men in love with one woman, quarrelling about her, and shouting their love, not one behaving in a rational manner; they challenge one another in their hatred and agree only in seeking one another's destruction." It is hardly to be wondered that Victor Hugo was not best pleased with this highly melodramatic version of his drama, in which all the situations are exaggerated and the details that would make them at all credible are omitted owing to the need for compression. *Ernani* is the first of many examples among Verdi's operas of the mistake of attempting to turn a stage play into an opera without reorganizing the whole material from the very start. The same sort of error is made by film producers who use dramas for the screen. The medium of opera is distinct from that of the spoken drama, and a libretto must be constructed expressly to meet its special needs, not merely adapted as best as may be from a dramatic script. An opera cannot successfully present all the complexities that go to the making of the kind of romantic melo-drama that was in vogue and of which Hugo was the leading exponent. The music takes too long to unfold the essential situations, leaving the details to be taken for granted and so emphasizing to the point of making them ridiculous all the coincidences and improbabilities of the original plot. Moreover in opera the characters as presented by the librettist have to be simplified; it is the com-poser's business to reclothe them with flesh and blood. It proved beyond Verdi's powers at this stage of his development to transform into a semblance of hu-man reality Piave's naive simplifications of Hugo's already stagy persons and improbable situations. Yet the composer of *Ernani* was hailed by a Venetian critic as possessing "an abundant and felicitous imagination, equalled only by his good taste," which is the last quality a modern audience would find in an opera conspicuous for its violence and brutality of expression.

The Italian public, however, took *Ernani* to its heart, once more identifying itself with the outlawed hero, sharing in the stage conspiracy against his op-pressor, and substituting for "Carlo Quinto" in the chorus "A Carlo Quinto sia gloria ed onor" the name of Pio Nono, when that liberal pope was elected three years later. If the strength of its patriotic appeal won for *Ernani* an immediate success in Italy so great that Verdi's publishers soon had twenty copies of the score out on hire at one time, the finer quality of the music as compared with that of *I Lombardi* has secured it a longer life than any of its predecessors, though in England it is known nowadays only by the cavatina, "Ernani, involami," to which we are occasionally treated by sopranos desirous of showing off their *fioriture*.

Indeed, *Ernani* did more than enhance Verdi's popularity at home; it brought him international fame. Within six months of its first performance it was given in Vienna, under the supervision of Donizetti, who was director of the Italian opera, and won the praise of young Hans von Bülow, who rec-ognized Verdi's "richness of melodic invention and genius for theatrical effect." In Paris, where Verdi's reputation was long in making headway, there was trouble with Hugo, who insisted on a change of title in order to dissociate the opera from his play. It was the first of Verdi's operas to reach London, where it was given at Her Majesty's Theatre in 1845, the year after its original pro-duction. Although, according to Henry Chorley, the critic of *The Athenaeum,* it "shared the fate of Bellini's and Donizetti's first works in England," and "was received with curiosity rather than with sympathy," it remained in the repertory the following year and brought with it as companions *I Lombardi* and *Nabucco,* which was given as *Nino* in order to meet English prejudices about Biblical subjects in the theatre. Chorley, a conservative admirer of the older style of opera, was no lover of Verdi's music, but he acknowledges that *Ernani* struck his ear "by a certain rude force and grandeur," and writes of the "dignity and passion" of the "great" finale, "O sommo Carlo," and the final trio. He records also that the Elvira "was, in every sense of the word, a stout singer, with a robust voice—a lady not in the least afraid of the violent use to which the latest Italian *maestro* forces his heroines, but able to scream in time,* and to shout with breath enough to carry through the most animated movement of those devised by him." It may have been due to the singer's want of personal attraction, which then, as now, carried great weight with a London audience, that the opera, like the soprano, "did not enjoy a success such as singers (and operas) far inferior have commanded."

Chorley was even more critical of *Nabucco,* challenging the appearance in the theatre of "the personages of Holy Writ," and expatiating again upon the "screams" of the soprano in "Amazonian attire." *I Lombardi,* on the other hand, "had the aid of Mme. Grisi and Signor Mario," but even so "the music betrayed the wear of the lady's voice. . . . The sickly *cavatina* for the tenor, which the barrel-organs made us hate ere 'Il balen' was thought of, was given delightfully by Signor Mario; and the rude vigour of certain concerted pieces made itself felt—but the opera did not stand." *Ernani* was, according to the same critic, doomed by the miserable company of singers. Despite these strictures, the operas remained in the repertory the following year together with two new ones, including *I Masnadieri,* which was composed for London. So they cannot have so completely failed "to stand" as Chorley suggests.

Within a fortnight of the production of *Ernani* in Venice, Verdi was back in Milan writing to Vincenzio Flauto of the San Carlo Theatre, Naples, stating his terms for the composition of a new opera.

D. H.

In a very short time, *Ernani* was given in Vienna . . . in Paris, in London, and in New York, where, after being first heard at the Park Theater, on April 15, 1847, it was used, on the following November 22, to open the first season of the Astor Place Opera House (whose orchestra was notoriously unruly and unwilling to co-operate), the principal lessee of which was Salvatore Patti, father of the famous Adelina. *Ernani,* too, reached San Francisco in 1853, the first grand opera to be sung there. It was not produced at the Metropolitan until January 28, 1903, when Marcella Sembrich headed a cast that included Scotti and Édouard de Reszke. After three performances, it was dropped until December 8, 1921, being revived then for Rosa Ponselle, with Martinelli, Danise, and Mardones. . . . It was as the heroine Elvira that the eighteen-year-old Pauline Lucca, one of the most individual singing talents of the mid-nineteenth century, made her debut, at Olmütz, on September 14, 1859.

W. B., H. W.

* *Sic.* Possibly a misprint for "in tune."

Macbeth

OPERA IN 4 ACTS

Book by the Composer, with verses by Francesco Piave and minor
contributions by Andrea Maffei, after Shakespeare

First performance: Teatro della Pergola, Florence, Mar. 14 or 17, 1847

CHARACTERS

Lady Macbeth, SOPRANO
Macbeth, a general, BARITONE
Banquo, a general, BASSO
Macduff, a Scottish nobleman, TENOR
Duncan, King of Scotland

Lady-in-waiting to Lady Macbeth,
SOPRANO
Malcolm, son of Duncan, TENOR
Fleance, son of Banquo
Doctor, BASSO

The action takes place in medieval Scotland

In the opening scene a chorus of witches on a blasted heath hails Macbeth as
thane of Cawdor and king of Scotland and greets Banquo, who accompanies him,
as the father of kings to come. Presently a messenger arriving from King Duncan
brings Macbeth information that the thane of Cawdor has been executed for treason.
A dance and chorus of witches concludes the scene.

In the next scene Lady Macbeth learns from Macbeth's letter of the witches and
their prophecy. When Macbeth enters she tells him of her project for putting Duncan out of the way, and thence the tragedy proceeds to the midnight murder of the
sleeping king. To the terror of Macbeth a knocking is heard. It is Macduff. With
Banquo beside him, he discovers what has happened. Banquo arouses the dwellers
in the castle.

The second act brings the murder of Banquo and the escape of his son and ends
with the banquet scene and the appearance of Banquo's ghost to Macbeth. The
third act introduces the witches again—their pantomimic invocation of Hecate, a
dance around the caldron, and the summoning of the apparitions for Macbeth. When
he tells his wife of what he has seen and heard, she becomes so enraged over the
vision of Banquo's descendants as kings of Scotland that she joins him in an oath
to put sternly out of the way all who are unfriendly to themselves and their dynasty.

The last act takes us to the vicinity of Birnam Wood, where Scottish exiles in
a particularly fine chorus lament the sad lot of their country under the Macbeth
tyranny, and Macduff sings of the death of his wife and children at the behest of
the tyrant. Lady Macbeth's sleepwalking scene (a superb page) follows, then Macbeth's meditations on his own lot and on the death of his wife, and finally the
battle, with the slaying of Macbeth by Macduff and a concluding chorus of liberated
Scots.

P. S.

Verdi's political preoccupation may well have retarded his musical development, making him complacent with easy successes due to the non-musical elements in his operas. But the experience gained in the composition of so many operas to order in a short space of time must nevertheless have contributed not only to his facility in writing, but to the development of that sense of theatrical effectiveness which was to be the conspicuous quality of his mature work. Journalism, which is what these early operas amount to, is no bad exercise for a young writer, provided he can resist the temptation of the second-rate and the second-hand. Verdi may not always have avoided clichés and meretricious effects; but in the end he rose triumphantly above them, creating an original and individual style, which, for all its frankly popular character, bears the stamp of true greatness.

In [Macbeth] . . . he almost achieved that greatness, and it has been argued that, but for his experience of operatic journalism, he might have risen higher. It is doubtful, however, whether at the age of thirty-four his genius had sufficiently developed for him to do justice to so magnificent a tragedy as Shakespeare's Macbeth. But, apart from any question of the composer's own qualifications for the task, the contemporary view of Shakespeare, especially in a foreign country, must be taken into account. Even in England he was regarded rather as a romantic dramatist than as a great poet, and this view of him, accentuated in countries where his actual language, now regarded as his most precious quality, could even less be appreciated at its true worth, inevitably militated against the transformation of one of his greatest tragedies into an opera that would accord entirely with modern taste. Even if we cannot see eye to eye with Verdi in his attitude towards the poet, his enthusiasm for Shakespeare is in itself sufficiently remarkable. It was of long standing and he had, as has been mentioned, already considered the possibility of writing an opera on the far more difficult subject of "King Lear."

The choice of Macbeth was, in the event, accidentally determined by the fact that a good tenor was not available at Florence, where the opera was produced in the spring of 1847, and that the tenor could be given a subsidiary part. The libretto—or rather its versification—was entrusted to Piave; for Verdi himself provided the complaisant poet with a complete version in prose in order to ensure that his ideas about the treatment of the subject should be strictly carried out. He adhered closely to the action of Shakespeare's play, and, although some of the minor characters, including Macduff and Malcolm, are reduced to the merest shadows of their real selves, all the more important features of the tragedy are retained.

In one vital respect Shakespeare's scheme is modified. In the tragedy Macbeth is the protagonist, for all that he is dominated by his wife. We are shown a man of potentially noble character and a great soldier, as well as a man in whom ambition leads to crime, remorse and neurotic weakness. In the opera, owing to the compression of the first scenes, Macbeth's nobility is not defined at all and his hesitations in the face of temptation are barely touched upon. As a character he is reduced to the stature of a conventional melodramatic villain. . . . Verdi was curiously blind to the need for creating a character completely in the round, with all the mingled qualities, good and bad, of a real human being. It was not until he came to write *Otello* that, with Boito's help, he created a genuinely convincing tragic hero comparable with his Shakespearian prototype.

In his opera it is Lady Macbeth who occupies the centre of the stage, and even here Verdi misses the opportunity of her tremendous invocation:

> Come, you spirits
> That tend on mortal thoughts! unsex me here,
> And fill me from the crown to the toe top full
> Of direst cruelty . . .

which, one would have thought, should have inspired him to something more impressive than Lady Macbeth's first aria. If he failed here, he does not seem to have attempted to make any effect of the fight between Macbeth and Macduff. Here was an opportunity, if ever there was, for one of those grand tenor-baritone duets that are among the special glories of his later operas. Yet in this scene the two characters are given no more than one sentence apiece to sing, and the whole thing is over in a few bars. Perhaps Verdi felt that he could not entrust an important movement to the second-rate tenor cast for Macduff.

Apart, however, from the initial failure, Lady Macbeth's character is finely drawn. Her aria, "La luce langue," with its tremulous accompaniment, is a sensitive expression of dawning doubt in Lady Macbeth's mind, and although the succeeding *allegro vivo,* in which doubt is dismissed and she exults in her newly acquired royalty, smacks too much of the jumpy conventional *cabaletta,* the melody has a bold vigor that makes it very effective in the theatre. Her *brindisi,* or drinking song, in which she toasts the guests at the banquet, again looks on paper no more than the trumpery kind of music that so often serves for social occasions in the early operas of Verdi. Yet in the hands of a good singer it can make a tremendous effect. The ludicrous melody then takes on the nervous energy of a factitious gaiety assumed for the occasion. It is the exact expression of a neurotic temperament unsure of itself. And when, after Macbeth has been unmanned by the first appearance of Banquo's ghost, Lady Macbeth repeats her song, lifting her cup to the absent guest, the detached notes and elaborate *fioriture* take on a new meaning and become the faltering accents of a soul shaken to the core. It may be that Verdi did not himself realize the tremendous effect of this piece, that he was not conscious of writing anything but a conventional drinking-song. I can find no reference to it in his letters revealing his intention to create this vivid dramatic effect. But the effect remains and the experience of it must make one chary of dismissing as trivial any passage in Verdi's operas until one has seen them on the stage.

If the *brindisi* was, perhaps, in the nature of a fluke, there can be no question of the genuine mastery of the *gran scena del sonnambulismo,* which must be numbered among the finest individual pieces in all Verdi's operas. This sleep-walking scene is set exactly as Shakespeare wrote it, with the doctor and gentle-woman in attendance, whose hearing of it adds so much to the horror and pathos of its effect upon the audience. Here, at any rate, the composer rises to the level of the poet and gives the full equivalent in music of the spoken word. Verdi has not attempted to relate this scene musically to the previous scene after Duncan's murder—a wonderfully effective duet carried through in under-tones—as he would almost certainly have done in his later years. A chromatic *ostinato* in the bass with a quick *staccato* figure above it to depict Lady Mac-beth's rubbing of her hands serves to create the mood and define the action. Out of her muttered phrases a fine melody grows until the end is reached with the hurried repetitions of "andiam" ("to bed") followed by a lovely slow cadenza that with *un fil di voce* touches D flat above the treble stave and thins out to nothing.

If Macbeth is, by comparison with his lady, too flatly drawn, he is not with-out his moments of greatness. The "dagger speech" is set to expressive music and the horror-stricken panic of Macbeth, in contrast to his wife's nervous at-tempt to pretend that nothing is amiss, is admirably portrayed. It cannot be said, however, that any of his airs rise to the same poetic heights as the Shake-spearian soliloquies whose place they take, and his best music is contained in the duets with Lady Macbeth and in the scene of the apparitions, which is imaginatively handled. It is impossible to accord the same praise to the Witches' music. Verdi had already shown his incapacity for handling the fantastic or the supernatural in the angel and demon choruses of *Giovanna d' Arco.* The *Mac-beth* Witches show no advance in this direction. At their best they use the idiom of liturgical responses in church. At their worst they are no more than the conventional bogy women of the nineteenth-century theatre. The chorus of murderers lying in wait for Banquo is no better. Its presentation of the "cat-like tread" provides a smile at its artlessness. It is a relic, surviving in *Rigoletto* and even in the music of Tom and Sam in *Un ballo in maschera,* of an operatic style that is outworn because it was never, either dramatically or musically, very convincing, and was made for ever ridiculous by Sullivan's parody in *The Pirates of Penzance.* The other choral movements are on a different plane altogether. That which ends the first act after the discovery of Duncan's mur-der is a splendid piece of music, static in feeling, but wholly admirable as a musical summing-up of the dramatic situation. The banquet-scene chorus is more dynamic and brings the second act to an effective climax. But best of all is the reflective chorus of Scottish exiles at the opening of the last act, which portrays their home-sickness in a most poignant way and shows an enormous advance in subtlety upon the straightforward Bellinian manner of the famous "Va pensiero" in *Nabucco*.

Of the minor characters Banquo alone has any individuality. His aria, "Come dal ciel precipita," is in the direct line of bass arias that runs through Verdi's operas from Zaccharia's Prayer in *Nabucco* to such things as "Il lacerato spirito" in *Simon Boccanegra*. Yet it has a pathetic character of its own which admirably fits the situation of the doomed man. Malcolm is but a shadow of his Shakespearian prototype and Macduff's air, a charming enough melody, is a poor substitute for

> What! all my pretty chickens and their dam
> At one fell swoop?

Verdi himself was intensely enthusiastic about *Macbeth* and, as a result, more than usually exacting about the details of its performance. He dictated exactly how Banquo's ghost should appear and was very angry when the singer of the part apparently proposed that a super could take his place in this scene. Verdi pointed out that the ghost must resemble Banquo in face and form, and asked whether operatic artists were not paid to act as well as sing. The ghost, he insists, must appear from underground, clad in ashen veils so fine as to be barely visible, and with his hair matted about his wounds. These ideas, he assured the impresario, came from London, "where this tragedy has been performed continuously for two hundred years and more."

When the opera was in rehearsal for performance at the San Carlo Theatre, Naples, in 1848, Verdi appended to a letter to Cammarano about the libretto of *Luisa Miller* the following interesting postscript, which proves how close *Macbeth* was to his heart and how advanced were his ideas of dramatic propriety in opera:

> I understand that you are rehearsing *Macbeth,* and as this opera interests me more than any other, I ask you to allow me to say a few words about it. Mme. Tadolini is, I believe, to sing Lady Macbeth, and I am astonished that she should have undertaken this part. You know how highly I think of Mme. Tadolini, and she knows it too; but in all our interests I think it necessary to remark that she has too great qualities for this part! This may seem an absurdity! Mme. Tadolini has a beautiful face and looks good, and I would have Lady Macbeth ugly and wicked. Mme. Tadolini sings to perfection, and I would not have Lady Macbeth sing at all. Mme. Tadolini has a wonderful voice, clear, liquid and powerful, and Lady Macbeth's should be the voice of a devil. Please bring these comments to the notice of the directors, of Maestro Mercadente, who will understand my ideas better than any one, and of Mme. Tadolini herself, and do what you think for the best.
>
> Note that the two most important scenes in the opera are the duet between Lady Macbeth and her husband, and the sleepwalking scene. If these fail, the opera falls to the ground, and these scenes must not be sung:

Here is need of declamation
In a veiled and gloomy tone;
Else the whole effect is gone,
Note, the strings must have their mutes on.

The scene is very dimly lit. In the third act the apparitions should appear (as I saw it done in London) at an opening in the scenery with a thin, ashen veil in front of them. The kings must not be lay-figures, but men of flesh and blood, and the floor over which they pass should have a slant up and down, so that they appear to rise and descend again. The scene must be very dark, especially when the cauldron vanishes, and only lighted where the kings pass by. The band under the stage should be strengthened for a large theatre like the San Carlo, but mind that there are no trumpets or trombones. The sound must seem to come from afar off in a muffled tone, so the band should consist of bass clarinets, bassoons and contra-bassoons, nothing else.

He was also more than usually careful about the details of the orchestration, and when the opera was given in Paris in 1865, he complained about the substitution of key trumpets for valve trumpets in the fugue describing the battle of Dunsinane, which, he declared, detracted from the effect of dissonance representing the din of battle.

For the Paris production Verdi revised the opera—in itself a proof of the high regard he had for the work, since his revisions are extensive and important. It is in this new version that the opera is given nowadays, and the hearer must beware of attributing to the thirty-three-year-old Verdi excellences that are in fact the product of another eighteen years' experience. All the finest things in the opera are additions to or radical revisions of the original score and the rest was to a large extent touched up, both in the voice parts and the orchestration. One can only deplore that Verdi did not wholly rewrite the opera, for so he might have added a third Shakespearian masterpiece to *Otello* and *Falstaff*. As it stands, *Macbeth* is too uneven to be placed in that august class.

In Florence, whither Verdi went in order to supervise the production of *Macbeth* early in 1847, the composer was introduced by Alessandro Manzoni to a cultured society, which included Giuseppe Giusti, a poet who touched up Piave's verses, Gilbert Duprez, a sculptor, and Andrea Maffei, who was at work upon an operatic version of Schiller's "Die Räuber." Duprez showed him the sights of Florence, of which the sculpture of Michelangelo made the greatest impression on the composer. It is easy to imagine the appeal made upon a man of Verdi's virile temperament by the masculine power of those figures hewn in the white heat of excitement from the solid marble. In the theatre Verdi adopted a more than ever dictatorial attitude, and the rehearsals of *Macbeth* did not run too smoothly. But the opera pleased the public and Verdi's belief in its merits was justified. It is worth remarking that he dedicated it to his father-in-law, Antonio Barezzi, as though he considered that this was the first of his works worthy to repay the debt he owed to the man who had made his career as a musician possible. "For a long time," he wrote to Barezzi, "I have had it in mind to dedicate a work to you, who have been to me a father, a benefactor and a friend. . . . Here, then, is *Macbeth,* which I love above all my other works and for that reason deem it most worthy to be presented to you."

D. H.

[*Macbeth* was introduced to America, in Italian, at Niblo's Garden, New York, on April 24, 1850. On Oct. 24, 1941, the New Opera Company presented it at the 44th Street Theatre, N.Y., with Florence Kirk and Jess Walters. Fritz Busch conducted.]

Rigoletto

OPERA IN 3 ACTS

Book by Francesco Maria Piave, after Victor Hugo's drama *Le Roi s'amuse*

First performance: Teatro la Fenice, Venice, Mar. 11, 1851

CHARACTERS

Rigoletto, a hunchback, jester to the
Duke of Mantua, BARITONE
Gilda, his daughter, SOPRANO
Giovanna, her nurse, MEZZO-SOPRANO
Duke of Mantua, TENOR
Sparafucile, a hired assassin, BASS
Maddalena, his sister, MEZZO-SOPRANO

Count Ceprano, a courtier, BASS
Countess Ceprano, his wife,
    MEZZO-SOPRANO
Monterone, a noble of the court, BASS
Borsa, a courtier, TENOR
Marullo, a courtier, BARITONE
Chorus of Courtiers

The action takes place at Mantua during the sixteenth century

Mantua's duke is a Don Juan; his court a place of debauchery. Rigoletto, hump-backed court jester, panders to his master's depravity; suggests that Ceprano, whose wife he loves, be made away with; and insults Monterone, whose daughter the Duke has ruined. Knowing well his Duke, he keeps his own daughter Gilda hidden in a far quarter of town, her existence unknown. As Monterone is led to prison he curses fool and master. Gilda leaves her home only to visit a near-by church. Alas, there she meets, loves, and admits to her home a supposed student (the Duke in disguise). The courtiers who have suffered from Rigoletto's jibes, discover the house he visits. Sure its occupant is his mistress they plan to abduct her. Near his home the jester falls in with them. They blindfold him and, thinking Ceprano's wife is being carried off, he holds the ladder while his own child is dragged to the ducal palace!

When next the Duke seeks Gilda he finds an empty house, but when the laughing courtiers tell their tale he hastens to the girl—and gives orders that he be not dis-turbed. In vain the despairing father kneels before the locked door (he has admitted the girl is his child), pleading madly with his master to forbear. When the door opens and Gilda rushes into his arms, Rigoletto clasps the poor betrayed creature to his breast, vowing vengeance on her deceiver, whom she loves.

Monterone's curse now moves to tragic fulfillment. In vain Rigoletto lets Gilda witness the Duke's ardent attentions to the strumpet Maddalena, the *bravo* Spara-fucile's sister, his latest flame. She still loves her seducer. After the Duke's departure Rigoletto pays the ruffian to murder him, having sent his daughter home to prepare for their flight from the city. Gilda, storm-driven, returns to the *bravo's* den for shelter, and hears the sister beg her brother to spare the Duke. Sparafucile refuses:

537

his dagger stroke has been bought and paid for. Suddenly the door opens, and the *bravo,* mistaking Gilda, disguised as a youth—intent on saving her ducal seducer—for his appointed victim, strikes her down. When Rigoletto arrives, his heart swelling with gratified revenge, he is given the body wrapped in a sack. As he drags it from the house to cast into the river, he suddenly hears the Duke's carefree voice raised in a merry song, "La Donna è mobile" (Woman is changeable), tears open the sack, and recognizes his daughter. When the dying girl's last words have revealed her sacrifice he falls across her body with a cry of agony.

F. H. M.

None of Verdi's operas is more generally popular than *Rigoletto,* and this popularity was predictable from the night of its triumphant world première at the Teatro Fenice (Phoenix), Venice, March 11, 1851. Yet few operas have had a harder time passing the censors. In fact, the troubles of *Rigoletto* began not in 1851, but in 1832. The libretto is derived from Victor Hugo's famous melodrama, "Le Roi s'amuse" (The King Amuses Himself), and that play was forbidden by the censorship in Paris in 1832 after its second performance. The fact that that gallant French monarch, Francis I, and his pandering court fool, Triboulet, are the protagonists proved a stumbling block to censors wherever revolution was in the air and thrones imperilled. Incidentally, "Le Roi s'amuse" was long popular on the American stage under the title of "The Fool's Revenge," and in the character of the fool Edwin Booth, the great old-school tragedian, found one of his most effective roles.

In spite of the risks inherent in the subject, Verdi, with his sure instinct for the theatre, saw in Victor Hugo's play an operatic theme to his liking. On March 9, 1850, the management of the Teatro Fenice commissioned Verdi to write a new "serious opera." Here was a task which he could envisage with particular pleasure because the Fenice had brought him such luck in the past. Two of his operas had been produced there with conspicuous success—*Ernani* (after Victor Hugo, by the way) on March 9, 1844, six years to the day before the new commission, and *Attila* on March 17, 1846. "Le Roi s'amuse" he chose for the libretto, the writing of which he entrusted to the faithful and obliging Piave, and the name that was decided on for Italian uses was "La Maledizione" (The Curse).

Favorable as the auguries seemed, an immediate curse descended on the new work in the form of a militant censorship. Innumerable are the stories of what happened. None of them, perhaps, is more trustworthy or more succinct than the account given by Barrili. The first indictment was sweeping. The police would not have King Francis I on the stage, nor yet his buffoon, nor yet the plot of the French poet, nor yet the title chosen for the new lyric drama. Too many things at once were not wanted by these inconvenient police! But, after all, it was a case of the proverbial spear of Achilles, which healed the wound it had dealt. An employee of the police, a certain Martello, proposed a useful expedient to the impresario and the librettist. They should give up Francis I, whose illustrious name would lend itself to unpleasant allusions, substituting the name of some Italian prince of an extinct line, and give up "La Maledizione" as too sonorous and ringing a title and use instead the name of the court fool. This last should be changed from Triboulet, Francis' buffoon, to Rigoletto, which was obviously Italian and would "swallow as easily as, say, soup and soft bread."

Thus the matter was finally adjusted, though not without a good deal of trouble and fatigue, and Verdi, reconciled at length to the change, repaired to his home at Busseto, where in forty days and forty nights he wrote down the entire score from the first note to the last, and then betook himself to Venice for the rehearsals. In the first performance, on March 11, 1851, a Pons was in the cast, but unlike Lily Pons of the Metropolitan, this Pons was a bass and sang Sparafucile. For Gilda there was one of the singing quintet of Brambilla sisters. Signora Casaloni, a contralto described as "of beautiful voice and lively intelligence," appeared as Maddalena. Mirate was the Duke, Varesi the Rigoletto, the two constituting with Pons "an exceptional trio of male voices and dramatic temperaments."

Probably alone among operas, *Rigoletto* could not be rehearsed complete. Always one piece was lacking, whether the rehearsal was at the piano or on the stage. It was the song that the Duke of Mantua (no longer Francis I) was to sing in Sparafucile's hideout. The eve of the dress rehearsal arrived and the song in question was not yet forthcoming. The tenor Mirate complained to the composer: "How shall I sing it as I should if I haven't it in time?" "Don't worry, you will have it," the composer replied. "You will have it tomorrow morning." And in fact the following morning he entrusted the tenor with the music of the piece. The melody proved simple to learn and Mirate was highly pleased with it.

But be careful [added Verdi]; you must swear to me that you will not let anybody see or hear the melody of this little song. Don't hum it, don't whistle it, I beg of you, in the presence of anybody whatsoever. It is so easy to remember that anybody could steal it from your lips; and then good-bye!—they would be singing it all over the streets of Venice before the performance.

Mirate understood the importance of the request and jealously guarded the secret. But, nevertheless, he was obliged to sing the song at the dress rehearsal. And at the dress rehearsal Verdi made the same request to all who were present, on and off the stage. Once more the secret was kept. And at the first public performance, when Mirate had sung the piece, with its easy and popular rhythm, "La donna è mobile," the public burst out in a shout of admiration, wanted an encore, got it, and after the performance chanted everywhere in Venice the Duke's elegant and facile melody.

The outstanding masterpiece of Verdi's younger years reached New York at the Academy of Music on February 19, 1855. The language of the performance was the original Italian, but *Rigoletto* has also been sung in New York, with linguistic versatility, in English, in German, in French, and even in Russian. It entered the repertory of the Metropolitan Opera House on November 17, 1883, before the institution was one month old. Marcella Sembrich then sang Gilda, as she did, conspicuously again on November 23, 1903, when Caruso made his North American début as the Duke. Louise Homer was the Maddalena and Scotti the Rigoletto.

On account of the grateful character of the leading roles and the celebrated quartet in the last act for four of the chief personages, *Rigoletto* has always invited extraordinary casts. Caruso and Louise Homer took part in another memorable one on February 6, 1912, when Luisa Tetrazzini was the Gilda, Maurice Renaud the Rigoletto, and Léon Rothier the Sparafucile. Renaud had also exhibited his remarkable portrait of the jester at the Manhattan Opera House with Melba as Gilda and Bonci as the Duke.

It is interesting to recall, too, that at one of Rossini's famous Saturday Evenings in Paris the presence of Verdi was honored by a performance of the *Rigoletto* quartet with Adelina Patti, Marietta Alboni, Italo Gardoni, and Enrico delle Sedie as the singers—an all-star cast if there ever was one—plus the host himself as accompanying pianist.

                                                                              P. S.

Il Trovatore

[The Troubadour]

ROMANTIC OPERA IN 4 ACTS

Book by SALVATORE CAMMARANO, after a play by ANTONIO GARCIA GUTIERREZ

First performance: Teatro Apollo, Rome, Jan. 19, 1853

CHARACTERS

Leonora, a noble lady of the court of a princess of Aragon, SOPRANO

Azucena, a wandering Biscayan gypsy, CONTRALTO

Inez, Leonora's attendant, SOPRANO

Manrico, a young chieftain under the Prince of Biscay, of mysterious birth, and in reality a brother of the Count di Luna, TENOR

Count di Luna, a powerful noble of the Prince of Aragon, BARITONE

Ferrando, a captain of the guard, and under di Luna, BASS

Ruiz, a soldier in Manrico's service, TENOR

An Old Gypsy, TENOR

A Messenger, a Jailer, Soldiers, Nuns, Gypsies, Attendants, etc.

The action takes place in Biscay and Aragon, in the middle of the fifteenth century

In the fifteenth century in Aragon the Count di Luna has burned a woman at the stake for bewitching one of his sons. Azucena, the gypsy's daughter, wishes to avenge her mother by killing the Count's son, but kills her own in error. She kidnaps the Count's boy, and takes him to raise as her own. The young Count di Luna, years after these events, is in love with Leonora and jealous of Manrico, a troubadour whom Leonora loves. Leonora is informed falsely that Manrico is dead and decides to become a nun. Manrico snatches her from the altar, a kidnapping that Count di Luna intended to do but Manrico's men beat off those of the Count. Near Castellor, where Manrico has taken Leonora, the Count's guard capture Azucena, and she is condemned to be burned at the stake. Manrico rushes to his mother's rescue. Manrico is captured, and is to be executed with his mother. Leonora offers herself to the Count if he will let Manrico free. She takes a slow poison when this offer is accepted. Azucena is enraged because her mother's death will go unavenged. Leonora dies saying farewell to Manrico, and the Count, breaking his promise, sends Manrico to be executed. Azucena then has her revenge by pointing out to the Count that he has just killed his brother.

From the beginning *Il Trovatore* has been popular. The initial performance took place at the Teatro Apollo, Rome, on January 19, 1853. The moment was by no means auspicious, for the Tiber was threatening one of its periodic floods. The muddy stream began to overflow at the St. Angelo bridge, and in order to reach the Apollo people had to take a cross-street passing through the San Salvatore piazzetta, with the probability of going out of the theatre by means of an improvised bridge, as actually happened later on in both 1871 and 1875. However, no amount of wintry Tiber-water could dampen the ardor of the Romans bent on hearing the latest opera by the composer of *Ernani* and *Rigoletto,* nor were they discouraged either by the increase in the price of tickets.

Lines of prospective purchasers, though ankle-deep in the wet, were on hand by 8 A.M. awaiting the opening of the box office, and by noon the entire house had been sold out. What happened in the evening was reported as follows by the Roman correspondent of the *Gazzetta Musicale* of Milan:

Last night *Il Trovatore* was produced in a theatre crammed with people. . . . The music transported us to heaven; and, in truth, it could not be otherwise, because this is, without exaggeration, heavenly music. The composer deserved this splendid triumph, seeing that here he has written music in a new style imbued with Castilian characteristics. The public listened to every number with religious silence and broke out with applause at every interval, the end of the third act and the whole of the fourth arousing such enthusiasm that their repetition was demanded. My own opinion is that in this score Verdi has effected a combination of musical learning with true Italian fire, and that the fourth act in particular is unmatchable.

The specific criticism of this page and that strikes us as for the most part valid even today. Cordial praise, for instance, is given the "Miserere" and Azucena's narrative. Yet few would now be likely to complain of a lack of concerted numbers, even though no *Lucia* sextet or *Rigoletto* quartet is offered. It is surprising, too, that the Andante of Leonora's first aria should ever have been deemed a failure. It is rather the ensuing Allegro that we would do without, unless it is sung superlatively.

In general, audiences have been prevailingly enthusiastic about *Il Trovatore* from that inaugural January 19 on, and in recent years such high notabilities of music as Dame Ethel Smyth, the worshipful disciple of Brahms, and Arnold Schönberg, the redoubtable modernist, have paid glowing tributes to the genius of the score.

On May 2, 1855, *Il Trovatore* reached America and was presented at the New York Academy of Music. Richard Grant White, the operatic historian of the period, handles the singers without gloves. Of the best remembered of them today, Pasquale Brignoli, he says: "He had one of those tenor voices that seem like the bleating of a sheep made musical." He was as awkward as "the man that a child makes by sticking two skewers into a long potato; and he walked the stage hitching forward, first one side and then the other, much as the child would make his creature walk."

Amodio, the Count di Luna, White praises as a singer. "He had one of the most beautiful baritone voices ever heard. It was of almost unexampled richness and sweetness. . . . His vocalization was remarkably good, and his style pleasing—a serene, very simple cantabile style."

But alas, Amodio had little dramatic power, was corpulent and low of stature, and "looked like a plum-pudding set upon sausages"! Yet because of his voice and style "he was the favorite baritone in New York for some years."

The Leonora, Bina Steffenone, is commended by White for "her satisfying voice, her admirable style, and her pleasing, although notably ample, person." The most remarkable personality in the cast, however, was Felicita Vestvali, a native, some said, of Stettin, others of Warsaw.

Vestvali, the Azucena of the production at the Academy of Music, was greatly admired by White, who not only considered her a "formidably handsome woman," but once wrote of her contralto voice that it was "fresh, full, sympathetic, and of unusual compass"; and that it had, moreover, the "happiness to dwell in a body of such stately symmetry, and to be aided by a countenance so blooming with healthful beauty, so radiant and expressive, that her singing could not be judged with exact and impartial justice until her judges were smitten with blindness." The presence of this magnificent Amazon in the cast of the first American *Il Trovatore* (she was one of the tallest women ever seen in opera, and had a penchant for parts requiring men's costumes) must have compensated in no small degree for possible deficiencies in other respects.

Il Trovatore was the third work presented at the Metropolitan Opera House (on October 26, 1883), with Alwina Valleria (Leonora), Zelia Trebelli (Azucena), Roberto Stagno (Manrico), and Giuseppe Kaschmann (di Luna) in the cast, but perhaps the most distinguished production it has ever enjoyed there occurred on February 20, 1915, when after a season's disuse it was revived under the musical direction of Arturo Toscanini with the cast he himself had picked—Emmy Destinn as Leonora, Margarete Ober as Azucena, Giovanni Martinelli as Manrico, Pasquale Amato as di Luna, and Léon Rothier as Ferrando.

With regard to the intricate plot of *Il Trovatore,* it is well to ponder the words of one of Verdi's latest and most acute biographers, the eminent English musicologist, Francis Toye:

Cammarano's libretto is often dismissed as preposterous and unintelligible; it is neither. [And again:] Anyone who is prepared to devote an hour's study to the Italian libretto of *Il Trovatore* can follow its thread perfectly well. This is not done, partly because Verdi's music is so easy to follow, so immediately expressive of the individual emotions and situations therein portrayed, partly because study of Italian opera librettos is not considered a proper pastime for the intelligent!

P. S.

La Traviata

[The Strayed One]

OPERA IN 3 ACTS

Book by FRANCESCO MARIA PIAVE, after ALEXANDRE DUMAS'
La Dame aux camélias

First performance: Teatro la Fenice, Venice, Mar. 6, 1853

CHARACTERS

Violetta Valery, a courtesan, SOPRANO
Flora, Violetta's friend, SOPRANO OR
  MEZZO-SOPRANO
Alfredo Germont, Violetta's lover, TENOR
Giorgio Germont, his father, BARITONE
Baron Douphol, a rival of Alfredo,
  BARITONE

Gastone de Letorières, TENOR
Marquis d'Orbigny, BASS
Dr. Grenvil, BASS
Giuseppe, Violetta's servant, TENOR
Annina, Violetta's confidante and maid,
  SOPRANO

Ladies and Gentlemen, Masquers, Servants

The action takes place in Paris and environs circa 1840 (sometimes 1700)

A brilliant party is in progress at the home of the Paris demi-mondaine, Violetta, a very beautiful woman, who, however, feels already the first signs of a fatal illness. At this party she meets for the first time Alfredo Germont, a young gentleman of distinguished family. Alfredo and Violetta fall in love with each other and Violetta consents to leave town to live with Alfredo in the country.

Violetta and Alfredo have been living together for some time at their country home when Alfredo discovers that Violetta is selling all her belongings in order to pay their expenses. Conscience-stricken, he leaves for Paris to see whether he can get some money. During his absence his father calls on Violetta to implore her to give up Alfredo because the scandal resulting from their illicit relationship threatens to ruin the life of his daughter who is engaged to be married. Violetta is persuaded by the urgency of his request and consents to leave Alfredo. Georgio Germont tries to console his son when he learns of Violetta's departure.

Violetta appears at the masked ball given by Flora, with an old admirer, the Baron Douphol. Alfredo arrives and the jealous Baron challenges him to gamble; it is Alfredo who wins. Violetta succeeds in getting a word alone with Alfredo and she begs him to leave the party; he in turn asks her to come with him, but she refuses. Alfredo then accuses her of loving the Baron, which she affirms, although it is untrue. Alfredo, in a jealous rage, summons the guests to witness the repayment of his debt and hurls the money he has won at the stunned Violetta. At this moment Alfredo's father appears and reproves his son for his cruel and unjustified behavior.

Violetta, impoverished and close to death, receives a letter from Alfredo's father telling her that he has revealed her sacrifice to his son. Alfredo arrives and once more renews his vows of love; but Violetta, happy for only a few short moments, dies in Alfredo's arms to the horror of the remorseful Georgio Germont.

Although today one of the best-liked of operas wherever opera is given, *La Traviata* was shelved in 1853 as a failure. Its case-history is among the most curious in the annals of the stage. Before the opera was the play, and before the play was the novel. Alexandre Dumas, the younger, brought out the novel "La Dame aux camélias" (The Lady with the Camellias) in 1848. The play derived from it (usually called in this country "Camille") was produced in Paris in 1852. The unaccustomed character of the story and its fragile and ailing heroine caused a tremendous sensation.

Idealist and reformer that he was from the beginning, the youthful Dumas had dared in his first play to depict a Parisian demi-mondaine of the day without recourse to historical or other camouflage and, what was still worse, to present her as a fine-grained and sympathetic woman (quite apart from the consumption with which she is rather gratuitously afflicted). Of course the moral tories and the outraged prudes were up in arms. Marriage had been deliberately assailed, free love championed, and all that sort of thing. Dumas was an enemy of society, a dispenser of subtle poisons, a rank immoralist, and his play was anathema. Never a tory, Verdi, who happened to be in Paris at the time, seeing the play, not only admired it exceedingly, but was mightily impressed by its operatic possibilities. Nevertheless, he did not immediately go so far as to order a libretto made from it.

However, he soon afterwards signed a contract for a new opera with the management of the Teatro Fenice (Phoenix) at Venice, and though other subjects were considered for the work, "La Dame aux camélias" was finally chosen. Still, it was apparently not till the very end of 1852 that Verdi penned the first notes of the score which was to be named *La Traviata*. And in spite of his having to go to Rome for the world première of *Il Trovatore* on January 19, 1853, *La Traviata* was ready for production on the following March 6, 1853.

Because of the peculiar nature of this opera, dealing frankly with a special phase of contemporary life and in an intimate fashion, Verdi was even more concerned than had been his wont about the casting. Yet, for all his anxiety, the cast proved his undoing! First of all, to what soprano should be allotted the rôle of the phthisical heroine, Violetta? The management of the Fenice had engaged Salvini-Donatelli for the part. Verdi, however, had had bad reports of this singer from Paris and declared to the president, Marzari, that he would not accept her. He named three singers as the only ones who seemed to him to be suitable—Rosina Penco, who had just created Leonora in *Il Trovatore* at Rome; Luigia Boccabadati, who was singing Gilda in *Rigoletto* at Bologna, and Maria Piccolomini, then engaged at Pisa. Verdi adds in his letter of protest "La Penco (the only one of these that I know) I believe would be the best. She has a beautiful figure, animation, and appears well on the stage. Excellent qualities for *La Traviata*."

Nevertheless, Verdi was forced to put up with Salvini-Donatelli, who is reported to have been a good singer, but who as the impersonator of a consumptive woman suffered from excessive corpulence. Nor when it came to the first performance were the tenor and the baritone of any assistance. Graziani (Alfredo Germont) was hoarse and Varesi (Giorgio Germont) looked down on his rôle as unworthy of his abilities (little did he suspect the popularity his chief aria, "Di Provenza il mar," was to attain!). It may be said for the cast, though, that they felt out of place in a species of opera which was totally unknown to them and were awkward about following the instructions of the composer.

The exacting Venetian audience had plenty of fault to find with the production. In the first place, opera-goers unacquainted with *Louise* and *Jonny spielt auf* were somewhat upset by the sight of a serious opera presented in the dress of their own day. Then, the staging of the ballroom scene fell short of the standard prevailing at the Fenice, even to the point of provoking mild hilarity. Finally there was the incongruously robust Violetta. When the doctor remarked that she had only a few hours to live, the house went into gales of laughter just where it ought to have dissolved in tears!

The day after the première Verdi with characteristic stoicism wrote to his pupil and secretary, Emanuele Muzio, in Milan, " 'La Traviata' last night a fiasco. Is the fault mine or the singers'? I don't know at all. Time will decide." Verdi in Venice, however, was not so noncommittal about imputing the blame as has been generally inferred from his laconic note to Muzio and similar communications to Luccardi and the publisher Ricordi. The very evening of the fiasco, it seems, when Varesi came up to him to offer his condolences, Verdi replied brusquely: "Offer them to yourself and to your colleagues, who like you have not understood my music."

Though the opera was promptly withdrawn and Verdi returned to Busseto with a failure marked against him, he well knew where the fault lay, as did certain Venetian critics and, in particular, one devoted Venetian admirer, Antonio Gallo, who the following year revived "La Traviata" (the composer meanwhile had retouched some pages of act II) at his own Teatro San Benedetto. Appropriately cast, and with the costuming, pursuant to the taste of the time, set back two hundred years, "La Traviata," on May 6, 1854, triumphed in the very city where fourteen months previously it had gone down in defeat.

Further triumphs were speedily its portion in one Italian city after another, and before the end of 1856 it had been acclaimed also in London, St. Petersburg, New York, and Paris. Of course the England and the America of the eighteen-fifties were in the grip of Victorian prejudice, and the morals of "La Traviata" came in for horrified denunciation. The London *Times* thundered against the "foul and hideous horrors" of the libretto. . . . The incomparable Chorley, critic of the Athenaeum, was particularly scandalized by the Violetta—this time the very Maria Piccolomini of whom Verdi had written to Venice. He found her "little better than a comedy soubrette . . . born to make eyes over an apron with pockets" and he further declared that "never did any young lady, whose private claims to modest respect were so great as hers are known to be, with such self-denial fling off their protection in her resolution to lay hold of her public at all costs. Her performances at times approached offence against maidenly reticence and delicacy." Which is perhaps the oddest censure ever meted out to a Violetta! The pulpit, for its part, was even more shocked and shaken than the press.

Naturally the resulting publicity was of inestimable value to opera-givers. Lumley, manager of Her Majesty's Theatre in London, was temporarily saved from ruin by the immense vogue of "La Traviata." In his reminiscences he says: "Once more frantic crowds struggled in the lobbies of the theatre; once more dresses were torn and hats crushed; once more a mania possessed the public." Thus Verdi and his work enjoyed one of Time's revenges!

La Traviata, from the initial fiasco to the latest triumph, has always been pre-eminently a prima donna's opera, and no prima donna has been more consistently devoted to the role of Violetta than Adelina Patti. Famous Violettas have included, besides Piccolomini, Angiolina Bosio, Christine Nilsson (her debut, 1864, in Paris), Anna de Lagrange (the first in New York), Lilli Lehmann (her London debut in 1880), Lillian Nordica (her debut, 1879, at Brescia), Marcella Sembrich, Nellie Melba, Mary Garden (at the Opéra Comique, Paris, in French), Geraldine Farrar, Gemma Bellincioni, Rosina Storchio, Luisa Tetrazzini (her London debut in Nov., 1907; her New York debut in Jan., 1908), and Amelita Galli-Curci (who made her first appearance at New York's Metropolitan Opera House as Violetta Nov. 24, 1921, the opening night of the new season).

The first American performance of *La Traviata* took place at the New York Academy of Music, in the original Italian, Dec. 3, 1856, with Lagrange as Violetta. It entered the repertory of the Metropolitan Opera House Nov. 6, 1883, with Sembrich as Violetta. Recent Metropolitan Violettas to enjoy the favor of the public have been Lucrezia Bori, Claudia Muzio, and Rosa Ponselle.

Among tenors who have sung Alfredo at the Metropolitan the names of Enrico Caruso and Alessandro Bonci are conspicuous. Unlike Varese of the inaugural fiasco, subsequent baritones have shown a liking for the role of the virtuous father because of the opportunities provided in Act II for lyric singing. Probably none of them has surpassed in vocal and histrionic distinction the late Maurice Renaud, who took part with Melba, at Oscar Hammerstein's Manhattan Opera House in the winter of 1907, in the first presentations of the work in New York done with the costumes of its own day.

P. S.

Simon Boccanegra

OPERA IN A PROLOGUE AND 3 ACTS

Book by Francesco Maria Piave (later revised by Arrigo Boito), after a play by Antonio Garcia Gutierrez

First performance: Teatro la Fenice, Venice, Mar. 12, 1857

CHARACTERS

Prologue

Simon Boccanegra, corsair in the service of the Genoese Republic, BARITONE

Jacopo Fiesco, Genoese nobleman, BASS

Paolo Albiani, gold-spinner of Genoa, BASS

Pietro, Genoese commoner, BARITONE

Seamen, Commoners, Followers of Fiesco, etc.

The Play

Simon Boccanegra, first Doge of Genoa, BARITONE

Maria Boccanegra, his daughter, known as Amelia Grimaldi, SOPRANO

Jacopo Fiesco, known as Andrea, BASS

Gabriele Adorno, Genoese nobleman, TENOR

Paolo Albiani, favorite courtier of the Doge, BASS

Pietro, another courtier, BARITONE

A Captain of the Arbalisters, TENOR

Amelia's Maidservant, MEZZO-SOPRANO

Soldiers, Seamen, Commoners, Senators, Court of the Doge, etc.

The action takes place in and near Genoa, toward the middle of the fourteenth century

(Twenty-five years elapse between the Prologue and Act I.)

There is a prologue, which treats of a conspiracy fomented largely by workmen to make Simon Boccanegra, a corsair in the service of the Republic, doge. Among the conspirators are Paolo and Pietro.

In the first act Simon has become doge. Returning from the chase, he stops at the house of the Grimaldi, where in Amelia Grimaldi he recognizes his long-lost daughter. She is affianced to Gabriele Adorno, a Genoese nobleman. Paolo, whom we have met in the prologue and who stands high in the doge's favor, falls in love with Amelia and demands her hand of the doge. He is refused. Angered, Paolo, with the aid of his friend Pietro (also of the prologue), swears to bring about Simon's downfall. This enterprise they initiate by causing Amelia to be kidnaped. Andrea, Amelia's tutor and protector, who is in reality the Genoese noble, Jacopo

549

Fiesco, and Gabriele, her betrothed, accuse the doge of the deed. On the anniversary of Simon's coronation, Gabriele hurls himself upon him, dagger in hand, but Amelia, who has escaped from the kidnapers, arrives in time to declare the doge innocent.

In the second act Andrea and Gabriele are prisoners. Paolo and Pietro try to persuade them to kill Simon. Both, however, reject the proposition indignantly. But Paolo has aroused Gabriele's jealousy. The latter, hidden under a terrace, is witness to a tender scene between father and daughter. Dagger in hand once again, he leaps into the room to dispatch the doge. Amelia again intervenes. On learning that she is the doge's daughter, Gabriele implores his pardon, and receiving it vows to defend the doge against all his enemies.

In the third act preparations are under way for the wedding of Amelia and Gabriele. Paolo, for his part, has poisoned the doge, who dies blessing the lovers.

P. S.

Verdi returned to Busseto early in 1856 and occupied himself with the revision of *Stiffelio,* which was to be produced under the title of *Aroldo* at the opening of a new opera house at Rimini during the summer of 1857. Piave was summoned to join the composer and bring such literary material as he might require. "You know there are not many books here," he explains, "only a modest library." In the new version the nineteenth-century German pastor became an English crusader living in "Kenth," a transformation to which Verdi agreed against his better judgment. We may imagine, however, that he did not greatly care what happened to this tiresome piece.

He was much more interested in yet another proposal to produce *King Lear,* this time at Naples. The project only lapsed because Verdi could not get the singers he required. The soprano at the San Carlo Theatre was in his opinion unsuitable for Cordelia. He wanted Mme. Piccolomini, who had established the success of *La Traviata* by her performance as Violetta, despite the scandalized protests of men like Chorley against her lack of "maidenly reticence and delicacy." He wanted, as well he might, a "great" baritone for the part of Lear and, at this stage, a first-rate contralto to play the Fool. But it was not to be. He flatly refused to proceed unless his views about the casting of the opera were accepted. "I am not in the habit of allowing any artist to be *imposed* on me," he wrote to Naples, "not though Malibran herself should return from the grave."

In the midst of these preoccupations Verdi had to return to Paris in order to deal with a new dispute with Calzado, who was threatening litigation over the French translation of *Il Trovatore.* He remained in Paris until the end of the year, and had the satisfaction of seeing *La Traviata* make a resounding success, with Piccolomini in the part of Violetta.

On the abandonment of Lear, Verdi considered various other subjects, among them "Ruy Blas" and Scribe's "Gustave III," which was eventually to become *Un ballo in maschera*. Unfortunately for Verdi Scribe's drama centered upon the murder of King Gustavus of Sweden at a court ball, which did not commend the project to the authorities. Before the objections of the censorship to regicide could be overcome, Verdi turned his attention to another drama which, though it involved the poisoning of a Genoese doge, presented him as so magnanimous a figure that there was no offence in it. Besides, the victim was an Italian and a plebeian with republican ideas, and it all happened a very long time ago.

The new opera, *Simon Boccanegra,* was produced at the Fenice Theatre, Venice, on 12th March 1857. Like *La Traviata* it was a complete failure, and unlike *La Traviata* it has never won the position in the popular favour that is due to it on musical grounds. Verdi himself had a special affection for the opera, and in 1881 he revised it with the help of Arrigo Boito for the Scala Theatre. This revision was much more radical than that to which *Macbeth* was subjected. The orchestration was largely rewritten; Piave's original libretto was overhauled and new scenes were added in an attempt to clarify the obscurities of the intrigue and to give more interest to a work that even the composer felt was too monotonous and chilly. It is in this form that the work has lately been revived in Germany and Italy. But even now its success has been a *succès d'estime* with musicians and connoisseurs; the general public seems to have remained indifferent. At Florence, where the opera was given for the first time during the May Festival of 1938, the audience received it politely, but without enthusiasm.

The reason is not far to seek. *Simon Boccanegra* is hampered by a story that is not only gloomy and so obscure as to be quite unintelligible without a close study of the libretto, but is marred by a cardinal fault in its presentation. Simon is by definition a *condottiere,* the Italian equivalent of Sir Francis Drake, who freed Genoa from the pirates and, in the face of the opposition of the patrician families, was elected its ruler by the popular vote. Yet this man of action is never, except in the scene in the council chamber added by Boito, seen in action. In the prologue, which happens some twenty-five years before the first act, we are shown not a man of action, like Otello at his first entry, but a distraught lover who is only persuaded to stand for election because success means gaining possession of Maria Fiesco, daughter of the leader of the nobles, whom he has seduced and who has been shut up by her outraged father. Maria, however, is dead, and his election as doge comes to him as Dead-Sea fruit.

In the main action that follows (after an interval of twenty-five years) Simon remains, except in the one scene already mentioned, the more or less passive victim of intrigues and repeated futile attempts at revolution, the second of which happens off stage and so contributes nothing effective to the drama. He responds to every attempt upon him with a consistent clemency that rivals even that of Mozart's Titus. Magnanimity may be an admirable quality in a ruler, but it makes a poor dénouement to dramatic situations. In the end Simon dies of a slow poison taken in the middle of the second act. It is hardly surprising that Boito, who undertook the revision with reluctance, could do little beyond clearing up some of the obscurer points in Piave's libretto. But it is odd that Verdi, who felt the need for some contrast in the prevailing gloom, should not have done more to lighten its sombreness. Even the festivities that celebrate the suppression of the second insurrection are singularly bleak and the lovely lyrical scene between Maria Boccanegra, the doge's illegitimate daughter, and Gabriele Adorno, her lover, who, needless to say, belongs to the opposing political party, is the only ray of light in the general darkness.

Beside the failure to present Simon as a man of resolution in action and the gloominess of the libretto, the complexities of the story are of minor importance, though they certainly contribute to the failure of the opera to make its proper effect. *Simon Boccanegra* is based on a play by Gutiérrez, the author of *El Trovador,* who seems to have had a mania for lost babies and mistaken identities. The result is a plot that may be described as a hybrid, a real *lusus naturae* between *Othello* (without the jealousy motive) and *The Gondoliers.* Two of the main characters appear under assumed names, which adds to the confusion of an already tangled tale, though Maria's disguise as Amalia Grimaldi certainly provides a most moving recognition scene, when the doge discovers in her his long-lost child. But this beautiful duet, which should have ended with a curtain, is followed by a scene that seems once more to indicate that blind spot in Verdi's eye for theatrical effect.

Simon had come to tell the supposed Amalia that she must marry Paolo, the villain of the piece. After the recognition Amalia departs on a high B flat.

Enter Paolo.

Simon. Renounce all hope [of marrying Amalia].
Paolo. I cannot.
Simon. I wish it! [Exit.

That is all! Then Paolo, to music reminiscent of the conspirators in *Rigoletto,* plots with a friend the abduction of Amalia and the curtain falls. The little scene is necessary to the action, but both musically and dramatically it produces in performance a quite ludicrous effect of anticlimax after what has gone before. As we have noted in discussing *Macbeth,* Verdi sometimes attempted to embody an important dramatic idea in a couple of phrases, but unless those phrases are more telling than they are in the present instance, they are apt to go for nothing. The immediate establishment of Amonasro's identity at the first mention of his name in the messenger's scene in *Aida,* Act I, is a contrary example of how effective such a swift stroke can be.

For the music of *Boccanegra* generally, however, there can be nothing but the highest praise. The score as we have it represents Verdi at the full maturity of his powers. With the exception of the final chorus of the first act, acclaiming Simon's election, there is hardly a page of it that is not first-rate. As a whole the score produces an effect of sombre magnificence, like some richly woven tapestry in which there is a preponderance of dark and oppressive colour. In the midst stands the radiant figure of Amalia Grimaldi (alias Maria Boccanegra), a remarkable and individual creation, youthful, charming and delightfully human. Nowhere else in Verdi's operas do we find any similar character outside *Otello* and *Falstaff*. She is neither so tragic as Desdemona nor so light-hearted as Nannetta Ford—how could she be? But she shares with them the bloom of youth and innocence. Gilda might be thought of as a close relation. But Gilda's music is of a different type, less aristocratic and less subtle. Indeed the distance that Verdi's genius had travelled since the composition of *Rigoletto* may be measured by the difference between Gilda's music and Amalia's. But we must beware of attributing the creation of Amalia as we know her to the Verdi of 1857; she belongs to the period between *Aida* and *Otello* twenty years later. Something of her individuality and charm must nevertheless have appeared in the earlier version, and the next operas Verdi wrote provide sufficient evidence that there had been an advance in his powers and a change in his attitude to opera.

This change may be summed up as a move away from the lyrical style of his earlier works towards a more heroic type of opera. *Il Trovatore* had already given some indication of the direction in which he was moving. But both that opera and *I Vespri siciliani* depend much more upon the stimulation of the senses by passionate or graceful melodies than upon the more carefully planned and less intuitive handling of the material that is evident in *Boccanegra* and its immediate successors.

We must beware of the easy division of Verdi's works into "periods." Nothing, in one sense, could be planned with greater judiciousness than *Rigoletto,* and in the even earlier *Macbeth* there is much evidence of that kind of intellectual grasp which becomes more and more marked from *Boccanegra* onwards until it finds its ultimate expression in the supreme masterpieces of the composer's old age, where all his knowledge, experience and intuition are marvellously fused together.

But, if we are to see intellect at work in *Boccanegra,* how comes it that such a muddled libretto could have been for one moment considered as possible? The paradox may be explained by Verdi's deficient education and want of literary sensibility. Knowledge of a kind he had acquired, but, as Mr. Bonavia has well put it, not the art to use knowledge.

Verdi [he continues] had the knowledge, not the education. Had he had the advantage of a literary training he could never have accepted the librettos of *Trovatore* or *Boccanegra*. In *Trovatore* we see the effects of romanticism on a mind powerful and responsive but untrained, and therefore apt to err in judging the values of facts and words. His is the romanticism of the masses, ever ready to listen to a tale of adventure, awed by the supernatural, by mystery, by the glamour of valour and power. . . .

This limitation in Verdi's intellectual equipment accounts for his readiness to accept and indeed to suggest librettos that have served only to cripple some of his finest music. It was not until he found, in Boito, a poet who could supply his own deficiencies that Verdi's genius was able to put out its full strength. . . .

D. H.

The first performance of the opera in America took place at the Metropolitan Opera House, New York, Jan. 28, 1932. Tullio Serafin conducted, and the cast included Lawrence Tibbett (Simon), Giovanni Martinelli (Gabriele), Ezio Pinza (Fiesco), Claudio Frigerio (Paolo), Paul Ananian (Pietro), and Maria Müller (Amelia).

Un Ballo in Maschera

[A Masked Ball]

OPERA IN 3 ACTS

Book by Antonio Somma

First performance: Teatro Apollo, Rome, Feb. 17, 1859

CHARACTERS

Riccardo, Governor of Boston, TENOR
Renato, his friend and secretary,
  BARITONE
Amelia, Renato's wife, SOPRANO
Ulrica, a fortuneteller, CONTRALTO

Oscar, a page, SOPRANO
Silvano, a sailor, BARITONE
Sam, conspirator, BASS
Tom, conspirator, BASS

A Judge, Guards, Conspirators, Dancers, etc.

Riccardo (Richard), count of Warwick and governor of Boston, late in the seventeenth century, loves Amelia, the wife of his faithful secretary and friend, Renato (Reinhart). The governor is unaware that a conspiracy is brewing among the dissatisfied negroes. Amelia, who is troubled over the secret love—in reality an innocent one—consults the black sorceress, Ulrica. She seeks a drug that will make her forget Riccardo, and Ulrica informs her that a certain herb, plucked from a grave at midnight, can bring about the desired effect.

By chance Riccardo overhears the conversation. After being told by Ulrica that the first man who clasps his hand will slay him, Renato appears and the two friends shake hands. Despite Ulrica's warning, Riccardo laughs. At midnight the governor repairs to the graveyard where Amelia is looking for the magic herb. Renato interrupts the scene between the lovers. He has come to warn his friend of the rising feeling against him and he does not know that the veiled lady is his wife.

The grateful Riccardo requests Renato to escort the lady to safety without attempting to learn her identity, and makes his escape. Suddenly, husband and wife are surrounded by the black conspirators. In the scuffle that follows the veil drops from Amelia's face and Renato makes the staggering discovery. Swearing vengeance against the man who he thinks has betrayed him, he joins the plotters. Lots are drawn for the assassination of the governor, and it falls to Renato to be chosen to do the deed.

During the magnificent masked ball in the governor's mansion, Riccardo, scorning Amelia's exhortations to flee, tells her that he plans now to send both her and her husband back to England. Thus he will conquer his evil passions. Penetrating

Riccardo's disguise, Renato stabs him. The guests make for Renato, but the dying governor stops them, and with his remaining breath he assures his friend of Amelia's innocence.

P. S.

Verdi's work as a composer was immediately affected by the political unrest of the time. For the objections of the Neapolitan censorship to the libretto of his new opera based on Scribe's *Gustave III* were reinforced by Orsini's attempt on Napoleon's life. Was not the assassination of a reigning sovereign at a masked ball, it was argued, a deliberate incitement to anarchists to throw bombs at emperors on their way to the opera? The censors evidently wished to strangle this opera at birth, so ludicrous were the changes upon which they insisted.

The recent publication in Luzio's *Carteggi Verdiani* of the correspondence with Somma, the librettist entrusted with the task of turning Scribe's drama into an opera book, together with Verdi's detailed comments upon the libretto as revised by the censor, reveal the full extent of the censor's stupidity and lack of humour. *Una vendetta in domino,* the title originally proposed, was changed into *Adelia degli Adimari* which, as Verdi remarked, is meaningless. The period and scene were moved from seventeenth-century Sweden to Florence in 1385, the characters becoming leaders of the Guelph and Ghibelline factions. Even the names of the persons were needlessly altered, Amelia becoming Adelia, and the page, Oscar, who was in the event to be one of Verdi's most brilliant musical creations, became Arpini (or, by some strange association of ideas, Orsini), a young knight. Verdi's annotations upon these proposals are scathing. The whole character of the drama would be falsified by its transfer from the north to Italy and backwards in time over three centuries, when habits of thought were utterly different. Besides, the situations in the drama were often altered beyond recognition, and, in particular, the omission of the maskers at the ball would destroy the whole effect of this important scene. Verdi sums up with the statistical facts:

The *Vendetta in domino* consists of 884 verses, of which 297 are altered in *Adelia,* besides many additions and a great many omissions. Moreover what remains of my work in the drama as revised?

The title? No.
The poet? No. [Somma's name was omitted from the title-page.]
The period? No.
The place? No.
The characters? No.
The situations? No.
The drawing of lots? No.
The festival ball? No.

Had Verdi already been reading Falstaff's speech about honour, that he cast his exasperation in this form?

The upshot was that Naples did not have the privilege of seeing the first performance of the new opera, which was given in Rome on 17th February 1859. But not before other changes had been made in the libretto. Somma was permitted to retain the eighteenth century as his period and northerners as his characters, but at the price of transporting them to Boston, where Gustavus became the English colonial governor, and the Count Ankarström his creole (!) secretary. The Counts Horn and Warting lost their titles and assumed the homely names of Tom and Samuel, while the fortune-teller, Ulrica, became a black practitioner of the black arts. To make the matter more ridiculous the governor of Boston, about 1715, was dressed in puritan fashion, and to this day the opera is usually given in Van Dyck costumes, the scene being sometimes transferred to an Italian court—a procedure to which Verdi would have strongly objected.

These modifications were possibly accepted by the composer out of sheer weariness. But at least they did not interfere with the main principles of his dramatic scheme. Indeed, there is not the slightest reason that one can see why nowadays the original scene and names of the characters should not be restored . . . since the restoration would remove at one stroke several incongruities in the opera as a picture of English colonial administration and would enormously heighten its dramatic effect by the association of the action with the well-known historical figure of King Gustavus. . . .

Verdi arrived in Rome only a month before the first performance of *Un ballo in maschera,* having been detained in Naples for the production there of *Simon Boccanegra,* which was substituted for the new opera when the impossibility of satisfying both the censorship and the composer was realized. This visit was the occasion of the first of the series of caricatures made by Melchiorre Delfico, whose witty pencil has recorded some of the amusing incidents without which no opera can be produced. These drawings range from the impressive disembarkation of Verdi and Giuseppina accompanied by Lulu, their *cagnolino*—why has English no diminutive for dog?—to the general rehearsals, and, if one may judge from them, this visit must have been singularly happy. Even Verdi's moments of rage and depression seem but passing shadows that could be comically treated. Any one who can get access to Luzio's "Carteggi Verdiani," where the whole series is reproduced, will be well rewarded.

Arriving in Rome so soon before the first performance, Verdi seems to have had less say than usual in the production of *Un ballo in maschera.* Indeed, we may fancy that he was so weary of the struggle to get the work produced at all, that he was glad to have it off his hands anyhow, and took less interest than was his custom in the details of casting and staging. In the event he was dissatisfied with the performance, which had an unfavourable reception from a section of the press. To Vincenzo Jacovacci, the impresario, who had secured the production of the opera he wrote some months later:

> You are wrong to defend the *Ballo in maschera* from the attacks of the press. You should do as I always do: refrain from reading them and let them sing what tune they please. . . . For the rest, the question is this: is the opera good or bad? If it is bad and the critics say so, they are right; if good and they have not thought it so owing to their own prejudices, etc., one must let them have their say and not take it to heart. Besides, you should be defending yourself in certain matters connected with the spring season. The company you provided was unworthy of me. Listen to the voice of conscience and confess that I was a model of rare restraint in not taking my score away and going in search of dogs who would howl less painfully than those you offered me. But *post factum* and for what followed, etc.

Verdi was not the only composer to profess that he never read nor took any notice of criticism, and perhaps he was more sincere than most of his kind. The brutality of his own criticism of the company may, perhaps, be accounted for in the following paragraph of his letter, where he flatly declines Jacovacci's proposal that he should reduce the rate of his royalties in view of the failure of the opera to attract the public. Verdi was stern in the exaction of his rights and touchy about even a proposal for their curtailment.

The streak of rather cantankerous boorishness in Verdi's temperament made itself felt in another direction when he returned to Sant' Agata. The municipality of Busseto had decided to build a new theatre and not unnaturally desired to enlist the support of their most distinguished fellow-citizen. Verdi disapproved of the expenditure of money upon such a project at a time when every penny was needed for the furtherance of the national cause. In spite of his objection, the building was begun and, on its completion, in 1868, was named after the composer. In the meantime a tactless mayor had stated that the theatre was being built for Verdi's benefit and that he had promised to secure the engagement of the finest singers in Italy. Verdi was furious and refused ever to enter the new theatre, to the cost of which he did, however, subscribe 10,000 lire. He further exacerbated public opinion by pointedly giving away the box that was allotted to him for his own use. This hostile attitude towards the people of Busseto may have been due in part to a rankling memory of the dispute about his appointment to the organist's post in his early youth. But it is more probable that it was the unkind gossip of a country town about his living with a woman to whom he was not married that made Busseto so distasteful to him that he never entered the town if he could avoid it.

Yet he allowed himself, though only under pressure from Cavour himself, to be nominated in 1860 as a local candidate for the national Parliament which was to be convened in accordance with the new Constitution.

D. H.

New York's Academy of Music introduced *Un Ballo* to America Feb. 11, 1861, in Italian. It was presented in English at that theater in 1871. The first performance of *Un Ballo in maschera* at the Metropolitan Opera House took place Dec. 11, 1889, in German with Lilli Lehmann as Amelia. The first Italian showing at the Metropolitan occurred Feb. 23, 1903, with Johanna Gadski (Amelia), Fritzi Scheff (Oscar), Louise Homer (Ulrica), Emilio de Marchi (Riccardo), Giuseppe Campanari (Renato), Édouard de Reszké (Sam), and Marcel Journet (Tom).

La Forza del Destino

[The Force of Destiny]

OPERA IN 4 ACTS

Book by FRANCESCO MARIA PIAVE, after the Spanish play, *Don Alvaro, o La Fuerza del sino,* by the DUQUE DE RIVAS

First performance: Imperial Italian Theater, St. Petersburg, Nov. 10, 1862

CHARACTERS

The Marquis of Calatrava, BASS
Donna Leonora, his daughter, SOPRANO
Don Carlo, his son, BARITONE
Don Alvaro, a young nobleman, TENOR
Preziosilla, a gypsy, MEZZO-SOPRANO

Padre Guardiano, an abbot, BASS
Fra Melitone, a friar, BARITONE
Curra, Leonora's maid, MIME
An Alcalde, BASS
A Surgeon, TENOR

Spanish and Italian Peasants, Soldiers, Franciscan Friars, etc.

The action takes place in Spain and Italy, about the end of the eighteenth century

Don Alvaro, rejected as a suitor by Leonora's father, the old Marquis of Calatrava, flings down his pistol and asks the old noble to stab him. The pistol explodes, accidentally killing the Marquis, whereupon Alvaro flees and Don Carlo, the Marquis's son, swears vengeance on the man he believes to be his father's murderer and his sister's seducer. Leonora, in male disguise, takes refuge near a monastery as a hermit under protection of the monks, who call upon the Virgin to protect her with "La Vergine degli angeli," a calm and majestic invocation.

Now the plot moves through tortuous scenes of misunderstanding, in which Alvaro and Don Carlo meet and become friends until Don Carlo discovers through a picture that this man is his sworn victim. Five years pass and bring them to the neighborhood of Leonora's retreat, where she is discovered singing "Pace, Pace mio Dio," to be interrupted by the appearance of Alvaro and Don Carlo dueling savagely. Don Carlo is mortally wounded, and Leonora, running to them, discovers her lover, whom she believed long dead, and her wounded brother. Don Carlo, dying, stabs his sister to wipe out the stain of her supposed corruption by the supposed murderer of their father. Alvaro, doubly bereft, turns to the kind Padre Guardiano, who comes up from the monastery, and seeks consolation in the Padre's reminder of God.

W. H., P. Z.

In June 1861 Cavour died. Verdi was about to leave for Turin when the news reached him. He was so overcome with grief that he felt unable to attend the funeral and he confesses that at the memorial service at Busseto he cried like a child. He was already conscious of a growing disgust with politics and with the inadequacy of Cavour's successors, and from a letter of Giuseppina's * written at a rather later date it appears that he was beginning to be bored with shooting. Gardening alone survived as an abiding hobby till the end of his life. The arrival of Achille Tamberlik, son of the famous tenor, from St. Petersburg with a commission to write an opera for the Imperial Theatre was, therefore, opportune and Verdi once more turned eagerly to composition.

The contract was signed at Turin in June. "Ruy Blas" was suggested as a possible subject, but Verdi was given a free hand, the only restriction made (unofficially) being that he must not insist on the tsar's proclaiming a republic! Verdi rejected Victor Hugo's drama. He remembered having read some years before a romantic Spanish tragedy by the Duke of Rivas, "Don Alvaro, o La fuerza del sino," and the bookshops of Turin were vainly ransacked for a copy. In the end one was procured from Milan. That this subject had been in Verdi's mind at least ten years before is evident from a letter written in 1852 by de Sanctis who says: "I begged you to let me know, as a favour, what subject you have chosen for Venice, but you have not gratified me. Is it to be 'Faust' or 'Kean' or 'Pagliaccio,' or 'La forza del destino'?"

This tragedy, which Verdi justly described as "potente, singolare e vastissimo," was written by the duke, who was a liberal politician as well as a distinguished man of letters, during a period of exile in France, and was produced in Madrid shortly after his return to Spain in 1834. During his exile Rivas visited England, where he came under the influence of Walter Scott. "Don Alvaro" is an extreme example of romantic melodrama. The action concerns a noble Spanish family caught helplessly in the toils of fate. It is full of accidents and coincidences, none of them beyond the bounds of possibility, but producing in the sum an effect of extravagant improbability. The fantastic activities of Alvaro and the de Vargas family in pursuit of their vendetta was, however, set against a background of minutely observed Spanish life during one of the interminable civil wars that have been the curse of Spain. For this background Rivas had plenty of first-hand material, for he had served against the French in the Peninsular War and had no doubt witnessed many of the horrifying scenes that have been preserved for us by Goya's scathing pencil.

By July 1861 Verdi was at work with Piave at Busseto, and in September Giuseppina wrote to Tamberlik on his behalf—"he is absorbed in composition and has not a minute to spare"—about the production, "which is his province and not Piave's." By the end of October Verdi was able to announce that "this accursed *Forza del destino* is practically finished, apart from the orchestration,

* [Giuseppina Strepponi, an operatic soprano who was long Verdi's inseparable companion and later became his second wife.]

which is no great matter. Any quarter of an hour serves to get on with the work. I write to you in fret and fury and must run back to my martyrdom."

Early in the following year Verdi visited St. Petersburg to supervise the production of the new opera, but the illness of the *prima donna,* La Grua, and the impossibility of finding a substitute necessitated its postponement until the autumn. Verdi and his wife took the opportunity to visit Moscow, and returned to Sant' Agata, whence he wrote on 15th April:

I am here on business. To-morrow or the day after or the day after that I go to London to join Peppina, who has been there for the past fortnight. The bearer of this is a young man from the village, good, honest, very willing and exceedingly shy—so do look kindly on him or he will be scared out of his wits. . . . On the way back from London I shall stay in Paris: in September back to St. Petersburg. You see what an infernal life it is!

The occasion of the visit to London was an invitation to compose a work for the opening of the exhibition of 1862. Rossini having excused himself on the grounds of his age from representing Italy, Verdi was asked to take his place. His acceptance is rather surprising in view of his dislike of such commissions and his general disinclination to write occasional works. It is possible that Enrico Tamberlik had something to do with the matter. The tenor divided his time between St. Petersburg, where he sang in the winter, and London. The solo part in Verdi's festival work was designed for him. But undoubtedly patriotism was the chief motive that dictated acceptance. It was important that Italian claims to musical eminence among the nations should not go by default. England was to be represented by Sterndale Bennett who set an official ode by Tennyson; France by Auber who offered a march; and Germany, oddly enough, by Meyerbeer who wrote an overture. . . .

The summer of 1862 was spent at Sant' Agata upon finishing the orchestration of *La forza del destino,* and at the end of August Verdi and his wife set out for St. Petersburg via Paris and Moscow. The new opera was produced on 10th November, and four days later Giuseppina wrote gaily to the de Sanctis [a Neapolitan friend of Verdi's]:

I have been silent, thou hast been silent, he has been silent, we have been silent, and so on. It is true I have not written, Verdi has not written and you have mislaid pen, paper and inkstand. This reciprocal silence is no cause for reproach since, if sin there is, we are both guilty. However the silence of the pen does not imply silence in the heart, and I hope that you and your dear wife love us as we love and always have loved you. I hope you admire my skill in conjugation and the wealth of my vocabulary.

But to come to ourselves. The proverb says: "No news is good news," not always with accuracy. But I give you on this occasion news and good news! *La forza del destino* has been produced with great success. A good performance by every one, singers, chorus and orchestra. The emperor had an attack of bronchitis and severe ophthalmia, and was unable to be present until the fourth performance.

Your friend lost nothing on that account however, for the emperor applauded, himself called out his name and had him presented by the minister in his box. There he was, so to say, buried under an avalanche of compliments, especially from the empress who was most gracious and appreciative in all she said. You imagine that this presentation in the temple was the end of it? *Niett,* as they say in Russia; on Saturday Verdi received the imperial and royal order of St. Stanislas (the commander's cross to hang round his neck), and that without any suggestion or intervention from outside, but *per moto proprio* of the Emperor of all the Russias! Doff your hat and bow to the emperor, to the cultured public and to the Illustrious Nightgown, and so good-night!

We leave shortly for Spain where Verdi has accepted a pressing invitation to produce the new opera. . . . We shall be in Madrid at the end of December.

It was natural that Madrid should wish to see Verdi's setting of the popular Spanish drama, which had given a new impetus to national poetry and ousted the French classics from the Spanish stage.

The enthusiasm for *La forza del destino* in St. Petersburg was not unanimous outside the court. The Russian musicians, growing conscious of national ideals and impatient of the long domination of foreign composers, regarded Verdi as yet another interloper, and ruefully contrasted the large fee of 20,000 roubles he received with the 500 they were usually paid for an opera. This opposition even made itself audible in a demonstration at one of the performances. Nor was even the Italian press exactly enthusiastic, the critics concentrating on the progress Verdi displayed in his orchestration and on the beauty and originality of the choruses, and leaving unsaid the things that would indicate a high opinion of the opera as a whole.

D. H.

A generation ago *La Forza del Destino* was about as familiar to the average music lover as *Stiffelio, Alzira* or *I due Foscari.* In Italy the opera enjoyed a vogue of a sort. Not elsewhere. If anything kept its name alive it was a famous recording by Enrico Caruso and Antonio Scotti of the duet "Solenne in quest' ora"—and the appearance from time to time on concert programs of the soprano air "Pace, pace." Otherwise *La Forza* was just another occupant of that populous cemetery where a quantity of other Verdi works are interred.

Then suddenly, unexpectedly, things began to happen. A few days after the close of World War I the Metropolitan brought out the opera with Rosa Ponselle, Enrico Caruso and Giuseppe de Luca in the principal parts. People rubbed their eyes, not to say their ears. What ever had happened to the producers of opera all these years to ignore a work so incredibly full of music? Certainly the fault was not Verdi's. Neither was it the want of singers, for *La Forza* contained a full half dozen fat parts, roles that called for capable vocalists but not for generally unavailable specialists, like Norma, Donna Anna, Fidelio or the Queen of the Night.

Only a few years afterwards and thanks largely to the efforts of that Verdi enthusiast, the late novelist Franz Werfel, *La Forza del Destino* caught on in Central Europe and spread like a prairie fire from one opera house to another, becoming as inescapable as *Rigoletto* or *Aïda*. Over here, meanwhile, it remained steadily in and out of the repertory, disappearing for a few seasons owing to practical exigencies but always cropping up again, its status now undisputed.

Nevertheless, *La Forza* does not represent a clear-cut issue in Verdi's output, like *Traviata,* for instance, or *Trovatore*. Rather it shares something of the paradoxical destiny of *Don Carlos, Macbeth* or *Simon Boccanegra* without directly resembling them. When it was first produced in the city we now know as Leningrad it was neither a conspicuous success nor a conspicuous failure. It went well in Spain and it caught on in Italy, but otherwise it languished fitfully. It seems to have lain in a state of more or less suspended animation to await some liberating agency of popular need.

Much of the blame for the indecisive fate of *La Forza del Destino* has been charged to the confused libretto. Yet a work like *Trovatore* possesses a book certainly no less complicated and devious and the fact has never really prejudiced its universal triumph. Nevertheless, one writer after another has felt it his duty to deplore the weaknesses of the book which the unfortunate Piave made out of the tortuous Spanish play by the Duke of Rivas.

Verdi's sympathetic biographer, Ferruccio Bonavia, says: "Sad as is the destiny of Don Alvaro still sadder is that of a composer of Verdi's caliber in being fatally drawn toward such poor dramatic material. From time to time he fell victim to the glamor of the horrible; and in such moods he would have preferred Kyd's "Spanish Tragedy" and Ford's "Broken Heart" to any of the Shakespeare dramas. There are explanations for this partiality to sensationalism. During such stirring epochs as the *Risorgimento* in Italy the theatre inclines to be rather passionate and provoking than courtly and elegant. . . . Again, Verdi was [not] so much concerned with the details of the play as moved by the pity that often accompanies terror."

And another English biographer, Francis Toye, complains that "the psychology of the characters in the main drama is unintelligible to us without an effort of constructive imagination. . . . There are many weak points both as regards action and characterization. Coincidences of time and place throughout the play are too frequent."

What these critics and others like them steadily overlook is the type of inspiration the composer seeks and derives from such a piece, as well as the impact of an apparently extravagant and disorganized plot on his creative faculties. Weber once uttered a profound artistic truth and, incidentally, a judgment against hasty or superficial criticism, when he declared that "a good composer will not allow a libretto to be put in his hand, like an apple"—in other words, he has excellent reasons of his own for accepting even a highly fantastic text. Verdi, in the case of *La Forza,* certainly had, even if he found it advisable to make alterations some time after the work had first been given. And those reasons are the music with which he filled to overflowing the creaky dramatic framework, giving it life and purpose.

When the opera was first performed in Russia the correspondent of the French paper *Nord* wrote that "real music lovers are agreed that Verdi has never produced so conscientious a score or paid so much attention to the form in which his ideas are molded. The originality and beauty of the choruses are undeniable, that of the monks at the end of the second act and that of the *Rataplan,* in the third, being quite irresistible. How many fresh and new ideas are scattered in this so scholarly work! How many numbers so elevated in their style, so dramatic and sincere in their expression! The orchestration shows very steady progress and if a certain portion of the public felt disappointed it was because they expected something different. In place of a light opera in the ordinary manner the composer of *Rigoletto* has given us in this a work more akin to the productions of Meyerbeer and Halévy."

If the public was disappointed and expected lightness the answer must be sought, undoubtedly, in the lugubrious character of the drama and in the fact that the composer has not, as he did in *Trovatore,* served up a series of scenes of widely contrasted character and content. Indeed, it is this astonishing variety which has gained general acceptance for the complexities of *Trovatore.* In *La Forza* Verdi has sought to lighten the prevailingly somber nature of the main plot by the brightness and effervescence of Preziosilla; the monk, Melitone; and the exhilarating folk scenes. Yet what they do is chiefly to heighten the darkness of the tragic incidents.

The truth is that the virtues and jostling weaknesses of *La Forza del Destino* have substantially the same origin as those which in greater or lesser degree beset every Verdi opera after *La Traviata* and before *Aïda.* All of them are transitional works. New methods elbow the old without achieving a real uniformity. There are new and considerable advances in technic (incidentally, *La Forza* is probably the first opera which Verdi orchestrated in advance of the rehearsals and not during their progress), a richer, more expansive vein of melody, finer workmanship and warmer harmony, side by side with throwbacks into the earlier manner. There are tunes in this work which might almost be interchangeable with some from the *Masked Ball,* without being any the less attractive for that reason. If the characters of *La Forza* are less vividly pictured in music than those of *Un Ballo* the score, if less diverse, is quite as lavish.

H. F. P.

The first American production of *La Forza del destino* took place at the New York Academy of Music Feb. 24, 1865. At La Scala, Milan, Feb. 20, 1869, a revised version, the textual alterations by Antonio Ghislanzoni, was first presented, in which the bloody events are made to occur off-stage.

In this version the work was given at the New York Academy of Music in 1881 with a cast that included Marie Louise Swift (Leonora), Annie Louise Cary (Preziosilla), Italo Campanini (Don Alvaro), Giuseppe del Puente (Don Carlo), Galassi (Melitone), and Conrad Behrens (the Abbot).

Thirty-seven years elapsed before as good a cast, or better, was assembled in New York. The one to match it came with the first Metropolitan presentation, on Nov. 15, 1918, with Rosa Ponselle (her debut in opera), Alice Gentle, Enrico Caruso, Giuseppe de Luca, Thomas Chalmers, and José Mardones.

Don Carlo

TRAGIC OPERA IN 5 ACTS

Book by Joseph Méry and Camille du Locle

First performance: Opéra, Paris, Mar. 11, 1867

CHARACTERS

Philip II of Spain, BASS
Don Carlos, Infante of Spain, TENOR
Rodrigo, Marquis of Posa, BARITONE
Grand Inquisitor, BASS
A Friar, BARITONE
Elizabeth of Valois, SOPRANO

Princess Eboli, MEZZO-SOPRANO
Theobald, Elizabeth's page
Countess of Aremberg
Count of Lerna
A Royal Herald

Flemish Ladies, Inquisitors, Gentlemen and Ladies of the Courts of France and Spain, Members of the Populace, Pages, Guards, Familiars of the Holy Office, Soldiers, Magistrates, Deputies from the Various Provinces Constituting the Spanish Empire

The action takes place in France and Spain in the sixteenth century

Don Carlos, son of Philip II, King of Spain, is in love with the beautiful Elizabeth de Valois, daughter of Henry II, of France. She returns his affection, but for reasons of state is compelled to marry not Don Carlos, but Philip II himself; thus the young prince finds himself in love with his own stepmother. He confides in his friend, Rodrigo, who advises him to leave the Spanish court and obtain a commission from his father to go to the Netherlands and relieve the Flemings from some of the cruelties inflicted on them by their Spanish rulers. Don Carlos meets with Elizabeth, to gain her influence in obtaining the object of this request from Philip. But as the King is secretly in favor of the method of rule of the Spanish tyrants, the request only angers him and helps estrange father and son. Moreover, as a result of this meeting, the former passion between Don Carlos and Elizabeth returns with even greater intensity.

Don Carlos has a dangerous admirer in Princess Eboli, who learns that the Queen has by no means ceased to love him, and, overcome by jealousy, informs Philip of the state of affairs. At the beginning of the last act, we see the King alone in his library, thinking of his unhappy, loveless state. It is dawn, and his weary eyes long for sleep. "Yet," he meditates, "I shall sleep only in my royal mantle when the day of my doom shall have come," and sings the beautiful aria beginning with the words "Dormirò sol nel manto" ("I shall sleep").

Acting on the advice of the Grand Inquisitor, he orders Don Carlos to be thrown in prison. Princess Eboli repents her rash act and confesses to the Queen. Elizabeth orders her to leave the court . . . death or exile! Left alone, the Princess pours forth her grief in the air "O don fatale" ("Oh, fatal gift"), a melody of great beauty and dramatic force.

Rodrigo visits Don Carlos in prison and there is shot by order of the King, who suspects him of aiding the Flemings. He bids farewell to earth in the beautiful melody, "O Carlo, ascolta."

Carlos is freed, but, in keeping a tryst with Elizabeth before the tomb of Charles V in the Monastery of Yuste, is discovered by the King, and handed over to the officers of the Inquisition. However, a monk steps forth from the tomb, and, dressed as he is in the habit of the Emperor, all present take him for an apparition. In their surprise the officers release Don Carlos, who is led away by the strange figure into the monastery.*

Despite the failure of *Macbeth* and Verdi's dislike of "the big shop," "la grande boutique," as he called it, it was for the Paris Opéra that he wrote his next new work. He and his wife spent the winter of 1865-6 in the French capital, and the idea of producing *La forza del destino* was again debated. The project was abandoned, however, in favour of a new opera based upon Schiller's "Don Carlos" with a French libretto by Méry and du Locle, one of those pairs of theatre hacks by whom Verdi, as he remarked on an earlier occasion, seemed always to be haunted in Paris.

Schiller's tragedy is on a very different plane from that of the romantic melodramas of Gutiérrez and the Duke of Rivas, in which the springs of action are not a part of the mechanism of human character but high-flown abstractions, sentiments of love and honour and revenge put into the mouths of puppets with no inner life of their own. Whatever his faults of imagination as a poet—and they do not really concern us here—and whatever his position relative to Shakespeare and the Attic masters in that august line, Schiller belongs to the great tradition of tragic drama. He understood that a tragic action must arise from the conflict of personalities, real and convincing as presented within the conventions of the theatre, and that the sense of tragedy is created precisely by the web of circumstances, inevitable only because they are conditioned by the conjunction of these particular personalities, in which the actors are caught. This is from our point of view the most important fact about *Don Carlo,* and beside it the question of historical accuracy is irrelevant, and even a certain clumsiness in the construction of the drama is unimportant for the good reason that Schiller's structure had to be pulled to pieces and put together again by the librettists. Schiller's drama provided Verdi with a genuinely tragic theme and with a set of, for the most part, psychologically convincing characters at a moment when his craftsmanship as a musician had

* From "The Victor Book of Operas."

become equal to the greater strain that such a subject, as compared with that of, say, *Il Trovatore,* put upon it. He might have been able to compose *Don Carlo* five years earlier, perhaps, but certainly not in 1857, as the earlier version of *Simon Boccanegra* shows.

Although historical accuracy is irrelevant in poetic drama, which is concerned not with the facts as they occurred in life, but with their reaction upon the creative imagination of the poet, the poet is on that very account laid under a great responsibility. His invention need not square with the history books, but it must square with the imagined "facts" of the ideal world in which we live in the theatre. It must be, in a word, convincing. And paradoxically the poet may carry least conviction when he is keeping most closely to the spirit, if not to the established facts, of the historical period he has chosen. It is possible, for instance, to believe that a king of Spain in the sixteenth century might, for political reasons, marry the bride intended for his own son—though, even so, it is not easy to see why marriage with the king should put an end to a war more surely than marriage with his heir. But while this is historically possible, it is unconvincing and, what is worse, repellent to a modern audience. We may suspect Schiller of an obsession with the classic Oedipus-Jocasta theme, which he was inhibited by contemporary notions of propriety from handling frankly in all its horror; so he cast over it a cloak of romance that may have sufficed for his audience, ready to be moved by a spectacle of suffering innocence. But in the process the tragic motive is weakened and the whole situation becomes false. In his part of lover Carlos makes an unsatisfactory tragic hero, though Schiller manages to arouse our interest and sympathy with him as a political idealist. It is not surprising, therefore, that some of Carlos's music in the opera, where the librettists were obsessed by the same idea of the importance of a "love-interest" that preoccupies the film producer, is by comparison with the rest conventional.

The real interest of Schiller's drama lies, however, not in Carlos and Isabella (Elisabetta in the opera), but in Philip and Posa. It is their tragedy that holds us, however much we may pity the unhappy queen. In order to make this clear the facts must be briefly narrated. The action of the opera takes place in Spain about 1559. In that year Philip II, already twice widowed and having failed to persuade Queen Elizabeth of England to take the place of her sister Mary as his consort, married Elizabeth (Isabella in Spain), daughter of the French king. There is no historical warrant, as I have said, for Schiller's idea that Don Carlos, the king's son by his first wife, had been affianced to Isabella. Carlos was, in fact, a malformed epileptic, but we need not complain of his transformation into a personable, if rather neurotic young man whose humanity sets him in opposition to the ruthless policy of his morose father. For this is the Philip of the Inquisition, the Spain of El Greco, the period of the cruel oppression of Flanders by the Duke of Alva. . . .

On its merits, which far outweigh its defects, *Don Carlo* deserved a resounding success, especially as those defects, arising as they do from an adherence to the popular conventions of the time, would be (and were) less apparent to a contemporary audience than they are to us. The *auto-de-fé* was, indeed, acclaimed even by critics like Reyer and Théophile Gautier, who acknowledged the superior musical quality of the scene between Philip and the Inquisitor. But, in spite of the praise lavished upon the opera by the more intelligent writers, Verdi writing . . . on the morrow of the first performance (11th March 1867) had to admit that *Don Carlo* was not a success. Various explanations have been given of its failure to please the Parisian public. The heretical doctrines of the Marquis of Posa were said to have offended the Catholics headed by the Empress Eugénie, who turned her back to the stage at the fall of the curtain, to show her disapproval. The Italians, as a nation, were suffering from one of their periodic bouts of unpopularity with the French. And there was the usual feeling of jealousy among native musicians aroused by the fuss made about even so distinguished a foreigner.

Apart from these external considerations, the general feeling seems to have been that the opera was consistent neither in style nor in musical quality. For this judgment there is, as we have seen, a solid basis. But it seems that the quality of the performance contributed, more than anything else, to the opera's failure to achieve a resounding success—for complete failure it certainly was not. Verdi complained of a lack of real enthusiasm on the part of the singers. The opera went better in London under Costa's direction, though it had to wait for a revival at Covent Garden until 1933, when it was given three poor performances, and failed to achieve any real popularity here until it was given, for the first time in English, at Sadler's Wells in 1938. Mariani [the conductor], who had expressed his dissatisfaction with the Parisian performance, produced it with great success at Bologna in the summer of 1867, and the opera subsequently went the round of the Italian cities, but, like the other products of this period in Verdi's career, it never achieved the wide popularity of his three earlier masterpieces. Like *Boccanegra,* it has always been rewarded with the respect and admiration of musicians rather than with the affection of the larger public.

Don Carlo was certainly composed under trying circumstances. Verdi was in poor health at the time and was compelled now and again to knock off all work upon it. Giuseppina writes of the anxiety and extreme fatigue induced by its composition. It was a sad time, too, for Verdi's father was seriously ill, and his death, which occurred in January 1867 while Verdi was in Paris, affected him so deeply that for a time the rehearsals had to be abandoned. Yet it would be a mistake to take too sombre a view of Verdi's mood at the time. He could write gaily enough to his intimate friends, and there is an amusing letter purporting to come from his dog, Black, to Arrivabene's dog, Ron-ron. Without the companionship of Black, the successor to the faithful

Lulu, he wrote later, *Don Carlo* could not have been written. At the same time Giuseppina was writing in the best of humours to Cesare de Sanctis [a friend of Verdi's], whom she addresses with affectionate abuse as "Animal, assassin, brigant-scellerato."

D. H.

The first performance in America took place at the New York Academy of Music on April 12, 1877, in the Italian version. Also in Italian *Don Carlo* entered the repertory of the Metropolitan Opera House Dec. 23, 1920. The chief singers were Rosa Ponselle, Margaret Matzenauer, Giovanni Martinelli, Giuseppe de Luca, and Adamo Didur. Marie Sundelius sang the Celestial Voice. Gennaro Papi conducted. The scene between the king and the Grand Inquisitor was among the omissions, but the Ballet of Pearls was performed at great length.

On Dec. 2, 1922, Feodor Chaliapin revealed for the first time to a Metropolitan audience his incomparable impersonation of Philip II, and the performance gained further distinction from the participation of Léon Rothier as the Grand Inquisitor in the restored scene between king and cardinal archbishop.

Aïda

OPERA IN 4 ACTS

Book by Antonio Ghislanzoni, aided by the Composer, from the French
of Camille du Locle, after a prose sketch by the
Egyptologist Mariette

First performance: Opera, Cairo, Dec. 24, 1871

CHARACTERS

Aïda, an Ethiopian princess, soprano
The King of Egypt, bass
Amneris, his daughter, contralto
Rhadames, captain of the guard, tenor

Amonasro, King of Ethiopia, baritone
Ramfis, high priest, bass
A Messenger, tenor

*Priests, Priestesses, Ministers, Captains, Soldiers, Officials, Ethiopian Slaves and
Prisoners, Egyptians, etc.*

The action takes place at Memphis and Thebes during the epoch of the Pharaohs

In Memphian Pharaoh's palace, Rhadames, captain of the guard, is loved by Aïda,
an Ethiopian slave (daughter of Amonasro, king of Ethiopia), and by Amneris,
Pharaoh's daughter. Rhadames loves Aïda. Amneris, suspecting the slave girl's passion, feigns friendship for her to confirm her suspicions. When Rhadames, invested
with consecrated armor in the temple of Pthah, leads the Egyptian army against the
Ethiopians, Aïda mourns the fate which makes her lover her father's foe.

While Moorish slaves dance before Amneris, Aïda enters, mourning her father's
defeat. When Amneris falsely tells her Rhadames has been killed, Aïda betrays her
love for him; and Amneris makes Aïda crouch on the steps of the throne when
Pharaoh and his daughter receive the victors before the gates of Thebes, and Pharaoh
rewards Rhadames with the unwelcome gift of Amneris' hand.

As Aïda waits for Rhadames to keep a nocturnal tryst on the banks of the Nile,
her father Amonasro appears and threatens to disown her unless she makes Rhadames
disclose the road the Egyptian army will take when it invades Ethiopia on the morrow. Then he hides. Rhadames now appears, tells Aïda he will refuse Amneris' hand
and demands her own instead. Aïda assures him Amneris will not consent to be
jilted. Rhadames promises to fly with her. Unwittingly he mentions the road the
Egyptian army will take, Amonasro breaks triumphantly from his hiding place, and
Rhadames realizes he has betrayed his country. About to flee with Aïda and her
father, he is discovered by Rampis, the high priest, and Amneris, who raise the
alarm. Aïda and Amonasro escape; Rhadames is made prisoner.

Golden light fills the judgment hall in Pthah's temple; gloomy darkness shrouds
the subterranean vault of punishment opening from it (the stage shows both floors).

While the priests above seal the tomb, Rhadames, condemned to be buried alive as a traitor, calls on Aïda—who comes to him out of the shadows. She has crept in to share his fate, not caring to live without him. The lovers expire in each other's arms, singing their swan song "O terra addio!" while above their sealed sepulcher the sighs of repentant Amneris mingle with the solemn chant of the temple priestesses.

F. H. M.

The Suez Canal is responsible for the existence of *Aida*. Incidentally, *Aida* is one of the rare examples of "occasional" music that have proved to be immortal music. As a rule music of any kind commissioned and written for a definite occasion, such as the opening of a canal or the inauguration of a World's Fair, turns out merely official and temporary. *Aida,* like Beethoven's overture "The Dedication of the House," written for the opening of the Josephstädter Theater in Vienna, and Handel's "Utrecht" and "Dettingen" "Te Deums," has in it the stuff that lasts.

However, *Aida* was destined to follow a difficult path, as so many another masterpiece has done, before it reached the stage. The first step is a bit mysterious. In 1869, it seems, somebody asked Verdi to "write an opera for a very distant country." Verdi refused, and he did so without informing even his publisher, Ricordi, what country was meant and whence the invitation had come. We now know, of course, that the source of the invitation was the Khedive of Egypt, who desired the opera for his new theatre at Cairo to celebrate the opening of the Suez Canal.

Although in November, 1869, the canal was opened without benefit of *Aida,* but in the presence of such dignitaries as the Khedive, the Emperor of Austria, the Empress of the French and the Crown Prince of Prussia, the matter of a new opera by Verdi was not dropped. The composer visited Paris in the spring of 1870, and while he was there Camille du Locle, who had already collaborated with him on *Don Carlos,* broached the subject again and even offered a handsome sum of money if Verdi would now consent. Verdi, however, was not in the mood for writing music. He reiterated his refusal and departed for his home in Italy.

Du Locle, however, was a man of resource and tact. This time he baited his hook in another way. Shortly after Verdi had gone, he sent him a summary of the story of the proposed opera, together with a request that he at least read it. The summary occupied only four pages. Verdi read them and immediately recognized the rare potentialities of the plot. Thus the old war horse was provoked to engage in a new battle. Now Verdi accepted the commission and, shrewd business man that he was, named as his fee 150,000 francs (some say 100,000, generously increased a half by the Khedive), reserving his rights for all countries excepting only Egypt.

The plot that had turned the trick so neatly Verdi, though doubting, seems to have been given to understand was furnished by the Khedive himself. Such, however, was by no means the case. The real author was one Mariette Bey, a French archaeologist employed at the Louvre museum in Paris. He had been sent to Cairo to look for Coptic manuscripts, but had preferred the ruins of ancient cities and, after getting permission to stay in Egypt for four more years to be devoted to archaeological research, had been appointed Inspector-General of Egyptian monuments and honored with the title of Bey.

The plot sketched by Mariette is said to have an authentic historical basis, and whether fact, fiction, or a mixture of both, it soon absorbed all of Verdi's attention. Du Locle went to Italy to visit Verdi and together they studied the scenario carefully. Verdi, though already he suggested changes, seems to have felt then that the job of the Italian librettist would be little more than a translator's. He wanted the libretto made at his own expense so that it would be his personal property, and he was ready to pay well for it. Antonio Ghislanzoni seemed to him the man indicated, and Ricordi obtained Ghislanzoni for the task.

Little did Ghislanzoni realize, however, what he was in for. Verdi himself took an unprecedented interest in the text, informing himself on the subjects of Egypt and Ethiopia; altering Ghislanzoni's verses; insisting on the "scenic word"; editing drastically, as in the case of the judgment of Radames; sometimes in the heat of composition pouring out the music of a scene and afterwards bidding Ghislanzoni find the words to go with it. It has been well said of this case that words and music grew up side by side.

Originally the world première at Cairo had been set for January, 1871, but the previous July the Franco-Prussian war had begun and Mariette Bey, who had been entrusted with the supervision of scenery and costumes, found himself beleaguered in Paris. Consequently the production had to be postponed. Meanwhile Verdi was exceedingly concerned over details of casting and conducting, and only ten days before the initial performance he, further, provided a revised version of the latter part of the duet between Aida and Amneris in act II!

At length the time for the première arrived. The Khedive and his suite attended the dress rehearsal, which lasted from 7 P.M. to 3 A.M., and at the end the potentate was so delighted that he wanted to telegraph his congratulations to Verdi. The actual première, on Christmas Eve, 1871, was received with acclaim, and European observers were greatly impressed not only by the brilliant colors worn by Copts and Jews in the audience, but by the sight of three first-tier boxes in which ladies of the seraglio sat in veiled state.

Thus auspiciously launched, *Aida* proceeded in triumph the world over. It was given at La Scala, Milan, on February 8, 1872, and at the Academy of Music, New York, on November 26, 1873. The first New York cast— one of the strongest the work can have had anywhere—included Ottavia

Torriani in the name part, Annie Louise Cary as Amneris, Italo Campanini as Radames, Victor Maurel as Amonasro, and the bass Nannetti as Ramfis.

Aida was not presented at the Metropolitan Opera House till November 12, 1886, and its great vogue there dates from Caruso's assumption of the role of Radames (his second appearance in New York) on November 30, 1903.

Again it made Metropolitan history, and in a big way, when on November 16, 1908, it inaugurated the twenty-seven-year managerial reign of Giulio Gatti-Casazza. On that occasion no less a musical magnate than Arturo Toscanini made as conductor his North American début. Emmy Destinn, a soprano already famous in Europe, sang, as Aida, for the first time on this side of the Atlantic, beginning a distinguished American career. Conspicuous also in the cast were two singers who had been established for some time in the good graces of Metropolitan audiences, Louise Homer, the Amneris, and Antonio Scotti, the Amonasro, as well as the now indispensable Caruso. In number of performances *Aida* now leads the entire Metropolitan list.

P. S.

Otello

[Othello]

LYRIC DRAMA IN 4 ACTS

Book by Arrigo Boito

First performance: La Scala, Milan, Feb. 5, 1887

CHARACTERS

Otello, a Moor, general in the Venetian army, TENOR
Iago, his aide, BARITONE
Cassio, lieutenant to Otello, TENOR
Roderigo, a Venetian gentleman, TENOR
Lodovico, Ambassador of the Venetian Republic, BASS

Montano, predecessor of Otello as Governor of Cyprus, BASS
A Herald, BASS
Desdemona, Otello's wife, SOPRANO
Emilia, Iago's wife, MEZZO-SOPRANO

Soldiers and Sailors of the Venetian Republic; Venetian Ladies and Gentlemen; Cypriot Men, Women, and Children; Heralds; Greek, Dalmatian, and Albanian Soldiers; an Innkeeper, and Four Servants

The action takes place at a seaport of Cyprus toward the end of the fifteenth century

Otello, victor over the Saracens, is acclaimed by the Cypriots in the harbor of Famagusta. At once Iago's demoniac machinations begin. Plying young Cassio, newly made a captain, with drink, he leads him to toast Desdemona, Otello's wife, and draw sword on Rodrigo. Degrading Cassio to the ranks, Otello makes passionate love to his wife beneath the stars.

Cassio at Iago's suggestions begs Desdemona to intercede for him with her husband, then Iago rouses Otello's jealousy. In the garden, where women, children, and Dalmatian sailors bring her flowers, Desdemona asks her husband's mercy for the offender, but Otello angrily flings to the ground the handkerchief she tries to bind round his forehead to assuage his pain. Iago tells Otello Cassio murmurs Desdemona's name in dreams, and claims to have a handkerchief she gave him. And Iago produces it.

Questioned by her husband, Desdemona says she has lost her handkerchief, and again pleads for Cassio. But the jealous Moor thinks his wife untrue. When a Venetian embassy arrives appointing Cassio in his place, and Desdemona drops a harmless word in the latter's favor to the ambassador Lorenzo, Otello ill-treats his wife in his rage.

Desdemona dons her bridal robe—divining it will be her shroud—and singing the affecting "Song of the Willow Tree," commends her soul to the Virgin, and falls asleep. Long the Moor stands watching her, then wakes her with kisses to tell her she must die. His blind rage will listen to no plea for mercy and he strangles her, her last words protesting her innocence. Otello's cries bring Iago, Lodovico and men at arms into the chamber where Iago's wife, despite her husband's threats, tells how he ruined Desdemona. Yielding up his sword (Iago flees) Otello steps to the bed of his innocent victim and stabs himself with his dagger.

F. H. M.

Despite revisions, despite depression, the idea of *Otello* lurked always at the back of Verdi's mind. During the year 1881 and sporadically during the ensuing years he was in correspondence with his friend the painter Morelli about the characters and costumes of the play. Apparently Morelli would have liked Othello himself to be dressed as an ordinary Venetian, but Verdi replied that, as Shakspere had chosen to make a Moor out of Giacomo Moro (a Venetian general in the original Italian story on which the play is based), a Moor he would have to remain. His chief preoccupation was with Iago. Morelli's idea of Iago was a small man of cunning aspect, dressed in black. Verdi approved the black, but confessed that his own idea of Iago was quite different.

If I were an actor [he wrote] and had to act Iago, I should like to portray rather a spare, tall man with thin lips, small eyes set close together like a monkey's, a high, receding forehead, and head well developed at the back. His manner should be vague, nonchalant, indifferent to everything, skeptical, pungent. He should throw off good and evil sentiments lightly, as if he were thinking of something quite different from his actual utterances. Thus, if somebody reproached him, saying: "What you propose is infamous," he would reply: "Really? . . . I did not think it was . . . don't let us talk about it any more!" A man like this might deceive anybody, even his own wife to a certain extent. A small malevolent-looking man arouses suspicion in everybody and deceives no one.

Morelli was told that he ought to paint a picture of Othello prostrate on the ground after the terrible insinuations of Iago, and he in fact made a sketch for such a picture, which Boïto vainly tried to describe to Verdi in March 1884; but the picture itself had not even then materialized. There is no doubt that the figure of Iago, in whom he saw an embodiment of the kind of priest he so much disliked, especially fascinated Verdi. It was no mere coincidence that for a long time he intended to call the opera "Iago."

The whole project nearly came to grief in 1884. After the production of *Mefistofele* at Naples, a banquet was given to Boïto, at which he was reported by a newspaper to have said that he was sorry not to be setting "Iago" himself. Verdi, in his touchy mood, thought that Boïto implied that his music would not be satisfactory and offered to restore the manuscript as a free gift, "without the slightest resentment." Boïto, whose relations with Verdi had been growing steadily more intimate, had no difficulty in proving that he had been misreported. He refused point-blank to accept Verdi's offer, and the storm blew over. Verdi, however, refused to guarantee to complete the opera, writing to Boïto on the 26th of April 1884 that there had been too much talk about it, that he had worked and lived too long, that the years not only of his life but of his labor were excessive: "Heaven forbid that the public should have to say to me too openly: 'Enough.'" Ten days later he wrote to Franco Faccio [conductor and composer] in much the same strain: "So, in your opinion, I ought really to finish this *Otello*? But why? And for whom? It is a matter of indifference to me and still more to the public."

Verdi speaks of "finishing" the opera, but it is, to say the least, doubtful whether he had as yet composed much of the music. He certainly told Giulio Ricordi [the music publisher] in March 1883 that he had not written a note at that time. Checchi* makes the definite statement that he did not begin writing the score until November 1885 (and, incidentally, that he scored the whole of the first act during the fortnight that he passed at Montecatini during the summer of 1886, working not more than two or three hours a day); but this seems scarcely possible in view of the fact that Verdi wrote to Maurel on the 30th of December 1885 to the effect that *Otello* "is not completely finished, as has been stated, but is well advanced towards completion. I am in no hurry to finish it, because up to now I have not made up my mind to produce it"— his hesitation being due, apparently, to the impossible economic conditions prevailing in the theater.

Besides, he informed the publisher Leduc in January 1886, "my *Otello* (no longer 'Iago') is not finished. True, I did a lot of work on it toward the end of last winter and at the beginning of the autumn, but many things still have to be done to complete the score." Knowing Verdi's habitual procedure, we may surmise that he had most of the music in his mind before he started to write it down. He may even have made definite sketches; in any case it would be perhaps unwise to take his denials to Ricordi and Arrivabene too literally. Where his compositions were concerned, Verdi always showed himself extraordinarily secretive even with his most intimate friends.

Rumor became busy with his intentions. As early as March 1883 Verdi was surprised to read in a paper that "Maurel has again told us that Verdi is preparing a huge surprise for the musical world and in his 'Iago' will give the young 'musicians of the future' a very stiff lesson." He was not at all pleased. "Heaven forbid!" he wrote to Ricordi; "it never has been and never will be my intention to give lessons to anybody. I admire everything I like without prejudice for or against any particular school. I am guided by my own tastes and I let everybody else do as he pleases."

As the facts with regard to the progress of the opera became known, interest not only in Milan but in Paris increased. Maurel wrote, reminding Verdi of a promise to entrust to him the part of Iago. Verdi, though protest-

* [E. Checchi, an Italian biographer of Verdi.]

ing that he never could have made a promise that he was not absolutely sure of being able to fulfill, replied that he could imagine no better interpreter possible, and for the time being closed the subject. A year later, in January 1886, Maurel again returned to the charge, this time trying to persuade Verdi to allow *Otello* to be produced at the Paris Opéra Comique under the direction of Carvalho, who was prepared to do everything conceivable to satisfy the composer's requirements. Verdi, though much pleased, politely refused.

You who know Boïto will not need to be told that in *Otello* he has fashioned a libretto wherein situations and verses alike are extraordinarily powerful. I have tried to give to these verses the most true and significant accents in my power. This quality (it may turn out to be a defect) would be largely lost in translation. It is imperative, then, that *Otello* should be given for the first time in Italian. . . . But, I repeat, any such consideration is premature.

Several celebrated singers wrote in the hope of procuring parts in the new opera, but on some excuse or other all were discouraged except Tamagno, who was told to come quietly to Genoa on his way back from Madrid to talk things over. The journalists began to take a hand in the game, tackling the notoriously reserved Boïto with no success at all and eliciting from Giulio Ricordi, afraid perhaps of his own expansiveness, only the deliberate misstatement that it was a thousand pities that Verdi would or could write no more music. Needless to say, the inscrutable composer himself vouchsafed no information. Outwardly his attention seemed occupied with quite other matters. For instance, he was considering the presentation to the village of Villanova of a tiny hospital with twelve beds, in order to save the poorer inhabitants the tiresome and often fatal journey to Piacenza; while the newspapers credited him with the further intention of restoring the church of the hamlet of Sant' Agata. Since Verdi, who regarded the report as tendentious, never had any such intention, this led to correspondence in which he complained that the newspapers seemed determined to make him out much richer than he was. "You must know better than anybody else," he wrote to Ricordi, "that when I composed a great deal, the price paid for operas was low; now that it is high I hardly compose at all." Even as late as March 1886 he found time to go to Paris for a week or two, "a little to hear Maurel, a little to see if they are madder than they used to be, a little just to have a change." In July he journeyed posthaste to Milan to be present at the deathbed of the Countess Maffei, his friend for forty-four years and the recipient of his most intimate confidences.

Nevertheless, on the 1st of November 1886 *Otello* was finished, the fact being announced to Boïto in the following laconic note:

DEAR BOITO,—
It is finished.
Here's a health to us . . . (and also to Him . . .).
Good-by.

G. VERDI.

On the 18th of December the last pages were sent from Genoa to the copyist. Verdi hated to see them go. He felt as if he had lost a friend. "Poor Otello!" he wrote to Boïto, "he will come back here no more."

The production was announced for the 5th of February 1887 at La Scala, but Verdi had reserved the right, though the public was unaware of the fact, to withdraw the opera at any time during rehearsal or even after the dress rehearsal.* Curiosity and excitement were rife in the city. The choice of subject, inseparably associated in the mind of the older generation with Rossini, provoked comment, not all of it favorable. With an insignificant exception, no new work by Verdi had been heard for nearly thirteen years. Some remembered his own declaration that he was too old to write any more, that "music needs youthfulness of the senses, impetuousness of the blood, fullness of life"; that the children of old men "are rickety, anæmic and worse." Others, pointing to Verdi's well-known vitality in comparison with his years, recalled the fact that Professor Fedeli, who looked after him during his annual cure at Montecatini, had declared that he was still perfectly capable of work. Nobody had the slightest idea what the new opera would be like as regards either nature or style, especially as the La Scala rule of exclusion from rehearsals had been enforced even more rigidly than usual.

Though the speculators took advantage of the situation to push up the price of seats to fantastic heights, the theater, with the exception of the royal box, was completely filled a quarter of an hour before the performance; the rush for the cheaper seats nearly ended in a free fight, and the approaches to La Scala were thronged throughout the evening by crowds of people unable to gain admission but determined to play some part, however vicarious, in such a historic event.

Monaldi,† who was present, gives an extremely vivid account of the scene in the theater, with its atmosphere of tense expectancy. The orchestra, under Faccio, numbered a hundred; so did the chorus. Managers and critics from all Europe were present in force, including Reyer from Paris, Bennett and Hueffer from London. What would their verdict be? As to the reception of the opera by the public there was soon no doubt. Twice in the first act, after the fire chorus and Iago's drinking song, they tried, though vainly, to call Verdi on to the stage. When, at the end of the act, Verdi took his call, "one immense simultaneous shout makes the theater rock. Verdi slightly bends his head and smiles, the frantic enthusiasm of the huge assembly bringing tears to his eyes. He seems to feel the necessity to retire, which the public, with a tardy respect for his age, finally permits him to do."

* This little-known fact is established by a letter to Giulio Ricordi that appeared in the *Berliner Tageblatt* and is included by Werfel in his collection of Verdi's letters. It is of importance as illustrating the sense of experiment felt by Verdi in his new venture.
† [G. Monaldi, an Italian biographer of Verdi.]

At the end of the opera renewed and even greater enthusiasm! When the composer left the theater, a crowd of admirers, who throughout the day had lined the streets to applaud his every appearance, unharnessed the horses from his carriage and drew it to the Hotel di Milano, where he always stayed. Bellaigue relates that here, in the midst of those he loved most . . . listening to the acclamations of the crowds outside, he was assailed by melancholy. "I feel," he said, "as if I had fired off my last cartridge. Oh, the solitude of Sant' Agata, hitherto peopled by all the creatures of my imagination whom, well or ill, I translated into terms of music! Tonight the public has torn away the veil that concealed my last mysteries. I have nothing left."

And as they spoke of his glory, he continued: "Oh, glory, glory! I so loved my solitude in the company of Otello and Desdemona! Now the crowd, always greedy for something new, has taken them away from me, leaving me nothing but the remembrance of our secret conversation, our dear, past intimacy." But the mood, which will readily be understood by anyone who has experienced the vicissitudes of artistic creation, soon passed, and with a smile on his austere face the old man said: "My friends, if I were thirty years younger I should like to begin a new opera tomorrow, on the condition that Boïto provided the libretto."

F. T.

In *Otello* Verdi achieves a musical style that approaches a perfect fusing of the old *opera seria* elements of measured recitative and set number in a flexible, coherent, and continuous tonal flow. At one time it was usual to speak of Wagner's influence on this score. As a matter of fact, Verdi's idiom is almost purely Italian and it might best be described as an enormously resourceful and expert development of the style devised two and a half centuries earlier by Monteverdi.

It seems that at first there was some idea of naming the new opera "Iago," out of deference to the memory of Rossini's *Otello,* which, however, by this time had virtually disappeared from the stage. Verdi, with characteristic courage, rejected the idea as an unworthy subterfuge. He declared it would seem to him hypocrisy not to call it *Otello* for fear of comparison with Rossini: "I prefer that they should say 'He wanted to match his strength with a giant and has come back beaten,' rather than 'He wanted to hide behind the title of *Iago.'"*

Of course, as one of the dramatis personae the villain Iago is of equal importance with the hero Othello, and there was never a question of assigning the role in the inaugural performance to any other artist than the great dramatic baritone, Victor Maurel. For Othello himself Francesco Tamagno of the ultrapowerful tenor was the inevitable choice. Romilda Pantaleoni, a soprano who was a close friend of Franco Faccio, was allotted Desdemona. Faccio, as a matter of course, conducted.

Italo Campanini, beyond his prime as a tenor, ventured as an impresario to bring the new *Otello* to New York with a specially organized company. The *première* took place at the Academy of Music on April 16, 1888, with Marconi in the title role, Antonio Galassi as Iago, Eva Tetrazzini as Desdemona, and Sofia Scalchi as Emilia. Cleofonte Campanini conducted.

Tamagno made his initial appearance in the United States March 24, 1891, when *Otello* opened a spring season of opera in Italian under the direction of Henry E. Abbey and Maurice Grau at the Metropolitan Opera House, New York. Besides Tamagno as the Moor, the cast included Giuseppe del Puente as Iago, Emma Albani as Desdemona, and Sofia Scalchi as Emilia.

The first performance of *Otello* at the Metropolitan by the regular troupe took place Jan. 11, 1892, when Jean de Reszké, for one performance only, essayed the name part. Camera was the Iago, Albani the Desdemona, Scalchi the Emilia. At length, on Dec. 3, 1894, *Otello* was presented at the Metropolitan with a cast of the first order throughout. Tamagno and Maurel were both of it, as well as Emma Eames (Desdemona) and Eugenia Mantelli (Emilia). Luigi Mancinelli conducted.

On Nov. 24, 1902, *Otello* opened the Metropolitan season with Albert Alvarez in the name part, Antonio Scotti as Iago, Eames as Desdemona, and Louise Homer as Emilia. Oscar Hammerstein revived *Otello* at his Manhattan Opera House on Dec. 25, 1908. In the cast were Giovanni Zenatello (Othello), Mario Sammarco (Iago), and Nellie Melba (Desdemona). The conductor was again *Otello's* first for New York: Cleofonte Campanini.

Arturo Toscanini conducted the revival of *Otello* at the Metropolitan under the Gatti-Casazza regime on Nov. 17, 1909. Leo Slezak, a Bohemian, made his American debut as the Moor and Florence Wickham, an American, made hers as Emilia. The Desdemona was Frances Alda; the Iago, Scotti. After Slezak left the Metropolitan no tenor engaged there attempted the part of Othello until Lauritz Melchior on March 19, 1935, appeared in the fourth act with Elisabeth Rethberg as Desdemona in the course of the program of a special gala evening. [Since then the role of the Moor has been sung at the Metropolitan by Giovanni Martinelli, Torsten Ralf, and Ramon Vinay; Desdemona, Rethberg, Helen Jepson, Stella Roman, and Daniza Ilitsch; Iago, Lawrence Tibbett and Leonard Warren.]

Though the American presentations of *Otello* mentioned so far were all given in the original Italian, the work was presented in New York in English as early as 1903—at the Brooklyn Academy of Music on Oct. 6, at the West End Theater on Dec. 21.

P. S.

Falstaff

LYRIC COMEDY IN 3 ACTS

Book by Arrigo Boito

First performance: La Scala, Milan, Feb. 9, 1893

CHARACTERS

Falstaff, BARITONE

Fenton, TENOR

Ford, BARITONE

Dr. Caius, TENOR

Bardolph, TENOR

Pistol, BASS

Mistress Ford, SOPRANO

Anne Ford, SOPRANO

Mistress Page, MEZZO-SOPRANO

Mistress Quickly, MEZZO-SOPRANO

The action takes place in Windsor, England, in the fifteenth century

Sir John Falstaff, plotting affairs with both Mrs. Page and Mrs. Ford, wishes to make them pay out financially. The ladies themselves, however, are in on the plot, thanks to Dame Quickly, and are attempting a counterplot. Anne Page, who is in love with the threadbare Fenton, it is hoped by her parents will marry much better. Sir John accepts the invitations to a tête-à-tête sent him by Mrs. Ford and Mrs. Page. Ford himself, dressed as a man named Fontana, delivers the invitations. Sir John attired in his best wooing garments goes to the Fords' house as Fontana (Ford) follows. There, to save Sir John from discovery, after a variety of horseplay, he is tumbled out the window into the Thames. Ford's anger is eased by seeing Sir John's humiliating situation. Wine revives Sir John, however, and he is ready to fall into another trap when Mrs. Ford again invites him to a rendezvous in Windsor Forest. He is to come disguised as a hunter. He arrives and this time elaborate preparations have been made to receive him. Mrs. Ford goes as the Queen of Fairies, Mrs. Page as a nymph, Dame Quickly as a witch, and scores of children as sprites and elves. Sir John, in the moonlit forest scene, is chased and hounded by all until he admits that he has been bested. All unmask for a last chorus together, not before, however, Anne has taken part in a mock marriage ceremony with Fenton, which, it develops, was no mockery but real.

Boito's libretto, though based chiefly on "The Merry Wives of Windsor," draws also on "Henry IV," with its appreciably nobler presentation of the Fat Knight. A special case in point is the monologue on honor. The main lines of "The Merry Wives" are followed in Boito's book, which, however, condenses the action to six scenes, omitting conspicuously the witch of Brentford

583

episode. Master Page is likewise deleted, and since his wife is reduced to secondary importance, their daughter—the sweet Anne Page of the original—who
cannot be so reduced, is kept dully in the foreground by being assigned filially
to Master Ford and his wife. Furthermore, Boito bestows the name of Alice
on Mrs. Ford and Meg on Mrs. Page. Anne is rendered in the Italian as Nannetta.

Musically *Falstaff* is the comic counterpart of *Otello*. Here the style blends
the traditional elements of *opera buffa,* from the half-spoken "dry" recitative
to the scintillant ensemble, in a thoroughly fused current of tone. It has been
deemed astonishing that a man just short of eighty should create a work so
overbrimming with youthful vivacity and humorous zest, but no less remarkable, if not so astonishing, in view of Verdi's untiring quest of perfection, is
the excelling workmanship, from the broad outlines to the finest detail, that
distinguishes this masterpiece. As a comedy in music *Falstaff* ranks with the
very greatest of the species—with *Le Nozze di Figaro, Il Barbiere di Siviglia,*
and *Die Meistersinger.*

P. S.

Verdi had retired to Sant' Agata and devoted himself to his hobby, the cul-
tivation of his estates. This time it really seemed that his career as a composer
was at an end. He would remain the venerable figure-head of Italian music,
to be celebrated in face of his own opposition on the jubilee of his first opera
or to lend his support, more willingly, to the celebration of other masters.
Much as he disliked such festivities, he permitted Joachim to number him
among the patrons of the Beethoven centenary celebrations at Bonn: "Where
Beethoven is concerned, we must all do reverence!" And when Rossini's centenary came round in 1892, Verdi even took an active part in the proceedings
and conducted the prayer from *Mosè.*

By that time the new cat was out of the bag. Once more there was a dinner
party and an indiscretion, this time calculated, on Boito's part. The poet gave
the toast, not of the aged guest of honour, but of "Pot-belly"—an allusion
promptly explained by Ricordi, who called out: "Falstaff!"

This was in November 1890. The earliest mention of *Falstaff* in Verdi's correspondence occurs rather more than a year before, by which time it appears
that the scheme of the opera had already been thoroughly discussed and settled. The manuscript of the text contains comparatively few emendations, from
which fact Luzio deduces a very thorough preliminary survey of the ground
by Verdi and Boito.* Even the new correspondence published in "Carteggi
Verdiani" throws no light upon the origins of the new project. But it is, perhaps, not stretching imagination far to suggest that one spur to Verdi's intent
was the desire to avenge once and for all the defeat of long ago, the disastrous

---

* It is not true that Verdi accepted the libretto as it stood without changing a word, but the
alterations amounted only to minor verbal adjustments and the excision of superfluous lines.

Il finto Stanislao, and to prove in the teeth of all the pronouncements, even of Great Jupiter Rossini himself, that he, Giuseppi Verdi, was capable of composing a comic opera. If there was a touch almost of quixotry in the venture, there was also a large measure of trepidation.

Do you realize [he wrote to Boito in July 1889], when you are drawing your portrait of Falstaff, the enormous number of my years? I know that in reply you will exaggerate the state of my health, saying it is robust and of the best. . . . That may be; none the less you will agree with me that it may be thought very rash of me to undertake such a task. Suppose I find the strain too great and cannot finish the music? Then your time and labour would have been wasted to no purpose. For all the wealth in the world I would not have that happen. Such an idea is intolerable, all the more so if, in writing *Falstaff,* you should find your mind distracted from *Nerone* (I will not contemplate the possibility of your giving it up) or its production delayed. I should be blamed for the postponement, and the lightnings of the public's anger would fall upon my head!

Verdi may be absolved of guilt in causing the delay in the long process through which Boito's *Neroni* went, a process which was not complete even when he died in 1918—unless we suppose that his contact with a far greater artist set up for Boito, always a man of the highest aspirations, a standard of excellence to which he felt he could not attain, but towards which, like the young man in Longfellow's poem, he struggled to the end of his life.

Verdi also felt that he could not end his career more triumphantly than with *Otello*—an argument of which Boito acknowledged the weight. But, he countered, it was valid for his contemporaries only, not for history, which assesses the whole worth of a man.

It is rare, indeed [he continues], for an artist's life to end with a worldly victory. Such a victory is *Otello*. All the other arguments about age, strength, your exhaustion or mine, etc., have no validity and present no obstacles to a new work. . . . I do not think that you would find the composition of a comic opera fatiguing. Tragedy makes its author genuinely suffer. His mind undergoes a painful experience and his nerves are unhealthily strung up. But the jests and laughter of comedy exhilarate both mind and body. . . . You have longed for a good subject for a comic opera all your life, which proves that you have a natural bent for the noble art of comedy. Instinct is a good guide. There is only one way of ending your career better than with *Otello,* that is to end it with *Falstaff.*

"The Merry Wives of Windsor" presented Boito with a very different and, on the whole, a less difficult task than *Othello*. In the one he was confronted with a poetic masterpiece whose form must be carefully handled if it was not to be distorted and ruined; in the other he was faced with a farce bearing every indication of having been hurriedly put together and consisting of a number of repetitive episodes loosely strung together round the paunch of Sir John Falstaff. And it is round his borrowed paunch that they are strung, for of the personality that makes the Falstaff of "King Henry IV" one of the great comic figures in our literature there is hardly a trace—only a fat man in a series of funny situations. The comedy is said to have been the result of a command from Queen Elizabeth to exhibit the fat knight in love—which is precisely what Shakespeare failed to do. Falstaff makes no pretence of being in love with either of the merry wives.

This is no occasion, then, for pulling long faces or talking of the iniquity of tampering with Shakespeare's text, as though it had the sanction of divine inspiration. Boito's first task was to reduce to a manageable form the sprawling, shapeless mass, to cut away the loose ends and irrelevant side-issues, and to rehabilitate Sir John Falstaff as a man of character. This task he carried out with the greatest skill, and no one who reads his libretto without prejudice can fail to acknowledge that, on its own merits as a comedy, it is a great improvement upon the original.

There were hardly any superfluous characters in *Othello* who could be dispensed with; there are nine in "The Merry Wives." Shallow, Slender, Evans and Caius could be rolled into one—their complaints against Falstaff and his minions, and the pretensions of two of them to Anne Page's hand, being concentrated in the person of Doctor Caius. Then Master Page was of no real use to the plot, so he could go; and to tighten up the unities his daughter Anne became Nannetta Ford. And, last major excision, the whole incident of Falstaff's disguise as Mother Prat, the fat woman of Brentford, which is but a weak repetition of the buck-basket episode, could be cut out bodily. Among the lesser figures Nym disappears—what is essential in his part being taken over by Bardolph—together with Rugby, Simple, and William Page. Robin, the boy, remains as a *persona muta*.

With these characters and the by-plots in which they figure Boito rejected all those topical allusions that make "The Merry Wives" such a mine for the historical annotator of Shakespeare's text. Gone are the references to deer-stealing and the Lucy Arms, to the idiosyncrasies of Ben Jonson and to the court of Queen Elizabeth. Out went "Cosen Garmombles" and the "Duke de Jaminie," and the curious affair of the post-horses of Maidenhead, Reading and Colnbrook. And, it must be confessed, with all these superfluities and obscurities, went also much that gives the play its immortal quality—the tang of English character and of the English countryside that makes Shakespeare's hand unmistakable, for instance, in the opening scene for Shallow and in the salt humour of Mrs. Quickly's speech.

The gains are greater, and not only in form and concentration. It would have been futile to concentrate upon a figure that was nothing more than a padded belly. By a piece of patient recension Boito has substituted for the dummy the real Shakespearian Falstaff of the histories in all his grand unscrupulousness and geniality. Bardolph refusing to play pander substitutes for Nym's original Jonsonian excuse of his "humour" that of his own "honour," and so provides the cue for the insertion of the great speech upon that topic from "Henry IV," Part I. Even more ingenious is the invention of a repetitive objurgation of the world's vileness in the very manner of the "plague of all cowards" speech in the same play, which serves to strengthen the scene of Falstaff's discomfiture after his ducking in the Thames. To this is added an excerpt from another of his *bravura* pieces—the speech on the effects of wine from the second part of "Henry IV"; and among other borrowings from the historical play may be mentioned the description of Bardolph's nose. In this way Boito reconstructed as far as was possible within the framework of the Shakespearian farce the great figure of the true Falstaff.

The resultant libretto consists of three acts, each containing two scenes. The location alternates between the Garter Inn and Ford's house (and garden) until at the end we reach the mock fairyland of Windsor Forest with Herne the Hunter's oak as the central feature. As an example of dramatic form the libretto is without superior. The action is swift, compact—indeed, an astonishing amount is compressed into a small space—and convincing, and it moves to its climaxes with an appearance of a natural ease that conceals a great skill in its handling.

Falstaff was composed slowly and methodically. Verdi worked at it for two hours, neither more nor less, each day. He had read somewhere a warning against the dangers of overwork to elderly people. Always timorous about the state of his health, he was determined to run no risks. His hypochondria did not grow less with the passing years. A visit to Montecatini, the spa in the Tuscan hills above Lucca, to take the waters, remained an annual fixture in the routine of his life.

Verdi enjoyed himself enormously in spite of his misgivings. He was, he said, composing *Falstaff* for the fun of the thing. He even suggested that it might never be given to the public. But that was only a saving clause to cover the risk of the work not turning out to his satisfaction. Nothing could be wider of the mark than the idea of Verdi writing an opera as an intellectual exercise, for his private amusement, or in order to create a work of art without regard to a possible audience. When he composed he had one eye always on the box-office, and not upon the stars or Mount Parnassus or a vague future in which he would find his reward. Those are, more often than not, the objects of the conscious gaze of minor and usually unsuccessful artists. As in everything that concerns artistic creation, there are exceptions. But if a refutation of the slogan "Art for Art's sake" is ever needed, it may be found in the operas of Verdi.

We may suspect, too, a mischievous delight in mystification for its own sake, to tease his friends and to bamboozle the press. Even as late as January 1891, and even to so close an associate as Giulio Ricordi, Verdi persisted in his coy refusal to come to terms about *Falstaff*:

To come to *Falstaff,* all projects for the future seem to me folly, absolute folly! I will expound myself. I am engaged on writing *Falstaff* to pass the time, without any preconceived ideas or plans; I repeat, *to pass the time!* Nothing else. All this talk, these proposals, however vague, and this splitting of words will end by involving me in obligations that I absolutely will not assume. I tell you again: *I am writing to pass the time.* I tell you the music is only about half finished, by which I mean half sketched. There remains the greater part of the work: the concerting of the parts, revisions and adjustments, besides the instrumentation, which will be most exhausting. In fine, to put it in a word, the whole of 1891 will not suffice to finish it. So why make plans and accept terms, however loosely worded? Besides, if I felt myself in any way, even in the slightest degree, tied, I should no longer be *à mon aise* and could do nothing well. When I was a young man, in spite of ill health, I could work at my desk for ten or even twelve hours without a break! And many is the time I have set to work at four in the morning until four in the afternoon with nothing but a cup of coffee inside me. . . . I can no longer do that, alas! . . . To conclude, it would be best to say now and later to every one, to every one, that I cannot and will not make any promises about *Falstaff.* If it will be, it will be; and it will be what it will be!

Six months later to the same correspondent he wrote:

You are joking, my dear Giulio! . . . How? For six or seven months no one has given a thought to *Falstaff* or to the Venerable Veteran of Sant' Agata. The theatres, too, have gone their way from failure to success (little enough of this!), and now you come and tell me that a subvention would be less badly needed [i.e., if *Falstaff* were to be produced]! It is inopportune to talk of *Falstaff,* which proceeds very slowly, and I am inclined to think that the vastness of the Scala might ruin the effect. In writing *Falstaff* I have thought neither of theatres nor of singers. I have written it to please myself, and I believe that it ought to be performed at Sant' Agata and not at the Scala.

I have already suggested that Verdi's protestations about writing to please himself without a thought for theatres or singers, by which he meant a particular theatre and individual singers, should not be taken too literally. In fact, a few days later Boito was writing to announce that he had discovered the right singer for Mrs. Quickly. Verdi's misgivings about the effect of *Falstaff* in so large a theatre as the Scala, on the other hand, were real and well founded. *Falstaff* requires for its proper effect the intimacy of a small auditorium; it is almost chamber music.

It is usual to regard *Falstaff* as a kind of miraculous "sport," bearing little relation to any other opera of Verdi's. That its production by a composer in his eighth decade deserves the adjective will hardly be disputed, and not the least astonishing thing about it is the complete freedom of its musical style from the conventions of Italian *opera buffa.* Verdi's admiration for Rossini coupled with his total inexperience (apart from the unhappy experiment of fifty years before) of comic opera might reasonably have produced a work in the accepted and still popular style of *Il Barbiere di Siviglia* and *Don Pas-*

quale. But Verdi, by adapting the style he had developed for tragedy and carrying it to the extreme limit of which it was capable, produced a comic masterpiece as unique and original in its own way as *Die Meistersinger.* At the same time, once we get below the surface of its unique musical style, *Falstaff* is seen to be in the true succession of the *opera buffa.* Its roots may, indeed, be traced back to the old Italian Comedy, which in fact provided the original bare bones of Shakespeare's plot. Pistol, at least, among the characters has Latin blood in him and one of his collateral descendants may be found in the braggart Rodimarte in Alessandro Scarlatti's *Il trionfo d'onore.* . . .

What fun Verdi had, too, with the orchestration! His mastery of instrumental effect, like his feeling for the right setting of words and for the balance of voice and accompaniment, had developed even beyond the consummate skill of *Otello.* And he uses this mastery with a gusto that is never allowed to degenerate into showing off for its own sake, still less to lapse into vulgarity. The underlining of Falstaff's repeated "No's" in the monologue on honour with staccato chords emphasized by an *acciaccatura,* the airy whiffling of the woodwind at "What is in that word honour? Air," and the great shake of the whole orchestra that accompanies his description of the effect of wine, are famous points in a score that has in almost every bar some happy touch of beauty or stroke of wit.

The swiftness of movement, the quick play of wit, the subtlety and restraint of the comedy, the aristocratic air of it all combine to make Falstaff one of the most difficult operas to appreciate, though its richness of humour and robust vitality save it from being merely recondite. The composer who had made the greatest popular reputation of his time ended by producing the musicians' opera; the romantic had turned pure classicist; and the master of theatrical effect said farewell to the theatre in strict fugue.

Falstaff, produced at the Scala Theatre on 9th February 1893, brought Verdi the homage of the whole civilized world. Musicians from all parts of Europe and from America gathered in Milan, and the anticipatory excitement was not lessened by the fact that Verdi firmly refused to intervene with the management to waive the rule against admitting strangers to rehearsals. Telegrams of congratulation poured in from the great, among them one from King Humbert, who expressed his regret at being unable to witness "this new manifestation of an inexhaustible genius." Acting up to its name, *La Perseveranza* continued its indiscretions and published a rumour that Verdi was to be created a marquis. Verdi promptly begged a friend in the Ministry to use his good offices to avert so unwelcome an honour.

When *Falstaff* set out on its triumphal career through Italy, Verdi followed its fortunes with an eager interest and, indeed, pursued the conductor, Edoardo Mascheroni, with good-humoured sallies. He had borrowed from "Farfarello," as he affectionately called him, the cost of his fare from Rome to Genoa, and chaffed him, with mocking quotations of the laughter of the Merry Wives, about the prospect of losing his hundred lire. Verdi was persuaded to go to Rome for the first performance of the opera in the capital by Boito, who was anxious about its success. He was afraid that in a theatre with such strict academic traditions of elegance and sentimentality, William Shakespeare would be like a bull in a Dresden-china shop. He also feared, contrariwise, that the full-blooded humour of *Falstaff* might be refined away. In the event, the Rome production was a complete success. King Humbert was present at the head of a brilliant audience, and after it was over "Farfarello" and the orchestra serenaded the composer at his hotel with a selection of his music, including the overture from his first success, *Nabucco*.

If the old lion could roar with laughter, he could also still roar with anger in defence of his rights. When there was a question of making cuts in *Falstaff* at the Opéra-Comique, he showed his claws, not for the first time on this same account, and insisted either that the opera should be performed as written or that it should be withdrawn altogether. "I make this formal demand of you," he wrote to Ricordi, "as the publisher and owner of the score. As my friend, I beg you to attend to this matter, for I am not disposed to endure what I regard as an artistic outrage." Needless to say the Opéra-Comique did as it was told, and Verdi actually graced the first performance with his presence.

Generally, the note was more genial, even when his scorn was aroused. His temper mellowed with age. There was more of irony than wrath in his astonished exclamations at the proposal to give *Otello* in Italian at the Paris Opéra. Writing in French to the director, he declared that he was unable to reconcile the idea of an Italian work with the Opéra ("your great National Theatre"). If they wanted to give *Otello,* they must give it in French; and he instructed Ricordi in the same sense. The Opéra, too, bowed to the imperious will, and was rewarded for its obedience with a simplified version of the finale to Act III, the original being too complicated for the Parisian chorus, and the ballet music to which reference has already been made. The Opéra wanted something to offset the attraction of the production of *Falstaff* at the Opéra-Comique, and both operas were given for the first time in Paris during the season of 1894.*

The following extracts from the letter-book of this period are characteristic:

To the president of a committee for the celebration of the twentieth anniversary of the liberation of Rome:

In my youth I could never write music for poems, hymns, and so forth on some particular occasion, though I did write a cantata in 1861 or 62 for an exhibition in London—and wrote it badly!

---

* There had been talk of producing *Otello* at the Opéra three years before, but Verdi objected that he "did not see the right person" to sing the title-part. Marchesi had written to suggest that his wife's most famous pupil, Nellie Melba, who had lately made her brilliant debut as Gilda, should visit the composer in order to study the part of Desdemona with him. Verdi received the suggestion coldly and expressed his usual dislike of the discussion of his affairs by third parties. "I do not like people talking of my concerns before the time has come. Oh! this publicity! I hate it."

Now my pen is dry, and I could not possibly write anything worthy of the high solemnity and of the really splendid poem by Carducci.

To a German publisher:

Never, never will I write my memoirs!

It is quite enough for the musical world that it should have had to put up with my music for all these years! Never will I condemn it to read my prose!

To Mascheroni, on various occasions:

I have had no letter from you from Vienna. The last was dated 12th May [1893] from Trieste. Since then I have had no news of *Falstaff;* and I am not sorry. From my own annoyance I can picture yours: all the wearisome gossip, the caprices and, you will add, the *villainies!* It is bad, very bad; but do not delude yourself. . . . The theatre is like that, and so it must be. . . .

We are born to suffer! And you believe that it is possible to be a composer or an orchestral conductor without having to eat your heart out every day, a bit at lunch, another helping at dinner—and always a little left over for to-morrow! . . .

"So that's that," as the man said when he had murdered his father! Not that we have murdered anybody; at most, we have flayed the ears of the good public. . . . Anyhow, my compliments to every one, my—what can I say? Well, I shout to you all: Bravo! ladies; bravo! gentlemen, and to yourself: *ten points!*

So ended the tour of *Falstaff,* which had not been without the squabblings and intrigues that seem inseparable from any operatic enterprise. Nor had it been, from the financial point of view, an overwhelming success, and in the letters to Mascheroni there is a reflection of Verdi's disappointment at the falling of the mercury in "that infallible thermometer, the box-office."

Other things increased the natural melancholy of old age, that sees in each farewell a final parting. Verdi was deeply distressed by that sorest affliction of the ageing—the loss, one by one, of his old friends. Emmanuele Muzio, his only pupil and his companion on his first visit to London in the dim past, had died shortly before the production of *Otello.* Faccio was struck down by mental disease during the composition of *Falstaff,* and his condition preoccupied Boito, who took him to Krafft-Ebing's sanatorium at Graz in the vain hope of a cure. The passing of mere acquaintances ("poor Catalani") or total strangers of eminence in the world (like Wagner or Delibes) moved Verdi to sorrow. Then, in November 1897, the closest and dearest of them all left him.

Giuseppina had been ailing for some time, but she herself thought her illness no worse than a cold, whose most annoying symptom was that it deprived her of enjoying the scent of the flowers Verdi brought her. He bore her death with courage, but in silence. He could not bring himself to speak of the partner of his whole working life, who had encouraged his youthful efforts and advised him about his business even before friendship ripened into love. She had watched over his health, borne with his waspish irritability which could make him an exacting companion when he was in the throes of composition, and, for all that these moments of exasperation sometimes made her wish that he might never write another opera, never failed to stimulate and support him in each new venture. She showed neither jealousy nor ill will towards the women, chief among them Teresa Stolz, who were on terms of intimate friendship with her husband, and the fact that she had no cause for jealousy does not detract from the virtue. At the same time she was no "doormat," no meek Egeria content to be the mute inspiration of her husband's muse; she was a woman of spirit and character and wit. The gracious sweetness of her mind and her sense of fun are the traits that most impress the reader of her letters.

It is not surprising that her death shattered the health of a man so sensitive to loss as Verdi. The almost undiminished vigour of his mind gave way under the shock to a pathetic senility. He wandered from room to room, complaining that "Peppina" was gone. Yet, even so, though his heart became affected at this time, his physical strength carried him on through three more years of ebbing vitality.

D. H.

The cast of the world *première* of *Falstaff* included besides Maurel, Emma Zilli as Mrs. Ford, Virginia Guerrini as Mrs. Page, Adelina Stehle as Anne, Giuseppina Pasqua as Dame Quickly, Edoardo Garbin as Fenton, and Antonio Pini-Corsi as Ford. The conductor was Edoardo Mascheroni.

Falstaff was introduced to South America at Buenos Aires July 9, 1893; to North America at the Metropolitan Opera House, New York, Feb. 4, 1895. Maurel's presence at the Metropolitan gave special distinction to an extraordinary cast which could boast also Emma Eames (Mrs. Ford), Jane de Vigne (Mrs. Page), Zélie de Lussan (Anne), Sofia Scalchi (Dame Quickly), Giuseppe Russitano (Fenton), and Giuseppe Campanari (Ford). Luigi Mancinelli conducted. There were five performances of the work at the Metropolitan that season.

The following season it was presented again four times, now with Mme. Kitzu as Mrs. Page, Lola Beeth as Anne, and Giuseppe Cremonini as Fenton, and the rest as before.

Falstaff was next heard in New York when Giulio Gatti-Casazza revived it at the Metropolitan March 20, 1909, under the direction of Arturo Toscanini. Antonio Scotti appeared as Sir John, and his chief associates were Emmy Destinn, Maria Ranzenberg, Frances Alda, Maria Gay, Rinaldo Grassi, and Campanari. The next season Jeanne Maubourg succeeded to the role of Mrs. Page, Louise Homer to that of Dame Quickly, Edmond Clément to that of Fenton, and Antonio Pini-Corsi to his original role of Ford.

Falstaff then lapsed from the repertory until Mr. Gatti-Casazza revived it again Jan. 2, 1925, with Tullio Serafin as conductor and Scotti, Lucrezia Bori, Kathleen Howard, Mme. Alda, Marion Telva, Beniamino Gigli, and Lawrence Tibbett in the leading parts. The evening was notable in particular for an ovation accorded Mr. Tibbett after the first scene of Act II which made him overnight a national figure. With the six performances of that season *Falstaff* again disappeared from the New York stage.

Meanwhile, at the Lexington Theater, the visiting Chicago company had given *Falstaff* a single presentation, Feb. 6, 1920. Giacomo Rimini essayed Falstaff. With him were Rosa Raisa, Irene Pavloska, Myrna Sharlow, Maria Claessens, Tito Schipa, and Désiré Defrère. Gino Marinuzzi conducted.

The language of all the aforesaid performances was Italian. On Feb. 1, 1935, at the Philadelphia Academy of Music, *Falstaff* was presented in English in the course of the Philadelphia Orchestra's operatic series. The text used was the translation made by Charles Henry Meltzer and revised by Fritz Reiner, the conductor.

P. S.

Richard Wagner

(Leipzig, May 22, 1813–Feb. 13, 1883, Venice)

If it is difficult to determine which was the dominant bent of Wagner's genius—the musical, the dramatic, or the poetico-picturesque—one can hardly escape recognizing the dominant trait of his character to have been combative energy. He was a born fighter; with his well-nigh excessive craving for human sympathy, his character was distinctly militant. Adverse criticism hurt him sorely; it seemed to him a wanton refusal of that sympathy which, his whole nature told him, he had a right to demand of the world. But it spurred him on, was the stimulant which his militant genius most needed. Indeed, one can hardly help suspecting that the opposition he met with during the better part of his life may have been for something in shaping his work, and that much therein might have been different without it. He was not in the least an intellectual hermit, could not live happily out of communion with the rest of mankind. Not that his thirst for sympathy ever led him to alter his course by an iota for the sake of winning it—there was not a grain of diplomacy in his composition, and he carried firmness to the pitch of obstinacy—but that, he looking instinctively upon sympathy as his natural right, it set his moral teeth on edge to find that, where he had asked for bread, he was offered a stone. He found the whole world out of joint, and was fully persuaded that he was the predestined man to set it right. Opposition was but fuel to his energy. With every successive work he brought forth, he seemed to say to the world: You found that, in my last work, I had gone too far in my chosen direction; well, here you will see that I have gone still farther!

W. F. A.

The life of Richard Wagner was a continuous and undaunted struggle for the attainment of one objective: a fusion of dramatic poetry and music into an artistic whole—the music-drama. Wagner's convictions on the application of music to the drama amounted almost to an obsession. This monomania drove him relentlessly forward to the composition of gigantic operatic works which, judged by the standards of the period, possessed no possibilities whatever of being performed. Wagner's works, literary as well as musical, stirred up a hornet's nest of discussion and engendered violent displays of partisanship. No other composer was so enthusiastically praised or so bitterly condemned during his lifetime. In the face of all this, Wagner not only completed a great series of music-dramas, but also built a theater to be devoted exclusively to their production. Grandiose as Wagner's conceptions were, all were successfully realized on the operatic stages of Europe during his lifetime. The music-dramas are now the very foundation of the operatic repertory, and excerpts from them are among the works most frequently performed at orchestral concerts.

Wilhelm Richard Wagner . . . was the ninth child of Friedrich Wagner, a clerk in the local police court. Wagner's father had shown some dramatic inclinations, and a brother and two sisters were actively engaged on the stage during his youth. The father died not long after Wagner's birth, and in the same year the widow married Ludwig Geyer, an artistically-minded individual, gifted not only as an actor but also as a painter and a dramatist. Wagner's youth was spent in Dresden, where he conceived an intense admiration for the local Kapellmeister, Carl Maria von Weber, and his works. He had as yet not demonstrated any strong musical bent; as a student his interests were predominantly literary, and before his fifteenth birthday he had made some translations from Homer and had written a tragedy, modeled largely after Shakespeare. Piano studies were pursued with much indifference. Wagner, like Berlioz, was not an instrumental virtuoso; nevertheless, he possessed in later years a pianistic ability adequate for the performance of extracts from his own works in the privacy of his home.

In 1827 the family, which had again been left fatherless, returned to Leipzig. Wagner's conversion to music dates from the following year, when he heard a Beethoven symphony, the Seventh, for the first time. He at once borrowed a textbook of harmony from a local lending library, neglected school, and devoted himself avidly to rather amateurish efforts at composition. An eccentric "Concert-Overture," played in 1830 at a concert given in the Leipzig Theater, was his first composition to be given a public performance. In 1831 he enrolled as a *studiosus musicae* at the University of Leipzig and for some time gave himself over to the excesses in which students of the time were prone to indulge. But his stay at the university was soon terminated in favor of his all-absorbing interest in music.

Wagner now placed himself under the tutelage of an able theorist, Christian Theodor Weinlig, who as Cantor of St. Thomas' Church occupied the position which had been held by Johann Sebastian Bach in the previous century. Wagner was subjected to a severe contrapuntal discipline by Weinlig, who at the end of six months dismissed him with the remark that he had nothing more to impart to him. The compositions of this period of Wagner's life were almost entirely instrumental works of a not particularly promising nature.

Wagner's active musical career commenced in 1833 when he became chorus master at the opera theater at Würzburg. Subsequently he directed operatic performances at Magdeburg and at Königsberg, where in 1836 he married the actress Minna Planer. In the following year Wagner and his wife journeyed to the distant city of Riga (then in Russia), where he became Kapellmeister at the German Theater. Here he composed the first two acts of his first important opera, *Rienzi,* whose libretto he had adapted from the novel of Bulwer-Lytton. But Wagner was forced to flee from Riga because of the huge burden of debt which his extravagances had incurred. This unfortunate habit of continually accumulating debts that he could not possibly ever repay persisted throughout his lifetime.

The harassed Kapellmeister and his wife took passage on a small sailing vessel bound for London; but the boat was blown far off its course by storms, and the voyage which normally consumed eight days lasted for three and one half weeks. Episodes on this journey later found their way into *Der Fliegende Holländer* (The Flying Dutchman). The pair stayed in London for only a brief period and then headed directly for Paris, where Wagner hoped to make a name for himself in what was then the center of the operatic world. He was unsuccessful in his plans, however, and for two and one half years he earned a miserable living by journalistic hack writing and such lowly musical tasks as arranging operatic tunes for cornet and piano. While in Paris he completed *Rienzi* and *Der Fliegende Holländer. Rienzi* was accepted for performance by the Dresden opera in 1841, and the composer returned to Germany to supervise its production (October 20, 1842). The work was a great success, and in the following year Wagner was appointed to the comparatively well-paid post of Kapellmeister at Dresden. Here he gave fine performances of the operas of Mozart and Gluck. In 1846 he conducted what was to all intents and purposes a "revival" of the Ninth Symphony of Beethoven, the result of which was to restore to an important place in the repertory what had been a neglected and undervalued work. The operas *Tannhäuser* and *Lohengrin* were composed at Dresden, the former being performed in 1845. Wagner, despite the fact that he was a Royal Kapellmeister, had taken an important part in the political agitation then current in Dresden, and when the popular unrest broke out in street riots, a warrant was issued for his arrest. He fled in 1849, taking refuge for a few days with Liszt at Weimar and eventually making his way over the border into Switzerland.

For the next eleven years Wagner was an exile from his native land. He settled in Zurich where his principal activity for the first few years was the writing of his great theoretical treatise "Oper und Drama" (Opera and Drama), completed in 1851, and the composition of the dramatic poem "Der Ring des Nibelungen" (The Ring of the Nibelungen), which was to be the libretto for the cycle of four operas of the same name. The poem was finished and privately printed in 1852. The musical setting of it was begun in 1853, after a period of six years in which Wagner had written only a very small amount of music, and during which his style had undergone a complete metamorphosis. *Das Rheingold,* the first opera of the *Ring* cycle, was finished in 1854 and *Die Walküre,* the second, in 1856.

About this time Wagner became intimate with Mathilde Wesendonk, the wife of a wealthy Swiss merchant. In 1857 he was forced to cease work on

Siegfried because of straitened finances. He now turned to the composition of what he naïvely believed would be a "simple" opera, easy to perform and consequently financially remunerative. The "simple" opera turned out to be one of his most difficult works—*Tristan und Isolde,* finished in 1859 and not performed until 1865. *Tristan und Isolde* was in many respects the direct result of his hopeless love for Mathilde Wesendonk. His relationship with Frau Wesendonk served to accelerate what had been going on for years—his drifting away from his wife Minna. They separated in 1861 after twenty-five years of a union in which neither had found happiness. *Tristan und Isolde* was followed by the great comic opera, *Die Meistersinger von Nürnberg* (The Mastersingers of Nuremberg), which was commenced in 1861 but was not completed until 1867. In the interim he had, in 1861, revised and added a scene to *Tannhäuser* for a performance of the work in Paris. After six months of heart-breaking rehearsals, the revised opera was finally given three presentations at which the fashionable members of the Jockey Club, incensed because Wagner had not written a second-act ballet, created so much disturbance that the work was withdrawn. His enforced exile from Germany was terminated in 1860 when he received a partial amnesty which excluded him from Saxony only. This restriction was removed two years later.

The long series of disappointments which had been Wagner's fate since his flight from Dresden came to an end when Ludwig II, the young King of Bavaria, became interested in him after hearing a performance of *Lohengrin.* In 1864 he dispatched a messenger to find Wagner and bring him to Munich. Ludwig now took him under his protection, and for a long time supplied him with funds. Cabals were formed against Wagner in Munich, and as the result of much criticism of the King's partiality to him, he withdrew to Switzerland. But the King's interest, both financial and artistic, served to sustain him for many years.

From the year 1864 dates also the beginning of Wagner's relationship with the daughter of Franz Liszt, Cosima Liszt von Bülow, then the wife of the celebrated pianist-conductor Hans von Bülow. In 1866 Cosima left von Bülow to live with Wagner at Triebschen on Lake Lucerne. They were married in July, 1870. Three children had already been born to them, the youngest a son, Siegfried. Wagner's conduct with Cosima for a long time estranged him from his father-in-law and best friend, Liszt, and also caused an abatement of the King's interest in him. In his new-found happiness Wagner completed *Die Meistersinger von Nürnberg* and turned again to the long-neglected *Siegfried.* It was not until 1874 that the composition of the music for *Der Ring des Nibelungen* was brought to an end with the completion of *Götterdämmerung* (The Twilight of the Gods).

From the commencement of his labors on *Der Ring des Nibelungen* Wagner had been convinced that it could not be mounted in any of the theaters of Europe. At first he planned to erect a theater for the performance of the Ring operas in Zurich; at another time he mentioned locating it on the banks of the Rhine. The contact with King Ludwig resulted in the drawing up of plans for a festival theater to be erected in Munich, but these were abandoned when the popular opposition to Wagner's presence at the Bavarian Court caused his withdrawal to Switzerland. In 1871 Wagner decided to build his own theater at Bayreuth, a small Bavarian town centrally located in Germany, yet far enough away from a city and in the heart of a beautiful countryside. To raise the necessary funds, Wagner Societies were established in the principal cities of Germany and even in London and New York. The cornerstone of the Festspielhaus was laid in 1872 on Wagner's fifty-ninth birthday, and the event was celebrated by a magnificent performance of Beethoven's Ninth Symphony with Wagner conducting. After herculean labors on the part of all concerned, the theater was opened to the public on August 13, 1876, and *Der Ring des Nibelungen* was performed on four nights (August 13, 14, 16, 17) before a distinguished audience. While the first festival was an unqualified artistic success, the financial results were disappointing, and the season ended with a large deficit.

A desire to wipe out this deficit was responsible for Wagner's journey to London in the following year. Here he directed eight concerts comprising extracts from his operas. His works met with an enthusiastic response, but the expenses were large and the profits small. Shortly after his return to the Continent Wagner finished the poem of his last opera, *Parsifal*. This work was completed in January, 1882, and Bayreuth reopened its doors for the première in July of the same year. At the same time an excellent travelling company under the impresario Angelo Neumann was busy performing *Der Ring des Nibelungen* in the principal German cities. Audiences flocked to the presentations, and Wagner's name was on every tongue. The composer's success was now complete, but the exertions attendant upon the mounting of *Parsifal* at Bayreuth had seriously undermined his health. He died in Venice in February, 1883, and was buried in the garden of his villa "Wahnfried" in Bayreuth.

It is doubtful if the personality of any other artist rivalled in complexity that of Richard Wagner, yet probably no other artist has so completely revealed himself. Wagner left no stone unturned in the expression of his ideas. Not only did he write the text and the music for thirteen operas, but he also penned ten volumes of prose, including wordy essays on many non-musical topics, and approximately six thousand letters. At social gatherings it was always Wagner who monopolized the conversation. Unlike Liszt, he was not particularly interested in the music of other composers, and he continually imposed upon such of his friends as were willing to put up with his demands. In short, he rode roughshod over everyone without feeling any qualms of conscience. But this cannot be attributed to vanity or conceit. It was, rather, the result of a limitless faith in himself and in his ideas, which would brook no opposition. This faith, which did not disdain to sacrifice the careers of others for the attainment of its own selfish purposes, also brought Wagner to create gigantic masterworks at a time when his cause seemed almost hopeless. Even when he was a young man he was convinced that he would become a person of importance. In 1835, when he was only twenty-two years old and still a fledgling operatic conductor, he commenced to keep careful notes for his autobiography.

The Fates were kind to Wagner and granted him a long life; he died a few months before his seventieth birthday. Yet he was never in perfect health, and suffered from various stomach disorders and painful facial eruptions. The life and the works of Wagner constitute a phenomenon so unusual and so provocative that more books have been written about him than about almost any other creative artist. He was, beyond doubt, one of the most important characters of the nineteenth century and one whose influence made itself felt in many non-musical fields.

M. B.

Rienzi, der Letzte der Tribunen

[Rienzi, The Last of the Tribunes]

OPERA IN 5 ACTS

Book by the COMPOSER

First performance: Hoftheater, Dresden, Oct. 20, 1842

CHARACTERS

Cola di Rienzi, last of the Roman
   Tribunes, TENOR
Irene, his sister, SOPRANO
Stefano Colonna, Head of the House of
   Colonna, BASS
Adriano, his son, MEZZO-SOPRANO

Paolo Orsini, head of the House of
   Orsini, BASS
Raimondo, Papal legate, BASS
Baroncello, citizen of Rome, TENOR
Cecco, citizen of Rome, BASS
A Messenger of Peace, SOPRANO

The action takes place in Rome during the fourteenth century

Based on the character of Rienzi, the Roman tribune of the fourteenth century, this is the story of the abduction of Irene, sister of Cola di Rienzi. Paolo Orsini, a noble, has captured her. His right to her is contested by Steffano Colonna. Adriano, Colonna's son, protects Irene from the warring factions. When Rienzi decides to overthrow the nobles and save the people, Adriano gives him his support. When this is an accomplished fact the nobles come to the Capitol to submit to his rule. Adriano is convinced that foul work is afoot, and warns Rienzi who prepares himself so that, when Orsini leaps upon him with a dagger, hidden armour protects him. Adriano's pleas for the release of his father, after all the nobles have been condemned to death, leads Rienzi to free them all. The nobles immediately betray their pardon, and battle the people. They are defeated, but Adriano's father, Colonna, is killed. Adriano serves warrant on Rienzi that the death must be avenged. Rienzi is Coronated and, almost immediately, it is rumoured that he is a partisan of the Emperor's. Adriano tries to assassinate him and, unsuccessful, goes to Irene and tells her of the danger Rienzi is in. He asks her to flee with him but she won't. She goes to the Capitol, and finds Rienzi in prayer. He pleads with her to leave with Adriano. She will not go, but stays with her brother in the Capitol, perishing with him. Adriano, who wants to be with her, dies in the flames trying to get to her.

THE EARLY OPERAS AND "RIENZI"

Wagner's first three operas belonged to his twenties. In none of them is the true Wagner more than vaguely and fleetingly foreshadowed, though in each of them there are intimations of what was to come. The music of his first completed opera,* *Die Feen* (The Fairies), was begun in 1832 or 1833, and finished in 1834, when he was twenty-one. It was never given in Wagner's lifetime. Its first performance took place five years after his death—at Munich, June 29, 1888; and during the next decade it had as many as seventy performances there.†

Wagner has left us his own account, in "A Communication to My Friends," written in later years, of the composition of the ingenuous opus.

"On the model of one of Gozzi's fairy tales ('La Donna Serpente')," he says, "I wrote for myself an opera text, in verse, *Die Feen*. The then predominant 'romantic' opera of Weber, and also of Marschner—who about this time made his first appearance on the scene, and that at my place of sojourn, Leipzig—determined me to follow in their footsteps. What I turned out for myself was nothing more than barely what I wanted, namely, an opera text. This I set to music, according to the impressions made upon me by Weber, Beethoven, and Marschner. However, what took my fancy in the tale of Gozzi was not merely its adaptability for an opera text, but the fascination of the subject itself: a fairy, who renounces immortality for the sake of a human lover, can become a mortal only through the fulfillment of certain difficult conditions, the non-compliance wherewith on the part of her earthly swain threatens her with the direst penalties. Her lover fails in the test, which consists in this: that however evil and repulsive she may appear to him (in an obligatory metamorphosis), he shall not reject her in his unbelief. In Gozzi's tale the fairy is now changed into a snake; the remorseful lover frees her from the spell by kissing the snake; thus he wins her for his wife. I altered this dénouement by changing the fairy into a stone and then releasing her from the spell by her lover's passionate song; while the lover—instead of being allowed to carry off the bride into his own country—is himself admitted by the fairy king to the immortal bliss of Fairyland, together with his fairy wife."

Wagner's lifelong preoccupation with the idea of redemption is indicated in *Die Feen;* and in the music there are foreshadowings of his subsequent works, half amusing, half startling—prophecies of the Wagner of *Tannhäuser, Lohengrin, Die Walküre,* even of the far-off *Tristan.* The music has charm and address. It is both juvenile and surprisingly mature, with flashes of arresting insight and impressive skill.

* Wagner's first attempt at an opera, which was to be a tragedy, *Die Hochzeit* (The Wedding), never got beyond a few fragments, composed and scored in 1832–33—an orchestral introduction, a chorus, and a septet. The fragments were published, in full score, in the "Gesamtausgabe" by Breitkopf and Härtel in 1912.

† *Die Feen* was revived in an elaborate production at the Württemberger Landestheater, Stuttgart, in the season of 1932–33, as part of a complete cycle of Wagner's stage-works given in commemoration of the fiftieth anniversary of his death; and on that occasion it was enthusiastically received. The Overture was performed in New York at concerts of the Philharmonic Society in 1915–16, and has since been repeated.

Wagner's second opera, *Das Liebesverbot* (The Ban on Love), was written between 1834 and 1836. Its subject, "transformed pretty freely," as Wagner puts it, was taken from Shakespeare's "Measure for Measure." It was meant, he says, as a protest "against puritanical hypocrisy," and "tended boldly to exalt unrestrained sensuality." It was produced at Magdeburg, March 29, 1836, under Wagner's direction. Inadequately prepared, the result was a dismal fiasco. The music remained in manuscript for eighty-seven years after it was written. The vocal and orchestral scores were published in 1922–23. In the latter year the opera was resurrected at Munich.

Wagner gave the score to King Ludwig II in 1866, proffering it, with a plea for indulgence, as a "youthful sin." For his patterns in composing the music he had turned from the German romantic composers to the more frivolous Italian and French opera of his time. His command of that style is sure and effective. The music is often delightful in its unpretentious and light-hearted way. It is astonishingly skillful; it has charm and wit and sprightliness and gusto. Some of its qualities are attributable to Wagner's models for the work—Donizetti and Auber, Bellini and Rossini. But that is of no great consequence, for Wagner puts something of his own unmistakable stamp upon them all. And we are not allowed to forget that a greater master is in the offing. Not only does the score include a theme that Wagner was afterward to use in *Tannhäuser* (the so-called Pardon motive), but the faint, far rumors of an unimaginable later music are audible at times in measures that sound like tentative experiments in the idiom of *Tristan,* and even of *Parsifal.*

Das Liebesverbot has been too summarily rejected by those who were impressed, not unnaturally, by Wagner's own disparagement of it. The work calls for reëxamination. One would like to hear it tried out in America. After all, a novelty by Wagner would be an engaging experience—even if it were not another *Meistersinger.*

It is not *Das Liebesverbot* that is Wagner's "youthful sin," but *Rienzi,* the third of the three works of his young manhood that preceded *The Flying Dutchman* (it was begun at Riga in 1838 and completed at Paris in the Autumn of 1840, in Wagner's twenty-eighth year). Over this Brobdingnagian setting of Bulwer-Lytton's historical novel, the loyal Wagnerian is tempted to draw the veil of sorrowful silence. This all-too-faithful imitation of the Parisian "grand opera," this swollen, pretentious blend of banality and bombast, is a sore trial for lovers of the godlike Wagner of the greater works.

Wagner says in his "Communication to My Friends" that at the time of conceiving *Rienzi* he desired to satisfy

an eager longing to begin something on a grand and inspiring scale. . . . This mood was fed and fostered by my reading Bulwer's *Rienzi*. From the misery of modern private life, whence I could nowhere glean the scantiest stuff for artistic treatment, I was borne away by the picture of a great historico-political event. . . .

In accordance with my particular artistic bent, however, I still kept more or less to the purely musical, or rather operatic standpoint. This Rienzi, with great thoughts in his head, great feelings in his heart, amid an entourage of coarseness and vulgarity, set all my nerves aquivering with sympathy and love. Yet my plan for an art-work based thereon sprang first from the perception of a purely lyric element in the hero's atmosphere. The "Messengers of Peace," the Church's summons to awake, the Battle-Hymns—these were what impelled me to the opera *Rienzi*.

Writing in the same "Communication," however, Wagner, with truly heroic candor and just a touch of inconsistency, says that in the preparation of this text he

took no thought for anything but the writing of an effective operatic libretto. The "Grand Opera," with all its scenic and musical display, its sensationalism and its massive vehemence, loomed large before me; and not merely to copy it, but, with reckless extravagance, to outbid it in every detail, became the object of my artistic ambition. However [he adds], I should be unjust to myself did I represent this ambition as my only motive for the conception and execution of my *Rienzi*. The subject really aroused my enthusiasm, and I put nothing into my sketch which had not a direct bearing on the grounds of this enthusiasm. My chief concern was Rienzi himself; and only when I felt quite contented with him did I give rein to the idea of a "grand opera." Nevertheless, from a purely artistic point of view, this "grand opera" was the pair of spectacles through which I unconsciously regarded my material. . . . I always fixed my gaze upon the material itself, and did not keep my eye open for certain ready-made effects which I might wish to father on it by hook or crook; only, I saw it in no other light than that of a five-act opera, with five brilliant finales, and filled with hymns, processions, and the musical clash of arms.

It is not impossible that Wagner, when he penned this mixture of confession and attempted self-vindication, was troubled by a guilty conscience. However that may be, *Rienzi*, as it survives for us, scarcely justifies Wagner's assertion that he was inspired by the historic character who is its central figure. This operatic hero of Wagner's is far from the authentic Rienzi—Rienzi the visionary, the dreamer, the lover of "sacred Italy," the warrior and the man of peace. The downfall of Wagner's Rienzi is brought about externally and melodramatically, by the machinations of his enemies and the treachery and instability of his former friends. The real Rienzi came to a more tragic and ironic end. "We are betrayed," said Meredith, "by what is false within." And that was Rienzi's tragedy. His head was turned by his success. He abandoned his lofty dreams, became gross and shifty and time-serving.

This human, tragical, and wholly credible figure was whitewashed and sentimentalized by that dubious young man, the Wagner of 1838–40. Rienzi is a lay figure in the opera, stuffed with sawdust and Meyerbeer, and tailored by Spontini. Studying this lamentable production, it is hard to avoid the conclusion that Wagner, despite his later attempts at self-justification, was deliberately trying, in his own words, to "outbid with reckless extravagance" the Parisian Grand Opera at its worst and most profitable. The poverty-stricken composer had his eye on Paris, that potential operatic gold-mine for all those who could qualify (had not Meyerbeer banked 300,000 francs by *Les Huguenots?*). In *Rienzi* we have the marketable thing in its perfection, with its clamor and glare and fustian, its orgy of choruses, grand marches, grand airs, duos, trios, ballets, heaven-storming finales; its blaring, incontinent trumpets; its festal processions and ecclesiastical pomp.*

And this was all, in the outcome, that the tragedy of Rienzi apparently meant to Wagner.

There is no denying the crude vigor of the music; and it has something of that quality which Wagner always possessed, the quality of salient invention. The musical ideas that he was willing to put on paper in his early manhood were often harrowing; but one remembers them. Take, for example, the Prayer theme from *Rienzi*. It is not a theme that even the most indulgent would call distinguished; yet it sticks in the mind; one wishes it would not.

L. G.

The American *première* of *Rienzi* took place at the New York Academy of Music March 4, 1878, in German. Charles R. Adams was the Rienzi, Eugenie Pappenheim the Adriano, Miss Human the Irene. Max Maretzek conducted. Likewise in German, the work entered the repertory of the Metropolitan Opera House, New York, Feb. 5, 1886, with Eloi Sylva in the name part, Marianne Brandt as Adriano, and Lilli Lehmann as Irene. Anton Seidl conducted. In the course of that season and the next and the third following *Rienzi* attained thirteen performances at the Metropolitan, the last of them occurring Feb. 26, 1890, when, with Walter Damrosch at the baton, it led off a Wagner "cyclus." The chief singers were Julius Perotti (Rienzi), Luise Meisslinger (Adriano), and Sophie Traubmann (Irene).

The only subsequent performance in New York, apparently, was given by the Wagnerian Opera Company at the Manhattan Opera House Dec. 26, 1923. Eduard Mörike conducted, and the cast included Heinrich Knote (Rienzi), Ottilie Metzger (Adriano), Luise Perard (Irene), and Editha Fleischer (the Messenger of Peace).

---

* But though *Rienzi* had been intended for Paris, Wagner came to realize that there was no immediate hope of its production there. "I decided," he wrote, "to complete it in German with a view to a German theatre, and I selected Dresden." *Rienzi* was given at Dresden, with enormous success, on October 20, 1842.

Der Fliegende Holländer

[The Flying Dutchman]

ROMANTIC OPERA IN 3 ACTS

Book by the COMPOSER

First performance: Hoftheater, Dresden, Jan. 2, 1843

CHARACTERS

Daland, a Norwegian sea captain, BASS

The Dutchman, BARITONE

Eric, a huntsman, a lover of Senta, TENOR

Daland's Steersman, TENOR

Senta, daughter of Daland, SOPRANO

Mary, Senta's nurse, CONTRALTO

Sailors, Maidens, Hunters, and Villagers

The action takes place in a Norwegian village in the eighteenth century

While the storm rages off the Norse coast, Daland's ship has hove to in the cove. He waits for fair weather to go ashore to his daughter Senta. Captain and crew are below, the boy at the wheel asleep when—with blood-red sails, black masts and spectral crew—the phantom ship, the *Flying Dutchman,* drops anchor beside the Norwegian fishing bark. Seven years have passed since the Dutchman has set foot on land. Again he has his chance to find a woman who, sacrificing herself, will free him from his curse. As the Dutchman despairs and, aboard Daland's ship, to which he has been rowed, longs for the Day of Judgment, Daland mentions Senta's name. He is willing to sell his daughter for the gold which fills the phantom ship, and the wind having shifted, the two are rowed ashore.

In Daland's home Senta is spinning (singing her famous ballad, the "Spinning Song"). But her thoughts are with the Dutchman whose picture hangs on the wall; on his vow by all the devils of hell to double the Cape of Good Hope though he sail till Doomsday, and of God's curse which makes him roam the seas till he finds a woman who will die to save him. Senta prays heaven to pity the unfortunate man. The huntsman Eric, Senta's lover, rebukes and leaves her, only to clear the way for the Dutchman himself, who comes in with Daland. When her father leaves the room the wanderer asks Senta to marry him. He is the hero of her dreams, she is his hope of salvation; they love each other at sight. Rejoicing at the prospect of lifting the curse, they plight their vows happily in Daland's presence.

In the bay lie the two vessels. Lights and festivity reign on Daland's ship; from the phantom craft rises a weird sepulchral chant, while blue flames hover on spars and masts. Eric, coming from the house with Senta, falls at the girl's feet and pleads passionately with her to give up the stranger. Senta refuses; she loves none but the Dutchman. The latter has seen Eric kneeling at Senta's feet. He thinks her untrue

606

and rushes aboard his ship, despairing that his curse ever will be raised. Yet as the wind fills the blood-red sails and the phantom ship is about to disappear, Senta proves the greatness of her love. Running to the near-by cliff, she casts herself into the waves, and, as they close about her, the curse is lifted. The phantom ship disappears beneath the water and Senta and the Dutchman, rising to the surface clasped in each other's arms, are transfigured by celestial radiance from the bosom of the sea.

F. H. M.

In his next opera, *Der fliegende Holländer,* he quite abandoned the French model, and turned back to Germany and Weber. To be sure, he gave up spoken dialogue—a far safer experiment in the 'forties than in the 'twenties—but, if there had never been a *Freischütz,* there never would have been a *Holländer.* Yet, notwithstanding the strong Weberish streak in this opera, there is less homogeneity of style in the music than in any other of Wagner's works; beside the Weber influence, there is, at times, distinctly that of French *opéra-comique.* All these borrowings are, however, recognizably coloured with Wagner's own individuality; now and then you even get Wagner pure and simple. Technically speaking, the musical forms are very considerably relaxed; more, upon the whole, than in any opera of Meyerbeer's. The separate numbers are often, so to speak, ravelled out at the ends, that they may be woven together into some semblance of a continuous whole; only a semblance as yet, but Wagner is plainly coming to himself.

W. F. A.

True to a predilection for the legendary, which began early and lasted, Wagner was attracted by the story of the Flying Dutchman, that pale "Ahasuerus of the ocean," who in his ghostly ship, black of mast, blood-red of sail, must voyage the seas over "without aim, without rest, without end." It was Heinrich Heine's version of the legend of the hapless Captain Vanderdecken which provided Wagner with the plot of the opera that was brought out at Dresden on January 2, 1843. But the overmastering impulse to write the opera really came from a sea voyage taken by Wagner himself—by all odds the most hazardous adventure of his diversified career.

Why Wagner took a sea voyage goes back to his early experiences in East Prussia and the Baltic Provinces of Russia. In 1836, when he was twenty-three, he followed the actress Minna Planer to Königsberg in East Prussia and there married her. After a disastrous sojourn, marked by Wagner's piling up debts, as he had a habit of doing wherever he lived, his wife first, and then he, fled to Dresden. In 1837 Wagner went to Riga, then under Russian rule, to be chief conductor at the German theatre. Minna joined him there, and the usual history of an agitated life and mounting debts ensued. The pressure in time became such that there seemed to be no alternative but flight. To

Paris, then the musical capital of Europe, he would go, to Paris where recognition and riches awaited him, and there teach the Germany of his creditors a merited lesson and with his works conquer the world!

First, however, came the sordid and unromantic problem of eluding his Russian creditors. The Cossack-guarded frontier, with its embarrassing ditch to be crossed, has been described as "almost hermetically sealed." Nevertheless, Richard, Minna and their devoted Newfoundland dog Robber survived the perils and hardships and, much the worse for wear, got through into East Prussia. Next came the problem of embarking without a passport in some craft or other en route for France.

At Pillau they were smuggled aboard the *Thetis,* a sailing vessel of no less than 106 tons! Though July was the month, the voyage turned out so stormy that instead of one week it consumed three and a half, and once the captain had to take refuge in the little Norwegian harbor of Sandwike, which Wagner adopted as the roadstead in the first act of *Der fliegende Holländer.*

While in Paris, Wagner, who found the French capital less ready to surrender to his siege than he had naïvely hoped, sketched the libretto for *Der fliegende Holländer* and submitted it to Léon Pillet, the director of the Opéra. Pillet liked it, but instead of commissioning Wagner to work it out and set it to music, he offered to buy it and turn it over to one of the various composers whom he was under agreement to supply with texts.

Wagner, much against his will, sold the sketch to Pillet for the exceedingly modest sum of five hundred francs. The sale of the sketch did not, of course, prevent him from developing his own German libretto for *Der fliegende Holländer* and setting it to music.

Having failed of his objectives in Paris, he returned to Dresden in April, 1842, to seek productions for his operas there. *Rienzi* was given in October; the *Holländer* in January. From the first it was evident that the rôle of the visionary and heroic Senta could not be allotted with confidence to just any prima donna, and the Holländer himself ought to be able to account to eye and ear for Senta's anticipatory fixation.

Wagner was fortunate in having at hand for Senta the great Wilhelmine Schröder-Devrient, but Michael Wächter, the baritone selected for the Holländer, has been described as an obese fellow always at a loss what to do with his awkward arms and legs. At a rehearsal when the heroine was about to implore heaven that she might be the Holländer's redeemer, Schröder-Devrient abruptly interrupted her singing with a despairing whisper to the composer: "How can I say it when I look into those beady eyes? Good God, Wagner, what a mess you have made!"

Der fliegende Holländer did not drop its posers with its first production. When on January 26, 1877, Clara Louise Kellogg, heading her own company, introduced the work to the United States (in an English translation) at the New York Academy of Music, she records in her "Memories of an American

Prima Donna" that to do so was a "tremendous undertaking." The chief case in point was the entrance of the Holländer in Act II:

The music, so far as Siegfried Behrens, my director at the time, and I could see, had no meaning whatever. . . . It was just a long, intermittent mumble. I had not yet been entirely converted to innovations such as this and did not fully appreciate the value of so extreme a pause. . . .

"For heaven's sake, Behrens," said I, "what is the public going to do while we stand there . . . ?"

"Wagner says," he explained, "not to be disturbed by long intervals. If both singers could stand absolutely still, this pause would hold the public double the length of time."

We tried to stand "absolutely still" [Miss Kellogg goes on]. It was an exceedingly difficult thing to do. In rôles that have tense moments the whole body has to hold a tense rigidity until the proper psychological instant for emotional and physical relaxation. The public is very keen to feel this without knowing how or why. A drooping shoulder or a relaxed hand will "let up" an entire situation.

The first time I sang Senta it seemed impossible to hold the pause until those eighteen bars were over. "I have *got* to hold it! I have *got* to hold it!" I kept saying to myself, tightening every muscle as if I were actually pulling a wire stretched between myself and the audience. . . . An inspiration led me to grasp the back of a tall Dutch chair on the stage. That chair helped me greatly, and as affairs turned out I held the audience quite as firmly as the chair! . . .

The Dresden public, which had liked the pomp and spectacle of *Rienzi,* found its successor gloomy and spare. There was a feeling, too, that legendary and supernatural subjects had had their day. Historical opera of the Meyerbeer type, so successfully copied by Wagner in *Rienzi,* was the genre of the hour. There were three more performances of *Der fliegende Holländer* before Schröder-Devrient herself forced it out of currency through celebrating April 1 by retiring from the Dresden company for a year.

The *Holländer* was the first of Wagner's operas to reach England (at Covent Garden, London, in March, 1870, in Italian, with Charles Santley and Ilma di Murska). It was the third of Wagner's operas to reach the United States, having been preceded by *Tannhäuser* and *Lohengrin.* The American *première* took place at the Philadelphia Academy of Music Nov. 8, 1876.

English was the language of the first *Holländer* in New York, at the Academy of Music, Jan. 26, 1877. Clara Louise Kellogg appeared as Senta to the Dutchman of William T. Carleton. In English it also figured in the repertory of the American Opera Company, with William Ludwig as the Dutchman, Helene Hastreiter as Senta, Whitney Mockridge as Erik, and Myron W. Whitney as Daland. Theodore Thomas conducted.

The work entered the repertory of the Metropolitan Opera House, New York, Nov. 27, 1889, in German. Theodor Reichmann sang the Dutchman; Sophie Wiesner, Senta; Paul Kalisch, Erik, and Emil Fischer, Daland. Anton

Seidl conducted, as he did on March 31, 1892, when the *Holländer* was presented in the same theater, in Italian, with Jean Lassalle, Emma Albani, Montariol, and Édouard de Reszké as the chief singers.

In subsequent performances by the Metropolitan company Milka Ternina or Johanna Gadski was the Senta, Theodore Bertram or Adolf Mühlmann the Dutchman, Andreas Dippel the Erik, and Lemprière Pringle or Robert Blass the Daland. Emil Paur or Walter Damrosch conducted. It is also noteworthy that the minor part of Mary was sung by Ernestine Schumann-Heink or Rosa Olitzka. A little earlier David Bispham had been an admired Dutchman with Walter Damrosch's own company.

P. S.

Tannhäuser

ROMANTIC OPERA IN 3 ACTS

Book by the COMPOSER

First performance: Hoftheater, Dresden, Oct. 19, 1845

CHARACTERS

Hermann, Landgrave of Thuringia, BASS
Tannhäuser, a minstrel knight, TENOR
Wolfram von Eschenbach, his friend and
  a minstrel knight, BARITONE
Elisabeth, niece of the Landgrave,
SOPRANO

Venus, SOPRANO or CONTRALTO
Walther von der Vogelweide, TENOR;
  Biterolf, BASS; *Heinrich der Schreiber,*
  TENOR; *Reinmar von Zweter,* BASS;
  minstrel knights
A Young Shepherd, SOPRANO

Thuringian Nobles and Knights, Ladies, Elder and Younger Pilgrims, Sirens, Naiads, Nymphs, Bacchantes

The action takes place in the vicinity of Eisenach at the beginning of the thirteenth century

Tannhäuser, a minstrel and singer, has deserted Wartburg, his native village, for Venusberg, on a near-by hill where the Goddess Venus holds him with her charms. When his desires are satisfied he longs to return to his home. He breaks Venus' hold on him when he mentions the Virgin Mary. He is found on the road by the singers of Wartburg, and his friend Wolfram tells him that Elisabeth, pious niece of Herrmann the Landgrave, loves him. He returns with them to Wartburg to sing in the prize contest. Elisabeth is to grant any wish of the winner. Wolfram sings of ideal love which incenses Tannhäuser who has known the sensual love of Venus. He answers with a hymn to Venus. The others uphold Wolfram, and draw swords on Tannhäuser, but Elisabeth protects him. Her father tells him to join the Pilgrimage to Rome to obtain forgiveness from the Pope. When the Pilgrims return Elisabeth asks for Tannhäuser but he isn't among them. Wolfram realises she is about to die. Tannhäuser comes back without the forgiveness of the Pope and calls for Venus. She appears but Wolfram shows him the funeral train of Elisabeth, and Tannhäuser, overcome, throws himself upon her bier. Messengers arrive from Rome to tell of the Pope's forgiveness, and Tannhäuser dies beside Elisabeth, saved from damnation.

In his next opera, *Tannhäuser,* [Wagner] makes a new experimental throw of the dice. [He] was essentially a man of vast ideas, most comfortably at home in "large frames," as the French say. In *Tannhäuser* we have what is intrinsically a romantic opera masquerading in the guise of Grand Opera; although only in three acts, it is on the largest French scale. Shortly before his death, Wagner called it: *"meine schlechtste Oper* (my worst opera)"; and not wholly without justice. The musical style is more homogeneous than in the *Holländer,* but Weber still stands largely in the foreground. A most strangely transmogrified Weber, however: at times pretty thoroughly Wagnerized, but, for the most part, washed over with a coat of the most bourgeois sort of German thoosy-moosy, redolent of the merely *Bänkelsänger* spirit of men like Franz Abt and F. W. Kücken! Never before nor since did Wagner strike so essentially vulgar a vein of melody. What saves *Tannhäuser* is the beauty of the story, the complete sincerity of the music, and Wagner's unerring dramatic touch—which last he had by nature. The technique, however, is still rather feeble, except in the matter of a skilful handling of material means—the orchestra and choral masses; the score is defaced by some mere school-boy clumsinesses, which were called Wagnerish at the time, but are now seen to be anything but that. Yet in *Tannhäuser* we do descry at times the beginning of Wagner's third manner; developed with no very conspicuous technical skill, but already wiping out all traditional musical forms; here the plastic form of the music is based upon nothing but the dramatic development of the scene.

W. F. A.

Paris played a special and sinister rôle in the career of Richard Wagner. Twice he laid artistic siege to the French capital and twice he withdrew defeated and dismayed. The first attempt occurred when Wagner was a very young man. He was twenty-six when he arrived in Paris in September, 1839.

When he returned to Paris for the second attempt, in September, 1859, he was a different Wagner. This time he had something very definite to offer the Parisian managers and public.

At first the prospects were rosy enough. Now the unknown German musician was become a personage. He had distinguished friends in the artistic world of Paris, and at the court of Napoleon III his cause was urged by men as powerful as the Maréchal Magnan; Count Pourtalès, the Ambassador of Prussia, and Count Paul Hatzfeld, his attaché, and by a woman who surpassed them all in ascendancy, the Princess Metternich, wife of the Ambassador of Austria.

Concerning her Wagner tells us in "My Life": "To the Princess, in particular, people attributed an almost omnipotent influence at the French Imperial Court." One evening at the Tuileries the group around the Emperor happened to be discussing Wagner. The Princess Metternich, joining the group, was asked what she thought. She answered so enthusiastically about *Tannhäuser,* which she had heard at Dresden, that the Emperor immediately promised her it should be staged at the Opéra.

Wagner plunged into the preparations with characteristic fire. He super-vised the translation of the text into French, he proceeded to revise the score, he busied himself with the casting and other matters of production. Besides, there was the crucial question of the ballet. For at that time it was de rigueur that every lyric drama presented at the Opéra should be equipped with a ballet. Now, let us remember that since the initial production of *Tannhäuser* in 1845 Wagner had written not only *Lohengrin,* which had been duly staged, but *Das Rheingold, Die Walküre,* a large part of *Siegfried,* and all of *Tristan und Isolde* as well. Consequently his talent was in its rich maturity, and he saw a splendid opportunity to give it scope in an amplification of the open-ing scene in the Venusberg. And here, of course, was the appropriate place for an elaborate ballet. The result of this strictly logical thinking was the superb "Parisian Bacchanale," which follows immediately on the rising of the curtain, and the more opulent version of the scene between Venus and Tann-häuser that follows.

The defect of this plan was that it ran contrary to the tastes of the Jockey Club. True, the aristocrats composing its membership were in great part bal-letomanes, but they were also devoted to their late and leisurely dinner. It was not their idea at all to hurry to the Opéra, after choking down a hasty meal, in order to see their favorite dancers disport themselves at the very be-ginning of the performance. Oh, no! The ballet should come no earlier than Act II! But they counted without Wagner, who was altogether too thorough and uncompromising an artist to disfigure the Wartburg scene with a pre-posterous interjection of dancing. Consequently, when the time for performance arrived, Wagner found arrayed against him a curious alliance of the "bald-headed row" with musical chauvinists and reactionaries.

The first performance took place on March 13, 1861, without effective hos-tility on the part of the audience. The second performance, on March 18, began most promisingly. The overture, Wagner recounts,

was loudly applauded without a note of opposition. Mme. Tedesco, who had eventually been completely won over to her part of Venus by a wig powdered with gold dust, called out triumphantly to me in the manager's box, when the "septuor" of the finale of the first act was again vigorously applauded, that everything was now all right and that we had won the victory. But when shrill whistling was suddenly heard in the second act, Royer, the manager, turned to me with an air of complete resignation and said, "Ce sont les Jockeys; nous sommes perdus."

It seems that on the initiative of the Emperor negotiations had been carried on with members of the Jockey Club looking to their permitting three per-formances of *Tannhäuser* to take place on the promise that afterwards the opera should be sufficiently shortened to serve as a curtain raiser for an en-suing ballet! The sagacious "Jockeys," however, had refused to agree, believ-ing that Wagner would never consent and fearing that if two more performances should go through without interruption *Tannhäuser* would score such a hit that "the friends of the ballet would be treated to repetitions of this work thirty times running." Accordingly the "Jockeys" were determined to make their protest in time. And the disgraceful riot went on, in spite of the moral support given Wagner by the attitude of Napoleon and Eugénie, "who stoically kept their seats through the uproars of their own courtiers."

At the third performance (on March 24) the "Jockeys" resumed their rioting, "Cheerfully whistling their hunting-tunes and playing their flageolets." In an entr'acte, Wagner records,

one of these gentlemen entered the box of a certain great lady who, in the excess of her anger, introduced him to one of her friends with the words, "C'est un de ces misérables, mon cousin." The young man, completely abashed, answered, "Que voulez-vous? I am beginning to like the music myself. But, you see, a man must keep his word. If you will excuse me, I will return to my work again." He thereupon took his leave.

The comment of the Princess Metternich was withering. To some of her best friends she was quoted as saying: "Away with your free France! In Vienna, where at least there is a genuine aristocracy, it would be unthinkable for a Prince Liechtenstein or Schwarzenberg to scream from his box for a ballet in *Fidelio*."

Although the management had announced a fourth and a fifth performance, they reluctantly allowed Wagner to withdraw his work after the third. Thus subsided the greatest scandal in the history of opera.

At the Dresden *première* of *Tannhäuser* Johanna Wagner, the composer's niece, appeared as Elisabeth, Wilhelmine Schröder-Devrient as Venus, Joseph Aloys Tichatschek as Tannhäuser, Anton Mitterwurzer as Wolfram, and Wilhelm Dettmer as Landgrave Hermann. At the Paris *première* the chief singers were Marie Sax, Fortunata Tedesco, Albert Niemann, Morelli, and Cazaux.

Tannhäuser inaugurated the German regime at the Metropolitan Opera House, New York, Nov. 17, 1884, with Auguste Kraus, Anna Slach, Anton Schott, Adolf Robinson, and Josef Kögel in the leading roles and Leopold Damrosch conducting. Not till Jan. 30, 1889, was the Paris version heard in New York, presented at the Metropolitan with Lilli Lehmann as Venus and Anton Seidl to conduct. A remarkable cast opened a Metropolitan season Nov. 29, 1898. Luigi Mancinelli conducted and the principal roles were allotted to Emma Eames, Lillian Nordica, Ernest van Dyck, Henri Albers, and Pol Plançon.

P. S.

Lohengrin

ROMANTIC OPERA IN 3 ACTS

Book by the Composer

First performance: Hoftheater, Weimar, Germany, Aug. 28, 1850

CHARACTERS

Henry the Fowler, King of Germany, BASS

Lohengrin, a Knight of the Grail, TENOR

Elsa of Brabant, SOPRANO

Frederick of Telramund, Count of Brabant, BARITONE

Ortrud, his wife, CONTRALTO

The King's Herald, BASS

Duke Godfrey, MIME

Saxon, Thuringian, and Brabantian Counts and Nobles, Ladies of Honor, Pages, Attendants

The action takes place at Antwerp during the first half of the tenth century

At Antwerp, Gottfried, the young Duke of Brabant, has disappeared. Count Telramund accuses Elsa, Gottfried's sister, of murdering him. King Henry calls Elsa beneath the oak of justice. Elsa tells of a dream she has had of a knight who will come to protect her, and marry her. Elsa prays, and the boat drawn by a swan appears with the Knight in the prow. He declares himself Elsa's champion on the condition that she never ask his name or origin. He bests Telramund in battle, but spares his life. Telramund and his heathen wife, Ortrud, plan vengeance. As Elsa is entering the church about to marry the Knight Ortrud tells Elsa she should know her husband's name. After the ceremony in the bridal chamber Elsa, her curiosity aroused, asks her husband's name. Telramund enters with drawn sword, and is killed by the Knight. Because of Elsa's question her husband now leaves her, and, before King Henry, he tells his story and that his name is Lohengrin. He kneels to pray, and the swan leading his boat sinks, Gottfried appearing in his place. A dove pilots Lohengrin's boat down the river out of sight as Elsa falls dead in her brother's arms.

———

With *Lohengrin* comes a magnificent change. It is still romantic Opera parading as Grand Opera; but . . . the musical style is distinction itself. Weber almost disappears; what there is left of him is no more than the little occasional touch of Haydn to be found in the works of Beethoven's second period. For the first time, Wagner succeeds in raising his music to the full level of his poetic conception; the vehicle is worthy of the load! The third manner crops up, too, in a far more developed condition in the opening scene of the second act (Ortrud and Telramund on the church steps by night). *Lohengrin* was emphatically Wagner's transition opera; after it, he left the "Opera" entirely for the Music-Drama.

It was *Lohengrin* that fully opened Wagner's eyes to what he wanted. And, now that we have followed him so far in his career, we can see how very purblind his vision in this matter had been. Taking the ground, both by instinct and rational conviction, that the Opera must be primarily a form of Drama, and only secondarily a form of Music, he was some time in discovering the way in which he personally could best make it a worthy form of Drama; *Rienzi,* the *Holländer, Tannhäuser,* and *Lohengrin* were but experiments to this end, and experiments, too, guided by no particularly definite theoretical hypothesis.

W. F. A.

Among the operas *Lohengrin* was Wagner's luck piece. Between 1842 and 1845 *Rienzi, The Flying Dutchman,* and *Tannhäuser* had been produced at Dresden, where Wagner was then conductor at the Court Opera, but it was not until Liszt brought out *Lohengrin* at Weimar on August 28, 1850, that the popularity of Wagner's operas outside of Dresden really began. Nor was the missionary work of *Lohengrin* confined to Central Europe. It was the first Wagnerian opera produced in Italy (Bologna, 1871) and in England (Covent Garden, London, 1875). True, *Tannhäuser* preceded it to the United States and to France, yet it was once more *Lohengrin* (Stadt Theater, New York, 1871; Eden Théâtre, Paris, 1887) that established the composer's stage works in the affections of both countries.

A red-letter night for Wagner in New York witnessed the first all-star production of one of his operas, *Lohengrin* again, at the old Academy of Music on March 23, 1874. A fabulous array of artists included Christine Nilsson, dubbed "the second Swedish Nightingale," as Elsa; the American Annie Louise Cary, one of the foremost contraltos of her time, as Ortrud, and three celebrated Italians, Campanini, tenor, Del Puente, baritone, and Nannetti, bass, as Lohengrin, Telramund, and King Henry, respectively. Naturally enough, the language was Italian, as it was nine years later in the Metropolitan's first *Lohengrin.*

Strange as it may seem, the early days of this opera were troublous. It was during a holiday at Marienbad in the summer of 1845 that Wagner shelved the subject of *Die Meistersinger von Nürnberg* in favor of *Lohengrin* and began work on the libretto. The following November he read the completed poem to a group of his friends in Dresden. They seem to have received it with faint praise, and none of them, especially Robert Schumann, could imagine it set to music. Hermann Franck even suggested that a happy ending would help the work, and it seems that Wagner actually considered a change which would send Elsa away with Lohengrin. This, however, was effectively opposed by the wise and cultivated Frau Lüttichau, wife of the Intendant at Dresden.

When it came to composing the music Wagner, surprising as it may appear to us, worked backwards. It seems that in spite of Frau Lüttichau's emphatic stand he remained somewhat disturbed about the ending of his opera, so he wrote the music for the last act first to set his doubts at rest. The first and the second acts followed, and the famous prelude, depicting the descent of the Holy Grail, was done last. The entire work, including the scoring, was finished in March, 1848. Yet, only one stage of the troubles was thus ended. Now came the question of a production.

Though three of Wagner's operas had been brought out in Dresden and he himself was still one of the Court conductors, *Lohengrin* in December, 1848, was refused a production at the Court Opera. Revolution was then in the air. Wagner sympathized with the revolutionists and the following May found himself forced to flee from German soil. He took refuge in Switzerland, but that country offered no opportunity for the production of his new opera. He had dreams of a French production in Paris, of an English production in London, which came to nothing. It is interesting to know, however, that immediately after leaving Dresden he wrote to Eduard Devrient in the Saxon capital:

My immediate object is to get my latest opera *Lohengrin* translated into English and first performed in London. Let us suppose that the present storm will pass and that I shall probably soon appear far less deeply compromised politically than is the case at the moment—then why should an artistic institution of Dresden dismiss me finally, pending a time when it may very likely contribute to its honour that one of its members should have won fame in the greatest cities of the world? I at least with my whole heart offer Dresden my hand on it to return later, and I think the latter would not have to regret having accepted that hand.

At length his friend and champion, Liszt, who was Kapellmeister at Weimar, undertook to stage *Lohengrin* in that small capital of a great artistic tradition. Liszt saw to it that a distinguished audience gathered for the event. Still, in spite of his best efforts there was some boredom because the opera ran from 6 p.m. till 11 p.m. Wagner himself, in a letter to Liszt, imputes the fault to dragging of the recitatives by the singers.

Such proportions has the legend of the Liszt régime at Weimar assumed that it is interesting to know the actual conditions under which *Lohengrin* was produced there in 1850. Weimar, for all its prestige, was then a town of some 12,000 inhabitants and the operatic forces were in proportion. The orchestra with which Liszt had to work numbered only thirty-eight; the choristers less than thirty. Compare these figures with the orchestra of ninety and the chorus of one hundred and fifty employed in performances of *Lohengrin* at the Metropolitan.

Liszt complained in a memorial to the Grand Duke of Weimar that his orchestra had been inadequate, that he had needed at least a dozen more choristers (which seems to us putting it mildly), that the scenery had been makeshift and dilapidated, that the costumes, without being too costly, could have been made of better stuff than what one is accustomed to find on the sofas of the hotels that rent furnished rooms, that there could be no procession in act II because he had had no "supers," and that four peasants had composed Lohengrin's personal following. Clearly the allegation is true that only Liszt's supreme efforts carried through the Weimar production.

At the Metropolitan Opera House *Lohengrin* has been sumptuously mounted and provided with noteworthy casts. During the first season of the house (1883–84) it was sung in Italian with Christine Nilsson (Elsa), Emmy Fursch-Madi (Ortrud), Campanini (Lohengrin), Kaschmann (Telramund), and Novara (the King). One of the most popular operas in the local repertory, it has had subsequent Metropolitan performances now in German, now in Italian, now in English.

P. S.

[The American première at Stadt Theatre, N.Y., occurred on April 3, 1871, the language being German; the Metropolitan première occurred on November 7, 1883.]

WAGNER'S THEORY OF MUSIC-DRAMA

Between the productions of *Tannhäuser* and *Lohengrin* came Wagner's exile, for participating in the revolutionary business of 1848, and flight to Switzerland. Here he had leisure to think, to account to himself for those artistic instincts for which he had hitherto found no adequate form of expression, and to formulate his theory of the Music-Drama. In this period fall the writing and publication of "Das Kunstwerk der Zukunft" and "Oper und Drama," his principal theoretico-controversial works. But what best helped to open his eyes was what he had done, and left undone, in writing *Lohengrin*. . . .

Stripped of its dialectic trappings, and with its metaphysical convolutions straightened out, Wagner's theory is briefly this. In any sort of Drama, whether musical or otherwise, the play's the thing; and, in the Music-Drama, the music must lend itself unreservedly and continuously to intensifying the emotional expression of the text, and to giving an illustrative colouring to the dramatic action. In the end,—aye, and even down to minute details,—it is the theory of the old Florentine *Camerata,* and nothing else under the sun.

As to the practical means by which Music can best fulfil this its allotted mission, two points in Wagner's theory are noteworthy; the first fundamental, the second more adventitious. The first point is that Music must abandon all those forms which were developed, not so much from its own intrinsic nature as from its first application to human uses—that is, from the Dance—and assume only such plastic forms as spring naturally and freely from the nature of the dramatic subject it seeks to illustrate. The second point is what is known as the *Leitmotiv*.

Be it said at once that the *Leitmotiv* idea—the association of a theme, or musical phrase, with a particular personage, idea, or incident in a drama—was not original with Wagner; neither do we find anything new in his use of it until we come to his third manner.

The episodic use of the *Leitmotiv* was no new thing; and all that distinguishes Wagner's use of it in his earlier operas—from *Rienzi* to *Lohengrin*—is that it is more frequent than is to be found in other composers. But, in the last struggle between Tannhäuser and Wolfram (in the third act of *Tannhäuser*), still more, in the scene on the Church steps between Ortrud and Telramund (in the second act of *Lohengrin*), we begin to find something of the use Wagner makes of the *Leitmotiv* in his later music-dramas. This use is no longer merely episodic, but distinctly functional. In Wagner's third manner, almost the whole web of the music is woven out of *Leitmotiven;* they come either singly and in succession, or else simultaneously and interwoven. There is no melodic constituent of the music that is not a *Leitmotiv*. This gives the music, if not greater dramatic force, at least an unflagging dramatic suggestiveness.

Such was Wagner's theory in its main outlines. This theory he applied fully in all the works of his third period—the *Nibelungen* tetralogy, *Tristan und Isolde, Die Meistersinger von Nürnberg,* and *Parsifal;* the practical artistic expression of it was his third manner.

W. F. A.

Tristan und Isolde

ACTION (*HANDLUNG*) IN 3 ACTS

Book by the COMPOSER

First performance: Hof-und-National-Theater, Munich, June 10, 1865

CHARACTERS

Tristan, a Cornish knight, nephew of King Mark, TENOR

King Mark of Cornwall, BASS

Isolde, Princess of Ireland, SOPRANO

Kurvenal, Tristan's servant, BARITONE

Melot, one of King Mark's courtiers, TENOR

Brangäne, Isolde's friend and attendant, SOPRANO

A Shepherd, a Steersman, a Sailor Lad; Chorus of Sailors, Knights, and Men-at-Arms

The action takes place during legendary times, at sea, in Cornwall, and in Brittany

Before the Drama. Morold, the Irish king's brother, was slain by Tristan, nephew of King Mark of Cornwall, and his head sent to Isolde, his betrothed, in lieu of tribute. Tristan, wounded in the combat and knowing Isolde's skill in healing, goes to the Irish coast as "Tantris," a wandering minstrel. Isolde tends his wound, but matching a notch in his sword with the steel splinter found in Morold's skull, knows he is her lover's murderer. As she is about to slay him, he looks into her eyes. Love fills her soul; she spares him. In Cornwall Tristan sings Isolde's praises. The nobles suggest King Mark marry her and Tristan sails to Ireland to bring back his uncle's bride. Isolde feels deeply wronged: Tristan, who knows she loves him, has come to woo her for another man. But she sails for Cornwall on his ship.

While a sailor sings, Isolde, on the deck section curtained off for her, grieves. Brangäne, her faithful servant, says Cornwall has been sighted. Invoking destruction on herself, Isolde gasps for air—the curtain hiding the deck is withdrawn, showing sailors, knights, and Tristan, with Kurvenal his squire looking at the fleeting waters. Isolde summons Tristan and swears never to wed King Mark, then bids Brangäne take the poison vial from her casket of drugs. Tristan, willing to die, knowing his love hopeless, shares the goblet's contents with Isolde. But Brangäne has poured a love instead of a death potion into the wine. As the waves of their passion overwhelm the lovers they cling together while the vessel makes its destination.

Hunting horns sound from the nocturnal forest to Isolde's tower above the palace gardens. Isolde signals her lover. They recline on a bank of flowers and murmur their vows. Vainly Brangäne and Kurvenal warn them. Then Melot, who has betrayed them, brings King Mark to the scene and the humiliated King reproaches his nephew. As he begs Isolde to follow him Tristan is attacked by Melot and severely wounded. While Kurvenal receives his falling body and Isolde flings herself upon it, King Mark restrains Melot.

In the garden of his Breton castle Tristan awaits the vessel bringing Isolde to him. When a shepherd pipe proclaims the glad news, Tristan, wild with sudden joy, rises from his couch and tears away his bandages. Blood pouring from his wounds, he hears Isolde's voice and staggers to meet her. As she clasps him in her arms, he sinks to the ground and with a supreme look of recognition dies at her feet. The clash of arms heralds King Mark's approach. He has come to forgive the errant lovers. Kurvenal, not knowing this, is slain by Melot barring the entrance to the castle, killing Melot as he himself is cut down. King Mark kneels sobbing at his nephew's feet, while Isolde, her gaze riveted on Tristan, sings the swan song of the greatest love the world has known, the "Liebestod" (Love-Death) and dies in Brangäne's arms.

F. H. M.

The writer of these lines has had a life time of experience listening to *Tristan* and inducing others to listen to it. In various opera houses of the the world he has heard it more than two hundred times. There is one thing above all else he would like to impress upon any who may be making his first acquaintance with the opera; and that is, if you imagine you do not understand it, that it is beyond you or even that you do not like it, hear it again and again and yet again! And if you lack the possibility of hearing performances, listen over and over to recordings of it, sit down to the piano with a score or, if you cannot play it yourself, try to get someone who can play it to you. The ideal way to hear *Tristan* is the unfortunately impractical one of hearing just one act at a sitting. It is not the music itself which is in any way difficult to absorb; it is the enormous, oceanic quantity of it and the emotional strain it imposes. "Completely good performances," once said Wagner half in earnest, half in jest, "are bound to set people crazy!" What Wagner meant by "completely good" is not what one frequently hears. But this apparently contradictory genius gave some other, and more comforting clues about how to listen to his music. For one thing he said: "The people who best understand me are the ones who do not even know that notes are written on a five-line staff!"

Tristan is, in a way, a singularly good work to hear over the air. Why? For the very reason that it offers little outward stage action. Its action is in the souls of its characters and hence in the music. Here, however, it is as boundless as the sea.

It may not be amiss to recall at this point an incident which happened at the Festival Theatre in Bayreuth during the rehearsals preceding the first Festival, in 1876. Seated in the auditorium, her eyes glued to a pair of opera glasses, Wagner's devoted admirer, Malvida von Meysenbug, diligently followed the happenings on the stage. Suddenly, from behind, a pair of hands were clapped over her face and she heard the voice of Wagner himself whispering in her ear: "Don't look so much; listen!" That sally of the composer's had to do with the *Ring*. But it applies better still, if possible, to *Tristan*. You lose perhaps less by not actually seeing *Tristan* than you would in the case of any other work in the Wagnerian repertory. Particularly the second act, which has not its like in the whole range of music! It has always been the writer's impression that one could best enjoy this act on a totally blacked-out stage, with no more furniture than a bench and the shadowy outline of a staircase. In the opera house the stage is almost invariably over-lighted and its physical trimmings disturb the celestial enchantment of the music, which for the greater part is more important here than anything else—more even than the text!

H. F. P.

Strange as it may seem, what impelled Wagner to compose *Tristan und Isolde* was a desire to resume contact with the stage. After the production of *Lohengrin* at Weimar in 1850, the composer, an exile from Germany, was mainly occupied for several years with theoretical writings and the composition of the vast epic which was to take final shape in the four related music-dramas of *Der Ring des Nibelungen*. Meanwhile, he was losing touch more and more with the actualities of the theatre and not taking the wished-for strides toward fame and fortune. Consequently, in August, 1857, he began work on the text of a new music-drama, choosing as subject a story that already had interested him, the Arthurian legend of the Cornish knight and the Irish princess whom he called Tristan and Isolde (in English literature these names oftenest appear as Tristram and Iseult). The composition of the music was interrupted by emotional and financial disturbances. Finally the score was completed in August, 1859.

Now came the question of a production, and here we realize the oddity of Wagner's hope that through this new work he should re-establish his immediate theatrical contact. In the interval between *Lohengrin* and *Tristan* Wagner's musico-dramatic theories had developed greatly and taken definite form. Moreover, he had actually completed *Das Rheingold, Die Walküre,* and part of *Siegfried*. Consequently, *Tristan und Isolde* embodied a musical philosophy, so to say, that represented a great advance over the procedure exemplified in *Tannhäuser* and *Lohengrin,* and through its novelty and its radical departures from previous accepted standards posed problems that the average opera singer and the ordinary conductor were quite unprepared to solve.

Wagner, in need of money and far from finding opera houses bidding against one another for the chance to produce this highly problematic work, was under the painful necessity of scouting around to beg an opening for it. At one time Karlsruhe seemed to promise well. There the chief tenor, Ludwig Schnorr von Carolsfeld, impressed Wagner as combining gifts and art enough to assure a satisfactory Tristan, but he objected to the soprano, Malwina Garrigues, for Isolde. In any event, the negotiations fell through. Nor was Wagner luckier in Vienna. There the Court Opera actually undertook a production and over seventy rehearsals were held. Just why, after such lengthy preparation, the project was dropped has been a matter of dispute. The long accepted story had it that the singers protested to the management that after learning one act they would forget it in the labor of learning the next. The fact seems to be, however, that though the company was divided into two camps, pro-Wagner and anti-Wagner, the performance would have gone through, thanks to the enthusiasm of Frau Luise Dustmann-Meyer for her role of Isolde (Wagner went on record to the effect that she was ideally suited to the part), if the good lady had not discovered a love affair in progress between the composer and her younger sister, Friederike. Whereupon she deserted the Wagner camp and threw her determining influence to his foes.

The years from 1860 to 1863 were a stormy time for Wagner, deriving their only brightness from the final amnesty that permitted the exile to return to Saxony as well as to the other German countries. The production of *Tannhäuser* in Paris proved a fiasco. It seemed out of the question to get *Tristan* done anywhere, and Wagner had to make his escape secretly from Vienna lest he be imprisoned for debt. Then the new king of Bavaria, the youthful and artistic Ludwig II, who was an ardent admirer of Wagner's music, intervened. Unasked, he sent for Wagner, provided him generously with money, and ordered that *Tristan und Isolde* be staged at the Hof-und-National-Theater of his capital, Munich. Wagner's devoted champion, Hans von Bülow, was the musical director of the production and the "one and only" Schnorr von Carolsfeld impersonated Tristan. What of it if the composer had to put up with the former Malwina Garrigues, now Frau Schnorr, as Isolde? No trivial objections were allowed to interfere! *Tristan und Isolde* really was produced!

But where in all this is Mathilde Wesendonck? Where is the lady whom Wagner called his "Muse" and to whom the world in general has ascribed the very existence of *Tristan und Isolde?* Wagner in the days of his exile lived much of the time at Zurich, and from April, 1857, till August, 1858, was the guest of the rich silk merchant, Otto Wesendonck, and his beautiful young wife, Mathilde. Wagner fell in love with Mathilde, and certain it is that Mathilde was associated with the composition of *Tristan.* But as to her being the inspiration, opinions differ.

Wagner's latest and shrewdest biographer, Ernest Newman, believes it less probable that he wrote the opera because he was in love with Mathilde than that he was in love with Mathilde because he was writing the opera. In other words, Wagner needed a personal love affair as obbligato to the tremendous lyric tragedy of love which he was evolving and conveniently invented it in his immediate entourage! The point is for the psychologists to argue: they will never settle it.

In spite of the production at Munich, the trials of *Tristan* were by no means over. Schnorr, fatigued by the strain of rehearsals, caught cold during the first performance, and after the fourth, on July 1, fell ill of rheumatic fever, which carried him off on July 21. The world was then without a performance of *Tristan und Isolde* for three years till another famous operatic couple, Heinrich and Therese Vogl, made possible a revival at Munich, and for some time thereafter Vogl was the world's only Tristan.

P. S.

The American *première* did not take place till Dec. 1, 1886, when the music drama was presented at the Metropolitan Opera House, New York, under the musical direction of Anton Seidl and with Albert Niemann as Tristan, Lilli Lehmann as Isolde, Marianne Brandt as Brangäne, Adolf Robinson as Kurwenal, and Emil Fischer as King Mark. There was a memorable revival of the work at the Metropolitan on Nov. 27, 1895, when Seidl again conducted and Jean de Reszké, Lillian Nordica, and Édouard de Reszké made their first appearances as Tristan, Isolde, and King Mark respectively, with Marie Brema as Brangäne and Giuseppe Kaschmann as Kurwenal.

Arturo Toscanini made known to America his conception of the score on Nov. 22, 1909. The cast included Karl Burrian, Johanna Gadski, Louise Homer, Pasquale Amato, and Robert Blass. When, following three *Tristan*-less seasons, the music drama was restored to the Metropolitan repertory after the World War, on Nov. 20, 1920, an English version of the text was used. The conductor was Artur Bodanzky, the chief singers Johannes Sembach, Margaret Matzenauer, Jeanne Gordon, Clarence Whitehill, and Robert Blass. The German text was brought back Nov. 28, 1921.

Die Meistersinger von Nürnberg

[The Mastersingers of Nuremberg]

OPERA IN 3 ACTS

Book by the COMPOSER

First performance: Hof-und-National-Theater, Munich, June 21, 1868

CHARACTERS

Hans Sachs, cobbler, BASS OR BARITONE
Pogner, goldsmith, BASS
Beckmesser, town clerk, BASS
Walther von Stolzing, a young
  Franconian knight, TENOR
David, apprentice to Hans Sachs, TENOR
Eva, Pogner's daughter, SOPRANO

Magdalena, Eva's nurse, SOPRANO
Vogelgesang, furrier; *Nachtigall,*
  buckle-maker; *Kothner,* baker; *Zorn,*
  pewterer; *Eislinger,* grocer; *Moser,*
  tailor; *Ortel,* soap boiler; *Schwarz,*
  stocking weaver; *Folz,* coppersmith

Burghers of all Guilds, Journeymen, Apprentices, Girls, and People

The action takes place in Nuremberg in the middle of the sixteenth century

A young Franconian knight, Walter von Stolzing—who reads the poems of others in his lonely castle in wintertime and writes his own in the greening spring-tide forests—falls in love and scrapes acquaintance with Eva, daughter of the wealthy Nuremberg goldsmith, Pogner, in St. Catherine's Church. When Walter learns Eva's hand in marriage goes to the winner in the morrow's Mastersinger contest he determines to break a vocal lance. David (apprentice of Hans Sachs, the popular cobbler) tries to teach Walter the endless pedantic rules governing singing as the Mastersingers practice it. Walter the next day sings his trial song—all of love and spring—but Beckmesser, the stupid, jealous, and malicious "official marker," covers his slate with Walter's violations of the rules. Though Hans Sachs sees the beauty of his heartfelt and untutored song, Walter is refused admission to the guild, and rushes from the hall in despair.

After David gives indignant Magdalena, Eva's maid, the news of Walter's defeat, and fights jeering fellow apprentices, Hans Sachs sits down in front of the cobbler shop. There Eva discloses that she loves Walter, and Sachs, though he loves the girl, determines to help his rival. Now Beckmesser sings beneath Eva's window, but Sachs insists on scanning the music with a hammer blow for every error. The noise wakens the neighbors. David thinks Beckmesser is serenading Magdalena and uses his cudgel on him. Townsfolk and apprentices pour into the street and fight, but Hans Sachs stops Eva and Walter as they try to elope under cover of the confusion.

He sends Eva home and takes Walter into his own house, while with the mellow sound of the watchman's horn the crowd disappears from the moonlit street.

To Sachs, brooding over the folly of man, comes Walter who has dreamed of a wonderful song. He sings it and at Sachs' request jots down the words on a bit of paper. Beckmesser, crawling in after Sachs and Walter have left, finds the paper, and is caught in the act of stealing. Sachs, however, tells him he can keep the poem. When Eva comes in Walter sings her a stanza of his dream song, and the arrival of David and Magdalena motives the famous Quintet. On the banks of the Pegnitz river the Nuremberg guilds and their families watch the Mastersingers move in procession to the platform. Sachs calls on Beckmesser to sing, and the pedant makes a pitiful botch of fitting Walter's new words to his old tune. Laughed from the platform, his place is taken by Walter, whose singing of the "Prize Song," the love melody to Eva, wins the laurel crown and his sweetheart's hand in marriage. Sachs, who has shown that Art's future lies in the happy union of the traditional and the inspired, is acclaimed by all.

F. H. M.

Though they all bear the unmistakable stamp of his style, Wagner's great music dramas differ markedly from one another. The music of each is so appropriate to the action that the two become an inseparable unit in our minds. Thus, we have the passionately throbbing *Tristan und Isolde,* the fervidly mystical *Parsifal,* and the mellow and humorous *Die Meistersinger.* This blend of humor and humanity in his great comedy quickly appealed to Wagner's growing public, and to this day the great comedy remains one of his most popular works.

The vast contrapuntal power of the music is never there for its own sake, but as a kind of inevitable flowering of the very theme of the opera, of the poetic idea embedded in the conflict of schools. This poetic, or aesthetic, idea is represented in the struggle between the liberal-minded Walther, rebelling against the doctrinaire tenets of the guilds, and Beckmesser, the scoundrelly pedant, opposed, like all hidebound custodians of the older ways, to any progress in the arts. As everyone knows, in this Beckmesser the composer pilloried forever Eduard Hanslick, the dreaded critical oracle of Vienna who had become the archenemy of Wagnerism. In the fair-minded Hans Sachs, Wagner represented enlightened public opinion, respectful of the great masters, yet willing to grant all innovators the right to be heard and, if genuine, to be accepted. The historic Sachs was, of course, somewhat different from Wagner's cobbler-poet. In a deeper sense, it is the aging Sachs' hopeless and self-denying love for the young and beautiful Eva that explains why *Die Meistersinger* is often called a "tragicomedy."

Instead of legendary sources, Wagner this time depends to a large extent upon actual history for the basis of his comedy. He conceived the work at first as a sort of humorous variation on the contest theme of *Tannhäuser.* In that opera Wagner had treated of the medieval minnesingers, nobles who sang of exalted love—the German counterparts of the French *trouvères,* or troubadours. Like the chivalry of which they were an expression, the minnesingers disappeared with the coming of the Renaissance. In their place there arose, among the middle-class trade guilds, bands of singers who, patterning themselves after the minnesingers, took the name "mastersingers" (*Meistersinger*). To become an enrolled member of one of these groups of "mastersingers," the ambitious youth, while learning his trade, was obliged to study the arts of singing and poetry, too. After passing various examinations, he then worked his way up through the several degrees of "Scholar," "Schoolman," "Singer," "Poet," and finally "Master." The purpose of the guild was to foster a love of the noblest ideals in art. However, in the course of time, the Mastersingers' Guild inevitably adopted a fixed dogmatic outlook. Excessive value was now given to pedantic and traditional rules. Most famous of the mastersingers was Hans Sachs, cobbler, poet, and dramatist, who lived at Nuremberg (1494–1576) and helped combat the pedantry of his colleagues.

Wagner made a thorough historical research before he penned this vivid picture of life in Nuremberg, crowded with its wealth of amusing and picturesque details. Two of the musical motives employed, "The Banner" and "The Art Brotherhood," were gleaned from some "Prize Master Tones" included in an old book by J. C. Wagenseil, printed at Nuremberg in 1697. Yet Wagner does not thrust this history upon us, but allows it to form a diverting and realistic background for the human and romantic story he has to tell.[*]

Among all the imposing array of Wagner's music dramas there is only one comedy, *Die Meistersinger von Nürnberg.* To be sure, in *Siegfried* the prevailing note is a note of happiness: no more than two characters die in the course of the three acts, and of them one is a miserly dragon and the other a malignant dwarf, both slain by the jubilant hero, who naturally goes scot free. But *Siegfried* cannot be considered of and by itself. It exists as a radiant interlude in the vast tragic panorama of *Der Ring des Nibelungen,* and even so the underlying motif of tragedy darkens the surface once and again.

It was while Wagner was taking a cure at Marienbad in July, 1845, that the Mastersingers of mediaeval and renaissance Germany first appealed to him as an operatic subject. He had lately been reading about them in Gervinus's "History of Germany Literature." Now he went so far in his enthusiasm as to sketch a scenario for a lyric comedy, with Nuremberg as locale. There is even a legend that he composed some of the music—the great quintet and the songs of Walter von Stolzing and Hans Sachs. Yet his real preoccupation at this time was with *Lohengrin. Die Meistersinger* he consequently put aside for a good many years.

[*] From "The Victor Book of Operas."

In the autumn of 1861 we find Wagner in anything but cheerful circumstances. The previous March *Tannhäuser* at the Paris Opéra—a production on which he had banked so much—had been a resounding fiasco. His hope of seeing *Tristan und Isolde* produced at either Karlsruhe or Vienna remained a hope deferred. Under these disheartening conditions he hankered after work that would distract him, that would quickly bring him into contact with the public again.

On October 30, 1861, he wrote as follows from Vienna to the publishing house of Schott at Mainz: "My creative work has long been interrupted. Oppressed by vexatious and long delays attending my attempts to get my works performed, I long to undertake some piece of artistic work which would occupy me pleasantly and distract my mind. At this time and to this end I do not feel that I can return to my great *Nibelung* cycle, preferring to postpone that to a period of public recognition."

Then he goes on to express a wish to apply himself to some "easier, less exhausting" task, especially in view of the obstacles he has had to contend with in getting his "serious" works performed. Whereupon the surprise follows:

I believe it is a happy thought, according with my mood and circumstances, to put in hand at once the execution of an earlier idea for a popular operatic comedy. The opera is called *Die Meistersinger von Nürnberg,* and the chief hero is the jovial poet Hans Sachs. The subject is extraordinarily full of kindly humor, and I flatter myself that this plan, which is all my own, is something striking and original. The style in poetry and music shall be thoroughly light and popular, and this time I shall need neither a so-called first-class tenor nor a great tragic soprano [At both Karlsruhe and Vienna there had been difficulty in casting *Tristan und Isolde* in a way that was acceptable to the composer]; a rapid circulation through all theatres may be anticipated.

Apparently Wagner had little notion of the dimensions which his "light and popular" operatic comedy would attain before he finished with it or of the exceeding exactions which he was in due course to impose on the singer of his tenor hero, Walter von Stolzing!

Shortly after this letter had been dispatched Wagner's friends the Wesendoncks invited him to meet them in Venice. So to Venice Wagner went. Though in "My Life" he describes his four days there as "dreary," he tells of visiting the Academy of Arts with Wesendonck and confesses that, in spite of all his indifferences, the "Assumption of the Virgin" by Titian exercised "a most sublime influence" upon him. "My old powers," he declares, "revived within me, as though by a sudden flash of inspiration. I determined at once on the composition of *Die Meistersinger."*

In fairness to Mathilde Wesendonck it should here be pointed out that she as well as Titian's "Virgin" had a deciding part in the resurgence of *Die Meistersinger.* In Venice Wagner told her of the trials and tribulations of his Viennese sojourn. Mathilde immediately recalled the *Meistersinger* scenario he had made at Marienbad and suggested that he now stop bothering about a production of *Tristan* and compose his Nuremberg comedy. Thus the well-beloved Mathilde was not only the Muse of *Tristan und Isolde,* but, in a sense, the Mother of *Die Meistersinger!*

On November 20, 1861, Wagner wrote (again from Vienna) in this exultant fashion to Franz Scott: "When I saw before me the prospect of a year wasted in every respect, I asked myself what I should do next. . . . Then suddenly my wonderful *Meistersinger* cropped up, and all in a moment I felt once more master of my fate. . . . A glance at the sketch will show you that my own characteristic note, even the tenderly sentimental, will be struck here round and full. In short, I think I can count, particularly at the moment, on having struck the most characteristic chord of German life." In December he went to Paris to devote himself to working out the *Meistersinger* libretto.

The composition of the music, however, was interrupted by the sharp vicissitudes of the next few years of Wagner's life. But at length he completed the work, and the world première took place on June 21, 1868, at the Hof-und-National-Theater in Munich.

P. S.

Immediately, *Die Meistersinger* took the town, then Germany. And why should it not have? This lusty, heartily created big comedy of manners evoked the soul of sixteenth-century Germany. Everything about it was right, beginning with the locale: Nuremberg is the most flavorsome of towns, where a seen past lingers on every stone, and where even the least imaginative can call up the late-medieval atmosphere of guilds, journeymen, and apprentices. Again, the libretto was right, though to be so it had to break with some of Wagner's pet theories: there is no element of myth in *Die Meistersinger,* which is all human and credibly everyday historical. To a poem that carried conviction and radiated charm, Wagner added music of varied but always surpassing beauty and life. It was music that he could not have used to body forth the doings of gods and goddesses or even of superlovers like Tristan and Isolde. In order to create such music at all, he had to recede some distance from the ironclad theorizing that had produced *Tristan* and, constricted into dogma, was to challenge dissent in the *Ring* and *Parsifal.* . . .

It was in German, on May 30, 1882, that *Die Meistersinger* was first given in London. That night, the Drury Laners heard Sucher as Eva, Winkelmann as Walther, and Eugen Gura, a famous *Ring* baritone at Bayreuth, in the leading role of Sachs. Richter conducted, and magnificently. Seven years later, to mark Jean de Reszke's growing interest in Wagnerian roles, Covent Garden staged an Italian version in which, according to Bernard Shaw, Jean's singing was far better than his understanding of the part of Walther. The top honors of this performance of *I Maestri cantori* went to Lassalle, the Sachs, and to

Albani, the Eva. Meanwhile, three years earlier, on January 4, 1886, the ambitious Seidl had trotted out an uneven cast for the Metropolitan *première* of the German version, which, because of its excessive length, was much cut—to this day a complete *Meistersinger* has never been heard at the Metropolitan. In the cast were Fischer (Sachs), Seidl-Kraus (Eva), and Brandt (Magdalena), with most of the other roles taken by relatively second-flight artists. The work was repeated seven times that season. Given twenty-eight times in German in the course of six seasons, it was kept in the repertoire when the Italian regime took over in the fall of 1891. Then New York heard almost precisely the same stars who had sung *I Maestri cantori* at Covent Garden in 1889. On March 25, 1901, the De Reszkes having for some time increased their fame by singing Wagner in German, the Metropolitan presented their first German *Meistersinger,* with Jean a more understanding Walther, and Édouard a lusty Sachs; Gadski was the Eva, Schumann-Heink the Magdalena, and Bispham the Beckmesser. This performance was just four days before Jean's Metropolitan farewell.

W. B., H. W.

Der Ring des Nibelungen

[The Ring of the Nibelung]

TETRALOGY IN A FORE-EVENING (*Das Rheingold*) AND 3 DAYS
(*Die Walküre, Siegfried,* and *Götterdämmerung*)

Book by the COMPOSER

First cyclic performance: Festspielhaus, Bayreuth, Aug. 13, 14, 16, and 17, 1876

After making use of both history and legend, Wagner decided that the true subject matter for the lyric drama was to be found in legend. While still at work on *Lohengrin* he had been strongly attracted by Northern mythology as found in the German, Scandinavian, and Icelandic epics and sagas. Though for his next opera he hesitated between the historical Friedrich Barbarossa and the mythical Siegfried, he eventually rejected the emperor in favor of the Volsung hero, and sketched the coming work in a poem entitled *Siegfrieds Tod* (Siegfried's Death). This was written in November, 1848. It then seemed to him that a prefatory opera would be necessary, so he expanded the poem backwards by writing *Der junge Siegfried* (Young Siegfried). But now the idea developed to such a degree that he prefaced *Der junge Siegfried* with *Die Walküre* (The Valkyr) and that in turn with *Das Rheingold* (The Rhinegold). The title of the third member of this tetralogy he shortened to *Siegfried* and that of the fourth member he changed to *Götterdämmerung* (Dusk of the Gods).

The four poems, composed so oddly in reverse order, he had printed for private distribution in 1853. And then came the music. *Das Rheingold,* begun that year, was composed in 1854. *Die Walküre* occupied him from the summer of 1854 to the spring of 1856. In the following autumn he began *Siegfried,* and by the next July the first act and part of the second were finished. But Wagner had no illusions as to the difficulty of obtaining a production for such a colossal venture. Consequently, having brought out no new lyric drama since *Lohengrin* in 1850, he determined to lay his tetralogy aside for a while and bring out a single work that would give the world proof of his continued activity. The result was *Tristan und Isolde,* than which nothing could have been less well suited to an immediate theatrical contact.

During the years that ensued Wagner was too thoroughly occupied otherwise to resume work on his Siegfried cycle until after *Tristan* and *Die Meistersinger* had been composed and produced. At length, in February, 1869, he

631

applied himself anew to the unfinished *Siegfried,* completing it the next autumn. Then he took up *Götterdämmerung,* which he finished in November, 1874. The entire tetralogy, collectively named *Der Ring des Nibelungen,* was produced, after Herculean efforts, in the specially constructed Festspielhaus at Bayreuth, in Aug. 1876, thus in a sense crowning Wagner's life work and vindicating all his claims before the world.

It should be borne in mind that when Wagner began to compose *Das Rheingold* he had not only brought out his earlier and more conventional operas, including *Lohengrin,* but had formulated and published his musico-dramatic theories. In the score of *Das Rheingold, Leitmotive* (leading motives) no longer recur merely from time to time, but constitute the very warp and weft of the music. Thus, the orchestra steadily provides the singers with an organic dramatico-sympathetic background, and such being the case the number of *Leitmotive* has been vastly increased.

Although from *Der fliegende Holländer* on each of Wagner's music dramas embodies a philosophical or moral idea, in *Der Ring des Nibelungen* the idea becomes universal. The individual tragedy of one and another is related and subordinated to the tragedy of the world that is their undoing. Wotan, king of the Norse gods, is avid for power, and in token of that power he has had constructed as the dwelling place for himself, his wife Fricka, and their kindred deities the mighty castle of Valhalla. But Wotan's greed remains unsatisfied, and greed it is that brings the downfall of his arrogant race.

From the Rhine Daughters deep in the river Alberich the Nibelung filches their gold and fashions from it a ring which is the symbol of all power. When the desperate Wotan obtains the ring from him by trickery, he curses the gold, which all who have it not shall covet and he who has it shall cling to as to his very life. To atone for Wotan's sin and divert the approaching dusk of the gods a free and fearless hero must arise as the untrammeled agent of reparation. Intent on the creation of such a hero, Wotan goes among the daughters of men and begets the race of Volsungs. To his twin children Siegmund and Sieglinde is born Siegfried, the free and fearless hero designate. With his adventures the rest of the story of the *Ring* is concerned.

P. S.

Das Rheingold

[The Rhinegold]

MUSIC DRAMA IN 4 SCENES

Book by the COMPOSER

First performance: Hof-und-National-Theater, Munich, Sept. 22, 1869

CHARACTERS

GODS:

Wotan, BARITONE-BASS
Donner, BASS
Froh, TENOR
Loge, TENOR

GIANTS:

Fasolt, BASS
Fafner, BASS

GODDESSES:

Fricka, SOPRANO
Freia, SOPRANO
Erda, CONTRALTO

THE RHINE-MAIDENS:

Woglinde, SOPRANO
Wellgunde, SOPRANO
Flosshilde, CONTRALTO

NIBELUNGS (GNOMES):

Alberich, BARITONE
Mime, TENOR

The action takes place during legendary times in the bed of the Rhine, at a mountainous district near that river, and in the subterranean caverns of Nibelheim

Alberich the Nibelung sees the Rhine Maidens bathing in the crystal flood and longs to possess them until the sunlight, piercing green depths, kisses awake the golden hoard which the Rhine Maidens guard. Hearing them tell of the boundless power the possessor of the Nibelungen hoard will enjoy, Alberich flings himself upon the gold and disappears with it, vainly pursued by its guardians.

The god Wotan and his wife Fricka resign their daughter Freia, goddess of beauty, to the giants Fafner and Fasolt, in payment for the castle they have built them. But when the giants offer to exchange Freia for the gold of the Nibelungs, Wotan and Loge, god of evil, descend to Nibelheim, Alberich's underground kingdom, where Mime, the dwarf's brother, has completed a helmet which makes its wearer invisible. Loge's flatteries lure from Alberich the secret of the helmet, and he and Wotan wrest it from him.

Before Wotan's castle, his heart filled with hatred and revenge, Alberich yielding helmet, ring, and gold as the price of freedom, calls down a terrible curse on the ring and the gold. The giants bring back Freia and receive the Nibelungen gold and ring. At once the curse goes into effect: Fafner slays his brother Fasolt for the sake of the treasure. Now the gods can enter the splendid castle bought at so terrible a price. The thunder rolls, the lightning flashes and over a gloriously colored rainbow bridge the gods enter their abode, which Wotan calls Valhalla. Yet as they enter the wailing of the Rhine Maidens, robbed of their hoard, rises to the ears of the gods.

F. H. M.

The poem "Kubla Khan" and the music of *Das Rheingold* are similar cases. Each resulted from a dream. Coleridge, though, never completed his poem. At the lines "He on honey-dew hath fed And drunk the milk of Paradise" the dream, or at least the memory of it, forsook him, and so he left the poem unfinished, a magnificent fragment. Wagner, of course, kept on.

In October and November, 1852, Wagner, who was then a resident of Zurich and in his fortieth year, wrote the libretto of *Das Rheingold*. But with regard to taking up composing again he felt a "peculiar disinclination" that amounted to fear, even as he had done previously "after protracted pauses in musical production." He also felt "very much exhausted" by all he had recently gone through.

Accordingly, as he tells us in "My Life," before undertaking the gigantic task of writing the music for *Der Ring des Nibelungen,* he was convinced that he must make one final effort to see whether he could not in some new environment attain an existence more in harmony with his feelings than he could possibly aspire to after so many compromises. Consequently he planned a journey to Italy, and Otto Wesendonck (the generous husband of that Mathilde Wesendonck who was to become his "Muse") placed the necessary money at his disposal.

But first, companioned by the poet Georg Herwegh, he went to St. Moritz, climbed about among the mountains of the Engadine, eagerly crossed glaciers, drank champagne that had been iced in the fissures, swallowed such quantities of "delicious milk" at one herdsman's cottage that both men were "perfectly amazed," and read vast amounts of Goethe. This recuperative jaunt took place in July and August. Before going on to Italy (without Herwegh) Wagner returned briefly to Zurich. Then, in September, he set out for the south by way of Geneva, crossing Mount Cenis in a "special" mail coach!

Two days were spent in Turin, where he found nothing to detain him longer. Thence he pressed on to Genoa. "The grand impression produced on me by that city," he tells us, "overcomes, even to this day, any longing to visit the rest of Italy. For a few days I was in a dream of delight." But loneliness claimed him. He was a stranger in a strange world.

A curious psychological condition supervened: "Absolutely inexperienced as I was in searching out the treasures of art on a systematic plan, I gave myself up in this new world to a peculiar state of mind that might be described as a musical one, and my main idea was to find some turning point that might induce me to remain there in quiet enjoyment. My only object still was to find a refuge where I might enjoy the congenial peace suited to some new artistic creation."

Alas, the eminent gentleman's digestive processes were upset by his "thoughtlessly indulging" in Genoese ices, and a "most depressing lassitude" succeeded the previous exaltation! For the time being the "grand impression" produced by the Ligurian city was appreciably diminished. Wagner had put up at an inn near the waterfront, and of a sudden the "tremendous noise of the harbor" got on his nerves and he wanted to flee from it and "seek the most absolute calm." It occurred to him that a trip to Spezia would be beneficial, so thither he went by steamer.

Though the voyage lasted only a night, there was a violent head-wind, and the commotion it kicked up made the disturbed composer violently seasick into the bargain. In the "most utterly exhausted condition," scarcely able to drag himself another step, we are assured, he made for the best hotel in Spezia, which, to his horror, was situated in an extremely noisy and narrow street.

All the sore travail, however, was slowly leading up to the creative moment. Here is Wagner's account of that in his own words:

After a night spent in fever and sleeplessness, I forced myself to take a long tramp the next day through the hilly country, which was covered with pine woods. It all looked dreary and desolate, and I could not think what I should do there. Returning in the afternoon, I stretched myself, dead tired, on a hard couch, awaiting the long-desired hour of sleep. It did not come; but I fell into a kind of somnolent state, in which I suddenly felt as though I were sinking in swiftly flowing water.

The rushing sound formed itself in my brain into a musical sound, the chord of E flat major, which continually re-echoed in broken forms; these broken chords seemed to be melodic passages of increasing motion, yet the pure triad of E flat major never changed, but seemed by its continuance to impart infinite significance to the element in which I was sinking.

I awoke in sudden terror from my doze, feeling as though the waves were rushing high above my head. I at once recognized that the orchestral overture to *Das Rheingold,* which must long have lain latent within me, though it had been unable to find definite form, had at last been revealed to me. I then quickly realized my own nature; the stream of life was not to flow to me from without, but from within.

I decided to return to Zurich immediately and begin the composition of my great poem. I telegraphed to my wife to let her know my decision and to have my study in readiness. The same evening I took my place on the coach going to Genoa along the Riviera di Levante.

On January 15, 1854, Wagner wrote from Zurich to Franz Liszt in Weimar: *"Das Rheingold* is finished—but I am finished too!!!"

Wagner exaggerated!

The Hof-und-National-Theater at Munich was the scene of the first performance on any stage of *Das Rheingold,* on September 22, 1869, as it was of *Die Walküre* the following June. Though these pre-Bayreuth productions were made against Wagner's wishes, Ludwig II of Bavaria was impatient to hear the works in question and he had the advantage of owning the copyright of the *Ring,* so the royal will prevailed.

However, the first performance of *Das Rheingold* in connection with the three related music dramas took place in the Festspielhaus at Bayreuth on August 13, 1876, as the initial event in the world première of the *Ring* as a whole. The American première was reserved for January 4, 1889, at the Metropolitan Opera House, New York.

It is interesting to note the emphasis laid by Wagner on the unprepossessing character of Alberich, who is so conspicuous in *Das Rheingold.* To Karl Hill, creator of the part at Bayreuth, he wrote:

I was very much prejudiced in your favor by your talented performance in *Der fliegende Holländer,* which I witnessed, and I assure you that I see no task even in my great tetralogy which I am not convinced you could accomplish excellently. I have, however, assigned you the most difficult rôle in every respect, one which it gave me great anxiety to cast, namely that of Alberich, a part filled with daemonic, passionate tragedy.

P. S.

Die Walküre

[The Valkyr]

MUSIC DRAMA IN 3 ACTS

Book by the Composer

First performance: Hof-und-National-Theater, Munich, June 26, 1870

CHARACTERS

Brünnhilde, soprano
Sieglinde, soprano
Siegmund, tenor

Wotan, baritone
Hunding, bass
The Eight Other Valkyries

Wotan, King of the Gods, begets Siegmund and Sieglinde in a union with a mortal woman. Separated at birth Sieglinde is unhappily married to Hunding, a savage fighter. She gives a stranger shelter in her house. Suspecting him to be Siegmund, her lost brother, she secretly tells him of a sword, Nothung, Wotan their father placed in a tree for Siegmund to use in his hour of need. The stranger pulls the sword from the tree, proving himself her brother. They embrace in love and flee to the forest, Hunding pursuing. Wotan tells Brünnhilde, one of the nine Walküre Maidens he created by a union with Erda the Earth Goddess, to protect Siegmund against Hunding. Fricka, his wife and Goddess of Marriage, makes Wotan reverse his order and protect Hunding, punishing Siegmund for uniting with Sieglinde in love. Brünnhilde disobeys and protects Siegmund. Fricka forces Wotan to interfere on Hunding's behalf, and he breaks Siegmund's sword, Nothung, with his spear. Hunding slays Siegmund, and for this Wotan kills him in return. Brünnhilde sends Sieglinde to the forest to bear the child of her lover. Wotan, angry at Brünnhilde's disobedience, punishes her by putting her to sleep on a rock surrounded by fire which only a fearless hero can penetrate, and who only with a kiss can awaken her.

If we take into account the ordinary span of man's life, *Der Ring des Nibelungen* seems little short of miraculous as an example of persistence and endurance in artistic creation. It was in November, 1848, that Wagner began the actual writing of the series of four music-dramas which came eventually to constitute the *Ring.* But it was not until August, 1876, that the tetralogy in its entirety was given to the world. Luckily Wagner could live through a long succession of interruptions and trials to complete his colossal work—interruptions and trials that would have wrecked a weaker nature, a nature less aware, if you like, of its unconquerable ego.

Relatively early Wagner was drawn to the northern sagas, German, Scandinavian, Icelandic. In the autumn of 1848 he sought to escape from the political turmoil of Dresden, where he was still a Court Conductor, into the worlds of distant history and more distant legend. Both the Emperor Frederick Barbarossa and the epic hero Siegfried appealed to him as subjects on which to expend his talent. Siegfried, however, prevailed, and Wagner, an undiscourageable rationalizer, accounted for his preference of legend to history by maintaining that legend is really superior to history itself as a source of history, being based on popular intuition rather than on written records, which are either conjectural or limited to the deeds of rulers.

Accordingly, in November, 1848, Wagner wrote a dramatic poem which he called "Siegfrieds Tod" (Siegfried's Death). In 1851 Liszt, emboldened by his success with *Lohengrin* the previous year, invited Wagner, then an exile from Germany at Zurich, to set "Siegfrieds Tod" to music for production at Weimar. In "My Life" Wagner tells us further: "I was to finish the work within a year and during that period was to receive a payment of fifteen hundred marks."

In Wagner's mind, however, the subject was expanding too rapidly to permit his accepting that invitation. First he decided to write also a "Junger Siegfried" (Young Siegfried), an heroic comedy "by way of prelude and complement to the tragedy of 'Siegfrieds Tod.' " Wagner goes on to tell us that, carried away by this conception, he tried to persuade himself that the resulting piece would be easier to produce than the other "more serious and terrible drama."

With this idea in mind [he continues], I informed Liszt of my purpose, and offered the Weimar management to compose a score for "Junger Siegfried," which as yet was unwritten, in return for which I would definitely accept their proposal to grant me a year's salary of fifteen hundred marks. This they agreed to without delay, and I took up my quarters in the attic-room evacuated the previous year by Karl Ritter, where, with the aid of sulphur and May-blossom, and in the highest spirits, I proposed to complete the poem of "Junger Siegfried," as already outlined in my original design.

Wagner's reference to "sulphur and May-blossom" was due to the fact that that spring he had suffered from an illness for which the doctor had prescribed daily sulphur baths and with this treatment had combined a walk to the town and back every morning, "surrounded by the fresh green and early spring flowers of May," which he tells us acted as a cheerful mental stimulant.

Even under these favorable conditions, however, Wagner did not now compose music for either "Siegfrieds Tod" or "Junger Siegfried" because his conception of his "Siegfried" epic had grown to such proportions that he felt the necessity of another drama as preface to "Junger Siegfried" and yet another as preface to the preface. Accordingly, still proceeding backward, he wrote the poem of *Die Walküre* (The Valkyr), finished by July, 1852, and the poem of *Das Rheingold,* finished in the following November. He now had in hand the text for his four-part cycle, subject to necessary editing and amplification to bring the two earlier-written pieces into harmony with the later two, and the title of "Siegfrieds Tod" became *Gotterdämmerung* (Dusk of the Gods) and that of "Junger Siegfried" became merely *Siegfried.*

His friends the Ritters had just inherited a large fortune, and Frau Julie Ritter offered Wagner an annuity of 2400 marks as long as he should need it. Thus relieved of immediate financial pressure, he could work as he willed.

When the task of editing and co-ordinating had been done, Wagner had a number of copies of the completed poem struck off for private distribution, but an unforeseen sorrow now overtook him. Despite "the indications of sympathetic interest" in the composition of his "great lyric work," most of the members of his circle of acquaintances at Zurich "regarded the whole thing as a chimera, or possibly a bold caprice."

Nevertheless, Wagner applied himself to the composition of the music, taking up the dramas in their proper order. *Das Rheingold,* begun in September, 1853, was completed in May, 1854. *Die Walküre,* begun the following month, was completed in March, 1856. *Siegfried* was begun in September of that year, and by the following July the first act and part of the second had been completed. Then came an interruption of more than ten years, crowded and fateful years, the years of *Tristan und Isolde* and *Die Meistersinger.* In 1868 we find Wagner settled at last with Cosima in the tranquil retreat at Triebschen, near Lucerne, resuming work on *Siegfried.* And before he finished the scoring he had begun the composition of *Gotterdämmerung,* which was completed on November 21, 1874.

There remained now the production, which took place triumphantly in the specially constructed Festspielhaus at Bayreuth on August 13, 14, 16, and 17, 1876.

However, it would be a mistake to suppose that the world première of *Die Walküre* took place at Bayreuth. The Hof-und-National-Theater at Munich was the scene of the event; the date June 26, 1870. Wagner's patron and former friend, King Ludwig II of Bavaria, in his impatience to hear *Das Rheingold* and *Die Walküre,* ordered them produced in Munich seven and six years, respectively, before the production of the *Ring* as a whole at Bayreuth. Wagner was opposed to these presentations, which he regarded as premature; but the King had acquired the copyright of the *Ring.*

At Bayreuth in 1876 the great Amalie Materna embodied Brünnhilde, along with such distinguished Wagnerian artists as Albert Niemann for Siegmund and Franz Betz for Wotan, and again Materna was the Brünnhilde when on January 30, 1885, *Die Walküre* entered the repertory of the Metropolitan Opera House, under the direction of Dr. Leopold Damrosch. But already New York had heard *Die Walküre,* for as early as April 2, 1877, it was staged at the Academy of Music with Eugenie Pappenheim as Brünnhilde.

                                                        P. S.

Siegfried

MUSIC DRAMA IN 3 ACTS

Book by the COMPOSER

First performance: Festspielhaus, Bayreuth, Aug. 16, 1876

CHARACTERS

Siegfried, TENOR

Mime, TENOR

Wotan, BARITONE OR BASS

Alberich, BARITONE OR BASS

Fafner, BASS

Erda, CONTRALTO

Brünnhilde, SOPRANO

Forest Bird, SOPRANO

In the magic forest wilderness, in the cave of Mime, Alberich's brother, Sieglinde died giving birth to Siegfried. As the boy grows up strong and savage in the dwarf's care, the latter plans to use him as a tool to overcome Fafner, and gain the ring. Mime cannot make a sword to slay Fafner; such a sword none but the fearless can forge; but young Siegfried, amid shouts of joy, welds together the fragments of his father Siegmund's sword, and tests it by splitting the anvil in twain.

Alberich is watching by Fafner's cave at night when Wotan, as a wanderer, wakes the sleeping dragon to warn him of the hero's approach, while Alberich vainly promises Fafner life in exchange for the ring. At dawn Siegfried and Mime appear. Siegfried revels in the charm of the forest, and failing to imitate the song of the birds, sends a merry blast of his horn to the tree tops. Fafner awakes and rolls his hideous length from the cave, but the hero thrusts his sword through the monster's breast. Dying, Fafner warns him against Mime, and the drop of Fafner's blood burning on the hero's finger makes him understand the song of the forest bird, bidding him take hoard, helm, and ring from the cave. Returning with them, treacherous Mime hands Siegfried the poison drink he had prepared while the hero welded his sword; but the bird warns him, and slaying the dwarf he hurries off, the bird leading the way, to find the sleeping bride within her circle of fire.

Wotan tells Erda, the All-Knowing, he hopes for the world's redemption once Siegfried and Brünnhilde have become the parents of a new race. Meeting Siegfried outside the ring of fire, he lets the hero beat down his spear. Sounding his horn Siegfried forces his way through the flames to the top of the hillock and rouses sleeping Brünnhilde with a kiss. At first Brünnhilde, who fell asleep a goddess, resents Siegfried's human passion. Yet she has awakened a mortal woman; she cannot resist the tenderness which overwhelms her, and yields herself to the hero's embrace. Valhalla's stress, the gods, and the world are forgot, for love's star fills her skies.

F. H. M.

If Wagner's third manner is found fully developed in *Das Rheingold,* we do not find his style completely matured and individualized, nor his technique fully grown, until we come to *Siegfried.* Completely Wagnerian though the method may be, there is not a little in *Das Rheingold* and *Die Walküre* that is not wholly Wagner's; not only are some of the themes appropriated from other composers, having not quite the true later-Wagner ring, but even up to far on in *Die Walküre* does one find now and then a distinctly Meyerbeerish detail. Wagner, like other great men, had a way of taking his own where he found it; but, with *Siegfried,* he began to find it only in himself.

Not the least merit of Wagner's third manner is its wondrous flexibility and adaptability. It can lend itself to every conceivable kind of drama, from the most exalted tragedy to the broadest farce. In its more colloquial phase it becomes the first German substitute for the Italian *recitativo quasi-parlando* ever discovered, a fit musical vehicle for homely dialogue. Nor does it lose caste amid the grandest and most elaborate musical developments. It is at once thoroughly dramatic and thoroughly musical.

W. F. A.

The Forest of Arden, according to Robert Louis Stevenson, is the most bird-haunted spot in literature. By similar token *Siegfried* is the most bird-haunted spot in music. In point of fact, a bird sings out with the voice of a woman! Listening to the second act of the work, we hear the caroling of many birds and the weavings of a forest which, if not Arden itself, cannot be far distant from Shakespeare's magical realm of a banished Duke, of the fair Rosalind, of Celia, Orlando, Audrey, and the rest, even to the right melancholy Jaques! No wonder *Siegfried* has been spoken of as the sunlit scherzo of the *Nibelung* symphony!

The summer of 1857 brought one of the happy interludes in Wagner's stormy life. In July Eduard Devrient, manager of the Hof-theater at Karlsruhe, spent three days with the exiled composer at Zurich. From Wagner's house Devrient wrote to the Grand Duke of Baden giving his impressions of his host—in Wagner's own words, "what he had found me like." Shortly after he had gone came an autograph letter to Wagner from the Grand Duke, "couched in very amiable terms." He thanked Wagner most profusely for the souvenir he had presented to the Grand Duchess for her album and at the same time declared his intention of championing the composer's cause and, above all, of securing his return to Germany.

From this time forward [Wagner tells us in his autobiography], my resolve to produce *Tristan* [planned, but not yet set down on paper] had to be seriously entertained, as it was written in plain letters in my book of fate. To all these circumstances I was indebted for the continuation of the favorable mood in which I now brought the second act of *Siegfried* to a close. My daily walks were directed on bright summer afternoons to the peaceful Sihlthal, in whose wooded surroundings I listened long and attentively to the song of the forest birds, and I was astonished to make the acquaintance of entirely new melodies, sung by singers whose forms I could not see and whose names I did not know. In the forest scene of *Siegfried* I put down, in artistic imitation of nature, as much as I could remember of these airs. At the beginning of August I had carefully sketched the composition of the second act.

Another and very different phase of *Siegfried* also owes its inception to the relation of sound to sense. During the summer and autumn before the fruitful walks in the Sihlthal the Wagners had several visitors in Zurich. First there was Richard's sister Clara Wolfram.

She was the musical one among my brothers and sisters [he writes], and I enjoyed her society very much. . . . In October I expected a visit from Liszt, who proposed to make a fairly long stay at Zurich, accompanied by various people of note. I could not wait so long, however, before beginning the composition of *Siegfried,* and I began to sketch the overture [sic] on the 22nd of September.

A tinker had established himself opposite our house, and stunned my ears all day long with his incessant hammering. In my disgust at never being able to find a detached house protected from every kind of noise, I was on the point of deciding to give up composing altogether until the time when this indispensable condition should be fulfilled. But it was precisely my rage over the tinker that, in a moment of agitation, gave me the theme for Siegfried's furious outburst against the bungling Mime. I played over the childishly quarrelsome "Polter" theme in G minor to my sister, furiously singing the words at the same time, which made us all laugh so much that I decided to make one more effort. This resulted in my writing down a good part of the first scene by the time Liszt arrived on 13th October.

With *Siegfried* thus "carefully sketched" through act II, Wagner laid his half-finished *Ring des Nibelungen* aside in favor of *Tristan und Isolde* and resumed work on it only in 1868. The next great step was the production in August, 1876, of the cycle of four music dramas in the Festspielhaus at Bayreuth, constructed on purpose to accommodate them. The preparations for that momentous event were superintended by Wagner with infinite solicitude and care. Naturally the selection of a Siegfried, the fearless forest lad who is also the "highest hero of worlds," was a matter of the utmost concern. The tenor he picked out was Georg Unger. Unger had studied theology before he turned to opera and had been on the stage only a few years, and without particular success. Nevertheless, the composer wanted him. As a preliminary to his undertaking the rôle of Siegfried, however, Wagner sent him to Julius Hey at Munich for further vocal study. In letters to Unger, Hey, and others the composer expressed himself in original fashion as regards both singing and singers, among the latter, of course, being Unger. To the publisher, Emil Heckel at Mannheim, who was president of the Richard Wagner Verein, he wrote on June 25, 1875: "Well, I am at it with Unger now. I have gone to great trouble to correct his Saxon vocalization, which made his voice wholly unintelligible, but I believe now that I shall do better with him than with any other tenor known to me."

To Unger himself he wrote on New Year's Day, 1876, both expressing satisfaction and proffering advice:

> It is comforting to turn my eyes on you. You are entered, together with Hey, in my book of hope. . . . Put your trust in me always! . . . I think of giving *Tristan* with you in Vienna late next autumn. If our divine Hey should wish to study it a little with you in advance, may I ask you not to do so until you are sure of Siegfried down to the tiniest muscle. For—in *one* part one can learn things of use in acting all other parts, but this *one* part must be fully assimilated! When you are as perfect as needs be in Siegfried, Tristan, for you, will be only a matter of memorising.

The sequel to these enthusiastic effusions is less rosy, though Unger was praised for his Siegfried at Bayreuth. But there was no *Tristan* in Vienna at the time mentioned and when the tenor accompanied Wagner to London the following May for the eight concerts of his music given in the Albert Hall in aid of Bayreuth, he was so often unable to appear that Wagner lost interest in him. From London he returned to his native Leipzig, where he sang in opera till 1881 and died in 1887. Further light on Wagner's ways with his singers is shed by no less an authority than the foresaid Julius Hey. Wagner at the piano had personally coached Unger for Siegfried in every nuance of color and expression, even to the point of trying to "influence his temperament." "Your whole outlook on life," he told him, "seems to be too heavy and black. It must become gay and sunny." And in a letter to Hey thanking the teacher for the good results of his "protracted efforts with Unger," and characteristically laying down the law about the fellow's voice, Wagner described the character of Siegfried as "distinguished by daemonic high spirits and impetuous self-confidence."

P. S.

The initial presentation of *Siegfried* in America occurred at the Metropolitan Opera House, New York, Nov. 9, 1887. The conductor was Anton Seidl. The cast comprised Lilli Lehmann (Brünnhilde), Auguste Kraus (Voice of the Forest Bird), Marianne Brandt (Erda), Max Alvary (Siegfried), Ferenczy (Mime), Emil Fischer (the Wanderer), Rudolph von Milde (Alberich), Josef Kögel (Fafner).

A historic revival took place at the Metropolitan Dec. 30, 1896, when Jean and Édouard de Reszké and Nellie Melba appeared for the first time as Siegfried, the Wanderer, and Brünnhilde, respectively. Again Anton Seidl conducted.

Götterdämmerung

[Dusk of the Gods]

MUSIC DRAMA IN A PROLOGUE AND 3 ACTS

Book by the COMPOSER

First performance: Festspielhaus, Bayreuth, Aug. 17, 1876

CHARACTERS

Brünnhilde, SOPRANO
Siegfried, TENOR
Alberich, BARITONE
Hagen, BASS
Gunther, Chief of the Gibichungs, BASS
Gutrune, his sister, SOPRANO
Hagen, son of Alberich and half-brother
    to Gunther, BASS

Waltraute, SOPRANO
Woglinde, SOPRANO
Wellgunde, SOPRANO
Flosshilde, MEZZO-SOPRANO
Three Norns: SOPRANO, MEZZO-SOPRANO,
    CONTRALTO

The three Norns (Fates of Northern mythology) break the golden rope of destiny as they pass it to one another. The Gods, seeing in this their doom, go down into the earth to their mother Erda. Brünnhilde sends Siegfried forth on a journey to the Rhine. Before he leaves he places the ring on her finger to give her strength. By the Rhine is the family of the Gibichungs, Gunther, head of the tribe, Gutrune, his sister, and Hagen, their half-brother. Hagen plans to unite Gunther and Brünnhilde, and Gutrune and Siegfried in marriage. Siegfried enters and, after drinking a potion which blots out his memory of Brünnhilde, he marries Gutrune, and sets out to bring Brünnhilde for Gunther. Brünnhilde refuses to give up Siegfried's ring to Wotan to save the Gods from destruction. Siegfried, disguised as Gunther, comes and takes the ring from Brünnhilde, and tells her she must be his wife. Siegfried returns to Gutrune, and they begin to celebrate a wedding feast. Gunther enters with Brünnhilde who is wild with anger when she sees Siegfried married to Gutrune. She and Hagen plan Siegfried's death and enlist Gunther's aid. She tells Hagen of the vulnerable spot in Siegfried's back. On a hunt Siegfried passes the Rhine, and the Maidens ask for his ring. When he refuses they predict his death. When the potion wears off and Siegfried regains his memory, he relates the story of his life and his love for Brünnhilde. Hagen stabs him in the back, and they bring him to Gutrune. Hagen and Gunther fight over the ring, and Gunther is killed. When Hagen tries to wrench it from Siegfried's finger the dead man raises his hand in warning. Brünnhilde enters, and takes the ring saying it will be restored to the Rhine Maidens after it has been purified by the fire that will burn Siegfried and herself. She lights the funeral pyre of Siegfried and mounted on her horse, Grane, rides into the flames.

The Rhine overflows and extinguishes the fire. The Rhine Maidens catch the ring when Brünnhilde flings it to them. Hagen drowns in the waters, and in the distance the Valhalla burns, destroying the Gods.

One of the longest of operatic works, as well as one of the greatest, *Götterdämmerung* (Dusk of the Gods) was in process of composition for a matter of twenty-six years. Wagner's preoccupation with the Scandinavian, Icelandic, and German sagas resulted in his writing in November, 1848, the dramatic poem, "Siegfrieds Tod" (Siegfried's Death), which was the text of *Götterdämmerung* in its first estate. This poem, finished on November 28, grew eventually into the series of four music dramas entitled collectively *Der Ring des Nibelungen* (The Nibelung's Ring). Work on the series was interrupted for years at a time, and only on November 21, 1874, did Wagner give the final touch to the last of the four, that being, of course, *Götterdämmerung*.

One of the most curious details of musical biography is the pleasure Wagner and his wife Cosima took while he was scoring *Götterdämmerung* in reading Xenophon's "Anabasis." Cosima herself has written of that experience: "It is as though one looked into a pure atmosphere, and he [Wagner] praises the naïveté, the complete unconsciousness of effect. How diffuse and colorless in comparison are our historians of today!"

When the November 21 arrived that witnessed the end of the colossal task begun so long before, it was clouded by one of those unfortunate domestic occurrences which were always impending owing to Wagner's excitable temperament. Cosima tells of it in her diary:

Thrice holy, memorable day! About noon Richard calls up to me that I might bring him the newspapers. Inasmuch as yesterday he complained to me of how overridden he is and declared he would not be done till Sunday, I supposed he was so tired he couldn't work any more. Shyly I avoided the question. To distract him I tossed him the letter I had just received from my father [Liszt] presuming him well disposed toward our going to Pest.

On reading the letter, Wagner wanted further information. Cosima told him what she was thinking of replying, purposely refraining from glancing at the scoresheet on the writing table in order not to offend him. Offended none the less, he informed her the score was completed, adding bitterly that whenever a letter from her father came, there was no further interest in him. For the time being she concealed her feelings, but when later Richard repeated the complaint, she burst into tears.

"That in pain I devoted my life to this work," she wrote, "did not earn me the right to celebrate its completion in joy. So I celebrated it in pain . . . I greet you eventful day, day of fulfillment! If the Genius can end his flight at such a height, what may the poor wife do! In love and rapture suffer."

The masterful Cosima, we may be certain, had dried her tears before the world première of *Götterdämmerung* took place in the new Festspielhaus at Bayreuth. That performance rounded out the first *Ring* cycle, on August 17, 1876. The magnitude of the four-part event attracted people from all corners of the earth, "a very Noah's ark company" of pilgrims, and the rumor of clashing opinions, the paeans of Wagner's champions and the philippics of his denigrators encircled the globe. Some of the views published at the time we read today with amusement, if perhaps not altogether with amazement. An English observer, the Reverend C. Halford Hawkins, wrote by no means unsympathetically in *Macmillan's Magazine:*

Here was a realization of an idealist's dream, so utterly alien to the spirit of the nineteenth century as commonly understood [Had the reverend gentleman, or had he not, heard of the "music of the future"?], that it will ever remain a marvel how a band of disciples could have been collected round the Master to carry it into effect. Yet the miracle, long postponed, has been performed; never, in the present writer's opinion, to be repeated. *Der Ring des Nibelungen* has been heard in its integrity, and probably will never be so heard again. It is a further illustration of the extraordinary activity and perseverance of the German nation.

Then the firm though kindly prophet of never-again throws off his mask of caution and boldly proceeds:

Here is the damning fact, that neither can orchestra be found to play, nor singers to declaim, nor audience to listen to the work as a whole again. Herein is chronicled the euthanasia of the magnum opus of the advanced school: for it is evident not even the riches of the score will induce the ordinary conductors or executants to rehearse frequently or perform unflaggingly; that no love of art or disdain of lucre will persuade singers to strain and sacrifice their voices to the caprice of a theorist, and finally no intellectual excitement, however supreme, will compel average audiences to study (as it must be studied) the minute development of tone and character painting which makes Wagner the George Eliot of music.

In spite of the thoroughness of this funeral oration, the *Ring* in its entirety has managed to survive innumerable repetitions; and if the analogy with George Eliot seems hardly apt, we at least know of the admiration the eminent novelist, on her side, entertained for Wagner's music. And in any event the reverend observer voiced the opinion of many another of his contemporaries who with regard to Wagner was really more pro than anti.

An American observer, John R. G. Hassard, writing in the *New York Tribune,* made no bones about his delight. At the end of *Götterdämmerung,* according to his account,

the whole audience rose in a transport of enthusiasm and shouted for Wagner until he came before the curtain and in a few words, spoken in a clear and pleasant voice, expressed his satisfaction with the efforts of the artists and the readiness of the people to sustain the highest efforts of art. He was called forward again, with shouts and cheers and the waving of hats, and then there were loud cries for the conductor [Hans Richter] who, however, did not respond.

You will have no difficulty in gathering from what I have written that the success of Wagner's experiment is not only complete, it is triumphant and unquestioned. . . . Some unnecessary criticism has been expended upon the singers and too much attention paid to little hitches (during the *Rheingold*) in the machinery and vagaries of the clouds. But we did not come 3500 miles to criticise a tenor or a steam-pipe.

January 25, 1888, was the date of the initial performance of *Götterdämmerung* in America, at the Metropolitan Opera House, minus the Norns and Waltraute. Anton Seidl conducted. In the cast were Lilli Lehmann as Brünnhilde and Albert Niemann as Siegfried.

P. S.

Parsifal

CONSECRATIONAL FESTIVAL STAGE PLAY IN 3 ACTS

Book by the COMPOSER

First performance: Festspielhaus, Bayreuth, July 26, 1882

CHARACTERS

Titurel, founder and retired King of the Knights of the Grail, BASS

Amfortas, his son and present ruler, BARITONE

Gurnemanz, a veteran Knight of the Grail, BASS

Parsifal, a "guileless fool," TENOR

Kundry, an enigmatic character, serving both the Brotherhood of the Grail and their enemy, Klingsor, CONTRALTO

Klingsor, a magician, BARITONE

Knights of the Grail, Klingsor's Flower Maidens, Esquires, and Boys

The action takes place during the Middle Ages in Spain, at Monsalvat, near and in the Castle of the Grail and in Klingsor's enchanted garden and castle

The action which has taken place before the play concerns the Spanish Pyrenees where the Knights of the Holy Grail live, guarding two sacred relics: the Spear with which the side of Christ was pierced, and the Cup of the Last Supper which also caught the blood from His side. They have refused Klingsor entry to their order. In a garden which he has created to tempt the Knights he contrives to ensnare Amfortas, King of the Grail, through the agencies of the fascinating Kundry. Amfortas is wounded by the Spear and can find no way to heal his wound. He must find an Innocent Fool, a man who can resist all temptation, and win back the Spear with which to cure Amfortas. He, then, will become the new King. The opera action opens at this point. Parsifal, a boy of the forest, is captured by the Knights for killing a swan. Gurnemanz believes this innocent lad may be the Fool for whom they are waiting. He shows no understanding of the service of the Eucharist which further convinces Gurnemanz. In the castle of Klingsor, Kundry is called to practice her wiles on Parsifal. He resists all temptations and finally, when Klingsor in anger hurls the Spear at him, Parsifal makes the sign of the Cross which protects himself, and destroys the garden. He wanders for some time until he gets back to the castle of the Holy Grail where he is received by Kundry who has repented and is now a servant of the Grail. With the Spear he heals Amfortas' wound. As Amfortas kneels before the new King, Kundry dies. Parsifal has become the Saviour of the Order of the Holy Grail.

Wagner, in January, 1882, a year and a month before his death, put the finishing touches to *Parsifal*. It was produced the following July at the Bayreuth Festspielhaus. The composer died suddenly in Venice on February 13, 1883. There are some who regard *Parsifal* as the richest, as well as the last, expression of Wagner's genius. Then, too, it stands apart from other music dramas. Though each of them from *Der fliegende Holländer* on is based upon a philosophic or moral idea—a thesis, in other words—*Parsifal* has also a religious element. Its "message," so to say, is derived from both Christian doctrine and Buddhism. Suffering, compassion, service, renunciation are of its component parts. The ethical core has been expressed thus: "Enlightenment coming through conscious pity brings salvation."

The brotherhood of knights who inhabit the Castle of the Holy Grail are the guardians of two sacred objects, the Spear that pierced the side of Jesus as He hung upon the Cross and the Cup from which He drank at the Last Supper and which received the blood from His wounded side. Only the pure in heart could belong to this brotherhood, whose mission was the doing of good with the help of the supernatural powers given them by the Grail.

The Grail myth is so much older than Christianity that its beginnings vanish in the mists of antiquity. A charm or talisman in the pagan world, the Grail, on Europe's being converted to Christianity, took its place as an element of Christian symbolism. In the latter estate two accounts of its origin prevailed. According to the earlier, when Archangel Michael smote the crown of Lucifer, a stone was dislodged which falling to the earth became the Grail. According to the later and more familiar version, the Grail was the sacred Cup of the Last Supper, in which Joseph of Arimathaea caught the Saviour's blood at the Crucifixion.

The legends clustering about the Grail have been related to a magic basin which, filled with wonder-working herbs, could bestow wisdom and even the gift of prophecy. It has been pointed out that in mediaeval Latin the word *gradalis* or *gradale* means basin or vase or cup. With the D changed to S or Z, in accordance with normal linguistic procedure, there exists today in some dialects of southern France *grasal* or *grazale* in the sense of basin.

Akin to the Grail are such conceptions as the Cup of Hermes (Egyptian) and the Basket of Dionysia (Greek), as well as the Black Stone of the Kaaba at Mecca, which is supposed to have been dropped from Paradise along with Adam and bears, among other names, that of "The Right Hand of God on Earth." The belief in a Redemption after the Fall is inherent in this body of myths. A curious variation identifies the basin with the charger that received the severed head of John the Baptist.

It was during the early conflicts in Gaul and Britain between the newly converted Christians and the priests of the ancient religion that the basin was fortified by the addition of the Lance or Spear. At first it signified resistance to the conquering foreigners; then it became the emblem of the persecuted. On the point of the spear the unconverted Celts, oppressed by the victors, took their oath of hatred and revenge. The sword that Siegfried in the northern epics forges anew is the sword that is wielded victoriously by him who possesses the requisite strength. In time this weapon came to be identified with the sword that struck off the head of John the Baptist, and eventually, thanks to the Crusades, the struggle to gain and hold relics of the Saviour gathered together in a definitive pattern the earlier and vaguer legends of cup, spear and sword.

Students of Wagner's texts may notice that in *Lohengrin* the name of the hero's father is given as *Parzival,* the ordinary German form. Why, when many years afterwards Wagner took Parzival as the subject of a music drama, should he have changed the spelling? It seems that a German philologist, one Goerres, bent on finding an Oriental origin for the Grail myth, pretended to derive the name of the Guileless Fool from the Arabic words *parseh,* meaning pure, and *fal,* meaning foolish, simple. Thus we should have "pure simple one" (that is Guileless Fool) in the very name Parsifal! And apparently Wagner was convinced by Goerres. But, according to Oriental scholars, in the bright lexicon of Arabic there is no such word as *fal!* So Wagner in his revised spelling went amiss.

Relatively early Wagner was obsessed with the idea of a religious drama—witness his project for a "Jesus of Nazareth" and his sketch of "Die Sieger" (The Victors). In 1845 he had made the acquaintance of the Parzival poem of the twelfth-century Minnesinger Wolfram von Eschenbach, the same who hymns the evening star in *Tannhäuser.* The upshot of that Wagner tells in his "Life." Late in April of 1857, he moved into the Asyl on the Wesendonck estate near Zurich.

Beautiful spring weather now set in [he writes]; on Good Friday [Wagner presumably had really in mind the Good Friday of 1858] I awoke to find the sun shining brightly for the first time in this house: the little garden was radiant with green, the birds sang, and at last I could sit on the roof and enjoy the long-yearned-for peace with its message of promise. Full of this sentiment, I suddenly remembered that the day was Good Friday, and I called to mind the significance this omen had already once assumed for me when I was reading Wolfram's "Parsifal." Since the sojourn in Marienbad, where I had conceived *Die Meistersinger,* and *Lohengrin,* I had never occupied myself again with that poem; now its noble possibilities struck me with overwhelming force, and out of my thoughts about Good Friday I rapidly conceived a whole drama, of which I made a rough sketch with a few dashes of the pen, dividing the whole into three acts.

Parsifal, however, had to wait its turn. Only in August, 1865, did Wagner sketch the libretto through, and it was not published in final form till December, 1877. Shortly before he had set to work on the score. A subscription performance at Bayreuth on July 26, 1882, was the occasion of the world première, followed by a public performance on July 30. The first public stage production outside of Bayreuth took place at the Metropolitan Opera House, under the management of Henrich Conried, on Christmas Eve, 1903. Great ceremony attended this performance, which was given uncut and at two sessions, the first beginning at 5 P.M. Alfred Hertz was the conductor, and the extraordinary cast included Alois Burgstaller as Parsifal, Milka Ternina as Kundry, Anton van Rooy as Amfortas, Robert Blass as Gurnemanz, Otto Goritz as Klingsor, Marcel Journet as Titurel, and to sing the five measures allotted to the mystic "alto voice" Louise Homer. There were eleven representations that season.

P. S.

At Bayreuth, every small detail was prearranged with an eye toward unity of effect, even the musical themes to be played for reassembling the audience after intermissions being stipulated by Wagner. He supervised everything about productions, with the exception of drilling orchestra and chorus—that function was, however, safely in the hands of men who had dedicated their very existence to the service of Wagner's ideals. Not content with being the first composer of operas to set only librettos of his own writing, and with having designed, down to the smallest acoustical detail, a great hall especially adapted to his music, Wagner ordered the scenery, designed the costumes, chose the singers, and made mandatory minutiae of voice and gesture. Applause and encores would have marred the continuity of the Wagnerian drama: they were banished. For the same reason, latecomers were not admitted until intermission. This was a long way, indeed, from the days when people had license to cook spaghetti in their loges, play chess, or indulge in chatter that drowned out whatever was coming from the orchestra pit and the stage. Unpermitted in Wagner's operas were the irrelevancies of virtuoso singers—even the spoiled Alvary could not sing an encore, add a special passage of vocal flourish, or interpolate some music he and the audience happened to like. The most practical commandments of Wagner in respect to conduct of both performers and audience still hold good in the best-run opera houses and concert halls, and thus guarantee to the modern music lover a chance to listen undisturbed. . . .

Because of its quasi-religious character, Wagner did not wish to have *Parsifal* performed outside Bayreuth: there the special facilities for its production had been brought into being under his own supervision, and there, too, a tradition of reverence had, from its first performance, clung to this last of the *Meister's* music dramas. Yet, there is evidence that, toward the end of 1882, he had so relaxed his point of view that he was willing to give Angelo Neumann a contract to take *Parsifal* on tour. He died, however, on February 13, 1883, without giving Neumann the precious document. Frau Cosima, *plus royaliste que le roi,* was fanatical in her efforts to restrict stage performances to Bayreuth. Oratorio versions and concert excerpts were another matter, and almost at once advantage was taken of this concession. During the Edmond C. Stanton regime at the Metropolitan occurred, on March 4, 1886, under Walter Damrosch, the first oratorio presentation of *Parsifal* in America, the principals, including Brandt and Fischer, singing in German; the Oratorio Society chorus sang in English.

Late in 1886, Stanton played with the idea of giving *Parsifal* as an opera, but was dissuaded by, among others, Lilli Lehmann, who considered the scheme a sacrilege. It was therefore shelved for fifteen years, when Conried, desiring something unusual for his first season at the Metropolitan, determined to brook all protest, and scheduled *Parsifal,* as a music drama, for Christmas Eve, 1903. It was a publicity move of genius: ministers thundered at him from their pulpits, Mayor Seth Low was asked to intervene, and the Wagner family, through their American representative, brought suit against Conried. But he was unmoved, confident in his knowledge that Wagner's operas were not protected by copyright in the United States. He won the suit, and produced the opera in an atmosphere of excitement comparable to that attending the election of a president. Fannie Bloomfield Zeisler, the pianist, chartered a special "Parsifal" Limited from Chicago, and the New York *Evening Telegram* brought out a "Parsifal" extra.

W. B., H. W.

Carl Maria von Weber

(Eutin [Oldenburg], Germany, Dec. 18, 1786–June 5, 1826, London)

Carl Maria von Weber has often been called the father of German opera. Like other musical paternities, the extent of this fatherhood is somewhat exaggerated, for the German people already possessed two great operas in their own tongue—Mozart's *Die Zauberflöte* and Beethoven's *Fidelio*. But while the language of these works was German, their libretti and the many Italian conventions to be found in them prevented their having popular appeal. The roots of von Weber's art are to be found more in the German "Singspiel" with its emphasis on folk life. In raising this form to a position of dignity, von Weber displaced the empty and shallow Italian opera and brought a truly indigenous German opera into being. Rooted in the people, in their folk-lore and their folk music, the "romantic opera" quickly established itself as a significant art form. In its later perfection at the hands of von Weber's most ardent disciple, Richard Wagner, it became one of the most important manifestations in the history of music.

Von Weber spent the first years of his life in the atmosphere of the theatre. His father, a former soldier, court official, and musician, now turned actor, had organized the several members of his family into a theatrical troupe which wandered through Germany performing in the principal towns. Von Weber received his first musical instruction from his father and an older step-brother; but as had been the case with both Haydn and Schubert, possession of a fine voice earned him a place in an institution, in this instance, the choirboys' school at Salzburg. Here he received thorough training at the hands of Michael Haydn, a younger brother of the more famous Joseph. In 1803 he journeyed to Vienna and placed himself under the tutelage of the celebrated Abbé Vogler. Vogler was an ardent student of folk music and directed von Weber's interest to it, an interest that was to have magnificent results.

Von Weber's active musical career commenced when he was nineteen years old; on Vogler's recommendation, he was given the post of opera conductor in the theater at Breslau. Operatic conducting was von Weber's principal activity throughout his lifetime, with the exception of an interval of six and a half years. Part of this time was spent as private secretary in the service of Duke Ludwig of Württemberg at his dissolute court at Stuttgart, and the rest in travel and concert appearances as a piano virtuoso. From 1813 to 1816 he directed operas in Prague, and from 1817 till his untimely death in 1826 he was Kapellmeister in charge of German opera at Dresden. As an operatic conductor, von Weber aroused antagonism in his colleagues because of his painstaking method of rehearsal and the meticulous care which he bestowed upon every aspect of an operatic presentation, including acting, costuming, and stage-setting as well as music. He was one of the first orchestral conductors to use a baton.

All of von Weber's great zeal as an operatic conductor was dedicated to one cause—the furtherance of German opera. Most of the important opera houses of the period were parts of the musical establishments of various royal houses, and the predominating taste of the sovereigns who dictated the destinies of these opera houses was Italian. Italian musicians were engaged to direct them and Italian operas were given preference. The two great German operas already in existence, *Die Zauberflöte* and *Fidelio*, were performed infrequently if at all. The German language was considered vulgar, and regular performances in the native tongue were usually given only in the smaller popular theaters. The situation which existed at the Saxon capital, Dresden, during von Weber's nine years of service there was thoroughly typical of the times. The King of Saxony had two Kapellmeisters in his employ, the Italian Morlacchi and the German von Weber. All the honors and royal approbation were bestowed upon the now-forgotten Italian. Despite the fact that von Weber had organized and conducted a splendid German opera company, his efforts were not appreciated, and he and the art for which he stood were almost completely ignored by the Royal House. The situation at Berlin paralleled that at Dresden, and in all of his relations with the Prussian king, von Weber, as the representative of German opera, met with a condescension and an apathy that bordered on insult.

Von Weber was catapulted into fame when his opera *Der Freischütz* was given in 1821. The applause at the first performance, which was unattended by the Prussian Court, was tumultuous; so great was the enthusiasm of the audience that the overture and one of the choruses had to be repeated. No other opera in the history of the German theater had ever met with such ready acceptance and with such popular demonstrations of approval. Within eighteen months there were fifty performances of the work in Berlin alone. The fame of the work spread quickly, and it was not long before it was heard not only on all the German stages, but in foreign capitals as well. A performance in English took place in New York as early as 1825. *Der Freischütz* was followed by *Euryanthe*, written for Vienna, and *Oberon*, written for London; but neither of these works, despite many features of merit, achieved the artistic level of their forerunner. The fame of von Weber rests almost entirely on his one masterpiece; of the two later operas only the brilliant overtures are regularly performed today. An earlier work for piano, "Invitation to the Dance," was salvaged from the fragments of an uncompleted opera and dedicated by von Weber to his wife. An orchestration of the work, frequently heard today, was made by Hector Berlioz in 1841 to be inserted as ballet music in the performances of *Der Freischütz* in Paris. Wholesale mangling of operas was not infrequent at that time, and garbled versions of works often appeared. At earlier Paris performances of *Der Freischütz* various liberties had been taken with the text, and the title of the work had been changed to *Robin des Bois*.

Like Mozart's and Schubert's, von Weber's life was tragically brief. While his music won him tremendous popular acclaim, the indifference of the ruling houses of Germany to one of the finest flowerings of their native art all but broke von Weber's heart. Continued exasperation slowly wore him down; and in a desire to provide for his wife and children he accepted an offer to compose *Oberon* for England, and to make the long and arduous journey to London to conduct the première of the work. The financial results of this London venture were disappointing, however, and von Weber's bitter sense of failure served further to undermine his already fragile constitution. He died of consumption in London on June 5, 1826, and was buried there. Eighteen years later his body was brought back to Germany, largely as a result of the efforts of Richard Wagner.

M R

He brought—as Cavalli did before him, in Venice, if not quite in the same way—the popular element into serious Opera, and the form itself closer to the hearts of the German people. This Mozart, one of the most intrinsically aristocratic geniuses in all Music, had never done; neither had Beethoven— notwithstanding the bourgeois quality of the *Fidelio*-text—done it much more than he. But in Weber's melody, no matter how broad in style or elaborately ornamented, you get all the romantic, out-of-door freshness of the Suabian folk-song, the peculiarly Teutonic sentimentality in its best expression; one might almost say he wrote in dialect. And if, in this, he did the Opera good service in Germany, he did other things, of a technical sort, the influence of which was farther-reaching. He effected a sort of interweaving of the *scena* * with the aria that did much to relax strictness of conventional form, and rendered the form more scenically plastic. The so-called Incantation-scene in the *Freischütz* even reaches out toward the Wagnerian Music-Drama, almost as much as the Statue-scene in *Don Giovanni*. It positively terrified contemporary pedants; but, when someone showed it to Beethoven, that appreciative great man said: "If the scene was to be set to music, I don't see how it could have been done in any other way." In this scene Weber shows all his ro-

---

* The term *scena* is applied to an accompanied recitative of more than usual length and dramatic quality, often (but not necessarily) containing passages in the *arioso* style. Donna Anna's recitative "Era già alquanto avanzata la notte," which debouches into the aria, "Or sai chi l'onore," in the first act of *Don Giovanni*, is a transcendent example of the older form of scena. Leonore's "Ascheulicher! wo eilst du hin?" in *Fidelio*, is another. Of Weber's intermingling of the scena with the aria, Max's "Nein! länger trag' ich nicht die Qualen," and Agathe's "Nie nahte mir der Schlummer," in *Der Freischütz*, and Rezia's "Ocean! thou mighty monster," in *Oberon*, are conspicuous examples.

mantic deviltry; probably no other composer in the whole list ever supped with the Devil with so short a spoon. Upon the whole, the supernatural was an element very congenial to him; few composers have treated it so to the manner born, with so little of the melodramatic, as he. The fairy music in *Oberon* stands unapproached.

W. F. A.

Der Freischütz

[The Free-Shooter]

ROMANTIC OPERA IN 3 ACTS

Book by Johann Friedrich Kind, after a story in the *Gespensterbuch,* edited by Johann August Apel and Friedrich Laun

First performance: Schauspielhaus, Berlin, June 8, 1821

CHARACTERS

Ottokar, a Prince of Bohemia, TENOR
Kuno, head ranger to the Prince, BASS
Agathe, his daughter, SOPRANO
Ännchen, a relative and friend of Agathe, SOPRANO

Caspar, first huntsman, BASS; Max, second huntsman, TENOR; in the service of KUNO
Zamiel, the Black Huntsman, SPEAKER
A Hermit, BASS
Kilian, a peasant, TENOR

Bridesmaids, Huntsmen, and Attendants on the Prince, Peasants, Musicians, Spirits, Demons, and Various Apparitions

The action takes place in Bohemia, shortly after the termination of the Thirty Years' War

The plot makes use of an ancient tradition of German foresters—the demon who buys the souls of hunters with magic bullets. In this instance, Kaspar, attached to Prince Ottokar of Bohemia, has sold out to the demon Zamiel, and is about to lose his soul unless he can substitute a new victim. The prince's chief huntsman, Kuno, wishes to retire, and Max, who is in love with Kuno's daughter, Agathe, hopes her father will consent to their marriage if he is appointed to her father's position. Kaspar, aided by Zamiel, causes Max to appear a poor shot in the first contest. The despondent Max then gets entangled in Kaspar's wiles and arranges a midnight meeting with him in Wolf's Glen, where Zamiel will give him the magic bullets. Agathe, who has a premonition of impending evil, is presented by a holy hermit with a magic wreath, which will protect her from danger. Max, though Agathe would detain him, keeps the midnight rendezvous.

In a terrifying incantation scene in Wolf's Glen, seven magic bullets are cast, six to do what Max wants them to do, the seventh to obey Zamiel. Agathe, still full of misgivings, pays no heed to the comforting humors of her maid, Ännchen. She puts on the hermit's wreath when by mistake a funeral wreath is sent her instead of the expected bridal wreath. Max, at the ensuing contest, easily comes off victorious, thanks to the six magic bullets. But when Prince Ottokar asks him to shoot once

657

more, Zamiel compels him to aim at Agathe. The wreath, however, protects her, and the deflected bullet actually pierces Kaspar's heart, whereupon Zamiel claims his victim, and Max, when he has confessed and won pardon, is united to Agathe.

P. S.

The year 1817 was epochal in the career of German romanticism, for it was then that Friedrich Kind presented Carl Maria von Weber with the libretto of *Der Freischütz.* In certain fields, the movement was already in lush maturity, but it was awaiting a salient musical expression of sufficient proportions and popularity to challenge the efforts of classical and pseudo-classical musicians, native or foreign, plying their trade in the German states. Weber was marked from birth to sweep German music into the romantic camp: he was qualified by heredity, experience, and special talents. There were, of course, huge chunks of romanticism in Schubert and the later Beethoven, not to mention lesser men, but the work of the former was, except in his own small circle, unknown, while Beethoven's, except in *Fidelio,* was in classical forms. Schubert's songs were too delicately wrought and intimate to be effective rallying points. *Fidelio* might have served had it been more popular, more theatrical, more stageworthy. In effect, it was merely a huge straw in the wind.

Weber's training for his mission included a childhood in traveling theatrical companies and a young manhood in operatic work, ranging from prompting to directing (at the age of twenty-six) the Prague opera house. Further, his personal life, disordered by the unpredictable behavior of a rogue father who dabbled in music, playwriting, acting, politics, and lithography, was itself a timid romantic extravaganza. Weber felt the strong call of the new, still heterogeneous Germany, and in 1814 had composed a group of patriotic songs and choruses that had touched the hearts of millions of his countrymen. The next year came his fervidly nationalistic cantata, "Kampf und Sieg," about which an old Prussian fire-eater of high rank had been pleased to remark, "With you I hear nations speaking." It was only natural, then, that Friedrich Augustus, King of Saxony, seized upon this redoubtable patriot when, in 1816, he was looking around for a *Kapellmeister* for the German opera at Dresden. But this was a political appointment, pure and simple, and the King, who doted on Italian opera, may have thought that his new employee would not take his job too seriously. If so, Friedrich Augustus had mistaken his man.

From the first, Weber fought tenaciously for the prerogative of the German opera. Actually, the native fare was scanty, and the *Kapellmeister* had to content himself with staging Meyerbeer, then at his most Rossinian, and Méhul's *Joseph* (in German, of course), a cantatalike opera in a dignifiedly lyrical vein. Oddly enough, he waited six years to give a Dresden performance of *Fidelio,* which he had staged in Prague as early as 1814. In moments he could snatch from onerous official duties, petty squabbles, literary efforts, composition of ceremonial folderol, touring as a piano virtuoso, getting married, and begetting his first child, Weber was himself preparing to swell the German repertoire. He was not utterly without experience as an operatic composer: two, possibly three, of his efforts, including the delightful little Singspiel *Abu Hassan* (Munich, 1811), had reached the boards. Most characteristic of these (in a Weberian sense) was *Silvana,* a rewriting of a Singspiel he had composed and produced at the age of thirteen. *Silvana* was tried out at Frankfort on the Main in September, 1810, but as a female balloonist was making an ascent outside the town, not only was the house practically empty, but some of the singers, in their frenzy to get a glance at the spectacle, skipped whole arias. The *première* was therefore far from propitious, but Weber always had a tenderness for *Silvana* and in his palmier days revived it. The libretto was outrageously, absurdly romantic—and the heroine was a mute. The score abounds in effects instantly recognizable as Weber's.

After *Abu Hassan,* no new opera by Weber was mounted for ten years, and then it was one based on a story that he was actually thinking of setting when the idea for *Abu Hassan* struck him. *Der Freischütz,* the cornerstone of German romantic opera, was achieved in the most haphazard and vacillating manner. Far from seeming to be pursued by a Teutonic demon that would not let him rest from his task of destiny, Weber acted just the opposite of a man about to make history. He discovered the story in 1810, but it was not until seven years later that he began talking it over with Friedrich Kind. He then wrote excitedly to his wife: "Friedrich Kind is going to begin an opera book for me this very day. The subject is admirable, interesting, and horribly exciting. . . . This *is* super-extra, for there's the very Devil in it. He appears as the Black Huntsman; the bullets are made in a ravine at midnight, with spectral apparitions around. Haven't I made your flesh creep upon your bones?" This was February, 1817. Kind, doubtless fired by Weber's enthusiasm, produced a libretto in ten days. Immediately, the composer's interest seemed to flag. During the remainder of that year, he squeezed out only one aria and a few rough sketches. Three days were all of 1818 that he devoted to the score. In March, 1819, he sketched the first-act finale in one day, and then abandoned work for six months. Suddenly, he apparently regained his old enthusiasm, and completed *Der Freischütz* between September, 1819, and May, 1820, writing the overture last.

Piqued by Dresden's seeming indifference to the prospects of German opera, and infuriated by its officials' scurvy treatment of himself as an operatic composer, Weber promised *Der Freischütz* to Berlin, then the seat of a vast if undiscriminating expansion in all the arts. There he was evidently appreciated, for Count Brühl, intendant of the court theaters, pledged his word that the new opera would be the first to be sung at the Schauspielhaus. Weber stuck to his part of the bargain: when the opening of the Schauspielhaus was delayed for a year, he simply laid *Der Freischütz* aside, and went about his other business. Copenhagen heard a sample of the opera when Weber went there on tour: the ever-popular overture received its first acclamation. In 1821, when the Schauspielhaus was finally ready, *Der Freischütz* was billed for June 18.

Meanwhile, however, something had happened to depress Weber's friends: Gasparo Luigi Pacifico Spontini, a composer of vast operatic canvases, and extraordinarily honored in France, had secured the lucrative post of royal music director in Berlin in 1819. He had already tested, with flattering success, Prussian response to his music, and the Berlin *première* of his lavish *Olympie,* with a libretto translated by Hoffmann, was scheduled for May 14, little more than a month before *Der Freischütz. Olympie* was so magnificent as a spectacle that the Berliners were hypnotized into believing that the music was better than it really was. Weber alone kept his head, certain that his own opera was a masterpiece. So calm, indeed, was he that between rehearsals he composed the still-famous "Concertstück." When the Prussian capital heard *Der Freischütz* on that sixth anniversary of Waterloo, it was found that Spontini had met his Wellington.

Various operas have established the reputations of their composers overnight, but the wild acclamation that greeted *Der Freischütz* was something special. The excited temper of the audience was evident from the moment the overture was encored, the ardor being heightened by the fiery applause of the many members of the *Landswehr,* all of whom had, during the fateful years of the Napoleonic crisis, thrilled to Weber's patriotic songs and choruses. Representatives of the arts were there in force, including Hoffmann, Felix Mendelssohn, and Heine, nor was society less brilliantly shown off at this historic performance. From his peers Weber received the accolade he seems to have anticipated—after the opera was over, Hoffmann crowned him with a laurel wreath. But his final triumph came from a wider quarter. Before six months had elapsed, *Der Freischütz* had been presented to clamorous audiences throughout Germany and had become a loved favorite of the people, which it remains. In Vienna, even a truncated version caused by an imperial ban on the Devil himself, as well as on the guns and bullets that are essential to the salient scene, could not stem this wildfire. Finally, on January 26, 1822, Dresden was converted. And, on March 2, 1825, less than four years after its world *première,* New York heard *Der Freischütz,* in English, the first true opera to be heard there.

Although it is never presented as one, *Der Freischütz* was originally a Singspiel, with a great deal of the plot carried forward by spoken dialogue. While Tieck, the great spokesman of romanticism, sneeringly remarked that it was just another Singspiel, he could not deny that it was brimming over with true-blue romantic feeling. It was (and this was an aspect of *Der Freischütz'* success that Weber came to resent) the sort of thing that ordinary people, especially those without artistic sophistication, took to their hearts and kept there. It is tremulous with emotion (not excluding sentimentality), full of shudders, full of plot, and extremely proper—Agatha, the heroine, is more nicey-nice than Parsifal; not unnaturally, this role was chosen for the operatic debut of Jenny Lind, on March 7, 1838, at Stockholm. It is drenched with that quality for which only German has a word—*Gemüthlichkeit*—and the very fact that the peculiarly heart-warming and folksy Hunting Chorus, from Act III, was, and in its native land still is, the most popular number from the opera shows that it was this quality that first captivated Germany.

The overture sums up all these qualities, being an enormously clever patchwork not only of musical segments, but also of theatrical effects and moods. It is played constantly by both symphony orchestras and bands. Outside Germany, very little more of the opera survives in popular musical memory. Occasionally, a soprano with a big enough voice will revive the dramatically tender "Leise, leise," and even more rarely a tenor may be heard in the still fresh "Durch die Wälder," an ingenuous evocation of woodland spirit. . . .

Of the historical importance of *Der Freischütz* there can be no doubt. Meyerbeer and Wagner owed much to it, and so did lesser men, including Marschner and, in his own despite, Spohr. It is difficult not to hear echoes of it in Rossini's *Guillaume Tell*. What Weber passed on to those men was not only such specific things as new orchestral effects, both in general color and in the handling of separate instruments, but also a broad understanding of music definitely for the stage. He gave them a new atmosphere to play with, to draw out into subtleties, and, finally, to spiritualize. This new atmosphere was, of course, musical romanticism—the something that throbs through *Der fliegende Holländer, Tannhäuser, Lohengrin,* and *Die Meistersinger,* through Schumann's overture to "Manfred" and the "Symphonie fantastique" of Berlioz. Unfortunately, it also pulses blatantly through the overtures of Suppé and whole cohorts of imitators of that king of imitators. It is a currency that has become so debased that we thoughtlessly extend to the model the stigma of the counterfeit. Too much din of this variety has assailed our ears—too many challenging horns, too many slow, moon-bathed introductions and galloping finales—for us to be able to "hear" *Der Freischütz* as Weber conceived it (with its unquestionable originality) and as those first audiences heard it (with its unquestionable impact of novelty). . . .

Der Freischütz has been most widely retained of all the Weber operas. New York has heard it in German, French, Italian, and English. After a single performance at the Metropolitan in the season of 1884–85, a quarter of a century intervened; then sixteen repetitions were bunched into twenty years, the last in 1929, when Elisabeth Rethberg appeared triumphantly as Agatha. In France, the opera, though in an abominable distorted version that aroused the bitter maledictions of Berlioz, attained a success that at first rivaled its vogue in Germany. The perpetrator of this scandal was François-Henri-Joseph Blaze, better known as Castil-Blaze, a respectable enough musicologist but a fiendish

Procrustes to what he considered intractable operas, who in the course of his nefarious activities operated similarly on stage works by Mozart, Rossini, and Donizetti.

In 1824, Castil-Blaze prepared a translation and adaptation of both the book and music of *Der Freischütz,* called it *Robin des bois,* and had it presented at the Odéon. The performance was so sloppy that it was hissed off the stage, and Castil-Blaze wisely withdrew it for revision, particularly of the casting. But when it was staged again, many of those who had hissed the first performance of *Robin* returned to vent their spite on the refurbishment. When Castil-Blaze saw how the wind was blowing, he papered the house night after night for more than a week. At that point, popular curiosity was strained to such a point that demand broke through his all-sold-out artifice, and legitimate ticket sales forced 327 consecutive performances. Not realizing what they were seeing and hearing was a caricature, the French romantics—Victor Hugo among them—went into ecstasies over *Robin des bois.* Before the craze evaporated, articles of dress and other objects were named after *Robin.* Only Berlioz, the purist, continued to object, though it is worth noting that, years later, when he himself was in a position of authority at the Opéra, he felt called upon to adapt Weber's score to certain realistic exigencies of production.

W. B., H. W.

The sensitive Weber was well aware that his new opera had its bitter and sarcastic opponents. The poet Tieck spoke of *Der Freischütz* as "the most unmusical uproar I have heard upon a stage." Louis Spohr, an ultraconservative for whom Beethoven's Fifth Symphony had been incomprehensible, wrote: "As I never had a great opinion of Weber's talent as a composer, I wanted to hear this opera to discover the secret of its wonderful success; but this riddle was by no means solved, and I can only explain it by the gift possessed by Weber to write for the general masses." Zelter, writing to Goethe, made fun of *Der Freischütz* with the witticism that "out of a small nothing the composer had created a colossal nothing." Even E. T. A. Hoffmann, who had crowned Weber with a wreath of laurels and presided at a literary party after the performance, could not resist some pointed barbs. At the performance, printed verses were showered over the audience reminding them that whatever animals Weber had used he did not have to rely upon elephants for his success. Various stage contraptions had been introduced into the wolf glen scene of *Der Freischütz,* such as an owl of which one wing failed to flutter and whose gleaming eyes were too obviously a pair of oil lamps. There were also fireworks which failed to go off. Spontini's *Olimpia,* which had been produced on the previous May 14 and which was fastened upon by the advocates of Italian opera, had resorted to such spectacular features as live elephants for its success. Weber was distressed at this slight upon Spontini, and even more so by a *bon mot* circulated against his librettist and friend August Kind:

"Maria trägt das Kind," a word play upon the names of the composer and the poet especially annoying to the latter because he tended to appropriate the success of *Der Freischütz* to himself. His adherents answered, *"Was wäre Maria ohne Kind?"* This led to a break between the two.

J. N. B.

The American *première,* in English, occurred March 2, 1825, at the Park Theater, New York. A French version was performed at the same theater Aug. 13, 1827. The original German version reached New York Dec. 8, 1845, at Palmo's Opera House. At the Astor Place Opera House, Oct. 21, 1850, *Der Freischütz* was performed in Italian.

Der Freischütz has been presented in a number of places with various emendations and interpolations. The most recent performances at New York's Metropolitan Opera House, beginning with the revival of March 23, 1924, have been provided with recitatives by the conductor, Artur Bodanzky. Mr. Bodanzky refrained, however, from adding to Weber's score in the Wolf's Glen scene. Recitatives for production in French at the Paris Opéra in 1841 were provided by Berlioz. For an Italian production at Covent Garden, London, in 1850, Sir Michael Costa composed recitatives.

Euryanthe

ROMANTIC OPERA IN 3 ACTS

Book by Helmine von Chezy

First performance: Kärnthnerthor Theater, Vienna, Oct. 25, 1823

CHARACTERS

Louis VI, BASS
Adolar, Count of Nevers, TENOR
Euryanthe of Savoy, his bride, SOPRANO

Lysiart, Count of Forêt, BARITONE
Eglantine de Puiset, captive daughter
of a mutineer, MEZZO-SOPRANO

The action takes place at the Castle Premery and burg of Nevers in the early twelfth century

The plot, which has been described as a mixture of "Cymbeline" and *Lohengrin,* is derived from an old French romance, "L'Histoire de Gérard de Nevers et de la belle et vertueuse Euryanthe, sa mie." The first scene takes place in the court of the French king. Count Adolar sings of the beauty and virtue of his affianced bride, Euryanthe, in the melodious aria, "Unter blühenden Mandelbäumen." Count Lysiart sneeringly replies that he knows he can gain her favor. Adolar demands proof.

There is a change of scene to the castle of Nevers, where we find both Euryanthe and the evil Eglantine, who also is in love with Adolar. Euryanthe unwisely confides to Eglantine the secret of the unhappy Emma, Adolar's sister. Emma has killed herself and from a near-by tomb her ghost has come forth and haunted Euryanthe and Adolar, informing them that she can never be at rest till tears of innocence have fallen on the ring which brought about her death.

Count Lysiart now appears bearing an order to take Euryanthe to the King. Eglantine remains behind, gloating over the secret of Emma's tomb.

In the next act, Lysiart is deploring his failure to win Euryanthe. He has a renewal of hope, however, when he encounters Eglantine coming out of the tomb with the ring. For now he can establish Euryanthe's indiscretion or at least her breaking her word not to tell the secret of Emma's death. At the royal palace he faces Euryanthe with the ring and she has to admit her breach of faith. The disillusioned and angry Adolar carries her off to a wilderness where he means to kill her. But there they are attacked by a serpent, which Adolar slays. Then, in pity, he refrains from killing Euryanthe, merely abandoning her to her fate.

The King, out hunting, comes upon her and learns from her of Eglantine's treachery. Whereupon he takes her back to the palace. Count Adolar, thinking things over, suspects that Euryanthe has been victimized by Eglantine, and he sets out for Nevers to get satisfaction from Count Lysiart. On the way, he comes across the wedding procession of Eglantine and Lysiart. It is interrupted, however, by the arrival of the King, who tells them that Euryanthe is dead. Immediately Eglantine discards her bridegroom, announcing her love for Adolar. Lysiart, in his rage, stabs her. Of course, Euryanthe has not died, but only fainted, and as she and Adolar are reunited, Lysiart is led off to execution.

P. S.

The composition of *Euryanthe* was the result of a commission given to Weber by Domenico Barbaja, manager of the Kärnthnerthor and the An der Wien theaters in Vienna, to write a new opera for the first-named house.

Weber was delighted with this commission, for his spirit, in spite of the enormous public triumph that had been gained in 1821 by *Der Freischütz*, had been wounded by the remarks of the professional critics to the effect that that masterpiece, being, they declared, merely a glorified "singspiel," * had not been able to compete in mastery of form with the works of other composers who had given the world grand operas. Now, in the very year of that triumph, the master decided that his new work should silence that criticism. Two essentials first had to be met—a librettist and an effective subject. Weber considered a number of stories. With his friend, Friedrich Kind (who had supplied the libretto for *Der Freischütz*) he discussed an opera on the Cid; but the two almost immediately quarreled, and their collaboration came to nothing. Ludwig Rellstab approached Weber with a text based upon the story of Dido, the legendary foundress of Carthage and the lover of Aeneas. But Dido had been made the subject of operas by innumerable composers, and Weber decided against her. It was just then that he met Frau Helmina von Chezy, who lived in Dresden, where also Weber officiated as conductor at the Dresden Opera. The lady had recited some of her poetical effusions at the Liederkreis, and the composer, who happened to be present, was sufficiently impressed by their quality to ask her to become his collaborator in the new work. A number of subjects were discussed, but finally it was decided to employ one—the story of Euryanthe—that would be likely to appeal to a public that was filled with admiration for romantic opera. This story was by no means the invention of Frau von Chezy. The original version of the tale is to be found in the "Roman de la Violette" by the 13th century writer, Gilbert de Montreuil. But the legend had been used by others.

It was not long before Weber discovered that he had vastly over-rated the abilities of the Dresden poetess. She had no idea of the exigencies of the theater, and her writing was as turgid as her plot. Moreover, Frau von Chezy was extraordinarily eccentric. She would descend upon Weber at all hours, her loud voice and unconventional attire evoking scarcely suppressed titters from visitors who might happen to be present. "Weber," wrote the composer's son,

---

* Singspiel was a German form of dramatic entertainment in which music was interspersed with dialogue. In French and Italian "grand opera" music was employed continuously throughout, recitative being employed instead of spoken text.

"often felt inclined to turn the 'Chez,' as he called this thing in petticoats, that was neither man nor woman, out of the house."

The text of the first act of *Euryanthe* was completed in December, 1821, and the composer, having patched up its weakest portions, set to work to write the music. Much of the opera was written at Hosterwitz, and, with the exception of the overture, was finished August 29, 1823. In September Weber departed for Vienna to begin the rehearsals of *Euryanthe,* and it was there that the overture was written in the three days, October 16–19, 1823. The production of the opera took place at the Kärnthnerthor Theater, Vienna, October 25. The great fame that had come to Weber with *Der Freischütz* insured a crowded house, and, indeed, great expectations had been evoked by the new work.

The overture was greeted with acclamation, and it was evident that the audience wished to hear it again. Weber refused to accede to this desire, for he was afraid that the performance would become too protracted. Perhaps, also, he was not too well satisfied with the performance; for his son, Max von Weber, testified (in the biography of his father) that the playing was by no means worthy of the music, and that, in addition to a faulty ensemble, the violins often played the passage-work incorrectly.*

When the curtain fell upon the close of the last scene there was an ovation for the creator of *Euryanthe;* but what appeared to be a success turned out to be merely the postponement of a failure. After Weber had conducted the third performance, and had left for Dresden, public attendance fell off in marked degree. It was generally felt that the plot was incomprehensible, and there were those who declared that Weber's music was too long and too noisy. In order to remedy the defects of the libretto Conradin Kreutzer was called in to make a revision of it. But the result of this was to cause *Euryanthe* to be more incomprehensible than ever. After twenty representations had been given, the opera was withdrawn. Schubert was present at one of them, but was unable to find anything in Weber's work that was to his liking. Beethoven was living in Vienna, but he did not attend the Kärnthnerthor Theater, for he was completely deaf.

F. B.

When Weber set out for Vienna in September [1823] he was a tired, ailing man. In his job, in the face of enmity from his coworkers, royal negligence,

---

* A grotesque incident occurred immediately before the performance. There was a tumult in the parterre of the opera-house. There was laughing, screaming, cursing. A fat, carelessly dressed woman, with a crushed hat and a shawl hanging from her shoulders, was going from seat to seat, screaming out: "Make room for me! I am the poetess, I am the poetess!" It was Mme. von Chezy, who had forgotten to bring her ticket and was thus heroically attempting to find her seat. The laughter turned into applause when Weber appeared in the orchestra, and the applause continued until the signal for beginning was given.

P. H.

and ceaseless petty annoyances, he had been burning up his energies, already sadly wasted by tuberculosis. Yet, he threw himself into the rehearsing of *Euryanthe* with his accustomed abandon and was not daunted by singers' complaints—requests for the insertion of special arias, star billing, and so on—and the adverse criticism of his friends, professional and nonprofessional. Except for certain reservations about the libretto, Weber seems to have been as complacent about the high quality of *Euryanthe* as he had been about that of *Der Freischütz*—he was certain that it was a good opera. True, young Franz Schubert, who had succumbed completely to the folk magic of the earlier opera, was cool about the new, which he heard in rehearsal and pronounced lacking in melody. This must have annoyed Weber, for when Schubert showed him the score of one of his own ill-fated operas, he said that first operas, like first puppies, should be drowned. This remark, in turn, must have incensed Schubert, for later he spoke even more acidly of *Euryanthe:* "This is no music. There is no finale, no concerted piece according to the rules of art. It is all striving after effect. And he finds fault with Rossini! It is utterly dry and dismal."

So too thought Vienna, which had just risen from a feast of its beloved Rossini. By comparison, *Euryanthe* was funeral meats. Although the three hours consumed by the *première* of the opera, on October 25, 1823, would not seem long by modern standards, they bored the local wits, who cruelly said that Weber was evidently writing for eternity. The critics were more forthright, but quite as harsh. Strangely enough, *Euryanthe* persisted for twenty performances that season before being retired for many years. It has never been a lasting success anywhere. The Metropolitan has given it only nine times in all, the last performance being in 1915. For, with reservations, Schubert and the Viennese were right: as a stage work, *Euryanthe* is an unmitigated failure. The reservations, then, are musical, not theatrical. It is impossible now to discover why Weber, who had smelled grease paint from his infancy, and who knew what was theatrically effective and what was not (his mountings of other composers' operas were notable for their point and taste), had not summarily tossed the libretto aside. Beside it, the rigmarole of *Die Zauberflöte* is Euclidean logic. Admitting that the libretto would throw any man, it is nonetheless odd that Weber, once having accepted it and perspired over its revisions, did not compose more apposite and telling music for the few dramatic high spots it has.

Actually, *Euryanthe* lives more dimly than *Der Freischütz*. Weber pieced together, in one of his précis overtures, the best of his purely musical inspirations, and that is still often heard. As for the rest, even the several pleasantly lyrical airs are never resurrected. Weber had failed in his chief purpose of writing a grand opera that would prove his position as a serious composer, and was left with the chill comfort of a studied encomium from Ludwig Tieck. Yet, again, *Euryanthe,* like *Der Freischütz,* exerted considerable influence on the course of opera, for from its elaborate first scene—a full-dress ceremonial at the court of Louis VI of France—stem those similar scenes of pomp and circumstance that Meyerbeer used in *Les Huguenots,* Wagner in *Tannhäuser, Lohengrin,* and *Die Meistersinger,* and Verdi in several operas, notably *Aïda.*

As early as the rehearsals of *Euryanthe,* Weber was in agonizing ill health. Now he began to die. Nothing could save him except complete inactivity, but the harrying duties of his position, as well as his neurotic financial fears, would not permit him to rest. For a time, public coldness to *Euryanthe* suspended his operatic activities, despite the fact that *Der Freischütz* was going on from success to success, abroad as well as in Germany. For fifteen months, Weber composed nothing.

Euryanthe has always been unfortunate, though Weber secured the seventeen-year-old Henriette Sontag for the title role, thus helping to launch one of the most brilliant operatic careers of the century—a career that brought this poor girl a countess' coronet and unstinted professional and domestic happiness.

W. B., H. W.

In the original German *Euryanthe* was presented at the Metropolitan Opera House, New York, Dec. 23, 1887. Whether this was the American *première* has not been established. There is an unsubstantiated report that *Euryanthe* was given at Wallack's Theater, New York, in 1863, but no record of such a performance or of any other in New York before 1887 has been found.

The chief singers in 1887 were Lilli Lehmann (Euryanthe), Marianne Brandt (Eglantine), Max Alvary (Adolar), and Emil Fischer (Lysiart).

On Dec. 19, 1914, there was a revival of *Euryanthe* at the Metropolitan conducted by Arturo Toscanini. The chief singers were Frieda Hempel, Margarete Ober, Johannes Sembach, and Hermann Weil. *Euryanthe* has not been presented in America since that season.

Oberon

ROMANTIC OPERA IN 3 ACTS

Book in English by JAMES ROBINSON PLANCHÉ, after the old French romance, *Huon de Bordeaux*, as adapted by the German poet WIELAND and translated into English by SOTHEBY

First performance: Covent Garden, London, Apr. 12, 1826

CHARACTERS

Oberon, King of the Fairies, TENOR
Titania, his Queen (ACTING PART)
Puck, his attendant sprite, CONTRALTO
Droll, CONTRALTO
Harun-al-Rashid, Caliph of Bagdad, BASS
Rezia, his daughter, SOPRANO
Fatima, her attendant, MEZZO-SOPRANO
Sir Huon de Bordeaux, Duke of
  Guienne, TENOR

Sherasmin, his squire, BARITONE
Babekan, a Persian prince, BARITONE
Mesrour, chief of the harem guards,
  (ACTING PART)
Almanzor, Emir of Tunis, BARITONE
Roschana, his wife, CONTRALTO
Abdallah, a corsair, BARITONE
Charlemagne, BASS

Elves, Nymphs, Sylphs, Genii, Mermaids; Spirits of the Air, Earth, Water, and Fire; Mermen; Retinue of the Caliph, Ladies Attendant on Rezia, Black and White Servants of the Harem, Slaves, Dancers of Both Sexes, a Janissary Band, Watchmen, Moorish Boys, Corsairs, Retinue of Charlemagne, Pages, Nobles, Priests, Choirboys, Halberdiers, etc.

The action is laid in France, Bagdad, and Tunis at the beginning of the ninth century

Three characters made familiar through Shakespeare's "A Midsummer Night's Dream" appear in this opera, Oberon and Titania, king and queen of the Fairies, and the sprite Puck.

The king and queen have had a falling out, and he swears no reconciliation will be possible until two lovers can be found who will remain faithful to each other through a variety of temptations and ordeals. The enterprising Puck brings word of Sir Huon of Bordeaux, who has been insulted by Charlemagne's son and has slain him in a duel and is condemned by the emperor to go to Bagdad to kill the man at the left hand of the caliph and to bring back with him the caliph's daughter, Rezia. Oberon decides that this is the indicated pair, so he brings it about that Sir Huon beholds Rezia in a vision and immediately falls in love with her. Oberon also gives Sir Huon a magic horn, which shall enable him always to summon the help of the fairy queen, and likewise a cup that fills at pleasure and detects any villainy in the drinker.

Thus equipped, Sir Huon sets out and does as he has been told to do at Bagdad. On the way back to Charlemagne's court, however, Sir Huon and Rezia have all sorts of misadventures including shipwreck, slavery, and condemnation to death by fire. But they remain unshakably faithful and finally are saved from dying by the magic horn. In the end, Titania forgives Oberon and Charlemagne pardons Sir Huon.

P. S.

When Weber composed *Oberon* he was a dying man and he knew it. To his anxious friend Gubitz he wrote: "Money must be made for my family—money, man. I am going to London to die there. Not a word! I know it as well as you." Yet the music in its sum total is cheerful, brilliant, abounding in vitality, keen for the high emprise. Chivalrously the doomed musician steps forth to face his chivalric theme, wearing bravely his gallant plume without a difference. We may well doubt whether an artist's physical state is necessarily mirrored in his work.

The writing of *Oberon* is a chronicle of courage and pathos. In 1824 the management of Covent Garden was in the hands of Charles Kemble of the famous theatrical family—an eminent actor himself and a brother of John Philip Kemble and Sarah Siddons, as well as the father of Fanny Kemble and thus the great-grandfather of the American novelist Owen Wister. Inspired by the immense vogue of *Der Freischütz,* he desired an opera by Weber expressly composed to please the British public. So in July, 1824, he went to Ems, where Weber, already consumptive, was taking the waters, to discuss the matter in person with the composer.

Kemble had two subjects for an opera in mind. One was Goethe's "Faust," the other Wieland's poem "Oberon" (derived from the *chanson de geste* "Huon de Bordeaux"). Weber had doubts concerning an operatic "Faust" but "Oberon" seized his fancy. Planché was selected to supply the book and Weber himself was to go to London to superintend the rehearsals and conduct the earlier performances. Then came the question of money.

Weber refused Kemble's first offer of £500, but when the manager doubled it, he accepted. True, his doctor told him frankly that if he were to go to London, between the climate and the work involved, the end would be a matter of months or perhaps weeks, whereas if he would spend one year in Italy he might live for four or five. Weber thought of his wife and children and their needs after his death. "As God wills!" he exclaimed and chose London.

In spite of his poor health, Weber's artistic conscience would not allow him to set an English text without first mastering the language. Consequently he set out to learn English thoroughly, taking one hundred and fifty-three lessons from an Englishman named Carey, and the astonishing progress he made can be gathered from his English letters to Planché.* The librettist sent Weber, who was in Dresden, the first and second acts early in January, 1825, and the composer began his musical sketches on the twenty-third. The score was not finished, however, when Weber started for England on February 7, 1826, accompanied by his devoted friend Kasper Fürstenau, the flautist.

In London he was the guest of Sir George Smart, conductor of the London Philharmonic Society. Though gravely ill when he arrived on March 5, and harried by the dampness and fog of London, he braced himself to go through with his task. "All the light and life and freshness and geniality of the work gushed forth from the brain of a weak, sick, bowed-down, irritated man, who was shattered by an incessant cough, who sat at his work table wrapped up in furs, with his swollen feet in wadded velvet boots, and yet shivered with cold in his heated room; as though the genius which created all had nothing in common with the poor suffering body." † Rehearsals began on March 9, and he had to be present at all fifteen. The overture, which, like not a few other overtures, was, paradoxical as it may seem, written last, Weber completed on April 9.

Three days later the première was a triumph. Benedict in his life of Weber, after recording that the overture was so wildly applauded that the composer-conductor had no choice but to repeat it, goes on to tell us that every other piece also received its full meed of approbation, "and without a single dissentient voice, to the last note of the opera. When the curtain fell, the entire audience, who had shown the composer their attention and regard by remaining in their places till all was over, rose simultaneously with frantic and unceasing calls for Weber, who at last appeared, trembling with emotion, exhausted, but happy."

After the performance Weber could write to his wife: "By God's grace I have had tonight such a perfect success as never before." And though dying, he conducted eleven more performances of *Oberon* and several concerts, including one of the Philharmonic Society and a benefit concert at the Argyll Rooms. His entire earnings in London amounted to the equivalent of $5,355.

On the evening of June 4, Weber had to be helped upstairs to bed. To Fürstenau he remarked: "God reward you for all your kind love to me. Now let me sleep." The next morning the maid informed Smart that she had knocked at Weber's door but there was no answer. Smart, who sent at once for Fürstenau and a doctor, relates in his diary: "On bursting open the bedroom door, we found Weber dead, lying tranquilly on his right side, his cheek in his hand."

Smart's house, at 91 Great Portland Street, was provided in 1894 with a

---

* When Planché sent him a French translation of the text, he answered: "I thank you obligingly for your goodness of having translated the verses in French; but it was not so necessary, because I am, though yet a weak, however, a diligent student of the English language."

† [Weber's son and biographer, Max Maria von Weber.]

memorial tablet, the gift of the Incorporated Society of Musicians, telling that there Weber had died. The house stood till 1907, when its old walls yielded to the march of progress.

P. S.

What *Oberon* would have been like had Weber lived to revise it, it is difficult to guess, but certainly in its present form it leaves much to be desired. Nor have its inadequacies been effectively masked by the fumbling remedies of the patchwork artists of varying degrees of grandeur, from Benedict to Bodanzky, who have sweated over the score. Unhappily, *Oberon* has a central organic disease—chronic rather than acute—that defies the blue pencilings and additions of learned musical doctors.

As Weber left it, *Oberon* is a bad play, preceded by his best overture, and interrupted by fine outbursts of song. There is a sort of mutual courtesy between the action and the music that does not allow them to get in each other's way—they alternate, but do not co-operate. The result is emulsion, not solution. The musical reflection of the drama's play and contrast is all in the overture, which, in addition to its sheer loveliness, is an adroitly calculated piece of stage music. The *scena* "Ocean, thou mighty monster," which already has been quoted copiously in the overture, is Weber's most brilliant writing for voice: symphonic in scope, epic in style, and too taxing for any but the strongest and most gifted of dramatic sopranos, it is of the lineage of *"Abscheulicher, wo eilst du hin?"* and the *Liebestod*. The rest of the opera is tuneful, with the separate numbers eloquent enough in illustrating the rather painful *tableaux vivants* that turn up.

Thus, the most famous German operatic composer of the early nineteenth century left three immortal operas that are almost never performed, even after —in two cases—most auspicious beginnings. *Oberon,* for instance, boasted an ideal cast for its *première:* Mary Anne Paton, its Rezia, and John Braham, its Sir Huon, were the idols of the English public, and almost as well liked was the Fatima, Lucia Elizabeth Vestris. Weber pronounced the orchestra the best he had ever heard. Yet, despite Weber's popularity in England both personally and as a composer—*Der Freischütz* had been a notable attraction there for some years—*Oberon* scarcely outlived the furore attending the performances the composer himself conducted. Similarly, although it reached New York two years after its London performance, it disappeared from the American stage for ninety years.

W. B., H. W.

Several attempts have been made to grand-operatize *Oberon*. In 1860 it was performed in London in an Italian translation with recitatives by Sir Julius Benedict and added numbers taken from *Euryanthe*. Gustav Mahler made a German edition with recitatives and Artur Bodanzky prepared recitatives and otherwise arranged the score for a production in English at the Metropolitan Opera House on Dec. 28, 1918. The cast of this first Metropolitan *Oberon* included Rosa Ponselle (Rezia), Alice Gentle (Fatima), Giovanni Martinelli (Sir Huon), Paul Althouse (Oberon), Marie Sundelius (a Mermaid), and Albert Reiss (Sherasmin). The American *première* of *Oberon* in the original version took place at the Park Theater, New York, Oct. 9, 1828.

Index

ABOUT THE AUTHOR

Born in New York City in 1907, Louis Biancolli was educated entirely in the Borough of Manhattan which has always been his home. He received his B.A. and M.A. degrees at New York University, and then did further graduate work at Columbia University.

While still at college he was assistant to the late Pitts Sanborn of *The New York World-Telegram,* where he is still employed as music critic. For several years he was co-annotator, with Robert Bagar, of the New York Philharmonic-Symphony Orchestra program books. With Mr. Bagar he also co-authored *The Victor Book of Operas* and *The Concert Companion.*

Other books by Mr. Biancolli include *The Book of Great Conversations* (later re-issued as *From Socrates to Shaw*), *Mary Garden's Story* (with Miss Garden), *The Analytical Concert Guide,* and *The Flagstad Manuscript.* He has also written monographs on Tschaikowsky and Prokofieff for the radio subscribers of the New York Philharmonic-Symphony Society. Among his translations is a literal version of the libretto of Moussorgsky's opera, *Boris Godounoff.*

Apart from world literature and music, Mr. Biancolli's main pursuit has been languages, inheriting two and acquiring perhaps six others. He is married and is the father of a sixteen-year-old daughter. Other than walking, he knows only one sport, swimming, and acknowledges only one vice—playing the accordion.

MU   O/y/R129JMK

BIANCOLLI